DATE DUE

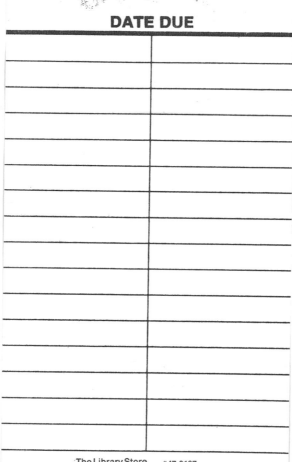

ABOUT ISLAND PRESS

Island Press is the only non-profit organization in the United States whose principal purpose is the publication of books on environmental issues and natural resource management. We provide solutions-oriented information to professionals, public officials, business and community leaders, and concerned citizens who are shaping response to environmental problems.

In 1994, Island Press celebrated its tenth anniversary as the leading provider of timely and practical books that take a multidisciplinary approach to critical environmental concerns. Our growing list of titles reflects our commitment to bringing the best of an expanding body of literature to the environmental community throughout North America and the world.

Support for Island Press is provided by Apple Computer, Inc., The Bullitt Foundation, The Geraldine R. Dodge Foundation, The Energy Foundation, The Ford Foundation, The W. Alton Jones Foundation, The Lyndhurst Foundation, The John D. and Catherine T. MacArthur Foundation, The Andrew W. Mellon Foundation, The Joyce Mertz-Gilmore Foundation, The National Fish and Wildlife Foundation, The Pew Charitable Trusts, The Pew Global Stewardship Initiative, The Rockefeller Philanthropic Collaborative, Inc., and individual donors.

ABOUT ISEE

Ecological economics is concerned with extending and integrating the study and management of nature's household (*ecology*) with humanity's household (*economy*). Ecological economics acknowledges that, in the end, a healthy economy can only exist in symbiosis with a healthy ecology. Ecological economics is the name that has been given to the effort to transcend traditional disciplinary boundaries in order to address the interrelationship between ecological and economic systems in a broad and comprehensive way. Ecological economics takes a holistic worldview with human beings representing one component (albeit a very important one) in the overall system. Moreover, human beings, play a unique role in the overall system because they can consciously understand their role in the larger system and manage it for sustainability. Ecological economics seeks to constitute a true marriage of ecology and economics so as to give meaning and substance to the idea of sustainable development. Mechanisms for achieving sustainable development will enable modern societies to develop and prosper within a natural world that is safeguarded from ecological destruction.

The International Society for Ecological Economics (ISEE) is a not-for-profit organization with more than 1,600 members in over 60 countries. Regional chapters have been established in Russia, Brazil, Canada, Australia-

New Zealand, Mexico-Latin America-Caribbean, Chile, Argentina-Uruguay and Europe, with efforts underway to organize chapters in China, Africa, and Southeast Asia. ISEE promotes the integration of ecology and economics by providing information through its membership journal, *Ecological Economics,* and the Ecological Economics Bulletin, and encourages the exchange of ideas by supporting major international conferences and smaller regional meetings on topics of interest to members, as well as research and training programs in ecological economics.

Costa Rica Counts the Future, a bilingual (English and Spanish) video providing an overview of ecological economics, and topics discussed at the conference can be obtained by contacting the ISEE Secretariat, P.O. Box 1589, Solomons, MD 20688, USA.

Getting Down
to Earth

Titles published by Island Press in the
INTERNATIONAL SOCIETY FOR ECOLOGICAL
ECONOMICS SERIES include:

R. Constanza, B.G. Norton, B.D. Haskell
(Editors), *Ecosystem Health,* 1992

A.M. Jansson, M. Hammer, C. Folke, R.
Constanza (Editors), *Investing in Natural
Capital,* 1994

Jeroen C.J.M. van den Bergh, Jan van der
Straaten (Editors), *Toward Sustainable
Development,* 1994

GETTING DOWN TO EARTH

Practical Applications of Ecological Economics

Edited by
Robert Costanza, Olman Segura,
and Juan Martinez-Alier

Technical Editors, Paula Hill Jasinski
and Sue Mageau

*Foreword by José María Figueres Olsen,
President of Costa Rica*

INTERNATIONAL SOCIETY
FOR ECOLOGICAL ECONOMICS

ISLAND PRESS

Washington, D.C. ■ Covelo, California

Library of Congress Cataloging-in-Publication Data

Getting down to earth: practical applications of ecological economics/
    edited by Robert Costanza, Olman Segura, and Juan Martinez-Alier:
    foreword by José María Figueres Olsen.
        p.   cm.—(International Society for Ecological Economics
    series)
    The product of a workshop held in Costa Rica, following a
conference of the International Society for Ecological Economics.
    Includes bibliographical references and index.
    ISBN 1-55963-503-7 (pbk.)
    1. Environmental economics. 2. Sustainable development.
I. Costanza, Robert. II. Segura Bonilla, Olman. III. Martínez
Alier, Juan. IV. International Society for Ecological Economics.
V. Series.
HC79.E5G478   1996
333.7—dc20   96-22628
                                                              CIP

Printed on recycled, acid-free paper ✖

Manufactured in the United States of America

10 9 8 7 6 5 4 3 2 1

CONTENTS

Contributors xiii

Foreword xv

Preface xxi

1.   Integrated Envisioning, Analysis, and Implementation of a
     Sustainable and Desirable Society 1
     Robert Costanza, Olman Segura, and Juan Martinez-Alier

PART I: VISION

2.   Socio-Ecological Principles for a Sustainable Society 17
     John Holmberg, Karl-Henrik Robèrt, and Karl-Erik Eriksson

3.   Consumption: Value Added, Physical Transformation, and
     Welfare 49
     Herman E. Daly

4.   Complexity, Problem Solving, and Sustainable Societies 61
     Joseph A. Tainter

5.   From Ecological Economics to Productive Ecology: Perspectives
     on Sustainable Development from the South 77
     Enrique Leff

6.   Social and Ethical Dimensions of Ecological Economics 91
     Anil Gupta

7.   Envisioning a Sustainable World 117
     Donella Meadows

PART II: ANALYSIS

8.   **Towards an Economics for Environmental Sustainability** . . . 129
     Paul Ekins

9.   **Ecological and Economic Distribution Conflicts** 153
     Juan Martinez-Alier and Martin O'Connor

10. **Technological Intensity, Technological Quality, and Sustainable
     Development** 185
     Gilberto C. Gallopín

11. **Renewable Resource Appropriation by Cities** 201
     Carl Folke, Jonas Larsson, and Julie Sweitzer

12. **Emergent Complexity and Procedural Rationality: Post-Normal
     Science for Sustainability** 223
     *Martin O'Connor, Sylvie Faucheux, Géraldine Froger, Silvio Funtowicz,
     and Giuseppe Munda*

13. **Integrating Spatially Explicit Ecological and Economic Models:
     Theory and Application in the Patuxent River Watershed,
     Maryland** 249
     Robert Costanza, Lisa Wainger, and Nancy Bockstael

14. **Ecological Economics: The Second Stage** 285
     Faye Duchin

15. **Modeling the Dynamics of Resource Depletion, Substitution,
     Recycling, and Technical Change in Extractive Industries** . . . 301
     Matthias Ruth and Cutler J. Cleveland

PART III: IMPLEMENTATION

16. **Institutional Change and Development Towards Sustainability** . . . 327
     Johannas B. Opschoor

17. **Creating the Institutional Setting for Sustainability in Latin America** 351
    Marc J. Dourojeanni

18. **Applying Agroecology to Improve Peasant Farming Systems in Latin America: An Impact Assessment of NGO Strategies** . . 365
    Miguel A. Altieri, Andres Yurjevic, Jean Marc Von der Weid, and Juan Sanchez

19. **Property Rights, People, and the Environment** 381
    Susan S. Hanna

20. **Will New Property Rights Regimes in Central and Eastern Europe Serve Nature Conservation Purposes?** 395
    Tomasz Zylicz

21. **Valuing Social Sustainability: Environmental Recuperation on Fevela Hillsides in Rio de Janeiro** 411
    Peter H. May and Marília Pastuk

22. **Resources Planning Should Integrate Conservation and Development Needs: The Case of Tegucigalpa's Water Requirements** 427
    Carlos A. Quesada-Mateo

23. **The Political Dimension of Implementing Environmental Reform: Lessons from Costa Rica** 439
    David Kaimowitz and Olman Segura

24. **Envisioning Sustainable Alternatives within the Framework of the UNCED Process** 455
    Alicia Bárcena and Diomar Silveira

Index 465

CONTRIBUTORS

Miguel A. Altieri — College of Natural Resources, University of California, Berkeley

Alicia Bárcena — The Earth Council, San José, Costa Rica

Nancy Bockstael — University of Maryland International Institute for Ecological Economics

Cutler J. Cleveland — Center for Energy and Environmental Studies, Boston University

Robert Costanza — University of Maryland International Institute for Ecological Economics

Herman E. Daly — School of Public Affairs, University of Maryland

Marc J. Dourojeanni — Chief, Environmental Protection Division, Inter-American Development Bank, Washington DC

Faye Duchin — Institute for Economic Analysis, New York University

Paul Ekins — Department of Economics, Birkbeck College, University of London

Karl-Erik Eriksson — Institute of Physical Resource Theory, Chalmers University of Technology and Göteborg University

Carl Folke — Beijer International Institute of Ecological Economics Royal Swedish Academy of Sciences

Sylvie Faucheux — Université de Versailles à Saint-Quentin-en-Yvelines, Guyancourt, France

Géraldine Froger — Université de Versailles à Saint-Quentin-en-Yvelines, Guyancourt, France

Silvio Funtowicz — Institute for Systems Engineering and Informatics, Varese, Italy

Gilberto C. Gallopín — Centro Internacional de Agricultura Tropical Cali, Columbia

Anil Gupta — Society for Research and Initiatives for Sustainable Technologies and Institutions and Honey Bee Network

Susan S. Hanna — Department of Agriculture and Resource Economics, Oregon Sate University

John Holmberg — Institute of Physical Resource Theory, Chalmers University of Technology and Göteborg University

David Kaimowitz — Center for International Forestry Research, Costa Rica

Jonas Larsson — Beijer International Institute of Ecological Economics Royal Swedish Academy of Sciences

Enrique Leff — United Nations Environmental Programme, Mexico

Juan Martinez-Alier — Department d'Economica i d'Història Econòmica, Universitat Autònoma de Barcelona, Barcelona, Spain

Peter H. May — Federal Rural University of Rio de Janeiro, Brazil

Donella Meadows — Dartmouth College, Hanover, New Hampshire

Giuseppe Munda	Department d'Economica i d'Història Econòmica, Universitat Autònoma de Barcelona, Barcelona, Spain
Martin O'Connor	Université de Versailles à Saint-Quentin-en-Yvelines, Guyancourt, France
Johannas B. Opschoor	Institute of Social Studies, The Hague Netherlands
Marília Pastuk	Eco-Eco Brazilian Society for Ecological Economics, Rio de Janerio, Brazil
Carlos A. Quesada-Mateo	Centro de Investigaciones en Desarrollo Sostenible (CIEDES), Universidad De Costa Rica
Karl-Henrik Robèrt	Institute of Physical Resource Theory, Chalmers University of Technology and Göteborg University and The Natural Step Foundation
Matthias Ruth	Center for Energy and Environmental Studies, Boston University
Juan Sanchez	Centro de Investigacion, Educacion y Desarrollo, Lima, Peru
Olman Segura	Universidad Nacional, Heredia, Costa Rica
Diomar Silveira	The Earth Council, San José, Costa Rica
Julie Sweitzer	Beijer International Institute of Ecological Economics Royal Swedish Academy of Sciences
Joseph A. Tainter	USDA Forest Service Rocky Mountain Forest Range Experiment Station, Albuquerque, NM
Jean Marc Von der Weid	Assesoría e Servicios a Proyectos un Agricultura Alternativa, Rio de Janerio, Brazil
Lisa Wainger	University of Maryland International Institute for Ecological Economics
Andres Yurjevic	Consorcio Latino Americano Sobre Agroecología y Desarrollo (CLADES) Santiago, Chile
Tomasz Zylicz	Warsaw Ecological Economics Center, Warsaw University

FOREWORD

It gives me great pleasure to fulfill the request of the International Society of Ecological Economics (ISEE) to write a foreword for the book produced from the world conference "Down to Earth: Practical Applications of Ecological Economics" which took place in our country in October 1994. I would like to share some ideas related to economic policy that we are implementing in Costa Rica. For Costa Ricans, our development style in the second half of the century has enabled us to make significant advances, both economically and socially. First and foremost, we are proud of abolishing the military more than four decades ago, having established the most mature and stable democracy in Latin America. Furthermore, we have relied on social indicators more similar to those used in industrialized nations than in developing countries. Economically, we are pleased to have the most successful and consolidated development model on the continent. However, we should lament that these advances have caused extensive and profound degradation to our natural systems, never before experienced in our history. Urban development, agricultural diversification, and industrialized growth have also accelerated the destruction of our natural forests, erosion of our soils, and contamination of our waters. Today we understand better than ever that the development style which has prevailed in recent decades cannot guide us towards a more just, more prosperous, and more harmonious Costa Rica. Instead, we have incubated a profound disequilibrium between social life and the environment whose cost remains underestimated. It is a cost we will have to pay sooner or later.

We understand that the gradual but persistent change towards a superior development style is an urgent necessity for Costa Rican society. We call this new national course 'sustainable development.' The term 'development' speaks to us of the eternal calling from the people to achieve higher levels of social welfare, economic progress and political democracy. And the term 'sustainable' reminds us that, in order for development to be accumulative and lasting in the long run, we need to preserve the great social, political, economical , and ecological equilibrium which gives it sustenance. Participatory democracy, social investment, macroeconomic balance and the alliance with the environment are the four elements which are of utmost importance to enrich national life, both materially and spiritually, generation after generation. In fact, every day it becomes clearer to us that the very survival of our national community in the long run depends on the success of this endeavor.

Nevertheless, we do not want to underestimate the large obstacles that we face in undertaking this national task. We know that environmentally destructive practices are inherent in the forms of production and consumption which prevail in our societies. In our national experience, it is evident that the price system, in its inability to transcend marketed costs and benefits in the short run, has left out the associated costs of deterioration, degradation, and extinction of natural capital. An exemplary case is the ridiculous price of wood which comes from our forests, because the price system treats forests like free resources whose only cost is the cost of extraction.

It is often the case that economic agents depend on the prevailing economic practices in order to exist and reproduce. For this reason, the interested groups which arise encourage its perpetuation, and in this way, generate resistance to change towards more sustainable forms of life. These interests are also expressed in our institutions and in daily policy decisions. The Costa Rican state has frequently created favorable conditions for the inappropriate use of natural resources. For example, we are reminded of state policies for credit and concession of idle land that, for years, has promoted the indiscriminate felling of natural forests.

To these difficulties, which have profound roots, we should add that our country is a poor nation with severe limitations when it comes to financing new conservation projects and the productive transformation that is essential to open new areas to sustainablity. Due to this, some are of the opinion that our national project for sustainable development is an illusion, and therefore, not viable. However, we believe that sustainability is the most viable option on which our society can rely to preserve its historic achievements and overcome the restrictive handicaps. Essentially, we think it is the only viable option we have.

Our confidence in the success of this national undertaking is based on the historic inclination of our country. Costa Ricans are accustomed to learning and adapting to great changes in order to expand our development options. Often these changes have gone against the grain of the dominant world tendencies. For example, we succeeded in abolishing the military at a time in which armaments and military violence were at a peak on the rest of the planet. We created a stable and harmonious democracy during a time in which government and military coups were occurring throughout the continent. We achieved high social development levels in a poor, small country while poverty and inequality were prominent in the region. Our present aspirations of sustainability are an expression of our ability to change.

Our confidence is also based on the basic fact that all people wish to improve their standard of living, and, sustainable development is, in essence, a way to truly improve. If we approach it intelligently, it will be, among other things, a source for excellent long term business. We are thinking, for example, about market opportunities open to us for agricultural exports which are 'environmentally friendly'. We are thinking about the potential increases in land productivity if we succeed in halting the rate of soil erosion, and the cost savings if we take better care of our natural water supply. We are thinking about the increased value that would result from a more intensive and less damaging use of inputs of natural origin.

Our national strategy to advance towards sustainability is inspired by a general principle that should permeate all our actions in this respect, and can be expressed as the following: fundamentally, the end and the means of our efforts for sustainability are the people of Costa Rica. Their well-being and their happiness, generation after generation is the central motivation in this great enterprise. The ability to organize around common goals, creativity, and capacity to change are the principal instruments of the process. In this sense, I recall something written by my father, José Figueres Ferrer, in 1955, when he occupied the same seat as I do today. He said, "It hurts us when the forests burn or the land erodes, or rivers flow without producing energy; but the greatest of resources, our people, our country, we frequently forget and even waste." We seek not to forget the general welfare, nor to waste the human resource of our people's potential. This is precisely our greatest aspiration.

In our strategy, there are at least five basic elements I wish to point out. First, the intensive use and the expansion of national technological and scientific means. These are essential in order to replace inefficient, less productive and environmentally damaging production methods with technology and methods that bring together high resource valuation and environmental conservation. Those means are also necessary to contribute to the technical basis of new conservation projects and the recovery of natural capital.

Second "the future is built today". We are seeking a solution to immediate problems oriented towards the achievement of objectives in the medium and long run. In this way we can deal with the urgency and the strategy as part of one process. But in addition, we are committed to investing efforts and resources in tasks that, by their nature, will not have visible results until after the present government has completed its term.

Third, the empowerment of forces for change that are contained in our civilian society. We know very well that in a democracy, such as ours, the advancement towards sustainability is not possible unless it is done in a holistic manner, advancing society as a whole. The role of government is not to substitute itself for civilian society, but to promote the advance of society itself with its own energy, as quickly as possible.

The success of our endeavor depends a great deal on our success in giving it the necessary political viability, which means that the different social and economic actors modify their practices, their perceptions and their values in such a way that they are more compatible with the laws which govern natural cycles. In this way, we are very interested in transcending the current representative democracy to advance towards new forms of participatory democracy, in which civilian society is enhanced like never before. Furthermore, we should explore new mechanisms of consultation, integration, and participation between civilian society and government spheres.

Fourth, state apparatus reform. In our experience, Costa Rica has been fortunate in being quite successful in its development efforts. We have mature institutions which have acquired technologically advanced levels in diverse areas related to natural resources and the environment, such as electricity, irrigation, water supply, agriculture, and nature conservation, among others. However, we need to revitalize and renovate these institutions to empower them with the ability to assume the new tasks of national development. In addition, we should advance towards more coordinated state actions, more oriented towards the integrated solution to problems. We are reminded that the undertaking of sustainable development requires an intersectorial and interdisciplinary effort which breaks from traditional divisions of functions among institutions.

Fifth, base ourselves in our own efforts, but take intelligent advantage of international cooperative support. Cooperative relations with friendly countries and international organizations that are of mutual benefit interest. Friendly countries have supported us in the past, with the bilateral debt for environment swap, and with the establishment of national parks and integrated rural development projects. In the future, we can explore new options, for example, taking advantage of our biodiversity in the development of new industrial and agricultural products. An exemplary experience of cooperation is the ambitious program for sustainable development that the Netherlands is developing with the countries of Benin, Butan, and Costa Rica. Nevertheless, we have not forgotten that the best, and most just international cooperation, is free access to markets for our products.

In conclusion, I want to emphasize that I am conscious that there are many challenges we have yet to face. However, I am sure we shall overcome all of them. In this manner, the day will arrive when we are so entrenched in the process of sustainable development that it will be more difficult to go back than to go forward. This is the dream that Costa Ricans share, and this is the cause to which this government is devoted with all of its energy.

To emphasize the Costa Rican experience and briefly share with you the strategy that we are developing, I attempt only to exemplify the optimism, conviction, and humility with which this small country is attempting sustainable development. We have the faith that we are constructing a better country, and in the end, a better world. It is our desire, that together we will construct this new idea of development, and that we research and initiate the same as soon as possible. In this sense, the work that is being accomplished by the International Center in Economic Policy for Sustainable Development at the Universidad Nacional de Costa Rica in conjunction with the International Society for Ecological Economics, by organizing the world conference in San José, and now this book, is worthy of my hearty congratulations and support. We are taking it as an important input in our national quest for sustainability.

José María Figueres Olsen
President of Costa Rica
February, 1996

PREFACE

This book is the product of a workshop held October 29–31, 1994 on the Pacific Coast of Costa Rica, near Herradura. The workshop immediately followed the third biannual conference of the International Society for Ecological Economics (ISEE), held October 24–28, 1994 in San José, Costa Rica. The theme of the conference was "Down to Earth: Practical Applications of Ecological Economics." Over 1,300 participants attended the five-day conference in San José, and 24 invited participants attended the subsequent three-day workshop on the coast.

The idea behind the workshop was to bring together the plenary speakers from the conference and other selected participants, and allow them to more fully discuss the ideas in their papers. They could also inject other ideas gleaned from the larger conference, and organize and revise their contributions into a coherent publication. Because of this "synthesis workshop" format, the papers in this book have benefited from more interaction between the authors than is usually found in a volume of contributed chapters. Hopefully, this has produced a volume which more closely approaches the consistency of style and organization of content found in a single-authored book, while still allowing a range of different perspectives to be represented. We have tried to limit jargon and define terms as they appear so that the text will be as accessible as possible to a broad audience. The introductory chapter synthesizes and summarizes these many perspectives and serves as a guide to the rest of the book. In addition to the general discussion of common themes at the workshop, each paper was formally reviewed by two other workshop participants and by one additional outside reviewer, and revised accordingly. Based on these reviews, some of the contributed papers were not included in the book.

This book is intended to be part of a coordinated set of three publications and a video. The book in your hands is intended for advanced readers and graduate courses. There is also a version aimed more for a popular, lay audience and a short "executive summary" aimed at the policy community. Both of these are currently in production. Finally, there is also a bilingual (English and Spanish) video entitled *Costa Rica Counts the Future*. We thus hope to address the full spectrum of audiences that may be interested in these ideas by presenting them in the appropriate form for each audience. We also envision that many readers may want the entire set, since the different versions are designed to be mutually supportive.

Acknowledgments

Major sponsors of the conference included the International Society of Ecological Economics (ISEE), the Universidad National de Costa Rica, The Earth Council, IICA, Universidad Nacional, Earth Council, United Nations Environment Program (UNEP), Institute of Biodiversity–Costa Rica (INBIO), Banco Nacional de Costa Rica, University for Peace, Merck Family Fund, Government of Netherlands, Canadian Embassy, Danish Embassy, British Embassy, United States Embassy, Swiss Embassy in Costa Rica, Swedish International, Development Authority, Swedish Agency for Research Cooperation, University of Costa Rica, Universidad Estatal a Distancia, LACSA Airlines, United Nations Education Science Organization (UNESCO), Fondo de Beneficio Social, Universidad Nacional (UNA), Fundacion Universidad Nacional, Instituto Costarricense de Turismo, International Union for Conservation of Nature (IUCN), Commission of the European Community, Fundacion de Parques Nacionales de Costa Rica. We would also like to thank the following for their varied and valuable contributions: Janet Barnes, Jessica Beckles, Dean Button, Beatriz Castaneda, Laura Cornwell, Katia Coto, Paula Hill Jasinski, Paul Jivoff, Sandra Koskoff, Michael Mageau, Sue Mageau, Carlos Murillo, Ana Cecilia Perez, Carlos Pomareda y Eduardo Trigo, Rose Marie Ruiz, Leon Santana, Daniel Vartanian, Patricia Vindas, and Lisa Wainger.

Robert Costanza
Olman Segura
Juan Martinez-Alier

1 INTEGRATED ENVISIONING, ANALYSIS, AND IMPLEMENTATION OF A SUSTAINABLE AND DESIRABLE SOCIETY

Robert Costanza
Director, University of Maryland
Institute for Ecological Economics
Center for Environmental and Estuarine Studies
University of Maryland
Box 38, Solomons, MD 20688-0038

Olman Segura
Universidad Nacional de Costa Rica
Maestria en Politica Economica para
Centroamerica y el Caribe
PO Box 555-3000
Heredia, Costa Rica

Juan Martinez-Alier
Departament d'Economica i d'Història Econòmica
Universitat Autònoma de Barcelona
Bellaterra 08193, Barcelona, Spain

OVERVIEW

Ecological economics represents a new, transdisciplinary way of looking at the world that is essential if we are to achieve sustainability. Getting "down to earth" and making sustainability operational requires the integration of three elements: (1) a practical, shared *vision* of both the way the world works and of the sustainable society we wish to achieve; (2) methods of *analysis* and modeling that are relevant to the new questions and problems this vision embodies; and (3) new institutions and instruments that can effectively use the analyses to adequately *implement* the vision.

The importance of the *integration* of these three components cannot be overstated. Too often when discussing practical applications we focus only on the implementation element, forgetting that an adequate vision of the world and our goals is often the most practical device to achieving the vision, and that without appropriate methods of analysis even the best vision can be blinded. The importance of *communication* and *education* concerning all three elements also can not be overstated.

INTRODUCTION

This introductory chapter is a synthesis and overview of the major ideas contained in the other chapters of the book, which is divided into three major sections dealing with vision, analysis, and implementation. The book was developed in part at a workshop which followed the third international conference of the International Society for Ecological Economics (ISEE) held in San José, Costa Rica in October, 1994. It is an unusual, diverse, and far-ranging collection, both in content and in style. We see this as a major strength of the book, because it expresses the diverse points of view that make up ecological economics.

But within this diversity, there are some basic points of consensus, including: (1) the vision of the earth as a thermodynamically closed and non-materially-growing system, with the economy as a subsystem of the global ecosystem. This implies that there are limits to biophysical throughput through the economic subsystem; (2) the future vision of a sustainable planet with a high quality of life and fair distribution of resources for all its inhabitants (both humans and other species) within the material constraints imposed by 1 (above); (3) the recognition that in the analysis of complex systems like the earth at all space and time scales, fundamental uncertainty is large and irreducible and certain processes are irreversible, requiring a fundamentally precautionary stance; (4) that institutions and management should be proactive rather than reactive and should result in simple, adaptive, and implementable policies based on a sophisticated understanding of the underlying systems which fully acknowledges the underlying uncertainties. This forms the basis for policy implementation which is itself sustainable.

VISION

There are several elements we have combined under the heading of "vision," some of which are "positive" having to do with theories and understanding about how the world works, and some of which are "normative," having to do with how we would like the world to be. The relationship between positive and normative, like the relationship between basic and applied science or between mind and body, or logic and emotion is best viewed as a complex interaction across a continuum, rather than a simple dichotomy. To some extent, we can change the way the world is by changing our vision of what we would like it to be. Likewise, the strict dichotomy between basic and applied science has often proven to be more a hindrance than a help in developing useful understandings of complex systems, as has the mind-body dichotomy.

Visionaries and theorists have often been characterized as mere impractical dreamers. People become impatient and desire action, movement, measurable change and "practical applications." But we must recognize that action and change without an appropriate vision of the goal and analyses of the best methods to achieve it can be worse than counterproductive. In this sense a compelling and appropriate vision can be the most practical of all applications.

This need for appropriate vision applies to every aspect of human endeavor. Far from being immune to this need for vision, science itself is particularly dependent on it. In the words of Joseph Schumpeter (1954):

> In practice we all start our own research from the work of our predecessors, that is, we hardly ever start from scratch. But suppose we did start from scratch, what are the steps we should have to take? Obviously, in order to be able to posit to ourselves any problems at all, we should first have to visualize a distinct set of coherent phenomena as a worthwhile object of our analytic effort. In other words, analytic effort is of necessity preceded by a preanalytic cognitive act that supplies the raw material for the analytic effort. In this book, this preanalytic cognitive act will be called Vision. It is interesting to note that vision of this kind not only must precede historically the emergence of analytic effort in any field, but also may reenter the history of every established science each time somebody teaches us to see things in a light of which the source is not to be found in the facts, methods, and results of the preexisting state of the science.

The first six chapters in this book address the envisioning aspect of the problem of operationalizing sustainability and making it practical. They also serve to differentiate ecological economics from more conventional visions. One of the major differences between ecological economics and conventional academic disciplines is that it does *not* try to differentiate itself from other disciplines in terms of its content or tools. It is an explicit attempt at pluralistic integration rather than territorial differentiation. This is admittedly confusing for those bent on finding sharp boundaries between academic disciplines, but we believe it is an essential revisioning of the problem.

Ecological economics does not aim at analyzing or expressing ecological, social, and economic relationships in terms of the concepts and principles of any one discipline. It is thus not merely ecology applied to economics, nor is it merely economics applied to ecology. It is a transdisciplinary approach to the problem that addresses the relationships between ecosystems and economic systems in the broadest possible sense, in order to develop a deep understanding of the entire system of humans and nature as a basis for effective policies for sustainability. It takes a holistic systems approach that goes beyond the normal narrow boundaries of academic disciplines. This does not imply that disciplinary approaches are rejected, or that the purpose is to create a new discipline. Quite the contrary. What ecological economics rejects is the "intellectual turf" model that unfortunately still holds sway in much of academia.

Instead of this "win-lose," "either-or" approach, which is ill-suited to the problem of understanding our world as an integrated complex system, ecological economics encourages a pluralistic, "win-win" approach that incorporates many different disciplines simultaneously (Norgaard 1989). This transdisciplinary approach could be described as an "orchestration of the sciences" (to use Otto Neurath's term). Scholars from various disciplines collaborate side-by-side using their own tools and techniques, and in the process develop new theory, tools, and techniques as needed to effectively deal with sustainability. Ecological economics focuses more directly on the problems facing humanity and the life-supporting ecosystems on which we depend. These problems involve: (1) assessing and insuring that the scale of human activities are ecologically sustainable; (2) distributing resources and property rights fairly, both within the current generation of humans, between this and future generations, and between humans and other species; and (3) efficiently allocating resources as constrained and defined by 1 and 2 above, and including both marketed and non-marketed resources.

HOW THE WORLD WORKS: BIOPHYSICAL CONSTRAINTS

The first five chapters by Holmberg et al., Daly, Tainter, Leff, and Gupta address different aspects of the "positive" side of the vision–how the world works, from both biophysical and social perspectives. In chapter 2, John Holmberg, Karl-Henrik Robèrt, and Karl-Erik Eriksson use a holistic systems perspective, the laws of thermodynamics, and the basic shared values of society to develop four basic principles that are necessary "system conditions" for a sustainable society. These are (paraphrased slightly):

1. Mined substances must not systematically accumulate in the ecosphere.
2. Anthropogenic substances must not systematically accumulate in the ecosphere.
3. Natural capital must be preserved and conserved.
4. Resource use must be efficient and fair with respect to meeting human needs.

System conditions 1, 2, and 3 relate to maintaining an ecologically sustainable scale of the economy within the ecosphere, while condition 4 relates to the requirements for a fair distribution of wealth and resources and an efficient allocation as described above. Holmberg et al. describe the implications of these four conditions and their use by the Natural Step Foundation in Sweden in a pedagogy that has proven remarkably successful in altering business and government practices toward sustainability.

Herman E. Daly extends this line of reasoning in chapter 3 to address the issue of the optimal size or scale of the human economy within the ecosphere. He points out that "consumption" is the dissipation of ordered matter, and that natural systems and natural capital represent a primary source of the value added to products. At some point the transformation of natural into human-made capital costs us more in terms of natural capital services lost than it gains us in terms of human-made capital services gained. Material growth in the economy beyond this point is "anti-economic." Sustainability requires that at this point we shift from natural capital consuming material growth to natural capital preserving qualitative development. As the economy matures, like an ecosystem changing from early, weedy, succession to mature forest, the emphasis shifts to producing as much value per unit of consumption as possible, rather than producing and consuming as much as possible.

Another perspective on this problem is provided by Joseph A. Tainter in chapter 4. He takes an historical perspective and shows that civilizations have tended to collapse in the past because their increasing complexity led to decreasing marginal returns to complexity and ultimately to negative returns to complexity. We have created an aversion to this history by focusing only on the positive benefits of economic growth (and increasing complexity) and ignoring the negative effects like natural capital depletion increasing crime, congestion, etc. Hopefully, the ecological economics vision will help us to change this cavalier attitude toward history, to learn where we are in this process of evolving complexity, and to develop in such a way as to remain sustainable rather than collapsing as so many of our predecessor civilizations have done.

Enrique Leff in chapter 5 emphasizes that while in the North the vision of the environmental problem has focused on global environmental change, the relationship between population and resources, intergenerational equity, and the internalization of environmental costs, in the South the problems have been seen as more focused on poverty, massive ecological degradation, and intragenerational equity. These differences are relevant, but, like Daly, he emphasizes the general importance of natural processes in adding value to the economy and the common need to minimize throughput while maximizing ecological productivity if the goal is sustainability. Different social structures will be required to meet these goals in the North and in the South. This idea is further elaborated by Anil Gupta in chapter 6 who points out the benefits of drawing upon indigenous/local ecological knowledge systems and the experience of grassroots organizations. They conserve and use nature respectfully as a cultural contribution to other species and themselves. Their vision of how the world works will be essential in generating the technological and institutional innovations necessary for sustainability.

SOCIAL GOALS: HOW WE WOULD LIKE THE WORLD TO BE

A broad, overlapping consensus is forming around the goal of sustainability. Movement toward this goal is being impeded not so much by lack of knowledge, or even lack of "political will," but rather by a lack of a coherent, relatively detailed, shared vision of what a sustainable society would look like.

Developing this shared vision is an essential prerequisite to generating any movement toward it. The default vision of continued, unlimited increases in material consumption is inherently unsustainable, but we cannot break away from this vision until a credible alternative is available. The process of collaboratively developing this shared vision can also help to mediate many short term conflicts that will otherwise remain irresolvable.

Donella Meadows in chapter 7 lays out: 1) why the processes of envisioning and goal setting are so important (at all levels of problem solving); 2) why envisioning and goal setting are so underdeveloped in our society; and 3) how we can begin to train people in the skill of envisioning and begin to construct shared visions of a sustainable society. She tells the personal story of her own discovery of that skill and her attempts to use the process of shared envisioning in problem solving. From this experience, several general principles emerged, which she elaborates in her chapter. They include:

1. In order to effectively envision, it is necessary to focus on what one really wants, not what one will settle for. For example, the lists below show the kinds of things people really want, compared to the kinds of things they often settle for.

Really Want	Settle For
Self esteem	Fancy car
Serenity	Drugs
Health	Medicine
Human happiness	GNP
Permanent prosperity	Unsustainable growth

2. A vision should be judged by the clarity of its values, not the clarity of its implementation path. Holding to the vision and being flexible about the path is often the only way to find the path.
3. Responsible vision must acknowledge, but not get crushed by, the physical constraints of the real world.
4. It is critical for visions to be shared because only shared visions can be responsible.
5. Vision has to be flexible and evolving.

Probably the most challenging task facing humanity today is the creation of a shared vision of a sustainable and desirable society, one that can provide permanent prosperity within the biophysical constraints of the real world in a way that is fair and equitable to all of humanity, to other species, and to future generations. This vision does not now exist, although the seeds are there. We all have our own private visions of the world we really want and we need to overcome our fears and skepticism and begin to share these visions and build on them until we have built a vision of the world we want. We have sketched out the general characteristics of this world—it is ecologically sustainable, fair, efficient, and secure—but we need to fill in the details in order to make it tangible enough to motivate people across the spectrum to work toward achieving it. The time to start is now.

ANALYSIS

Even the fragmented and vague vision of a sustainable and desirable world which we can currently articulate begins to change the kinds of analysis that are most appropriate for operationalizing it. In particular, we need models that:

1. Acknowledge the biophysical constraints on economic systems;
2. Analyze the linkages between ecological and economic systems at several interacting scales;
3. Acknowledge the fundamental uncertainties in our ability to predict the behavior of complex adaptive systems.

Chapters 8–16 address the analysis of complex adaptive systems in light of the emerging ecological economics vision of sustainability.

Paul Ekins in chapter 8 provides a review of the basic principles of resource economics (optimal use of environmental resources) and environmental economics (efficient levels of pollution), demonstrating that these principles do not guarantee sustainability. In addition, he shows how the conventional cost-benefit framework can actually make decision-making less manageable rather than more so. "It is economist's task" in his words, "not to define the goal of sustainability, but to advise on ways of minimizing the cost of achieving it." He lays out six fundamental conditions (similar and overlapping with the four system conditions elaborated in Holmberg et al.) which must be meet to assure sustainability. Ecological economics is then seen as the economics of meeting these sustainability conditions.

In chapter 9, Juan Martinez-Alier and Martin O'Connor analyze the interconnections between allocative efficiency and distribution of wealth and property rights. They introduce the idea of "ecological distribution" (the distribution of the benefits of present patterns of environmental exploitation) and compare it with more conventional "economic" distribution. They also show how the distribution of endowments and property rights determines the economic values of environmental goods and services, so that the problems of distribution and efficiency are inseparable.

Gilberto C. Gallopín builds on this theme in chapter 10 and shows that the current trajectory of development is clearly unsustainable. Poverty is rising and ecological life support systems are being seriously and irreversibly damaged.

Change from the current trajectory is not an option—it is a necessity. The problem cannot be solved by small incremental corrections, as many economists and politicians recommend, but requires fundamental changes in the goals of society and the rules of the game. He analyzes the distribution issue from the perspective of the distinction between material economic growth and real improvements in the quality of life. In the North, quality of life may actually be decreasing with increased material consumption while in the South, poverty requires material growth to at least some minimum standards. He lays out some strategies for achieving sustainable improvement of quality of life in this broader context, which is dependent on changing the distribution of resources.

In chapter 11, Carl Folke, Jonas Larsson, and Julie Sweitzer look at one important aspect of the material dependence of economies on ecological systems by investigating the "ecological footprint" of cities in the Baltic Sea drainage basin. This footprint, caused by the cities' need for energy, wood, paper, fibers, food, etc. is estimated to be 200 times the area of the cities themselves. They conclude that this dependence of cities on ecosystem services needs to be made more apparent to city dwellers if the goal is sustainability.

POST NORMAL SCIENCE

In chapter 12, Martin O'Connor, Sylvie Faucheux, Géraldine Froger, Silvio Funtowicz, and Guesippe Munda look at the prospects for applying "post normal science" to the problem of sustainability. This implies a science with changed roles to include community and political decisions regarding the redistribution of economic opportunity and access to environmental services. This "science of emergent complexity" is inseparable from considerations of ethics and politics. The chapter also develops the idea of a "sustainability tree" for analysis of the potential paths to joint ecological, economic and social sustainability in both a static and dynamic case. The dynamic sustainability tree incorporates the two key principles of the procedural rationality described in the chapter—the identification and appraisal of sub-goals and the satisfying principle used iteratively over time. This framework does not provide an "optimal" solution in the conventional sense. Rather it provides a structuring of information for use in decision making. It is particularly useful in conjunction with simulation models of the type discussed below, which display scenarios for decision makers under a wide variety of assumptions.

INTEGRATED ACCOUNTING AND MODELING

Several of the chapters in this section pursue the goal of integrated ecological economic accounting and modeling, at several different space, time, and complexity scales. The chapters describe in some detail current developments in this rapidly evolving field. In chapter 13, Robert Costanza et al. describe theoretical issues concerning integrated ecological economic modeling and a practical application in the Patuxent River Basin, Maryland. In chapter 14, Faye Duchin describes her work in structural economics (an extension of input-output analysis) as an integrated, formal evaluation framework for analysis of changing technologies and sustainable development options at both the national and global scale.

In chapter 15, Matthias Ruth and Cutler J. Cleveland describe a dynamic computer simulation model they constructed to assess the relative strength of two opposing forces in resource extraction. The first is the tendency for resource quality to decrease as extraction proceeds leading to increasing extraction costs. The second is the tendency for substitutes and technological advances to decrease extraction costs. They use the example of copper mining to explore the dynamic, systems level balance between these opposing forces. They conclude that, while technical change and substitution are important, "all processes on Earth are bounded by fundamental physical laws that cannot be overcome by technical change."

IMPLEMENTATION

The final section consists of nine chapters concerning the implementation of the ecological economics vision, including various institutional changes necessary for sustainability. These cover a broad spectrum including: property rights regimes, NGO activities, community-based management, and implementing UNCED. In fact the biggest challenge put to the conference, "Down to Earth: Practical Applications of Ecological Economics" in San José, Costa Rica, was to present some "practical applications." Participants from around the world, including scientists, managers, and national and international policy makers, presented examples of ideas on how to implement ecological economics. These attempts are in various stages of development, some just starting, some fairly far along.

Johannas B. Opschoor begins the section with an overview of the kinds of failures which occur in the current system and the kinds of institutions that are necessary to fix them. His chapter 16 offers a typology of three basic types of failures: (1) transaction failures; (2) empowerment failures; and (3) government failures. Each of these have several sub-types and reasons for the failure. For example, transaction failures are due to either: (1) market system failures caused by missing markets or market performance failures; (2) negotiation failures due to missing parties or asymmetries in bargaining power; or (3) preference failures due to missing knowledge or incomplete preferences or time preference bias. Of these, only the first sub-type has been given much attention by economists, and empowerment and government failures are hardly recognized at all. Institutional reform is necessary to address all of these failures in an integrated way in order to achieve sustainability. In chapter 17, Marc J. Dourojeanni elaborates on these ideas and offers some specific recommendations relative to the Latin American situation and the role of multi-lateral development banks. In chapter 18, Miguel A. Altieri et al. add additional depth by looking at the role of NGO's in establishing the agroecological approach to rural development in Latin America.

PROPERTY RIGHTS REGIMES

Susan S. Hanna in chapter 19 and Tomasz Zylicz in chapter 20 both look at property rights regimes as key institutions necessary for implementing sustainability. Hanna discusses the role of property rights regimes in the inter-action of human and natural systems. Property rights regimes cover a large and diverse spectrum which differs in the nature of ownership (i.e., private, common, state, and various hybrids), the rights and duties of owners, the rules of use, and the locus of control. Appropriate, well designed and well functioning property rights regimes which are consistent with the ecological systems they are embedded in at the appropriate scale are necessary (but not sufficient) conditions for sustainability.

Zylicz looks at a specific case study in Central Europe of a national park being threatened by urban development to illustrate how changing property rights regimes have influenced the social context of ecosystem protection. He concludes that the fate of ecosystem protection in this case depends on the ability to demonstrate economic benefits from investing in natural capital rather than allowing it to be degraded.

CASE STUDIES IN LATIN AMERICA

Chapter 21, by Peter H. May and Marília Pastuk, chapter 22, by Carlos A. Quesada-Mateo, and chapter 23, by David Kaimowitz and Olman Segura all look at case studies in Latin America concentrating on the importance of the equity issue. May and Pastuk look at favelas in Rio de Janeiro and a municipal program to reforest them, concentrating on the socio-political forces involved in the environmental and equity issues. Quesada looks at water supply in Tegucigalpa, Honduras as an integrated social, economic, cultural and ecological development problem. Kaimowitz and Segura look at the importance of interest groups in the adoption and success of policies in Costa Rica related to deforestation, pesticides, and air pollution. They conclude that effective implementation requires both substantial pressure from interest groups and a lack of a major threat to important existing activities.

IMPLEMENTING UNCED

The final chapter, 24, by Alicia Bárcena and Diomar Silveira looks at the challenges of implementing the recommendations of the UNCED conference within the vision and analysis of ecological economics. The challenge is to balance the four important dimensions of social equity, ecological integrity, changing the economic paradigm and increased public participation and consensus in decision making. They end their chapter with ten specific recommendations for implementing UNCED that strike a balance between these four dimensions. They include: empowering people; breaking the link between mass media and transnational corporations; reinforcing public accountability; exploring new more sustainable forms of trade; making the Brenton Woods organizations more democratic, transparent and accountable; opening new avenues for arbitration of conflicts at local, national, and international levels; and developing better indicators of environmentally sound development.

CONCLUSIONS

Integrating a shared vision of a sustainable and desirable world with adequate analysis and innovative implementation is the "full package" necessary to achieve sustainability. All three aspects of this task need much improvement, but their integration is lagging furthest behind. Ecological economics (through activities such as the conference and workshop that produced this book and a host of other activities) is helping to foster the transdisciplinary dialogue necessary to pull the package together and more forward toward the newly articulated goals. The remaining chapters of this book comprise a small step in that direction, but many more steps are needed.

REFERENCES

Barbier, E. B. 1987. The concept of sustainable economic development. *Environmental Conservation* 14: 101–10.

Borgström, G. 1967. The Hungry Planet. New York: Macmillan.Common, M., and C. Perrings. 1992. Towards an ecological economics of sustainability. *Ecological Economics* 6: 7–34.

Costanza, R. ed. 1991. Ecological Economics: The Science and Management of Sustainability. New York: Columbia Univ. Press.

Costanza, R. and L. Cornwell. 1992. The 4P approach to dealing with scientific uncertainty. *Environment* 34: 12–20.

Costanza, R. and H. E. Daly. 1987. Toward an ecological economics. *Ecological Modeling* 38: 1-7.

Costanza, R. and H. E. Daly. 1992. Natural capital and sustainable development. *Conservation Biology* 6: 37–46.

Costanza, R., H. E. Daly, and J. A. Bartholomew. 1991. Goals, agenda and policy recommendations for ecological economics. In Ecological Economics: The Science and Management of Sustainability, ed. R. Costanza. New York: Columbia Univ. Press.

Costanza, R., L. Wainger, C. Folke, and K-G Mäler. 1993. Modeling complex ecological economic systems: Toward an evolutionary, dynamic understanding of people and nature. *BioScience* 43: 545–555.

Cleveland, C. J. 1991. Natural resource scarcity and economic growth revisited: Economic and biophysical perspectives. In Ecological Economics: The Science and Management of Sustainability, ed. R. Costanza. New York: Columbia Univ. Press.

Daly, H. E. 1984. Alternative strategies for integrating economics and ecology. In Integration of Ecology and Economics: An Outlook for the Eighties, ed. AM. Jansson. Department of Systems Ecology. Stockholm: Stockholm University. Reprinted in Daly, H. E. 1991. Steady-State Economics. Covelo, CA: Island Press.

Daly, H. E. 1987. The economic growth debate: What some economists have learned but others have not. *Journal of Environmental Economics and Management* 14: 323–36.

Daly, H. E., and J. B. Cobb. 1989. For the Common Good: Redirecting the Economy Toward Community, the Environment and a Sustainable Future. Boston: Beacon Press.

Daily, G., and P. R. Ehrlich. 1992. Population, sustainability, and Earth's carrying capacity. *BioScience* 42: 761–71.

de Groot, R. S. 1992. Functions of Nature: Evaluation of Nature in Environmental Planning, Management and Decision-Making. Groningen, The Netherlands: Wolters-Noordhoff BV.

Ehrlich, P. R. 1989. The limits to substitution: Meta-resource depletion and a new economic-ecological paradigm. *Ecological Economics* 1: 9–16.

Folke, C. 1991. Socioeconomic dependence on the life-supporting environment. In Linking the Natural Environment and the Economy: Essays from the Eco-Eco Group, eds. C. Folke, and T. Kåberger. Dordrecht: Kluwer Academic Publishers.

Folke, C., and N. Kautsky. 1992. Aquaculture with its environment: prospects for sustainability. *Ocean and Coastal Management* 17: 5–24.

Gadgil, M., F. Berkes, and C. Folke. 1993. Indigenous knowledge for biodiversity conservation. *Ambio* 22: 151–6.

Gren, I-M., C. Folke, R. K. Turner, and I. Bateman. 1994. In press. Primary and secondary values of wetland ecosystems. *Environmental and Resource Economics.*

Hall, C. A. S., C. J. Cleveland, and R. Kaufmann. 1986. Energy and Resource Quality: The Ecology of the Economic Process. New York: Wiley.

Hammer, M., A. M. Jansson, and B-O. Jansson. 1993. Diversity change and sustainability: implications for fisheries. *Ambio* 22: 97–105.

Holdren, J. P. 1982. Energy risks: what to measure, what to compare. Technology Review (April): 32–8.

Holling, C. S. 1992. Cross-scale morphology, geometry and dynamics of ecosystems. *Ecological Monographs* 62: 447–502.

Homer-Dixon, T., J. Boutwell, and G. Rathjens. 1993. Environmental change and violent conflict. *Scientific American* (February): 38–45.

Ludwig, D., R. Hilborn, and C. Walters. 1993. Uncertainty, resource exploitation, and conservation: Lessons from history. *Science* 260: 17-36.

Mäler, K-G. 1991. National accounts and environmental resources.*Environmental and Resource Economics* 1: 1–15.

Norton, B. G., ed. 1986. The Preservation of Species. Princeton: Princeton Univ. Press.

Odum, E. P. 1989. Ecology and Our Endangered Life-Support Systems. Sunderland, MA: Sinauer.

Ostrom, E. 1990. Governing the Commons: The Evolution of Institutions for Collective Actions. Cambridge, U.K.: Cambridge Univ. Press.

Pearce, D., A. Markandya, and E. B. Barbier. 1989. Blueprint for a Green Economy. London: Earthscan.

Pearce, D. and K. Turner. 1990. Economics of Natural Resources and the Environment. London: Harvester Wheatsheaf.

Perrings, C., C. Folke, and K-G. Mäler. 1992. The ecology and economics of biodiversity loss: The research agenda. *Ambio* 21: 201–11.

Rapport, D. J. 1993. Book review of Man, Nature, and Technology. *Ecological Economics* 7: 79–83.

Reiger, H. A. and G. L. Baskerville. 1986. Sustainable redevelopment of regional ecosystems degraded by exploitive development. In Sustainable Development of the Biosphere, eds.W. C. Clark and R. E. Munn. London: Cambridge Univ. Press.

Repetto, R. 1992. Earth in balance sheet: Incorporating natural resources in national income accounts. *Environment* 34 (7): 12–20.

Robinson, J., G. Francis, R. Legge, and S. Lerner. 1990. Defining a sustainable society: Values, principles and definitions. *Alternatives* 17: 36–46.

Schumpeter, J. 1954. History of Economic Analysis. Allen and Unwin, London.

Vitousek, P. M., P. R. Ehrlich, A. H. Ehrlich, and P. A. Matson. 1986. Human appropriation of the products of photosynthesis. *BioScience* 36: 368–73.

PART I

VISION

2 SOCIO-ECOLOGICAL PRINCIPLES FOR A SUSTAINABLE SOCIETY

John Holmberg

Institute of Physical Resource Theory
Chalmers University of Technology and
Göteborg University S-41296, Göteborg, Sweden

Karl-Henrik Robèrt

Institute of Physical Resource Theory
Chalmers University of Technology and
Göteborg University S-41296, Göteborg, Sweden
and
The Natural Step Foundation, Amiralitetshuset
Skeppsholmen, S-1149 Stockholm, Sweden

Karl-Erik Eriksson

Institute of Physical Resource Theory
Chalmers University of Technology and
Göteborg University S-41296, Göteborg
Sweden

OVERVIEW

A long-term sustainable global society must have stable physical relations with the ecosphere. This implies sustainable material exchange between the society and the ecosphere as well as limitations on society's manipulation of nature. Physically, sustainable development then means: (1) development towards such a sustainable relation and, after this has been reached, (2) development within the boundaries of sustainable relation.

Applying a systems perspective and putting our focus early in the causal chain, we derive four principles for a sustainable society that at least must be fulfilled:

1. Substances extracted from the lithosphere must not systematically accumulate in the ecosphere.
2. Society-produced substances must not systematically accumulate in the ecosphere.
3. The physical conditions for production and diversity within the ecosphere must not be systematically deteriorated.
4. The use of resources must be effective and just with respect to meeting human needs.

The principles require deep changes of paradigm and culture, and a thorough discussion of cultural roots—our values. The values that should be honored in a sustainable society are the value of human life and dignity and the value of life on Earth. The former implies that human welfare and justice are societal goals. The latter implies that life and life-supporting systems are valued in their own right and not only for their support of the human society.

The four socio-ecological principles have been worked out in close contact with a wide pedagogical practice. They have been found to function well in teaching situations and many actors within business and local administration in Sweden have adopted them as the basis for their strategies towards sustainable development. To promote the use of the four principles in business and politics, an organization called The Natural Step has been initiated.

INTRODUCTION

The discussion of environmental issues is often dominated by specific isolated problems, and results in a number of very difficult questions, (e.g., how to determine critical loads for different substances emitted from the society). There is lack of systems perspective, and the focus is put late in the cause-effect chain.

The need for early warning signals and a systems perspective is even more urgent now that the character of the environmental problems has changed and they have become more global, more diffuse, more delayed and more complex (Holmberg and Karlsson 1992). This means that it has become more difficult to draw conclusions from changes in nature—apart from the conclusion that society has acted wrongly. We need theoretical tools to formulate criteria that must be satisfied in a society having sustainable relations with nature.

The concept of 'sustainable development', was widely spread in connection with the report from the World Commission on Environment and Development (WCED 1987), which started the ongoing discussion on criteria for sustainability on the societal level. In this report, sustainable development was defined as: "meeting the needs of the present without compromising the ability of future generations to meet their own needs."

Sustainable development can be considered as a process consisting of two phases. In the first phase, the global human society develops towards sustainability; in the second phase, society continues to evolve within the boundaries given by sustainability.

Nature is a very complex system and we probably do not know every critical function. The solution to this problem that we seek is to move the focus backwards in the causal chain—from studying effects in nature to studying what constraints have to be put on the societal metabolism to avoid any systematic increases of society's impact on nature. The essential constraint is that the societal metabolism should be embeddable in the biogeochemical cycles.

This involves a change from environmental pathology to societal prevention. Since problems do not originate in the environment but in society, this seems to be a reasonable change.

In terms of the biogeochemical cycles, society is no longer small in comparison to nature. One important influence is the extensive human interference with land photosynthesis. Society also induces several one-way flows that do not fit into the cycles, or as is the case with nitrogen and sulphur, causes the flows to run much faster. No one can evaluate the risks involved. A general rule is therefore not to allow deviations from the natural state that are large in comparison to natural fluctuations. In particular, deviations should not be allowed to increase systematically. This means for example, that society must not allow systematic accumulation of substances that destroy the stratospheric ozone layer which protects the biosphere against ultraviolet radiation, or substances that induce changes in the climate. It also implies maintenance of biodiversity.

Using this general rule, the laws of thermodynamics, including the principle of conservation of matter, and the fact that the space for life on Earth is limited, we have formulated four socio-ecological principles for a sustainable society. The principles define a frame for discussing and evaluating the societal metabolism. It can be used for the design of ecologically and economically effective strategies for change: each step must be part of a path towards sustainability, as defined by the socio-ecological principles.

Our formulation of socio-ecological principles is structured in a way that differs from other formulations. We shall discuss below how our principles relate to Daly's five principles (Daly 1991), to principles of Jacobs (Jacobs 1991), and to the principles of Holdren, Daily, and Ehrlich (1992).

This chapter deals fundamentally with pedagogy. The socio-ecological principles are developed from basic science. The strength of the pedagogy developed around these principles depends on their being among the most venerable and solid tenets in science. In pedagogy we are interested in truth and clarity, not originality. Readers should not feel offended if we take time to explain things which most of them will surely know. We explain what we have found is essential for citizens to understand in order for them to accept and internalize the principles as the compass for orienting policy. Since nations systematically violate those principles, even though they are minimal criteria for sustainability, the problem must be one of inadequate pedagogy. Therefore, we do not apologize for our emphasis on pedagogy—we believe this is where the emphasis belongs. Since the principles are designed as the framework for sustainability, it enables the creation of concrete action programs for systematic change. In those, actors who want to contribute to sustainability can undertake measures that build on each other in a step-by-step fashion to meet the conditions. Defining the frame of the goal as a guidance for today's measures provides a superior approach in planning to gain control in relation to traditional forecasting. Such a strategy is referred to as "back-casting" (Robinson 1990), and is particularly useful when (Dreborg and Steen 1995):

- The problem to be studied is complex.
- There is a need for major change.
- Dominant trends are part of the problem.
- The problem to a great extent is a matter of externalities.
- The scope is wide enough and the time horizon long enough to leave considerable room for deliberate choice.

In the next section we describe flows of energy and matter in nature. The following section deals with societal flows and with the physical interaction of society with nature. Next we suggest four socio-ecological principles for a sustainable society and describe them each in greater detail. Then we discuss values in relation to culture and go on to briefly review our experiences from practical use of the four principles in business and politics. Finally, we conclude by summarizing the major results and discussing the practical use of the principles.

GEOPHYSICAL BASIS

Thermodynamics is that part of physics which deals with conversions of energy and matter. Conservation laws allow balance accounts to be set up for conserved quantities, such as energy or the chemical elements. Also for ordered energy, exergy,[1] which is destroyed when order is lost in irreversible processes, a balance account can be set up. This then has to include an exergy loss flow.

The Earth receives short-wave electromagnetic radiation from the sun and converts it into long-wave radiation emitted into space. The radiation thus connects the Earth to a "battery" (Eriksson 1992), which has the hot sun as one pole and the cold interstellar space as the other. The flow of energy leaving the Earth is very closely equal to the incoming energy. First, the fraction of the incoming energy which is stored for a long time on Earth is very small. At present such stored energy (fossil fuels) is turned into heat much faster than the storage rate, but even this flow is very small in comparison to the solar energy received. Secondly, the loss of nuclear energy and heat from the interior of the Earth is very small in comparison with the flow of solar energy, and so is the gravitational potential energy lost in tidal motions. Thus, according to the first law of thermodynamics, the energy content of the Earth is nearly constant. Also, the inflow or outflow of matter is nearly zero; thus the matter content of the Earth is also nearly constant.

The radiation going out from the Earth has a lower temperature than the incoming radiation; it is spread over a larger number of photons: the outgoing radiation is more disordered and has a higher entropy. Thus, there is a net outflow of entropy from the Earth. This implies that the Earth receives a flow of exergy from the sun/space battery. The exergy flow from this battery has powered the evolution on Earth (Eriksson and Robèrt 1991). It still helps to maintain energy and material flows on Earth and to charge secondary batteries on Earth. The great biogeochemical cycles of water, carbon, and oxygen, (i.e., including the life processes), take part in this. Biomass in chemical disequilibrium with the atmosphere and hydropower dams near steep gravitational potential slopes are then examples of secondary batteries.

The ecosphere[2] is that part of the Earth which directly or indirectly maintains its structure and flow using the exergy flow from the sun/space battery. With this definition the ecosphere contains the biosphere, the atmosphere (including the protective stratospheric ozone layer), the hydrosphere, and the pedosphere (the free layer of soils above the bedrock).

The lithosphere is the rest of the Earth, (i.e., its core, mantle, and crust). Processes in the lithosphere are mainly driven by radioactive decays of its heavy elements. The formation and concentration of minerals in the lithosphere is so slow that these resources, as viewed from the society, can be considered as given finite stocks. There is a natural flow from the lithosphere into the ecosphere through volcanoes and through weathering processes and there are reversed flows through sedimentation. However, compared to the flows within the ecosphere, the exchange of energy and matter between the ecosphere and the lithosphere is much smaller.

THE PHYSICAL INTERACTION OF SOCIETY WITH NATURE

The lithosphere, the pedosphere, the hydrosphere, and the atmosphere constitute the geophysical system that supports the biosphere. All these spheres are the basis for the sociosphere (human society). Within the sociosphere one can distinguish a material supporting part, the technosphere (constructions, machines, tools etc.), and an immaterial part, here called the human sphere, (emotions, wishes, thoughts, ideas, traditions, institutions, etc.). The human sphere performs the ultimate control of the technosphere. In the technosphere exchange of energy and materials with the ecosphere and the lithosphere are used to produce services to the human sphere. The services are delivered in various final-use processes, which normally also imply a conversion of energy and materials, even if we dispose materials over certain time periods, we only consume the qualitative aspects, (e.g., the exergy or structure). Energy and materials are degraded, but do not disappear (Ayres and Kneese 1969; Ayres 1978).

The laws of thermodynamics discussed in the previous section can be applied to the use of energy and materials. They make it clear that what can be consumed is quality in the form of structure, purity and/or exergy, but not energy or matter. Energy is often, but not always, easy to get rid of—it can for instance be spontaneously radiated into space—but matter stays on the Earth's surface. The thermodynamic laws are ideologically neutral, but when combined with the concept of sustainability, they have far-reaching consequences. In particular, this is true of the law of matter conservation, since many environmental questions concern the problem how to handle or how to avoid unwanted forms of matter.

When matter is taken into society in a form considered to be a resource, it is in a state where it has high physical value, but after it has been used, it has often lost structure, purity and/or exergy and gone into a form of lower value, often considered to be of no value or negative value, usually called waste.

As long as societies could consider themselves to be small, surrounded by vast nature from which they borrowed materials that were used and returned in forms not very foreign to nature, then societal use of matter did not cause much damage. Natural systems had sufficient capacity to reprocess the materials that society returned to them. This is no longer the case, we shall return to this later.

Societies construct, operate, maintain, and change the technosphere by using structures, flows, and functions in the ecosphere and the lithosphere. There are two main mechanisms for the physical influence of society on nature (Holmberg and Karlsson 1992). Activities in society imply, in various proportions a combination of:

1.   Exchange, (i.e., influence through flows of energy and materials be tween nature and society); and
2.   Manipulation, (i.e., influence by displacement or control of subsystems of the ecosphere).

These mechanisms are illustrated in Figure 2.1.

1.   The exchange takes place in the form of flows of energy and materials. Energy and materials are extracted from nature for use in the society. The return flow back into nature consists of refuse material and energy from society.

The extraction of energy and materials from the ecosphere and the lithosphere into society is based on structure-creating processes in nature, secondary (or tertiary) batteries in the terminology of the next section. These processes create, or have created in the past, various resources. The resources can be of three kinds: (1) natural flow resources, (2) funds, or (3) deposits. The natural flow resources are continuously flowing resources (sunlight, winds, ocean currents, etc.), from which society can deflect a flow. The funds (forests, fish populations, etc.) are systems using natural flows to maintain themselves. When parts of the funds are harvested, they decrease temporarily but will regenerate themselves if not irreversibly damaged. The deposits (oils, minerals, metals, etc.) have no (or very limited) regrowth possibility within the time horizon of planning and are therefore gradually depleted when extracted.

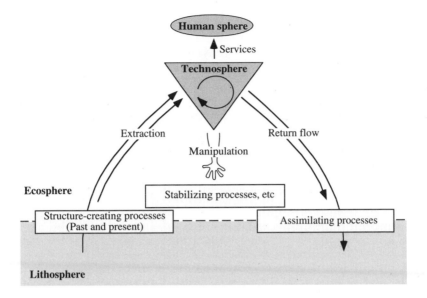

Figure 2.1. General mechanisms for the physical influence of society on nature, based on Holmberg and Karlsson 1992.

Since matter is conserved, materials taken from nature that are not stored in the technosphere, must be returned to nature. Many substances are taken by society from the lithosphere but when society returns them to nature, they are returned not to the lithosphere but to the ecosphere. The ecosphere has a limited capacity for assimilating the return flows of energy and materials from society. The assimilating processes rely on functions like transportation and transformation processes such as dilution or sedimentation, etc. Used material from a fund resource may be circulated through incorporation in the biogeochemical cycles. When deposit resources are used in a society, material is transported from the lithosphere into the technosphere, but there is usually no proper recipient available for processing the used material, the waste. The ecosphere and the living systems in the ecosphere are not adapted to systematically increasing concentrations of materials that were earlier stored in the Earth's crust. The same is true for most non-natural materials created in the extensive transformation processes of materials and structures taking place in the technosphere.

Because of this, we must now look at the entire process of conversions, including the assimilation by the natural systems of the material flows returned to them. In fact, it is reasonable to look upon all use of matter and energy as well as land use as a leasing relation with nature. Since we do not want to be left with increasing amounts of low-quality matter (waste), we want nature to reprocess it into new high-quality matter (resources). Then it is reasonable that nature does what any leasing company would do. It sets conditions for the proper form and place to return matter for reprocessing. If used resources are not allowed to lose quality unnecessarily, for instance if the mixing of used materials is avoided, then more can be recycled within society than would otherwise be the case. Similarly, what is handed over to nature for reprocessing can then be a smaller amount that is more suitable for natural processes.

2. Society also influences the ecosphere by manipulation, which can imply:

- A displacement of the ecosphere (The artifacts and societal activities of the technosphere force away or disturb ecological systems or geographical functions; much of the societal infrastructure has this effect);
- A reshaping of the structures of the ecosphere (e.g., damming of rivers, ditching, ploughing); and
- A guiding of processes and flows (e.g., agricultural practices, manipulation of genes).

There are different degrees of manipulations of areas, ranging from cities and roads, hydropower dams, agricultural areas and highly manipulated forests, to oceans and remote mountain areas. In fact, according to an often cited estimate, nearly 40% of the potential terrestrial net primary productivity is used directly, co-opted, or foregone because of human activities (Vitousek et al. 1986). Now eight years later, the situation has become even more serious. The question of scale of economic activities, previously neglected in economic theory has been brought onto the agenda of the economic debate by Daly (Daly and Cobb 1989; Daly 1991).

Human society depends on stabilizing processes in nature for the exchange of matter and energy with nature and for the use of nature (manipulation). These stabilizing processes consist of different functions in the ecosphere, such as energy transport through the water cycle, photosynthesis, biodegradation processes, and photochemical processes in the stratosphere. Some of the stabilizing processes thus coincide with structure-creating or assimilating processes. Many of these functions are dependent on a high biodiversity (Tilman and Downing 1994).

FOUR SOCIO-ECOLOGICAL PRINCIPLES FOR A SUSTAINABLE SOCIETY

In our attempt to make the concept of sustainable development operational, we focus directly on the source of the problems—early in the causal chain. This means that we focus on society's influence on nature through exchange of materials and manipulation, as discussed above. Based on knowledge of this influence and on the laws of thermodynamics together with the fact that we inhabit a limited area (the surface of the Earth), we have formulated four principles for a sustainable development. The foci of these principles are marked in Figure 2.2. Principle 1 deals with the exchange of substances with the litho-

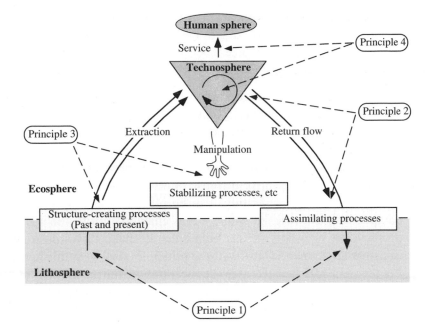

Figure 2.2. The foci of the socio-ecological principles.

sphere. Principle 2 concerns molecules and nuclides that are produced within society. Principle 3 deals with the manipulation of the ecosphere and the use of funds and flows in the ecosphere, and Principle 4 concerns the societal metabolism and the production of services to the human sphere. In this section, we formulate the socio-ecological principles, and in the following section, we discuss them more in detail and relate them to the work of others.

Principle 1. Substances Extracted from the Lithosphere Must Not Systematically Accumulate in the Ecosphere.

Substances from the lithosphere must not be spread in the ecosphere faster than the sedimentation processes return them to the lithosphere.[3] If the input to the ecosphere exceeds the sedimentation processes, these substances will eventually accumulate in the ecosphere (in accordance with the principle of matter conservation and the second law of thermodynamics). Because of the complexity and delay mechanisms in the ecosphere, it is extremely hard to say what level will cause an effect. In fact, every substance has a limit (often unknown), above which it will cause damage in the ecosphere. Increasing amounts of carbon dioxide in the atmosphere, of sulphur oxide leading to acid rain, of phosphorous in lakes and of heavy metals in soils and in our bodies are all examples of such accumulation.

Deleterious effects in the ecosphere occur when accumulation has resulted in increases in concentration of substances beyond a certain level which is difficult to foresee. We can identify three levels of complexity in the risk-assessment following accumulation of waste.

1.   Accumulation of waste occurs when emissions are higher than the assimilation-capacity of the recipient.

2.   The relative increase in concentration from the accumulation is the emitted amounts minus the amounts that are assimilated, divided by the base-line amounts in the recipient. As a general principle, damage is correlated to the relative increase in concentration. Moving focus upstream, these concentrations can be estimated already before the compounds have reached nature. This enables priorities in society's prophylactic measures already before the mechanisms for destruction in nature are known. Our first three principles deal with this level.

3.   For the same relative increases in concentration, the magnitudes of deleterious effects vary with different compounds and different levels and sites in the ecosphere. This complex problem is layered on top of level 2.

Problems inherent to assessment of the effects on level 3, do not justify negligence to assess levels 1 and 2. In fact, any problem concerning the difficulties to assess complexity—or trusting data—on levels 1 and 2 is severely magnified on level 3. Furthermore, it is only considerations on levels 1 and 2 that make it possible to avoid future damage of cause-effect chains that are hitherto unknown. Consequently, measures should be performed on all levels, and at least on levels 1 and 2. In spite of this, reality often shows us the opposite: Most work is performed on levels 3 instead of levels 1 and 2.

Principle 2. Society-Produced Substances Must Not Systematically Accumulate in the Ecosphere.

In the technosphere, molecules, and atomic nuclei of different kinds are produced, some of them long-lived, in amounts previously unknown to the ecosphere. If they are produced faster than they are transformed into molecules or nuclides that can be integrated in the biogeochemical cycles, such substances accumulate somewhere in the ecosphere. CFC-molecules destroying the ozone layer, increasing amounts of DDT and PCB in biota, and radioactive inert gases in the atmosphere are all examples of such accumulation.

For this principle, a similar discussion for risk assessment as for principle 1 can be applied.

Principle 3. The Physical Conditions for Production and Diversity Within the Ecosphere Must Not Be Systematically Deteriorated.

Society must not reduce systematically the physical conditions for production capacity in the ecosphere or the diversity of the biosphere. Society must neither take more resources from the ecosphere than are regenerated nor reduce natural productivity or diversity by manipulating natural systems. Deforestation, soil erosion, land degradation (with desertification as an extreme form), extinction of species of plants or animals, exploitation of productive land for asphalt roads and refuse dumps, destruction of fresh-water supplies are examples of such reduction.

Society is dependent on the long-term functions of the ecosystems. Even if Principle 1 and Principle 2 are fulfilled, society must be careful with its manipulation of the resource base not to lose the productive capacity for supply of food, raw materials, and fuel. This dependence will become more obvious when the use of fossil fuels or uranium is reduced (according to Principles 1 and 2). A more careful and efficient use of land, especially of high-productive areas, is an immediate consequence of this principle.

Principle 4. The Use of Resources Must Be Efficient and Just with Respect to Meeting Human Needs.

Principles 1, 2, and 3 constitute the external conditions for a sustainable metabolism of society. The assimilation capacity as well as the available resource flows are limited. In order to fulfil human needs for a growing global population the resources and services obtained from nature must be used efficiently within the society. Socially, efficiency means that resources should be used where they are needed most. This leads to the requirement of a just distribution of resources among human societies and human beings.

The socio-ecological principles formulated here describe a stationary state. They give a frame within which the societal metabolism must take place. This leads to the requirement that all actions taken should be part of a strategy directed towards sustainability, (i.e., fulfillment of the principles). From the principles it also follows which activities can only be transient, (e.g., extensive burning of fossil fuels according to Principle 1). They can also guide carefully prepared changes, which in turn can make it possible to revise the stationary state. An example may be cultivation of the deserts to make it possible for the ecosphere to carry a larger material turnover.

DISCUSSION OF THE PRINCIPLES

There have already been several attempts to make the concept of sustainability operational. [4] Herman E. Daly (1991) has formulated five principles for sustainable development.

1. Human scale (throughput) should be limited to a level which is within carrying capacity.
2. Technological progress for sustainable development should be efficiency-increasing rather than throughput-increasing.
3. Harvesting rates should not exceed the regeneration rate.
4. Waste emissions should not exceed the renewable assimilative capacity of the environment.
5. Non-renewable resources should be exploited, but at a rate equal to the creation of renewable substitutes.

Daly's first and most general principle is connected to our first three principles. We shall comment on this below. His second principle is related to one aspect of our fourth principle, which requires an increase in efficiency. Besides technological processes we discuss organization, demands and justice. His third principle concerns the maintenance of the ecosystems which is contained in our third principle. Besides harvest rates our third principle also includes manipulation of the ecosphere, qualitative aspects, and biodiversity. Daly's fourth principle contains our first and second principle but it is a little less explicit. Finally, his fifth principle concerns the transition, and is related to our requirement that all actions taken should be part of a strategy directed towards sustainability. His fifth principle also concerns our first principle, but we state that the assimilation capacity is more restrictive than the quantities of resources.

Jacobs (1991) has formulated principles for sustainability starting from three economic functions of the nature: (1) the provision of resources, (2) the assimilation of waste materials, and (3) the performance of environmental services. For the provision of services he has suggested one principle for renewable resources and one for non-renewable resources. The principle for renewable resources is similar to Daly's third principle but for non-renewable resources, Jacobs states that "the depletion of a given resource may be said to satisfy the principle of intergenerational equity if it occurs at the same rate as demand for the resource declines". Although the absolute stock level of the resource is reduced, the stock level relative to the demand is then kept constant. Maintaining the relative stock of non-renewables is a function of three activities: the development of new economically available reserves; reuse and recycling; and a reduction in demand, including substitution by other materials. This principle is thus less restrictive for the use of non-renewable resources than Daly's fifth principle.

For the assimilation of waste Jacobs suggests one principle for "flow waste" that can be assimilated by natural environment through biological and geochemical processes and one principle for "stock waste", such as nuclear waste and certain heavy metals, which can only be stored. Jacobs' sustainability criterion for "flow waste" is that the rate (and concentration) of flow waste discharges should not exceed the assimilative capacity of the recipient medium. For "stock waste" Jacobs states that, in a ideal situation, such waste should not be emitted to the environment at all, but since this is not at present practical Jacobs states that production of "stock waste" can be allowed if safe repositories are available.

For the performance of environmental services, Jacobs has not formulated any specific principle even though he discusses indicators such as the average global temperature and the intensity of incident ultraviolet radiation.

Jacobs' formulation that "sustainability requires that neither pollution, nor damaging effects, increase over time" is very close to the general rule that is the basic idea of our socio-ecological principles: "not to allow deviations from the natural state that are large in comparison to natural fluctuations. In particular, deviations should not be allowed to increase systematically".

Jacobs starts from the economic functions of nature, whereas our starting point is society's influence on nature.

Holdren, Daily, and Ehrlich (1992) make a distinction between non-substitutable resources (essential resources) and resources that can be substituted. They argue that renewable substitutable resources could be sustainably exhausted on the same basis as non-renewable substitutable resources. The "assimilative capacity", (i.e., the capacity to assimilate pollution without any adverse effects on human health or welfare), is probably zero for many kinds of pollutions. According to them, no harm from pollution is not a useful condition of sustainability; the question is rather what level of harm is tolerable on a steady-state basis, in exchange for the benefits of the activity that produces the harm. Because of the difficulties of measuring actual and potential benefit flows, and because of the conceptual and practical problems of insisting on no degradation "forever", they suggest as a practical decision rule, a half-life of 500 to 1,000 years of the magnitude and quality of environmental "stocks". They express this in the following way: constrain the degradation of monitorable environmental stocks to no more than 10% per century.

Holdren, Daily, and Ehrlich (1992) also discuss dangers to sustainability within the global society itself: poverty, the possibility of war, and oppression of human rights. All of these involve waste of human potential, which, at present, also takes place in many other forms.

The 10% exhaustion per century which is suggested as a limit for the near future, is intended as a provisional rule for a limited time. Daly's and Jacobs' principles for the use of non-renewable resources are of the same kind. Daly's and Jacobs' principles and Holdren, Daily, and Ehrlich's decision rule both relate to the transition towards sustainability. We have chosen instead to suggest principles that refer to a stationary sustainable situation and thus describe the goal in more absolute terms. Since the transition cannot take place at once, both kinds of recommendations are needed. One reason for using our principles and pointing out the goal in pedagogical situations, is that it may be simpler as well as more comprehensible and therefore more inspiring. It also makes it easier to take control of the transition process. Of course, one cannot avoid dealing with the complications of the transition, but in doing so, it helps to have a relatively clear idea about where to go.

Our three first principles can be seen as putting general physical limits on society's handling of energy and materials. They refer to three different rules which the human society should follow in order not to exceed Daly's Plimsoll line (Daly 1991). The first two principles are very concrete and directly related to physics; for Principle 3, referring to the manipulation of the natural systems, a vital and responsible discussion is needed. In Daly's metaphor, Principle 4 deals with the load of the ship. If the ship is not carefully loaded, the balance of the ship is upset, and the Plimsoll line is reached with a less than optimal load and at a lower level of security. The boundaries that we have to avoid, come closer, if the whole task is carried out inefficiently.

Below, each of the four principles will be discussed separately.

Discussion of Principle 1

When substances from mines, oil deposits, and other deposits in the lithosphere are used in the technosphere, society controls them for a while but in the very long run, almost all matter will be dispersed into the ecosphere. This means that in the long run there has to be a balance between mining, final depositing, and sedimentation.

Cycling of substances with a minimal leakage is a way to reduce the need for mining below the levels, set by natural sedimentation. Nevertheless, for some substances now in use, such as cadmium, even a very small amount leads to accumulation, and they are so toxic that they should not be recycled at all. These substances should be returned to a safe repository in the solid lithosphere as soon as possible. Cadmium was discussed in this context by van der Voet and Kleijn (1992).

The concentration of a substance in the ecosphere is dependent on the import into the ecosphere (mining and later outflow from the technosphere) and the export out from the ecosphere (sedimentation). What concentration can be accepted in the long run depends on properties such as ecotoxicity, here taken in a broad sense to include effects on the geophysical systems, and bioaccumulation. As noted already, due to the complexity and delay mechanisms in the ecosphere, it is generally impossible to say what concentration will lead to an ecotoxic effect. Therefore, what must at least be achieved is a stop to systematic accumulation. A starting point can be to compare the human-induced concentrations with the natural background concentration. For each substance, two measures are essential: first, the net inflow to the ecosphere, second, the quantity or the concentration within the ecosphere.[5] The average rate of mining minus final depositing must therefore not exceed the capacity for sedimentation. Moreover, the human-induced quantity or concentrations should stay within limits related to the corresponding natural quantities. One consequence of this is that mining will have to be reduced drastically. More efficient use of minerals, recycling, and substitution with renewable resources must be viewed in this context (see the discussion of Principle 4). Due to the first principle, describing the primary events in the causal chain, there will be no long-term benefit from recycling of metals unless this is linked to decreased mining.

Both measures discussed here can be used when deciding which substances are the most urgent to reduce through recycling, substitution, etc. Since the substances will eventually be degraded and will eventually leak from society into the ecosphere, more abundant substances should be substituted for less abundant ones. There are two main reasons for this.

1. The risk for damage in the ecosphere is usually larger if less abundant substances (e.g., copper) leak into the ecosphere than if more abundant substances (e.g., iron) leak to the ecosphere, (see Table 2.1). Biological systems react on concentrations rather than total amounts. The concentration of a rare substance may increase fast in the ecosphere if the society begins to use it. Furthermore, the biological enzyme systems and transport mechanisms are often less adjusted to rare substances than to common substances.

2. The resources within the lithosphere are finite, which means that society, due to the leakage, is forced to extract resources that are more and more difficult to get at. The question of what quantities can be extracted during a certain period of time is therefore relevant for justice between the generations. This is affected by the possibility of substitution by resources from the ecosphere, the development of new technologies for extraction and the further handling of the extracted substances within society, for example how available they are for future generations.

To be more concrete, we have chosen to discuss the situation concerning metals somewhat more in detail.

In Table 2.1 the static reserve life is listed for some metals. The reserve is the economically extractable part of the metal content in the Earth's crust. This part will increase due to higher metal prizes and new technology. Skinner (1987) claims that between 0.001 and 0.01% of the scarce metals in the continental crust is present in separate ores and the rest is present in solid solution in silicate minerals. For the abundant metals there are no such mineralogical barriers. The mean thickness of the continental crust is 36.5 km and the depth to which metal resources can be detected and recovered has been estimated to

Table 2.1. Anthropogenic Stocks and Flows of Metals

Element	Amount in Continental Crust Eg[a]	Static Reserve Life (Year) [b]	Static Sink Life (Year)[c]	Global Future Contamination Index (FCI)[d]	Global Mining Index (GMI)[e]
Abundant metals					
Aluminium	1200000	220	2400	0.01	0.02
Iron	720000	120	29	1.0	1.4
Titanium	82000	70	710	0.02	0.06
Magnesium	15000	9500	15000	<0.01	<0.01
Scarce metals					
Zinc	1200	21	4.9	6.9	8.1
Chromium	1200	100	2.5	2.6	16
Nickel	920	55	13	2.0	3.0
Copper	760	36	1.7	23	24
Lead	200	20	3.4	19	12
Molybdenum	17	50	5.3	4.2	7.5
Cadmium	8.3	27	11	3.0	3.8
Mercury	1.2	25	10	17	3.8

[a]$Eg = $ Exa gram $= 10^{18}$ gram.
[b]Static Reserve Life is the number of years the economically extractable material in the reserve base will last with present mining rate.
[c]Static Sink Life is the number of years it should take to double the amount of the metal in the top soil layer (to 0.2m depth) of land used for the technosphere if all mined metal should be spread there. Vitousek et al. (1986) call this 2 million km[2] area 'the human area'.
[d]Future Contamination Index is the ratio of accumulated global mining to the natural abundance of the same metal in the top soil layer of land used for the technosphere (Wallgren 1992).
[e]Global Mining Index is the ratio of global mining to global weathering.

Sources: Skinner 1987; Sposito 1989; Nriagu 1990; Crowson 1992; and Wallgren 1992.

4.6 km. This means that the theoretical resource life for the scarce metals and the abundant metals are 2–30 times and 6–60 million times greater than the reserve life, respectively.

As mentioned before, almost all mined matter will eventually be dispersed into the ecosphere. It is reasonable to suppose that the metals will accumulate in the soil close to the technosphere, the 'human area'. As a crude measure, we have chosen to define the static sink life as the number of years it would take to double the amount of the metal in the top soil layer (to 0.2 m depth) of the human area if all mined metal should be spread there. A comparison between the reserve life and the sink life shows that the sink capacity and the mining waste rather than the accessibility can be expected to restrict the use of metals.

The metals that are extracted from the lithosphere are accumulated in the technosphere before they leak into the ecosphere. Therefore, there is also good reason to keep accounts of the accumulation in the technosphere. To get a crude picture of the magnitude of the danger from the intake of metals into society, one can compare the accumulated amount of a certain metal (mined from year 1900) in the technosphere with the natural abundance of the same metal in the human area. Wallgren (1992) has studied this ratio for Sweden, the Future Contamination Index (FCI). The global FCI for some metals are given in Table 2.1 FCI can be compared with the critical concentration (lowest concentrations for measurable adverse effects) of heavy metals in forests mor that are three to five times the current baseline values for Cd, Cu, Pb, Zn, Hg, Ni (Tyler 1993).

The global mining index in Table 2.1 relates the anthropogenic weathering (mining) to the natural weathering. The anthropogenic flows exceed the natural flows for all scarce metals. The main conclusion from Table 2.1 is that wherever possible, the industrial society must substitute abundant light metals for scarce metals, mainly because of the limited sink capacity. The light metals are abundant and relatively non-toxic. The fact that they are light is also an important factor to reduce the need for energy supply in many applications.

Besides metals, there are other lithospherical substances that cause large environmental problems. Society has increased the amount of CO_2 in the atmosphere by 25%. Of this increase about 75% is caused by the use of fossil fuels and the remaining 25% is mainly caused by manipulation of forests (Holdren 1990). The latter is covered by Principle 2 and 3. Acidification is another consequence of the extensive burning of fossil fuels. Society has more than doubled the flows of SO_2 in the ecosphere (Holdren 1990). The uranium that is used by the nuclear industry causes risks and damages connected to the mining waste, the enrichment waste, the use in reactors, and the management of spent fuel as waste.[6]

As mentioned earlier the assimilation capacity is probably more restrictive than the limited supply of most of the substances extracted from the lithosphere. Phosphorus is one likely exception from this rule, the main restriction being that no other substance can substitute for phosphorus in the living cell. It is true that phosphorus contributes to the eutrophication of water systems and that the societal extraction of phosphorus from the lithosphere also leads to associated flows of pollutants (the most serious problem is the accumulation of cadmium in the cultivated fields). But these problems can probably be handled by more efficient fertilizing and purification of the phosphorus fertilizer. Phosphorus is an essential macro-nutrient and 90% of the extracted phosphorus is used as fertilizer in agriculture. Phosphorus can be used more efficiently (e.g., through recycling), but the extraction of phosphorus has increased drastically (4.8% per year since 1900) and the static reserve life can be estimated to 150 years[7] (Sheldon 1987; Fantel et al. 1989).

Several substances from the lithosphere are used in the chemistry of life, (e.g., carbon, sulphur, phosphorus, and iron and other essential trace substances, but in carefully regulated quantities). This means that we can allow a net transportation of a limited amount of these kinds of substances from the lithosphere to the ecosphere, if these substances can be incorporated in a sustainable way into an increasing amount of organic material. This implies a careful revision of the stationary state (compare with the example of cultivation of deserts discussed earlier).

Discussion of Principle 2

In the same way as for substances from the lithosphere, the concentrations of society-produced molecules and nuclides in the ecosphere are dependent on the inflow into the ecosphere (production of molecules and nuclides in the technosphere) and the export out from the ecosphere (the rate of breakdown or decay or sedimentation or final depositing). If the concentration of a certain molecule or isotope increases in the ecosphere, so does the amount that breaks down or decays during a certain time period. As for lithospheric materials, besides the flow, the concentration of the molecule or isotope must therefore also be considered. One should make sure that there is no gradual increase. This means that the average rate of producing molecules must not exceed the rate of breakdown and that the corresponding must hold for isotope production. Secondly, the human-induced quantities or concentrations should be related to natural background measures.

The assimilation capacity of the ecosphere is often smaller for persistent substances foreign to nature (e.g., DDT) than for substances from the lithosphere (e.g., metals), because the ecosphere has never adapted to those new substances. Their persistence implies that after being used they accumulate in the ecosphere if they are not destroyed within the technosphere. Thus, continued production of such substances cannot be allowed. In practical terms this means that we have to phase out the use of such compounds completely.

In nuclear power plants, new radioactive nuclides are produced, some of which, (e.g., plutonium), are so dangerous, that they have to be kept separate from the ecosphere until they have decayed, (i.e., for hundreds of thousands or millions of years). The accumulated amount of nuclear materials in nuclear arms and in waste from nuclear power must be deposited in safe repositories in the bedrock. Because of the risk for future nuclear arms, from long-lived highly radioactive waste, a deep enough repository is required, so that the material is practically irretrievable (Swahn 1992). Besides radioactive waste, there may be other society-produced substances which are dangerous and hard to transform and which therefore should be considered for final storage in repositories.

Another important question concerns the flows of new materials that can be important in more efficient technology or in solar technology, such as photovoltaics, electric batteries or super-conducting ceramics. One aspect of these substances is that they are used for capital equipment and not in flows like the present use of oil. Still, it is important that the flows of such materials are carefully planned in agreement with principle 1 and 2. The balance accounts previously discussed are instruments to be used in this planning.

Discussion of Principle 3

Principle 3 concerns the physical conditions for the production capacity within the ecosphere. Society influences this production capacity either through the exchange of substances or through manipulation. The exchange of substances extracted from the lithosphere and substances produced within society is contained in the Principles 1 and 2, respectively. The third principle mainly considers the extraction of resources from the ecosphere and the manipulation of the ecosphere. If the extraction of deposit resources from the lithosphere is restricted according to Principle 1, the society will be even more dependent on the productivity of the ecosphere. This implies that we cannot systematically reduce the production capacity of the ecosphere either through harvesting more than the regeneration rates admit nor through manipulation. On the other hand, the Earth receives 13,000 times more exergy from the sun than is used by the global society. This means that it is not the supply of exergy but rather the material turnover that will set the limit for society's metabolism (Holmberg 1992).

Besides the requirement that the production capacity must not be systematically reduced, it is important to preserve the stability of the ecosphere. High biodiversity is, as mentioned in section 3, an important factor to preserve the stabilizing functions of the ecosphere. The term biodiversity can be used to summarize three types of biological variation: (1) genetical variation within a specific species, (2) the number of species within an ecosystem, (3) the variation of ecosystems (biotopes) within a geographical area.

There is a close connection between the soils and their vegetation. The quality of the soils is often more fundamental than the production of the vegetation on the soils, since soil is more difficult to restore. The vegetation can often be reintroduced if the production capacity of the soil is not damaged and if the specific species are not extinct. It is usually considerably harder to restore eroded slopes (for example, in the Mediterranean region) or salinated soils (for example by the Aral Sea). The production capacity of the pedosphere can be recorded in geographical balance accounts, where quantitative and qualitative measures of the soils are recorded. If a certain areal element changes, for instance, if farmland is turned into highway, then it is removed from one account and inserted into the other. Aspects in such geographic balance accounts are: (1) the biotopes (the diversification of the area), (2) the diversity of species, and (3) the harvest of a biological fund compared to the natural regeneration.

Here (1) and (2) are mostly related to the stability within the area and (3) is related to the biological productivity within the area.

Society's manipulation of land areas often affect the supply of fresh-water. Manipulation of land can decrease the natural refilling. It is therefore important to have a balance account concerning the hydrosphere, (e.g., the extraction from a water reservoir and its natural refilling).

Discussion of Principle 4

The first three principles constitute the external conditions for a sustainable society. If we want to integrate the society within these external conditions, we have to restrain several inflows of natural resources into society in order to limit the outflows which have already outgrown the assimilation capacity of nature. To increase the service flow to the human sphere without increasing the exchange and manipulation, the efficiency of the technosphere must increase, (i.e., more service must be delivered for each unit of exchange and manipulation). To fulfill more human needs and obtain better benefits from the resource use, one can use the resources better through more efficient technology or better organization. Another aspect of efficiency is that resources should be used where they are most needed, (i.e., basic human needs should be given priority over luxury). To contribute to this one can also restrain one's life style and this would imply more moderate demands. Thus, in a societal context, efficiency implies justice. The reason for this is, of course, that efficiency makes sense only if related to a goal, a value, in this case fulfillment of human needs.

Technology

It is obvious that more efficient technology can substitute for energy and other natural resources. The energy efficiency in industrial processes is on the average improved by 1–1.5% every year (Spreng 1993). By studying the exergy efficiency in different processes, one can observe the gap between the actual efficiency and the maximum theoretical efficiency and get a view of the potential for improvements (Wall 1986). This is relevant also for material efficiency. It is desirable that products last long, that the material leakage is small during their use, that they can be reused, and that they are designed so that after use and reuse, different materials can be separated and recycled.

Organization

How technology is handled and organized is often more important than the specific technological efficiency. This is for instance obvious for transportation. It is more important to organize transports so that trains carry cargo in both directions than making the electric motor more efficient. It is also the case for the use of water in households: the way to wash the dishes is often more important than how the taps are constructed.

Certain substances can be used according to Principles 1, 2, and 3 only if closed material cycles are organized within the society. Cycles could be closed within the production process, or in the exchange between producers and consumers. An important condition for successful recycling of materials is that flows are sufficiently pure or separable. Unnecessary mixing of different kinds of materials can destroy this, and should therefore be avoided. The effects of the inevitable loss of quality in materials can be minimized through a cascading use, where each step involves a drop in quality requirements. After each recycling step of a certain material, it should be used in such a way that the quality can be kept on the highest possible level. There are mainly three qualities that are interesting: (1) purity, (2) structure and (3) exergy. For instance a special steel should not be used as reinforcing iron after only one cycle if one wants to save the purity. The bulk structure of wood, for instance, can be utilized, if wood is first used as a construction material, before the fibre structure is used in paper of stepwise declining quality and, finally, the chemical structure is utilized in chemical industry or fuel production and combustion. In the energy sector, one can also improve the exergy efficiency through cascading use of energy, where each step involves a drop in temperature. Besides matter and energy accounts, exergy accounts serve as one instrument to analyze and monitor technical and organizational efficiency.

Since each flow depends for its maintenance on other flows, a reduction in one flow can be expected to have multiplicative effects and lead to reduction also in others.

The localization of infrastructure, industries, and buildings is important to minimize the transportation demand and to create the necessary conditions for more efficient transportation, through work places closer to residence areas, paper mills based on waste paper close to cities, coordinated planning of residential areas, public transport systems, etc.

Closed material flows involve transports. Therefore local recycling is often preferable because the ecological costs of transports are lower. If energy and material exchange is organized locally, it is often easier to control the flows and local conditions can be taken into account in a more optimal way. Local resources may be used, that would not even be considered otherwise, and the need for transports can be reduced.

Local organization of energy and materials exchange can either be maintained for a concentrated settlement or for a spread-out settlement. Concentration can be preferable in activities involving costly equipment and competence (economy of scale) and where the products are valuable but not bulky, so that transportation costs are relatively small. Often central operations can be run more efficiently. Concentration can also be preferable, if for instance, steelworks for scrap iron, paper mills based on waste paper, breweries which handling returnable bottles are placed close to cities. Still, there are factors that restrain the level of concentration for example the assimilation capacity of the ecosphere close to these big cities and substances and products that are dependent on agriculture and forestry (access to large areas), for instance food, biofuel, phosphorus, etc. These examples of opposite cost relations indicate that there probably is some optimal level of concentration.

Demands (expectations)

Of importance are also the human expectations on access to large flows of energy and materials. They are linked to life-style patterns, for instance the possibility of convenient and comfortable travelling, large heated and air-conditioned residential floor area, or the option to amuse oneself with a fast motorboat.

The amount and the type of services that we demand in the end have consequences for the use of resources. The use of services varies a lot despite the fact that the fundamental human needs are the same in all cultures and in all historical periods. Max-Neef (1986) considers those needs to be few and classifiable. He suggests the following classification: permanence (or subsistence), protection, affection, understanding, participation, leisure, creation, identity, (or meaning) and freedom. What changes, both over time and through cultures is not the needs but the forms or the means by which these needs are satisfied. Since many of the fundamental human needs are not directly associated with any large turnover of natural resources, a plausible conclusion is that the society can increase the fulfillment of those needs at the same time as it decreases its use of natural resources.

After we have discussed technology, organization, and demand we want to conclude this section with a discussion of substitution. Principle 4 deals with substitution on different levels namely, the possibilities to substitute more efficient technology, more efficient organization and more moderate demands for natural resources in order to fulfill Principles 1, 2, and 3 and at the same time to meet human needs. Substitution can be realized on different levels,[8] (see Table 2.2).

The two first levels in Table 2.2 deal with the society's choice of material resources (Principles 1, 2, and 3). Level three and four are connected with technology, level five and six are connected with organization and level seven is connected with demands.

One aspect of efficient use of resources is that resources should be used for purposes that are as valuable as possible. As we stated above, this means that they should be used where they are most needed. This, in turn, means that they should be used in a way that is as just as possible. This is standard welfare economics. When money is used as a numeraire, one neglects the fact that the value of money varies according to people's needs. This variation is taken into account in the index of sustainable economic welfare (ISEW), suggested by Daly and Cobb (1989). Thus, the condition of efficiency leads us out of the field that can be analyzed within the field of science and into the field of values.

Table 2.2. Levels of Substitution, Based on Earlier Works (Ayres and Noble 1972; Svedin 1977; Holmberg 1992; Månsson 1993).

Level of substitution	Example
1. The raw material level.	The same material may be obtained from different raw materials with different environmental characteristics, (e.g., hydrocarbons from biota or fossil fuels).
2. The material level.	Aluminium can substitute for copper in electrical power transmission.
3. The component level.	One type of battery may have better properties than one currently in use.
4. The subsystem level.	Electric motors may at one time replace internal combustion engines for cars in local traffic.
5. The system level.	Private cars may be largely replaced by trains for medium and long-distance travelling.
6. The strategic level.	Different strategies can lead to the same goal. If the goal is "clean" environment, then there can be a shift in scientific strategy from environmental pathology to societal prophylaxis.
7. The value level.	Cultural and individual values decide what strategy to chose. Moreover, if people want a sustainable development, this will lead to consequences on all other levels.

Besides societal and human values, there is also an intrinsic value to be attached to life itself and the life supporting systems. This means that even if something is judged as valuable within society, its costs in terms of negative effects on those systems could be so large as to make the total balance negative.

CULTURAL ASPECTS[9]

So far we have defined three external conditions which are physical restrictions for a sustainable exchange of resources and waste between society and nature, and a fourth condition concerning a sustainable mode by which the available resources are metabolized within the society. These conditions imply so large changes in technical and economic judgement that they must be viewed as a shift of paradigm. For this shift to take place and for the practical measures connected to it to be implemented there must be support in the culture and in peoples' values. Therefore we shall pursue the value discussion a little further. This is all the more necessary, since the problems originate in the sociosphere, not in the ecosphere.

For any system to be sustained, there must be a limit to its internal disintegrative forces. Usually they are balanced by controlling forces. Within a society such forces are often exerted by a central authority with access to coercive means. What history tells us is that if coercion is the main mechanism, it works only for a limited time. Then it may come to a clash between the controlling and the splitting forces leading to societal disintegration or reorganization.

The other main method of control is cultural. It is usually connected to religious or other beliefs and to values. Moral rules and taboos have a controlling function, strengthened by rituals, traditions and social control. The basic beliefs and values can be seen as expressions of a common cultural experience. As such they often carry a truth, even if the beliefs are false or meaningless taken literally. To strengthen the foundation of the belief, reference is often made to a divine authority. The necessity of a common secular basis for common global values independent of religious beliefs was stressed in a profound paper by Wole Soyinka (1988).

Sustainability puts restrictions on society's exchange with the surrounding natural systems but also on the structure of society itself. In order to act in a concerted and a consistent way and with a shared responsibility, a society must have a structure that can be seen as legitimate by its citizens. If this is analyzed carefully, such an analysis will probably reach results not very far from those of John Rawls in his classical treatise (Rawls 1971) with the required generalizations. In the context considered here, it is a society valuing not only the present generation but also generations to come; it is a society with global responsibility and solidarity as well as responsibility towards the life and the life-supporting systems of the planet. The responsibility for the planet requires global solidarity and a global cultural base. This must be tied to local development, (i.e., to knowledge of local conditions and possibilities and to local responsibility).

Traditional cultural systems can be quite stable, if external conditions do not change too quickly. Often, however, they lack methods for explicit criticism, and they have often been overthrown by the quasi-rationalism of the modern industrial society. In many cases, the invasion of modern society has been quite destructive.

There is no way back to traditional beliefs, but the traditional knowledge content can be studied scientifically and become part of a general cultural heritage. With the scientific method available, it is possible to revise previous views in the light of new facts. Also the world picture and basic values can be open to a rational discussion. It is then clear that the views still prevailing in the modern industrial society rest on the false image of a small society in an infinite nature. Environmental adaptations have taken place, but they do not concern the society as a whole, only an increasing number of details. The relevant world picture is a more complex one, but, as we have shown elsewhere (Eriksson and Robèrt 1991; Holmberg 1992), also this picture has simple forceful elements.

Values Are Related to Identity

We value what we are, and traditionally the identity related to the family and to the local society has been as strong as or even stronger than the personal identity.

In recent historical times, much effort has been put in fostering a national identity, and manifestations and repressions of this kind of identity have been excessively cruel. Now national identity has lost its dominant function, and a global human identity is needed. The values connected to this identity are the universal human values (UN 1948, for a thorough discussion of justice see Rawls 1971) that have been preached for a long time now, but colonialism, slavery, and more recent forms of exploitation show that these values have not been taken seriously even by the societies that have been preaching them. We have chosen value of human life with dignity as our first value.

The human society is embedded in the ecosphere, and the humans in the global human society are living beings among other life forms in this ecosphere. This gives no reason to deny our human identity, but it makes us realize that the human identity is not sufficient, that standing alone, it leads to a destructive anthropocentrism. In order to take into account human citizenship in the society of living beings, we must value also life as such and, consequently, those systems that support life. Therefore we have chosen continued life on Earth as our second value.

This is nothing radical. It should be possible to reach a wide consensus on the value of human life with dignity and the value of life on Earth. Such a consensus is already manifest in many political declarations but, unfortunately, not in political praxis. The report of The Brundtland Commission (WCED 1987) and the Rio Declaration (UN 1992) may be important steps in this direction. Taken seriously, they would imply a revolution in the global human life. Ecologically sustainable fulfillment of basic human needs would be a primary concern. Development would be much more than a business for special experts; it would involve a widespread co-operative effort between people in different societies all over the globe. Solidarity, justice, and freedom for everyone would become realistic ideals. Nature would be valued for its own sake and not just as a source of raw materials and a processor of waste. There would be serious joint efforts to organize the technosphere within the limited area of $5 \cdot 10^8$ km^2 as efficiently as possible and still to give room to natural systems to continue their lives undisturbed.

Clearly, these values disagree with economic ideas as they are commonly interpreted (For critical reviews, see Etzioni 1988; Daly and Cobb 1989; Max-Neef et al. 1989). However, they clearly agree with the socio-ecological principles stated earlier in this chapter. They give immediate support to Principle 3 and Principle 4. Moreover, they give a purpose to societal actions taking place within the boundaries of the four principles.

THE CREATION OF AN ORGANIZATION TO PROMOTE THE FOUR PRINCIPLES

To initiate and support the necessary paradigmatic change on various levels in the Swedish society a special organization has been created. It identifies corporations and local authorities that would like to take a lead, and then supports them to benefit from the change. The phrase "think globally—act locally" underlines our present urgent need for good examples, to inspire the necessary global cultural change by demonstrating practical steps to go forward. An activity that fulfills all four socio-ecological principles, does not contribute to the build-up of garbage, neither visible garbage nor invisible "molecular" garbage. It does not damage the life-support systems of the ecosphere, and it meets human needs. To achieve this requires a strategy to overcome the short-term contradiction between today's practical economical reality and the four principles of sustainability. The key is to merge economic aspects (such as savings and sound investments in a given economic environment) with the socio-ecological principles into a programme of measures to be taken over a period of time.

These measures must be improvable so that neither economic nor ecological reasons will block the subsequent changes into complete fulfillment of the four principles. Thus, a successful systematic substitution process can change the appearance of the socio-ecological principles from painful restrictions into fascinating challenges that open new possibilities. It is rather so that if a consistent program of change in accordance with the principles, is violated, then this will render costs in the future. Such costs may show up as lost credibility due to sudden changes in the public opinion, "unforeseen" fees or costs or taxes due to legislation, unnecessary expensive changes due to lack of time, limited access to competence/experience, etc. The exemplary organization which starts its training right away, will be prepared when the time comes and thus, will have fewer and less expensive panic solutions.

What is the rationale for an individual corporation or a municipality to take on an active role towards sustainability? The answer is actually quite simple: Savings and investments that are undertaken to reduce the violation of the socio-ecological principles will pay off individually, if they are skilfully performed. The total societal metabolism is now violating the socio-ecological principles. Waste is steadily accumulating and the productive ecosystems are diminishing. This means that the resource potential for health and economy is systematically decreasing. At the same time, the Earth's population is rapidly increasing. This non-sustainable development could be visualized as entering deeper and deeper into a funnel, in which the available space becomes narrower and narrower. To a company, a municipality, or a country—the crucial thing must then be to direct its investments towards the opening of the funnel, rather than into the wall. In reality this means, that the wise investor makes herself/himself less and less economically dependent on a continued process in violation of the principles. The wall of the funnel will make itself more and more visible in the daily economic reality as: more environmental concern among customers, stricter legislation, increasing costs for resources and increasing fees for pollution, tougher competition from other companies who wisely invest themselves towards the opening of the funnel, (i.e., in accordance with the socio-ecological principles).

In concrete terms this means, that the socio-ecological principles should be expressed as a check-list, guiding any investment strategy.

1. Does your organization systematically decrease its economical dependence on underground metals, fuels, and other minerals? Yes? No?
2. Does your organization systematically decrease its economical dependence on persistent unnatural substances? Yes? No?
3. Does your organization systematically decrease its economical dependence on activities which encroach on productive parts of nature, (e.g., long road transports?) Yes? No?
4. Does your organization systematically decrease its economical dependence on using a large amount of resources in relation to added human value? Yes? No?

The exact sizes of different total material flows of matter that are allowed by the socio-ecological principles still remain to be determined. However, one doesn't have to await a detailed analysis of this before applying the principles. For some substances the "permitted" flows per capita are so close to zero, for instance concerning the use of cadmium (Principle 1), that the lack of concrete figures is no problem for strategic planning. And when the "total permitted" flows are much higher, for instance concerning emissions of N_2O (Principle 2), relevant questions can be raised without a detailed quantitative analysis: "Is it possible that we—in our business corporation or municipality—are investing ourselves into a dependence of N_2O emissions that exceeds our "permitted" share of the total assimilation capacity of N_2O?" And even more intriguing: "Knowing that today's total emissions of N_2O cause accumulation of this gas in the atmosphere, are the margins to very severe problems related to further accumulation of N_2O, large enough to give us a secure life-span for this investment?" In this way, the burden of proof is shifted from the public to the participants and their investments. Clear and intellectually solid definitions are helpful, even if they do not immediately imply numerical limits.

Until now, environmental planning at all levels of society, has usually been dealing with limited problems "downstream" in the causal chain. However, it is easier to gain an overview upstream than downstream, due to the smaller complexity.

In consequence with this reasoning, courses on the four principles are offered to companies, local authorities and state authorities through an organization The Natural Step (Robèrt 1992), initiated by one of us (Karlsson, Holmberg, or Robèrt). This organization writes scientific consensus documents on various environmental issues, initiates and supports networks of professional groups, and launches cooperative environmental projects. Experiences from the work with the Natural Step show that there are advantages in describing the goal (a sustainable society), in a consistent and systematic way, and in focusing "upstream" in the causal chain.

Professionals have detailed knowledge within their own fields, but they often lack an overview of what restrictions sustainability implies for their own activities. By giving them a comprehensible picture of the goal and asking them what this implies for their specific activities today, it is possible to inspire them to direct their creativity in a sustainable direction instead of forcing them into a defensive position by confronting them with a limited environmental problem connected to their activity.

This model has been applied for strategic planning in 25 Swedish corporations, and has created investments in the magnitude of more than a thousand million USD. It is applicable in corporations of differing fields of activities for instance manufacturers like Electrolux or JM Constructions, trading-companies like IKEA or Hemköp and service-companies like Swedish McDonald's or Scandic Hotels. The model is also systematically applied by 40 Swedish municipal authorities.

The Natural Step organizations are now being launched also in other countries such as USA, UK, and Australia.

CONCLUSION

We have used basic physical laws, such as the principle of conservation of matter, and the fact that the space for life on Earth is limited, to formulate four socio-ecological principles for a sustainable society aiming at human welfare.

1.   Substances extracted from the lithosphere must not systematically accumulate in the ecosphere.
2.   Society-produced substances must not systematically accumulate in the ecosphere.
3.   The physical conditions for production and diversity within the ecosphere must not systematically be deteriorated.
4.   The use of resources must be effective and just with respect to meeting human needs.

The socio-ecological principles thus deal with the physical limits for society (Daly's Plimsoll line) and the efficiency of society within those limits. But efficiency is meaningful only if related to purpose and value. The values that must be honored in a sustainable society are the value of human life with dignity and the value of life on Earth. The first implies that human welfare and justice are societal goals. The second implies that life and life-supporting systems are valued in their own right and not only for their support of human society.

When studying society's influence on nature, it is very hard to reach a scientific consensus about effects late in the causal chain, (e.g., what concentration of PCB gives a specific effect in nature). But if the focus is moved earlier in the causal chain, it can often be easier to reach a consensus, (e.g., whether a persistent ecotoxic substance should be allowed to leak from society and accumulate in nature). The socio-ecological principles do not lead to precise answers about critical loads of specific substances but they define a qualitative goal. This goal can be used to structure the discussion on a higher system level.

Our principles and values thus refer to a stationary sustainable situation and describe a goal (a sustainable society). One reason to use these principles and values and to point out the goal in pedagogical situations, is that it is simple and inspiring. Also for dealing with the complications of the transition (the first phase of a sustainable development), it is useful to have the goal stated as clearly as possible. As long as one knows the main path one can, when necessary, allow oneself some small deviations along the way.

The principles stated here and slightly modified forms of them have been tested in different pedagogical situations and found to function well. Our experience within the organization The Natural Step is that they are well suited to function operationally when applied to evaluate project plans for business enterprises or political bodies. Questions to be asked in such situations are: "Is the purpose and operation of this project in agreement with the basic values?" "Is it a step towards the fulfillment of the socio-ecological principles?" For an ongoing activity which does not violate the values, the first question to be asked is: "Could we change our way of operation at zero or negligible, or even negative, cost, in such a way that we conform better with the principles of sustainability?" Any actor who decides to honor sustainability should make up a plan for the activity in accordance with the values and the principles.

As we have tried to show, our chapter is also a step in a scientific development, where the agenda is set not primarily by intrinsic scientific interest, but where this interest still plays a very important role in structuring the discussion.

ACKNOWLEDGMENTS

We are grateful to all persons in the business-corporations, municipalities and in other organizations within The Natural Step's network, who have taken part in the dialogue and started to apply the socio-ecological principles in their concrete planning.

We express our gratitude to Christian Azar, Herman E. Daly, Sten Karlsson, and Kristian Lindgren for critical reading and constructive suggestions to our manuscript.

Financial support from The Swedish Council for Building Research, The Swedish Waste Research Council and The Bank of Sweden Tercentenary Foundation is gratefully acknowledged.

NOTES

1. *Exergy* is a thermodynamic quantity closely related to the first law of thermodynamics as well as the second law. It is *a measure of ordered energy* (Gibbs 1973 and Rant 1956; Wall 1986; Eriksson et al. 1987). The exergy of a certain system is the amount of perfectly ordered energy, such as mechanical work, that can, in principle, be extracted from the system in an ideal reversible process. In irreversible processes, where entropy is being produced, exergy disappears; *the exergy loss is proportional to the entropy production*. Often, exergy is a more useful measure than entropy.
2. These definitions have earlier been used by Holmberg and Karlsson (1992). They deviate from current usage. The reason is that society influences more than the biosphere, and depends on more than is traditionally included in the concept of biosphere (the part of the planet where life is active). An example is the deterioration of the ozone layer.
3. In some cases, materials from the lithosphere may have to be returned by society rather than by natural processes. This is the case with nuclear waste.
4. There has been many attempt to develop principles for sustainability on a more general level, of which the nine principles for sustainable living from The World Conservation Union (IUCN), The United Nations Environment Program (UNEP) and The World Wide Fund For Nature (WWF) probably are the most widely spread (IUCN/UNEP/WWF 1991). However, in this paper we focus on complementary principles, (i.e., principles that do not mix goals and means, but focus on what that has to be fulfilled in a sustainable society (the goal)).
5. If the concentration of a certain substance increases in the ecosphere, so does the sedimentation of this substance. Therefore, besides the inflow, the concentration of the substance must also be considered.
6. The static reserve life of uranium is only about 70 years using the present once-through nuclear fuel "cycle" (OECD 1990). This includes resonably assured resources and estimated additional resources at cost less than $130/kg U. However, if alternative fuel cycles based on plutonium recycling were introduced the static reserve life of uranium would be more than one hundred times greater. But in such a "plutonium economy" the risks and potential damages are considerably higher than those of the present use of nuclear energy.
7. Estimated global reserves of phosphorus are 2 200 Tg (Sheldon 1987) and the use of phosphorus for fertilizers is estimated to 15 Tg in 1985 (Fantel et al. 1989).
8. This discussion is based on a number of earlier works (Ayres and Noble 1972; Svedin 1977; Holmberg 1992 and Månsson 1993). One can also classify substitution according to types of substitution, (e.g., material for material, material for energy, labor for natural resources, capital for natural resources and time for natural resources).
9. Part of the discussion below was reported in a paper to a UNESCO conference (Eriksson 1993).

REFERENCES

Ayres, R. U. and A. V. Kneese. 1969. Production, consumption, and externalities. *American Economic Review* 59: 282.

Ayres, R. U. and S. Noble. 1972. Materials Scarcity and Substitution, IRT-302-R.

Ayres, R. U. 1978. Resources, environment and economics: Application of the Materials/Energy balance principle. New York: John Wiley and Sons.

Crowson, P. 1992. Minerals Handbook 1992-93. New York: Stockton Press.

Daly, H. E. and J. B. Cobb Jr. 1989. For the Common Good. Redirecting the Economy Toward Community, the Environment and a Sustainable Future. Boston: Beacon Press.

Daly, H. E. 1990. Towards some operational principles of sustainable development. *Ecological Economic* 2: 1–6.

Daly, H. E. 1991. Elements of environmental macroeconomics. In Ecological Economics, ed. R. Costanza. New York: Colombia University Press.

Dreborg, K-H and J. B. Steenx. 1995. Rationale of backcasting, Draft, fms 25, National Defense Research Establishment, Stockholm, Sweden.

Eriksson K. E., K. Lindgren, and B. Månsson. 1987. Structure, Context, Complexity, Organization. Singapore: World Scientific.

Eriksson K. E. 1992. Physical Foundations of Ecological Economics In Human Responsibility and Global Change, eds. Hansson and Jungen. (International Conference on Human Ecology, Göteborg 1991), University of Göteborg.

Eriksson, K.-E. and K. H. Robèrt. 1991. From the Big bang to cyclic societies. *Acta Oncol: Reviews in Oncology* 4: 2, 5.

Eriksson, K.-E. 1993. Science and research for a global cultural development. Note prepared for the meeting on UNESCO Chairs for Sustainable Development, University of Parana, Curitiba, 1-4 July, 1993.

Etzioni, A. 1988. The Moral Dimension: Toward a New Economics. New York: The Free Press.

Fantel R. J., R. J. Hurdelbrink, and D. J. Shields. 1989. World phosphate supply. *Natural Resources Forum*, Aug. 1989, 178–190.

Gibbs, J. W. 1873. Collected Works, Vol I, p 53. Yale University Press, New Haven 1948; Originally published in *Trans Conn Acad* Vol II, 382–404.

Holdren, J. P. 1990. Energy in Transition. *Scientific American* September 1990.

Holdren, J. P., G. C. Daily, and P. R. Ehrlich. 1992. The Meaning of Sustainability: Biogeophysical Aspects. Expanded version of a keynote presentation at the International Conference on the Definition and Measurement of Sustainability: The Biophysical Foundation, Washington, DC, 22-25 June 1992.

Holmberg, J. 1992. Resource-Theoretical Principles for a Sustainable Development. Licentiate Thesis. Institute of Physical Resource Theory, Chalmers University of Technology and University of Göteborg. (In Swedish)

Holmberg, J. and S. Karlsson. 1992. On designing socio-ecological indicators. In Society and Environment: A Swedish Research Perspective. eds. U. Svedin and B. Hägerhäll Aniansson. Dordrecht: Kluwer Academic Publishers.

Jacobs, M. 1991. The Green Economy. London Pluto Press.

Max-Neef, M. 1986. Human-scale economics: The challenges ahead. In The Living Economy, ed. P. Ekins. London: Routledge and Kegan Paul.

Max-Neef, M., Elizalde, and M. Hopenhay et al. 1989. Human scale development: An option for the future. *Development Dialogue* 1989: 1.

Månsson, B. 1993. Environment and Sustainability. Liber-Hermods, Malmö. (In Swedish)

Nriagu, J. O. 1990. Global metal pollution - Poisoning the biosphere? *Environment* 32: (7) 7–33.

OECD, 1990. Uranium—Resources, Production and Demand, OECD, Paris, France.

Rant, Z. 1956. Exergie, ein neues Wort für 'technische Arbeitsfähigkeit', Forschung auf dem gebiete des Ingenieurswesens 22(1) :36.

Rawls, J. 1971. A Theory of Justice, Cambridge MA: Harvard University Press.

Robèrt, K. H. 1992. The Necessary Step, Ekerlids förlag, Stockholm, Sweden (In Swedish)

Robinson, J.B. 1990. Future under glass—A recipe for people who hate to predict. *Futures* October.

Sheldon R. P. 1987. Industrial Minerals—with emphasis on phosphate rock. In Resources and World Development, eds. D. J. McLaren and B. Skinner. Wiley.

Skinner, B. J. 1987. Supplies of Geochemically Scarce Metals. In Resources and World Development, eds. D. J. McLaren and B. J. Skinner. New York: John Wiley and Sons.

Soyinka, W. 1988. Religion and Human Rights, Index on Censorship 17: 5, 82.

Sposito, G. 1989. The Chemistry of Soils. Oxford: Oxford University Press.

Spreng, D. 1993. Possibilities for substitution between energy, time and information. *Energy Policy* January.

Swahn, J. 1992. The Long-term Nuclear Explosives Predicament: The Final Disposal of Militarily Usable Fissile Material in Nuclear Waste from Nuclear Power and from the Elimination of Nuclear Weapons. Ph.D. Thesis. Chalmers University of Technology, Göteborg.

Svedin, U. 1977. Substitution processes, analyzed according to type and level in Substitution — to change resources, The Secretariat for Futures Studies, Stockholm.

Tilman, D. and J. A. Downing. 1994. Biodiversity and stability in grasslands. *Nature* 365: 363–365.

Tyler, G. 1993. Critical Concentrations of Heavy Metals In the Mor Horizon of Swedish Forests. Department of Ecology, Soil Ecology, University of Lund, Östra Vallgatan 14, S-223 61 Lund.

United Nations. 1948. The Universal Declaration of Human Rights. 10 December.

United Nations. 1992. The Rio Declaration and Agenda 21.

van der Voet, E. and R. Kleijn. 1992. Cadmium recycling: For better or worse?, Paper for ISEE confrence, August 3-6 1992, Stockholm.

Vitousek, P. M. et al. 1986. Human appropriation of the products of photosynthesis. *Bioscience* 36: 368–373.

Wall, G. 1986. Exergy — a Useful Concept. Ph. D. Thesis. Institute of Physical Resource Theory, Göteborg.

Wallgren, B. 1992. Basis of the Ecocycle Society, The Environmental Advisory Council, Ministry of the Environment and Natural Resources, Stockholm. (In Swedish).

WCED. 1987. Our Common Future, The World Commission on Environment and Development. Oxford: Oxford University Press.

3 CONSUMPTION: VALUE ADDED, PHYSICAL TRANSFORMATION, AND WELFARE[1]

Herman E. Daly
School of Public Affairs
University of Maryland
College Park, MD 20742

OVERVIEW

Consumption is the disarrangement of matter, the using up of value added that inevitably occurs when we use goods. We consume not only value added by human agents of labor and capital, but also value previously added by nature. We are consuming natural value added, converting raw materials into waste, depleting and polluting, faster than nature can absorb the pollutants and regenerate the resources. Consumption, that is, the transformation of natural capital into manmade capital and then ultimately into waste, leads to the basic question of what is the optimal extent of this transformation. What is the optimal scale of the economic subsystem (population times per capita resource consumption), the scale beyond which further transformation of natural into manmade capital costs us more in terms of natural capital services lost than it benefits us in terms of manmade capital services gained. Growing beyond the optimum is by definition anti economic. The North's over-consumption and the South's overpopulation are the consequences of anti-economic growth.

INTRODUCTION

The total of resource consumption (throughput), by which the economic subsystem lives off the containing ecosystem, is limited—because the ecosystem that both supplies the throughput and absorbs its wastes products is itself limited. The Earth ecosystem is finite, non-growing, materially closed, and while open to the flow of solar energy, that flow is also non growing and finite. Historically these limits were not generally binding, because the subsystem was small relative to the total system. The world was "empty". But now it is "full", and the limits are more and more binding—not necessarily like brick walls, but more like stretched rubber bands.

The total flow of resource consumption is the product of population times per capita resource consumption. Many people have for a long time urged the wisdom of limiting population growth—few have recognized the need to limit consumption growth. In the face of so much poverty in the world it seems immoral to some to even talk about limiting consumption. But populations of cars, buildings, TVs, refrigerators, livestock, and yes, even of trees, fish, wolves, and giant pandas, all have in common with the population of human bodies that they take up space and require a throughput for their production, maintenance, and disposal. Nevertheless, some think the solution to human population growth lies in increasing the growth of populations of all the commodities whose services we consume. The "demographic transition" will automatically stop population growth if only per capita consumption grows fast enough. Arguing that one term of a product will stop growing if only the other term grows faster, is not very reassuring if it is the product of the two terms that is limited. Will the average Indian's consumption have to rise to that of the average Swede before Indian fertility falls to the Swedish level? Can the eroding and crowded country of India support that many cars, power plants, buildings, etc.?

Never fear, the same people who brought you the demographic transition are now bringing you the Information Reformation, (a.k.a. the "dematerialized economy"). McDonalds™ will introduce the "info-burger", consisting of a thick patty of information between two slices of silicon, thin as communion wafers so as to emphasize the symbolic and spiritual nature of consumption. We can also dematerialize human beings by breeding smaller people—after all if we were half the size there could be twice as many of us—indeed we would have to dematerialize people if we were to subsist on the dematerialized[2] GNP! We can eat lower on the food chain, and we can be more resource-efficient, but we cannot eat recipes. The Information Reformation, like the demographic transition before it, expands a germ of truth into a whale of a fantasy.

While all countries must worry about both population and per capita resource consumption, it is evident that the South needs to focus more on population, and the North more on per capita resource consumption. This fact will likely play a major role in all North/South treaties and discussions. Why should the South control its population if the resources saved thereby are merely gobbled up by Northern over consumption? Why should the North control its over consumption if the saved resources will merely allow a larger number of poor people to subsist at the same level of misery? Without for a minute minimizing the necessity of population control, it is nevertheless incumbent on the North to get serious about consumption control. Toward this end, a reconsideration of the meaning of consumption is offered below.

CONSUMPTION AND VALUE ADDED

When we speak of consumption, what is it that we think of as being consumed? Alfred Marshall reminded us of the laws of conservation of matter/energy and the consequent impossibility of consuming the material building blocks of which commodities are made.

Man cannot create material things—his efforts and sacrifices result in changing the form or arrangement of matter to adapt it better for the satisfaction of his wants—as his production of material products is really nothing more than a rearrangement of matter which gives it new utilities, so his consumption of them is nothing more than a disarrangement of matter which destroys its utilities (Marshall 1964).

What we destroy or consume in consumption is the improbable arrangement of those building blocks, arrangements that give utility for humans, arrangements that were, according to Marshall, made by humans for human purposes. This utility added to matter/energy by human action is not production in the sense of creation of matter/energy, which is just as impossible as destruction by consumption. Useful structure is added to matter/energy (natural resource flows) by the agency of labor and capital stocks. The value of this useful structure imparted by labor and capital is called 'value added' by economists. This value added is what is "consumed", (i.e., used up in consumption). New value needs to be added again by the agency of labor and capital before it can be consumed again. That to which value is being added is the flow of natural resources, conceived ultimately as the indestructible building blocks of nature. The value consumed by humans is, in this view, no greater than the value added by humans—consumption plus savings equals national income— which in turn is equal to the sum of all value added. In the standard economist's vision we consume only that value which we added in the first place. And then we add it again, and consume it again, etc. This vision is formalized in the famous diagram of the isolated circular flow of value between firms (production) and households (consumption), found in the initial pages of every economics textbook.

For all the focus on value added one would think that there would be more discussion. But modern economists say no more about it than Marshall. It is just matter, and its properties are not very interesting. In fact they are becoming ever less interesting to economists as science uncovers their basic uniformity. As Barnett and Morse (1963) put it: "Advances in fundamental science have made it possible to take advantage of the uniformity of matter/energy—a uniformity that makes it feasible, without preassignable limit, to escape the quantitative constraints impose by the charter of the earth's crust".

That to which value is being added are merely homogeneous, indestructible building blocks—atoms in the original sense—of which there is no conceivable scarcity. That to which value is added is therefore inert, undifferentiated, interchangeable, and superabundant—very dull stuff indeed, compared to the value-adding agents of labor with all its human capacities, and capital that embodies the marvels of human knowledge. It is not surprising that value added is the centerpiece of economic accounting, and that the presumably passive stuff to which value is added has received minimal attention (Daly and Cobb 1994).

Three examples will show how little attention is given to that to which value is added, which for brevity I will refer to as "resources". Some Philistines (non-economists as they are now called, with even greater condescension) have questioned whether there are enough resources in the world for everyone to use them at the rate Americans do. This ignorant fear is put to rest by Professor Lester Thurow (1980), who points out that the question assumes that "the rest of the world is going to achieve the consumption standards of the average American without at the same time achieving the productivity standards of the average American. This of course is algebraically impossible. The world can consume only what it can produce."

You can only disarrange matter (consume) if you have previously arranged it (produced). Resources are totally passive recipients of form added by labor and capital. Value added is everything, and it is impossible to subtract value that was never added. So if you are consuming it you must have produced it, either recently or in the past. More and more high consuming people just means more and more value was added. Where else could the arrangements of matter have come from? It is "algebraically impossible" for consumption to exceed value added, at least in the economist's tight little abstract world of the circular flow of exchange value.

A second example comes from Professor William Nordhaus, who said that global warming would have only a small effect on the U.S. economy because basically only agriculture is sensitive to climate, and agriculture is only 3% of total value added, of GNP. Evidently it is the value added to seeds, soil, sunlight, and rainfall by labor and capital that keeps us alive, not the seeds, soil, and sunlight themselves. Older economists might have asked about what happens to marginal utility, price, and the percentage of GNP going to food, when food becomes very scarce, say, due to a drought? What about the inelasticity of demand for necessities? Could not the 3% of GNP accounted for by agriculture easily rise to 90% during a famine? But these considerations give mere stuff a more than passive role in value, and diminish the dogmatic monopoly of value added by human agents of labor and capital.

The importance of mere stuff is frequently downplayed by pointing out that the entire extractive sector accounts for a mere 5-6% of GNP. But if the 95% of value added is not independent of the 5% in the extractive sector, but rather depends upon it—is based on it— then the impression of relative unimportance is false. The image this conjures in my mind is that of an inverted pyramid balanced on its point. The 5-6% of the volume of the pyramid near the point on which it is resting represents the GNP from the extractive sector. The rest of the pyramid is value added to extracted resources. That 5% is the base on which the other 95% rests, that to which its value is added. Value cannot be added to nothing. Adding value is more like multiplication than addition—we multiply the value of stuff by labor and capital. But multiplying by zero always gives zero. Indeed, since the value of the extracted resources themselves (the 5-6% of GNP) represents mostly value added in extraction, practically the entire pyramid of value added is resting on a tiny point of near zero dimension representing the *in situ* value of the resources (user cost). This image of a growing and tottering pyramid makes me want to stop thinking exclusively about value added and think some more about that to which value is being added. What, exactly, is holding up this pyramid of value added? The size of the pyramid tells us nothing about the size of the resource base upon which it rests.

A third example comes from the theory of production and the customary use of a multiplicative form for the production function, the most popular being the Cobb-Douglas. Frequently production is treated as a function of capital and labor alone—resources are omitted entirely. But now economists have taken to including resources. However, the welcome step toward realism thus taken is very small, because, although resources are now necessary for production, the amount of resources needed for any given level of output can become arbitrarily small, approaching zero, as long as capital or labor are substituted in sufficient quantities. And it is implicitly assumed that the extra capital and labor can be produced without extra resources! Georgescu-Roegen (1979) referred to this paper and pencil exercise as Solow's and Stiglitz's "conjuring trick".

CONSUMPTION AND PHYSICAL TRANSFORMATION

The vision sketched above, that of Marshall, of Barnett and Morse, and of all textbooks founded on the circular flow of value added, is entirely consistent with the first law of thermodynamics. Matter/energy is not produced or consumed, only transformed. But this vision embodies an astonishing oversight— it completely ignores the second law of thermodynamics (Georgescu-Roegen 1971; Soddy 1922). Matter is arranged in production, disarranged in consumption, rearranged in production, etc. The second law tells us that all this rearranging and recycling of material building blocks takes energy, that energy itself is not recycled, and that on each cycle some of the material building blocks are dissipated beyond recall. It remains true that we do not consume matter/energy, but we do consume (irrevocably use up) the capacity to rearrange matter/energy. Contrary to the implication of Barnett and Morse, matter/energy is not at all uniform in the quality most relevant to economics—namely its capacity to receive and hold the rearrangements dictated by human purpose, the capacity to receive the imprint of human knowledge, the capacity to embody value added. The capacity of matter/energy to embody value added is not uniform, and it wears out and must be replenished. It is not totally passive. If the economic system is to keep going it cannot be an isolated circular flow. It must be an open system, receiving matter and energy from outside to make up natural value added as a subsidy, a free gift of nature. The greater the natural subsidy, the less the cost of labor and capital (value added) needed for further arrangement. The less the humanly added value, the lower the price, and the more rapid the use. Oil from East Texas was a much greater net energy subsidy from nature to the economy than is offshore Alaskan oil. But its price was much lower precisely because it required less value added by labor and capital.[3] The larger the natural subsidy, the lower its price and the faster we use it up!

Thanks in part to this natural subsidy, the economy has grown relative to the total ecosystem to such an extent that the basic pattern of scarcity has changed. It used to be that adding value was limited by the supply of agents of transformation, labor and capital. Now, value added is limited more by the availability of resources subsidized by nature to the point that they can receive value added. Mere knowledge means nothing to the economy until it becomes incarnate in physical structures. Low-entropy matter/energy is the restricted gate through which knowledge is incorporated in matter and becomes manmade capital. No low-entropy matter/energy, no capital—regardless of knowledge.[4] Of course, new knowledge may include discovery of new low-entropy resources, and new methods of transforming them to better serve human needs. But new knowledge may also discover new limits, and new impossibility theorems. New knowledge must always be a surprise. To assume that it will be always a pleasant surprise is unwarranted.

The physical growth of the subsystem is the transformation of natural capital into manmade capital. A tree is cut and turned into a table. We gain the service of the table; we lose the service of the tree. In a relatively empty world (small economic subsystem, ecosystem relatively empty of human beings and their artifacts) the service lost from fewer trees was nil, and the service gained from more tables was significant. In today's relatively full world fewer trees mean loss of significant services, and more tables are not so important if most households already have several tables, as in much of the world they do. Of course continued population growth will keep the demand for tables up, and we will incur ever greater sacrifices of natural services by cutting more and more trees, as long as population keeps growing. The size or scale of the economic subsystem is best thought of as per capita resource consumption times population (which of course is the same as total resource consumption). The point is that there is both a cost and a benefit to increasing the scale of the subsystem (total consumption). The benefit is economic services gained (more tables); the cost is ecosystem services sacrificed (fewer trees to sequester CO_2, provide wildlife habitat, erosion control, local cooling, etc.). As scale increases, marginal costs tend to rise, marginal benefits tend to fall. Equality of marginal costs and benefits define the optimal scale, beyond which further growth in scale (total consumption) would be anti-economic.

As we come to an optimal, or mature scale, production is no longer for growth but for maintenance. A mature economy, like a mature ecosystem (Odum 1969), shifts from a regime of growth efficiency (maximize P/B, or production per unit of biomass stock) to a regime of maintenance efficiency (maximize the reciprocal, B/P, or the amount of biomass stock maintained per unit of new production). Production is the maintenance cost of the stock and should be minimized. As Boulding (1945) argued almost fifty years ago, "Any discovery which renders consumption less necessary to the pursuit of living is as much an economic gain as a discovery which improves our skills of production. Production—by which we mean the exact opposite of consumption, namely the creation of valuable things—is only necessary in order to replace the stock pile into which consumption continually gnaws."

CONSUMPTION AND WELFARE

Welfare is the service of want satisfaction rendered by stocks of capital, both manmade and natural. The proper economic object is to transform natural into manmade capital to the optimal extent (i.e., to the point where total service — the sum of services from natural and manmade capital is a maximum). As discussed in the previous section, this occurs where the marginal benefit of services of more manmade capital is just equal to the marginal cost of natural services sacrificed when the natural capital that had been yielding those services is transformed into manmade capital. The theoretical existence of an optimal scale of the economic subsystem is clear in principle. What remains vague are the measures of the value of services, especially of natural capital, but also of manmade capital. But if economic policy is anything it is the art of dialectically reasoning with vague quantities in the support of prudent actions. We can have reasons for believing that an optimum scale exists, and that we are either above it or below it, without knowing exactly where it is. For policy purposes a judgment about which side of the optimum we are on is what is critical. Reasons are offered below for believing that we (both the U.S. and the world as a whole) have overshot the optimal scale (i.e., that the marginal benefits of growth are less than commonly thought; that the marginal costs are greater than commonly thought; and that the marginal costs are on the whole greater than the marginal benefits).

Welfare is not a function of consumption flows, but of capital stocks. We cannot ride to town on the maintenance costs, the depletion and replacement flow of an automobile, but only in complete automobile, a member of the current stock of automobiles. Once again Boulding (1949) got it right fifty years ago," I shall argue that it is the capital stock from which we derive satisfactions, not from the additions to it (production) or the subtractions from it (consumption): that consumption, far from being a desideratum, is a deplorable property of the capital stock which necessitates the equally deplorable activities of production: and that the objective of economic policy should not be to maximize consumption or production, but rather to minimize it (i.e., to enable us to maintain our capital stock with as little consumption or production as possible)."

This shift from maximizing production efficiency toward maximizing maintenance efficiency is the exact economic analog of the shift in ecosystems mentioned earlier, as they reach maturity (i.e., from maximizing P/B to maximizing the reciprocal, B/P). As a mature scale is reached, production is seen more and more as a cost of maintaining what already exists rather than the source of additional services from added stock. The larger something has grown, the greater, are its maintenance costs. More new production, more throughput, is required just to keep the larger stock constant against the entropic ravages of rot, rust, and randomization.

Boulding's and Odum's insights can be expressed in a simple identity (Daly 1991).

$$\frac{\text{Service}}{\text{Throughput}} = \frac{\text{Service}}{\text{Stock}} \; \text{X} \; \frac{\text{Stock}}{\text{Throughput}}$$

Stocks are at the center of analysis. On the one hand it is the stock that yields service; on the other it is the stock that is regrettably consumed and consequently requires maintenance by new production, which in turn requires new throughput and new sacrifices of natural capital with consequent reductions of the service of natural capital. We can define growth as increase in throughput, holding the two right-hand ratios constant. Service thus increases in proportion to throughput as a result of growth. Development can be defined as an increase in service from increases in the two right-hand efficiency ratios, holding throughput constant. 'Economic growth', growth in GNP, is a conflation of these two processes: (1) growth (physical increase) and (2) development (qualitative improvements that allow more stock maintenance per unit of throughput, and more service per unit of stock). Since physical growth is limited by physical laws, while qualitative development is not, or at least not in the same way, it is imperative to separate these two very different things. Failure to make this distinction is what has made "sustainable development" so hard to define. With the distinction it is easy to define sustainable development as "development without growth—without growth in throughput beyond environmental regenerative and absorptive capacities."[5] So far the politicians and economists are so wedded to growth that they insist that economic growth is itself the main characteristic of sustainable development, and therefore speak in muddled terms like "sustainable growth" (e.g., the President's Council on Environmental Quality).

If we accept that it is the stock of capital that yields service (capital in Irving Fisher's sense, including the stock of consumer goods as well as producer goods), for that which is dissipated to the outside. What is outside? The environment. What is the environment? It is a complex ecosystem that is finite, non growing and materially closed, while open to a non growing, finite flow of solar energy.

Seeing the economy as an open subsystem forces us to realize that consumption is not only disarrangement within the subsystem, but involves disarrangements in the rest of the system, the environment. Taking matter/energy from the larger system, adding value to it, using up the added value, and returning the waste, clearly alters the environment. The matter/energy we return is not the same as the matter/energy we take in. If it were, we could simply use it again and again in a closed circular flow. Common observation tells us, and the entropy law confirms, that waste matter/energy is qualitatively different from raw materials. Low-entropy matter/energy comes in, high-entropy matter/energy goes out, just as in an organism's metabolism. We irrevocably use up not only the value we added by rearrangement, but also the preexisting arrangement originally imparted by nature, as well as the very energetic capacity to further arrange, also provided by nature. We not only consume the value we add to matter, but also the value that was added by nature before we imported it into the economic subsystem, and that was necessary for it to be considered a resource in the first place. Capacity to rearrange used up within the subsystem can be restored by importing low-entropy matter/energy from the larger system and exporting high-entropy matter/energy back to it. But the rates of import and export, determined largely by the scale of the subsystem, must be consistent with the complex workings of the parent system, the ecosystem. The scale of the subsystem matters.

From this perspective value is still being added to resources by the agents of labor and capital. But that to which value is added is not inert, indifferent, uniform building blocks or atoms. Value is added to that matter/energy which is most capable of receiving and embodying the value being added to it. That receptivity might be thought of as "value added by nature". Carbon atoms scattered in the atmosphere can receive value added only with the enormous expenditure of energy and other materials. Carbon atoms structured in a tree can be rearranged much more easily. Concentrated copper ore can hold value added, atoms of copper at average crustal abundance cannot. Energy concentrated in a lump of coal can help us add value to matter; energy at equilibrium temperature in the ocean or atmosphere cannot. The more work done by nature, the more concentrated and receptive the resource is to having value added to it, the less capital and labor will have to be expended in rearranging it to better suit our purposes.

From a utility or demand perspective value added by nature ought to be valued equally with value added by labor and capital. But from the supply or cost side it is not, because value added by humans has a real cost of disutility of labor and an opportunity cost of both labor and capital use. We tend to treat then we still must ask how much extra welfare do we get from extra manmade capital stock, say in the U.S. at the present time?   How much extra cost in terms of sacrificed service of natural capital is required by the transformation of natural capital into the extra manmade capital?[6] We do not have good measures of costs and benefits of aggregate growth, so we must rely on common sense "dead reckoning", plus those preliminary measures that we do have, such as the Index of Sustainable Economic Welfare (ISEW) which certainly suggests that growth in GNP in the U.S. has passed the optimum in terms of welfare (Daly and Cobb 1994; Cobb and Cobb 1994).

CONCLUSION

We consume not only value added by human agents of labor and capital, but also value previously added by nature. We are consuming value added, converting raw materials into waste, depleting and polluting, faster than nature can absorb the pollutants and regenerate the resources. Economists who tell us not to worry because it is algebraically impossible for us to consume more value than we added have studied too much algebra and not enough biology and physics.   Consumption, that is, the transformation of natural capital into manmade capital and then ultimately into waste, leads to the basic question of what is the optimal extent of this transformation. Growing beyond the optimum is by definition anti-economic. Currently growth is anti-economic, as indicated by our "dead reckoning" considerations and the ISEW. The future path of progress therefore is not growth, but development—not an increase in throughput, but increases in the efficiency ratios (maintenance efficiency and service efficiency).

The consumer society must pay attention to what Al Gore (1992) said in his excellent, but too soon forgotten book, *Earth in the Balance*: ".....our civilization is, in effect, addicted to the consumption of the earth itself."   We absolutely must break that addiction. Economists can help break the addiction by remembering and finally taking seriously what Boulding (1949) taught us fifty years ago: "Consumption is the death of capital, and the only valid arguments in favor of consumption are the arguments in favor of death itself".

NOTES

1. This essay is dedicated to the memory of Kenneth Boulding (1910-1993)—great economist, inspiring teacher, and generous friend. I am grateful for the helpful suggestions from Paul Ekins and Tom Tietenberg.
2. However, some very good work is being done by groups who, unfortunately in my view, have adopted this term (e.g., the Wuppertal Institute).
3. Differential rent would equalize the price of both oil sources if demand were sufficient for them to be used simultaneously. But they are used sequentially, and the differential rent is never charged against the earlier subsidy. The energy rate of return on investment in petroleum has been declining, so that the real subsidy to the economy has been declining, even while the

contribution of higher priced petroleum to the GNP has been rising (Gever et al. 1986; Cleveland et al. 1984).

4. As geologist Earl Cook, (1982) wrote: "without the enormous amount of work done by nature in concentrating flows of energy and stocks of resources, human ingenuity would be onanistic. What does it matter that human ingenuity may be limitless, when matter and energy are governed by other rules than is information?"

5. This is the definition of a sustainable scale. Sustainability does not imply optimality—we may prefer another sustainable scale, one with more or less natural capital, but still sustainable. I think it would be reasonable to consider sustainability as a necessary but not sufficient condition of optimality. But in current economic theory sustainability is not implied by optimality—maximizing present value at positive discount rates implies writing off the future beyond some point and liquidating it for the benefit of the present and near future.

6. Reasoning in terms of broad aggregates has its limitations. Converting natural into manmade capital embraces both the extravagant conversion of tropical hardwoods into toothpicks, and the frugal conversion of pine trees into shelters for the homeless. The point is not that all conversions of natural into manmade capital simultaneously cease being worthwhile, but rather that ever fewer remain worthwhile as growth continues.

REFERENCES

Barnett, H. and C. Morse. 1963. Scarcity and Growth. Baltimore: Johns Hopkins University Press.

Boulding, K. 1945. The consumption concept in economic theory. *American Economic Review* May: 2.

Boulding, K. 1949. Income or Welfare? *Review of Economic Studies* 17: 79–81.

Cleveland, C. et al. 1984. Energy and the U.S. economy: A Biophysical perspective. *Science* 225: 890–897.

Cobb, C. W. and J. B. Cobb. Jr. 1994. The Green National Product: A Proposed Index of Sustainable Economic Welfare. Lanham, MD: University Press of America.

Cook, E. 1982. The Consumer as creator: A criticism of faith in limitless ingenuity, Energy. *Exploration and Exploitation* 1(3): 194.

Daly, H. 1991. Steady-State Economics, 2d. Washington, DC: Island Press.

Daly, H. and J. Cobb, 1994. For the Common Good, 2d. Boston: Beacon Press.

Georgescu-Roegen, N. 1971. The Entropy Law and the Economic Process. Cambridge, MA: Harvard University Press.

Georgescu-Roegen, N. 1979. Comments.... In Scarcity and Growth Reconsidered, ed. V. K. Smith. Baltimore: RfF and Johns Hopkins Press.

Gever, J. et al. 1986. Beyond Oil. Cambridge, MA: Ballinger .

Gore, A. 1992. Earth in the Balance. Boston: Houghton Mifflin Co.

Marshall, A. 1961. (originally 1920). Principles of Economics. 9d. New York: Macmillan.

Nordhaus, W. 1991. Ecological Economics: *Science* September: 1206.

Odum, E. P. 1969. The Strategy of Ecosystem Development. *Science* April: 262–270.

Soddy, F. 1922. Cartesian Economics: (The Bearing of Physical Science upon State Stewardship) London: Hendersons.

Thurow, L. 1980. The Zero-Sum Society. New York: Penguin Books.

4 COMPLEXITY, PROBLEM SOLVING, AND SUSTAINABLE SOCIETIES

Joseph A. Tainter
USDA Forest Service Rocky Mountain Forest and Range Experiment Station
Albuquerque, NM 87106

OVERVIEW

Historical knowledge is essential to practical applications of ecological economics. Systems of problem solving develop greater complexity and higher costs over long periods. In time such systems either require increasing energy subsidies or they collapse. Diminishing returns to complexity in problem solving limited the abilities of earlier societies to respond sustainably to challenges, and will shape contemporary responses to global change. To confront this dilemma we must understand both the role of energy in sustaining problem solving, and our historical position in systems of increasing complexity.

INTRODUCTION

In our quest to understand sustainability we have rushed to comprehend such factors as energy transformations, biophysical constraints, and environmental deterioration, as well as the human characteristics that drive production and consumption, and the assumptions of neoclassical economics. As our knowledge of these matters increases, practical applications of ecological economics are emerging. Yet amidst these advances something important is missing. Any human problem is but a moment of reaction to prior events and processes. Historical patterns develop over generations or even centuries. Rarely will the experience of a lifetime disclose fully the origin of an event or a process. Employment levels in natural resource production, for example, may respond to a capital investment cycle with a lag time of several decades (Watt 1992). The factors that cause societies to collapse take centuries to develop (Tainter 1988). To design policies for today and the future we need to understand social and economic processes at all temporal scales, and comprehend where we are in historical patterns. Historical knowledge is essential to sustainability (Tainter 1995a). No program to enhance sustainability can be considered practical if it does not incorporate such fundamental knowledge.

In this era of global environmental change we face what may be humanity's greatest crisis. The cluster of transformations labeled global change dwarfs all previous experiences in its speed, in the geographical scale of its consequences, and in the numbers of people who will be affected (Norgaard 1994). Yet many times past human populations faced extraordinary challenges, and the difference between their problems and ours is only one of degree. One might expect that in a rational, problem-solving society, we would eagerly seek to understand historical experiences. In actuality, our approaches to education and our impatience for innovation have made us averse to historical knowledge (Tainter 1995a). In ignorance, policy makers tend to look for the causes of events only in the recent past (Watt 1992). As a result, while we have a greater opportunity than the people of any previous era to understand the long-term reasons for our problems, that opportunity is largely ignored. Not only do we not know where we are in history, most of our citizens and policy makers are not aware that we ought to.

A recurring constraint faced by previous societies has been complexity in problem solving. It is a constraint that is usually unrecognized in contemporary economic analyses. For the past 12,000 years human societies have seemed almost inexorably to grow more complex. For the most part this has been successful: complexity confers advantages, and one of the reasons for our success as a species has been our ability to increase rapidly the complexity of our behavior (Tainter 1992, 1995b). Yet complexity can also be detrimental to sustainability. Since our approach to resolving our problems has been to develop the most complex society and economy of human history, it is important to understand how previous societies fared when they pursued analogous strategies. In this chapter I will discuss the factors that caused previous societies to collapse, the economics of complexity in problem solving, and some implications of historical patterns for our efforts at problem solving today. This discussion indicates that part of our response to global change must be to understand the long-term evolution of problem-solving systems.

THE DEVELOPMENT OF SOCIOECONOMIC COMPLEXITY

Complexity is a key concept of this essay. In an earlier study I characterized it as follows:

> Complexity is generally understood to refer to such things as the size of a society, the number and distinctiveness of its parts, the variety of specialized social roles that it incorporates, the number of distinct social personalities present, and the variety of mechanisms for organizing these into a coherent, functioning whole. Augmenting any of these dimensions increases the complexity of a society. Hunter-gatherer societies (by way of illustrating one contrast in complexity) contain no more

than a few dozen distinct social personalities, while modern European censuses recognize 10,000 to 20,000 unique occupational roles, and industrial societies may contain overall more than 1,000,000 different kinds of social personalities (McGuire 1983; Tainter 1988).[1]

As a simple illustration of differences in complexity, Julian Steward pointed out the contrast between the native peoples of western North America, among whom early ethnographers documented 3,000 to 6,000 cultural elements, and the U.S. Army, which landed 500,000+ artifact types at Casablanca in World War II (Steward 1955). Complexity is quantifiable.

For over 99% of the history of humanity we lived as low-density foragers or farmers in egalitarian communities of no more than a few dozen persons (Carneiro 1978). Leslie White pointed out that such a cultural system, based primarily on human labor, can generate only about 1/20 horsepower per capita per year (White 1949, 1959). From this base of undifferentiated societies requiring small amounts of energy, the development of complex cultural systems was, *a priori*, unlikely. The conventional view has been that human societies have a latent tendency towards greater complexity. Complexity was assumed to be a desirable thing, and the logical result of surplus food, leisure time, and human creativity. Although this scenario is popular, it is inadequate to explain the evolution of complexity. In the world of cultural complexity there is, to use a colloquial expression, no free lunch. More complex societies are costlier to maintain than simpler ones and require higher support levels per capita. A society that is more complex has more sub-groups and social roles, more networks among groups and individuals, more horizontal and vertical controls, higher flow of information, greater centralization of information, more specialization, and greater interdependence of parts. Increasing any of these dimensions requires biological, mechanical, or chemical energy. In the days before fossil fuel subsidies, increasing the complexity of a society usually meant that the majority of its population had to work harder (Tainter 1988, 1992, 1994a, 1995a, 1995b).

Many aspects of human behavior appear to be complexity averse (Tainter 1995b). The so-called "complexity of modern life" is a regular complaint in popular discourse. Some of the public discontent with government stems from the fact that government adds complexity to people's lives. In science, the Principle of Occam's Razor has enduring appeal because it states that simplicity in explanation is preferable to complexity.

Complexity has always been inhibited by the burdens of time and energy that it imposes, and by complexity aversion (which is no doubt related to cost). Thus explaining why human societies have become increasingly complex presents more of a challenge than is customarily thought. The reason why complexity increases is that, most of the time, it works. Complexity is a problem-solving strategy that emerges under conditions of compelling need or perceived

benefit. Throughout history, the stresses and challenges that human populations have faced have often been resolved by becoming more complex. While
a complete review is not possible here, this trend is evident in such spheres as:

1. Foraging and agriculture (Boserup 1965; Clark and Haswell 1966;
   Asch et al. 1972; Wilkinson 1973; Cohen 1977; Minnis 1995; Nelson
   1995);
2. Technology (Wilkinson 1973; Nelson 1995);
3. Competition, warfare, and arms races (Parker 1988; Tainter 1992);
4. Sociopolitical control and specialization (Olson 1982; Tainter 1988); and
5. Research and development (Price 1963; Rescher 1978, 1980; Rostow
   1980; Tainter 1988, 1995a).

In each of these areas, complexity increases through greater differentiation,
specialization, and integration.

The development of complexity is thus an economic process: complexity
levies costs and yields benefits. It is an investment, and it gives a variable
return. Complexity can be both beneficial and detrimental. Its destructive
potential is evident in historical cases where increased expenditures on socio-
economic complexity reached diminishing returns, and ultimately, in some instances, negative returns (Tainter 1988, 1994b). This outcome emerges from
the normal economic process: simple, inexpensive solutions are adopted before more complex, expensive ones. Thus, as human populations have increased,
hunting and gathering has given way to increasingly intensive agriculture, and to
industrialized food production that consumes more energy than it produces (Clark
and Haswell 1966; Cohen 1977; Hall et al. 1992). Minerals and energy production move consistently from easily accessible, inexpensively exploited reserves to
ones that are costlier to find, extract, process, and distribute. Socioeconomic organization has evolved from egalitarian reciprocity, short-term leadership, and generalized roles to complex hierarchies with increasing specialization.

The graph in Figure 4.1 is based on these arguments. As a society increases
in complexity, it expands investment in such things as resource production,
information processing, administration, and defense. The benefit/cost curve
for these expenditures may at first increase favorably, as the most simple, general, and inexpensive solutions are adopted (a phase not shown on this chart).
Yet as a society encounters new stresses, and inexpensive solutions no longer
suffice, its evolution proceeds in a more costly direction. Ultimately a growing
society reaches a point where continued investment in complexity yields higher
returns, but at a declining marginal rate. At a point such as B1, C1 on this chart
a society has entered the phase where it starts to become vulnerable to collapse.[2]

Two things make a society liable to collapse at this point. First new emergencies impinge on a people who are investing in a strategy that yields less and

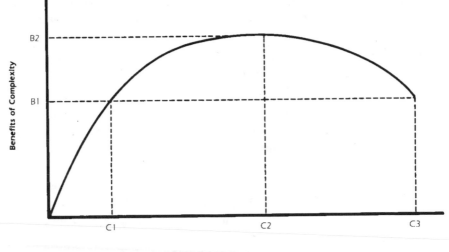

Figure 4.1. Diminishing returns to increasing complexity (after Tainter 1988).

less marginal return. As such a society becomes economically weakened it has fewer reserves with which to counter major adversities. A crisis that the society might have survived in its earlier days now becomes insurmountable.

Second, diminishing returns make complexity less attractive and breed disaffection. As taxes and other costs rise and there are fewer benefits at the local level, more and more people are attracted by the idea of being independent. The society "decomposes" as people pursue their immediate needs rather than the long-term goals of the leadership.[3]

As such a society evolves along the marginal return curve beyond B2, C2, it crosses a continuum of points, such as B1, C3, where costs are increasing, but the benefits have actually declined to those previously available at a lower level of complexity. This is a realm of negative returns to investment in complexity. A society at such a point would find that, upon collapsing, its return on investment in complexity would noticeably rise. A society in this condition is extremely vulnerable to collapse.

This argument, developed and tested to explain why societies collapse (Tainter 1988), is also an account of historical trends in the economics of problem solving. The history of cultural complexity is the history of human problem solving. In many sectors of investment, such as resource production, technology, competition, political organization, and research, complexity is increased by a continual need to solve problems. As easier solutions are exhausted, problem solving moves inexorably to greater complexity, higher costs, and diminishing returns. This need not lead to collapse, but it is important to understand the conditions under which it might. To illustrate these conditions it is useful to review three examples of increasing complexity and costliness in problem solving: the collapse of the Roman Empire, the development of industrialism, and trends in contemporary science.

The Collapse of The Roman Empire

One outcome of diminishing returns to complexity is illustrated by the collapse of the Western Roman Empire. As a solar-energy based society which taxed heavily, the empire had little fiscal reserve. When confronted with military crises, Roman Emperors often had to respond by debasing the silver currency (Figure 4.2) and trying to raise new funds. In the third century A.D. constant crises forced the emperors to double the size of the army and increase both the size and complexity of the government. To pay for this, masses of worthless coins were produced, supplies were commandeered from peasants, and the level of taxation was made even more oppressive (up to two-thirds of the net yield after payment of rent). Inflation devastated the economy. Lands and population were surveyed across the empire and assessed for taxes. Communities were held corporately liable for any unpaid amounts. While peasants

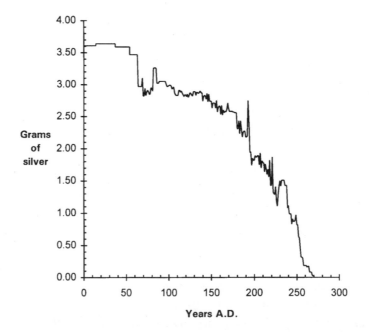

Figure 4.2. Debasement of the Roman silver currency, 0-269 A.D. (after Tainter 1994b with modifications). The chart shows grams of silver per denarius (the basic silver coin) from 0 to 237 A.D., and per 1/2 denarius from 238-269 A.D. (when the denarius was replaced by a larger coin tariffed at two denarii).

went hungry or sold their children into slavery, massive fortifications were built, the size of the bureaucracy doubled, provincial administration was made more complex, large subsidies in gold were paid to Germanic tribes, and new imperial cities and courts were established. With rising taxes, marginal lands were abandoned and population declined. Peasants could no longer support large families. To avoid oppressive civic obligations, the wealthy fled from cities to establish self-sufficient rural estates. Ultimately, to escape taxation, peasants voluntarily entered into feudal relationships with these land holders. A few wealthy families came to own much of the land in the western empire, and were able to defy the imperial government. The empire came to sustain itself by consuming its capital resources; producing lands and peasant population (Jones 1964, 1974; Wickham 1984; Tainter 1988, 1994b). The Roman Empire provides history's best-documented example of how increasing complexity to resolve problems leads to higher costs, diminishing returns, alienation of a support population, economic weakness, and collapse. In the end it could no longer afford to solve the problems of its own existence.

Population, Resources, and Industrialism

The fate of the Roman Empire is not the unavoidable destiny of complex societies. It is useful to discuss a historical case that turned out quite differently. In one of the most interesting works of economic history, Richard Wilkinson (1973) showed that in late-and post-medieval England, population growth and deforestation stimulated economic development, and were at least partly responsible for the Industrial Revolution. Major increases in population, at around 1300, 1600, and in the late 18th century, led to intensification in agriculture and industry. As forests were cut to provide agricultural land and fuel for a growing population, England's heating, cooking, and manufacturing needs could no longer be met by burning wood. Coal came to be increasingly important, although it was adopted reluctantly. Coal was costlier to obtain and distribute than wood, and restricted in its occurrence. It required a new, costly distribution system. As coal gained importance in the economy the most accessible deposits were depleted. Mines had to be sunk ever deeper, until groundwater came to be a problem. Ultimately, the steam engine was developed and put to use pumping water from mines. With the development of a coal-based economy, a distribution system, and the steam engine, several of the most important technical elements of the Industrial Revolution were in place. Industrialism, that great generator of economic well-being, came in part from steps to counteract the consequences of resource depletion, supposedly a generator of poverty and collapse. Yet it was a system of increasing complexity that did not take long to show diminishing returns in some sectors. This point will be raised again later.

Science and Problem Solving

Contemporary science is humanity's greatest exercise in problem solving. Science is an institutional aspect of society, and research is an activity that we like to think has a high return. Yet as generalized knowledge is established early in the history of a discipline, the work that remains to be done is increasingly specialized. These types of problems tend to be increasingly costly and difficult to resolve, and on average advance knowledge only by small increments (Rescher 1978, 1980; Tainter 1988). Increasing investments in research yield declining marginal returns.

Some notable scholars have commented upon this. Walter Rostow once argued that marginal productivity first rises and then declines in individual fields (1980). The great physicist Max Planck, in a statement that Nicholas Rescher calls 'Planck's Principle of Increasing Effort, observed that "...with every advance [in science] the difficulty of the task is increased" (Rescher 1980). As easier questions are resolved, science moves inevitably to more complex research areas and to larger, costlier organizations (Rescher 1980). Rescher suggests that "As science progresses within any of its specialized branches, there is a marked increase in the overall resource-cost to realizing scientific findings of a given level [of] intrinsic significance..." (1978). Exponential growth in the size and costliness of science is necessary simply to maintain a constant rate of progress (Rescher 1980). Derek de Solla Price noted that in 1963 science was, even then, growing faster than either the population or the economy, and of all scientists who had ever lived, 80–90% were still alive at the time of his writing (Price 1963). In the same period, such matters prompted Dael Wolfle to publish a query in *Science* titled "How Much Research for a Dollar?" (Wolfle 1960).

Scientists rarely think about the benefit/cost ratio to investment in their research. Yet if we assess the productivity of our investment in science by some measure such as the issuance of patents (Figure 4.3), the productivity of certain kinds of research appears to be declining. Patenting is a controversial indicator among those who study such matters (Machlup 1962; Schmookler 1966; Griliches 1984), and does not by itself indicate the economic return to the expenditures. Medicine is a field of applied science where the return to investment can be determined more readily. Over the 52-year period shown in Figure 4.4, from 1930–1982, the productivity of the United States health care system for improving life expectancy declined by nearly 60%.

The declining productivity of the United States health care system illustrates clearly the historical development of a problem-solving field. Rescher (1980) points out: Once all of the findings at a given state-of-the-art level of investigative technology have been realized, one must move to a more expensive level.... In natural science we are involved in a technological arms race: with every victory over nature the difficulty of achieving the breakthroughs which lie ahead is increased.

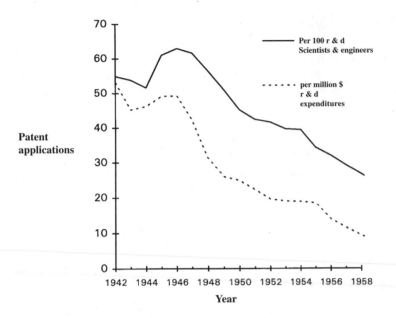

Figure 4.3. Patent applications in respect to research inputs, 1942–1958 (data from Machlup 1962).

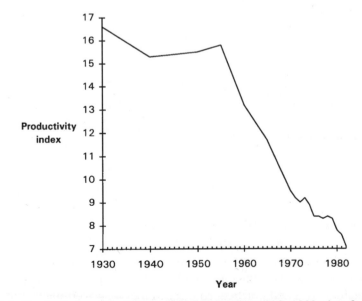

Figure 4.4. Productivity of the U.S. health care system, 1930–1982 (data from Worthington 1975; U.S. Bureau of the Census 1983). Productivity index = (Life expectancy)/(National health expenditures as percent of GNP).

The declining productivity of medicine is due to the fact that the inexpensive diseases and ailments were conquered first (the basic research that led to penicillin costing no more than $20,000), so that those remaining are more difficult and costly to resolve (Rescher 1978). And as each increasingly expensive disease is conquered, the increment to average life expectancy becomes ever smaller.

Implications of the Examples

The Roman Empire, industrialism, and science are important, not only for their own merits, but also because they exemplify: (1) how problem solving evolves along a path of increasing complexity, higher costs, and declining marginal returns (Tainter 1988), and (2) some different outcomes of that process. In the next section, I discuss what these patterns imply for our efforts to address contemporary problems.

PROBLEM SOLVING, ENERGY, AND SUSTAINABILITY

This historical discussion gives a perspective on what it means to be practical and sustainable. A few years ago I described about two dozen societies that have collapsed (Tainter 1988). In no case is it evident or even likely that any of these societies collapsed because its members or leaders did not take practical steps to resolve its problems (Tainter 1988). The experience of the Roman Empire is again instructive. Most actions that the Roman government took in response to crises—such as debasing the currency, raising taxes, expanding the army, and conscripting labor—were practical solutions to immediate problems. It would have been unthinkable not to adopt such measures. Cumulatively, however, these practical steps made the empire ever weaker, as the capital stock (agricultural land and peasants) was depleted through taxation and conscription. Over time, devising practical solutions drove the Roman Empire into diminishing, then negative, returns to complexity. The implication is that to focus a problem-solving system, such as ecological economics, on practical applications will not automatically increase its value to society, nor enhance sustainability. The historical development of problem-solving systems needs to be understood and taken into consideration.

Most who study contemporary issues certainly would agree that solving environmental and economic problems requires both knowledge and education. A major part of our response to current problems has been to increase our level of research into environmental matters, including global change. As our knowledge increases and practical solutions emerge, governments will implement solutions and bureaucracies will enforce them. New technologies will be developed. Each of these steps will appear to be a practical solution to a specific problem. Yet cumulatively these practical steps are likely to bring increased complexity, higher costs, and diminishing returns to problem solving.[4] Richard Norgaard has stated the problem well: "Assuring sustainability by extending the modern agenda...will require, by several orders of magnitude, more data collection, interpretation, planning, political decision-making, and bureaucratic control" (Norgaard 1994).

Donella Meadows and her colleagues have given excellent examples of the economic constraints of contemporary problem solving. To raise world food production from 1951–1966 by 34%, for example, required increasing expenditures on tractors of 63%, on nitrate fertilizers of 146%, and on pesticides of 300%. To remove all organic wastes from a sugar-processing plant costs 100 times more than removing 30%. To reduce sulfur dioxide in the air of a U.S. city by 9.6 times, or particulates by 3.1 times, raises the cost of pollution control by 520 times (Meadows et al. 1972). All environmental problem solving will face constraints of this kind.

Bureaucratic regulation itself generates further complexity and costs. As regulations are issued and taxes established, those who are regulated or taxed seek loopholes and lawmakers strive to close these. A competitive spiral of loophole discovery and closure unfolds, with complexity continuously increasing (Olson 1982). In these days when the cost of government lacks political support, such a strategy is unsustainable. It is often suggested that environmentally benign behavior should be elicited through taxation incentives rather than through regulations. While this approach has some advantages, it does not address the problem of complexity, and may not reduce overall regulatory costs as much as is thought. Those costs may only be shifted to the taxation authorities, and to the society as a whole.

It is not that research, education, regulation, and new technologies cannot potentially alleviate our problems. With enough investment perhaps they can. The difficulty is that these investments will be costly, and may require an increasing share of each nation's gross domestic product. With diminishing returns to problem solving, addressing environmental issues in our conventional way means that more resources will have to be allocated to science, engineering, and government. In the absence of high economic growth this would require at least a temporary decline in the standard of living, as people would have comparatively less to spend on food, housing, clothing, medical care, transportation, and entertainment.

To circumvent costliness in problem solving it is often suggested that we use resources more intelligently and efficiently. Timothy Allen and Thomas Hoekstra, for example, have suggested that in managing ecosystems for sustainability, managers should identify what is missing from natural regulatory process and provide only that. The ecosystem will do the rest. Let the ecosystem (i.e., solar energy) subsidize the management effort rather than the other way around (Allen and Hoekstra 1992). It is an intelligent suggestion. At the same time, to implement it would require much knowledge that we do not now possess. That means we need research that is complex and costly, and requires fossil-fuel subsidies. Lowering the costs of complexity in one sphere causes them to rise in another.

Agricultural pest control illustrates this dilemma. As the spraying of pesticides exacted higher costs and yielded fewer benefits, integrated pest management was developed. This system relies on biological knowledge to reduce the need for chemicals, and employs monitoring of pest populations, use of biological controls, judicious application of chemicals, and careful selection of crop types and planting dates (Norgaard 1994). It is an approach that requires both esoteric research by scientists and careful monitoring by farmers. Integrated pest management violates the principle of complexity aversion, which may partly explain why it is not more widely used.

Such issues help to clarify what constitutes a sustainable society. The fact that problem-solving systems seem to evolve to greater complexity, higher costs, and diminishing returns has significant implications for sustainability. In time, systems that develop in this way are either cut off from further finances, fail to solve problems, collapse, or come to require large energy subsidies. This has been the pattern historically in such cases as the Roman Empire, the Lowland Classic Maya, Chacoan Society of the American Southwest, warfare in Medieval and Renaissance Europe, and some aspects of contemporary problem solving (that is, in every case that I have investigated in detail) (Tainter 1988, 1992, 1994b, 1995a). These historical patterns suggest that one of the characteristics of a sustainable society will be that it has a sustainable system of problem solving—one with increasing or stable returns, or diminishing returns that can be financed with energy subsidies of assured supply, cost, and quality.

Industrialism illustrates this point. It generated its own problems of complexity and costliness. These included railways and canals to distribute coal and manufactured goods, the development of an economy increasingly based on money and wages, and the development of new technologies. While such elements of complexity are usually thought to facilitate economic growth, in fact they can do so only when subsidized by energy. Some of the new technologies, such as the steam engine, showed diminishing returns to innovation quite early in their development (Wilkinson 1973; Giarini and Loubergé 1978; Giarini 1984). What set industrialism apart from all of the previous history of our species was its reliance on abundant, concentrated, high-quality energy (Hall et al. 1992).[5] With subsidies of inexpensive fossil fuels, for a long time many consequences of industrialism effectively did not matter. Industrial societies could afford them. When energy costs are met easily and painlessly, the benefit/cost ratio to social investments can be substantially ignored (as it has been in contemporary industrial agriculture). Fossil fuels made industrialism, and all that flowed from it (such as science, transportation, medicine, employment, consumerism, high-technology war, and contemporary political organization), a system of problem solving that was sustainable for several generations.

Energy has always been the basis of cultural complexity and it always will be. If our efforts to understand and resolve such matters as global change involve increasing political, technological, economic, and scientific complexity, as it seems they will, then the availability of energy per capita will be a constraining factor. To increase complexity on the basis of static or declining energy supplies would require lowering the standard of living throughout the world. In the absence of a clear crisis very few people would support this. To maintain political support for our current and future investments in complexity thus requires an increase in the effective per capita supply of energy—either by increasing the physical availability of energy, or by technical, political, or economic innovations that lower the energy cost of our standard of living. Of course, to discover such innovations requires energy, which underscores the constraints in the energy-complexity relation.

CONCLUSIONS

This chapter on the past clarifies potential paths to the future. One often-discussed path is cultural and economic simplicity and lower energy costs. This could come about through the "crash" that many fear—a genuine collapse over a period of one or two generations, with much violence, starvation, and loss of population. The alternative is the "soft landing" that many people hope for—a voluntary change to solar energy and green fuels, energy-conserving technologies, and less overall consumption. This is a utopian alternative that, as suggested above, will come about only if severe, prolonged hardship in industrial nations makes it attractive, and if economic growth and consumerism can be removed from the realm of ideology.

The more likely option is a future of greater investments in problem solving, increasing overall complexity, and greater use of energy. This option is driven by the material comforts it provides, by vested interests, by lack of alternatives, and by our conviction that it is good. If the trajectory of problem solving that humanity has followed for much of the last 12,000 years should continue, it is the path that we are likely to take in the near future.

Regardless of when our efforts to understand and resolve contemporary problems reach diminishing returns, one point should be clear. It is essential to know where we are in history (Tainter 1995a). If macroeconomic patterns develop over periods of generations or centuries, it is not possible to comprehend our current conditions unless we understand where we are in this process. We have the opportunity to become the first people in history to understand how a society's problem-solving abilities change. To know that this is possible yet not to act upon it would be a great failure of the practical application of ecological economics.

ACKNOWLEDGMENTS

This chapter is revised from a plenary address to the Third International Meeting of the International Society for Ecological Economics, San José, Costa Rica, 28 October 1994. I am grateful to Cutler J. Cleveland, Robert Costanza, and Olman Segura for the invitation to present the address, to Maureen Garita Matamoros for assistance during the conference, to Denver Burns, John Faux, Charles A. S. Hall, Thomas Hoekstra, Joe Kerkvliet, and Daniel Underwood for comments on the plenary address, and to Richard Periman and Carol Raish for reviewing this version.

NOTES

1. In some literature of the physical sciences, striving for a definition as objective as possible, the complexity of a system is considered to be the length of a description of its regularities (Gell-Mann 1992, 1994). This is compatible with the definition employed here. A society with fewer parts, less differentiated parts, and fewer or simpler integrative systems can certainly be described more succinctly than can a society with more of these (Tainter 1995b).
2. Collapse is a rapid transformation to a lower degree of complexity, typically involving significantly less energy consumption (Tainter 1988).
3. This is part of the process responsible for contemporary separatist movements in the U.S.
4. I have not considered so-called "green" alternatives in this analysis. There are two reasons why these appear to be impractical in the short-term. Firstly, industrial economies are closely coupled to the existing production system and resource base, including conventional energy (Hall et al. 1992; Watt 1992). The capital costs of massive, rapid industrial conversion would be very high. Secondly, experience since 1973 indicates that most members of industrial societies will not change their consumption patterns merely because of abstract projections about the long-term supply of energy or other resources. They will do so only when the prices of energy, and of goods and services that rely on energy, rise sharply for an extended time. It takes protracted hardship to convince people that the world to which they have been accustomed has changed irrevocably. Hardship that is minor or episodic merely allows leaders to exploit popular discontent for personal gain. Economic growth has become mythologized as part of our ideology, which makes it particularly difficult to discuss objectively in the public arena (Giarini and Loubergé 1978).
5. Coal of course was not the only element that promoted industrialism. Other factors included declining supplies of fuelwood (Wilkinson 1973), changes in land-use laws, and availability of laborers who could be employed in manufacturing.

REFERENCES

Allen, T. F. H. and T. W. Hoekstra. 1992. Toward a Unified Ecology. New York: Columbia University Press.

Asch, N. B., R. I. Ford, and D. L. Asch. 1972. Paleoethnobotany of the Koster site: The Archaic horizons. Illinois State Museum Reports of Investigations 24. Illinois Valley Archeological Program, Research Papers 6.

Boserup, E. 1965. The Conditions of Agricultural Growth: The Economics of Agrarian Change Under Population Pressure. Chicago: Aldine.

Carneiro, R. L. 1978. Political expansion as an expression of the principle of competitive exclusion. In Origins of the State: the Anthropology of Political Evolution, eds. Ronald Cohen and Elman R. Service. Philadelphia: Institute for the Study of Human Issues.

Clark, C and M. Haswell. 1966. The Economics of Subsistence Agriculture. London: MacMillan.

Cohen, M. N. 1977. The Food Crisis in Prehistory: Overpopulation and the Origins of Agriculture. New Haven: Yale University Press.

Gell-Mann, M. 1992. Complexity and complex adaptive systems. In The Evolution of Human Languages, eds. J. A. Hawkins and M. Gell-Mann, pp. 3–18. Santa Fe Institute. Studies in the Sciences of Complexity, Proceedings Volume XI. Reading: Addison-Wesley.

Gell-Mann, M. 1994. The Quark and the Jaguar: Adventures in the Simple and the Complex. New York: W. H. Freeman.

Giarini, O. ed. 1984. Cycles, Value and Employment: Responses to the Economic Crisis. Oxford: Pergamon.

Giarini, O. and H. Loubergé. 1978. The Diminishing Returns of Technology: An Essay on the Crisis in Economic Growth. Oxford: Pergamon.

Griliches, Z. 1984. Introduction. In Research and Development, Patents, and Productivity, ed. Zvi Griliches, pp. 1–19. Chicago and London: University of Chicago Press.

Hall, Charles A. S., C. J, Cleveland, and R. Kaufmann. 1992. Energy and Resource Quality: The Ecology of the Economic Process. Niwot: University Press of Colorado.

Jones, A. H. M. 1964. The Later Roman Empire 284–602: A Social, Economic and Administrative Survey. Norman: University of Oklahoma Press.

Jones, A. H. M. 1974. The Roman Economy: Studies in Ancient Economic and Administrative History. Oxford: Basil Blackwell.

Machlup, Fritz. 1962. The Production and Distribution of Knowledge in the United States. Princeton: Princeton University Press.

McGuire, R. H. 1983. Breaking down cultural complexity: inequality and heterogeneity. In Advances in Archaeological Method and Theory, Volume 6, ed. Michael B. Schiffer, pp. 91–142. New York: Academic Press.

Meadows, D., H. Dennis, L. Meadows, J. Randers, and W. W. Behrens III. 1972. The Limits to Growth. New York: Universe Books.

Minnis, P. E. 1995. Notes on economic uncertainty and human behavior in the prehistoric North American southwest. In Evolving Complexity and Environmental Risk in the Prehistoric Southwest, eds. J. A. Tainter and B. B. Tainter, pp. 57–78. Santa Fe Institute, Studies in the Sciences of Complexity, Proceedings Volume XXIV. Reading: Addison Wesley.

Nelson, M. C. 1995. Technological strategies responsive to subsistence stress. In Evolving Complexity and Environmental Risk in the Prehistoric Southwest, eds. J. A. Tainter and B. B. Tainter, pp. 107–144. Santa Fe Institute, Studies in the Sciences of Complexity, Proceedings Volume XXIV. Reading: Addison-Wesley.

Norgaard, R. B. 1994. Development Betrayed: The End of Progress and a Coevolutionary Revisioning of the Future. London and New York: Routledge.

Olson, M. 1982. The Rise and Decline of Nations. New Haven: Yale University Press.

Parker, G. 1988. The Military Revolution: Military Innovation and the Rise of the West, 1500–1800. Cambridge: Cambridge University Press.

Price, Derek de Solla. 1963. Little Science, Big Science. New York: Columbia University Press.

Rescher, N. 1978. Scientific Progress: a Philosophical Essay on the Economics of Research in Natural Science. Pittsburgh: University of Pittsburgh Press.

Rescher, N. 1980. Unpopular Essays on Technological Progress. Pittsburgh: University of Pittsburgh Press.

Rostow, W. W. 1980. Why the Poor Get Richer and the Rich Slow Down. Austin: University of Texas Press.

Schmookler, J. 1966. Invention and Economic Growth. Cambridge: Harvard University Press.

Steward, J. H. 1955. Theory of Culture Change. Urbana: University of Illinois Press.

Tainter, J. A. 1988. The Collapse of Complex Societies. Cambridge: Cambridge University Press.

Tainter, J. A. 1992. Evolutionary consequences of war. In Effects of War on Society, ed. G. Ausenda, pp. 103–130. San Marino: Center for Interdisciplinary Research on Social Stress.

Tainter, J. A. 1994a. Southwestern contributions to the understanding of core-periphery relations. In Understanding Complexity in the Prehistoric Southwest, eds. G. J. Gumerman, and M. Gell-Mann, pp. 25–36. Santa Fe Institute, Studies in the Sciences of Complexity, Proceedings Volume XVI. Reading: Addison-Wesley.

Tainter, Joseph A. 1994b. La fine dell'amministrazione centrale: il collaso dell'Impero romano in Occidente. In Storia d'Europa, Volume Secondo: Preistoria e Antichità, eds. Jean Guilaine and Salvatore Settis, pp. 1207–1255. Turin: Einaudi.

Tainter, J. A. 1995a. Sustainability of complex societies. *Futures* 27: 397–407.

Tainter, J. A. 1995b. Introduction: prehistoric societies as evolving complex systems. In: Evolving Complexity and Environmental Risk in the Prehistoric Southwest, eds. J. A. Tainter and B. B. Tainter. pp 1–23 Santa Fe Institute, Studies in the Sciences of Complexity, Proceedings Volume XXIV. Reading: Addison-Wesley.

U.S. Bureau of the Census. 1983. Statistical Abstract of the United States: 1984 104d Washington, DC: U.S. Government Printing Office.

Watt, K. E. F. 1992. Taming the Future: A Revolutionary Breakthrough in Scientific Forecasting. Davis: Contextured Webb Press.

White, L. A. 1949. The Science of Culture. New York: Farrar, Straus and Giroux.

White, L. A. 1959. The Evolution of Culture. New York: McGraw-Hill.

Wickham, C. 1984. The other transition: From the ancient world to feudalism. *Past and Present* 103: 3–36.

Wilkinson, R. G. 1973. Poverty and Progress: An Ecological Model of Economic Development. London: Methuen.

Wolfle, D. 1960. How much research for a dollar? *Science* 132: 517.

Worthington, N. L. 1975. National health expenditures, 1929–1974. *Social Security Bulletin* 38(2): 3–20.

5 FROM ECOLOGICAL ECONOMICS TO PRODUCTIVE ECOLOGY: PERSPECTIVES ON SUSTAINABLE DEVELOPMENT FROM THE SOUTH

Enrique Leff
United Nations Environment Programme
Boulevard de los Virreyes 155
11000, Mexico, D.F.

OVERVIEW

Ecological economics has opened a dialogue between economics and ecology in the search for integrative analytic tools and pluralistic approaches to sustainable development. Political ecology is emerging from power strategies in knowledge, social practices, institutional organizations and political activity, to deal with ecological distribution, social appropriation of nature and an alternative rationality for production. These two approaches are welded into different visions and practices of sustainable development approaches to sustainability in the North have focused on global environmental changes, limits to growth, carrying capacity of ecosystems, population/resources relations, intergenerational equity and internalization of ecological costs. They have privileged a managerial approach to solve environmental problems without attempting to deconstruct economic rationality.

In the South, poverty, ecological degradation, and intra-generational equity appear as predominant environmental issues. Social environmentalism is legitimizing the rights of indigenous peoples and peasant societies to reappropriate their patrimony of natural and cultural resources, blend modern science and technology with their traditional practices, and self-manage their productive processes, offering new perspectives for sustainable development .

The construction and application of a new theory of production that integrates ecological potentials, cultural diversity, and technological productivity with the principles of participatory democracy will be discussed. This productive ecology supports a new bioeconomics based on technological enhancement and social control of natural biomass formation through photosynthesis, a negentropic process that can counterbalance the unsustainable trends towards ecological degradation, entropic decay, and resource depletion driven by economic growth.

INTRODUCTION

As a response to environmental crisis driven by economic growth, new methods are being developed to analyze the relations between nature and society within different scientific fields. This crisis of civilization questions the foundations of economic rationality as well as the ethical values and political systems of modern society. Thus, different approaches have emerged from conservationist philosophies of nature to radical social movements that attempt to integrate participatory democracy with economic decentralization and reappropriation of nature as productive ecosystemic resources. Distinct from environmental economics that intends to internalize ecological externalities through market mechanisms, ecological economics and political ecology are emerging as new fields of scientific inquiry and political action.

Economics, founded in principles of mechanics, expelled life and nature from its intended system, generating a process of production and circulation of market values that has undermined the ecological conditions for sustainable development. However, the institutionalization of economic rationality has generated its empirical referent in reality. Human behavior and the actual productive process have been shaped to resemble its theoretical construct. Today, the overflow of economic externalities to the social and environmental system makes it necessary to reconstruct the process of production from a new basis.

Copernicus produced his theoretical revolution by removing the Earth from the center of the Universe, transforming the foundations of the cosmic order of his time and shaking the social and religious hierarchies that supported them. A parallelism exists today with the paradigmatic conclusion of economic rationality. Economists and non economists are confronted with the choice, either to transform the unsustainable paradigm of economics or to trust that liberating market forces will reestablish ecological balance and social equity. Resistance to this paradigmatic changes in science, social institutions, and human behavior reflects in the attempts of neoclassical economics to adjust the economic cycles and market orbits of an ill-founded economic rationality by assigning values to nature through market prices, so that commodities can continue to circulate around a perfect sphere of economic order.

Ecological economics is moulding a new theoretical paradigm, establishing its interdisciplinary frontiers with different scientific fields, to integrate the ecological and cultural conditions for sustainable development. Different ideological visions, methodological approaches and conceptual strategies are being welded in the melting pot of sustainability, guided by conflicting political interests.

Theoretical responses to sustainability expand from neoclassical environmental economics that intends to internalize ecological externalities through economic instruments (shadow prices, environmental taxes), to human ecology, where a colorful bouquet of scientific ideologies find fertile soil. Thus, neo-Malthusian perspectives on the environment are flourishing that view sustainability as technological fixes and carrying capacity limitations to economic and population growth. An ecological approach in anthropology is reducing the rationality of cultural appropriation and productive transformation of nature to energy accounting; social Darwinism and sociobiological synthesis are ecologizing the symbolic and social orders.

Georgescu-Roegen's bioeconomics (1971) developed a critique to the foundations of economic rationality from the standpoint of thermodynamics and the ineluctable death end of technological processes and economic growth; from the consciousness that economy is undermining its own ecological basis for sustainable production, new approaches have emerged, that intend to subsume economics in ecological theory considered as a more comprehensive theory, the science *par excellence* of interrelations (Passet 1979). The connections between economy, ecology, and culture open up interdisciplinary linkages with ethnology and anthropology to analyze the processes of signification, valorization and legitimation that cross social practices for the appropriation and management of natural resources.

Among such theoretical approaches, ecological economics is settling in its academic niche, not yet definable by a precise theoretical paradigm or research program (Costanza 1989). It overlaps with neoclassical economics of natural resources, but its boundaries are open to political ecology, as the ecological conditions of sustainability cannot be delinked from issues of social equity, ecological distribution, and political democracy that determine the social appropriation of natural resources and environmental services. Thus, different perspectives to sustainability are emerging, from environmental managerialism and economic pragmatism, to new theories that internalize nature and culture as environmental conditions and potentials for sustainable development.

Sustainable Development: The Dispersion of the Concept by Conflicting Interests

The environmental question has become a political issue that goes beyond the purpose to internalize the ecological conditions for a sustainable economic growth. Socio-environmental problems cannot be accounted for nor regulated by the economic system. Poverty, environmental degradation, loss of cultural values, and intergenerational equity; natural productivity and ecological regeneration, entropic degradation of matter and energy, risk and uncertainty—all these externalities—cannot be reabsorbed by standard economics by assigning to these processes a common measure of value through market prices (Kapp 1983).

Theoretical developments in Latin America have produced a concept of the environment (different from the standard discourse on sustainability) to analyze the interrelations of ecological degradation and poverty. The environment is being perceived as a productive potential that arises from the synergetic integration of ecological, cultural, and technological processes (Leff 1994a, 1995a). The environment appears as a complex system demanding the articulation of different sciences and a social transformation of knowledge to guide a participatory and sustainable management of resources (Leff et al. 1986).

In the North, intervention on the environment is oriented mostly to problems of waste disposal and pollution that appear as ecological costs to be internalized by the economic system and the concept of ecology is being generalized in the domains of theory, policy making and social action. Environmental issues have been politicized and a new field of political ecology has emerged. Ecological awareness is spreading from theoretical discourse over to social organizations in defense of the environment and is being extended to sociology and philosophy of nature (Bookchin 1991).

In the North, the ecological conditions of production are considered a limit to growth and environmental preservation is treated as a cost. While in the South the dominant discourse on sustainability has turned to the capitalization of nature, internalizing ecological costs by assigning market values to natural resources, in the Third World tropical regions a new paradigm of production is emerging based upon their ecological potentials and cultural identities. It promotes sustainability from the ground through decentralization of the economy and diversification of development styles, mobilizing society for the reappropriation of their patrimony of natural resources and self-management of their productive processes.

Environmentalism in the North is oriented by leisure values of a post-scarcity society, while a green and conservationist movement rejects the modern capitalistic production system and lifestyle. Environmentalism in the South is surging as a rebellion of the poor for survival; thus peasant and indigenous peoples are mobilizing because of extreme poverty generated by degradation of the environment, their resistance to margination and their claims to recover their cultural rights and control over their natural resources. These social struggles for poverty alleviation involve strategies for the reappropriation of knowledge productive processes and livelihoods.[1]

In the North, sustainability is concerned with maintaining the ecological conditions for sustainable economic growth through managerial practices, technological means and international agreements. A good example is that of the connection between biodiversity and biotechnology, whereby the North intends to control deforestation and preserve biodiversity as a potential source of new profitable investments, capitalizing nature, and legitimating the ownership over the resources of biodiversity through intellectual property rights on biotechnology (Hobbelink 1992; Martinez-Alier 1994).

In the South, urban dwellers, peasant societies, and indigenous peoples associate sustainability with democracy, ethnic rights, and cultural autonomy to reappropriate their patrimony of natural resources and generate alternative styles of development delinked from economic rationality and unidimensional technological development.

Sustainability has thus emerged as the need to reestablish the place of nature in economic theory and development practices, internalizing the ecological conditions of production. Yet, this general purpose is not supported by an homogenous paradigm of sustainability and does not guide a smooth transition towards a "common future" (WCED 1987) for the whole of humanity. From the claim for the capitalization of nature through liberation of market forces, to a decentralized economy based in non-market principles (ecological potentials, intragenerational equity, democracy, and cultural diversity), sustainability is defined by different social meanings and political strategies.[2]

Equity, Distribution, and Sustainability: The Challenge for Ecological Economics

Ecological economics appears as a paradigm under construction, with new conceptual and methodologic approaches and alternative productive practices, driven by social interests and power strategies that circulate across institutions, political organizations and social movements.

Ecological economics questions the foundations of economics from the perception of its ecological and entropic limits, and opens theoretical inquiry on the ecological conditions of production. However, it has centered its inquiries on energy and resource scarcity, on pollution problems and the capacity of technology to solve them. Issues of sustainability, equity and distribution are considered problems about limits (Costanza 1989). These problems arise from the pressure exerted by a growing population over scarce resources and the unequal impact on ecological degradation. The concept of scarcity has been expanded to include meta-resource depletion (Ehrlich 1989) as the multiplying effect of particular scarcities in the environmental services and productive potentials of ecosystems. However, ecological scarcity is not set by natural conditions, but is determined by forms of social appropriation and economic exploitation of nature. Problems of equity and distribution were clearly generated by capital accumulation before any ecological limits were reached. Economic growth destroys the ecological and cultural conditions of sustainability by increasing throughput of matter and energy, generating resource scarcity as the result of socio-environmental degradation (O'Connor 1988; Leff, 1995a).

Beyond the ecological limits (Meadows et al. 1992) of growth and scarcity, of managerialism and technological solutions, power structures constrain social access and legal rights to appropriate natural resources. As Martinez-Alier (1992) has stated, "science has no criteria to evaluate... the distributive conflicts that are at stake". Such criteria cannot emerge from an ecological rationality "because to compare costs and benefits we need to assign values, and ecology cannot offer such valuation system independently from politics".

By naturalizing the limits of growth, political ecology is expelled from the field of ecological economics. Ecological conditions are reduced to environmental and demographic problems, where the distribution of ecological and social costs fade out of theoretical and political focus. As a result ecological economics is concerned with the theoretical difficulties to give present values to future consumer preferences, but exclude the problem of intragenerational equity, based on two false assumptions.

1. That the issue has been already solved in Western affluent societies (everybody has food, shelter, and two cars); and
2. That the issue of social justice has been displaced by that of sustainability of social institutions (Proops 1989).

Thus, ideologies of post-scarcity and dematerialization of production have invaded the approaches of ecological economics to sustainability.[3]

Egalitarian Environmentalism and Political Ecology

Contrasting with ecological economics, political ecology recognizes in the "environmentalism of the poor" the struggle for equity and democracy, and their cultural relation to nature; by claiming direct control of their patrimony of natural resources, environmental movements oppose the capitalization of nature by the market system and State control over natural resources (Leff 1994a, 1995a; Martinez-Alier 1992).

Social resistance to environmental degradation mobilizes the internalization of ecological costs which cannot be accounted for by economic instruments and ecological norms. Environmental movements to reappropriate nature are important not only for their conservationist effects and their contribution to more equitable and democratic conditions for sustainable development. Grassroots movements go beyond claims for ecological conservation and social participation. These new social actors are transforming the productive rationality imposed by the "enlightened" scientific and industrial revolutions, revaluing natural and cultural diversity, as well as traditional practices and wisdoms (Toledo 1992; Leff 1994b).

This is the profound sense of environmentalism in the South. Through the reaffirmation of communal rights to reappropriate and self-manage their patrimony of natural and cultural resources, these emergent environmental movements are internalizing the environmental conditions for sustainable production, based on the productivity of nature and the values of social equity and cultural diversity. As these movements deploy their power strategies to construct an alternative productive rationality, resources will be removed from the sphere of market economy, imposing a limit to the capitalization of nature.

Ecological economics recognizes the importance of natural conservation and ecological balance, however, nature's productive potential has been undervalued, particularly in the richly complex biodiverse tropical ecosystems. While the productive strategies developed by the Mesoamerican civilizations before the colonial conquest and capitalist expansion were overthrown by the industrial revolution and the instrumental rationality of modernity, the attempts of the Physiocrats to view nature as the source of values faded with the irruption of capital and its technical means to capitalize nature and culture, interrupting the coevolution of alternative paradigms of eco-ethno-development.

The new actors of grassroots environmentalism are adjusting the discourse on sustainability to their own interests and values (Instituto Indigenista Interamericano 1990) and many indigenous and peasant movements are introducing new agroecological tools to their productive practices. The internalization of ecological content to the political strategies of grassroots movements is developing as new struggles arise over the reappropriation of their patrimony of natural and cultural resources (Leff 1994b).

Bioeconomics, Productive Ecology, and Negentropic Economy

Economics is facing the problem of having been left without a theory of value. The economic system has no objective means to measure the equivalence of use-values to be exchanged. Market (or pseudo-market) prices are false signs of resource scarcity; they cannot serve as indicators for a rational allocation of productive factors nor to internalize environmental costs. Thus, economics must be reconstructed. This opens the question about the foundations of a new theory of production that can account for environmental processes in time and space, and internalize the ecological conditions of sustainable development.[4] These conditions include the ecotechnological potential of each region, mediated by the cultural values and the social interests of the people: the symbolic systems, ethnic styles, and productive practices through which nature is valued as resources; the social rules that establish the rights for appropriation and the rates of exploitation of natural resources; the technological patterns that allow for resource renewal and waste recycling.

Georgescu-Roegen developed a critique of standard economics from the standpoint of the second law of thermodynamics. However, the analysis of production in terms of flows of matter and energy, and entropy decay in throughput, cannot yield a new yardstick to measure value. Low entropy is a necessary, but not a sufficient condition to transform matter into use-values. Bioeconomics is based on the assertion that the economic process increasingly produces higher entropy that limits economic growth,[5] centering its attention on the technological transformation of matter. Altvater (1993) suggests that entropy growth can be controlled by "social modeling". Society would then be able to limit entropy production, but could not reverse it. Thus, the self-organizing character of nature and the primary productivity of ecological processes has been underestimated; the possibility of constructing bioeconomics on the negentropic potentiality of natural productivity has been widely ignored.

Georgescu-Roegen argued that the use of solar energy was an "illusory path".[6] By restricting his assessment of the potential of solar radiation to solar technologies, other perspectives were blocked to analyze the capacity of the biodiverse tropical forests and agroforestry systems as solar collectors to transform radiant energy into biomass, and of ecological agriculture to reduce the inputs of non-renewable sources of matter and energy. However, the energy intake from the environment has different effects in the production of entropy and a sustainable productive process if it comes from the sun (with no disturbances to the Earth's environment), or from exhaustible resources and polluting processes like the extraction and transformation of fossil fuels.

The potential for biomass formation through photosynthesis can become the basis for an alternative paradigm of production in the tropical regions. Natural net primary productivity can reach annual sustainable yields of about 8-10% (Rodin et al. 1975).[7] These levels of primary productivity may seem low compared with artificialized agrosystems. Nonetheless, when the productive efficiency of these crops are evaluated as a long-term process, a sharp decline in yields and a pronounced increment in their conservation costs is observed (Rosenzweig 1971).[8] In contrast, the productive management of biodiverse ecosystems and multiple croppings can be enhanced by appropriate technologies to generate a sustainable production of goods to satisfy the basic needs of a population. The primary productivity of ecosystems can be increased with biotechnologies that enhance the capacities of the biological processes to transform solar radiation into biomass to yield a significant output of use-values and consumer goods (Leff 1994a, 1995a).[9]

The approaches from ecological economics to the management of the primary productivity of ecosystems have focused on the environmental impact of present patterns of human appropriation of the products of photosynthesis and its limits to provide basic needs to a growing population. Recent research has assessed the amount of biomass that is presently produced and used by human beings through dominant agronomic practices.[10] However, no concrete analysis exists today of the ecotechnological potential of a new approach to production in the tropical regions.

By valuing the importance of photosynthesis as a negentropic process, bioeconomics can build a positive theory of production that can balance the natural production of biomass with the ineluctable entropic decay of matter and energy in the metabolism of living organisms and industrial or technological process of production. This open system's approach to sustainable production and ecological equilibrium offers more interesting perspectives as a productive ecology in the tropical regions. This new economy should consider the ecological potential of biomass formation through photosynthesis as a basis to develop a high yield of vegetal matter, enhancing ecological productivity to balance biotechnological processes in the metabolism of living matter in trophic chains, and technological transformation of raw materials in industry. The overall ecotechnological productive process would contribute to establish ecological balance while generating a sustainable yield of culturally defined use-values. Thus a new economy can be forged, blending a natural economy (primary productivity) with a moral economy (cultural values) and an industrial economy (technological productivity).

CONCLUSIONS

The Emergence of a Grassroots Productive Ecology

New approaches to sustainability are emerging from the social appropriation of nature. In this perspective, I have suggested the construction of a new paradigm of ecotechnological sustainable productivity that aims to reduce ecological degradation, entropic decay, and resource depletion and to enhance ecological productivity, developing the negentropic productive process provided by nature (Leff 1986, 1994b, 1995a). This paradigm is being internalized by indigenous groups and peasant movements in their struggles to regain control over their biological diversity and traditional biotechnologies to reconstruct self-managed productive economies, based on a more equitable and sustainable use of natural resources.

The inquiries from ecological economics to these social processes are limited by a rigid and reductionist assessment of carrying capacity and technological fixes, rather than envisioning the potential of nature to derive an alternative rationality to production through the sustainable management of complex biodiverse ecosystems, enhancing natural ecosystemic productivity with appropriate sustainable biotechnologies. The basic question is not how many people can live on the direct appropriation of natural productivity based on present limits to per capita biomass use. The basic point is to recognize natural ecosystems as productive ecosystems that can undergo a process of selection and transformation to yield an increasing sustainable production of natural use-values.

Ecotechnological productivity is geared to enhance instead of destroy the ecological conditions for resource renewal and recycling and for a sustainable process of production. Thus, the high primary productivity recognized and measured by ecologists in the tropical regions, should be viewed as a potential (rather than a limit) to yield increasing output of consumer goods.[11] The socio-environmental processes triggered by the social construction of this alternative paradigm of production will establish new balances between population growth and natural resources. Only with the materialization of this process will we be able to compare the potential of this sustainable production and consumption of biomass with present trends of unsustainable agronomic practices. My hypothesis is that the ecotechnological paradigm offers better alternatives to alleviate poverty and solve the needs of the majority of the people, to establish ecological equilibrium, and to root sustainable development on ecological and social basis, than the dominant economic rationality and the capitalization of nature.

This project cannot be centrally planned nor be left to market mechanisms. The ecotechnological paradigm can only be constructed as a creative and innovative process based on the appropriation of the natural resources, ecological potentials, and biotechnological means of production by peasant and indigenous communities, to self-manage their productive processes. This emergent environmental rationality is based on cultural diversity and oriented towards a decentralized economy. This process is open to conflict over the appropriation of biodiversity but also to freedom and creativity, to scientific and technological innovation, and to a more equitable, sustainable, and democratic management of natural resources.

NOTES

1. Martinez-Alier (1992) has labeled these two tendencies the "environmentalism of affluence" and "ecologism of survival".

2. As the environment has become internationalized, it has been transformed. As it is transformed social struggles are mounted for the control and ownership of natural resources. The attempt to import solutions to environmental problems from developed countries, in the form of orthodox environmental management, therefore assumes more importance as the ecological crisis of development deepens. For indigenous cultures, sustainable development is not so much the invention of the future as a rediscovery of the past, even when the practical mechanics of how to combine modern technologies with a concern for sustainable livelihood creation remains largely unexplored" (Redclift 1987).

3. In its more perverse strategies, criticized by Herman E. Daly (1991) and other ecological economists, the discourse on sustainability pretends that economic growth can be maintained in the long-run by liberating market forces; that the mechanisms of an ecologically extended economic rationality are the key to ecological balance and social justice.

4. As Christensen (1989) has rightly argued, "what has been missing in all of the various critiques [of economics] is a reconstruction of the biophysical foundations of economic activity. Modern economic theories have neglected the implications of the basic physical principles governing material and energy use for an economic theory of production, for the operation of a production based price system, for macroeconomic (disequilibrium) dynamics and for longer run growth processes and prospects".

5. "Although the law of entropy increase is inexorable, its actual effect in the reshaping of nature can be affected by human social behavior. Changes in the total entropy of the system are made up of entropy increase within the system as a result of materials and energy transformation, and interchange with the environment through energy intake and entropy

discharge. Thus, the limitation of entropy increase is above all a question of social modeling" (Altvater 1993).

6. This conclusion is drawn from the evaluation of the environmental and economic costs of presently available solar technologies, "that require so much space and so many inputs that the gain in useful energy would be outweighed by the investment in energy and materials" (Altvater 1993).

7. Leigh (1975) estimated the Net Primary Production of the planet at 1.76×10^{11} annual tons in dry weight, equivalent to 8×10^{18} kilocalories (of which, terrestrial ecosystems contribute with 1.21×10^{11} tons, and marine ecosystems with 5.5×10^{10} tons). For a comprehensive compendium of methods and evaluations on the primary productivity of the biosphere see Lieth 1978). Empirical analyses of traditional practices in tropical ecosystems show that biomass accumulation in relation to harvestable crops can reach annual rates of 16 to 22 tons per hectare, in dry weight of organic material; traditional agricultural techniques, such as chinampas, can reach a daily productivity of 900 kgs per hectare (Gliessman et al. 1981). More recent studies carried out in Latin America have characterized the terrestrial ecosystems of the region according to its NPP with the purpose of identifying their potential for sustainable use. Gilberto Gallopin et al. estimated the aerial annual NNP per hectare in dry weight in humid tropical and subtropical forests to be of 10–15 tons; 5–12 in humid tropical, subtropical and temperate mountain forests; 3–19 tons in dry tropical and subtropical forests; 5–9 tons in tropical and subtropical savannas; and less than 5 tons in deserts and arid zones (I.A. Gomez and G. Gallopin 1989).

8. Clapham (1973) expresses the limits of modern technological inputs to increase the productivity of these ecosystems in the following terms: "Technology can allow these ecosystems to remain viable and productive, but only at considerable cost. There are clearly limits to which technology can overcome the tendency of ecosystems to revert to natural equilibrium, and the instability and uncertainty of the system's capacity to produce products useful to man increase greatly as these limits are approached".

9. Research studies have discovered a highly efficient enzyme in tropical plants responsible for photosynthetic assimilation (Slack and Hatch 1967; Bjîrkman and Berry 1973).

10. Vitousek et al. (1986) have assessed the human appropriation of the products of photosynthesis. They estimate that human beings use approximately 40.4 petajoules ($1Pg=10^6$ kilo calories) of (NPP). This is being reduced from a potential production of 58.1 Pg because of human intervention that transform land use patterns (9.0 due to decreased NPP in agriculture; 1.4 to conversion of forest to pasture; 4.5 to desertification; and 2.6 to loss to urban areas). They conclude that present forms of "co-option, diversion and destruction of these terrestrial resources clearly contribute to human-caused extinctions of species and genetically distinct populations..." and suggest that "with current patterns of exploitation, distribution and consumption, a substantially larger human population... could not be supported without co-opting well over half of terrestrial NPP." Their argument is that 40% of the potential NPP is used, co-opted or foregone because of human activities, while it could otherwise enhance biodiversity as a condition for sustainability and a source of economic value.

11. This potential is not limited by the primary productivity of natural ecosystems, nor by the present efficiency of available biotechnologies. These environmentally sound biotechnologies must not be conceived as a new green revolution that minimizes ecological degradation while increasing yields of monocroppings, but rather as a technological means to manage-integrated and multiple patterns biodiverse ecosystems. Their carrying capacity will not depend on any ecological fixes but on innovative productive practices and human settlement designs that will establish new demographic dynamics arising from new life styles and consumption patterns.

REFERENCES

Altvater, E. 1993. The Future of the Market. London: Verso.

Bjîrkman, O. and J. Berry. 1973. High Efficiency Photosynthesis. *Scientific American.* 229(4): 80–93.

Bookchin, M. 1991. The Philosophy of Social Ecology. Montreal: Black Rose Books.

Clapham, W. B. 1973. Natural Ecosystems. New York: Macmillan.

Christensen, P.C. 1989. Historical Roots for Ecological Economics—Biophysical versus allocative approaches. *Economical Economics* 1(1): 17–36.

Copernic, N. 1970. Des Revolutions des Orbes Celestes, Paris: Librairie Scientifique et Technique A. Blanchard.

Costanza, R. 1989. What is Ecological Economics. *Ecological Economics* 1(1): 1–7.

Costanza, R. et al. 1991. Ecological Economics: The Science and Management of Sustainability. New York: Columbia University Press.

Daly, H.E. 1991. Steady-State Economics. Washington: Island Press.

Ehrlich R.P. 1989. The limits to substitution: Meta-resource depletion and new economic-ecological paradigm. *Ecological Economics* 1(1): 9–16.

Ehrlich, P. R. and A. H. Ehrlich. 1991. Healing the Planet. USA: Addison-Wesley Publishing Co.

Georgescu-Roegen, N. 1971. The Entropy Law and the Economic Process. Cambridge, Mass: Harvard University Press.

Gliessman, S.R. et al. 1981. The ecological basis for the application of traditional agricultural technology in the management of tropical ecosystems. *Agro-Ecosystems.* 7: 173–185.

Gomez I.A. and G. Gallopin. 1995. Oferta Ecologica en America Latina: Productuvudad y Production de los Grandes Ecosistemas Terrestres. In El Futuro Ecologico de un Continente: una vision prospectiva de America Latina, eds. G. Gallopin. et al. Mexico: UNU/Fondo de *Cultura Economico* 1 (79): 445–496.

Hobbelink, H. 1992. La Diversidad Biologica y la Biotecnologica Agricola. Conservacion o Acceso a los Recursos? *Ecologica Politica* 4:57–72. Barcelona: ICARIA.

Instituto Indigenista Interamericano 1990. Politica indigenista 1991-1995. *America Indigena* 50(1).

Kapp, W. 1983. Social Costs in Economic Development. In Ullmann, J.E. (Comp.), Social Costs, Economic Development and Environmental Disruption, Lanham, Mass: University Press of America.

Leff, E. 1986. Ecotechnological productivity: A conceptual basis for the integrated management of natural resources. *Social Science Information* 25(3): 681–702.

Leff, E. et al. 1986. Los Problemas del conocimiento y la Perspectiva Ambiental del Desarrollo, Mexico: Siglo XXI.

Leff, E. 1994a. Ecologic a y Capital. Racionalidad Ambiental, Democracia Participativa y Desarrollo Sustentable, Mexico: Siglo XXI/UNAM.

Leff, E. 1994b. The concept of ecotechnological productivity: Implications and applications for sustainable development. Second International Conference of the European Association for Bioeconomic Studies. Palma de Mallorca. (unpublished manuscript).

Leff, E. 1995a. Green Production. Toward an Environmental Rationality. New York: Guilford.

Leff, E. 1995b. Los Nuevos Actores Sociales del Ambientalismo en el Medio Rural, in UNAM/ INAH/UAM-AZ., La Sociedad Rural frente al Nuevo Milenio, Mexico: Plaza y Valdez (in print).

Leigh, H. 1975. Primary productivity in ecosystems: Comparative analysis of global patterns. In: Unifying Concepts in Ecology, eds. W. H. van Dobben, and R. H. Lowe-McConnell. The Hague: W. Jung B.V. Publishers, Centre for Agricultural Publishing and Documentation.

Lieth, H. F. H. 1978. Patterns of Primary Production in the Biosphere, Stroudsbourg. PA: Dowden, Hutchinson and Ross.

Martinez-Alier, J. 1994. The merchandising of biodiversity. *Etnoecologica* 3: 69–86.

Martinez-Alier, J. 1995. De la Economa Ecologica al Ecologismo Popular, Barcelona: ICARIA.

Martinez-Alier, J. and K. Schlupmann. 1987. Ecological Economics. New York: Oxford.

Meadows, D. H., D. L. Meadows, and J. Randers. 1992. Beyond the Limits, Post Mills. Vermont: Chelsea Green Publishing Company.

O'Connor, J. 1988. Capitalism, nature, socialism: A theoretical introduction. *Capitalism, Nature, Socialism* 1(1): 11–38.

Passet, R. 1979. L'Economique et le Vivant. Paris: Payot.

Proops, J. L. R. 1989. Ecological Economics: Rationale and Problem Areas. *Ecological Economics* 1(1): 59–76.

Redclift, M. 1987. Sustainable Development: Exploring the Contradictions. London: Rutledge.

Rodin, L. E., N. I. Bazilevich, and N. N. Rozov. 1975. Primary productivity of the main world ecosystems. In: Unifying Concepts in Ecology, eds. W. H. van Dobben, and R. H. Lowe-McConnell. The Hague: W. Jung B.V. Publishers, Centre for Agricultural Publishing and Documentation.

Rosenzweig, M. L. 1971. Paradox of Enrichment: Destabilization of Exploitation of Ecosystems in Ecological Time. *Science* 171: 385–387.

Slack, C. R. and M. D. Hatch. 1967. Comparative studies on the activity of carboxilases and other enzymes in relation to the new pathway of photosynthetic carbon dioxide fixation in tropical grasses. *Biochemical Journal* 103: 660–665.

Toledo, V.M. 1992. Toda la Utopia: El nuevo movimiento ecologico de los indigenas y campesinos de Mexico. In Autonomia y Nuevos Sujetos Sociales en el Desarrollo Rural, eds. J. Moguel et al. Mexico: Siglo XXI /CEHAM.

Vitousek, P.M. et al. 1986. Human appropriation of the products of photosynthesis. *Bioscience* 36(6): 368–373.

WCED 1987. Our Common Future. Report of the World Commission on Environment and Development. UK: Oxford University Press.

6 SOCIAL AND ETHICAL DIMENSIONS OF ECOLOGICAL ECONOMICS

Anil Gupta
Society for Research and Initiatives for Sustainable
Technologies and Institutions and Honey Bee Network
c/o Indian Institute of Management
Ahmedabad - 380 015, India

OVERVIEW

The ethical values underlying the behavior of those people who conserve natural resources individually or collectively have to be explicitly incorporated into ecological economics. Instead of arriving at values of scare resources only through opportunity cost in the market place, we should also assign weights to the kind of future socio-ecological order that we wish to see in place. These weights should reflect our preferences and, therefore, help us make decisions that contribute towards sustainable society. To identify these weights, I suggest we draw upon dynamics of innovators. Most of these innovators, generating technological and institutional innovations for sustainable resource management, have resolved ecological economic trade-off by balancing the time and discount rate.

In this chapter, I begin with the arguments in favor of incorporating ethical values in the calculation of economic weights for ecologically sustainable outcomes. Then I discuss the process of value addition in local innovations and describe the Honey Bee Network, and goals of the Society for Research and Initiatives for Sustainable Technologies and Institutions (SRISTI). Later in the chapter I discuss the logic of extending time-frame and reducing discount rates: the key to translating ethical concerns into economic values. I discuss modified socio-ecological paradigms for understanding interplay between ecological, economic, and ethical trade-offs for household survival system in high risk environments. I also discuss the conceptual relationship between conservation of resource and knowledge around it in intra- and inter-generational time-frame to identify strong and weak sustainability outcomes. Finally, I deal with the process of institution building for rejuvenating indigenous ecological knowledge system, as well as the norms and values created by different institutional conditions.

The illustrations are presented about specific innovators at grassroots level whose ethical values have led them to remain poor despite being rich in ecological knowledge. It is unlikely that this knowledge system will survive without breaking the close nexus that exists between existence of poverty and high biodiversity and associated knowledge systems.

INTRODUCTION

The conservation of natural resources particularly biodiversity involves making judgments about what to conserve, how much, for how long and at what and whose cost.[1]

The crucial link between biodiversity and cultural diversity (McNeely 1988; Gupta 1991; 1992; Gupta and Ura 1992; Gupta 1995a; 1995c) indicates that we have to look at deeper processes that are affected when decisions about conserving biodiversity are made. Cultural and social institutions provide a context in which technological choices regarding use of biodiversity have to be made. Making these choices involves making judgments and trade-offs. Judgments about natural resources performing ecological functions do not have to be resolved only in the realm of philosophy and morality. Though moral judgments cannot be avoided altogether. My contention is that values underlying the behavior of those people who conserve natural resources individually or collectively have to be explicitly incorporated into the ecological economics. Instead of arriving at values of scarce resources only through opportunity cost in the market place, we should also assign weights to the kind of future socio-ecological order that we wish to see in place. These weights would reflect our preferences and, therefore, help us make decisions that contribute towards sustainable society. To identify these weights, I suggest we draw upon the dynamics of indigenous/local ecological knowledge systems as well as the experience of grassroots innovators. Most of these innovators, generating technological and institutional innovations for sustainable resource management, have resolved ecological/economic trade-off by balancing the time-frame and discount rate.

In this chapter I present the arguments in favor of incorporating ethical values in the calculation of economic weights for ecologically sustainable outcomes, I discuss the process of value addition in local innovations. I describe the Honey Bee Network and goals of Society for Research and Initiatives for Sustainable Technologies and Institutions (SRISTI). I present the logic of extending time-frame and reducing discount rates: the key to translating ethical concerns into economic values. I discuss modified socio-ecological paradigm for understanding interplay between, economic and ethical trade-offs for a household survival system in high risk environments. I also discuss the conceptual relationship between conservation of a resource and knowledge around it in intra- and inter-generational time-frame to identify strong and weak sustainability outcomes. I deal with the process of institution building for rejuvenating indigenous ecological knowledge system. I provide examples from actual situations in which individual as well as institutional innovations for conservation of resources have evolved. I analyze the norms and values created by different institutional conditions, and then I summarize the key ideas of the chapter.

ETHICAL FOUNDATIONS OF ECONOMIC CHOICES: SUSTAINING OPTIMAL ECOLOGICAL OUTCOMES

The incentives or disincentives for using resources in a manner that these can be renewed in a reasonable period of time emerge not only in the market place but also through public policy and private moral judgments. When biological diversity got reduced in the high growth green revolution regions because of availability of high yielding varieties and chemical inputs, it was considered necessary at that time to meet the goals of food production. Even at that time, planners knew that the regions which provided the precious biodiversity were inhabited by some of the poorest communities. The absence of any premium for conservation of diversity was compatible with the short-term calculus of market place for using resources in a non-sustainable manner. It is important to understand the link between pricing of natural resources through such calculus and the contrasting behavior of communities in high risk environments such as drought prone areas, hill areas, forest regions, and flood prone regions which are poor in economic infrastructure but rich in biological diversity and associated knowledge systems. Today, when the link between poverty and biodiversity is pursued in a normative manner, many times people ignore the implicit ethical judgments.

In the high-growth low-biodiversity regions, farmers use ground water in a non-sustainable manner because the state prices electrical power on the basis of horse power of the engine of the pump sets/tube well and not on the basis of actual consumption of power. There is no reason why farmers should be judicious in the use of power and water. Likewise, when the price of irrigation does not reflect scarcity value of water, farmers do not economize its use. That is why in many of the drought prone regions in India, some farmers grow sugar cane (which is a water wasting crop), whereas many others cannot get life saving irrigation even to grow millets. Similarly, by reducing custom duty and other taxes on chemical pesticides, farmers are encouraged to use this input rather excessively thereby triggering a treadmill effect.

Merely by getting the prices right, allocation of resources could not have been corrected. Most governments have faced the dilemma of increasing the resource use intensity to meet the goals of food self-reliance. And ironically, one notices at the same time that the institutions providing these inputs have become non-viable because of inability to cover the costs. Therefore, while state folds back, market institutions fill in the gap and further intensify the distortions in the prices of natural resources as well as the process of their non-sustainable use.

The withdrawal of state affects some regions and communities more than others. The slow-growth or low-growth regions with high diversity are inhabited by some of the most disadvantaged communities. These communities get affected most adversely, thereby, sharpening the cleavages in society. The erosion of the natural resource base is not stemmed by the state because banks use high discount rates to appraise their investments. Only enterprises with higher rates of return in the shortest period of time can attract capital. Obviously, most such enterprises externalize the environmental costs to maintain their profitability within the short time-frame. Since market penetration is not necessarily accompanied by evolution of institutions for collective management of externalities, the costs of internalization becomes the barrier for technological transformation in favor of sustainable resource use. These barriers are stronger or more evident in well endowed regions. But the costs are significant even in high risk environments. The conclusion reached earlier by Martinez-Alier (1991), "because of big, diachronic, invaluable 'externalities', economic commensurability does not exist separately from a social distribution of moral values regarding the rights of other social groups" is still valid. The relationship between ecological context and economic implications mediated by public administration are indeed political in nature as also argued by Martinez-Alier (1991). The people in regions rich in natural resources but poor in economic infrastructure feel bewildered when they are told to conserve these resources for larger social good despite remaining poor themselves and dependent upon government subsidies or money order economies. Intensification of social unrest in many of these regions in the recent past clearly explains that the patience of the people is running out.

The occupationary niches in most urban regions with least social and economic status are filled by emigrants from the high risk environments lacking local employment opportunities. This emigration also implies that the proportion of households headed or managed by women is much higher in the regions from where males emigrate. Obviously, there can be no ethical or moral justification for a social order which institutionalizes different developmental tracks for different socio-ecological and economic groups. And yet one of the most precious ecological resource (i.e., biodiversity is also found most abundantly in these impoverished regions) (Gupta 1991).

Political Economy of Alienation of High Risk Regions

Why do regions with high biodiversity contain the most economically disadvantaged people? Politically, most democracies run on the basis of constituencies created out of a minimum number of people in one region. Therefore, the number of representatives elected from hill areas, drought prone areas, and forest regions with low population densities are far lesser than developed regions. The political alliances can survive by alienating the representatives from these regions. The political support, or lack of it, manifested in the choice of economic criteria for allocation of resources. If mineral and forest resources are not valued properly, it may appear that state has to subsidize the economic systems in the regions. Patronizing attitudes evolve out of subsidy culture. The entire public policy is based on what people do not have rather than what they have. The employment programs are based on the assumption that people in these regions are unskilled. Therefore, the food-for-work program during the period of drought in arid regions or forest areas may involve breaking stones and making roads. Ironically, the same roads make the exploitation of natural resources more efficient and fast.

There are many other reasons for close association between poverty and richness in natural resources.

1.   The biodiversity evolves and grows in regions of ecological heterogeneity. Variation in micro soil-climatic interactions creates conditions for biological diversity to evolve. Variations in ecological endowment mean that the local land use systems cannot respond to market input based technologies suitable for uniform endowments. This implies low and uncertain productivity level in agriculture and fluctuating and low prices for non-agricultural biodiverse products or forest products.

2.   Given diversity in color, taste, shape and quality of natural products, markets are often unable to generate consumer demand for these products. The logistics of transporting, storing and displaying diverse varieties of vegetables, grains, fruits, etc., are also very costly. In the absence of consumer willingness to bear extra cost, markets shy away from providing channels for their consumption. The result is that producers of such products do not have much purchasing power and rely on local demand which is limited. The impoverishment is an obvious consequence.

3.   The lack of purchasing power also results from low value or no value attached to the biodiversity prospecting skills of the local communities by the outsiders. Once the knowledge system is devalued, the cultural and social decline follows. The tenuous relationship with nature is ruptured. The erosion of knowledge goes hand-in-hand with erosion of resources. The eco-degradation spurred by external forces is abetted by the poor, as well as the not so poor people. This further decreases the prospects of capital generation and accumulation. Even the social communities start breaking down. Once the social structure breaks down, the communal safety nets for the poor are no longer available; poverty becomes socially a humiliating experience.

4.   The ethical values of local communities which conserve biodiversity despite remaining poor also reinforce material poverty. There are many medicine men and women who believe that the power of their potion

would go down if they charged a price for it. There are large number of such people who even do not accumulate medicines. Instead they collect a plant only when need arises. Some others who do accept payment demand such a low price that only poor people use their services. The well-off people generally believe that anything which is cheap is also less effective and safe. There are various institutions which prohibit extraction of a resource beyond a reasonable limit lest a deity supposed to protect that resource gets annoyed. Religious mechanisms merely symbolize the constraints a culture imposes on the use of given resource. There are many other ways in which extraction of a resource is restrained and thus opportunities for generating economic surplus are foregone.

Thus, a combination of political, economic, institutional, and ethical factors leads to the nexus between poverty and richness in biodiversity.

How does one break this nexus without generating an economic weight for ethical values? Thus, if a community decides not to extract a resource beyond a minimum quantity, should it be punished for upholding its values? At present, that seems to be the message. There are at least three specific instruments through which economic weightage for these values can be generated.

1.   *The non-actionable subsidies for disadvantaged regions*

Under GATT, Part Four, Article 8, the assistance to disadvantaged regions which are contiguous geographical area and where per capita income is not above 85% of the average for the territory and where unemployment rate is at least 110% of the average measured over three-year period is non-actionable. Thus, weights can be assigned to the conservation practices and levies can be charged on various products or services to subsidize these regions for a comprehensive development policy. It is assumed that in view of the various factors mentioned earlier, the local regional councils may not have enough surplus to undertake these investments themselves. New ecological enterprises requiring value addition in natural products of these regions can be subsidized so that additional cost due to locational disadvantages can be set off. These industries might enable higher value addition through better technologies and with smaller quantities of the raw material. This will generate incomes and employment without creating stress on ethical values preventing excessive extraction of a given resource. Domestic support also provide a basis for supporting research in connection with environmental programs, plant protection, extension besides infrastructural development. Support for the disadvantaged regions is accepted under this annexure as well. It is not my argument that states will indeed do so. What I am implying is that should a political commitment materialize, doing so will not be impeded by at least the new world trade order despite much popular beliefs to the contrary.

2. *Compensation for local creativity, innovation, traditional knowledge of ethnomedicinal and ethno-agricultural uses of plants.*

Various arrangements for compensation will be discussed later but this instrument certainly can enable providing weights to the knowledge and resource conserving practice. Under TRIPS, patent protection can be extended to the products based on plants, animals, micro organisms, etc., provided they meet the conditions of newness, non-obviousness and inventiveness besides utility. Despite controversy on the patentability of traditional knowledge held by a community, it is possible to file applications on behalf of large communities either through their representatives or collectively for a specific contributions. In addition to traditional knowledge, contemporary innovations for pest control, veterinary medicine, etc., can also be protected. State can buy these patents and make them available freely to investors after paying the local communities a reasonable license fee or other forms of compensation. Under this provision, the local communities do not have to feel obliged or be under patronizing pressure.

3. *The weightage to local institutions, practices, sacred sites etc., may improve the prospects of local communities conserving their resources.*

Since additional gains accrue only so long as resources are conserved, these incentives may encourage conservation. Tourism is another function through which non-extractive resource use can generate incentives for conservation.

For all the three instruments to work, several institutional changes would be required. Necessary changes range from curricula and pedagogy in the educational systems at different levels to changing the nature of discourse around developmental projects in high biodiversity rich areas. The value formation takes place in the early stages of life. There is very little in the educational curriculum which generates respect in the mind of learners towards resource conserving disadvantaged communities and grassroots innovators. In a recent study, I found that in some cases children who dropped out of school knew more than enrolled children in terms of local ecological knowledge. In any case there was not a clear correlation between the rank achieved by children in biodiversity contests and academic exams. Apparently, in the early stages, some of the children who have an aptitude for ecological knowledge, and can grow as ecologists, are rejected by the formal academic system (Chand et al. 1994).

The rehabilitation policy for the ecologically skilled and economically less skilled tribal people (many of whom conserve resources very well) in the event of displacement due to dams and industrial projects leaves considerable scope for improvement. The valuation of the cultural ties of local communities with resources is done so poorly that the disruption does not appear costly.[2]

Similarly, the policy of drawing up strict boundaries around sanctuaries and parks keeping people out may imply a very low value and weight on the survival options of the people living in those regions. The ethical values that may have guided the conservation of wildlife may have become weaker. But as many native groups have explained, the commonalities of the same spirit among human and animal systems require that the hunting and other such activities are performed with considerable restraint. One does not deny that in some cases, poaching may have taken place even by local people, the incentives often arise through external valuation. When an animal in the wild generates less revenue for local communities due to poorer returns from tourism, hunting for selling the skin or other parts may take place.

Valuation and compensation thus are required in various ways to modify the consumer preferences, societal values and economic calculus. The discourse on development will undergo a fundamental shift if opportunities of economic improvement were to evolve through respect and responsiveness towards local knowledge, ethics, institutions and creativity. How we have tried to do that is discussed in the next part.

VALUE ADDITION IN LOCAL CREATIVITY AND INNOVATION: TRANSFORMING ECONOMICS OF CONSERVATION AND SUSTAINABLE RESOURCE USE

The options of sustainability depend upon the conditions of conservation of knowledge as well as resource. As evident from the following matrix (Table 6.1), sustainability is highest in cases where knowledge and resource both have been conserved in single as well as multiple generations. If knowledge is conserved and resource is eroded within a single generation, the sustainability is weak to moderate. If knowledge is not used and reproduced over generations, it is likely to be lost. Similarly, if resource is conserved but knowledge is not within single generation, the resource is endangered. Many parks and sanctuaries come under this category. By keeping people out, the knowledge may not get renewed. After a while when ecological complexities increased or perturbations increase, the local knowledge may not be available for regeneration. The possibility of resource being conserved for several generations without conserving associated knowledge system is remote. It is a different matter that under certain situations, the managers of such a resource may generate lot of local knowledge. In any case, it is like a map in which the legend is lost. Much of the biodiversity in such regions can be accessed only randomly.

If knowledge is conserved and resource has been degraded even for more than one generation, the regeneration is possible. This is precisely the context in which Honey Bee Network operates.

Table 6.1. Scope for Regeneration

	Generational Time Framework	
	Single	Multiple
Eroded Resources	1	2
Conserved	3	4
Eroded Knowledge	5	6
Conserved	7	8

HONEY BEE NETWORK ON INDIGENOUS KNOWLEDGE, CREATIVITY, AND INNOVATION

Global Networking: Honey Bee
The Honey Bee Network draws its philosophical principles from the conduct of the honey bee.

- The network believes that we should collect the knowledge of the people, as the Honey Bee collects pollen, without making the flowers poorer.
- We should connect people to people as innovators with other innovators as the Honey Bee connects different flowers through pollination.

We insist in our work that two principles are followed without fail: one, whatever we learn from the people must be shared with them in their language; and two, every innovation must be sourced to individuals/communities with names and addresses, to protect the intellectual property rights of the people.

The Honey Bee Network newsletter is brought out in six languages in India (Hindi, Gujarati, Malayalam, Tamil, Kannada, and Telugu) and Zonkha in Bhutan, so that dialogue with the people takes place in their own languages. Creative people from one place should be able to communicate with similar people elsewhere to trigger mutual imagination and fertilize respective recipes for sustainable natural resource management.

Sustainability Combination of Cell of Regeneration

a)   *Poor* (1 and 5) – This is so because within one generation, as in our times both the resources and the associated knowledge base get eroded. The knowledge may only be available in old book shops or waste paper markets, or pavement stores. The folk knowledge having been eroded may be almost to reconstruct or rejuvenate. Erosion of knowledge was never so rapid, as in our generation, because of declining intergenerational communication. We have no time for our own elders or those of others.

b)   *Very poor* (2 and 6) – In this case the situation is even worse because the resources and the knowledge have been degraded for more than one generation. Only rare repositories of knowledge may exist among some by-passed communities.

c)   *Medium* (1 and 7) – This situation can occur if local knowledge is incorporated in strategies of regeneration. The knowledge will also be eroded if not used.

d)   *Sustainable* (3 and 7, 4, and 8).

e)   *Endangered* (3 and 5) – This can happen when state-controlled conservation of resources through park or sanctuary is attempted, keeping people out of the resource. If knowledge is eroded, the erosion of resource cannot be far behind.

f)   *Not easily possible* (4 and 6) – This is because a resource cannot be sustained over generations without drawing upon local knowledge at all. Under conditions of no human intervention or access, certain resources like forests may be conserved over generations without incorporating local knowledge. But with increasing influence of human factors on the survivability of forests through acid rains, global warming, erosion of upper catchments, etc., and increasing population pressure, it would be difficult to pursue this possibility.

g)   *Possible* (2 and 8) – If knowledge has been documented through efforts like Honey Bee and is available to people, regeneration of resources is possible within a long time-frame.

I realize that technological innovations cannot survive without institutional innovations and support structures. Hence, I have been documenting the ecological institutions which have been evolved by the people to manage knowledge and resources as common property.

It is also possible to take the current global debate on biodiversity and peasant knowledge beyond rhetoric. Our network extends to sixty four countries at present. Some colleagues have started similar documentation in their respective regions. Offers have been received for Nepali, Sri Lankan, Ugandan,

Fulfuldi (Mali) and Bangla versions of the newsletter.

The Honey Bee Network is headquartered at SRISTI, c/o Indian Institute of Management, Ahmedabad.

Society for Research and Initiatives for Sustainable Technologies and Institutions

There is a recognized need, not only in developing countries but also in developed countries, for reorienting research and education processes to incorporate greater sensitivity towards nature. While transformation of this kind cannot be achieved through a centralized lab to land model as followed by the CG system (Consultative Group on International Agricultural Research - CGIAR), the need for a coordinating centre for networking autonomous and independent initiatives still remains. Society for Research and Initiatives for Sustainable Technologies and Institutions (SRISTI) seeks to provide such a hub. Thus, its key aim is to establish links between formal or reductionist or institutional science and the holistic or informal science underlying local ecological knowledge systems. Following from this aim, the key objectives of SRISTI are:

- Strengthening the capacity of grassroots innovators and inventors engaged in conserving biodiversity through;
- Protecting their intellectual property rights;
- Experimenting in order to add value to their knowledge;
- Developing entrepreneurial ability in order to generate returns from this knowledge; and
- Enriching their cultural and institutional basis for dealing with nature.

In due course, an international centre may be developed which, apart from networking, may provide a global forum for authentic and accountable discourse on indigenous ecological knowledge. The centre would also provide a registering facility for innovations and inventions, so that patent protection can be invoked in favor of the individuals or communities developing these innovations.

It is also hoped that SRISTI and its associated institutions will be governed by the grassroots innovators. A lot is often said about accountability and transparency. But usually, even basic documents such as balance sheets are never shared with the people with whom organizations work. SRISTI would try to set standards in this regard.

The entire modernization paradigm builds upon what people do not know, rather than what people know. The ecological, technological, institutional, and cultural knowledge of the nature conserving communities is the basic building block of our work.

We hope that future initiatives in not just the agricultural sector, but in every other sector of the global economy will be based on the existing knowledge of nature-dependent communities.

In passing, one may add that if global climatic changes do indeed take place, and environmental fluctuations dominate the regions which have managed without much fluctuation, then the skills of people used to dealing with wide fluctuations would be in greatest demand. Who would these people be if not the inhabitants of forests, hill areas and drought and flood prone regions? For this reason too we need to understand the logic of survival of disadvantaged communities, creatively.

There are several concrete initiatives that have been taken up to generate economic opportunities without impairing ethical and value basis of the communities conserving natural resources. Ethical principles underlying external access or exploration of biodiversity and associated knowledge systems have been articulated recently (Gupta 1995a) and guidelines have been suggested through collective efforts of Pew Conservation Scholars (1995b).

Recognition and Respect for Ecological Entrepreneurs, Experimenters, and Innovators

We have several examples of artisans, farmers, and pastoralists who combine their need to solve problems through local materials with an urge to pursue that in a larger social, spiritual, and cultural context. The ethics underlying this context makes their material acts more meaningful. There are many implicit mechanisms of dealing with complexity of nature.

Amratbhai, an innovative artisan who developed several creative bullock drawn implements works to improve the efficiency of these implements so that the pressure of the harness on the bullocks shoulders is reduced. In his calculus, the productivity of the implement may justify the decision of other farmers to purchase it. But the possible blessings he may get from the bullocks who would suffer less, provides him the motivation and drive to pursue more solutions.

Karimbhai is a potter, but a very perceptive herbalist at the same time. He is very poor and has not been able to send his son to school regularly. And yet, there is hardly any plant in the nearby forest in a semi-arid region of Gujarat which he does not know use of. When we organized a biodiversity contest among children and requested him to give away the prizes, being the most knowledgeable person, he was embarrassed but happy to oblige. However, when we offered a token gift to him after the function, he refused. He could not accept any gift or compensation which was linked to his ecological knowledge. This knowledge was supposed to be used for larger social good without any cost. He would accept payment if we purchased his pots. But not if we offered gifts unconnected with his knowledge. In a way, he was right. He was invited to distribute the prizes because of his knowledge and thus gifts could have had a corrupting influence.

On another occasion we were trying to make a film of our dialogue with him on the subject. While discussing the issue of biodiversity, we talked about a plant. He showed the plant to the photographer who immediately went and plucked it. This shocked Karimbhai. He felt sorry that the plant had been plucked without having to be used for solving someone's problems. This injury to nature was obviously not to his liking. We learned our lesson hard way.

Rahmatbhai is a animal healer in another village of semi-arid Gujarat. He cures various external and internal maladies of animals through numerous plant diversity based medicines. This region is inhabited by the pastoral communities. People in this village and around call him Gopalbapa out of respect and reverence. Despite being Muslim, he has been given a name of Hindu God who was known for taking care of animals and animal rearing communities. Such a cultural fusion brings out a functional aspect of local knowledge system, as well as the ethereal dimensions of social networks in which knowledge is tested, produced, and reproduced.

Rehmatbhai, alias Gopalbapa, does not charge for his services though accepts offering made by the beneficiaries. He has no other major means of livelihood. It is said that animals respond to his touch with greater submission and satisfaction than they would to their own masters. Such is the ability of Gopalbapa to communicate with animals.

Haribhai is a farmer but with a difference. He has been growing groundnut without application of any pesticide. And yet, his yields are comparable if not better than the farmers who use chemical pesticides. He does not allow water from his well to be used even for washing the pesticide sprayers. He does not claim much distinction for this, but is quite knowledgeable about the entire ecological chain which helps him keep his crop healthy.

There are a large number of other technological and institutional innovations that we have documented from different parts of India as well as other countries. Honey Bee Network and SRISTI database provides strong evidence of an ongoing social and institutional experimentation at grassroots level for generating sustainable alternatives. The question arises as to how many of these innovators make sense of their practices when they have access to more "efficient" though less environment friendly alternatives. To understand the ethical basis of ecological economic evaluation, we will have to understand the conceptual basis of their local ecological knowledge systems.

LOGIC OF EXTENDING TIME-FRAME AND REDUCING DISCOUNT RATES: THE KEY TO TRANSLATING ETHICAL CONCERNS INTO ECONOMIC VALUES

I have shown earlier in the social ecological paradigm (Gupta 1981, 1985, 1985a, 1986, 1987, 1989) how ecological conditions define the range of economic enterprises which can be sustained in a give region. However, the scale at which different enterprises are managed and the combination in which these are pooled in a portfolio is a function of access to factor and product markets, formal and informal institutions, non-monetized exchange relations, etc. The modified framework presented in Figure 6.1 illustrates the dynamic interactions between ecological endowments, perception of risks, relative scarcity or abundance of difference resources, response to various opportunities generates different kinds of household budgets and consequent stakes in resource conservation.

The ecological context in terms of soil, climate, micro-flora and fauna, etc., in a given watershed defines the range of enterprises such as crop, livestock, trees, grasses, and even some of the crafts. The ecological adaptability of species particularly in refined environments is quite localized. That in fact, is the reason why biodiversity is high. The niche specificity was confirmed through

Socio-ecological Paradigm

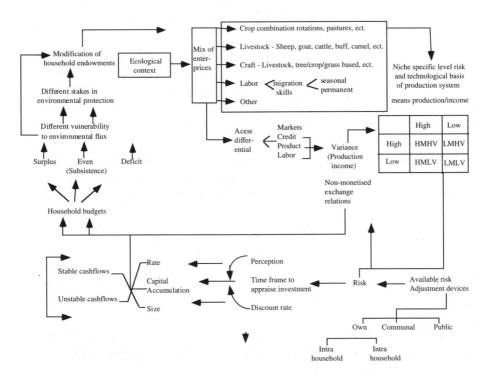

Figure 6.1. Socio-ecological paradigm.

a rotated factor analysis of the village-wise endowments of livestock species, irrigation sources, land use, etc. (Gupta 1981, 1985, 1990). The niches of sheep and goat, for instance, were quite different from niches of water buffalo.

The ratio of different species can also be a good indicator of the land use potential and prospect. For instance, in a semiarid region when ratio of small ruminants to large ruminants increases, the extent of degradation may be enhanced. This is not because people are unaware of the consequences. It happens because as the degradation increases, only small ruminants can survive. Other factors which accentuate household choices in this direction are dependent upon the nature of portfolio that households evolve.

The conventional measures of portfolio are risk and return. There are four kinds of portfolios which can emerge in a given ecological region.

1. high mean-high variance (HMHV)
2. high mean-low variance (HMLV)
3. low mean-high variance (LMHV)
4. low mean-low variance (LMLV)

It is obvious that these portfolios evolve through historical experience of the functioning of various markets and non-market institutions. The most vulnerable subset is that of the households with LMHV portfolios. People with very low average income and with very high fluctuations survive on the margin of the system. Their survival is also a function of their innovativeness and inventiveness. This is not to say that farmers in other groups are not innovative. But the innovations for survival are likely to be quite different from innovations for accumulation (Gupta 1987, 1988, 1989).

The access to factor and product markets and other formal and informal institutions do influence the way innovations are pursued. Where markets and state both are weak, the probability of evolving low external input technological innovations is rather high. Similarly, in view of greater reliance on common property resource management institutions in these areas, innovations requiring group action may also be high.

The most vulnerable households have LMHV portfolios and from the pure economic rationale, should have highest propensity to privatize commercial or open access resources. However, the presence of ecological ethic among such people demonstrates the way values modify perceptions and preferences of economic outcomes. Values are obviously not shared by everyone uniformly. In many cases, we have noticed that innovators using alternative ways of pest control, for instance, do not bother to disseminate their ideas. To them, it is satisfactory if they can apply their own techniques.

In regions where negative externalities of actions of others make such choices difficult, innovators, like Haribhai mentioned earlier, persist with their practice quite fortitudinously. But there are many people who are so vulnerable that they only work as laborers in rural or urban areas. Since reproduction of labor requires minimum consumption which they cannot afford, they age faster and develop many disabilities associated with malnutrition. Because of the emigration of males from such households, the role of women in managing households becomes crucial. Since women cannot take animals for grazing as far as men can, the grazing pressure in the neighborhood regions becomes more excessive. At the same time, grazing pressure from the livestock of the well-off people is also no less serious. Under such conflicting demands and pressures, the ethics underlying common property resource institutions comes under strain. In some areas, the institutions survive because the non-emigrating communities derive only a small share of their requirements from the common properties. They can afford to be indifferent. In other cases, the values of the institution builders seem to have been strongly carried forward through traditions and norms.   In any case, the preferences of households, vulnerable as they are, indeed influenced by the institutional contexts in which resources have to be used. If institutions are strong and uncertainties about future supplies of a scarce resources low, the time-frame may get extended.

The perception and response to risk is influenced not only by the economic portfolios and ecological institutions but also by the existing repertoire of risk adjustment strategies. Three kinds of risk adjustments have been proposed.

1. *Household level.* Intra- as well as inter-household level risk adjustments.
2. *Institutional.* Common property institutions, collective safety mechanisms.
3. *Public interventions.* Food-for-work type of employment programs or other relief measures.

Household Level Risk Adjustments

The intra-household risk adjustments (intra-HHRA) imply such options which can be exercised within the household. These options require making social, ethical, and moral trade-offs. For instance, three major intra-household choices are migration, disposal of assets, and modification or reduction of household food consumption. In the case of migration, generally only the male migrates but whole families also migrate. Education of children under such circumstances is ruled out. Once that happens, the future options are modified.

Similarly, choices about disposal of assets have to be exercised in terms of gender and social status. Women consider certain kinds of jewelry very sacred and would like to dispose of these only in the periods of acute crisis. The modification of consumption often implies priority to children followed by men with women last. Though in terms of work and responsibility, women may share no less burden. While making economic calculations of the costs and benefits of different kinds of household decisions, the moral pain that a family has to go through during periods of scarcity and crisis is not looked into. These pains may disrupt family structures. In many parts of Africa, men abandon their families either out of shame or because of opportunistic behavior. The economic choices by such households are significantly different from the rest. Since the emigration of males or their abandoning the families takes place much more in some region than in others, the aggregate effects of intra-household adjustments manifest more in those regions. The ecological costs of such social pressures remain to be properly worked out.

The inter-household risk adjustments (inter-HHRA) imply those options in which at least two or more households are involved. For instance, tenancy, credit, labor, and product contracts. In credit market, the options for women borrowers may not be same as for men borrowers. Accordingly, the investment options and their ecological consequences also could vary. In product market, various kinds of contracts for supply of forest products or minor forest products influence the rate of extraction of natural resources and the time-frame in which these extractions are made.

The forward trade of trees has also been reported from some of these high risk regions. The buyers negotiate a price for a tree growing near the homestead or in the farm and then after having paid the price offer to harvest the tree as and when they need. Until then the seller has to take care of the tree as an obligation. The ecological implications of forward trade in trees are also influenced by the nature of households (i.e., whether these are managed by men or women). The vulnerability of women in negotiating these contracts may influence the choice of species and the relative allocation of time for this purpose.

The common gruel kitchen during drought or floods, common reserve of fuel wood or water, or any other resource provides considerable cushion for risk adjustment to the households. The sacred basis of some of the common institutions and their secular function, I propose can be analyzed through an inter-twined double helical structure of institutions. The ethical values may be rooted in the sacred beliefs but the economic risks may require secular rules for the working of these institutions. Anybody who violates rules of common property institutions may receive sanctions evolved through either participative or coercive institutional decisions.

The public relief mechanisms modify the perception of and response to risk. The emigration rates can be modified, the carrying capacity can undergo a great shift because of lack of livestock migration in the period of drought and accordingly the short-term relief can have long-term ecological and economic consequences. In the absence of relief, great human misery may follow. With the availability of relief, the great ecological misery follows. A compromise between ecological, economic, and social goals requires institution building.

Otherwise there are examples in arid regions when people do not deepen or desilt their own private tanks, or wells, before rains. They anticipate government to start relief works. Perception of risk in such situations is quite different and, therefore, short-term and long-term choices for people exposed to risks in the presence of relief would vary. The nature of relief itself can modify the perception of risks. If relief could be in the form of capital for creating permanent assets for conserving soil and water, time horizon ensuing such investments would be different if such was not the case.

The non-monetized exchange relations imply option of sending one's children to relatives or friends during drought and famines. A household would take different risks in the absence or presence of such safety nets.

The variation in the perception of risks modify the time-frame as well as the discount rate. Greater the horizontal and vertical assurance a household has the longer the time-frame may be. And with a longer time-frame, technological options with smaller but sustained returns become viable. The sustainability therefore requires reduction in discount rate and/or extension of the time-frame.

Many times people argue that poor people have shorter time-frame and by implications therefore may chose non-sustainable alternatives. In some cases, it might indeed be the case. But it cannot be generalized. Some households may have different time preferences in different resource markets (Gupta 1981). In resource markets in which a household has greater confidence, or a more intimate knowledge, a longer time-frame may be chosen. On the other hand, in a resource market in which the uncertainties are high, de facto property rights are ill-defined and in management of which, institutions play marginal role, the time- frame is likely to be shorter.

Thus a very poor household can grow very slow growing species of trees (much against what donor supported agro-forestry programs may advocate) which may mature at the time of a daughter's marriage. In the deficit budget households, to accumulate savings in liquid forms is often very difficult. Such time bound maturity oriented savings may allow a household to meet its strategic objectives.

On the other hand, in case of temporary lease of land or water body, a household may choose non-sustainable technologies because they desire a short term investment return. In the absence of clearer property rights, but de facto recognition of boundaries of local claims, households may evolve norms of not killing fish during spawning period. But when access rules are changed, despite previous ethical values, the choice of technology may become non-sustainable.

Household budgets can be surplus, subsistence, or deficit depending upon the rate and size of capital accumulation given varying preferences for time horizon and perception of risk.

The stakes of households in preserving environment and modifying choice of economic enterprise may be influenced by the nature of household budget.

Simultaneously, the local institutions and cultural and spiritual beliefs may counteract the pressures for reducing time-frame and increasing discount rates.

In the era of economic liberalization, there is a genuine danger that many local communities, which had conserved resources for that long might decide to liquidate historical assets in favor of short-term benefits. Unless the existence value and the option values of resources start getting reflected in the household budgets through carefully crafted incentives, the unfortunate prospect of resource degradation is likely to follow.

One way in which time-frame can be extended, which I have argued in this chapter, is by adding value to local innovations and knowledge system so that households recognize economic benefits of conserving resources. Since conservation of knowledge requires maintaining institutions of social interaction, along with economic incentives, thus, we will also have to invest in institution building. I discuss the framework for institution building next. It may be added here that I do realize that all economic values signal some people's ethical assumptions. I may not share those ethical values but the ethics is embedded in all economic transactions. What distinguishes one set of ethical values from another may be the institutional context of the belief systems. Although as E. O. Wilson noted, "an enduring environmental ethic will aim to preserve not only the health and freedom of our species, but access to the world in which the human spirit was born" (Wilson 1992). The only point I am adding here is that opportunities for human spirit to articulate itself and assert itself in market place are not evenly available to various socio-ecological groups. The asymmetry of opportunities is precariously balanced today because of asymmetry of ethical values. It may not remain so in future because of the obvious injustice inherent in keeping people with superior ethical values as poor.

INSTITUTION BUILDING FOR REJUVENATING INDIGENOUS ECOLOGICAL KNOWLEDGE SYSTEM

The restoration of ecological ethics in the communities where they have become weak, due to either declining common properties or shortening timeframes, may require careful blending of formal and informal institutions. How local knowledge systems can sometimes prove inadequate in meeting the challenges of ecological or economic or even a combined crisis is apparent in many areas. A very large number of step wells or water conservation structures which worked for a long time have been abandoned or abused in many dry regions where half-hearted government interventions generated false hopes. I do not argue that local knowledge systems by themselves can resolve all kinds of dilemma in resource use. I have earlier demonstrated that people can do the right things for wrong reasons just as they may do right things for right reasons. Under what conditions local knowledge systems grow and become liberating influence rather than a constraint depends upon the term at which we under-stand its boundaries, nature of sense making process and identify symbols of appropriation or distribution of benefits and costs.

The eco-institutional framework of blended knowledge systems is presented in Figure 6.2.

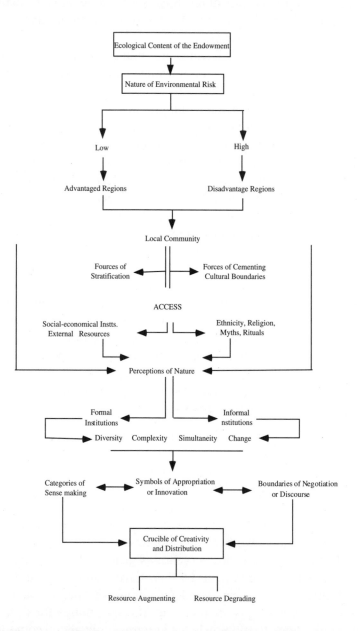

Figure 6.2. The eco-institutional framework of blended knowledge systems.

The ecological context in a given region or for a given community defines the nature of environmental risks or threats. A drought, a flood, erosion of biodiversity, or increase in salinity levels in coastal areas due to ingress of sea water may be different kinds of threats. The regions which have very low level of threats are preferred by markets and even state and, therefore, are advantaged in most respects. Given low transaction costs of exchanging resources in these regions, the adaptive response of the households is fast. At the same time, in view of the prevalent value system, the social structures are also different compared to the disadvantaged regions having higher perceived risks or threats. In Table 6.2 I have enumerated the key contrasts that characterize the advantaged (market dependent) and disadvantaged (nature dependent regions). The market dominated communities are the ones in which most exchanges are mediated through markets, institutions and instruments. The commoditization of labor, product and skills is quite high. In contrast, the communities which draw their major sustenance through use of natural resources often without much value addition are defined here as nature dependent communities. The regions where each type of communities predominate are also contrasted here. The market dependent regions are the high growth green revolution regions. On the other hand, the nature dependent regions are rainfed drylands, hill areas, or forest fringe areas.

The nature of local community is therefore quite different though affected by similar processes of stratification as well as cultural homogenization. The access to resources may be unequal due to property rights sanctified by culture,

Table 6.2. Market Dependent and Nature Dependent Region

	Market dominated	Nature dominated
1. Communication system	Digital	Analogical
2. Pooling of resources	Very low	Very high
3. Reliance on common properties	Low	Very high
4. Settling of books of account	Very short term	Long term
5. The proportion of women headed or managed households	Very low	Very high
6. Women participation rates	Very low	Very high
7. Reciprocities	Specific	Generalized
8. Empowerment	Material resource-based	Knowledge resource- and culture-based

Source: Gupta 1992, 1995.

state, or sometimes just the local usurper. The stratification may also occur due to inter-generational transfer of property, bad luck in discriminating good from the bad opportunities, or specific biases in public policy.

The unifying tendency could similarly be strong or weak, among different subsets of a community. Religion, caste, ethnicity, myths, rituals, etc., may contribute to the centripetal forces. Since the units which are unified may not completely overlap with the units which are stratified, they remain subsets which are fragmented. I have argued that most institutions of resource management have fuzzy boundaries. In each group, there are people who agree only partly with the rules and therefore play the game half-heartedly. The pluralism of this kind is a guarantee against too quick an agreement or for too long (in either case, the rules will be eventually aborted for want of periodic rejuvenation, reaffirmation or revalidation).

The perception of nature is mediated by the formal institutions as well as informal institutions and through the stratified prisms as well as through unified lenses. The prisms refract light. The perceptions through stratified prisms thus are fragmented, fractioned, and in many cases, contentious. On the other hand, the perceptions through cultural or religious lenses tend to be homogenized within a cultural boundary. The contest between differentiated meanings as well as shared meanings takes place in every society. In the nature dependent society, the unifying spirit of the nature apparently provides an outer limit within which differences can be articulated. In the market dependent communities, such unifying forces, are unfortunately guided by great degree of expedience and opportunism. We are in some sense seeing the contradiction between the interest of groups with short or long time-frames.

The perceptions of nature essentially require making sense of four facets of a natural phenomena known as diversity, complexity, simultaneity, and change. These facets of any natural system describe the basic aspects of ecological systems. It is not our submission that diversity is always accompanied by complexity or change. The limited point being made here is that the perception of nature has to include the inherent complexity and simultaneity of changes taking place in different subcomponents of a diverse system. It is for this reason that defining boundary of a system becomes very crucial for understanding it.

The perception of nature mediated by formal or informal institutions are distinguished on the basis of the categories of sense making. Once certain categories become powerful in defining the boundaries of a phenomena, the system of appropriation gain legitimacy. This they do through the efficiency with which resources are extracted.

To illustrate, the crop and weed are two such categories. A plant out of its place is called weed. Obviously, in nature there is not ever a plant which can be out of its place. And yet, once we define the companion plants in the crop field as weeds, the next step is to find ways of eliminating them. The so-called weeds may perform a whole host of functions. Some of these might attract predators of the pest, prevent certain insects from completing their life cycle, move nutrients from the lower level of soil to the surface through deep roots, fix nitrogen in the soil, etc. Some of the weeds are mulched in the soil to conserve moisture, still others may have allelopathic interactions. Similarly, there are companion plants (weeds) which may compete with the crop and take away its nutrient and moisture.

The point is that boundary of a system in terms of crop or weed may prevent looking at certain interactions which may hold the key to sustainability. There are very few studies, which look at the positive or negative impacts of biodiversity on the field bunds, roadside or swamps, etc. on the cultivated systems. What part of nature is relevant for a particular purpose is essentially decided by the categories of sense making. These in turn influence the way we define the boundary of a system.

If we take another case of soil classification, we notice similar contradictions. The soil classification based on the USDA system may mask more information than it reveals. Indigenous soil classification may provide valuable clues about the micro-environmental niches and the suitability of specific sites for different species and varieties. Sustainability would require precision farming (i.e., an attempt for need based input use).

There are large number of other examples in which the classification of a natural resource may not provide sufficient clues for augmenting renewability of resource through various feedback loops in the ecological systems. By drawing artificial boundaries, and classification criteria we may create symbols of appropriation which alienate us from nature. To extract returns without supporting various ecological requirements of a system one needs economic calculus and an ethical position which justifies making these boundaries. Thus, if birds are only a pest, companion plants are only weeds and biodiversity around the fields or water bodies a nuisance, the judgments have been made and categories created.

Many times, in the process of doing so, we incur ecological costs which feedback in the long run and impair the viability of the systems. However, there are processes through which we may avoid these eventualities.

The local knowledge systems act as crucible of creativity and innovation. Various institutions, rituals, technologies, and practices may be generated which augment a resource or deplete it. However, an '*ought*' may follow from differences in what Rolston calls the *case is* (Rolston 1988). But whether a moral '*ought*' about responsible behavior of poor communities will follow may also depend upon the ecological, economic, and political '*is*' about unfair valuation of resources and corresponding opportunities (Rolston 1988). Local ecological knowledge systems can merely provide a basis for such corrections to be made. But the corrections themselves will follow only in the political-economic field.

CONCLUSION

In this chapter, I have provided a framework in which blending of culture and technology with ecological ethics happens through autonomous and independent technological and institutional innovations but in a historical perspective. The fact that many of these innovations draw upon biodiversity and resources in the neighboring regions implies that the concept of so-called weed is very different for these people. Unfortunately, the modern systems of intellectual property rights do not recognize rights in so-called wild plants. The nature of diversity created through selection pressures is wild only if anything non-cultivated could be called wild. Otherwise, the management of grazing, collection of various plant products and other interactions with the non-cultivated lands and water bodies generates specific niches for diversity to evolve. The migration routes provide boundaries, local names provide indigenous categories of sense making and local customs and cultural values in which people knowledgeable about the plants often do not charge, provide the symbols of appropriation or lack of it.

I realize that a marriage between reductionist and holistic system of knowledge is not easy to come about. But numerous resource management programs today are recognizing that sustainability requires blending of formal and informal institutions which in turn means that perceptions of nature need to be modified. Ethical foundations of ecological economic exchanges may bring about such changes in our perception of nature as well as the values underlying technological and institutional innovations by the communities which still continue to live with it harmoniously.

But whether it will actually so happen may just as well depend upon the political space 'little innovations' may get. The space for these solutions evolved by local communities at grassroots level in our own intellectual discourse may finally determine the legitimacy of moral discourse on ethics of ecological economics.

NOTES

1. Whenever environmentalists asked for certain parts of the forests to be saved from logging since these might have species of unknown future value, the conventional economists always questioned the prudence of such a judgment. To them things of unknown value were not worth bothering about. They did not see a moral dilemma in such a situation. The trade-off was seen as a choice between foregoing an opportunity of generating wealth now and waiting for a possible wealth which may arise in future if at all and nobody knew when (through better ecological care).
2. It is true at the same time that despite all the kinship ties remaining intact in the native regions, the tribal people could not prevent land alienation. Other social forces were apparently more powerful.

REFERENCES

Chand, V. S., S. Shukla, and A. K. Gupta. 1994. Incorporating Local Ecological Knowledge in Primary Education. Ahmedabad: Ravi J Mathai Centre For Educational Innovations, Indian Institute of Management, Mimeo.

Gupta, A. K. 1981. Viable Projects for Unviable Farmers - An Action Research Enquiry into the Structure and Processes of Rural Poverty in Arid Regions. Symposium on Rural Development in South Asia. IUAES Inter Congress. Amsterdam

Gupta, A. K. 1985. Socio-ecological paradigm for analyzing problems of poor in dry regions. *Ecodevelopment News* No. 32 33: 68–74.

Gupta, A. K. 1985a. On organising equity: Are solutions really the problem? *Journal of Social and Economic Studies*, 2 (4): 295–312.

Gupta, A. K. 1986. Socio Ecology of Stress: Why Do Common Property Resource Management Projects Fail?: A Case Study of Sheep and Pasture Development Project in Rajasthan, India. Paper presented at conference on Management of CPR. Washington DC: National Research Council. April 21–26, 1985.

Gupta, A. K. 1987. Why poor don't Cooperate: Lessons from traditional organizations with implication for modern organizations. In Research Relationship Politics and Practice of Social Research, ed. C. G. Wanger. George Allen and Unwin, London.

Gupta, A. K. 1989. The design of resource-delivery systems: A Socio-ecological perspective. *Int. Studies of Management and Organization* 18(4): 64–82.

Gupta A. K. and M. Shroff. 1990. Rural Banking: Learning to Unlearn - An Action Research Enquiry. New Delhi: Oxford and IBH.

Gupta, A .K. 1990. Survival Under Stress: Socio Ecological Perspective on Farmers' Innovation and Risk Adjustments. W.P. No. 738, International Congress on Plant Physiology, New Delhi, 1988.

Gupta, A. K. 1991. Why Does Poverty Persist in Regions of High Biodiversity?: A Case for Indigenous Property Right System. Paper for the International conference on Property Rights and Genetic Resources, IUCN, UNEP and ACTS, Kenya, June 10–16.

Gupta, A. K. 1992. Sustainability Through Biodiversity: Designing Crucible of Culture, Creativity and Conscience. Presented at International Conference on Biodiversity and Conservation, Danish Parliament, Copenhagen, November 8, 1991. IIMA Working Paper No.1005.

Gupta, A. K. and U. Karma. 1992. Blending Cultural Values, Indigenous Farming Technology and Environment: Experience in Bhutan. In: Sustainable Mountain, eds. N. S. Jodha, M. Banskota and Tej Partap. New Delhi: Oxford and IBH Publishing Company Pvt.Ltd.

Gupta, A. K. 1993. Biodiversity, poverty and intellectual property rights of Third World peasants: A case for renegotiating global understanding. In Biodiversity: Implications for Global Food Security, eds. M. S. Swaminathan, and S. Jana. Madras: MacMillan.

Gupta A. K. 1995a. Ethical dilemmas in conservation of biodiversity: Towards developing globally acceptable ethical guidelines. *Eubios Journal of Asian and International Bioethics* 5: 40–46.

Gupta, A. K. 1995b. Suggested ethical guidelines for accessing and exploring biodiversity - A Pew Conservation Scholars initiative. *Eubios Journal of Asian and International Bioethics* 5: 38–40.

Gupta, A. K. 1995c. Sustainable institutions for natural resource management: How do we participate in peoples' plans? In People's Initiatives for Sustainable Development: Lessons of Experience, eds. S. A. Samad, T. Watanabe, and S.-J. Kim. Kuala lumpur: Asian and Pacific Development Centre.

Martinez-Alier, J. 1991. Environmental policy and distributional conflicts. In Ecological Economics, ed. R. Costanza. New York: Columbia University Press.

McNeely, J. A. 1988. Economics and Biological Diversity: Developing and Using Economic Incentives to Conserve Biological Resources. Gland: IUCN.

Rolston, H. III. 1988. Environmental Ethics: Duties To and Values in the Natural World, Philadelphia: Temple University Press.

7 ENVISIONING A SUSTAINABLE WORLD

Donella Meadows
Environmental Studies Program
Dartmouth College
Hanover NH 03755

OVERVIEW

Vision is necessary to the policy process. If we have not specified where we want to go, it is hard to set our compass, to muster enthusiasm, or to measure progress. But vision is not only generally missing from policy discussions; it is missing from our culture. We talk easily and endlessly about our frustrations, doubts, and complaints, but we speak only rarely and with difficulty about our dreams and values.

Environmentalists in particular have a reputation (only partially deserved) for communicating more about the polluted world they are trying to avoid than about the sustainable world they are working toward—a world in which people live in a way that meets human needs while not degrading natural systems. Few of us can imagine that world with clarity or communicate to others what it might be like.

Building a responsible, desirable vision of a sustainable world is partly a rational process, subject to analysis of what is possible over what time frame. But it is also a non-rational or perhaps supra-rational task of imagination, one that comes not only from logic but from values. The skill of visioning is one that can be developed, like any human skill, through practice. This chapter tells the personal story of one analyst's discovery of that skill, and it provides an opportunity to practice.

INTRODUCTION

To bring our world toward sustainability—or any other goal—we need to take different kinds of steps, which require different kinds of knowledge, talent, skill, and work.

We need, for example, to make things happen—pass laws, make budgets, find resources, hire people, establish and manage organizations, invent technologies, build, restore, protect, tax, subsidize, regulate, punish, reward. Implementation is the active, visible phase of achieving a goal, and therefore it is the most discussed phase. Most public discourse involves arguing about implementation. Most policy debates start and end with this phase, unfortunately.

I say unfortunately, because any talk of implementation is necessarily based on models, which explain how we got to whatever state we are in, and what we should do to get to a better state. Models may be in computers, on paper, or in our heads. They may be sophisticated, but usually they are very simple—for example, "freeing the market from regulation will make things better," or "new technology is all we need." We expose, examine, debate, and challenge our models far too little, especially the models in our heads. Most of them are too narrow, too linear, too lacking in understanding of feedback, time-lags, exponentiality, variability, diversity, and other aspects of real system complexity. Obviously, if our models are faulty, all the skillful and well funded implementation measures in the world will not get us to sustainability or any other goal.

There are at least two more steps in the policy process that precede and are even more important than modeling. One of them is information gathering. We need to know with accuracy where we are and where we have been, before we develop models. Information not only validates or disproves our models, it helps us form them and turn them into action. If information about our history and present situation is biased, delayed, incomplete, noisy, disorganized, denied, or missing, our models will be wrong, and our implementation will be untimely and misdirected. Improving information means, among other activities, monitoring, organizing data, choosing good indicators, educating, communicating, and—an issue vital to ecological economics—removing bias, especially from price signals.

If most of policy discussion focuses on implementation, virtually all the rest focuses on modeling and information. That leaves just about no room for the remaining step of policy formation, which should be first—the establishment of clear, feasible, socially shared goals. What do we want? Where would we like all these models, this information, this implementation to take us? What is our vision of the world we are trying to create for ourselves, our children, and our grandchildren?

Environmentalists have failed perhaps more than any other set of advocates to project vision—which may be as much a statement about the culture into which environmentalists are trying to communicate as it is about their communication ability. The general public associates environmentalism with restriction, prohibition, regulation, and sacrifice. When I ask people what they think a sustainable world might be like, I usually hear about tight, centralized control, low material standard of living, and no fun. I do not know whether that impression is so common because puritanism is the actual, unexpressed, maybe subconscious model in the minds of environmental advocates, or whether the public, deeply impacted by advertising, cannot imagine a good life that is not based on wild consumption. Whatever the reason, hardly anyone seems to envision a sustainable world as one that would be nice to live in. The best outcome of reaching sustainability that the public perceives, is the avoidance of catastrophe. Survival, but not much more.

That is a failure of vision. There may be motivation in escaping doom, but there is much more in creating a better world. It is pitifully inadequate to describe the exciting possibilities of sustainability in terms of mere survival— at least that is what my vision of sustainability tells me.

But I did not always have such a vision. I had to learn, or perhaps I should say relearn, to create and express vision. In our industrial culture, particularly in the cultures of science and economics, envisioning is disparaged. We rarely see it demonstrated; we rarely get to demonstrate it ourselves; many of us are so unused to being in the presence of vision that we are ill at ease with the whole concept. We are badly out of practice with what President Bush uncomfortably called "the vision thing."

Perhaps if I tell you the story of my own experience with vision, you will understand what I mean.

A WORLD WITHOUT HUNGER

About ten years ago I ran a series of workshops intended to figure out how to end hunger. The participants were some of the world's best nutritionists, agronomists, economists, demographers, ecologists, and field workers in development — people who were devoting their lives in one way or another to ending hunger.

Peter Senge of MIT, a colleague who helped design and carry out the workshops, suggested that we open each one by asking the assembled experts, "What would the world be like if there were no hunger?" Surely each of these people had a motivating vision of the goal he or she was working for. It would be interesting to hear and collect these visions and to see if they varied by discipline, by nationality, or by personal experience.

I thought this exercise would take about an hour and would help the participants get to know each other better. So I opened the first workshop by asking, "What is your vision of a world without hunger?" Coached by Peter, I made the request strongly visionary. I asked people to describe not the world they thought they could achieve, or the world they were willing to settle for, but the world they truly wanted.

What I got was an angry reaction. The participants refused. They said that was a stupid and dangerous question. Here are some of their comments.

- Visions are fantasies, they do not change anything. Talking about them is a waste of time. We do not need to talk about what the end of hunger will be like, we need to talk about how to get there.
- We all know what it is like not to be hungry. What is important to talk about is how terrible it is to be hungry.

- I never really thought about it. I am not sure what the world would be like without hunger, and I do not see why I need to know.
- Stop being unrealistic. There will always be hunger. We can decrease it, but we can never eliminate it.
- You have to be careful with visions. They can be dangerous. Hitler had a vision. I do not trust visionaries and I do not want to be one.

After we got those objections out on the table, some deeper ones came up. One person said, with emotion, that he could not stand thinking about a world without hunger, when he was so painfully aware of the suffering all around him. The gap between what he longed for and what he knew to exist was too great to bear. So he escaped the pain by forgetting about what he longed for.

Finally another person said what may have come closer to the truth than any of our other rationalizations: "I have a vision, but it would make me feel childish and vulnerable to say it out loud. I do not know you well enough to do this".

That remark struck me so hard that I have been thinking about it ever since. Why is it that we can share our cynicism, complaints, and frustrations with perfect strangers without hesitation, but we cannot share our dreams? How did we arrive at a culture that has labeled vision as "childish" and that constantly, almost automatically, ridicules visionaries? Whose idea of reality forces us to "be realistic?" When were we taught, and by whom, to suppress our visions?

Whatever the answers to those questions, the consequences of a culture that does not tolerate vision are tragic. If we can not speak of our real desires, we can only marshal information, models, and implementation toward what we think we can get. We only half-try. If, in working for modest goals, we fall short of them, for whatever reason, we reign in our expectations still further and try for even less. If we exceed our goals, we take it as an unrepeatable accident, but if we fail, we take it as an omen. That sets up a positive feedback loop spiraling downward. The less we try, the less we achieve. The less we achieve, the less we try. Without vision, says the Bible, the people perish.

Children, before they are squashed by their elders, are natural visionaries. They can tell you clearly and firmly what the world should be like. There should be no war, no pollution, no cruelty, no starving children. There should be music, fun, beauty, and lots and lots of nature. People should be trustworthy and grown-ups should not work so hard. It is fine to have nice things, but it is even more important to have love. As they grow up, children learn that these visions are "childish" and stop saying them out loud. But inside all of us, if we have not been too badly bruised by the world, there are still "childish" visions.

We discovered that in the hunger workshop. Having vented all the reasons why we should not and would not share our visions, we shared our visions. Once we got going, it took us a whole day for 16 people to express the visionary richness inside them. It was the first time I had been in a shared visionary space. As we constructed together a picture of the world we wanted, our mood lifted, our faces softened, our bodies woke up, we gained energy and clarity and solidarity.

The vision we pulled out of each other that day has gone on powering me for years. It was not just a picture of the hungry fifth of the world's people becoming exactly like the rest of us, with all our stresses and strains. It did not include massive, constant, expensive transfers of food from the rich to the poor. It did not require soaking ecosystems in agricultural chemicals, or letting populations explode, or centralized control of anything. I list all these things that were not in our vision, because they are what the world seems to expect of the end of hunger, if the world thinks of ending hunger at all. More people, more chemicals, more stress, more control, forceful redistribution—it is no wonder that we do not work very hard to achieve a future like that. But that is a future based on what we might expect or settle for; it's not a vision of what we want.

To summarize what we did see in our workshop vision, in the world without hunger that we actively want to live in, every child is born wanted, treasured, and lovingly cared for. Because of that, many fewer children are born. The world is physically beautiful, cultures are diverse and tolerant, information flows freely, untainted by cynicism. Food is raised and prepared as consciously and lovingly as are children, with profound respect for nature's contribution as well as that of people. In a world without hunger we can take care of our own nearby community and be taken care of by it, knowing that other people in other communities are also doing their caring close at hand. Because of the strength of local community, there is no need for over-weening world government—though we did see an ongoing world conversation, and a great willingness, when communities fall into trouble, for the world to help. There would be plenty of problems to solve (we decided that we want and need problems to solve) but we could travel anywhere in the world without encountering deprivation, terror, or ugliness.

I could go on. I can see this vision clearly and in detail. I can see the sustainable farms; I can see the kitchens where fresh ingredients are turned mindfully and skillfully into healthy, beautiful meals. But you get the point. Maybe you are already filling in your own details, or maybe you are squirming in the presence of such utopian language. Whatever your reaction, just notice it, notice what has been laid upon you by your culture, and notice that there is a place inside you, close to the surface or deeply buried, that desperately wants something like what I have just sketched out. I have noticed, when I can get a visionary discussion going anywhere in the world, that in different disciplines, languages, nations, and cultures, our information may differ, our models disagree, our preferred modes of implementation are widely diverse, but our visions, when we are willing to admit them, are astonishingly alike.

We do not believe that, by the way. We do not believe in common values. Nearly everyone with whom I have talked about vision informs me with great certainty that visions, or values are the one thing human beings will never agree upon. I thought that too, before I began dabbling in vision. I was taught that by a culture that is so inept with visions that it can sustain beliefs like that without ever testing them. My experience now, in many different parts of the world, is that visions and values (I have come to use those two words almost interchangeably) are amazingly, astonishingly congruent.

SOME GENERALIZATIONS ABOUT VISION

So I have been honing my capacity to envision. I rarely start a garden, a book, a conference, or an organization, without formally envisioning how I want it to come out—what I really want, not what I am willing to settle for. I go to a quiet place, shut down my rational mind, and develop a vision. I present the vision to others, who correct and refine it and help it to evolve. I write out vision statements. When I lose my way, I go back to those statements.

I still feel silly doing all this. I was raised in a skeptical culture, after all, and worse, I was trained as a scientist, with "soft-mindedness" drummed out of me. But I keep practicing vision, because my life works better when I do. Here are some things I have learned about the way vision works. It would be best to consider the following a list of hypotheses, which you can test for yourself.

- Envisioning does not seem to come from the part of me that does rational analysis. It comes from whatever part of me informs my values, my conscience, my sense of morality. Call it heart, call it soul, call it conscience, whatever is the source of vision, it is not rational mind.
- I have to keep filtering out remnants of past disappointments, fear of failure, tinges of negativism, warnings of "reality." (In this chapter, when I put quotation marks around "reality," I mean mental models based on fear, whether or not soundly based, that are routinely used to undercut vision.) I have to work actively to focus on what I want, not what I expect.
- I have stopped challenging myself, or anyone else who puts forth a vision, with the responsibility of laying out a plan for how to get there. A vision should be judged by its clarity of values, not by the clarity of its implementation path.
- In my experience the implementation path is never clear at first. It only reveals itself, step by step, as I walk along it. It often surprises me, because my computer and mental models are inadequate to the complexities and possibilities of the world. Holding to the vision and being flexible about the path is the only way to find the path.
- Vision is not rational, but rational mind can and must inform vision. I can envision climbing a tall tree and flying off from its top, and I might very much want to do that, but that vision is not consistent with the

laws of the universe; it is not responsible. I can envision the end of hunger, but careful modeling tells me that it can not be accomplished overnight; it will take decades. I use every rational tool at my disposal not to weaken the basic values behind my vision, but to shape it into one that acknowledges, but does not get crushed by, the physical constraints of the world.

• One essential tool for making vision responsible is sharing it with others and incorporating their visions. Only shared vision can be responsible, because many people are needed both to encompass what is known about physical reality and to incorporate morality. Julian Simon, Herman Kahn, and other "cornucopians" have a materialistic, industrial vision that is simply not compatible with the physical constraints of the earth. Hitler had an immoral, genocidal vision that was certainly not shared by his victims, the Jews, the Gypsies, and most of the peoples of Europe.

• Staying in touch with vision prevents me from being seduced by cheap substitutes. If what I really want is self-esteem, I will not pretend to achieve it by buying a fancy car. If I want human happiness, I will not settle for GNP. I want serenity, but not the kind that comes from drugs. I want permanent prosperity, not unsustainable growth.

• Vision has an astonishing power to open the mind to possibilities I would never see in a mood of cynicism. Vision widens my choices, shows me creative new directions. It helps me see good-news stories, pockets of reality that could be seeds of a wider vision. I see what I should support; I get ideas for action.

• Vision has to be flexible and evolving. The path toward a vision reveals new information, models, and possibilities as one moves along. The sustainable world we can see from this moment in history may be primitive compared to what we will be able to see as we move closer and gain experience. We can not stick with old visions; we have to keep "re-visioning."

• People who carry responsible vision become, in some sense I cannot explain, charismatic. They communicate differently from cynical people. Even if the vision is not overtly expressed, it is there and it is noticeable. Inversely, many progressive, dedicated, "realistic" people unconsciously a communicate their underlying hopelessness. Being around them is downer; being around visionaries is an inspiration.

• I have rarely achieved the full expression of any of my visions, but I have learned not to be discouraged. I get much further with a vision than without it, and I know I am going the right direction. I can take comfort in my progress, even while I continue to bear the tension of knowing I am not there yet.

I am a practical person. I think of myself as relentlessly realistic. I want to create change in the world, not visions in my head. I am constantly amazed, but increasingly convinced, that visioning is a tool for producing results. Olympic athletes use it to make the difference between the superior performance their trained bodies can achieve and the outstanding performance their inspired vision can achieve. Corporate executives take formal classes in vision. All great leaders have been visionaries. Even the scientific, systems-analyst side of me has to admit that we can hardly achieve a desirable, sustainable world, if we can not even picture what it will be like.

ENVISIONING A SUSTAINABLE WORLD

So I invite you to join with me in building a vision. What kind of sustainable world do you *want* to live in? Do your best to imagine not just the absence of problems but the presence of blessings. Our rational minds tell us that a sustainable world has to be one in which renewable resources are used no faster than they regenerate; in which pollution is emitted no faster than it can be recycled or rendered harmless; in which population is at least stable, maybe decreasing; in which prices internalize all real costs; in which there is no hunger or poverty; in which there is true, enduring democracy. But what else? What else do *you* want, for yourself, your children, your grandchildren?

The best way to find your answer to that question is to go to a quiet place, close your eyes, take a few deep breaths, and put yourself in the middle of that sustainable world. Do not push, do not worry, and do not try to figure it out. Just close your eyes and see what you see. Or, as often happens for me, hear what you hear, smell what you smell, feel what you feel. Many of my visions are bright, detailed, and visual, but some of the most profound ones have come not through "seeing," but through sensing in other ways.

In short, relax, trust yourself, and see what happens. If nothing happens, do not worry, try again sometime, or let your visionary talent surface in your sleeping dreams.

But keep asking yourself: What would my home be like in a sustainable world? What would it feel like to wake up there in the morning? Who else would live there; how would it feel to be with them? (Remember this is what you *want*, not what you're willing to settle for.) Where would energy come from, and water, and food? What kinds of wastes would be generated and where would they go? How are these physical flows kept sustainable within the earth's carrying capacity?

When you look out the window or step out the door, what would your community look like, if it looked the way you really want? Who else lives near you (human and non-human)? How do you all interrelate? Go around your visionary neighborhood and see it as clearly as you can. How is it arranged so that the children and the old people and everyone in between will be surrounded by security and happiness and beauty?

What kind of work do you do in this sustainable world? What is your particular and special role? With whom do you do it? How do you work together and how are you compensated? Are you compensated more or less than other people? Does it matter? Do you want it to matter?

How do you get to work? Do you have to *get* to work? Is *work* a distinguishable activity in your ideal world? Is it separate from the rest of life?

Travel farther in your vision, to surrounding communities. Look not only at the physical systems that sustain them—water, energy, food, materials—but look at how they relate, what they exchange with each other, what they know of each other. How do they make joint decisions? How do they resolve conflicts? (How do you *want* them to resolve conflicts?) How do they treat different kinds of people, young and old, male and female, intelligent and talented to different degrees and in different ways? How do they fit within nature? How do they think about plants and animals, soils and waters, stones and stars?

Look at your nation (if your visionary world has nations, if it does not, what does it have?). How does it meet its physical needs sustainably? How does it make decisions, resolve conflicts within and without its borders? What do your people know of other people, and how do they think about them? How much and what kinds of people and goods and information travel between your place and other places? Is your nation and your world diverse or homogeneous (the way you want it, not the way you expect)?

How does it feel to live in this world? What kind of consciousness or worldview, or tolerance of diverse worldviews do people use to keep things sustainable? What changes in this world, and what stays the same? What is the pace of everyday life? How fast, if at all, do people travel and by what means? What fascinates them? What kinds of problems do they work on? What do they regard as progress? What makes them laugh?

Whatever you can see, or cannot see, keep looking. *Not* being able to see something in a vision may be as meaningful as seeing it. Once when I did a visioning session with some German engineering students, they had no trouble seeing sustainable farms, sustainable forestry, even "sustainable chemistry." (That, seen by a chemist, was interesting. It involved minimizing rather than maximizing the amount of chemical needed to do any job, deriving chemicals from nature, making them the way nature does—at low temperatures in small batches with no harmful emissions—and recycling them as nature does.)

But none of these engineers could envision a sustainable transportation system that they really *wanted*, though some of them actually worked on designing solar vehicles, and most of them, being German men, loved fast cars. (They had to admit that what they loved was being the driver of a single fast car on an open roadway; they hated the noise and pollution of fast cars, they did not want to live anywhere near places where fast cars drive; and they hated the consequence of too many people crowding onto the Autobahns in their fast cars. The 'fast car vision', to their utter regret, was not shared, not responsible, not sustainable, not in fact what they really wanted. That led to an interesting discussion of what men really want, for which fast cars are a temporary substitute!)

Finally they concluded that transport is a means, not an end, a cost, not a benefit, that it's inevitably noisy, disrupting, energy- and time-consuming, and that it would be best if everyone were already where they wanted to be, with whom they wanted to be. (Except, they wanted to have in their sustainable world sailboats, horses, and hang gliders, not for travel, but for fun!) In a sustainable society, they concluded, some travel would still be necessary, but it would be minimal. And then they saw that sustainability has at least as much to do with land-use planning, the physical arrangement of settlements, the ability to live, work, recreate, shop, visit loved ones, and walk in nature without long-distance travel, as it does with solar cars.

CONCLUSIONS

Of course having a vision is not enough. Of course it is only the first step toward any goal. The grandest vision will get nowhere without proper infor-mation and models and implementation (and resources, labor, capital, time, and money). There are great difficulties in all these steps of social change and much work to do. I am by no means advocating that we become nothing but flaky visionaries. I think what I am advocating is simply that we make the world safe for vision.

That means, at the least, that we take a mutual vow not to go around squash-ing vision, our own, or anyone else's, and especially not that of young people. That we do not try to protect our colleagues, our loved ones, or ourselves from disappointment or from looking silly by urging them to "be realistic."

Beyond that we could occasionally take the social risk of displaying not our skepticism but our deepest desires. We could declare ourselves in favor of a sustainable, just, secure, efficient, sufficient world (and you can add any other "value word" you like to that list), even at the expense of being called idealis-tic. We could describe that world, as far as we can see it, and ask others to develop the description further. We could give as much credit to the times when we exceed our expectations as to the times when we fall short. We could let disappointments be learning experiences, rather than fuel for pessimism.

Above all, we could strengthen ourselves to endure the tension of the enor-mous gap between the world we know and the world we profoundly long for. I believe that it is only by admitting, permitting, and carrying that tension that we can gather the information, develop the models, and insist upon the actions that can gradually move our world away from its present suffering and unsustainability and toward our deepest values and dearest visions.

PART II

ANALYSIS

8 TOWARDS AN ECONOMICS FOR ENVIRONMENTAL SUSTAINABILITY

Paul Ekins
Department of Economics
Birkbeck College
University of London
Gresse St., London W1P 2LL, UK

OVERVIEW

This chapter briefly surveys some of the principal ways in which the environment has been dealt with in the mainstream economics literature. It notes, in particular, that, in resource economics, the optimal use of environmental resources can be quite consistent with environmental unsustainability; in environmental economics the efficient level of pollution is also consistent with environmental unsustainability, and the use of cost-benefit analysis for complex environmental problems can render decision-making less manageable rather than more so. Some initial conditions for environmental sustainability are then introduced, together with an outline of the kinds of actions that will be necessary in order to move towards complying with them. It is suggested that the economist's role in analyzing environmental issues be redefined as helping society to achieve environmental sustainability at least cost. In contrast to environmental and resource economics, such an approach might be characterized as an economics for sustainability.

INTRODUCTION

The principal concerns of mainstream resource and environmental economics are the optimal use of resources and the treatment of environmental externalities. Input into decision-making is normally formulated in terms of cost-benefit analysis, in which attempts are made to express costs and benefits in monetary terms.

For some environmental issues and problems these approaches may yield useful insights and policy-making guidance. However, where the issues under consideration are pervasive in time or space, subject to uncertainty or irreversibility, involve complex ecosystems or natural processes, or are concerned with resources or environmental effects that are unpriced and of socio-cultural importance, these techniques do not work well. In particular, resource and environmental economics can describe as optimal resource allocations that are environmentally unsustainable, and the use of cost-benefit analysis can make an issue less manageable rather than more so.

These mainstream approaches are, therefore, of only limited use when seeking to generate understanding and advice concerning 'sustainable development', which has in recent years become the dominant organizing concept in the use of natural resources and the environment. This concept demands an explicit concern with environmental sustainability that is physically based and therefore lies outside conventional economic treatment. However, once physical sustainability objectives have been articulated, economic analysis has an important role in illuminating how they may be achieved at least cost.

The first half of this chapter briefly outlines the mainstream approaches to environment and resource issues, discussing the kinds of problems that arise with such approaches. The second half explores the alternative approach based on seeking to achieve sustainability.

RESOURCE AND ENVIRONMENTAL ECONOMICS: A BRIEF OVERVIEW

Resource Economics

The conventional analysis of the use of environmental resources seeks to determine the 'optimal' path of such use, where optimality here involves the maximization of the present value of the profits or consumption from the use of the resource. For both non-renewable and renewable resources it is easy to derive plausible models whereby it is optimal to exhaust non-renewable resources and to drive renewable resources to extinction.

For non-renewables, from the point of view of the resource owner, the core theoretical result was that of Hotelling (1931), who showed that in a competitive market the depletion of the resource would be such that the resource's net price, or rent, would increase at the rate of interest. The intuition behind 'Hotelling's Rule' is easily seen. Were the resource's rent to be rising more slowly than the rate of interest, its price would fall, as owners sought to acquire alternative assets instead. This would tend to restore the resource's rate of rent increase to parity with the interest rate. Were the rent to be rising faster than the rate of interest, the opposite would happen: people would seek to buy stocks of the resource, the net price of which would rise, slowing its rate of rent increase, again until it was equal to the interest rate.

Theoretical results for perfect markets have been modified to try to take into account market imperfections such as non-exclusive ownership (e.g., an oilfield that extends under differently-owned plots and is tapped into by differently-owned wells) or varying degrees of monopoly. As would be expected, the former condition leads to more rapid depletion than the optimal rate, as each owner tries to maximize their private return; the latter condition leads to slower depletion than the optimal rate, due to the restriction of output that the concentration of ownership brings about. Other studies have considered the influence of uncertainty, extraction costs, and economies of scale. Dasgupta and Heal (1979) is the classic work that reviews and derives results in such areas.

Smith (1981) attempts an empirical evaluation of Hotelling's Rule, with the important qualification that lack of data prevented him from using figures of net price, or rent, of the resources considered. Instead, the price used was that of "natural resources of uniform quality in their rawest form at a uniform distance to markets" (i.e., inclusive of extraction costs). The study does not support the practical validity of Hotelling's Rule, after examining the price movements of twelve non-renewable resources (four fossil fuels and eight metals) through the use of five different economic models incorporating arbitrage behavior, including the simple Hotelling model. For four of the metals, none of the models used had any explanatory power. Hotelling's Rule was only accepted by the data for two of the resources. While the best performing model, Heal and Barrow (1980), was accepted by eight of the resources, in all but three cases even it was outperformed by a simple autoregressive model that related the resource's current price to that in the previous time period. Smith's conclusion is that variables not entering the models, such as extraction costs, new discoveries, and changes in market structure and their institutional environment, for which data is not generally available in suitable form, must also be important in explaining price movements.

The poor empirical performance of the Hotelling model is corroborated by a review of other studies (Slade 1992; Farrow 1985). Farrow's careful application of the Hotelling Rule to the actual behavior of a mining firm, using confidential proprietary data from the firm, found that the Rule was not consistent with the firm's behavior. Eagan (1987) considers that, at best, the Hotelling Rule is a special case of very little practical application in a real-life situation dominated by institutional, distributional and political considerations, from which it abstracts. At worst the Hotelling Rule may be based on the 'chimera of intertemporal arbitrage', the theoretical application of which has more to do with mathematical tractability than relevance to firms' behavior.

Where privately optimal depletion seeks to maximize the present value of profits from a resource over its lifetime, socially optimal depletion is concerned with maximizing the social utility to be derived from it. Utility is normally identified with consumption, so the problem then becomes one of maximizing the present value of the consumption of the resource through time. Several conditions affect the optimal depletion path: whether the resource is essential to the production of the consumption good; whether, and to what extent, forms of produced capital can be substituted for the resource; whether technological change either economies on the use of the resource or develops a substitute that renders it inessential; whether a new resource will be discovered that serves the same purpose; and the size of the discount rate, the relative value that is given to present and future consumption.

The core theoretical result in this area is that if the discount rate is positive (i.e., if future consumption is worth less than present consumption), if the resource is essential to consumption, and no technological breakthrough, discovery of substitutable resources or substitutability with produced capital (formally, that the elasticity of substitution, is such that $0<\sigma<1$) stop it from being so, then it can be optimal to drive future consumption towards zero through the exhaustion of the resource (Dasgupta and Heal 1974). Improvements in the efficiency of resource use (the yield of more consumption goods per unit of resource use), or a reduction in the discount rate, will prolong consumption but will not prevent its eventual decline. This can only be achieved by rendering the resource inessential for consumption by the development or discovery of substitutes. In this case, the resource may still be fully depleted but, as far as the maintenance of consumption is concerned, it will not matter.

The difference between a renewable and non-renewable resource is the capacity of the former for self-regeneration. Provided the harvest-rate does not exceed the rate of regeneration, the stock of the resource will be undepleted. Pearce and Turner (1990) have set out the basic economics of renewable resources, on which the following treatment is based.

In Figure 8.1, Q_0Q_{max} shows a curve relating the stock of a renewable resource to its growth rate, G. Below Q_0 and above Q_{max} no net regeneration takes place. The regeneration rate rises to a maximum at Q_{msy} and then falls. The vertical axis also gives the harvest rate, h. The curve then also represents the equilibrium sustainable harvest rate, H, at any stock level. Inside the area bounded by the curve and the horizontal axis, $h < G$, and the stock will increase. Outside this area $h > G$ and the stock will decrease. H_{msy} represents the maximum sustainable yield.

The lines E_1 to E_6 show increasing levels, or effectiveness, of harvesting effort. It may be that the harvesting technology is improving, so that with the same effort the harvest at a given stock level is increased; or it may be that more effort (more labor, more capital equipment) is being applied such that $E_6>E_5>E_4>E_3>E_2>E_1$. For efforts E_1 to E_4, and for stock levels above the points where each line first cuts Q_0Q_{max}, an equilibrium at the maximum sustainable harvest corresponding to that effort (e.g., H_1 for E_1) will tend to result. Thus, if for effort E_1 the stock is initially above Q_1, then harvest above the growth rate will reduce it to Q_1; if the initial stock level is below Q_1, the harvest below the growth rate will allow the stock to grow to Q_1.

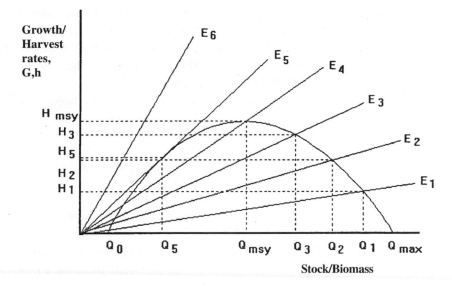

Figure 8.1. Growth, harvest, effort, and the stock of biomass.

Effort E_5 yields a knife-edge equilibrium. If the stock is initially above Q_5, the excess harvest rate over the growth rate will reduce it to Q_5, with equilibrium harvest H_5. However, if a natural or anthropogenic disturbance reduces the stock level below Q_5, then continuing effort E_5 will deplete the stock to extinction. At effort E_6 extinction at any stock level will occur. Where E_1 to E_6 simply represent changes in technology, it can be seen how such changes by themselves can extinguish a resource.

To arrive at the optimum stock level and harvesting rate, the cost of harvesting needs to be taken into account, so that the marginal cost of harvesting effort may be equated with the marginal revenue yielded by the effort. Furthermore, unless it is assumed that the resource owner is indifferent with regard to present and future profits (i.e., that the implicit discount rate is zero) a non-zero discount rate must be allowed for. Here the analysis becomes much more complex (see Pearce and Turner 1990), and only its conclusions can be summarily rehearsed here.

- Clearly defined property rights and profit maximization, with a zero discount rate, will tend to result in a yield that is lower and a stock that is higher than that at maximum sustainable yield.
- Open access conditions will reduce the stock from the level in A, but will not result in extinction provided that the sustainable yield is not exceeded.
- A positive discount rate will tend to result in a stock level between that of A and B. The higher the discount rate the closer will the stock level be to B.

- If the discount rate exceeds the net rate of return from the resource as an asset, the resource will be liquidated, perhaps to extinction.
- Increasing the price of the resource, or reducing the cost of harvesting it, will reduce the stock level. If the price is above the cost at low population levels, then extinction becomes likely.
- The calculated costs of harvesting the resource should include the externalities of both attendant environmental damage costs and foregone option and existence values. They frequently do not do so, increasing harvesting beyond the social optimum.

It is clear from the above that, in conditions of open access, if the price of the resource received by the harvester is high, if the cost of harvesting is low, or if the discount rate is high, then it can be optimal to drive the resource to extinction. The experience of Antarctic whaling, (Clark 1990), provides a clear example: stocks of the blue whale fell from 150,000 to probably below 1,000 and the whale's extinction was only prevented by regulation, in this case a moratorium imposed by the International Whaling Commission in 1965. Even so, Clark notes "whether the population has increased significantly in the intervening quarter century remains in doubt". Of course, extinction can also occur non-optimally due to uncertainty about stocks or sustainable yields.

While these results yield useful insights, their relevance to the actual production of renewable resources by ecosystems may not be very great. Concerning many ecosystems there are profound·uncertainties about stocks and the basic processes that give an ecosystem stability and resilience, which are fundamental to the maintenance of sustainable yields. It may not be possible to compute the maximum sustainable harvest for any given stock size (even where the stock is known) with any degree of accuracy, so that attempts to achieve such harvests run the perpetual risk of actually exceeding them. If, for example in Figure 8.1, the real stock/growth relationship is a curve that lies well inside the curve shown, then an effort level E_4, far from giving a maximum sustainable yield harvest, could actually drive the resource to extinction. Given the scientific uncertainties, and the incentives of economic agents to exaggerate the growth potential of a resource in order to justify a greater harvest, there is a very real risk of this happening. Without being able to assign probabilities to the uncertainties, which is often the case, an optimal solution cannot be derived. One possible response to this problem is the adoption of the safe minimum standards approach, or the precautionary principle, which fall outside the conventional territory of resource economics and are discussed further below.

Leaving incalculable uncertainties aside, the analysis above leads to the conclusion that for both renewable and non-renewable resources, optimal use or depletion can be environmentally unsustainable. This was made explicit by Smith (1977), who concluded from four control theory models of natural and environmental resource use, involving renewable, nonrenewable and amenity resources, that: "Just as exhaustion can be optimal, extinction can be optimal". Optimality and unsustainability are very much compatible in the mainstream resource economics literature.

Environmental Economics

The central organizing insight of environmental economics is the existence of "externalities", a phenomenon first analyzed by A.C. Pigou (1932). Although Pigou never used the term 'externality', his description of the effect remains definitive to this day: "The essence of the matter is that one person A, in the course of rendering some service, for which payment is made, to a second person B, incidentally also renders services or disservices to other persons (not producers of like services), of such a sort that payment cannot be exacted from the benefited parties or compensation enforced on behalf of the injured parties".

Environmental externalities arise because property rights to the use of environmental resources are either non-existent—the resources are treated as 'free goods'—or ill-defined. In principle, as suggested in a celebrated paper by Ronald Coase (1960), the externality problem may be solved by the clear legal delineation of these rights, so that environmental conflicts may be resolved through private negotiation. In practice, it may not be feasible for political or other reasons to give strict definition to property rights over natural resources. It is not clear, for instance, what system of private ownership could realistically encompass the atmosphere or the stratospheric ozone layer. Alternatively, it may be that, even if such resources could be privately owned, their degradation would affect so many people that the transaction costs involved in negotiations would be so great as to prohibit the negotiations taking place. Consequently the property rights approach to the resolution of the problem of externalities, while theoretically appealing, is often practically infeasible. Furthermore, there is nothing inherent in private ownership *per se* that will guarantee the sustainable use of resources, which requires the adoption of sustainability as a specific objective and the evolution of institutions and implementation of measures to achieve it, as discussed below.

Another theoretically attractive approach to resolving the externality problem is to seek to "internalize" the cost by levying a charge or tax on the activity concerned. This approach is illustrated in Figure 8.2.

Private producers gain benefits from an activity which causes pollution, as shown by the marginal net private benefit (MNPB) curve. Left to themselves, they will produce until the MNPB falls to zero, when the level of emissions is Q. Associated with this pollution is a cost, external to the producers, shown by the marginal external cost (MEC) curve, which rises with the pollution level. At Q the external cost is C.

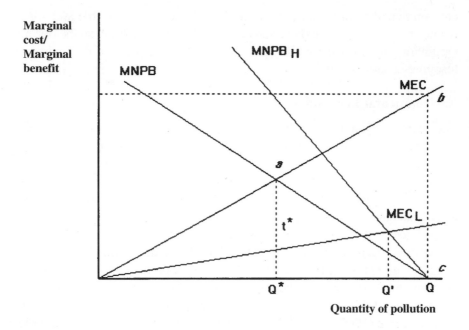

Figure 8.2 External costs of pollution and a Pigouvian tax.

Now it can be seen that at all levels of production that cause emissions higher than Q*, at which MNPB = MEC, the marginal external cost is greater than the marginal net private benefit. In other words, although production causing emissions greater than Q* makes the producers better off, society as a whole is worse off. At Q, the total excess cost to society of the externality-induced over-production is the area abc.

The policy problem is to persuade producers to reduce their production such that their emissions fall to Q*. This can be achieved by levying a tax, called a Pigouvian tax, equal to t* per unit of emissions, which will cause the producer either to cut production or to abate emissions so that they fall to the efficient level Q*. This efficient level is unlikely to be a zero level of pollution. Its position will be determined exclusively by the interaction between the MNPB and MEC curves.

The MNPB curve will be unproblematic to derive if, as is often the case, the benefit derives from economic activity which is marketed and therefore priced. The MEC curve, however, will often be representing or including unpriced, external effects, the value of which must be derived from techniques of environmental valuation. Where no surrogate markets exist to assist with this valuation, contingent valuation, usually based on willingness-to-pay (WTP) surveys, is generally the technique employed. Because WTP survey replies are supposed to be based on existing budget constraints, the use of this method ensures that poor people's valuation of external effects is lower than rich people's.

Again, in Figure 8.2, consider an economic activity with a high MNPB ($MNPB_H$) but involving serious external environmental effects, which primarily or exclusively affect poor people, who may or may not be the beneficiaries of the activity. Contingent valuation surveys may well reveal that these people have a low willingness to pay to avoid these effects, because they have a low ability to pay to do so. The MEC curve will be correspondingly low (MEC_L), so that the optimal level of environmental damage, where the curves intersect (Q'), could be relatively high. There is certainly no guarantee that such optimality will be environmentally sustainable.

Cost-Benefit Analysis

The efficiency and optimality calculations of resource and environmental economics are brought together in cost-benefit analysis in order to compare the discounted streams of costs and benefits through time. To do so, all the costs and benefits of resource use and environmental impact must be expressed in monetary terms. Much ingenuity has been employed in devising techniques to achieve this for the myriad impacts involved (e.g., in Cropper and Oates 1992). These techniques have their uses, but they are simply unequal to the task to giving any kind of coherent valuation of the multiple moral, spiritual, cultural, and survival values inherent in the environment. Two examples from global warming economics illustrate the kinds of problems that can arise.

The first concerns the valuation of the lives that are likely to be lost as a result of climate change due to global warming. Fankhauser (1995) estimates that a 2.5°C average global temperature increase due to a doubling of the atmospheric concentration of CO_2-equivalents of greenhouse gases would result in 137,727 extra mortalities per year, of which 22,923 are in OECD countries, 7,722 in the former USSR, and the rest in the so-called developing world. In the literature of valuations of statistical lives (VOSLs) in industrial countries, values range from $200,000 to over $16 million, with an average around $3 million; Fankhauser chooses a "fairly conservative" figure of $1.5 million. He chooses an "arbitrary value" of $100,000, one fifteenth of the industrial country valuation, as the VOSL in low-income developing countries, such as China, which is envisaged to lose 29,376 lives per year, more than in all the OECD countries together.

Economists are quick to point out, as Fankhauser does, that VOSLs do not measure what human lives are "worth". Rather they are derived either from considerations of lifetime production, or from willingness to accept risk as shown in differential wages. Either way it is "right" that poor people's lives are valued at less than rich people's. Fankhauser explains: "[the different valuation] merely reflects the fact that the willingness-to-pay for increased safety (a lower mortality risk) is higher in developed countries".

This may be true, but the fact remains that the purpose of the calculation is to ascertain whether investments should be made to save the lives in question by, in this case, abating emissions of greenhouse gases. Moreover, if it were possible to discriminate over which lives were saved (as, with global warming, it is not) the valuation method ensures that it is the lives of the rich which should be saved first. Whatever the *a priori* theoretical motivation, the practical result of such valuation is to make the lives of poor people worth less than those of rich people and so more easily traded off against the benefits from economic activity. This was precisely the argumentation used by Lawrence Summers, (Economist 1992) when, as Chief Economist of the World Bank, he concluded: "I think the economic logic behind dumping a load of toxic waste in the lowest wage country is impeccable". The situation is rendered even more problematic morally when, as with global warming, the benefits from the causal activity (largely the combustion of fossil fuels) accrue largely to rich people, while the poor are likely to be the worst affected by the ensuing negative physical impacts. This situation, in which rich people benefit from activities which kill poor people, can be deemed 'efficient' in cost-benefit analysis by ascribing very low values to poor people's lives.

Such a procedure is controversial even within economics. For example, Lockwood (1992) considers that "in the interests of intercountry equity, it is desirable to cost statistical lives in different countries equally, but it is not sensible to use valuation of statistical life for a high-income country such as the U.K.". Instead he divides the valuation for the U.K. by the ratio of UK GDP to world GDP, arriving at a uniform valuation of statistical life of £540,000 in both industrial and developing countries. But this seriously undervalues industrial country lives according to VOSL techniques which are routinely used when effects in developing countries are not involved. It seems a strange logic to infer that the loss of an industrial country life is worth less when people in developing countries are to be killed as well.

The figure used for the VOSL in a global cost-benefit analysis of global warming is of crucial importance to the final result obtained. Using Fankhauser's figures for the loss of life, and his valuations of the loss, yields a figure of $49.2 billion, which contributes to an overall cost of global warming of 1.4% of gross world product (GWP) (Fankhauser 1995). Valuing all the lives at Fankhauser's "fairly conservative" industrial country value increases the value of the lost lives to $207 billion and the overall cost of warming to 2.2% of GWP. Depending on the MNPB schedule, this could make a considerable difference to the amount of abatement that is "efficient" and, therefore, to the number of lives that are saved. Funtowicz and Ravetz (1994) in any case consider that "The practice of valuing a lost life is legitimate in the context of conservation *post hoc*, but ... it is fraught both morally and legally if done *ante hoc* in a design and costing exercise."

The use of cost-benefit analysis for such problems as global warming would therefore seem dubious on at least four counts. First, it is morally questionable in that it permits the conclusion that, provided the benefits to one group of people (in this case relatively rich people) are high enough, then the taking of the lives of another group of people (in this case relatively poor people) can be justified. Many would call such a conclusion, and the methodology that led to it, simply immoral (e.g., Adams 1993). Second, it is scientifically flawed in that the premises and methodology that generate the numbers do not sanction the uses to which they are then put. Third, it is of very doubtful practical value, in that an enormous range of values can be generated, which can be used to justify a very large range of actions; Fankhauser (1993) has himself admitted that, in global warming economics: "(T)hrough the choice of appropriate parameter values almost any abatement policy can be justified". And fourth, it is politically unhelpful. Developing countries are not likely to respond positively to the suggestion that their citizens are worth one tenth of those in industrial countries, so that such valuations will positively hinder the development of the global consensus on global warming and emission abatement that is necessary if the issue is to be adequately addressed.

The valuation of human life illustrates one kind of problem in seeking to derive monetary estimates of the non-monetary costs of seriously destructive environmental effects, namely the difficulty in justifying monetary valuation, in general and an adequately narrow range of figures, in particular. Another kind of problem, where market goods are involved but where their current price may not be an accurate reflection of the value of their loss, is illustrated by the treatment of agriculture in global warming damage estimates.

Nordhaus (1991) in one of the first and most influential cost-benefit analyses of global warming, based his cost analysis of agricultural damage on the assumption that in 2050 the structure of the world economy would be the same as the structure of the U.S. economy in 1990, when agriculture comprised less that 3% of U.S. output. He then estimated the net damage to U.S. agriculture in 2050 from global warming as 6.7% (central figure) and used the structural assumption to apply this figure, as a percentage of GWP, to the whole world.

Such a procedure is at best only valid for very small changes in agricultural output. If carried beyond this it implies that the total loss of the world's agriculture would involve a cost of only 3% of GWP, leaving 97% to be enjoyed, whereas, as Cline has noted: "If world agricultural production fell to zero, so would world population. The economic loss would equal the entirety of GDP, not just the *ex-ante* share attributable to agriculture" (1992).

Food is a basic human need, with a consumer surplus that rises very fast once supply falls below a basic level of sufficiency. At present there is enough food for the human population, but its distribution is such that in 1988–1990 20% of people in developing countries, 786 million people, were "chronically undernourished" (World Resources Institute 1994), with many of these actually starving. Moreover, by 2050 on current trends population is likely to have doubled and there are some doubts whether, even without global warming, the global food supply will be able to expand enough to meet this new level of need (e.g., Brown et al. 1993). Furthermore, to avoid disruption it is not enough for average supply levels to be broadly maintained. Extreme weather events that destroy particular crops in particular places in particular periods could have an impact quite out of proportion to their effect on such averages.

In short, it is clear that the world's food supply is currently precarious as far as millions of people are concerned, that this situation may well not improve and could deteriorate further, and that even a relatively small (in percentage terms) contribution to such deterioration could result in chaos, misery, and starvation beyond all human experience. Even Nordhaus' 6.7% damage could have a disproportionate effect, but some other estimates of damage are much higher. Cline's (1992) estimate of damage from long-term warming puts agricultural losses at 35% of agricultural output ($212 billion out of $603 billion). Rosenzweig et al. (1993) put Egypt's aggregate yield losses at 25-50% for only one doubling of atmospheric CO_2 concentrations. Hohmeyer and Gärtner (1992) calculated that an extra 900 million deaths from hunger could be caused in the period 2010-2030, due to global warming damage to agriculture. Such an estimate for hunger-related deaths alone is an order of magnitude higher than the Fankhauser figures for all global warming induced fatality, and makes the overall result of the cost-benefit analysis even more dependent on how these lives should be valued.

Such uncertainties overwhelm the careful weighing of costs and benefits that give cost-benefit analysis its aura of scientific method. A continuing commitment to such analysis in the face of such imponderables may provide the argument "with an image of quantitative science rather than of doctrine reinforced by guesswork" (Funtowicz and Ravetz 1994), but the image is false, and the doctrine and guesswork predominate. This undermines the technique's principal purpose and usefulness,

Cost-benefit analysis is intended to facilitate decision-making by giving values to different effects using a common metric (money) so that the values may be more easily compared and the aggregate outcome more easily appreciated. According to a standard text on the subject, cost-benefit analysis has "a fundamental attraction of reducing a complex problem to something less complex and more manageable" (Pearce 1983). But it can only fulfill this function if the basis of valuation commands a wide consensus.

Where this is not the case, and the methodology of valuation itself becomes disputed ground, especially if the dispute centres on concerns with justice or morality, then the use of cost-benefit analysis is likely to inflame an issue rather than illuminate it. This can be easily seen by referring again to Fankhauser's numbers of deaths from global warming. His first-stage calculation, that the number of deaths in OECD countries and the rest of the world could be 22,923 and 114,804 respectively is informative and meaningful. It gives clear insight into the scale and distribution of the problem. His second-stage calculation that, on the basis of values differing by factors of ten to fifteen, these lives are "worth" $34.4 billion and $14.8 billion respectively, cannot help but cause rage and a deep sense of injustice in those who believe developing country lives to be as valuable as industrial country lives. Certainly such calculations do not make global warming "more manageable". They arouse passions, and will make it very difficult, as mentioned earlier, to forge the global consensus that will be required if global warming is to be controlled and at least some of the lives in question are to be saved.

In summary, then, there is no question but that conventional resource and environmental economics can aid analysis and understanding of environmental problems. But they can also classify as 'optimal' patterns of resource use that are unsustainable; and the central decision-making aid of welfare economics, cost-benefit analysis, can, when applied to the environment, intensify controversy rather than diminish it. There is an evident need, if environmental sustainability is the objective, to adopt modes of analysis that amend the traditional derivation of optimality, and assign values (not necessarily monetary values) to environmental resources and services that ensure their sustainable provision and use. It is to some preliminary arguments toward this end that the next section is devoted.

TOWARDS AN ECONOMICS FOR SUSTAINABILITY

Environmental sustainability is a condition which entails the maintenance into the indefinite future of important environmental functions. These functions have been extensively analyzed and classified (see De Groot 1992), and can be grouped into three distinct categories: functions of resource-provision; functions of waste-absorption and naturalization; and functions providing environmental services from amenity to climate-regulation. Environmental sustainability derives its legitimacy as a fundamental objective of public policy from a number of sources, (Perrings et al. 1995). Most importantly, perhaps, is the issue of intergenerational equity, whereby it is perceived that present generations have an obligation to leave future generations no worse off in terms of environmental functions, in acknowledgment of the fact that these functions provide the basis for wealth-creation and economic activity, for human welfare and ways of life, and, indeed, for life itself.

The environmental functions produced by complex ecosystems are in many cases not substitutable by human-made alternatives. Moreover, such ecosystems are often characterized by threshold effects and irreversibilities that make unwelcome changes impossible both to predict and undo. As Perrings et al. (1995) observe: "Ecosystems typically continue to function in the short-term even as resilience declines. Indeed, they often signal loss of resilience only at the point at which external shocks at previously sustainable levels flip these systems into some other basis of attraction and so some other regime of behavior". Other regimes of behavior may be substantially less hospitable to humans than the present one. Munasinghe and Shearer (1995) consider that "sustaining the global life support system is a prerequisite for sustaining human societies". They go on to say, however, "The increasing concentration of greenhouse gases in the atmosphere, the weakening ozone shield, increased local and regional pollution, and the decreasing capability of the atmosphere to oxidize biogenic and anthropogenic emissions are symptoms of progressive and unsustainable deterioration of the life-support system provided by the global atmosphere".

The importance of environmental functions for human welfare justifies the adoption of environmental sustainability as an important, and perhaps preeminent, policy objective. Even so, not all environmental functions everywhere can be sustained. Some assessment must be made of those functions that play a particularly important role in life support and policy for sustainability must be geared towards these. Ekins (1994) posited that this implies at least the following six sustainability principles:

1. Destabilization of global environmental features must be prevented. Most important in this category are the maintenance of biodiversity (see below), the prevention of climate change, by the stabilization of the atmospheric concentration of greenhouse, and safeguarding the ozone layer by ceasing the emission of ozone-depleting substances.

2. Important ecosystems and ecological features must be absolutely protected to maintain biological diversity. Importance in this context comes from a recognition not only of the perhaps as yet unappreciated use value of individual species, but also of the fact that biodiversity under pins the productivity and resilience of ecosystems. Resilience, defined as "the magnitude of the disturbance that can be absorbed before the system changes its structure by changing the variables and processes that control its behavior" (Folke et al. 1994) depends on the functional diversity of the system. This depends in turn, in complex ways, not just on the diversity of species but on their mix and population and the relations between the ecosystems that contain them. "Biodiversity conservation, ecological sustainability and economic sustainability are inexorably linked; uncontrolled and irreversible biodiversity loss ruptures

this link and puts the sustainability of our basic economic-environmental systems at risk" (Barbier et al. 1994).

3. The renewal of renewable resources must be fostered through the maintenance of soil fertility, hydrobiological cycles and necessary vegetative cover and the rigorous enforcement of sustainable harvesting. The latter implies basing harvesting rates on the most conservative estimates of stock levels, for such resources as fish; ensuring that replanting becomes an essential part of such activities as forestry; and using technologies for cultivation and harvest that do not degrade the relevant ecosystem, and deplete neither the soil nor genetic diversity;

4. Depletion of non-renewable resources should seek to balance the maintenance of a minimum life-expectancy of the resource with the development of substitutes for it. On reaching the minimum life-expectancy, its maintenance would mean that consumption of the resource would have to be matched by new discoveries of it. To help finance research for alternatives and the eventual transition to renewable substitutes, all depletion of non-renewable resources should entail a contribution to a capital fund. Designing for resource-efficiency and durability can ensure that the practice of repair, reconditioning, re-use and recycling (the 'four R's') approach the limits of their environmental efficiency.

5. Emissions into air, soil and water must not exceed their critical load, that is the capability of the receiving media to disperse, absorb, neutralize and recycle them, nor may they lead to life-damaging concentrations of toxins. Synergies between pollutants can make critical loads very much more difficult to determine. Such uncertainties should result in a precautionary approach in the adoption of safe minimum standards.

6. Risks of life-damaging events from human activity must be kept at very low levels. Technologies, such as nuclear power, which threaten long-lasting ecosystem damage at whatever level of risk, should be foregone.

Of these six sustainability principles, 3, 4, and, to some extent, 2 seek to sustain resource functions. Five seeks to sustain waste-absorption functions; 1 and 2 seek to sustain life-supporting environmental services; and 6 acknowledges the great uncertainties associated with environmental change and the threshold effects and irreversibilities mentioned above. The principles give clear guidance how to approach today's principal perceived environmental problems as classified in, for example, OECD (1994). They may need to be supplemented as new environmental problems become apparent.

The principles are also reflected in a number of international treaties, conventions, and principles, including the Montreal Protocol to phase out ozone-depleting substances (2 above), the Convention on International Trade in Endangered Species and the establishment of World Biosphere Reserves to maintain biodiversity (3 above) and the Precautionary Principle, endorsed by the United Nations Conference on Environment and Development in Agenda 21, to limit environmental risk-taking (5 and 6 above). None of these international agreements was the outcome of cost-benefit analysis. They rest on a simple recognition that they represent the humane, moral, and intelligent way for humans to proceed in order to maintain their conditions for life, and are argued for on that basis.

Moving systematically towards environmental sustainability as set out in the above conditions will, of course, not be easy. Targets will have to be set, over specific timescales and with defined budgets, which will demand sacrifices in some areas. In order to remedy the fact that hitherto the social and economic institutions that have guided modern development, including the market, have given low or no value to ecological sustainability, new institutions will be need to be created and old institutions will need to be imaginatively transformed or retired.

The process of institutional creation and change has already begun. Examples of important new institutions are the Global Environmental Facility, administered under the auspices of the World Bank, and the conventions on climate change and biodiversity established by the Rio Summit. Institutions undergoing transformation are the systems of accounting at both the national and corporate levels. Work on national accounts is now in many places seeking to adjust them for environmental effects; while corporate environmental reporting is becoming commonplace and is likely to be established in the future on an increasingly formal, quantitative, and statutory basis, so that a company's environmental accounts will come to contain the level of detail and sophistication of its financial accounts.

More profoundly, because the use and experience of the environment are inextricably linked to the deepest social and cultural processes, the pursuit of environmental sustainability will, if it is to be successful, have to be accompanied by a concern for economic, social, and cultural sustainability: the maintenance of the fundamental means of wealth-creation, the social cohesion and the cultural integrity that will themselves be necessary if the environmental challenges are to be effectively addressed. All this implies something close to a revolution in the way humans perceive the environment, the place of and the links between human societies within it, and the aspirations of those societies and the individuals they contain.

It has to be admitted that the present human situation is not particularly propitious for such a revolution. Durning (1991) has characterized the world's population as divided into broadly three groups: 20% of "overconsumers", who "live in unprecedented luxury"; 20% living in poverty, whose desperation to survive often leads them to degrade or destroy the resources on which they depend; and 60% currently living nearest to a sustainable lifestyle. However, not only do the 80% of non-overconsumers possess a powerful aspiration to enter into that category; but the overconsumers themselves show no sign of achieving sufficiency and are driven equally powerfully to seek to consume more, despite the fact that, as Durning says: "Overconsumption by the world's fortunate is an environmental problem unmatched in severity by anything but perhaps population growth." In such a world unsustainability does indeed present a formidable challenge: to governments, to business, to other social institutions and, particularly for overconsumers, to lifestyles.

However, it is increasingly clear what needs to be done to address the challenge, even if the difficulty of doing it must be acknowledged. In the last two decades, research, environmental activism, and common sense have identified very clearly the causes of environmental unsustainability. In particular, it is now known beyond doubt that:

- Environmental damage is principally the result of dominant patterns of energy use, agriculture, transport, some industrial processes, tourism and the disposal of producer and consumer wastes.

- Practically every marketed activity or product that uses environmental resources is underpriced, and there is a wide variety of instruments to remedy this.

- Much environmental damage is caused by subsidized economic activity, especially involving the use of energy, water, forests, and agrochemicals, thus compounding economic with environmental inefficiency.

- If people are to use resources sustainably, there must be justice in the allocation of those resources, and rights that guarantee those who invest in them access to them in the future.

- If people have access to so few or such poor resources that their sustainable use will not yield them subsistence, then they will use them unsustainably.

- Sustainable food production involves building up rather than depleting soil fertility; it is also broadly known what crops on what land with what inputs using what techniques will contribute to this objective, while producing good yields of healthy food.

- New techniques are available to reduce environmental impacts per unit of production very substantially, most importantly the new "ecotechnologies" (e.g., Mitsch and Jorgenson 1989), through which production and consumption work in synergy with ecosystem processes and functions. It is also known what technologies need to be developed for sustainability, most importantly all those technologies that can be powered by solar energy.

- Competitive pressures through global and local markets can provide powerful incentives for unsustainable resource use and the loss of biodiversity, and they can prevent governments from implementing environmental policy to remedy this. There have been many suggestions as to how the new World Trade Organization could relieve these pressures and give positive encouragement to moves towards sustainability (e.g., Esty 1994; Ekins 1995).

- Developing countries with high foreign indebtedness cannot both continue to repay debts and have the resources to invest for the transition to sustainability.

- Certain aspects of industrial country lifestyles are particularly environmentally damaging, including high levels of private motoring or aircraft travel, diets intensive in meat and packaged beverages, home environments requiring high inputs of fossil or nuclear energy for heating, cooling or power, or a fashion-driven approach to living that requires a high turnover of consumer goods and appliances. Such behavior is not only occupying more than its fair share of environmental space. It is also foreclosing options for future generations, while simultaneously stimulating the consumer appetites of the 80% of the world's population that cannot yet do these things, but is increasingly desirous of doing them in the future. Turning towards sustainability requires that consumers start to feel the full implications of these aspects of their lifestyles and to find ways of feeling good about sustainable alternatives to them.

In short, it is very largely known what needs to be done and how to do it in order to move decisively towards sustainability. It is clear that sustainability cannot be achieved overnight; it will be a process of decades, but the process needs to be started with determination now. However, as in 1989 with the end of the Cold War, transformations can happen quickly, which calls for preparedness to take opportunities as they arise. Vested interests or power structures that have thrived on unsustainability will need to be transformed or overcome. This will involve establishing new vested interests and building up the power of those who will benefit from sustainability; tackling issues one by one where winners from sustainability can overcome the beneficiaries from unsustainability; putting together coalitions for sustainability and building momentum towards it.

What role will economists have in this political-ethical-social-economics of sustainability? First, they will not have the responsibility of deciding whether it is economically efficient or optimal for people, individually or collectively, to live or die. For some economists this will come as something of a relief. Second, they will move beyond models of optimality that generate unsustainability, and, where issues of sustainability are concerned, will give up using discount rates that render insignificant any impacts more than a few decades away. Third, they will work with natural and other social scientists, philosophers, politicians, lawyers, and business-people to generate understanding and prescription appropriate for environmental sustainability in a complex reality. Fourth, and perhaps most particularly, they will use their concern with efficiency to advise on least-cost approaches to sustainability. The crucial message from economists must be that sustainability does not come with a fixed price tag. How fast societies decide to move towards sustainability, especially before the idea really catches on, depends to a large extent on how much it is perceived to cost. It is economists' task, not to define the goal of sustainability, but to advise on ways of minimizing the cost of achieving it, within an institutional framework that recognizes the pervasive and profound, if uncertain, links between ecosystems and the socio-economy, and the dangers of attempts at partial maximization or optimization in such a context.

This will require economists to be what Keynes (1972), at any rate, wanted them to be, "humble, competent people—on a level with dentists". Dentists prevent and relieve excruciating pain in the human body, often with simple and inexpensive means. It is to be hoped that economists can do the same for the body economic, by developing an analytic and practical economics of environmental sustainability effectively to address current unsustainability, which is probably the most pressing and intractable problem of the present time.

ACKNOWLEDGMENTS

I would like to thank Cutler J. Cleveland, Carl Folke, and Karl Steininger for their helpful comments and suggestions. The responsibility for the final text is, however, mine alone.

APPENDIX ON MEASURES OF SCARCITY

While Hotelling's Rule describes the expected movement of resources' net prices under perfect market conditions, the reason for such a price movement is the resource's actual or possible scarcity. Scarcity is, of course, the raison d'etre of rent, as Ricardo developed the concept. Marshall argued that "all rents are scarcity rents" (Marshall 1959). A resource that was not scarce would command a rent, or *in situ* price, of zero. Economic agents would not bother to hold it at all. This being so, it is to be expected that the increasing scarcity of an exhaustible resource, without a perfect, less scarce, substitute, would cause its rent and market price to rise, whether or not the increasing scarcity resulted in an increase in extraction costs. The rise in price would encourage both the economization of the use of the resource and the development of substitutes, thereby mitigating the increasing scarcity. However, while it may be acknowledged, with Dasgupta and Heal (1974) that "This argument clearly has force", Their qualification "In the absence of a well-articulated temporal plan, or a satisfactory set of forward markets, it is not all plain that market prices will be providing the correct signals", is equally valid as far as an increase in scarcity or otherwise is concerned.

There has been a sustained effort over the last thirty years to test the hypothesis of increasing scarcity by analyzing the movement of resource prices, beginning with Barnett and Morse's classic 1963 investigation, which, using a unit cost indicator, found no increase in scarcity since the late nineteenth century over a wide range of resource, with the exception of forest products. Barnett (1979) updated this work and came to the same conclusion, Hall and Hall (1984) found in contrast that coal increased in scarcity on a unit cost test, but on a relative price test oil, gas, electricity and timber all exhibited scarcity increases through the 1970s.

In the same volume reporting Barnett's updated results, Brown and Field (1979) present compelling arguments why both unit cost (the Barnett and Morse measure) and product price are ambiguous measures of scarcity. In contrast, "a rising rental rate always portends increasing scarcity and eventual exhaustion, unless there is a 'backstop technology' (Brown and Field 1979). Unfortunately, they also note that rental rates for most resources are not readily available. Furthermore, in the same volume Fisher presents a model in which "rent as an indicator of scarcity has the disturbing property of sometimes decreasing as the resource-stock decreases" (Fisher 1979). Such considerations, theoretical and empirical, suggest that Barnett and Morse's reassuring 1963 conclusions, and Barnett's 1979 restatement of them, should be treated with a great deal of caution.

Other work has confirmed the difficulty of using economic measures to test for increasing environmental scarcity. Slade (1982) seemed to have found a promising specification using a quadratic model, whereby price decreases due to technological progress initially dominated, but were later dominated by, price increases due to increasing scarcity. In this model, "fitted trends for prices of all the major metals and fuels showed the predicted convex curvature—initially falling but eventually rising—and all but one of the estimated coefficients of the squared terms were statistically significant at the 90% confidence level" (Slade 1982). However, in subsequent work on volatile price behavior in the 1980s (Slade 1991), the author did not even mention increasing scarcity as a possible contributory factor and concluded the following year that "there is little evidence of a sustained trend" (Slade 1992).

Three factors can be responsible for price decreases during the depletion of an exhaustible resource: large, new unanticipated discoveries of stocks of the resource, technical change, and the development of substitutes. Slade (1992) considers that "ultimately, the exhaustibility underlying Hotelling's Rule should reassert itself", but this does not by any means seem inevitable. In particular, it is perfectly possible that continuous incremental technical change could yield a rate of price decrease that constantly outweighs any price increase due to scarcity. This, in contrast to the quadratic timepath exhibited in Slade (1982), which suggests that new technologies are introduced as one-off improvements that eventually exhaust their price-reducing potential and that no further technological improvements are implemented to prevent scarcity-induced price increases from becoming dominant. In this way it is perfectly possible for physical exhaustion, or the extinction of commercial, marketed species (e.g., passenger pigeon in the U.S.) (Brown and Field 1979), to occur in the absence of price increases.

Dissatisfaction with economic measures of scarcity, and with other aspects of conventional approaches to environment and resource issues, has led to the emergence of a 'biophysical' approach to these issues, the proponents of which "generally argue that basic physical and ecological laws constrain our economic choices in ways that are not accurately reflected in existing economic models" (Cleveland 1991). This approach has resulted in the development of a biophysical indicator of scarcity, the physical output of an industry per unit of energy (direct and indirect), input (output per energy input, or OEI). For the energy industry this indicator is called the energy return on investment (EROI) and is the ratio of the energy produced to the energy consumed by the industry.

There are three reasons why an extractive industry's OEI might change over time. First, where the extracted resource is exhaustible, depletion of the resource may make further extraction more difficult, inter alia requiring more energy. This is a classic scarcity effect which would tend to reduce OEI, as well as increase the cost and price of extractive output. Second, the discovery or greater availability of new energy sources may result in a substitution in the production process towards energy and away from other inputs (labor and capital). Georgescu-Roegen (1975) observed that "economic history confirms a rather elementary fact—the fact that the great strides in technological progress have generally been touched off by a discovery of how to use a new kind of accessible energy. The substitution of energy for labor will reduce OEI unless it gives rise to a proportional increase in output that is equal to or greater than the proportional increase in energy use. However, assuming the substitution leads to cost-reduction (and in a competitive environment there is no other reason why it should take place), it will lead price and other economic measures of scarcity to indicate a decrease in scarcity, despite an underlying change in the availability of the resource and greater depletion of energy. This is one of the reasons why the biophysical and economic indicators of scarcity may tell opposite stories and why price has been criticized as a measure of scarcity.

Third, the more efficient use of energy by an industry is likely to cause its OEI to increase. Energy efficiency, in turn, is likely to be encouraged by high energy prices, which may come about due to a scarcity of energy. Therefore the increasing scarcity of an essential input into the extraction of a resource may lead to a perception that the resource itself is becoming less scarce. This is a perverse result, which can be further illustrated by considering a situation in which an extreme physical shortage and consequently high price of energy led to a collapse in output of some energy-intensive extractive resource. Despite the fact that the extracted (as opposed to in situ) resource would now be scarce in the sense of being in short supply, its OEI would increase, provided that the energy efficiency of its production increased, suggesting that its biophysical scarcity had decreased.

This leads to two conclusions: that the effective scarcity of a resource depends not only on its own abundance, but on the scarcity of the inputs that are essential to extract it; and, that the extractive importance of energy gives it a primacy among resources. If energy became extremely scarce, many other resources would effectively become extremely scarce too, no matter how energy efficient their extraction (how high their OEI) became. Paradoxically, cost and price measures of scarcity (though not rent) perform better than the biophysical, energy-based OEI on this score, because extreme scarcity of energy would result in a high price of energy and energy-intensive resources.

Cleveland (1991) calculates OEI time trends in the 20th century for the U.S. for many minerals and renewable resources. The results are mixed and few conclusions can be drawn. Metals as a whole show a decreasing OEI from about 1950; for non-metal minerals overall the OEI increases almost continuously from 1920–1980. For agriculture, the OEI fell almost continuously through the century to about 1970, and then rose, exhibiting the efficiency effect discussed above. For forestry, OEI declines from 1950–1974 and then rises a slightly greater amount to 1986. For fisheries OEI declined by 80% between 1968 and 1988.

For fossil fuels the results are more interesting and show a clear change of trend in the 1960s, from rising to falling EROI, for oil from 23 to 12, for coal from 60 to 30. Moreover, this biophysical indication of scarcity is confirmed by the economic measures: both the price of crude oil and the cost of US petroleum extraction rise from about 1970 (Cleveland 1993). Hall and Hall's (1984) analysis on the basis of relative prices and unit costs led them to conclude: "the most basic (conclusion) is that all primary fuels became more scarce in the 1970s". It remains to be seen whether this conclusion survives the oil-price collapse of the mid-1980s and the lower level of oil prices since.

REFERENCES

Adams, J. 1993. The emperor's old clothes: the curious comeback of cost-benefit analysis. *Environmental Values* 2: 247–260.

Barbier, E., J. Burgess and C. Folke. 1994. Paradise Lost? The Ecological Economics of Biodiversity. London: Earthscan.

Barnett, H. 1979. Scarcity and Growth Revisited. In: Scarcity and Growth Reconsidered, ed. V. Smith. Baltimore: Johns Hopkins University Press.

Barnett, H. and C. Morse. 1963. Scarcity and Economic Growth: the Economics of Natural Resource Availability. Baltimore: Johns Hopkins University Press.

Brown and Field 1979. The adequacy of measures for signalling the scarcity of natural resources. In Scarcity and Growth Reconsidered, ed. V. Smith. Baltimore: Johns Hopkins University Press.

Brown, L.R. et al. 1993. State of the World 1993. London: Earthscan.

Clark, C. 1990. Mathematical Bioeconomics: The Optimal Management of Renewable Resources, 2d. New York: John Wiley.

Cleveland, C. 1991. Natural resource scarcity and economic growth revisited: Economic and biophysical perspectives: In Ecological Economics: The Science and Management of Sustainability, ed. R. Costanza. New York: Columbia University Press.

Cleveland, C. 1993. An exploration of alternative measures of natural resource scarcity: The case of petroleum resources in the U.S. *Ecological Economics* 7: 123–157.

Cline, W. 1992. The Economics of Global Warming. Washington DC: Institute for International Economics.

Coase, R.H. 1960. The problem of social cost. *Journal of Law and Economics* 3: 1–44.

Cropper, M. and W. Oates. 1992. Environmental economics: A survey. *Journal of Economic Literature* 30: 673–740.

Dasgupta, P. and G. Heal. 1974. The optimal depletion of exhaustible resources. Review of Economic Studies, Symposium on the Economics of Exhaustible Resources: 3–28.

Dasgupta, P. and G. Heal. 1979. Economic Theory and Exhaustible Resources. Cambridge: Cambridge University Press.

De Groot, R. 1992. Functions of Nature. Groningen: Wolters-Noordhoff.

Durning, A. 1991. Asking how much is enough. In State of the World 1991 by L.R. Brown et al. London: Earthscan.

Eagan, V. 1987. The optimal depletion of the theory of exhaustible resources. *Journal of Post Keynesian Economics* IX (4): 565–571.

Economist. 1992. Let them eat pollution. *The Economist* February.

Ekins, P. 1994. The environmental sustainability of economic processes: A framework for analysis. In Toward Sustainable Development: Concepts, Methods, and Policy, eds. J. van den Bergh and J. van der Straaten. Washington DC: Island Press.

Ekins, P. 1995. Harnessing Trade to Sustainable Development. Green College Centre for Environmental Policy and Understanding. Oxford: Green College.

Esty, D. 1994. Greening the GATT: Trade, the Environment and the Future. Washington DC: Institute for International Economics.

Fankhauser, S. 1993. Global Warming Economics: Issues and State of the Art. CSERGE Working Paper GEC 93-28. London: CSERGE, University College London.

Fankhauser, S. 1995. Valuing Climate Change: The Economics of the Greenhouse. London: Earthscan.

Farrow, S. 1985. Testing the efficiency of extraction from a stock of resources. *Journal of Political Economy* 93(3): 452–487.

Fisher 1979. Scarcity and Growth Reconsidered, ed. V. Smith. Baltimore: Johns Hopkins University Press.

Folke, C., C. S. Holling, and C. Perrings. 1994. Biodiversity, Ecosystems and Human Welfare. Beijer Discussion Paper Series No.49. Stockholm: Beijer International Institute of Ecological Economics.

Funtowicz, S. and J. Ravetz. 1994. The worth of a songbird: Ecological economics as a post-normal science. *Ecological Economics* 10: 197–207.

Hall, D. and J. Hall 1984. Concepts and measures of natural resource scarcity, with a summary of recent trends. *Journal of Environmental Economics and Management* December: 363–379.

Heal, G. and M. Barrow. 1980. The relationship between interest rates and rental price movements. *Review of Economic Studies* 47: 161–182.

Hohmeyer, O. and M. Gärtner. 1992. The Costs of Climate Change, Report to the Commission of the European Communities. Karlsruhe: Fraunhofer Institut für Systemtechnik und Innovations-Forschung.

Hotelling, H. 1931. The economics of exhaustible resources. *Journal of Political Economy* 39(2): 137–75.

Keynes, J. M. 1972. Economic possibilities for our grandchildren. In Essays in Persuasion, Vol. 9   of The Collected Writings of John Maynard Keynes. London: Macmillan.

Lockwood, B. 1992. The Social Costs of Electricity Generation. CSERGE Discussion Paper GEC 92-09. Norwich: CSERGE, University of East Anglia.

Mitsch, W. J. and S. E. Jörgenson, eds. 1989. Ecological Engineering: An Introduction to Ecotechnology. New York: John Wiley.

Munasinghe, M. and W. Shearer, eds. 1995. Defining and Measuring Sustainability: The Biogeophysical Foundations for the United Nations University and World Bank. Washington DC: World Bank.

Nordhaus, W. 1991. To slow or not to slow: The economics of the greenhouse effect. *Economic Journal* 101 (July): 920–937.

OECD. 1994. Environmental Indicators: OECD Core Set, Paris: OECD.

Pearce, D. 1983. Cost-Benefit Analysis, 2d. London: Macmillan.

Pearce, D. and R. K. Turner. 1990. Economics of Natural Resources and the Environment. Hemel Hempstead: Harvester Wheatsheaf.

Pigou, A.C. 1932. The Economics of Welfare 4d. London: Macmillan.

Perrings, C., K. Turner and C. Folke. 1995. Ecological Economics: The Study of Interdependent Economic and Ecological Systems. Beijer Discussion Paper Series No.55 Stockholm: Beijer International Institute of Ecological Economics.

Rosenzweig, C., M. Parry, K. Frohberg, and G. Fisher. 1993. Climate Change and World Food Supply. Oxford: Environmental Change Unit.

Slade, M. 1982. Trends in natural-resource commodity prices: An analysis of the time domain. *Journal of Environmental Economics and Management* 9: 122–137

Slade, M. 1991. Market Structure, Marketing Method and Price Instability. *The Quarterly Journal of Economics* November: 1309–1340.

Slade. M. 1992. Do Markets Underprice Natural-Resource Commodities? Background Paper for the World Development Report 1992, WPS 962. Washington DC: World Bank.

Smith, V. K. 1981. The empirical relevance of Hotelling's model for natural resources. *Resources and Energy* 3: 105–117.

Smith, V. L. 1977. Control theory applied to natural and environmental resources. *Journal of Environmental Economics and Management* 4: 1–14.

World Resources Institute, UNDP, and UNEP. 1994. World Resources, 1994–1995. Oxford/New York: Oxford University Press.

9 ECOLOGICAL AND ECONOMIC DISTRIBUTION CONFLICTS [1]

Juan Martinez-Alier
Departament d'Economica i d'Història Econòmica
Universitat Autònoma de Barcelona
Bellaterra 08193, Barcelona, Spain

Martin O'Connor
Centre d'Economie et d'Ethique pour l'Environnement et le
Développement (C3ED), Département de Sciences
Economiques,Collège Vauban, Université de Versailles
à Saint-Quentin-en-Yvelines
72 boulevard Vauban, 78280 Guyancourt, France

OVERVIEW

This chapter analyzes the non-separability between allocative efficiency and distribution and its implications for environmental valuation and management. First, noting that most environmental resources and services are not in the market, the chapter introduces the concept of 'ecological distribution' (i.e., the social, spatial, and temporal asymmetries in the access to natural resources or in the burdens of pollution, and considers the relations between economic distribution and ecological distribution). Then it analyzes how the economic values that non-traded, and traded, environmental goods and services, or negative externalities, will depend (in different ways) on the endowment of property rights and on the distribution of income. This is shown at a practical level by some examples from Ecuador, and at the analytical level through didactic use of neoclassical general equilibrium (as a corollary of the fundamental welfare theorems) and of neo-Ricardian modeling (where the distribution of income and of property rights will determine the 'production prices' of traded items of 'natural capital'). Finally, implications for time-discounting, the valuation of natural capital, and sustainability are discussed.

INTRODUCTION

Since, in ecological economics, we see the market economy as embedded in a physical-chemical-biological system, the question arises of the value of such natural resources and environmental services for the economy. Is it possible to translate such environmental values into money values? And if so, for what purposes and with what effects (social justice, distribution of economic opportunity, ecosystem conservation, and so on)? There are important differences with regards to distributional issues between conventional economics and ecological economics. In the ecological economy, future human generations, and the existence values attributed to other species play a role because the time horizon of the ecological economy is much longer, as we take into account slow biogeochemical cycles, and irreversible thermodynamics. Also, many natural resources and environmental services are not in the market, because they have no owner. Attribution of property rights and inclusion in the market, would change the distribution of power and of income, and hence the pattern of prices in the market economy embedded in the ecological economy.

Our purpose in this chapter is to demonstrate, in both theoretical and empirical terms, the importance in ecological economics of distribution issues as determinants of environmental valuation. By 'ecological economics' we mean the study of the compatibility between the human economy and the environment, in the long run. A common understanding is that this compatibility is not assured by the valuation of environmental resources and services in markets. Moreover, we should not expect that this failure may be overcome by introducing ancillary mechanisms for 'internalization' (for example through markets in pollution, waste disposal, and genetic stocks; or contingent valuations of environmental amenities). Some of the "failures" of real markets—notably the absence from them of future generations and of members of other species—are not really failures, but rather part and parcel of what we all understand by markets (actual or surrogate) as practices, institutions and conventions for exchange.

Starting from the recognition that most environmental resources and services are not in the market, the chapter introduces the concept of 'ecological distribution' (i.e., the social, spatial, and temporal asymmetries in the access to natural resources, or in the burdens of waste disposal and pollution traded or not). We then discuss the relations between economic distribution and ecological distribution, in other words, the relations between political economy and political ecology. The economic values which non-traded, and traded, environmental goods and services, or negative externalities, might be given, depend (in different ways) on the endowment of property rights and on the distribution of income. This is shown at a practical level by some examples from Ecuador, and then at the analytical level, both in a neoclassical general equilibrium framework, and through neo-Ricardian modeling where the distribution of income (and of property rights) will determine (in a Sraffian-like manner) the value (or rather, the 'production prices') of traded items of 'natural capital'.

In effect, we present a number of different ways of interpreting and analyzing theoretically this dependency of valuation on distribution. In neoclassical equilibrium theory, a zero price for an environmental good would signal non-scarcity of that good relative to the demands on it over the time horizon considered (e.g., abundant air and water.) Changed perceptions, that the good is scarce, should result in a positive price. But alternatively, we may choose to look directly at the power relations that underlie pricing. A zero-price may then signal not non-scarcity *per se*, but a relation of power in a situation of conflict. For example a good may be plundered by an act of an invasive force, or may be appropriated by a dominant social group who define for themselves the terms of legitimate possession. Similarly, pollutants or toxic wastes may be discharged in ways that degrade the living habitat of others who are unable to stop the event. Although such situations may be interpreted as *de facto* rights/liability inequalities, it is more lucid to offer an interpretation directly in terms of power, namely the capacity of the dominant social groups to ignore or discount the demands of the other groups who claim an interest in the resources or services in question but who cannot give practical effect to this claim. The Sraffian joint production theory is a convenient framework with which to give a mathematical expression of relative prices (i.e., valuation) as outcomes of unequal power relations.

We will thus establish as a robust theoretical result that prices of environmental resources and services formed by transactions among humans who are alive at present, will depend on the existence (or non-existence), and the endowment of property rights on "natural capital", and they will depend also on the distribution of income already within the present generation of humans. Consequently, the question of rights and income distribution has central theoretical, as well as empirical, importance. We then trace the consequences of this contention in application to the question of the time-discount rate appropriate for an ecological economy, that is, a rate corresponding to the sustainable productivity of capital. In particular, we point out that the measures of sustainability potential offered in recent work adopting a neoclassical perspective, the 'weak sustainability test' are critically sensitive not only to assumptions about substitutability between natural and economic capitals, but also to the prices used for the measure of depreciation of natural capital. The question of substitutability must be resolved largely outside the confines of neoclassical axiomatic theory. The distribution-sensitivity of relative prices, and hence of environmental values may by contrast be established within the neoclassical theory itself. That is, the relative prices for measure of natural capital will depend, in various ways, on the endowment of property rights, and on the distribution of income. So the use of existing prices, or of willingness-to-pay (WTP) estimates based on existing distribution, for estimates and indicators relating to sustainability is theoretically incoherent as well as empirically wrong.

Having established and illustrated these results, we conclude by discussing briefly, the links between distributional issues, valuation, and incommensurability, and the practical implications for resource use decisions aimed at sustainability.

SOME EXTERNALITIES FROM ECUADOR: TEXACO/BANANAS/MANGROVES/BIODIVERSITY

Today's exploitation of nature in Ecuador, as in many other places in the world, raises the issue of the internalization of externalities. Empirically, the value of such externalities is clearly related to outcomes of distributional conflicts. What is the true value of a barrel of Texaco oil, of a bunch of bananas, or of a box of shrimps from Ecuador? According to recognized economic theory, the answer depends on the value of the damages caused. As such, there are no "true" values. So-called "ecologically-correct" prices do not exist, although there might be various sorts of ecologically-corrected prices. The value of the perceived negative externalities is, both in theory and empirically, a product of social institutions and social conflicts. In general, if the people damaged are relatively powerless and poor (or, moreover, members of future generations), then the externalities will be lower-valued relative to market goods. But this also means that the internationalization of environmental conflicts, when it involves significant shifts in real power or standing of formerly disadvantaged groups, may yield a very high valuation for the externalities—the apparent exceptions that prove the general rule.

Texaco extracted oil from the northern part of the Amazonian territory of Ecuador since the early 1970s until 1990. Damages have been claimed of $1,500 million, arising from oil spills, deforestation, and disruption of the life of local indigenous communities.[2] The case is now under consideration at a court in New York.[3] Texaco extracted about 1,000 million barrels of oil during that period, meaning that the damages claimed are about $1.50 per barrel, which would be about 10% of the gross value of sales. The government of Ecuador (which made the original agreement with Texaco), is not an actor in the class-action suit in the New York court. On the contrary, the government is pushing for an out-of-court settlement, by which Texaco would pay for the restoration of some restorable damages and would pay some indemnities (in the form of health posts, etc.) to the communities damaged. Some of the Indians and other plaintiffs involved have not much experience either with the generalized market economy or with the U.S. legal system. The out-of-court settlement being discussed in the fall of 1994 (by which the government of Ecuador was trying to stop the court case), seemed to imply a payment by Texaco of about $15 million, one hundred times less than the damages being sought in court. Indian groups across the border in Peru, downstream in the river Napo, are also claiming damages in the same court case because of oil spills by Texaco. Texaco is a U.S. company. Should the case be tried in New York, the court will be have to decide, as would have been the case for Bhopal, on the appropriate price for the externalities. Should it pay according to U.S. values, that is, according to the marginal value of the extra oil obtained per unit of spillover damage; or according to Ecuador values, that is, the value indicated by the victim's willingness-to-accept (WTA) a proposed compensation package? If there is an out-of-court settlement, as happened in the civil case for Bhopal, perhaps damages will be paid of only one cent per barrel of oil extracted? Why the cheap price? This would seem to be a real-world example of the principle 'the poor sell cheap', also called 'Lawrence Summers' principle' (Martinez-Alier 1993).

There is another court case being brought by unions from Ecuador and other countries, in a court in Texas, against Shell, Standard Fruit, Dow Chemical and others, because of a pesticide applied to banana plantations (DBCP) which has caused male sterility. This case first arose in Costa Rica (Thrupp 1991; Faber 1993).[4] In Ecuador, the banana farms are owned by Ecuatorians, but they produce under contract, and were induced to spread this chemical by the trading firms. How much is a case of male sterility worth? The existence of externalities for which compensation might be paid, depends on whether property rights, real or claimed, have been damaged. We might assume that wage-workers own their own health, although this is contradicted by many actual practices, but even so, the *value of the externality* depends, in neoclassical theory, on the distribution of income. As Lawrence Summers (1992) put it, "the measurement of the costs of health impairing pollution depends on the foregone earnings from increased morbidity and mortality. From this point of view a given amount of health impairing pollution should be done in the country with the lowest cost, which will be the country with the lowest wages."

Should we be concerned with WTP to avoid sterility, or the lowest payment they are WTA in exchange for sterility? Should a value on the margin be estimated with reference to banana value at U.S. prices, or sterility at Ecuatorian banana workers' prices? Will these various valuations diverge, by how much, and why?

The banana workers' case is, in fact, a relatively "easy" externality to analyze because (if we ignore lives that will not be born because of sterility) the damages are apparently to humans only, and of the present generation only. In the case of Texaco, on the contrary, irreversible damages to biodiversity (which could be valued as use and option values, and also as existence values) could become an issue; and perhaps also Texaco's direct contribution to the increase in global warming (by the decision made to burn the gas from the oil wells). In this case, property rights are unclear, moreover damages to future generations and other species become relevant. Such international cases are marvellous examples of the social, institutional, non-market influences on the valuation of externalities. In Ecuador, as in Colombia, there could be similar cases for damages to health in the production of flowers for export.

A third Ecuatorian case is that of shrimp against mangroves in the Pacific coast. Here there is, as yet, no court case. Possible plaintiffs would be people who use the mangroves sustainably and outside the market, and who are damaged by their destruction by the shrimp industry. Property rights over the mangroves are unclear. Although the demands for shrimp is international, the industry itself is owned by nationals. How much are the externalities involved worth, at present value? Present value for whom? Factors to be taken into account are the period of regeneration of the mangroves after being destroyed by shrimp farming, and the discount rate to be applied to benefits of shrimp farming and costs of mangrove destruction. Beyond this, pseudo-market valuations of damages, in terms of WTA compensation, for instance would depend on income levels.[5]

A fourth case worth studying in Ecuador, as in many other countries of the South, is that of a positive environmental good provided by poor people, namely their investments embodied in agricultural genetic resources. What are they worth? Here the poor do not only sell cheap, they have given away such genetic resources gratis. *In situ* agricultural biodiversity (which is not yet properly investigated and recorded) will lose its potential for coevolution as traditional agroecology disappears. The Biodiversity Convention in 1992 abolished the idea of genetic resources being the common patrimony of humankind, it gives States sovereignty over them, and leaves questions of ownership to national legislation. Who are now the owners of agricultural or wild genetic resources? The attempted implementation of Farmers' Rights, sponsored by the FAO, is becoming almost meaningless. It will mean setting up a small fund geared to the preservation of a few *in situ* "museums" of traditional agriculture. Current proposals from the FAO, instead of being based on a general defence of agroecology, boil down to a policy of a few reserves of traditional farmers (inappropriately applying the theory of optimal portfolio of assets to the conservation and coevolution of agricultural biodiversity). Thus, in Southern Mexico, if NAFTA becomes reality, agroecological maize growing may disappear, submerged by the inflow of maize from the United States (produced with Mexican genetic resources, and cheap Mexican oil). Perhaps some money will be available, under the Fund for Farmers' Rights, for the preservation of a few samples of milpa agriculture around San Cristobal de las Casas, for the ecotourists to see. [6]

ECOLOGICAL DISTRIBUTION AND EXTERNALITY VALUATION

Political economy was the historic name for economics, but nowadays it is used to refer, more particularly, to the study of the emergence and resolution of economic distribution conflicts. Sraffian economics is political economy. The field known as 'welfare economics' and social choice theory constitutes neo-classical political economy. Institutionalist approaches to the negotiation of income distribution also belong to political economy. The parts or branches of ecological economics (or human ecology) which focus on ecological distribution could, comparably, be called political ecology.

Thus, the peaceful functioning of the neoclassical economic *perpetuum mobile* circuit may be disrupted not only because it can run out of energy or because of the excessive burdens of the pollution it throws onto the surrounding biophysical system, but also by internal distributional conflicts. This is the field of study of political economy, which we now want to re-situate in the context of ecological concerns. For instance, firms are individually inclined not to pay high wages, meaning that there might be a lack of effective demand from households in the aggregate to buy all the goods and services which would be available with production running at full capacity utilization. This is a well known internal contradiction of capitalism. The regulation of the economy in a 'Fordist' pattern (mass-production, and mass-consumption goods) could elimi-nate or adjourn for a time this conflict. But, for instance, in a period of full employment, wages might increase more than productivity, and if there is strong internal or international competition among firms, it would be difficult to trans-late such pressure into higher prices, and there might occur a profit squeeze, and a crisis from the supply side. Similarly, if natural resources and environ-mental services become more scarce, and if such scarcity comes to be reflected in costs, then there might also occur a profit squeeze. James O'Connor (1988, 1994) has referred to this as the "second contradiction" of capitalism. In social terms, this means asking what is the role of environmental movements acting outside the market in pushing up prices which firms (or governments) have to pay for their use of environmental resources and services (Enrique Leff 1986). Or, in other terms, environmental movements may be seen as the social expres-sion of non-internalized externalities.

Political economy studies economic distribution conflicts. Political ecol-ogy would study ecological distribution conflicts. For instance, human ecolo-gists and ecological economists would be interested in the relation between ecological distribution and the human pressure on the environment. There are then clear links from the study of ecological distribution to studies of carrying capacity of humans on Earth. However, humans have no genetic instructions on the exosomatic consumption of energy and materials; and while our demography may follow in a general way the logistic curve of populations of other species, it is more self-conscious and it depends on changing social institutions; similarly, our territoriality is politically and socially constructed. Ecological distribution thus refers to the social, spatial, and temporal asymmetries or inequalities in the use by humans of environmental resources and services, for example, in the depletion of natural resources (e.g., the loss of biodiversity), and in the burdens of pollution. An unequal distribution of land, and pressure of agricultural exports on limited land resources, may cause land degradation by subsistence peasants working on mountain slopes (compare Stonich 1993; Faber 1993). The inequalities in per capita exosomatic energy consumption would be an instance of social ecological distribution; the territorial asymmetries between SO_2 emissions and the burdens of acid rain (as portrayed in the European RAINS model), of spatial ecological distribution; the intergenerational inequalities between the enjoyment of nuclear energy (or emissions of CO_2), and the burdens of radioactive waste (or global warming), of temporal ecological distribution.

Some of these asymmetries are beginning to have names, but the transfers to which the names refer have no agreed prices. For instance, 'environmental racism' in the U.S. means locating polluting industries or toxic waste disposal sites in areas of Black or Hispanic or Indian population. Correspondingly we find a movement for 'environmental justice' in the U.S. reacting against such environmental racism. There is also some discussion on 'ecologically unequal exchange' and on the "ecological debt", with both spatial and temporal aspects Robleto and Marcelo 1992; Azar and Holmberg 1995; Borrero 1994; O'Connor and Martinez-Alier 1996). For instance, work has been done on the environmental space that is effectively occupied by some economies, both for procuring resources and for disposal of emissions. Europeans, Japanese, and North Americans pay nothing for the environmental space they are using in order to dispose of emissions of CO_2. In this case, such countries act as owners of a sizeable chunk of the planet outside their own territories, but few are yet complaining, or trying to charge us a fee. So-called "joint implementation", by which rich countries would buy cheap tropical forest sinks for their carbon dioxide, might run into the difficulty of identifying whose carbon dioxide is being sequestered, since carbon dioxide from different sources and countries looks very much alike.

Should the European eco-tax, or the (failed) U.S.A. BTU tax be implemented, then, apart from the direct and indirect effects on energy demand, there would be effects on the price of imported oil as demand would decline. If energy taxes were collected at the point of extraction, and not of consumption, the effects on international income distribution would be quite different. And, as institutional economists such as Samuels (1972, 1991) have argued for some time ago, the correct valuation of externalities (even within neoclassical theory) depends on the allocation of property rights. For this reason, the allocational effects of environmental policies cannot be disentangled from the pattern of property rights and the distribution of income. Should Agarwal and Narain's 1991 proposal for equal per capita emission quotas of greenhouse gases, and tradable permits be implemented, then the redistribution of income would have, in its turn, an influence on demand for energy and other goods. For instance, extra money received by the population in India could perhaps support a movement up the hierarchy of domestic fuels, away from dung and fuelwood into kerosene or gas.

Ecological distribution refers, therefore, to the following questions: What is the distribution of the benefits of present patterns of natural resource and environmental exploitation? Who carries the principal burdens of the unwanted side-effects of these exploitations? Which social groups suffer most from the impairment of life-support functions and from the loss of environmental amenities resulting from environmental degradation? How are they distributed across societies, across space, and time? Finally, how are these asymmetries valued (or devalued)?

Among economists, valuation usually means relative prices. The proposition that prices depend on the distribution of income is, in fact, common ground to conventional neoclassical economics and Sraffian economics, although for different reasons. In neoclassical economics, the distribution of income is a by-product of the formation of the prices for the services of production factors. If the distribution of income is changed (for instance, by fiscal redistribution), then the pattern of demand and therefore the pattern of prices would change. For the Sraffian political economy, distribution (between wages and profits, and sometimes also land rent) determines from the supply-side (jointly with the technical specificities of the production), the prices of production.

In the domain of political ecology it is not so obvious what roles can be played by price analysis. In a general way, we are dealing with problems of cost-shifting (Beckenbach 1989), but typically in the absence of prices, so that natural resources and services are treated as free gifts and free disposals (O'Connor 1994a). One can think of the exploitation of nature by modern industry and consumer society as having two complementary senses: first, as predations, and second as impositions of unwanted burdens. Other things being equal, competitive enterprises may be expected to seek lower input costs and to off-load costs onto other parties such as government, the community at large, future generations. The social, ideological, and technical mechanisms for achieving a shifting of social and environmental costs may vary a lot. Some of the mechanisms are quite subtle. For instance, Schultz (1993) describes, for the current situation in Germany, how women in particular are being coerced or co-opted, as the caregivers in the household, to increase their unpaid labors in sorting and recycling of materials under the Duales System Deutschland. These gestures of environmental concern constitute a sort of gender-biased social subsidy to commercial waste management and to the recycling of materials for the benefit of industry.[7]

Such environmental costs cannot, in general, be convincingly translated into prices. What is really at stake is the redistribution of burdens and benefits, short and long-term, immediately tangible or speculative and uncertain, across and within societies, spatially, and through time. Economic price theory and formal mathematical models cannot be expected to have high predictive power in these respects. They can, however, still help sharpen insight into the character of such economic and ecological distribution conflicts, as we will now show.

NEO-RICARDIAN MODELING OF ECONOMIC AND ECOLOGICAL DISTRIBUTION

The Sraffian political economy (which has a *reproductive* approach to the economy, not an *allocative* approach), studies the formation of production prices from the supply side, and it shows that they depend on distribution. A Sraffian system is a system of production of commodities by means of commodities, or an input-output system, the analytical objective of which is to ascertain how much it costs to produce the different commodities (the "prices of production"), and the political objective of which is precisely to show that such prices depend on the distribution of income (as between wages and profits). Therefore the values of the capital stocks depend on the class struggle, so to speak. The remuneration to the owners of capital has nothing to do with the marginal productivity of capital (as in elementary neoclassical economics), because capital is a heterogeneous collection of items, the produced means of production, the value of which depends on the results of the distributional conflict between waged workers and capital owners.

This idea of capital as a heterogeneous collection of produced means of production, the valuation of which *in toto* presents some difficulties, was a main ingredient in debates of the 1960s and 1970s on capital theory and income distribution. Natural capital is still more heterogeneous (Victor 1991; Victor et al. 1996). Most of it is not in the market, yet it seems natural to ask what sorts of insights the Sraffian approach might give concerning valuation of natural capital stocks and flows. In a classical Sraffian economy, so-called natural capital appears only as Ricardian land, and there is no analysis of whether it is in open access and therefore unpriced; or in communal property and therefore perhaps administered outside the market; or already privately owned and in the market. Sraffa's political economy has a "reproductive" approach in social terms, but not a fully-fledged "biophysical" approach (Christensen 1989).

However, it is readily possible to 'ecologize' the Sraffian approach, through a generalization of joint production theory to include ecological production and economy-ecosystem exchanges of natural resources, environmental services, and waste products.[8] Though we are sceptical towards the use of terms like natural capital or ecological capital, we may nevertheless proceed to develop a Sraffian ecological economics, in order to present models which show social conflicts of interests concerning the appropriation and use of ecological capital.[9]

For Sraffian ecological economics, we need first to decide how to make environmental stocks and flows appear in the production-reproduction picture, and in what terms the identified items belong to natural capital (i.e., are appropriated for what purposes and by whom). We may then proceed to explore how their valuation depends, one way or another, on the distribution of income. The distributional conflicts may be between different societies and between groups within society, or over access to depletable resources, or concerning reproduction versus destruction of ecological necessities or life-support systems or environmental amenities. They may be conflicts also concerning which cultural projects will or will not be served by appropriation of environmental services and resources such as biodiversity (O'Connor 1993a). This opens up a range of questions about institutional forms and so on. However, we should emphasize that Sraffian economics (even if ecologized in this way) is still economics, and as such it still attempts to explain economic values in classical terms of prices of production and reproduction (Erreygers 1995). It does not deal with wider social/cultural issues such as political arrangements and incommensurability of values and systems of legitimacy.

What we will try to bring out here, with a simple example, is how conflicts over natural capital are interdependent with economic conflicts over the shares of surpluses produced within an industrial commodity economy. Different outcomes of such ecological and economic conflicts will also determine different outcomes for the growth of the economy. We take the case of disposal of waste, which, we assume, involves ecological opportunity costs in the forms of:

1. Input requirements of scarce natural capital into pollution treatment processes, where this natural capital could be used as an input elsewhere in the economy, or
2. Degradation of ecological capital having *in situ* amenity value.[10] These are "environmental costs" of pollution disposal, in the sense that, one way or another, economic waste disposal results in degradation of ecological capital.

For simplicity, suppose an aggregate economy (Process 1) that does not use ecological capital directly as an input to production of economic capital (resource 1), but that produces an economic waste (resource 2) as a by-product requiring disposal. Suppose that Process 3 achieves simple accumulation of an ecological capital (resource 3). Insertion of economic waste (resource 2) by economy propri-etors into the environment brings degradation of some ecological capital. This is represented by Process 2, describing the disappearance of economic waste and ecological capital (into a sink or wasteland, not represented in the model). In Sraffian style, the rows (representing processes) and columns (representing resources) of the technology input and output coefficient matrices have the form of A, B as follows:

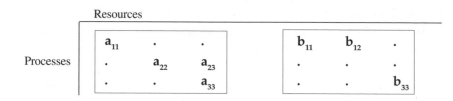

The economy depends, for waste disposal, on the ecological capital gener-ated in Process 3, but Process 3 regenerating ecological capital is self-suffi-cient. We now search for a price-vector with non-null values for resources 1, 2, and 3, assuming an equalized rate of return for all processes with valorized inputs and outputs. The value equations have the simple form:

(1) $Ap(1+\pi) = Bp.$

There will be three eigensolutions π-p. From the second row of Equations (1), we get: $[a_{22}p_2 + a_{23}p_3](1+\pi) = 0$. The three solutions are associated with, respec-tively: $\pi = -1$; $p_2 = p_3 = 0$; $a_{22}/a_{23} = -p_3/p_2$. The case $\pi = -1$ has little interest, as it signifies the vanishing of the system. For the other two solutions, the equilibrium profit rate is codetermined with the relative price p_1/p_3.

One solution is associated with a value-growth rate of $\pi_1 = g_1 = (b_{11} - a_{11})/a_{11}$, and has the price vector (written in transpose form) of p+ = [1,0,0]. This solu-tion signifies a zero price for the natural capital, (i.e., a putative free gift, free disposal (FGFD) regime for the economy). It is noteworthy that the associated activity vector has strictly positive elements only if the ecological capital own-growth rate, defined by $g_3 = (b_{33} - a_{33})/a_{33}$, satisfies $g_3 > g_1$. If this condition is satisfied, then this solution means that ecological capital (resource 3) accumulates at the rate g_1 which is lower than its own growth rate in Process 3, and there is sustainable growth of both economic and ecological capitals. But if $g_3 < g_1$, the associated activity vector is not non-negative, and this solution signifies myo-pic unsustainable economic growth.

The other solution is associated with value-growth rate of $p_3 = g_3 = (b_{33} - a_{33})/a_{33}$, and yields a negative p_2 relative to p_1 and p_3, and a corresponding y = [0,0,1]. This latter eigen-solution specifies that only Process 3 operates. In effect, the ecological sector (Process 3) can grow uninhibited, at its natural rate g_3, only if the economy (Process 1) has zero activity.

The model situation can further be interpreted in terms of a social value-system contest, where the outcome of distributional conflict between consumerists and conservationists over possession of ecological capital determines whether or not economic and ecological sustainability are achieved.

The solution relating to π_1 corresponds to free disposal by treating ecological capital as a free gift. This is consistent with a situation where resource allocation is controlled by myopic 'consumerists" who care nothing about ecological capital and act as if unwanted economic by-products can be ignored after being disposed of into the environment. Perhaps this is the sort of degradation risk facing, for example, parts of Southern Europe, where pollution and tourism-related development is imposing a large-scale degradation of farmlands, water supplies, and life-supporting ecosystems and landscapes. Not only does the ecological capital cherished by 'conservationists' get depleted, but also the predator economy will collapse once deprived of its natural capital base.

The π_3-p solution lends itself to interpretation as a set of signals in two different ways. The first, as already mentioned, is to signal the possible unimpaired growth of ecological capital, in the absence of the economy. This is a regime of activity that might be favored by extreme conservationists. The second refers to a time-path of unbalanced physical growth with equilibrated value-accumulation at rate-of-return π_3 across both Process 1 and Process 3. If $\pi_3 < \pi_1$, the relative prices for both economic and ecological capital are positive, but this is an unsustainable regime since the ecological capital is progressively depleted till eventually the economy no longer has a site for its waste disposal. Let us take a numerical example, chosen with $g_3 = 0$ and $g_1 > 0$, meaning $g_3 < g_1$. Suppose A, B are:

3	0	0
0	1	2
0	0	1

4	2	0
0	0	0
0	0	1

Writing $1/(1+\pi) = \lambda$, we have as the two solutions of interest for Equations (1):

$\lambda_1 = 3/4 \Rightarrow \pi_1 = 33\%$, with relative prices $(p_1, p_2, p_3) = (1, 0, 0)$.
$\lambda_3 = 1 \Rightarrow \pi_3 = 0$, with relative prices $(p_1, p_2, p_3) = (4, -2, 1)$.

The first case, $\lambda_1 = 3/4$, with $p_2 = p_3 = 0$, is the one signalling the free waste disposal economic growth regime, where we presume consumerists have possession of the ecological capital.

The second case, $\lambda_3 = 1 \Rightarrow \pi_3 = 0$, is associated with $y = [0,0,1]$ which signifies the possibility of in situ reproduction of the ecological capital. Suppose, however, that rather than there being a balanced (zero-)growth of Process 3 alone, there is an unbalanced activity in which economic activity is also continuing, with the requisite waste disposal. The prices p+ = [4, -2, 1] corresponding to $\pi_3 = 0$ provide for equalization of the rate-of-return at π_3 (= 0) on inputs across all processes for each period. Owners of economic capital must, in effect, relinquish one unit of economic capital in exchange for every four units of ecological capital they need for waste disposal purposes. Ownership of this economic capital passes to the owners of the ecological capital. Conversely, these latter (conservationists) accept to forego, for each unit of economic waste disposed of, the possible reproduction of two units of ecological capital, in exchange for acquiring ownership of a $^1/_2$-unit of economic capital in exchange.

The alternative model solutions portray different possible resolutions of economic and ecological distribution. Resolution of value-system conflict is portrayed at two levels. The first is the definition of what shall be the prevailing price system; and the second is contest over the distribution of any surplus-value defined in terms of this price system. At the two extremes, we can imagine a contest as to which accumulation regime signalled by the two distinct π-p solutions shall have force:

- Either economic growth, whether sustainable or unsustainable, at π_1 based on appropriation as "free gifts" of ecological capital; this reflects a relation of simple dominance by "consumerists" over "conservationists"; or
- Uninhibited ecological capital accumulation at π_3 with zero economic activity, which presumes dominance of "conservationists" over "consumerists" in ecological capital allocation policy.

Any intermediate situation within the bounds of these two extremes is also conceivable. One intermediate outcome has been described above, namely the myopic compensation regime with equalization of rates-of-return across both sectors. The three solution time-paths are, plainly, very different from each other with respect to:

- Rate of accumulation of economic capital;
- The rate of accumulation (or depletion) of ecological capital;
- The respective shares (which may change from period to period) of economic capital between consumerists and conservationists; and
- The inter-temporal distribution of both economic and ecological capital (i.e., whether or not there is economic and ecological sustainability).[11]

What is the meaning and limits of such economic models? The classical economic distribution conflict in the capitalist economy is over the size and division of the surplus from an expanding commodity economy between capital owners, land owners, and labor. Rapid economic growth depends partly on a substantial share of the economic surplus being appropriated (as profits) and reinvested for accumulation of capital. This appropriation represents the exploitation (in the Marxist sense) of industrial labor power. However, we know that there are also relations of dominance and exploitation over domestic labor, over peasant (subsistence) labor in non-commodity domains, over communal work of social repair and regeneration, and so on. That is, capitalist accumulation and the market economy depend, for their viability, on the exploitation not just of labor power in industrial production and of the physical habitat through raw material appropriation and waste disposal, but also of non-capitalist social domains and publicly provided infrastructures. These non-commodity domains, the domains of intertwined human, communal and natural activities of repair, renewal, regeneration, and reproduction, furnish the necessary material and social conditions for commodity production, market exchange, and capital accumulation.

Ecological distribution struggles of this sort are not resolved in isolation. Indeed, there always exist a wide range of qualitatively distinct (but cross-cutting) exploitation or unequal exchange relations within and between societies. Some of these are narrowly "economic", including industrial class conflict but also conflicts over the payments by peasants to landowners (as tenant farmers or sharecroppers), and conflicts between the money economy and the domestic economy. Other conflicts are social, in the sense of being asymmetries along ethnic, gender or comparable lines; many are simultaneously economic and social, for examples the complicated inter-relations between formal and informal economic activity and its social organization. All these axes of more or less unequal exchange may, evidently, become axes for distributional conflict within and between societies. It is not surprising, therefore, to find that very often demands for access to natural resources or for environmental quality improvements criss-cross with struggles for improvement in working conditions, or in the provision of social welfare services, or other social rights issues. Such material-communal conditions, as much as wages and workplace conditions, become the privileged terrain of political contest in the advanced economies, or regain importance (in the form, for instance, of struggles for indigenous, communitarian territorial rights, or rights on indigenous knowledge systems) in less developed economies. New social alliances are being formed along lines which are communal as much as industrial, extending not just over workplace solidarities on such matters as occupational health and safety, working conditions, hours of employment and wage levels, but also to the maintenance and enhancement of collective livelihood—including such matters as toxic waste control, respect of habitat as a cultural as well as ecological milieu.

It would be a formidable, and relatively useless, task to model in an integrated way all these different axes of distributional conflict. The value of the model-ing is that some fundamental ideas can readily be identified. Extensions might be made in the same heuristic spirit. The traditional Neo-Ricardian approach to representation of distributional conflict is to suppose that different rates of return are characteristic of each distinct class of factors of production, on the presumption that they are controlled by distinct social classes of proprietors who are in conflict. Such an approach was systematically developed in the Sraffian models of class-based economic distributional conflict, where there is a contest between wage levels, profit rates, and land rents. It would be possible to apply this sort of framework to include domestic labor as a social category distinct from industrial labor, and also to consider a variety of distinct ecologi-cal capital categories as a generalization from the single category of land in the traditional Neo-Ricardian literature.

For example, as seen in the simple model of pollution and ecological degra-dation given above, the outcomes of exploitation/conservation conflicts are di-rectly related to resolution of conflicts over the size and distribution of the economic pie. Now, as is well known from the Sraffian literature results, a change in the economic distributional parameters (i.e., wage rate, profit rate, rent rate) will generally imply a change in the value of the capital stock, in the relative prices of produced commodities, and in the economy's product mix. So, making the assumption that different commodities have unequal direct and indirect requirements for ecological capital (i.e., raw materials and waste dis-posal services), we also have the result that changes in economic distribution may entail changes in the pressures on the environment. These effects will also depend on characteristics of technologies and on consumption patterns. If more sectoral detail were introduced, various ecological-economic trade-offs open to, or forced upon, different classes of economic actors could thus be identified. To proceed usefully, the formal model results would then have to be supplemented by real institutional economic analysis.

NON-SEPARABILITY OF EFFICIENCY AND DISTRIBUTION IN GENERAL EQUILIBRIUM MODELS

Much work in environmental economics and environmental policy is concerned with the internalization of negative external effects—that is, with the problem of market failure. Of course, market failure is also cost-shifting success from the point of view of those parties benefiting from the non-internalization. The usual norm for correction is to achieve allocative efficiency in resource use, so that the marginal costs of the activity in question are equal to the marginal benefits obtained. It is often proposed that the effect of a correction of the market failure is that the size (in value terms) of the economic pie is maxi-mized, and that questions of the cost/benefit distribution can be dealt with in terms of political decisions about how the gains from the internalization come to be shared out. But this formulation is fundamentally flawed.

First, although much rhetoric in policy circles is about efficiency of resource use and opportunity cost, in most policy calculations we are dealing, at best, only with cost-effectiveness—and in this respect, only with effectiveness in relation to those environmental objectives for which policy impacts can reasonably be predicted and physically quantified which is not always the case. Second, even in the very restrictive world of 'first best' as expressed within a general equilibrium framework, for a given production possibility frontier the wealth-maximizing output-mix (and hence the input resource use pattern) is a function of the relative prices; and the vector of correct prices (signalling relative opportunity costs) is a function of consumers' preferences in conjunction with the distribution of ownership (property rights). When preferences differ between groups across society, to speak of wealth-maximization is indecisive, because the equilibrium prices at which total wealth is evaluated depend on income distribution. The decisive question is: What is the allocative efficiency relative to what underlying wealth, rights, or income distribution?

Neoclassical economics focuses on the efficiency of the allocation of scarce resources to alternative present and future ends, with opportunity costs supposed to be signalled through the price system. The simultaneous determination of relative prices and output mix in general competitive equilibrium means that, within the logic of the model, welfare distribution (in the sense of relative and absolute purchasing power of consumers) can be determined only simultaneously with equilibrium prices and output levels. Consumers' welfare levels depend on their respective income levels and relative prices of goods; in general equilibrium, a vector of equilibrium relative prices for inputs and outputs will be determined simultaneously with a Pareto-efficient output mix; the consumer-efficient output mix will, in general, depend on the relative income distribution across consumers; and these relative incomes will in turn depend on the distribution of input endowments among consumers-as-owners and the relative prices of inputs (O'Connor and Muir 1996). In particular, when preferences are non-homothetic and/or differ across social groups, a change in distribution of income would influence prices, from the demand side, jointly with the technical determinants of opportunity cost on the production margins. The demand for different environmental goods and services thus varies according to the distribution of income, or the relative levels of income between distinct social groups. By deciding distribution of property rights and/or income, we are simultaneously deciding output mix; by determining output mix we determine opportunity costs, thus equilibrium relative prices, and vice versa.

It follows that there is no unique determination possible of correct prices for doing a cost-benefit calculation. The correct prices will depend on distributional choices, including rights of future generations, as we shall see below. If the question of the income redistribution effects of a policy change (e.g., a new ecotax) is addressed when equilibrium relative prices depend significantly on the distributional choices, it is logically invalid to utilize pre-change prices to calculate post-change effects. These costs and benefits cannot be correctly evaluated without knowing the redistributions of wealth and income that are to take place, and the new prices producers and consumers will face. In other words, the distribution of property rights and incomes matters for the valuation of opportunity costs associated with resource use, including the valuation of externalities. [12]

For instance, in Ecuador again, a more egalitarian distribution of income would make it possible to express preferences for some environmental goods (e.g., WTP for potable water), but it would perhaps decrease demand for other environmental goods (e.g., travel to the Galapagos islands, which is quite expensive). Within neoclassical theory, two compatible explanations are possible.

1. That in one income redistribution takes place between groups with different intensities of relative preferences for drinkable water and tourist travel;
2. That some types of environmental goods are "necessities," while others are "luxuries," signalling that preferences are non-homothetic.

If the latter is true, then this suggests we should classify environmental goods and services into two broad groups—perhaps amenities of the rich, and necessities or conditions of livelihood for everybody, but especially the relatively less mobile poor would be appropriate names (Martinez-Alier 1995a).

SUSTAINABILITY, THE TIME-DISCOUNT RATE, AND FUTURE GENERATIONS

The general equilibrium methodology, although useless in order to analyze the real march of the economy and its impact on ecosystems, can nevertheless be put to good counter factual or paradoxical use, as we have just seen. Let us now pursue further this line, introducing future generations. The problem of missing markets is central to the externality problem as treated in the equilibrium methodology. As no prices exist for the benefits or disservices provided, these latter go unheeded by actors in the market. If future interests are regarded as having standing, then there are missing markets meaning, *prima facie*, a source of Pareto-inefficiency or market failure. The alternative is to assert that the future has no rights, hence no demand of its own, and simply receives whatever we, the present, see fit to pass on to them.

The traditional remedy to market failure has been to augment the market through defining appropriate tradable rights, or proxying these through a

Pigovian tax. If creating new or pseudo-markets is problematical enough for many static or localized spillover problems, it is insuperable in regard to inter-temporal choice problems. Frank Hahn (1973) made the following pertinent remarks: "The Arrow-Debreu equilibrium is very useful when for instance one comes to argue with someone who maintains that we need not worry about exhaustible resources because they will always have prices which ensure their proper use. Of course there are many things wrong with this contention but a quick way of disposing of the claim is to note that an Arrow-Debreu equilibrium must be an assumption he is making for the economy, and then to show why the economy cannot be in this state."

The argument of counter-factuality for our purposes would turn on the absence of futures markets, and on the inadequate treatment of time and uncertainty in the general equilibrium construction. Hahn concludes, "This negative role of the Arrow-Debreu equilibrium I consider almost to be sufficient justification for it, since practical men and ill-trained theorists everywhere in the world do not understand what they are claiming to be the case when they claim a beneficent and coherent role for the invisible hand."

In short, there are uses of the equilibrium construction quite distinct from its employment in the sense of defining an actual state, or time-path of an economy. These are negative, critical or paradoxical uses, by which, relative to an equilibrium construction, it can be explained where an argument for a coherent role for the market—such as its virtues for allocative efficiency, or as a vehicle for social wealth creation, or as a mechanism for valuation of welfare impacts and opportunity costs—breaks down.

So, in this counter-factual spirit, let us momentarily set aside real uncertainty and historical time, and examine the construct of inter-temporal general equilibrium. In the intergenerational context, we obtain again the result that the relative prices supporting an efficient equilibrium will depend on the endowments of property rights (and the distribution of income) between social groups with differing preferences. Central to the contemporary debates on sustainability, are questions of the rights of future generations and of inter-temporal equity in endowments of environmental necessities and amenities. It is intuitively obvious that different generations of consumers living in different periods, may be expected to have different relative preferences for goods differentiated by the period in time. (A person born in 50 years has little personal interest in goods consumed today). So, in the context of inter-temporal general equilibrium analysis, there will be certainly some sort of endowment effects on relative prices and output mix. In particular, there will be *interdependency between the inter-generational rights distribution and the relative prices of goods within each production period and between periods.*

Work by Howarth and Norgaard (1990, 1992, 1993) and Muir (1995, 1996) has shown, in overlapping generations (OLG) general equilibrium models, how the relative valuation of an externality, and the relative price of a good from one period to the next (that is, the interest rate from one period to the next) will be functions of the endowment of property rights across generations (and, hence, of the income distribution), and also a function of the preferences of each generation. Moreover, since any policy to internalize environmental spillover effects involves a redistribution of entitlements, the externality valuation and the time-discount rate from period to period will also be functions of the way in which rights and liabilities (e.g., pollution taxes paid and received) are distributed across the affected generations.

Howarth and Norgaard have considered a number of different model specifications, some involving depletable natural resources (Howarth 1991, 1992), others an environmental externality related to natural resource use (Howarth and Norgaard 1992). The basic model is a closed economy, and the question of time preference is structured by assuming overlapping generations. Each generation lives for two time periods (say, t and t+1), and maximizes utility $U_t = U_t(C_t, C_t+1)$; where (C_t) is consumption during period (t) when the generation is young, and C_t+1 is consumption during period t+1 when the generation is old. Within each generation, if individuals are assumed to be identical, the model emphasis is on aggregate consumption each period, and no questions of intra-generational equity are addressed. This assumption may then be relaxed in order to consider within-generation redistributional issues (Muir 1995, 1996). Markets for natural capital (resources or environmental amenity), consumer goods, and labor are assumed to be "competitive" in the sense of equalization of opportunity costs on all margins. Labor is an initial endowment distributed equally across all generations; each generation supplies labor only while young. Inter-generational transfers are possible through exchange of income for natural capital held as initial endowments.

The inter-temporal distribution issue is here explored in terms of alternative choices of social welfare rule which determine the socially optimum distribution of income subject to the production constraints of the particular model. Thus, the model solution obtained will be sensitive to the assumptions made or implied about, inter alia, the inter-temporal natural capital endowment (property rights) distribution. This is an example of well-known results associated with the Second Welfare Theorem from the theory of general competitive equilibrium. Under the appropriate assumptions (e.g., convexity). This theory states that any allocatively efficient model equilibrium can be obtained as a competitive equilibrium through suitable choice of initial endowments. It is often said that, for inter-temporal efficiency, the price of natural capital such as minerals or energy resources or fish or forest products, should correctly reflect the inter-temporal opportunity cost (viz., the user cost).

If sustainability is an objective, we must therefore add the condition that this has to be the opportunity costs as evaluated along an inter-temporal efficient path that also satisfies the sustainability criterion. With this formulation, a number of important points are clearly brought out.

1. Sustainability in the sense of indefinitely non-declining consumption from one generation to the next, is not guaranteed by the competitive rule of maximizing present-value of total consumption over time (equivalent, in these OLG models, to achieving inter-temporal allocative efficiency). On the contrary, when the property rights over natural capital are placed in the hands of the present generation, and then exchanged between generations to enable the old of each period to consume optimally, the typical result is monotonically declining utility levels beyond some period into the future.

2. Achieving an equilibrium characterized by the sustaining of consumption levels requires that, one way or another, present generations care enough about future generations. This caring for the future can be expressed, in an OLG model, by a variety of mechanisms, notably: (1) the imposition of a maximin social welfare function; (2) the requirement of non-negative change in utility from one generation to the next (Faucheux et al. 1996); (3) the assumption of a sufficiently high level of individual altruism of each generation towards the generation immediately following; (4) the assumption of an ethical "obligation" on the part of each generation to provide for a utility level of the generation immediately following at least as high as its own, resulting in a "chain of obligation" indefinitely into the future (Howarth 1992); or (5) the explicit award of property rights over natural capital or the benefits obtainable from it as initial endowments distributed equitably to all generations.

3. Such models allow formal demonstration of the possible significance of groups having divergent preferences within a given generation. If income distribution is shifted towards groups whose preferences are for goods that are less demanding of capital exploitation or who care more about the future, this will tend to favor sustainability of the model equilibrium (Muir 1995, 1996).[13]

4. Each Pareto-efficient equilibria for a given model has a distinct time-trajectory, not just for capital stocks and consumption, but also for relative prices including the time discount rate (generally itself a function of time, but sometimes time-invariant for a given model or class of equilibria). In model economies allowing both utility-sustaining and non-sustaining PV-optimizing timepaths, all else being equal it is typically the case that relative to a reference non-sustainability solution,

a lower time-discount rate will mean that the economy trajectory is closer to sustainability. Similarly, sustainable development timepaths will typically be characterized, early in the timepath, by relatively higher relative prices for a scarce (and depletable) natural capital, reflecting a higher weighting given to the opportunity costs imposed for the future by over-consumption of the natural capital in the present (Faucheux et al. 1996).

This recent theoretical work casts light on some old debates about the discount rate and inter-temporal valuation. One justification offered for a positive discount rate, which some economists since Ramsey (1928) have dismissed, is pure time preference. The inter-temporal equilibrium models make it clear that, while individual preferences do play a decisive role in optimizing choices in the market, the interest-rate that is faced by the individuals (as price takers) is itself a function of endowment distribution. Thus pure time preference alone is not decisive. Another traditional explanation for a positive discount rate is the decreasing marginal utility our descendants will obtain from their abundant consumption, on the assumption that they will be richer than we are. But from the point of view of ecological economics, of the sort that does not make brash assumptions about high elasticities of substitutability, there is no reason to believe that future generations are going to be richer. In the OLG general equilibrium models, a typical result when the assumption is made of a high social time-discount rate, is a boom-and-decline consumption timepath (Faucheux et al. 1996). This illustrates the intuition (Page 1977,1991; Clark 1991) that discounting future consumption may mean that the present generation will optimally consume exhaustible environmental resources and services in a non-sustainable way, leaving future generations irreversibly poorer.

The model results also bring some important clarification about the correct valuation of changes in capital stocks, as required for application of the 'weak sustainability criterion.' In theory, the sustainable national income (SNI) for an economy would be the value of goods and services that may be consumed in a given period while the economy-system still furnishes the basis for providing at least the same level of real consumption in every period through the future. In fact this can only be defined within the confines of a chosen model (Common 1993), so it is important that the assumptions of the model being used, are understood correctly. The idea of using the change in aggregate capital stock as an indicator of sustainability prospects was initiated by Solow (1986) who put forward the proposition that existence of a non-declining level of capital stock from one period to the next may coincide with having non-declining consumption (that is, utility) levels forever. However, the feasibility of non-declining consumption cannot be deduced from the sign of the change in value of total capital stock in an inter-temporal equilibrium. This means that, as pointed out by Pezzey (1994) and demonstrated further by Faucheux et al. (1996), the criterion of "non-negative change in the total capital stock" cannot be used as an indicator of sustainability potential for an economy. It is a valid indicator only if, making the substitutability assumptions characteristic of this genre of model, the changes in capital stocks are being valued using equilibrium prices corresponding to a sustainable development timepath.[14] The Solow-interpretation of the 'weak criterion' thus makes a double presumption: first, that the prices and discount rate *correctly* signal high substitutability between economic and natural capital; and second, that the opportunity costs of natural capital use are measured consistently with movement along a sustainable development equilibrium timepath. These presumptions are not valid *a priori*; indeed they may both be considered *prima facie* wrong.

Moreover, acting as if these prices are right for policy design and evaluation imposes a grave tort on the disadvantaged future generations, and also on present-day poor dependent on ecological assets valued only for their commercial functions but not for subsistence outside the national accounts. If natural capital is not even inventoried (e.g., the loss of biodiversity because of wood extraction in Amazonia, or in the Pacific Coast of Esmeraldas, Ecuador), or if natural capital has a low price because officially it belongs to nobody, or it belongs to poor and powerless people who sell it cheaply, then the destruction of nature is undervalued compared with a national sustainable development path. The use of market prices and interest rate thus means the systematic mis-measurement of prospects for sustainability, and the entrenchment of bias against those who, powerless in the market for reasons of lack of money or lack of presence, would perhaps favor a more sustainable resource use pattern.

The rate of discount appropriate for an ecological economy should be a rate at which investment maintains or increases *sustainable* production capacity. In principle, within neoclassical theory, the sustainability rate of time-discount would be the marginal productivity of capital, or the inter-temporal opportunity costs of investment, along a sustainable time-path. We accept this argument (within the neoclassical theory), and therefore we do not, here, go along with a fundamentalist zero rate of discount. It may be admitted that investment sometimes increases productive capacity. Consider, for instance, when in the Andes, consumption and/or leisure were sacrificed in order to build terraces and irrigation systems. This increased the capacity to use sun energy for photosynthesis, and crops increased. A genuine investment under the Inca empire. With an exogenous zero discount rate, (i.e., with equal valuation of units of present consumption—sacrificed and units of future consumption—increased, present value maximization would imply indefinitely increased investment, with all successive generations sacrificing their consumption while saving to the benefit of the last generation(s), which seems somewhat absurd).

The problem is whether or in what sense this sustainability interest rate can be defined and measured? When investment in economic capital does not mean simple accumulation on the base of an indestructible environment (as in Ricardo's view of economic growth), but consists, as it is really the case with industrial societies, not in a simple increase of productive capacity but in a mixture of production and destruction (some of the destruction being irreversible), then the basis for defining the appropriate rate of discount is in doubt. In a general equilibrium framework, an efficient equilibrium that internalizes all external effects, will assure that the opportunity costs of investment are equalized across all sectors. This assumes substitutability on all margins, making it possible to estimate in what respects the increase in economic capital will provide for an increase in sustainable production, and in what respects this production contributes to the destruction of natural capital, and to set these in compensation for each other. This is what Solow's 'weak sustainability criterion', correctly understood and used, purports to appraise. But it is an unrealistic framework. Once real time is introduced, once the complexity and heterogeneity of natural capital (e.g., biosphere cycles and living ecosystems) is admitted (and, correspondingly, easy substitutability is rejected), and once geographical barriers and institutional rigidities are acknowledged, it may seem more satisfactory to leave the enchanted world of 'first best', and return to real ecology, real geography and problems of power.[15]

The Texaco case (above), for instance, provides illustrations of attempts to put present money values on the unknown loss of biodiversity and other damages from oil development in Amazonia. Equally, one could try to measure the money values of the (lost) mangroves of Ecuador, and try a retrospective cost-benefit analysis of the shrimp industry. Or one could quantify the benefits provided by *in situ* conservation of agricultural biodiversity. But what does adding together such arbitrary and disparate numbers for a corrected national product really achieve? Aggregate measures of economic performance using market prices or contingent valuation based on *status quo* power structures and wealth distribution obscure the indeterminacies of inter-temporal valuation issues, and also obscure the questions of economic and ecological distribution within each generation.[16]

CONCLUSIONS

We have discussed how, in theory and in reality, valuations of today's externalities and also valuations of future externalities (and of environmental resources and services) will depend on the distribution, not only of property rights, but also of income, and also of power in social-institutional terms. The absence of future generations and of other species from markets has often been remarked upon. In this chapter we have emphasized the social background to the valuation of negative externalities and environmental resources and services, both in a general equilibrium framework and in Neo-Ricardian analysis.

Lawrence Summers was perhaps right (as an empirical observation and as a piece of positive economics) when he asserted that the price (market price or shadow-price) put on the damage caused by pollution was likely to be lower when the damaged were poor, than when they were rich. However, to accept such low prices for externalities is a political decision precisely because negative externalities (and also many environmental goods) are either not valued in markets, or, if they are valued, their value depends on prevailing power structures and previous decisions on property rights and income distribution. If surrogate market techniques were used to investigate the way people, in such situations, actually valued the pollution impacts, we might actually find—following Sagoff's interpretation corroborated by several studies since—a high rates of refusals to put a price in terms of WTP or even WTA among poor people, whose best chance of influencing events is not as consumers in the market, or surrogate consumers in the surrogate market, but as citizens acting in politics, through the vote or through direct action.[17]

We may conclude that, from our political economy point of view, there is no such thing as a set of right prices because, first, values of environmental resources and services, and of externalities, always depend on the property rights endowment and on the distribution of income, and second, these real valuations cannot plausibly be reconciled within an equilibrium system of value. Rather, the existence of conflicts and indeterminacies about economic and ecological distribution has, for a practical result, the incommensurability (or, at least, incomplete commensurability) between different dimensions of the economic and ecological goods and bads. In fact this feature has been recognized in the tradition of institutional/ecological economics for a long time. For example, Kapp (1970) wrote:

> To place a monetary value on and apply a discount rate to future utilities or disutilities in order to express their present capitalized value may give us a precise monetary calculation, but it does not get us out of the dilemma of a choice and the fact that we take a risk with human health and survival. For this reason, I am inclined to consider the attempt at measuring social costs and social benefits simply in terms of monetary or market values as doomed to failure. Social costs and social benefits have to be considered as extra-market phenomena; they are borne and accrue to society as a whole; they are heterogeneous and cannot be compared quantitatively among themselves and with each other, not even in principle.

Some decades earlier, Neurath (1919) had observed the indeterminacy inherent in inter-temporal valuations:

> The question might arise, should one protect coal mines or put greater strain on men? The answer depends for example on whether one thinks that hydraulic power may be sufficiently developed or that solar heat might come to be better used, etc. If one believes the latter, one may *spend* coal more freely and will hardly waste human effort where coal can be used. If however one is afraid that when one generation uses too much coal thousands will freeze to death in the future, one might use more human power and save coal. Such and many other non-technical matters determine the choice of a technically calculable plan .... we can see no possibility of reducing the production plan to some kind of unit and then to compare the various plans in terms of such units.

Neurath might already, in 1919, have included in his discussion the enhanced greenhouse effect, and nuclear energy. His example shows awareness that social decisions with regard to provisioning for future generations (in his example, whether future generations will have access to coal) would have an effect on today's values for all inputs. The non-separability between efficient allocation and intergenerational distribution, led Neurath to his conclusion on economic indeterminacy, and therefore, to the need for accounting in biophysical terms.

We suggest that rather than reducing ecological assets, values, functions and services of all sorts to a common money unit expressed in present-value terms, rational decisions could better be reached by discussion where different methods of analysis, different interests and different points of view are put forward, and the decisions reached give transparent weights to the different priorities or criteria. Sustainability potential needs to be assessed through biophysical indicators that incorporate consideration of spatial and social dimensions of ecological distribution. In this respect, multi-criteria evaluation is a scientific base for applied political ecology, a formal decision aid procedure in the study of what has been called above ecological distribution.[18] Such an approach would be able to consider distributional issues first, and investment prospects in service of distributional goals (O'Connor and Martinez-Alier 1996).

Multi-criteria perspectives admit incommensurability between value systems, or different units of measure. However, as explained by John O'Neill (1993), comparability need not presuppose commensurability. We can analyze ecological and economic systems, and compare their performance, constraints, and potentials, using a wide variety of concepts and units of measure. We can, for instance, rationally discuss sources of energy, transport systems, agricultural policies, patterns of industrialization, and the preservation of tropical rainforests, taking into account economic costs and benefits, and also social and ecological (present and future) costs and benefits, as they impinge on different groups of people, now and in future, without an appeal to a common chrematistic unit of measurement. The dimensions of comparability are multiple, and the incommensurability refers to the non-existence of a meaningful single dimension to which all these dimensions of comparability can be reduced (Martinez-Alier 1995b). So there is rationality beyond (actual or surrogate) chrematistic rationality; indeed it is irrational not to move beyond single-dimension chrematistic valuation methodology.

NOTES

1. Financial help from the D.G.XII, European Commission, under contracts EV5-CT-92-0084 and CT-92-00139 is acknowledged.
2. See for instance, *HOY* supplement, Blanco y Negro, Quito, 23 Oct. 1994. This newspaper compares such damages with those already awarded after the Exxon Valdez oil spill, of over 7 billion US$. A comparison could be made with damages at Tabasco and Campeche, in Mexico. In Mexico, the oil company is national, not foreign, although the consumers of Mexican oil, as of Ecuatorian oil, are to a large extent foreigners.
3. One lawyer involved is Judith Kemerling, the author of the report Amazon Crude, Spanish edition, Crudo amazónico, Abya Yala, Quito, 1993.
4. The Costa Rica case in 1991 was considered a great success by the plaintiffs. (Thrupp 1991).
5. Attempts have been made to give biophysical measures of benefits from shrimp farming and of damages to mangroves, which would be independent of the endowment of property rights and the distribution of income (Odum and Arding 1991). These analyses yield interesting insights into the functioning of the ecosystems and their economic exploitation, but the decision-making significance of the "eM-value" measures is not certain.
6. Cf. Martinez-Alier (1994). On recent developments, cf. Commission on Plant Genetic Resources, First Extraord. Session, Rome 7/11 Nov. 1994, Revision of the International Undertaking on Farmers' Rights. (CPGR. Ex1/94/5 Supp. Sept. 1994).
7. Waring (1989) indicates the general parallel between the occultation of "women's work" behind conventional national income statistics, and the non-inclusion of "environmental costs" of resource depletion and pollution damages. See also O'Connor (1994b) and Salleh (1994).
8. See work by Perrings (1985, 1986, 1987), and by M. O'Connor (1993a, 1993b, 1995).
9. For some years, we have expressed reservations about the use of the notion of natural capital, which inevitably means "nature as capital". First, nature cannot really be thought as capital which can be appropriated (e.g., unknown biodiversity, or the water cycle). Second, the monetary value of such natural capital as there is, will depend on the endowment of property rights, on the distribution of income (in a Sraffian manner, and also from the demand side), and more particularly on the distribution of power. The pre-existing and autonomous complexity of ecological systems renders doubtful the allocative virtues of putting (scraps of) nature in the market, and the social results are highly suspect. (M. O'Connor 1993c; Sachs 1993).
10. Here we ignore the prospect that uncontrolled (and generally disruptive) feedback impacts of waste disposal back to the economy from the environment may take place—and generally will, unless there is segregation of a "sink" from those processes of the environment from which raw materials and amenities are obtained (Perrings 1986, 1987; O'Connor 1993b).
11. The interpretation of the ratio $p_3/p_1 > 0$ as a bribe or compensation to conservationists, is a mathematically tidy outcome for the distribution of the value-surpluses obtainable over both processes at the common rate-of-return $\pi_3 < \pi_1$, for as long as (unsustainable) economic capital

accumulation persists. But, in a situation of contested possession, assuming a common rate of return is arbitrary, as the resolution will be the outcomes of military and/or social-political negotiation processes. In the model, we can express this idea by supposing that differential rates of return to exist for different sub-sets of production processes (O'Connor 1993a). Here the non-equalization of returns is established not between resources, but between distinct sets of processes that embody distinct use-values to the respective proprietor groups, or that are in asymmetrical power relationship to each other. Then, the rate(s)-of-return (influencing the relative prices that actually prevail), can be thought of as kinds of distributional parameters indicating the outcome of the contest over purposes of productive activity and over appropriation of the surpluses.

12. The key ideas are readily demonstrated using simple general equilibrium models allowing parametric variation of property rights endowment, or of income distribution, between two groups of consumers having contrasted consumption preferences. O'Connor and Muir (1996) present the simplest possible case (with two inputs, two goods, two consumers); and Muir and O'Connor (1996) give the extension to include a production externality, showing how valuation is sensitive not just to input endowments but also to decisions about rights and liability *vis-à-vis* the damages imposed by the externality.

13. This result is implicit in Howarth and Norgaard's (1992) work, and can be inferred from Pezzey's (1994) work, though it was not systematically brought out by these analysts.

14. The feasibility of a sustainable development model timepath usually depends, inter alia, on the elasticity of substitution between natural and economic capital being unity or greater (or else on some *deus ex machina* assumption about technological progress). For his demonstration, Pezzey (1994) considers the class of "present-value optimizing" timepaths in a model with a non-renewable natural capital where substitutability for natural capital (along with other technical parameters) makes feasible a timepath with non-declining consumption forever. He proves that, contrary to Solow's assertion, along a PV-optimal single-peaked timepath (which is a path of nonsustainability according to the non-declining utility definition), there will always be a portion where the aggregate wealth (the value of the total capital stock) is rising – prior to a subsequent monotonic decline. Faucheux et al. (1996) demonstrate the analogous result with numerical solutions to an OLG model.

15. Some recent literature concerned with applying the "weak sustainability" test as an indicator of national economic performance and potential, *pro forma* presumes the possibility of substitution between natural and economic capital, (Pearce and Atkinson 1993; Proops and Atkinson 1996). This work would have been more robust if the authors had examined the sensitivity of results to alternative hypotheses about substitutability, as for example has been attempted by Serôa da Motta (1995). Equally, the discussions neglect the significance of incorrect prices. For catalogues, doubtless incomplete, of some of the empirical and theoretical reasons, see Victor et al. (1996); Martinez-Alier (1995a, 1995b); Faucheux and O'Connor (1996); and Kaufmann and Cleveland (1995).

16. The Texaco case in Ecuador is mild compared with the externalities caused by Shell in Ogoniterritory in Nigeria, where once again the monetary valuation has been low although it is a heavily populated land. It was a social movement (the MOSOP, led by writer Saro-Wiwa) that made such externalities visible to the outside world. Seen from Shell's perspective, "the investment in Nigeria represents an important long-term commitment which can be clearly distinguished from the – probably short-lived – furore over the executions" (Financial Times, 15 November 1995). More on the theoretical plane than the execution of Saro-Wiwa and his colleagues, another furore was recently sparked off by the low monetary value attributed to human life in Poor countries in cost-benefit analysis of global warming; economists David Pearce and R.K. Pchauri faced considerable flak at IPCC meetings over this issue (Down to Earth, 14 September 1995). Sometimes the inseparability of property rights, distribution of income, and international allocation of externalities does make the news.

17. For example Guha (1994). For a similar view on landscape valuation, see Vadnjal and O'Connor (1994).
18. A discussion relating ecological distribution problem-solving to methods of non-monetary evaluation and multi-criteria decision support, in terms of the practice of Post-Normal Science, is found in the essay in this volume by O'Connor et al. (1996).

REFERENCES

Azar, C. and J. Holmberg. 1995. Defining the generational environmental debt. *Ecological Economics* (Forthcoming).

Beckenbach, F. 1989. Social costs of modern capitalism, *Capitalism, Nature, Socialism* 3 (Fall 1989).

Borrero, J. M. 1994. La deuda ecológica. Testimonio de una reflexión, FIPMA, Cali.

Christensen, P. 1989. Historical roots for ecological economics: Biophysical versus allocative approaches. *Ecological Economics* 1.

Clark, C. 1991. Economic biases against sustainable development. In *Ecological Economics*: The Science and Management of Sustainability, ed. R. Costanza. New York/Oxford: Columbia University Press.

Common, M. 1993. A cost-effective environmentally adjusted performance indicator. Discussion Papers in Environmental Economics and Environmental Management 9307, DEEEM. United Kingdom: University of York, Heslington.

Faber, D. 1993. Environment under fire: Imperialism and the ecological crisis in Central America. New York: Monthly Review Press.

Faucheux, S. and M. O'Connor, eds. 1996. Valuation for Sustainable Development: Methods and Policy Indicators. (Forthcoming), Edward Elgar.

Faucheux, S., E. Muir, and M. O'Connor. 1996. Neoclassical Natural Capital Theory and Weak Indicators for Sustainability. In: Cahiers du C3ED, Paris: Centre d'Économie et d'Éthique pour l'Environnement et le Développement, Université de Versailles à St-Quentin-en-Yvelines, Guyancourt 78280.

Guha, R 1994. The Environmentalism of the poor. Presented at the conference Social Dissent and Direct Action. Guggenheim Foundation; Otavalo, Ecuador, June 1994.

Hahn, F. 1973. On the Notion of Equilibrium in Economics. Inaugural Lecture. Cambridge University Press.

Howarth, R. 1992. Inter-generational justice and the chain of obligation. *Environmental Values* 1(2): 133–140.

Howarth, R. B. and R. B. Norgaard 1990. Intergenerational resource rights, efficiency, and social optimality. *Land Economics* 66: 1–11.

Howarth, R. B. and R. B. Norgaard 1992. Environmental Valuation under Sustainable Development. American Economic Review Papers and Proceedings 80: 473–477.

Howarth, R. B. and R. B. Norgaard 1993. Inter-generational transfers and the social discount rate. *Environmental and Resource Economics* 3: 337–358.

Kapp, K. W. 1970. Social Costs, Economic Development, and Environmental Disruption, ed. J.E. Ullmann. Lanham, Maryland: University Press of America.

Kaufmann, R. and C. Cleveland 1995. Measuring Natural Capital and Sustainable Development: Lessons from Ecology, Thermodynamics, and Economics. Boston University: CES.

Leff, E. 1986. Ecología y Capital, UNAM, Mexico, 1986. (2d) Siglo XXI, Mexico, English version: 1994. New York: Ecology and Capital, Guilford Publications.

Martinez-Alier, J. 1989. Ecological Economics and Eco-Socialism. *Capitalism Nature Socialism* 1(2): 109–122.

Martinez-Alier, J. 1991. Environmental Policy and Distributional Conflicts. In Ecological Economics: The Science and Management of Sustainability, ed. R. Costanza. New York/ Oxford: Columbia University Press.

Martinez-Alier, J. 1993. Distributional obstacles to international environmental policy: The failures at Rio and prospects after Rio. *Environmental Values* 2 (Summer 1993): 97–124.

Martinez Alier, J. 1994. The Merchandising of Biodiversity. *Etnoecologica* 3.

Martinez-Alier, J. 1995a. The environment as a luxury good, or too poor to be green. *Economie Appliquée XLVIII* 2: 215–230.

Martinez-Alier, J. 1995b. Political Ecology, Distributional Conflicts, and Economic Incommensurability. *New Left Review* 211: 70–88.

Muir, E. 1995. The Question of Value: Price and Output Distribution Sensitivities in General Equilibrium. Master's Thesis. New Zealand: University of Auckland.

Muir, E. 1996. *Journal of Income Distribution (*Forthcoming).

Muir, E. and M. O'Connor. 1996. Rights and Liability Assignments in the Policy Valuation of Environmental Externality: A Simple General Equilibrium Exposition. Paris: Cahiers du C3ED, Université de Versailles St-Quentin-en-Yvelines.

Neurath, O. 1919. Empiricism and Sociology.

Norgaard, R. B. and R. B. Howarth 1991. Sustainability and discounting the future. In Ecological Economics: The Science and Management of Sustainability, ed R. Costanza. New York/ Oxford: Columbia University Press.

O'Connor, J. 1988. Capitalism, nature, socialism: A theoretical introduction. *Capitalism, Nature, Socialism* 1(1): 11–38.

O'Connor, J. 1994. Is Sustainable Capitalism Possible. In *Is Capitalism Sustainable?*, ed. M. O'Connor. New York: Guilford Publications.

O'Connor, M. 1993a. Value system contests and the appropriation of ecological capital. *The Manchester School* 61 (4): 398–424.

O'Connor, M. 1993b. Entropic irreversibility and uncontrolled technological change in economy and environment. *Journal of Evolutionary Economics* 3: 285–315.

O'Connor, M. 1993c. Le Disavventure della Natura Capitalistica. *Capitalismo Natura Socialismo, Anno Terzo* 2 (June): 45–79; English version: On the misadventures of capitalist nature. *Capitalism Nature Socialism* 4(3): 7–40.

O'Connor, M. ed. 1994a. Is capitalism sustainable? Political Economy and the Politics of Ecology. New York: Guilford Publications.

O'Connor, M.1994b. The material/communal conditions of life. *Capitalism Nature Socialism* 5(3): 95–104.

O'Connor, M. and E. Muir. 1996. Endowment Effects in Competitive General Equilibrium: A Primer for Policy Analysts. *The Journal of Income Distribution* (Forthcoming).

O'Connor, M. and J. Martinez-Alier. 1996. Ecological distribution and distributed sustainability? In: Sustainable Development: Concepts, Rationalities and Strategies, eds. S. Faucheux, M. O'Connor, and J. van der Straaten. Kluwer: Dordrecht.

O'Connor, M., S. Faucheux, G. Froger, S. Funtowicz, and G. Munda. 1996. Emergent complexity and procedural rationality: Post-normal science for sustainability. In Getting Down To Earth, this volume.

Odum, Howard T. and Jan E. Arding. 1991. Emergy analysis of shrimp mariculture in Ecuador. Working Paper, Gainesville: University of Florida.

O'Neill, J. 1993. Ecology, policy, and politics. London: Routledge.

Page, T. 1977. Conservation and Economic Efficiency. Baltimore: John Hopkins University Press.

Page, T. 1991. Sustainability and the problem of valuation. In: Ecological Economics: The Science and Management of Sustainability, ed. R. Costanza. New York/Oxford: Columbia University Press.

Pearce, D. and G. Atkinson. 1993. Capital theory and the measurement of sustainable development: An indicator of "weak" sustainability, *Ecological Economics* 8: 103–108.

Perrings, C. 1985. The natural economy revisited. *Economic Development and Cultural Exchange* 33: 829–850.

Perrings, C. 1986. Conservation of mass and instability in a dynamic economy-environment system. *Journal of Environmental Economics and Management* 13: 199–211.

Perrings, C. 1987. Economy and Environment: A Theoretical Essay on the Interdependence of Economic and Environmental Systems. Cambridge: Cambridge University Press.

Pezzey, John 1994. The optimal sustainable depletion of non-renewable resources. Presented the 5th Annual Conference of the EAERE, 22–24 June 1994, Dublin.

Proops, J. and G. Aktinson. 1996. A Practical Sustainability Criterion when there is International Trade. In: Sustainable Development: Concepts, Rationalities and Strategies, eds. S. Faucheux, M. O'Connor, and J. van der Straaten. Dordrecht: Kluwer.

Ramsey, F. 1928. A Mathematical theory of saving. *Economic Journal* (December).

Robleto, M. L. and W. Marcelo. 1992. Deuda Ecológica, Instituto de Ecologia Politica, Santiago de Chile.

Samuels, W. J. 1972. Welfare economics, power, and property. In: Perspectives of Property, eds. G. Wunderlich and W. L. Gibson. Institute for Research on Land and Water Resources, Pennsylvania University.

Samuels, W. J. 1991. *Essays on the Economic Role of Government*: Vol.I Fundamentals; Vol.II Applications. London: Macmillan.

Sachs, W. ed. 1993. *Global Ecology: A new arena of political conflict.* London: Zed Books.

Salleh, A. 1994. Nature, woman, labor, capital: Living the deepest contradiction. In Is Capitalism Sustainable?, ed. M. O'Connor. New York: Guilford Publications.

Schultz, I. 1993. Women and waste. *Capitalism Nature Socialism* 4(2): 51–63.

Serôa da Motta, R. 1996. Sustainability Principles and Depreciation Estimates of Natural Capital in Brazil. In Sustainable Development: Concepts, Rationalities and Strategies, eds. S. Faucheux, M. O'Connor, and J. van der Straaten. Dordrecht: Kluwer.

Solow, R. M. 1986. On the inter-temporal allocation of natural resources. *Scandinavian Journal of Economics* 88: 141–149.

Stonich, S. 1993. I am Destroying the Land!".- The Political Ecology of Poverty and Environmental Destruction in Honduras. Boulder, Colorado: Westview Press.

Summers, L. 1992. Let them eat pollution. *The Economist* 8 (February).

Thrupp, L. A. 1991. Sterilization of workers from pesticide exposure: The causes and consequences of DBCP-induced damage in Costa Rica and beyond. *International Journal of Health Services* 21(4): 731–757.

Vadnjal, D. and M. O'Connor 1994. What is the value of Rangitoto Island? *Environmental Values 3* (December): 369–380.

Victor, P. 1991. Indicators of sustainable development: Some lessons from capital theory. *Ecological Economics* 4: 191–213.

Victor, P., J. E. Hanna, and A. Kubursi. 1996. How strong is weak sustainability? In Sustainable Development: Concepts, Rationalities and Strategies, eds. S. Faucheux, M. O'Connor, and J. van der Straaten. Dordrecht: Kluwer.

Waring, M. 1989. Counting for Nothing. Sydney: Unwin.

10 TECHNOLOGICAL INTENSITY, TECHNOLOGICAL QUALITY, AND SUSTAINABLE DEVELOPMENT

Gilberto C. Gallopín
Centro Internacional de Agricultura Tropical (CIAT)
Apartado Aereo 6713
Cali, Columbia

OVERVIEW

A Venn diagram representation of development, underdevelopment and mal-development on the basis of quality of life and economic growth (material and non-material) is introduced. Desirable and feasible transitions towards sustainable development for rich and poor countries are mapped in the diagram.

The Ehrlich and Holdren equation is generalized to include environmental impacts of both consumption and production (as well as non-economic activities); the relevance of the distinction is discussed.

Using a simple illustrative model of environmental worth embodying basic properties common to many self regenerating environmental systems, it is shown that coupled general ecological economic systems may exhibit bimodality, discontinuity, and hysteresis.

On the basis of the conceptual model, the technological factor is partitioned into the dimensions of intensity of use (representing the direct effects of extraction, consumption, or destruction upon environmental worth) and technological quality (representing the effects of the technology used upon the basic parameters of the environmental system).

Attributes of the current technological revolution embodying strategic opportunities for sustainable development are identified. The possibility of constructive technologies and new symbiotic relationships between society and nature, provided the adequate social choices that are made, is highlighted.

INTRODUCTION

It is increasingly recognized that prevailing development patterns are seriously flawed in the South and in the North, and they are failing dramatically in at least two fundamental realms: poverty not only has *not* been eradicated but it is rising, and the ecological life-support and natural resource systems are being seriously damaged from the local to the global level. (WCED 1987; The

South Commission 1990; Norgaard 1994). The current trajectory is clearly unsustainable.

Many of the proposals to improve the situation really are not much more than mitigating (sometimes merely cosmetic) measures (such as increasing efficiency in car engines while continuing to increase the total number of cars). However, it is becoming more and more apparent that attaining sustainable development involves much more than marginal adjustments and mitigating measures.

While recognizing that technology is, albeit important, only one of the relevant factors, in this chapter I attempt to develop a general conceptual framework for the analysis of the relationships between technology and sustainable development, drawing from a number of perspectives and including the unfolding of the current technological revolution.

I start by introducing a generic representation that allows us to map the relevant combinations of economic growth and human development, as well as to depict desirable and undesirable transitions between situations in terms of the sustainability of development.

This analysis identifies dematerialization of the economy as one possibility for indefinite development with non-zero economic growth.

This leads to the second section where, using a modified form of the well known Ehrlich equation, I discuss the environmental impact of human activities, distinguishing those associated to production from those associated to consumption. One of the basic dimensions generating the impacts (either positive or negative) is the technology used.

The technological factor is further partitioned into the dimension of intensity of use, representing the direct effects of extraction, consumption, or destruction upon the quantity or quality of the environmental good or service considered (or conversely, the addition or improvement by subsidies or other additive influences), and a technological quality dimension. Traits of the current technological revolution that represent important opportunities in terms of generating environmentally sustainable technologies are identified.

The final section summarizes the main conclusions obtained from the analysis.

THE DIFFERENT GUISES OF DEVELOPMENT

Figure 10.1 represents the basic relation between development, economic growth, and material economic growth in the form of a Venn diagram familiar in set theory. Sustainability (in principle) increases along the axis material economic growth - non material economic growth - no economic growth (the latter can be consistent with development in the form of qualitative transformations). The figure is useful to map the possible different combinations of economic growth and changes in the quality of life.

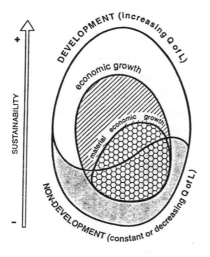

Figure 10.1. A Venn diagram representation including quality of life, material economic growth, and non-material economic growth.

Development is about increasing the quality of life of the human beings, and not necessarily about increased GNP (not even of "greened" GNP accounting for depletion of ecological capital).

Quality of life embodies the satisfaction of material and non-material human needs and the fulfillment of human desires and aspirations (Mallmann 1980; Gallopín and Oberg 1992). Human needs, desires and aspirations can be met through a variety of alternative material and non-material satisfiers. Many of those satisfiers are obtained directly or indirectly from the environment and therefore environmental quality is a component of quality of life (Gallopín 1981).

Economic growth is not necessarily synonymous with material growth. Material economic growth is now confronting both source limitations (scarcity of natural resources) and sink limitations (saturation of the natural capacity for dilution and neutralization of pollutants and wastes). Non-material economic growth has been increasing in the recent past; this relative dematerialization of the economy is evident in (a) the increasing share of the services sector in the GNP (although not all services are non-material, many are much less material-intensive than the primary and secondary sectors of the economy); and (b) the higher energy and resource efficiency of the new and emerging knowledge intensive technologies.

Nevertheless, such dematerialization of the economy can never be complete and besides, "angelized GNP" (Daly 1990) will not feed the poor, and therefore the question of redistribution of wealth and of intra-generational equity is inescapable.

One could say that under development occurs when neither quality of life increases nor economic growth takes place, a situation that affected many developing countries during the eighties and continues to plague many countries and groups of people mostly in the South.

The situation where there is material economic growth, but quality of life does not increase can be defined as mal-development it occurs both in the North and in the South, and it may be of particular relevance for some of the fast growing Asian countries and perhaps for some of the former socialist European countries.

The combination of non-development with non-material economic growth is rare, but it could characterize the situation of some fiscal heavens, or countries with service-based economies and exhibiting a stagnant quality of life for the majority of the population.

The combination of increasing quality of life with material economic growth is what is usually viewed as development. It currently occurs mostly in the North, but also in some countries in the South. However, in the long-term this situation is unsustainable, and in some instance critical environmental thresholds may have been already surpassed.

In a finite planet (and even allowing for rapid technological change) a basic sustainable level of per capita material consumption will have to be reached, both from below (increasing the material consumption of the billions [1] of people living now in poverty) and from above (reducing material over consumption by the rich minority by reducing individual consumption levels or by increasing the overall material and energetic efficiency of the economy, or both). Similarly, the global population will have to stabilize eventually. The issue is not whether this double stabilization is necessary, but how long can we continue in the current trajectory.

Ultimately, there are two basic types of truly sustainable development situations: 1) increasing quality of life together with non-material economic growth (but no net material economic growth) and 2) zero-growth economies (no economic growth at all). Sustainable development need not imply the cessation of economic growth: a zero-growth material economy with a positively-growing non-material economy is the logical implication of sustainable development. While demographic growth and material economic growth must eventually stabilize, cultural, psychological, and spiritual growth is not constrained by physical limits. Those different situations are represented in Figure 10.2.

The challenge of sustainable development lies in how to move from non-development to development in a sustainable way.

Rich countries (in the material sense), are in a good position to aim for a trajectory leading from mal-development or from development with material economic growth, to development with non-material economic growth (or to zero-growth economies, if this is the societal choice made).

Under-developed countries, however, in most cases will be unable to move from non-development to development without material economic growth or

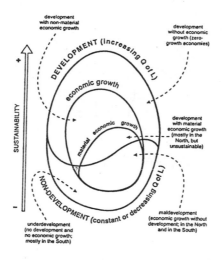

Figure 10.2. Different combinations of changes in quality of life, material and nonma-
terial economic growth defining different forms of development and non-
development.

to zero-growth economies, because a minimum level of accumulation and material economic activity is required to sustain development. The path from
under-development to what is called here mal-development is possible, but
obviously inappropriate. It is, nevertheless, one that has been fostered in the
past and is currently pursued by many countries.

Therefore, the only path appropriate for developing countries is the one that
goes from under-development to development with material economic growth,
and then to development without material economic growth. Similarly, moving from mal-development to unsustainable development with material economic growth is an option which should be discarded by rich countries *vis a vis*
the trajectory leading to development with non-material economic growth, although it could be justified temporarily for poor countries if minimum necessary levels of material accumulation have to be reached.

Those trajectories, and the alternatives available in principle to rich and
poor countries, are depicted in Figure 10.3.

Sustainable development requires reducing the total environmental impact
of the human activities (Equation 1). In this sense, dematerialization of the
economy is important as long as it contributes to reduce the negative environmental impact. Besides changing the non-economic actions and reducing population size, this can be obtained either by a reduction in per capita material
production/consumption, or by reducing the technological coefficient (ecological
impact per unit production/consumption). While per capita consumption/

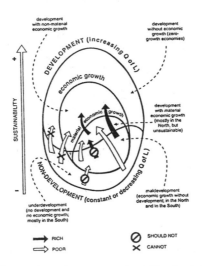

Figure 10.3. Alternative trajectories to sustainability in rich and poor countries.

production can never be negative, the technological coefficient, at least theoretically, could be negative in some cases and for some forms of production or consumption, implying an environmentally enhancing effect of economic activities.

THE ENVIRONMENTAL IMPACT OF HUMAN ACTIVITIES

In general terms, the total environmental impact can be represented as the product of the per capita impact times the total human population size. Usually, the per capita impact is calculated as the per capita consumption, multiplied by the impact per unit consumption (Ehrlich and Holdren 1974).

However, environmental impacts are produced by both consumption and production activities, and it is important to be able to differentiate the cases of over and under consumption from the cases of over or under production.

Furthermore, some human activities impacting the environment cannot be categorized as consumption nor as production activities, and they may be unconnected to population size. Those include war actions, environmental damage generated as forms of social protest (such as forest burnings), etc.

The Ehrlich and Holdren equation can then be generalized as:

(1) $I = N \times [\, C_n \times T_c + P_n \times T_p\,] + DA$

where:

I = Total environmental impact;
N = Population size;
C_n = Per capita consumption;
T_c = Environmental impact for unit of consumption (depending on the technology of consumption as well as on existing ecological conditions);

Pn = Per capita production;

Tp = Environmental impact for unit of production (also depending on the technology of production and ecological conditions);

DA = Non-economic human actions.

In general, the type of impacts and technological coefficients of consumption and production activities are not the same.

For instance, Japan and China had roughly the same per capita production of commercial energy in 1991, about 25 giga joules. However, Japan consumed 141 giga joules per person, as much as 6 times the Chinese per capita consumption. The per capita consumption of Venezuela was 105 giga joules (75% of that of Japan), but its production per person was 343 giga joules, 14 times that of Japan. Other countries, such as the U.S., have both a high per capita consumption (323 giga joules) and production (272 giga joules) (calculated from World Resources Institute et al. (1994).

A country with low production and high energy consumption such as Japan externalizes part of the environmental cost of energy production; an oil exporter country such as Venezuela externalizes part of the environmental cost of energy consumption. Developing countries that import polluting industries are importing the environmental costs of production. This also applies to agriculture: The Netherlands produces its agricultural output by exploiting more than twice agricultural land outside the country than within the country. By importing most of its feed for animals, and exporting milk and other agricultural produce, the production of manure increased so much that it surpasses the country's ability to process it (VROM 1991).

The relative importance of production and consumption, and of the "technological coefficient" indicating impact per unit of production or consumption, varies according to the item considered. The impact of fossil fuel consumption is generally higher than that of production, but the reverse is true for nuclear energy. Production and consumption of industrial materials have also varying impacts according to the material considered.

As production activities are different from consumption activities, and both may have environmental impacts, there is no double counting involved in this formulation: both types of impacts should be added in the cases of countries that consume all their production.

As discussed in the next section, the technological coefficients (Tc and Tp), which can have a very important role in the determination of the total impact (as witnessed by the much higher per unit pollution produced by the countries of Eastern Europe in comparison with the other European countries, or the high engine combustion inefficiency of cars in many countries of the South) do not depend only on the technology but they may also depend upon the local and global ecological conditions. For instance, the same quantity and quality of domestic effluents per unit production of consumption can have a different impact if spilled in a small lake or in a large river.

THE WAYS TECHNOLOGY IMPINGES ON THE NATURAL ENVIRONMENT

Many kinds of environmental components and functions, or environmental goods and services, have a capacity for self-regeneration. This is the case of renewable natural resources, air and water quality, and the like.

However, it is also true that the self-regenerating capacity can be lost in many systems, if the ecological fabric is so severely damaged that no spontaneous recovery of the system becomes possible.

This behavior can be represented by a very simple model derived from the ecological sigmoid growth equation (Gallopín 1980):

(2) $dy/dt = B (y - T) (K - y); y \leq 0$

where:

y = Environmental worth, as represented by the quantity or quality of environmental goods and services, the abundance of renewable natural resources, etc.

K = Upper asymptote (in some cases, it represents the carrying capacity).

T = Extinction threshold.

B = Maximum growth (or regeneration) rate.

The behavior of the model is such that environmental worth (y) will tend to grow or regenerate itself if it is above the extinction threshold (T) until it reaches its upper equilibrium value (K). If environmental worth ever become higher

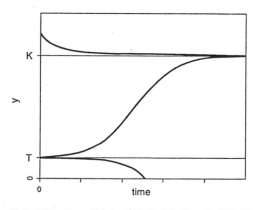

Figure 10.4. Behavior of the sigmoid equation with threshold; y = environmental worth; T = extinction threshold; K = upper asymptote. The three different curves represent the time trajectories for different initial values of (y).

than (K), it tends to spontaneously decrease towards (K). If environmental worth is reduced below the extinction threshold, it thereafter goes to zero and it does not recuperate spontaneously (Figure 10.4).

I want to emphasize that the analysis that follows does not depend on the exact mathematical details of the equation. The major conclusions hold, at least qualitatively, for any environmental system that has the described properties: a capacity to grow or self-regenerate, some kind of upper limit (even if it is not a constant value) and some threshold below which the self-regenerating capacity is lost. Those are rather general conditions applicable in principle to most environmental goods and services. The model used here is the simplest exhibit of these properties.

It is well known that the detailed behavior of real environmental systems under management is enormously more complex and often unpredictable, and that the sigmoid equation has predictive value for only very simple ecological systems such as the growth of bacterial populations. The modified sigmoid equation is used here not as a predictive tool, but as a convenient heuristic device to conceptualize and illustrate some relevant and seemingly general properties of the interaction between humans and nature, particularly in relation to the technological component.

This model represents the behavior of the environmental system in the absence of human perturbations.

Systems which have a threshold value of zero are systems that can regenerate even after complete depletion (e.g., through recolonization from the outside). Systems with (T) equal or higher than (K) cannot survive unless subsidized or otherwise supported (as is the case of most agricultural systems).

The effects of development (or of economic growth) upon the environment are often discussed in terms of rates of extraction, consumption, degradation, or emission. In terms of the model discussed here, the negative impact of the economy upon the environment is basically a reduction of environmental worth that can be represented as a minus term in the above equation depicting the rate of change in environmental worth. A positive influence of the economy upon the environment would be represented by an additive term in the equation.

This can be represented as:

$$(3) \qquad dy/dt = B\,(y - T)\,(K - y) - I; \quad y \leq 0$$

where:

I = Total environmental impact of production and consumption as defined before.

The effect of I upon the rate of change of environmental worth depends on its size in relation to the sustainable environmental production rate, y^*, the equilibrium of Equation 3. This rate is given by the non-zero positive solutions of B (y^* - T) (K - y^*) - I = 0 which depends not only on the intrinsic rate of growth or regeneration (B), but also on the current value of environmental worth (y), as well as the size of the extinction threshold (T) and the asymptote (K).

If the impact is very high, or the value of environmental worth is near the threshold, the environmental system may collapse catastrophically after a critical value is exceeded (Gallopín 1980).

The combined system including the impact variable (I) has new equilibria for each value of (I): a high stable equilibrium (whose value is y^* = K when I = 0), a low unstable equilibrium (adopting the value y^* = T when I = 0), and a low stable equilibrium when y^* =0. In Figure 10.5 the values of the equilibria of the system (3) are represented for each value of (I). All equilibria values lie along the parabola or the horizontal (zero) axis. Positive values of (I) imply positive (beneficial) impacts, adding to environmental worth; negative impacts imply subtraction, such as in Equation 3. Within the area enclosed by the horizontal parabola, the rate of change of the environmental system is positive and environmental worth (y) tends to increase towards the high stable equilibrium. Outside the limits of the parabola, environmental worth tends to decrease. This graph shows that the combined system has three basic properties: bimodality (because it has, for a range of values of (I), two stable equilibria); discontinuity (because it can exhibit a catastrophic or sudden jump, to be discussed later), and hysteresis (because the path followed by the system differs according to the direction of change, also discussed below). The properties of this model (including the case of the existence of feed backs from environmental worth to economic growth generating the impacts are discussed fully in Gallopín (1980). Holling (1973, 1986) has documented and modelled many cases of managed resources exhibiting this behavior.

If the original value of environmental worth (y) lies within the area enclosed by the parabola, environmental worth in the human natural coupled system will

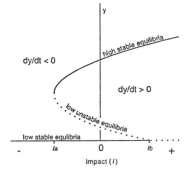

Figure 10.5. Equilibria of Equation 3 for different values of the impact. Continuous lines join stable equilibria; the dotted lines join unstable equilibria.

tend to growth to its high stable equilibrium. If the negative impact (I) increases (moves to the left in Figure 10.5) slower than the change in environmental worth, the latter will stay near its equilibrium, but the equilibrium itself will be moving slowly along the upper branch of the parabola. Therefore, in this region, a slight decrease in environmental worth will result from to a slight increase of the negative impact. However, eventually the extreme left point of the parabola will be reached, and for this value of the impact, $I = I_a$ a high stable equilibrium does not exist anymore, and the only stable equilibrium remaining is the low one ($y^* = 0$). Therefore, environmental worth (y) will drop suddenly following a further small increase in the negative impact. This is a "catastrophic jump" to the low equilibrium.

Moreover, the effect is not easily reversible. Even if the impact is now reduced, the system will be "locked" at its low equilibrium value (because the value of y tends to move away from the low unstable equilibria and it tends to be attracted by the low stable ones). In order to recuperate the system, it becomes necessary not only to reduce the negative impact, but to change the sign of the impact from negative to positive (subsidies, ecosystem restoration, etc.), moving to I_b. Therefore, to recover the environment from a condition of collapse will be much more costly and require more time than avoiding the environmental collapse in the first place. If the system has the basic properties assumed here (upper asymptote and lower extinction threshold) environmental recovery cannot be reached simply by going back a few steps, or reducing the impact to its value before collapse.

If the subtractive impact is low or moderate (i.e., constrained to the right of the apex of the parabola), and the values of (y) lies within the space enclosed by the parabola, then regeneration of environmental worth is maintained (e.g., the coupled environment/economic system is sustainable). However, the upper asymptotic value of the combined system will be reduced, in relation to the undisturbed environmental system represented by Equation 2, from (K) to a lower value.

Often the harvest or extraction rate is the variable of interest. In those cases, the optimum (in the sense that maximizes the total harvest over an indefinite period of time) sustainable harvest rate is the one that maximizes the actual rate of regeneration or growth dy/dt, which is higher at intermediate (higher than (T) and lower than (K) values of (y).

Within this framework, I define intensity of use of an environmental system as the ratio between the utilization rate and the sustainable production rate. Here utilization is used in a broad sense, implying reduction of environmental worth either by extraction, consumption, or destruction by pollution. Although additive influences upon the environmental systems could exist, they are not considered here as part of the concept of "use" of the environmental system.

Intensity of use can be characterized as nil, low, adequate (or sustainable) and excessive depending on whether that ratio is zero, less than one, one, or greater than one, respectively.

However, human activities may impinge upon the environment in other important ways besides addition or subtraction, depending on the technologies of production and consumption and the considered environmental systems.

The technologies may also affect the basic parameters of the environmental system: B, T, and K. This can be encapsulated in a classification of technology as destructive, conservative or constructive. This is a qualitative dimension of technology, based on its impact upon the parameters of the environmental system (Gallopín 1983).

Whether or not the sigmoid equation is strictly applicable, those parameters stand for some of the most basic properties of any self-regenerating environmental system: the intrinsic growth or regeneration rate, the threshold below which the system loses its regenerative capacity, and the highest level the system can maintain over the long-run.

Ecologically destructive technologies can affect environmental worth by reducing its carrying capacity (e.g., through agricultural soil degradation, pollution, habitat destruction, etc.) They can also increase the extinction threshold (e.g., through differential extraction of healthy individuals, through grazing treelings within the forests, etc.). And finally, the basic growth or regeneration rate may be reduced (e.g., by elimination of reproductive females, differential harvesting of faster-growing organisms, effects of pesticides upon individual growth, etc.).

Conservative technologies are defined as technologies that do not significantly affect the basic system's parameters. Their impact expresses itself primarily through the extraction or exploitation rates.

Ecologically constructive technologies are those including specific measures to increase the carrying capacity of the considered environmental system (e.g., through genetic improvement, habitat amelioration, etc.), to increase the regeneration rate (e.g., through protection of seedlings in the forests, selection favoring rapidly growing individuals, etc.) and to decrease the extinction threshold (e.g., through seeding fish spawn in lakes, reforesting fragile lands, etc.).

Other aspects related to the quality of the technologies, such as their resource or energy efficiency is reflected in the intensity of use (a resource efficient technology may allow a sustainable intensity of use in cases where an inefficient technology would overexploit the environmental system to obtain the same production).

Intensity of use can be qualified, in terms of human interests, as neglect, utilization, and overexploitation. Strictly from the viewpoint of utilization of the ecological goods and services, the use of low intensity technologies may imply under-utilization of the ecological system in relation to the sustainable utilization rate. Technologies that are too intensive lead to overexploitation and possibly extinction of the ecological system provider of goods and services. If critical limits are exceeded, the possibility of a catastrophic collapse of the ecological system arises, collapse that may be irreversible even if exploitation is suspended.

The destruction of the ecological system may also arise out of the application of destructive technologies, even at low intensities of extraction. This implies destruction with no or little economic or productive benefit.

In general, destructive technologies reduce or eliminate the future productive potential of the ecological systems, whether or not they provide an immediate economic benefit through the utilization of the systems, while constructive technologies increase the future potential, except in the cases where the intensity of use is excessive.

Combining the dimensions of intensity and quality of the technology, twelve combinations with different ecological and economic implications can be distinguished (Figure 10.6).

Each combination is characterized by the present benefit obtained by using the given ecological system (as indicated by the ratio of the current utilization rate to the sustainable production rate), the effects of the technologies upon the future productive potential of the ecological system, and by the ratio between the

		INTENSITY OF USE (UTILIZATION RATE/ SUSTAINABLE PRODUCTION RATE)			
		NIL (0)	LOW ($\ll$1)	ADEQUATE (=1)	EXCESSIVE ($\gg$1)
TECHNOLOGICAL QUALITY	DESTRUCTIVE	*Destructive neglect*		*Destructive utilization*	*Destructive overexploitation*
		Cp: nil / Fp: reduction	Cp: minimal / Fp: reduction	Cp: good / Fp: reduction	Cp: maximal / Fp: elimination
		$Cp/Fp \approx 0$	$Cp/Fp \gtrless 1$	$Cp/Fp > 1$	$Cp/Fp = \infty$
	CONSERVATIVE	*Conservative neglect*		*Conservative utilization*	*conservative overexploitation*
		Cp: nil / Fp: maintenance	Cp: minimal / Fp: maintenance	Cp: good / Fp: maintenance	Cp: maximal / Fp: reduction or elimination
		$Cp/Fp \approx 0$	$Cp/Fp < 1$	$Cp/Fp = 1$	$Cp/Fp \ggg 1$
	CONSTRUCTIVE	*Constructive neglect*		*Constructive utilization*	*Constructive overexploitation*
		Cp: nil / Fp: increase	Cp: minimal / Fp: increase	Cp: good / Fp: increase	Cp: maximal / Fp: decrease, maintenance or increase
		$Cp/Fp \approx 0$	$Cp/Fp \lll 1$	$Cp/Fp < 1$	$Cp/Fp > 1$

Figure 10.6. Categorization of technologies according to the intensity of use and technological quality.

two. The combination of intensity and quality characterizes the technologies (and by extension the patterns of development) in environmental terms. All those cells for which the ratio of current benefit to future productive potential is higher than one represent unsustainable situations.

In summary, the major environmental effects of technology are (a) magnifying or mitigating the additive/subtractive impacts of economic production and/ or consumption and, (b) affecting the basic parameters of the environmental systems. In the context of Equation 1 changes towards sustainable development may involve changes in total population size and density, changes in per capita volume of consumption or production (implying changes in lifestyles, patterns of consumption, industrial restructuring, etc.), technological changes in depletion or pollution rates per unit of production or consumption (increasing ecological efficiency), and reduction of the damaging non economic human actions. The analysis presented here also highlights the possibility of more basic changes directed to the identification and implementation of measures directed towards decreasing the extinction threshold, increasing the carrying capacity, and optimizing the basic growth or regeneration rate of the systems which provide ecological goods and services to society and the economy.

This includes radical technological innovations as well as the redesign of economic systems in order to go beyond corrective measures so as to make society intrinsically compatible with the preservation of its ecological base for development.

The new technological paradigm embodied in the unfolding "Third Industrial Revolution" exhibits strategically important differences with the technologies generated and diffused after WW II (those new and emerging technologies represent a complex led by micro-electronics and informatics and complemented by a constellation of science intensive technologies biotechnology, new materials, new energy sources).

First, it is ambivalent in the sense that it can be used to concentrate power and decisions, but also to decentralize decisions and increase participation; it is not inherently associated to economies of scale ("the larger the better"). The possibilities for flexible manufacture allowed by the new technologies imply that in many cases the scale of the plant becomes increasingly independent from the scale of the market, and productivity increasingly independent from the scale of the plant (Perez 1986).

Second, the flexibility of the new technologies allows in principle a better adaptation and adjustment to the local ecological and social conditions than is possible with the prevailing modern technologies.

Third, the new and emerging technologies tend to be much more energy and resource efficient than the prevailing ones, being typically knowledge intensive. This could foster a relative dematerialization of the economy, a saving of natural resources, and a reduction of pollution and wastes per unit production or consumption. Those characteristics favor the possibility of developing not only ecologically conservative technologies, but also truly constructive technologies, going beyond the reduction of environmental deterioration to environmental improvement in some cases. New socio-ecological configurations could be generated that incorporate symbiotic relationships between societies and nature.

However, the realization of this potential will depend upon the structure and organization of the societies, and on the social capacity and political will to implement the enormous institutional, political, and cultural changes required. Sustainable development is unlikely to be obtained through technological innovations alone (Goodland et al. 1994); changes in prevailing values, styles of consumption, social and economic equity and population stabilization will be essential.

CONCLUSIONS

Underdevelopment, mal-development, development, and sustainable development can be differentiated in terms of combinations of quality of life, material economic growth, and non-material economic growth. Transitions to sustainability may have to follow different trajectories in rich and poor countries.

Environmental impact associated with consumption should be, for some purposes, differentiated from impact associated with production. This may be particularly relevant in the context of the current process of economic globalization.

Technologies can be characterized environmentally in terms of intensity of use (a subtractive factor relating the actual utilization rate to the sustainable production rate), and in terms of technological quality (destructive, conservative, constructive) defined by the effects upon the basic parameters of environmental systems. This highlights the potential beneficial effect of constructive technologies upon environmental systems. This conceptualization may help to guide technogical research towards possible win-win situations.

In terms of sustainability, relevant attributes of many of the new and emergent technologies are the potential for tailoring to different scales, adaptability to specific social and ecological conditions, and material and energy efficiency. Dramatic increases in both environmental efficiency and quality of technology could be obtained through science and technology strategies optimizing those traits within the context of a new sustainable development.

While the technological factor is critical, the possibility of global sustainable development will be ultimately determined by social and political choices; technological change is unlikely to be sufficient (Taylor and Taylor 1992). It could be added that current trends showing increasing economic and technological gaps, the asymmetry of impacts of the techno-economic revolution upon high-income and low-income countries (Nochteff 1987), and the shift of development assistance to disaster relief (Mathews 1994), among other trends, suggest that, unless determinate policies are agreed and put in place, things will get worse before they get better even assuming rapid technological change.

NOTES

1. Three fifths of the world population receive 5.6% of the total world income; the richest fifth receives 82.7% (UNDP 1992). The poorest of the poor, living under absolute poverty, were estimated to reach more than one billion in 1985 (World Bank 1990).

REFERENCES

Daly, H. E. 1990. Sustainable growth: An impossibility theorem. *Development* 3(4): 45–47.

Ehrlich, P. R. and J. P. Holdren. 1974. Impact of population growth. *Science* 171: 1212–1217.

Gallopín, G. C. 1980. Development and environment: An illustrative model. *J. Policy Modeling* 2(2): 239-254.

Gallopín, G. C. 1981. Human systems: Needs, requirements, environments and quality of life. In: *Applied Systems and Cybernetics. Vol. I. The quality of Life: Systems Approaches,* ed. G. E. Lasker. Pergamon Press.

Gallopín, G. C. 1983. Technologia e sistemas ecologicos. *Informativo INT* 31: 17–29, Rio de Janeiro, Brazil.

Gallopín G. C. and S. Oberg. 1992. Quality of Life. In An Agenda of Science for Environment and Development into the 21st Century, eds. J. C. I. Doodge, G. T. Goodman, J. W. M. La Riviere, J. Marton-Lefebre, T. O'Riordan, and F. Praderie. Great Britinan: Cambridge University Press.

Goodland, R., H. Daly, and J. Kellenberg. 1994. Burden sharing in the transition to environmental sustainability. *Futures* 26(2): 146–155.

Holling, C. S. 1973. Resilience and staological systems. *Ann-Rev. Ecol. and Systematics* 4: 1–23.

Holling, C. S. 1986. The Resilience of terrestrial ecosystems: Local surprise and global change. In: Sustainable Development of the Biosphere, eds. W. C. Clark and R. E. Munn. IIASA/ Cambridge: Cambridge University Press.

Mallmann, C. A. 1980. Society needs and rights: A systemic approach. In: Human Needs. A contribution to the Current Debate, K. Lederer et al. Cambridge: Oelgeschlager, Gunn, and Hain.

Mathews, J. 1994. Robbing development to pay for disaster relief. *Washington Post*, July 6, 1994.

Nochteff, H. 1987. Revolucion tecnologica, autonomia nacional, y democracia. *Monografias Infromes de Investigacion* No. 59. Buenos Aires. Facultad Latinomericana de ciencias Sociales (FLACSO).

Norgaard, R. 1994. Development Betrayed. The End of Progress and a Coevolutionary Revision of the Future. London: Routledge.

Perez, C. 1986. Las nuevas tecnologias: Una vision de conjunto. In Latercera revolution industrial. Impactos internacionales del actual viraje tecnologico, eds. C. Ominami and Grupo. Buenos Aires: Latinoamericano.

South Commission. 1990. *The Challenge to the South*. Oxford: Oxford University Press.

Taylor, A. M. and A. M Taylor. 1992. Poles Apart. Winners and Losers in the History of Human Development. Ottawa: International Development Research Centre.

UNDP. 1992. Human Development Report 1992. New York: Oxford University Press.

VROM (Ministry of Housing, Physical Planning and Environment). 1991. Netherlands National Report to UNCED. The Hague: VROM.

WCED (World Commission on Environment and Development). 1987. Our Common Future. Oxford: Oxford University Press.

11 RENEWABLE RESOURCE APPROPRIATION BY CITIES

Carl Folke
Beijer International Institute of Ecological Economics
Royal Swedish Academy of Sciences
Box 50005, S-10405 Stockholm Sweden

Jonas Larsson
Department of Systems Ecology
Stockholm University, Sweden

Julie Sweitzer
Beijer International Institute of Ecological Economics
Royal Swedish Academy of Sciences
Box 50005, S-10405 Stockholm Sweden

OVERVIEW

It is projected that as much as 60% of the human population will live in an urban area in 2025. Urban areas need renewable resources. We estimate the consumption of wood, paper, fibers, and food, including seafood, by present the population of 22 million people living in the largest cities of the Baltic Sea drainage basin, and relate this consumption to the ecosystem area required to produce these resources. The results indicate that to satisfy their consumption of renewable resources the 29 major cities of the Baltic Sea drainage basin appropriate an area from ecosystems that is at least 200 times larger that the area of the cities themselves. We discuss the implications of our results in relation to the growth of cities, to trade with resources consumed in cities, and conclude there is an urgent need to develop social mechanisms and implement policies which reflect ecological scarcity and urban dependence on life-supporting ecosystems.

INTRODUCTION

Cities and nodal points of people and their activities. According to Nijkamp and Perrels (1994), cities are sustainable when socio-economic interests are brought together in harmony (co-evolution) with environmental and energy concerns in order to ensure continuity in change. This implies that cities will continue to develop without collapsing when faced with perturbations. It also implies that the institutions[1] which direct the development of cities, recognize the necessity of a functional ecological resource base for the long-run survival of the city. Such a recognition should not be taken for granted. On the contrary, it seems that the development toward larger cities, just as the development of many new technologies, tends to mentally alienate people from the natural capital on which they ultimately depend, and creates a world view, a preanalytic vision, which makes society insensitive in responding to environmental feedbacks (Daly and Cobb 1989; Berkes and Folke 1994).

Urban areas and cities are growing rapidly worldwide. In 1906, about 34% of the human world population lived in urban areas, in 1990 their share had grown to 44%, and it is projected that as much as 60% will live in an urban setting in 2025 (Simpson 1993). Concentrations of many people and a lot of activity in a small area such as a city, means intensive consumption of energy and resources in that area. Since cities tend to grow in a throughput manner, ecologists have compared them with large predators and even with parasites on their ecosystems (Odum 1971, 1989). Cities are sustained by a socio-economic infrastructure operating over vast ecosystem areas. Resources are extracted from ecosystems, often far outside national boarders, transported, upgraded, and refined into marketable commodities consumed by people living in the city, and when used up are released back into the ecosystems in concentrated forms as waste and pollutants. Every city draws on the material consumption and productivity of vast and scattered hinterland many times the size of the city itself (Rees 1992). Through the use of industrial energy (mainly fossil) resources are 'pumped' into the city and 'pumped' out in a linear flow as waste. In addition, cities depend on a variety of ecological services such as the capacity of ecosystems to produce drinking water and assimilate waste.

The energy and material demand of cities in the extraction, production, and consumption processes, and the impacts of by-products and waste from these processes alters the capacity of the ecosystem to support the socio-economy. Environmental problems of cities such as air and water pollution, waste handling, deterioration of coastal zones are extensively addressed in policy. But, solutions mainly focus on conventional technologies to cope with point source pollution, such as filters on chimneys, and the construction of sewage treatment plants.

There is a debate on how to improve living and working conditions and urban metabolism (Mega 1994), such as the use of energy and how to recycle resources within the city (e.g., Nijkamp and Perrels 1994). However, these solutions are generally concentrated on a few particular compounds. They do not look at the city and its development in the systems view of ecological economics. Cities not only affect their environment, but they are dependent on functional ecosystems, outside the borders of the city. Ecosystems produce the ecological goods and services which provide the biophysical foundations for people living in cities.

Functional ecosystems are becoming increasingly scare as a consequence of rapid human population growth, and human overexploitation and simplification of the resource base (Jansson et al. 1994). Increasing globalization of human activities and large scale movements of people mean that mankind in an era of novel co-evolution of ecological and socio-economic systems at regional and even planetary scales (Holling 1994; Anderson et al. 1995). It is no longer wise to take the ecological resource base for any city as given, since its productive potential is becoming increasingly fragile.

Odum (1989) discussed the "shadow" area of the U.S. cities and industrial areas (i.e., the spatial ecosystem area that they appropriate in order to be sustained). He used the concept of energy density (the amount of energy consumed per unit of area per year), and estimated that cities and industrial areas occupy 6% of the continental U.S., but when their shadow area is included they appropriate about 35% of this area. Rees and Wackernagel (1994) estimated what they called the "ecological footprint" for urban industrial regions with more than 300 people per km^2. Their results indicate that such regions use 10-20 times more forest and arable land for food, forest products, and to produce biomass energy equivalent to the per capita fossil energy consumption, than what is available in the regions themselves.

In this chapter we estimate the consumption of wood, paper, fibers, and food including seafood, by people in the major cities of the Baltic Sea drainage basin. We relate this consumption to the area required to produce the resources in agricultural, forest, and marine ecosystems. We do not estimate the ecosystem areas that would be required to process human wastes. The implications of the results are discussed in relation to the growth of cities, to trade with resources consumed in cities, and to ecological scarcity (Barbier et al. 1994).

RENEWABLE RESOURCE APPROPRIATION BY CITIES IN THE BALTIC SEA DRAINAGE BASIN

The Baltic Sea drainage basin covers land belonging to 14 countries as shown in Figure 11.1. Eleven of those have cities with populations of 250,000 or more (see Table 11.1). The 29 cities that are included in this study account for about 26% (> 22 million people) of a human population of about 85 million in the whole drainage basin (Sweitzer et al. in press).

Data Used for the Estimates

Data on food and fiber consumption and land use statistics, were obtained from the FAO computerized database Agrostat. This database contains national, continental and global statistics on cultivated area, production, imports, exports, and supply of all major categories of food and fibre products from 1961–1990,

Table 11.1. Large Cities in the Baltic Sea Drainage Basin (Population >250 000)

	City	Country	Population
1.	Karvina	Czech Republic	284,784
2.	Ostrava	Czech Republic	327,413
3.	Århus	Denmark	261,437
4.	Copenhagen	Denmark	1,359,000
5.	Tallin	Estonia	492,430
6.	Helsinki	Finland	497,542
7.	Kiel	Germany	315,000
8.	Lübeck	Germany	260,000
9.	Riga	Latvia	897,078
10.	Kaunas	Lithuania	422,600
11.	Vilnius	Lithuania	582,400
12.	Bialystok	Poland	256,000
13.	Bydgoszcz	Poland	370,000
14.	Czestochowa	Poland	251,000
15.	Gdansk	Poland	468,000
16.	Katowice	Poland	367,000
17.	Krakow	Poland	744,000
18.	Lodz	Poland	847,000
19.	Lublin	Poland	330,000
20.	Poznan	Poland	578,000
21.	Sosnowiec	Poland	258,000
22.	Szczecin	Poland	395,000
23.	Warsawa	Poland	2,422,000
24.	Wroclaw	Poland	640,000
25.	St. Petersburg	Russia	5,035,000
26.	Gothenburg	Sweden	704,000
27.	Malmö	Sweden	458,000
28.	Stockholm	Sweden	1,435,000
29.	L'vov	Ukraine	807,000

The numbers refer to their location in Figure 11.1. The years of population data for the 29 cities are 1986, and 1989–1992.

Sources: Statistical yearbooks of the Czech Republic, of Finland, and of Latvia; Estonian Statistics; Administrative map of Lithuania; Länderbericht Ukraine; Länderbericht Russische Föderation; Nordbas Database, Uppsala; Prof. Dr. I.B.F. Kormoss, Brugge.

Figure 11.1. The Baltic Sea drainage basin. The numbers show the locations of the 29
cities included in this study, as listed in Table 11.1.

except for some items for which 1989 is the last year of data. This implies that
consumption statistics were not available for the Baltic republics, Russia, or Ukraine
separately, but for the sake of preserving data consistency we have used former
USSR figures for all these countries. Since Russia is the dominant country in
terms of population and proportion of drainage basin, this approximation is unlikely to significantly affect the results.

   We have consistently used supply as defined by FAO as a measure of total
consumption, rather than direct or actual per capita consumption. This is preferable to consumption since supply also includes losses incurred on storage,
transport, processing, etc. Based on the FAO database we calculated supply
figures for non-food items as production + imports – exports. This calculation

does not take into account stock changes, which the FAO supply calculations do, but stock changes are relatively insignificant in the FAO supply categories of food and fibre (at the most a few percent). Therefore we assume that they have minor impact on the overall results.

Population data for the cities and land use in the region were obtained from Sweitzer et al. (in press). Data on shelf sea areas and marine exclusive economic zones were obtained from the World Resources on Diskette Database (WRI 1992). In addition various statistical sources were used. Their use is reported in the Appendix.

Estimating Resource Use and Appropriated Ecosystem Area

Appropriated ecosystem area (AEA or aea, using small case letters to denote per capita values) of a given product (i) is defined as the ecosystem area required to produce the amount of i that is consumed. This spatial ecosystem appropriation is obtained by dividing the consumption (c_i) of that product by its areal yield (Y_i):

(1) $\qquad aea_i = c_i / Y_i$

or, using supply of i (s_i) rather than consumption to account for waste and losses:

(2) $\qquad aea_i = s_i / Y_i$

Per capita ecosystem aea (aea_E) is then obtained by summing the aea's of products originating in that ecosystem:

(3) $\qquad aea_E = S\ aea_i$

Total per capita aea (aea_T) is the sum of the aea's in each ecosystem (E) required to produce the renewable resources that are consumed.

(4) $\qquad aea_T = S\ aea_E$

Agricultural ecosystems

The yield, or area required to produce each food or fiber resource, was calculated in different ways for vegetable and animal products.

For vegetable foods and most fibers, except wood, yield was obtained by dividing annual production (P) by area under cultivation (A) of each crop (i):

(5) $\qquad Y_i = P_i / A_i$

This was done for each country, or for imported crops for the most proximate major producer country or region. If no such region could be identified calculations were based on world production data. For a number of tree crops and some tropical crops no FAO data were available. For these resources world target (maximum) yields were obtained from a reference handbook on agriculture

(Hanson 1990). These yields are *ideal maximum yields* that can be obtained under optimal conditions and therefore the resulting AEA will be a conservative measure. Some products, such as vegetable oils and paper, are manufactured from raw materials. Conversion factors were estimated in order to account for this. For oils, the oil yield was calculated by dividing the yield of each oil crop by the average proportion of fat in that crop:

(6) $\qquad Y_{oil} = Y_{oilcrop} / pf_{oilcrop}$

where $(pf_{oilcrop})$ denotes the proportion of fat by weight in each oil crop. The actual yield is likely to be lower, which translates into a conservative estimate of oil crop AEA, since we assumed no losses in processing. A similar conversion was used to calculate grape AEA for wine consumption.

The areal requirement for animal (meat) products was calculated as the area (A) required to produce animal feed for domestically consumed livestock:

(7) $\qquad A_{animal} = A_{feed}$

We were interested in the quantity of feed used to produce domestically consumed livestock products, whether raised domestically or imported. This ideally requires not only identifying the sources of imported meat and other products but also, for each source region, characterizing the livestock feeding practices, herd sizes, age distribution, and so on. We deemed this amount of detail to be impracticable and likely to be inaccurate, since statistics for feeding practices are scant and do not necessarily reflect actual practices. It was also for our purposes beyond the scope of this chapter. For the same reason, we did not attempt to separate feed used in meat, milk, or egg production, since that would also require a detailed knowledge about feed use for the different categories of livestock at different ages, data which are difficult if not impossible to come by reliably even in countries for which good statistics exist. Instead we decided to chose a proxy for animal product consumption or supply that was readily available for the whole region. We decided that total meat consumption would be the most practical such measure. Using meat consumption as the proxy variable, we then assumed that the total annual domestic feed supply for livestock in a given country is required to sustain the total production of meat in that country the same year. We divided the supply (S_j) of each category of $(feed_j)$ (as specified in the FAO supply data) by total meat production $(\Sigma\,^P meat)$ to arrive at an estimate of feed use FU for each unit of meat produced:

(8) $\qquad FU_j = S_j / (\Sigma\,^P meat)$

These ratios were then multiplied by per capita total meat consumption:

(9) $\qquad c_j = FU_j * (\Sigma\,^c meat)$

The resulting figure corresponds to the amount of each feed category required to produce, on average, the amount of meat products consumed annually given the production conditions of the country in question. This approximation is more of a reflection of consumption relative to domestic production capacity than of actual production areas (which in the context of appropriation of ecosystems area may be a more relevant measure anyway). This estimate will however be reasonably accurate provided that meat product imports are not a major part of meat product supply or that such imports come from countries with not vastly different production systems. The estimates of total required feed use were subsequently added to supply figures (from which FAO feed supply amounts had been previously subtracted to avoid double counting).

(10) $S_j = C_j + S'_j$

where (S_j) denotes non-feed supply of crop (j). The resulting supply figures were used in the calculations of appropriated ecosystem areas.

The agricultural aea was calculated by dividing per capita supply of each crop (i) excluding supply for feed, calculated as described above, by the corresponding calculated or literature yield of that crop. Agricultural aea's by item were then summed to give a total per capita agricultural aea (^{aea}AG), which was subsequently used in the index calculations:

(11) $^{aea}AG = \Sigma\, ^{aea}i$

By identifying crops of temperate, tropical and Mediterranean origin it was possible to selectively sum the aea's of these products in order to estimate the total appropriation of temperate, tropical, and Mediterranean ecosystems, respectively.

Grazing land

The areal requirement for larger grazers (cattle and sheep) was calculated as required supplementary grazing land. The numbers of cattle and sheep consumed per capita (*n cattle* and *n sheep*, respectively) were calculated by dividing per capita cattle and sheepmeat consumption with carcass weight (CW) of cattle and sheep:

(12) $^{n}cattle = {}^{c}cattle\ meat\ /\ ^{CW}cattle$

(13) $^{n}sheep = {}^{c}sheep\ meat\ /\ ^{CW}sheep$

Carcass weight was obtained by dividing total cattle and sheep meat production (P) with number (N) of cattle and sheep slaughtered:

(14) $^{CW}cattle = {}^{P}cattle\ meat\ /\ ^{N}cattle$

(15) $^{CW}sheep = {}^{P}sheep\ meat\ /\ ^{N}sheep$

The number of sheep and cattle consumed per capita were then divided by values for the maximum grazing density (*GDmax*) of cattle and sheep on the most productive farmland in southern Sweden (Lärn-Nilsson et al. 1989), to avoid exaggerating the area required for grazing, and subsequently added to yield per capita grazing land aea, (^{aea}GR):

(16) $\qquad ^{aea}GR = (ncattle \,/\, GDmaxcattle) + (nsheep \,/\, GDmaxsheep)$

It is difficult to tell from the statistics to what extent cattle and sheep depend on grazing as opposed to feed. For this reason, we choose to calculate grazing aea only for the number of cattle and sheep actually consumed, as calculated above, rather than for the total stocks of sheep and cattle. We also present grazing AEA separate from other agricultural AEA to indicate the more tentative validity of this estimate.

Forest ecosystems

Wood yield was taken to be the annual growth rate of managed forests in (m^3/ha) for each country, either obtained from stand growth data derived from forestry statistical yearbooks of each country or calculated from production and forest area data from the same sources (see Appendix). For certain countries no forest growth data could be found, and as an approximation, yields of a neighboring country were used instead. Thus, for Czechoslovakia and Denmark, German forest yields were used, for the USSR, Estonian forest yields, and for Norway, Finnish data.

Instead of calculating paper and wood pulp per area "yield", these items were converted to wood equivalents using conversion factors. For wood pulp, the conversion factor WP_u for each country was obtained by dividing pulpwood supply by pulp production:

(17) $\qquad WP_u = {}^Spulpwood \,/\, {}^Ppulp$

and for paper similarly, denoting the pulp to paper conversion factor (PuPa), by dividing pulp supply by paper production for each country:

(18) $\qquad PuPa = {}^Spulp \,/\, {}^Ppaper$

The wood requirement for paper WPa was then obtained by multiplying the two factors:

(19) $\qquad WPa = WPu*PuPa$

Pulp and paper supply was multiplied by the conversion factors and the results were added to other wood supply to yield total wood supply s_w:

(20) $\qquad s_w = {}^Spulp*WPu + {}^Spaper*WPa + s'_w$

where s'_w is non-paper, non-pulp wood supply.

Wood product aea was then obtained by dividing per capita wood, pulp and paper consumption in wood equivalents by forest yield (Y_w) for each country:

(21) $^{aea}WP = s_w / Y_w$

Marine ecosystems

The marine product aea (^{aea}MP), was obtained by dividing fish supply per capita in the different countries by fish yield for shelf sea areas (North Sea data):

(22)   *aeaMP = sfish / Yfish, North Sea*

Yields were taken from Odum (1983). The FAO data differ between pe-lagic, demersal, and freshwater fish species consumption, but for some coun-tries not all categories are included. This inconsistency may reflect real con-sumption patterns, but may also be due to lack of data. Therefore, marine AEA calculations were made on the basis of shelf sea yields only, as these yields are intermediate between pelagic and freshwater yields. FAO catch data do not include discards, so the marine AEA calculated here is a conservative estimate.

Appropriated ecosystem area by cities

The area of the cities was estimated through the GIS database of the Baltic Sea drainage basin developed by Sweitzer et al. (in press). National per capita aea figures for each production ecosystem (E) were multiplied by the population (N) of each city included in the analysis (see Table 11.1) to give city-level appropriated ecosystem area, (AEA_{city}):

(23) $AEA_{city,}E = N * {}^{aea}E$

The different ecosystem AEA's were added to yield a total estimate, $(AEA_{city,}T)$:

(24) $AEA_{city,}T = \Sigma\ AEA_{city,}AG + AEA_{city,}GR + AEA_{city,}WP + AEA_{city,}MP$

The total city AEA was estimated by adding the cities' AEA, nation by na-tion (see Table 11.3). All calculations were made for 1989, the last year for which consistent data were available.

RESULTS

Our estimate indicates that the 29 major cities of the Baltic Sea drainage basin need an area from forest, agricultural and marine ecosystems for their con-sumption of wood, papers, fiber and food that is approximately 200 times larger than the area of the cities themselves (Figure 11.2). The total area of these cities was estimated to be 2,217 km². The appropriated ecosystem area (AEA) of forests was estimated to be 17 times larger, of agricultural land 50 times larger, and of marine systems 133 times larger than the total area of the cities.

If the resources were to be exclusively derived from ecosystems within the Baltic Sea drainage basin, the cities would appropriate about 5% of its forest ecosystems, 15% of agricultural land, and as much as 70% of the Baltic Sea area. Part of this appropriation comes from ecosystems outside the drainage basin. In Table 11.2, we provide the percentages of appropriated ecosystem area for vegetable products imported from Mediterranean and tropical climate countries, country by country.

The AEA results country by country are provided in Table 11.3. The cities' consumption of animal products, non-wood fibers, seafood, vegetable products, and wood products in tones, and country by country, is reported in Table 11.4.

Table 11.2. Percentage of Appropriated Ecosystem Area for Vegetable Products (V.P.) Imported from Tropical and Mediterranean Climate Countries, and Produced in Temperate Areas

Country	Category	% Tropical crops	% Mediterr. crops	% Temperate crops	% Imported (Trop.+Med.)
Denmark	V.P.	17	2	82	18
Norway	V.P.	12	1	86	14
Sweden	V.P.	13	2	85	15
West Germany	V.P.	17	4	80	20
Finland	V.P.	9	1	90	10
Czechoslovakia	V.P.	5	2	93	7
East Germany	V.P.	7	1	92	8
Poland	V.P.	2	0	97	3
USSR (former)	V.P.	2	1	97	3

Table 11.3. Appropriated Ecosystem Areas by Cities in the Baltic Sea Drainage Basin

Country	Cities Pop. >250,000	Grazing land AEA km²	Cropland AEA km²	Crop+pasture % of BDB open land	Forest AEA km²	% of BDB forest	Marine Shelf km²	% of Baltic Sea area
C	612,200	493	1,649	0.30	629	0.08	6,013	1.44
D	1,620,440	769	4,358	0.71	2,221	0.27	33,485	8.03
F	497,540	357	1,521	0.26	3,657	0.44	17,039	4.09
P	7,926,000	6,951	27,801	4.83	7,545	0.90	72,854	17.48
S	2,597,000	1,491	6,356	1.09	10,808	1.29	52,249	12.54
E	492,430	425	1,701	0.48	844	0.10	6,371	1.53
L	897,080	1,267	5,069	0.88	1,537	0.18	11,602	2.78

Table 11.3. Continued.

Country	Cities Pop. >250,000	Grazing land AEA km²	Cropland AEA km²	Crop+pasture %of BDB open land	Forest AEA km²	% of BDB forest	Marine Shelf km²	% of Baltic Sea area
Li	1,005,000	1,420	5,679	0.99	1,722	0.21	12,997	3.12
U	807,000	1,140	4,560	0.79	1,383	0.17	10,438	2.50
R	5,035,000	7,109	28,438	4.94	8,622	1.03	65,093	15.62
G	575,000	378	1,264	0.23	708	0.08	5,683	1.36
B	22,064,680	21,800	88,396	15.49	39,680	4.75	293,857	70.51

C = Czechoslovakia, D = Denmark, F = Finland, P = Poland, S = Sweden, E = Estonia, L = Latvia, Li = Lithuania, U = Ukraine, R = Russia, G = Germany, and B = Baltic drainage basin. The columns in km² show the estimated appropriated areas by the people living in Baltic cities. The columns in % indicate how much of available ecosystem areas within the Baltic Sea drainage that would be required for this appropriation. The % is not the actual appropriation, since there are renewable resources both exported and imported to the region.

Table 11.4. Consumption of Wood, Fibers, and Food, in Tons, by Cities in the Baltic Sea Drainage Basin with a Population >250 000 People, Country by Country

Country	Pop. major cities	Animal products	Non-wood fibers	Tons of: seafood	Vegetable products	Wood products
C	612,197	28,063	2,804	8,458	506,281	138,394
D	1,620,437	25,828	217	16,320	505,324	169,377
E	492,430	35,704	4,091	19,262	863,369	268,039
F	497,542	31,585	533	51,525	621,228	781,016
G	575,000	24,482	957	7,766	407,127	151,270
L	897,078	65,044	7,453	35,091	1,572,832	488,296
Li	1,005,000	30,641	3,511	16,531	740,937	230,029
P	7,926,000	19,167	1,352	6,977	580,597	58,688
R	5,035,000	365,068	41,833	196,955	8,827,780	2,740,645
S	2,597,000	27,648	218	27,865	627,635	664,745
U	807,000	58,512	6,705	31,568	1,414,899	439,265

C = Czechoslovakia, D = Denmark, E = Estonia, F = Finland, G = Germany, L = Latvia, Li = Lithuania, P = Poland, R = Russia, S = Sweden, and U = Ukraine.

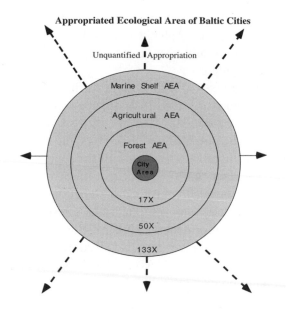

Figure 11.2. The ecosystem area appropriated by Baltic cities. This area only concerns
ecosystem appropriation to satisfy consumption of renewable resources
from forests, agricultural, and marine ecosystems.

DISCUSSION

Many renewable resources consumed by inhabitants in a city are produced by
ecosystems. As a result, the major cities of the Baltic Sea drainage basin appropriate a shadow area at least 200 times their actual area (under present
technology). This area is required to support the 22 million city inhabitants
with wood, paper, fibres, and food, including seafood. If the supply of these
renewable resources is reduced, or ceases, the inhabitants will suffer, as experienced in situations of crisis such as war. However, it is not widely recognized that inhabitants in a city need functional ecosystems for production of
their supply. The capacity of ecosystems to provide these resources is a fundamental and necessary 'factor of production' for cities, and socio-economic
development in general.

Our results indicate that the appropriated marine ecosystem area is much
bigger than the ones from agricultural and forested land (see Figure 11.2).
There are at least two major reasons behind this result. The first is ecological.
Fish and shellfish are consumers in their ecosystem. For example, the herring
in the Baltic Sea moves between three subsystems during its life cycle. It
feeds on zooplankton in the open water ecosystem during summer, switches to
microscopic shrimps near the sea bottom during fall, stops feeding during the
winter and forms large schools in the coastal ecosystem where it will spawn in

May (Hammer et al. 1994). The herring is dependent on the work of primary producers, such as algae, phytoplankton and their associated foodwebs. In contrast, agricultural crops and trees are primary producers and therefore need smaller areas for life-support.

The second reason relates to technology. Agriculture is a fairly intensive activity, where high yields of crops are maintained by inputs of fertilizers, machinery, pesticides, irrigation, etc. The use of fossil fuel based inputs means that higher yields can be obtained per area. To some extent this is also true in forestry. Yield is often used as an indicator of the state of the ecosystem. This is a serious mistake, since there seldom is a linear relationship between the flow of a resource and the health of the ecosystem (Dasgupta et al. 1994). Ecosystems are complex systems with non-linearities, thresholds, and discontinuities (Costanza et al. 1993). Unfortunately, higher yields are often maintained at the expense of a deteriorated resource stock, a well known fact in agriculture where soil erosion and salinization are serious problems (Kendall and Pimentel 1994). The estimate of appropriated agricultural area is based on yields achieved under present technology, a technology which is fossil fuel subsidized, fairly intensive, and causes environmental impacts. Intensive agriculture requires shadow areas for its own operation. We have not estimated such areas, and therefore the appropriated agricultural area is a partial estimate of the actual shadow area. This is also true for the marine appropriated ecosystem area, but for another reason. The FAO-data used in our calculations does not include discards, which may be as much as a third of recorded catches (Pauly and Christensen 1995; Rees W., pers. comm.).

Here, the appropriated ecosystem area concerns the consumption of renewable resources in cities. It does not reflect the areas needed to process the output from that consumption, such as sequestering of carbon dioxide, or assimilation of nutrients. The areas required for the water cycle are not accounted for. Hence, our calculated appropriated ecosystem area is a very partial one. On the other hand, one may argue that at least some of the ecological services (Ehrlich and Mooney 1983; Folke 1991; de Groot 1992) are partly covered by the estimate presented here. This is a consequence of ecosystems being multifunctional; a forest produces timber but also assimilate nutrients. Several resources and services are produced by the same ecosystem. The complex issue of joint products in ecosystems have been dealt with Costanza and Hannon (1989). To address it properly requires knowledge of the internal relationships of the ecosystem. Such detailed knowledge is often lacking. How to avoid double-counting of appropriated ecosystem areas for resource production and waste assimilation is an empirical issue which we are in the process of analyzing.

The methodology of this chapter is in many respect similar to the one developed by Rees and Wackernagel (1994) on the ecological footprint. They also derive estimates of the physical stocks of natural capital necessary to sustain a given human population and compare this to the population's home territory. They interpret human carrying capacity as the maximum rate of resource consumption and waste discharge that can be sustained indefinitely without progressively impairing the functional integrity and productivity of relevant ecosystems wherever the latter may be (Daily and Ehrlich 1992). We support this interpretation, but do not attempt to quantify carrying capacity. Our estimate of appropriated ecosystem area is more conservative that the appropriated carrying capacity of Rees and Wackernagel (1994). We based our quantitative analyses on existing national data from a large-scale region with varying standards of living. Although there may be errors in the statistics, we have used the best production data available, and have not made scenarios of potential resource production or waste assimilation.

We have shown that the Baltic cities depend on the productivity of large life support systems outside their borders. This dependence is seldom accounted for in city planning and development. If it is not recognized, and cities continue to damage their life-support ecosystems it implies that social norms and rules rely on technology, indicators of welfare, and world views which mentally alienate people from their dependence on functional ecosystems, and which take for granted that it is possible to substitute the loss of domestically produced goods and services for the imports of similar goods and services from other regions or countries. But the human population and the scale of human activity continue to increase and environmental damage does not only occur in local ecosystems. Humanity has entered the era of the 'full world economy', where natural capital worldwide is increasingly becoming the scarce resource for development (e.g., Goodland et al. 1992; Jansson et al. 1994). Many of the ecosystem modifications and the environmental effects that they cause, which today are regarded as of only local or national concern, are in fact already of regional and ultimately of global concern (Holling 1994). Local environmental problems may have their cause half a world away. The web of connections linking one ecosystem and one country with the next is intensifying across all scales in both space and time. Everyone is now in everyone else's backyard. We are facing ecological scarcity (Barbier et al. 1994).

Cities are embedded in this web of connections. Cities free themselves from local ecological boundaries by importing resources (raw or processed materials) and ecological services from elsewhere. Trade is a means by which cities expand their ecological footprint (Rees 1992). This is also the case of Baltic cities. They not only import goods from areas within the drainage basin, but also from countries in other regions. We have traced the percentage of vegetable products imported to the Baltic Sea drainage basin, as shown in Table 11.2. These imports vary between 3–20% of the total appropriated ecosystem area.

The market-based economies have a much higher share of tropical crops than the former planned economies of Eastern Europe, which means that they to a larger extent use trade as a mechanism for ecosystem appropriation far beyond their national boundaries.

However, relying on trade means that people in cities become dependent on their access to resources and ecosystem functions outside the boundaries of their own jurisdiction. They will have limited ability to influence the use of foreign ecosystems on which their city life depends. Furthermore, people often do not perceive that their consumption decisions may contribute to environmental degradation in other countries. For example, consumption of large shrimp imported from abroad, contributes to the chopping down of mangrove forests on the coasts of South America, Africa, and Asia. The ecosystem exploitation, for short term profit, results in decreased fish reproduction, and thereby fewer fishing catches, not only for subsistence economies, and domestic fisheries, but also for other countries exploiting the fish stocks (Bailey 1988; Primavera 1993). Prices of traded goods and services, do seldom reflect the ecosystem support needed to produce the goods and services (Hammer 1991), or the costs of natural capital deterioration caused by their production (Ekins et al. 1994). Even though trade dissolves domestic boundaries, it cannot eradicate ecological boundaries. Trade moves ecological boundaries outside national boundaries, and the ecological impacts of production and consumption are now shared by several nations (Andersson et al. 1995).

Sustainability implies that society remains within ecological boundaries. Local human influences on air, land, and oceans slowly accumulate to trigger sudden abrupt changes when ecological boundaries are challenged and thresholds reached, directly affecting the resource base of cities. Therefore, the ecological support to city development should no longer be taken for granted.

It is in this context that estimates of appropriated ecosystem area; the ecological footprint; become interesting. Although appropriated ecosystem area, a static measure, does not provide an estimate of carrying capacity (due to the dynamics of complex systems and associated true uncertainty of where ecological thresholds are) it illuminates the *hidden* human requirements for ecosystem work, and puts the scale of human activity in an ecological economics framework. The work of ecosystems, which forms the precondition for city life, is hidden because people and policy seldom perceive it, but nevertheless it is real.

If natural capital were superabundant estimates of appropriated ecosystem area would be of less value. Some people would even argue that we do not need to worry about ecological footprints, since trade makes it possible for cities to get their resources from elsewhere. However, the present situation of ecological scarcity, interdependence and novel co-evolution of ecological and economic systems at regional and even planetary scales, makes substitution merely an illusion (Folke et al. 1991 in press). It is an illusion since cities are not the only appropriators of the footprint. Other human activities use and abuse it as well, and cause changes in the capacity of natural capital to produce essential goods and services. A concept of 'environmental utilization space' is in development to reflect such interdependencies (Siebert 1982; Opschoor and Weterings 1994).

Policies dealing with urbanization should apply an integrated view of ecosystems and human settlements, asking questions such as how large can the city grow without challenging the capacity of natural capital to support it? Rees (1992) raises some policy issues in this context: Should dependent urban regions formalize their relationships with export regions to secure maintenance of essential natural capital stocks, thereby enhancing their ecological security, or should they develop policies explicitly to support and sustain local/regional agriculture, forestry, and fisheries, in order to reduce potentially unstable interregional dependencies? And what are the appropriate levels of institutions to deal with these matters?

Clearly, urbanization based on physical expansion will not be sustainable. It must take ecological constraints into account. Institutional frameworks for urban development, including its relation to economic development and trade, which account for the genuine uncertainty of the thresholds of life-support ecosystems must be introduced (Andersson et al. 1995). Fortunately, approaches towards avoiding ecological thresholds, through ecocyclic urban development are in progress (Anonymous 1992; Smit and Nasr 1992; Berg 1993).

CONCLUSION

Nearly 70% of the population inhabiting the Baltic Sea drainage basin live in urban areas. Of those about 35% live in the 29 cities of focus in this study (Sweitzer et al. in press). As mentioned in the introduction, it is projected that as much as 60% of the global human population will live in urban areas in year 2025 (Simpson 1993). In this chapter, we have stressed that development of cities and urban areas must account for the dependence on functional and healthy ecosystems for water, food, other resources, and a variety of ecological services. To be able to exist cities need large ecological shadow areas. We have estimated part of the appropriated ecosystem area for Baltic cities to be 200 times the spatial area of the cities themselves. It is in the self-interest of inhabitants in urban areas to make sure that ecosystems continue to produce the goods and services on which people live. There is an urgent need to develop social mechanisms and implement policies which reflect ecological scarcity and urban dependence on life-supporting ecosystems.

ACKNOWLEDGMENTS

We thank the three referees Marina Alberti, Cutler J. Cleveland, and William Rees for most valuable comments on the manuscript. The chapter is part of Baltic Sea Drainage Basin Project, of the Beijer Institute, with support from the European Union Environment Research Program 1991–1994, the Swedish Environmental Protection Agency, and the Swedish Council for Planning and Coordination of Research (FRN). Carl Folke's work is partly funded by the Swedish Council for Forestry and Agricultural Research (SJFR).

APPENDIX OF STATISTICAL SOURCES

Consumption and agricultural yield data:

FAO. 1990. FAO Agrostat Database Rome. Crop categories were the ones defined by FAO, with minor exceptions, and include food crops, feed crops, fiber crops, and stimulants such as tea, coffee, and tobacco (some spices and other products consumed in negligible quantitites were excluded).

Hanson, A.A. eds. 1990. Practical Handbook of Agricultural Science. Boca Raton, FL: CRC Press.

Conversion factors for oil crops and wine:

Jonsson, E. ed. 1993. Våra livsmedelsråvaror. Produktion, sammansättning, ochegenskaper. (Our raw foodstuffs. Production, constituents, and properties. In Swedish.) Tuna Tryck, Eskilstuna.

Lena Bergström, Livsmedelsverket (Swedish Foodstuff Agency) (pers. comm.) (for oil content of linseed, sesame seed, and safflower seed).

Lars Torstensson (personal communication), Domaine Rabiega, Clos Dière Méridional, 83300 Draguignan, France (for areal yield of grapes for wine production and conversion factors from grapes to wine).

Shelf sea areas and exclusive economic zones:

WRI. 1992. The World Resources Data Base on Diskette. The World Resources Institute. Oxford, UK: Oxford University Press.

Population data:

Sweitzer, J., S. Langaas and C. Folke. in press. Land use and population density in the Baltic Sea drainage basin: a GIS database. *Ambio.*

Forest yield data:

Estonia, Russia, and Ukraine: Pers comm, State Statistical Office of Estonia, 4 May 1993.

Latvia and Lithuania: Nordic Project Fund, Environmental Situation and Project Identification in Latvia, Helsinki. 1991.

Sweden: Skogsstatistisk årsbok 1992 (Yearbook of Forest Statistics). Statistiska centralbyrån (Central Bureau of Statistics Sweden).

Finland and Norway: Skogsstatistisk årsbok 1989 (Yearbook of Forest Statistics). Central Bureau of Statistics Finland.

Poland: Rozncik Statystyczny. 1993 (Statistical Yearbook of Poland). Central Statistical Office of Poland, Warsaw.

Environment Protection. 1992. Central Statistical Office of Poland, Warsaw.

Germany, Czechoslovakia, and Denmark: Statistisches Jahrbuch über Ernährung Landwirtschaft und Forsten 1993. Statistisches Bundesamt, Wiesbaden, 1993.

Land use:

Sweitzer, J., S. Langaas and C. Folke. in press. Land use and population density in the Baltic Sea drainage basin: a GIS database. *Ambio.*

NOTES

1. Institutions are the human devised constraints that shape human interaction. They structure incentives in human exchange, whether political, social, or economic, and shape the way societies evolve through time (North 1990).

REFERENCES

Andersson, T., C. Folke, and S. Nyström. 1995. Trading with the Environment: Ecology, Economics, Institutions and Policy. London: Earthscan.

Anonymous. 1992. Ecocycles: The Basis of Sustainable Urban Development. Environmental Advisory Council to the Swedish Government. SOU 1992:43. Swedish Ministry of the Environment and Natural Resources. Stockholm: Sweden.

Bailey, C. 1988. The social consequences of tropical shrimp mariculture. *Ocean and Shoreline Management* 11: 31–44.

Barbier, E. B., J. Burgess, and C. Folke. 1994. Paradise Lost? The Ecological Economics of Biodiversity. London: Earthscan.

Berg, P. G. 1993. Biologi och Bosättning: Naturanpassning i samhällsbyggandet. Stockholm: Institutet för Framtidssdtudier/Natur och Kultur.

Berkes, F. and C. Folke. 1994. Investing in cultural capital for a sustainable use of natural capital. In Investing in Natural Capital: The Ecological Economics Approach to Sustainability, eds. A.M. Jansson, M. Hammer, C. Folke, and R. Costanza. Washington, DC: Island Press.

Costanza, R. and B. Hannon. 1989. Dealing with the "mixed units" problem in ecosystem network analysis. In Network Analysis of Marine Ecosystems: Methods and Applications, eds. F. Wulff, J. G. Fields, and K.H. Mann. Heidelberg: Springer-Verlag.

Costanza, R., L. Wainger, C. Folke, and K.-G. Mäler. 1993. Modeling complex ecological economic systems: Toward an evolutionary, dynamic understanding of people and nature. *BioScience* 43: 545–555.

Daily, G. C. and P. R. Ehrlich. 1992. Population, sustainability and Earth's carrying capacity. *BioScience* 42: 761–771.

Daly, H. E. and J. B. Cobb. 1989. For the Common Good: Redirecting the Economy Toward Community, the Environment, and a Sustainable Future. Boston, MA: Beacon Press.

Dasgupta, P., C. Folke, and K.-G. Mäler. 1994. The environmental resource base and human welfare. In Population, Economic Development, and the Environment, eds. K. Lindahl-Kiessling and H. Landberg. Oxford, UK: Oxford University Press.

de Groot, R.S. 1992. Functions of Nature. Amsterdam: Wolters-Noordhoff.

Ehrlich, P. R. and H. A. Mooney. 1983. Extinction, substitution and ecosystem services. *Bio-Science* 33: 248–254.

Ekins, P., C. Folke, and R. Costanza. 1994. Trade, environment and development: The issues in perspective. *Ecological Economics* 9: 1–12.

Folke, C. 1991. Socioeconomic dependence on the life-supporting environment. In Linking the Natural Environment and the Economy: Essays from the Eco-Eco Group, eds. C. Folke and T. Kåberger. Dordrecht, the Netherlands: Kluwer Academic Publishers.

Folke, C., C. S. Holling and C. Perrings. in press. Biological diversity, ecosystems, and the human scale. Ecological Applications.

Folke, C., M. Hammer, and A.M. Jansson. 1991. Life-support value of ecosystems: A case study of the Baltic Sea Region. *Ecological Economics* 3: 123–137.

Goodland, R., H. E. Daly, and S. El Serafy. eds. 1992. Population, Technology, and Lifestyle: The Transition to Sustainability. Washington, DC: Island Press.

Hammer, M. 1991. Marine ecosystems support to fisheries and fish trade. In Linking the Natural Environment and the Economy: Essays from the Eco-Eco Group, eds. C. Folke and T. Kåberger. Dordrecht, the Netherlands: Kluwer Academic Publishers.

Hammer, M., A. M. Jansson and B.-O. Jansson. 1994. Diversity change and sustainability: Implications for fisheries. *Ambio* 22: 97–105.

Hanson, A. A. ed. 1990. Practical Handbook of Agricultural Science. Boca Raton, FL: CRC Press.

Holling, C. S. 1994. An ecologists view of the Malthusian conflict. In Population, Economic Development, and the Environment, eds. K. Lindahl-Kiessling and H. Landberg. Oxford, UK: Oxford University Press.

Jansson, A.M., M. Hammer, C. Folke, and R. Costanza. eds. 1994. Investing in Natural Capital: The Ecological Economics Approach to Sustainability. Washington DC: Island Press.

Kendall, H. W. and Pimentel, D. 1994. Constraints on the expansion of the global food supply. *Ambio* 23: 198–205.

Lärn-Nilsson, J., I. Bjäresten, and P. E. Sundgren. 1989. Lantbrukets Husdjur del 1(2). Stockholm: LT's Förlag.

Mega, V. 1994. Improving the urban environment: European challenges. *Ambio* 23: 451–454.

Nijkamp, P. and A. Perrels. 1994. Sustainable Cities in Europe. London: Earthscan.North, D.C. 1990. Institutions, Institutional Change and Economic Performance. Cambridge, UK: Cambridge University Press.

Odum, E. P. 1983. Basic Ecology. New York: Holt-Saunders International Editions.

Odum, E. P. 1989. Ecology and Our Endangered Life-Support Systems. Sunderland, Massachusetts: Sinauer Associates.

Odum, H. T. 1971. Environment, Power and Society. New York: John Wiley and Sons.

Opschoor, J. B. and R. Weterings. 1994. Environmental utilisation space: An introduction. *Netherlands Journal of Environmental Sciences* 9: 198–205.

Pauly, D. and V. Christensen. 1995. Primary production required to sustain global fisheries. *Nature* 374: 255–257.

Primavera, J. H. 1993. A critical review of shrimp pond culture. *Reviews in Fisheries Science* 1: 151–201.

Rees, W. E. 1992. Ecological footprints and appropriated carrying capacity: What urban economies leaves out. *Environment and Urbanization* 4: 121–130.

Rees, W. E. and M. Wackernagel. 1994. Ecological footprints and appropriated carrying capacity: measuring the natural capital requirements of the human economy. In Investing in Natural Capital: The Ecological Economics Approach to Sustainability, eds. A. M. Jansson, M. Hammer, C. Folke, and R. Costanza. Washington, DC: Island Press.

Siebert, H. 1982. Nature as a life-support system: Renewable resources and environmental disruption. *Journal of Economics* 42: 133–142.

Simpson, J. R. 1993. Urbanization, agro-ecological zones and food production sustainability. *Outlook on Agriculture* 22: 233–239.

Smit, J. and J. Naser. 1992. Urban agriculture and sustainable cities: Using wastes and idle land and water bodies as resources. *Environment and Urbanization* 4: 141–152.

Sweitzer, J., S. Langaas and C. Folke. in press. Land use and population density in the Baltic Sea drainage basin: A GIS database. *Ambio.*

WRI. 1992. The World Resources Data Base on Diskette. The World Resources Institute. Oxford, UK: Oxford University Press.

12 EMERGENT COMPLEXITY AND PROCEDURAL RATIONALITY: POST-NORMAL SCIENCE FOR SUSTAINABILITY

Martin O'Connor
Centre d'Economie et d'Ethique pour l'
Environnement et le Développement (C3ED)
Département de Sciences Economiques
Université de Versailles Saint Quentin-en-Yvelines
47 boulevard Vauban, Guyancourt 78280, France

Sylvie Faucheux
Centre d'Economie et d'Ethique pour l'
Environnement et le Développement (C3ED)
Département de Sciences Economiques
Université de Versailles Saint Quentin-en-Yvelines
47 boulevard Vauban, Guyancourt 78280, France

Géraldine Froger
Centre d'Economie et d'Ethique pour l'
Environnement et le Développement (C3ED)
Département de Sciences Economiques
Université de Versailles Saint Quentin-en-Yvelines
47 boulevard Vauban, Guyancourt 78280, France

Silvio Funtowicz
Commission of the European Communities, Joint Research
Centre, Institute for Systems Engineering and
Informatics, I-21020 Ispra, Varese, Italy

Giuseppe Munda
Department of Economics and Economic History
Universitat Autónoma de Barcelona
Bellaterra 08193, Spain

OVERVIEW

Reorientation of scientific practice is necessary if science is to well serve the role of aiding collective choices regarding risk management and the redistribution of economic opportunity and of access to environmental services and benefits. This chapter presents 'post normal science' practice in application to problem domains of ecological economics. Elements of the epistemological foundations for a 'science of emergent complexity' are presented, and related back to social requirements of conflict resolution. The chapter then describes application of this perspective in policy analysis, focussing successively on ecological distribution in the management of systems of natural capital; the epistemological basis for management of uncertainty; and procedural rationality in the setting of environmental norms or policy objectives. These themes are brought together with an illustration of multi-criteria decision aid methodology, called a 'sustainability tree' designed to display the inter-relationships between different dimensions of policy evaluation and to furnish an operating framework for employing procedural rationality to help decision-making for sustainability.

INTRODUCTION

Economic analysis as it developed in the 19th century, has tended to portray a human economy as a self-equilibrating mechanism, amenable to prediction and mechanical control. This bird's-eye instrumental vision of the economic system is, however, no longer appropriate as we come to deal with large-scale ecological economics problems. Here it becomes apparent that we are acting and observing from within complex natural-social systems, and these are not amenable to control along the lines of classical paradigms of mechanics, engineering design, and cybernetic regulation. The spaces of social-ecological action are characterized by high levels of indeterminacy and conflict, related to scarcity and to the extent of physical and social interdependencies (over wide ranges of space and time scales) of production and consumption processes and policy actions. Scientific analyses furnishing inputs for environmental policy and decision making fall within these contested spaces. So an epistemology and practice for science is needed that is suited to the social process requirements of effective conflict resolution.

In this chapter, we discuss the science of emergent complexity as it relates to ecological economics, and give illustrations of its application. We argue that fundamental reorientation of scientific practice is necessary if science is to perform adequately the changed roles required of it in environmental policy and decision-making. These changed roles include, in particular, to guide and inform collective choices (community and political decisions) regarding the redistribution of economic opportunity and of access to environmental services and benefits. The choices relate to present day questions of justice (such as North-South redistribution) and to the opportunities afforded to future generations—the equity, irreversibility, and uncertainty issues of sustainability. The science of emergent complexity (post-normal science) is inseparable from considerations of ethics and politics.

We explain the basis for 'post normal science' practice in application to problem domains of ecological economics and provide sketches for some of the epistemological foundations for a 'science of emergent complexity' and relates these to the social requirements of conflict resolution. Moreover, we show the application of this perspective in policy analysis, focussing successively on issues of: ecological distribution in the management of systems of natural capital; the epistemological basis for management of uncertainty; and procedural rationality in the setting of environmental norms or policy objectives. We then bring together these themes with an illustration of multi-criteria decision aid methodology, called a 'sustainability tree', and conclude with a recapitulation of the new roles and perspectives required of physical and ecological science.

Although the discussion necessarily remains formal and abstract in a short paper, we emphasize that this reorientation of science needs to permeate day to day practices, particularly with regard to uncertainties, to industrial and ecological risks that are part and parcel of modern times.

ECOLOGICAL ECONOMICS AND POST-NORMAL SCIENCE

In dialectical terms, environmental crisis may be understood as the encounter of industrial society with contradictions and inadequacies of the 19th century view of science and industrial production as essentially Progressive in character. These contradictions appear in the forms of, first, environmental scarcity and, second, the non-attainment of real control over nature (Norgaard 1994; O'Connor 1989, 1994c, 1994d). In the instrumental view of nature that has underlain dominant scientific practice of the past two centuries, the non-human world is represented as a freely available raw material merely waiting to be put to use. Through until the 1970s, it was usual in standard textbooks on macro- and microeconomics, and economic development, to have scarcely a mention of problems of waste disposal, pollution, ecological disruption, or natural resource depletion. The theory reflected the practice. For example, throughout the post-World War II period until the 1960s, the so-called "under-developed" territories of newly "independent" Third World nations were being opened up for agricultural and mineral raw material exploitation. The societies in question—or, at least, their dominant elites—were not immediately presented with biophysical "limits to growth" on a global scale. Thus, although there was an awareness that forests and oil reserves, for example, could be exhaustible, the exploitation of these territories, the depletion of particular mineral reserves, and the degradation of particular ecosystems by waste disposal, could nonetheless be seen as furnishing the platform for continued output growth, not as undermining the basis for future livelihood.

Correspondingly, the role of science was mainly to furnish the knowledge base for improvements in productive efficiency and for innovations in process technology and product types. Scientific progress and economic progress (improved productivity and output growth) thus walked hand in hand. Today, however, there are no *external* territories, whether social or biophysical, to be *opened up* to exploitation. The question of physical limits to sinks and sources has become a truly *global* issue, binding in material and political terms on almost all peoples interlocked through the worldwide commodity economy or fighting for their survival on the margins of the expanding commodity economy. The alliance between economic growth and science thus has spawned contradictions. Emphasis on economic output growth as a desirable collective goal and as a means of softening economic distribution conflicts (through public policies of redistribution or the 'trickle down effect' in mass consumer society), has been a powerful factor encouraging neglect of environmental costs associated with economic expansion. However, it is now perceived that economic growth and population growth place increasing stress on ecosystems but that it is not possible to expand physically the ecological pie upon which economic activity depends. So, science now informs us of the finiteness of our ecological capital, of the fragility of our biosphere as a collective habitat and life support system, and of the trade-offs between present and future associated with natural resource use, land degradation, and waste generation and disposal. Our resource extraction technologies can now lay waste vast tracts of land, and disrupt biosphere cycles upon which future generations' livelihoods will depend. We no longer have a simple equation between science, progress, and growth (Funtowicz and Ravetz 1992, 1993; Norgaard 1994).

The heightening of decision stakes under uncertainty, and the sharpening of distributional conflicts means a change in the roles required for science inputs to policy decision making. One outcome under such circumstances can be the management of science specifically in the service of military and political hegemonies. Another possibility is the emergence of post-normal science as developed by Funtowicz and Ravetz (1991, 1993, 1994b), in which scientific information is provided in the context of an enlarged decision-making framework aiming to help in resolving social conflicts and environmental distributional choices. In this earlier work, post-normal science has been presented as the problem-solving strategy appropriate to major contemporary environmental management issues. It is a perspective to be applied when, typically, facts are uncertain, values are in dispute, stakes are high, and decisions are urgent. We can visualize this situation as one where either systems uncertainties or decision stakes are large. When they are both small, traditional applied science is adequate; when either is medium, then we have 'professional consultancy' see Figure 12.1.

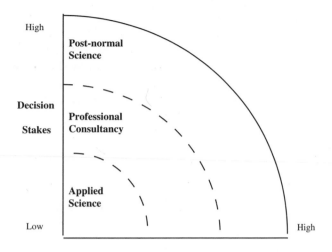

Figure 12.1. Systems uncertainties.

In this new class of problems, we require a new approach to the management of uncertainty and to the legitimacy of decision making participants. Funtowicz and Ravetz refer to an extended 'peer community', including all stakeholders in an issue who are prepared for a dialogue, regardless of their formal certification. Such an extension is necessary for the effective quality-assurance of the scientific inputs into the decision process. Here we discuss epistemological foundations for such scientific practice.

THE SCIENCE OF EMERGENT COMPLEXITY

The theory of 'systems' has, in recent years, been developed and enriched by a number of approaches in which dynamical and evolutionary properties have been grafted onto what were originally rather static concepts and simulation frameworks. Among the key new themes is 'complexity,' which is now seen as manifesting in many scientific contexts. This notion, developed in conjunction with new concepts of structure, growth, qualitative change, and chaos has provided powerful tools of analysis, guiding practice in many scientific fields including ecology (e.g., Hollings 1994; Schneider and Kay 1994). However, as such concepts and analytical techniques have expanded in their application from the abstract fields of their origin to the study of diverse phenomena in the biological and social worlds, the problem of their relation to external realities — the basic question of epistemology for science—arises once more.

In order to explain the way that we use the term "complexity", we draw on a distinction developed by Isabelle Stengers (1987), between two views about the character of explanation sought in science. The first, that we can call Laplacian, takes for its reference point and ideal, the formulation of a set of equations describing "perfectly" the behavior of the system in question, past, present, and future, as seen by an omniscient god (Laplace 1795). A *compli-cated* system may thus be deemed ultimately determined in its behavior, at the same time admitting that in practice (due to limitations of knowledge, lack of precision, computing power, etc.) it is unable to provide a description that captures this underlying determination. The ideal of scientific explanation is to achieve—even if only locally, partially, and imperfectly—the same sort of determinacy that is visible to Laplace's divinity. The second, that we designate *complexity* (Stengers 1987; O'Connor 1994b, 1994d), rejects determinacy and aims rather at the formulation of laws that express regularities characterizing many distinct levels of hierarchical structures and their inter-relations within specified phenomenal domains. It is asserted that reality displays an irreducible complexity of structure—a hierarchical, dynamically meta-stable, and mutable character being confronted at whatever level reality is interrogated.

In systems vocabulary, the fundamental distinction is thus made between systems viewed as unpredictable merely because they are complicated, and systems deemed to be inherently indeterminate in their behaviors by virtue of the real complexity of their organizational forms, functions and change. Within this epistemology of complexity, we may describe as "simple", those systems and models that, for the analytical horizons considered, are determinate in their behavior. However, explanatory models in the simple category are not considered to be steps towards a complete scientific body of knowledge in the deterministic sense described by Laplace. Rather, they are a special case, an impoverished mode of description that abstracts away from the enriching indeterminacy of our reality, and a sort of description that is possible and appropriate only for limiting situations. Complexity is the general case, and indeterminacy is a real feature of the world. So the movement from the general (complex) to a special (simple) case amounts to a qualitative alteration in the logical character of explanation sought. To say that a "simple" mode of explanation is applicable is tantamount to saying that we can, in the given situation and for the purposes of analysis, forget about (or abstract away from) the real "complexity" of the phenomena we are dealing with.

It is useful to further refine the notion of complexity through making a distinction between ordinary and emergent (Funtowicz and Ravetz 1994a, 1994b). In effect this is a methodological as well as ontological distinction, relating to the sorts of concepts required for explanation of the phenomena under consideration. The ordinary complex systems typically display features akin to a simple teleology. Taking biological organisms as examples, much of their behavior can be explained in terms of a functional teleology, with systems "goals" such as growth and survival (cf. the theory of autopoiesis of Maturana and Varela (1980)). Thus they tend to maintain a dynamic stability against perturbations until pushed to such extremes that they are overwhelmed. By emergent complex systems, we mean by contrast those systems in which at least some of the elements possess individuality, along with some degree of intentionality, consciousness, foresight, purpose, symbolic representations, and morality. Our logic of explanation must then take account of the dimensions of intentionality and ethical reflection. Emergent complexity can display resiliency and self-transforming capabilities of a qualitatively different order from simple functional teleology. Indeed, continuous novelty may be considered as a characteristic property, and such systems frequently evolve through oscillating between hegemony and fragmentation (which is a conflict among different purposes or among plural attempted hegemonies). Economic and ecological change will, in this view, be characterized not primarily in terms of growth, but in terms of the emergence, maintenance, and violation of distinctive system identities over time (Castoriadis 1975; Serres 1982). Indeterminacy, and incomplete predictability are regarded positively—that is, as inherent characteristics of reality that we recognize in the world (Baudrillard 1983; Latouche 1984).

The phenomena of emergent complexity are amenable to scientific analysis along a variety of spatial-scales and time-scales, according to a rich variety of investigative methods. In post-normal science, thus, there is an admitted plurality of legitimate perspectives. We may think of scientific research as a process of having conversations within material reality. These conversations may, by circumstance and temperament, be impassioned and dispassionate, violent and amiable, assertive and receptive, hostile and loving. Objectivity (which we characterize here as the will to learn about the reality) and subjectivity (the specificity of one's knowing, feeling and desires) are intertwined. It can be insisted that as far as economics and environmental management is concerned, there are few if any cases of pure ordinarily complex systems. Any natural system that is of interest to us has properties that affect our welfare. Our scientific priorities as well as our descriptions of these systems and their relations, will reflect our interests, our ethical preoccupations, and our passions. Valuation analyses are concerned with the interests of future generations, and long-term modeling studies such as scenario simulations, must take account of this "interminacy"—for example by comparative scenarios, by sensitivity analyses, by recognition of institutional and cultural variety, and by comparisons of the sensitivity of policy analyses to alternative assumptions about social preferences and environmental dangers.

NATURAL CAPITAL AND COMPLEXITIES OF ECOLOGICAL DISTRIBUTION

In our conception of emergent complexity, the systems under study include awareness as a crucial dimension. Scientific methods and practice need to become reflexive, so as to take account of the researchers' own roles and places in social-political reality. A feature of contemporary ecological management problems is that, in scientific practice aimed at informing decision-making processes, we can almost never forget about the complexity—both social and biophysical—of the phenomena being dealt with. Moreover, we will argue, on social and ethical planes we should not want to neglect this complexity, for it is synonymous with the possibilities of love and passion. What we want to do now is suggest some key themes for making scientific practice self-aware in a policy-relevant way. First we look at the entwinement of scientific and social conflict dimensions in analysis of ecological distribution issues for the management of systems of natural capital (cf. O'Connor 1994d).

In public policy as traditionally understood, distribution refers to the requirement of resolving competing claims in society by different persons/groups on available or potentially available goods/services or money. Therefore distribution is, generally, a matter of social conflict. The resolution of this conflict depends on the decision rules defined by society, or broadly speaking the institutions and norms of each society, and agreements between them. The rise to prominence of environmental issues in the public policy domain, and the emergence of the discipline of ecological economics, signals the necessity to resolve politically not only economic distribution conflicts (money income, and marketable property), but also conflicts over ecological distribution.

By ecological distribution, we mean the social, spatial, and intertemporal patterns of access to the benefits obtainable from natural resources and from the environment as a life support system (IÖW 1994; Martinez-Alier and O'Connor 1996). The determinants of ecological distribution are in some respects natural (e.g., climate, topography, land quality, minerals, rainfall patterns), and in other respects social and technological. We can speak of ecological goods and bads. For example, ecological goods and services include renewable and non-renewable resources, the pollution assimilation capacities of the environment, species diversity, and amenity values of all sorts. Ecological bads are the risks and burdens falling on people as a result of pollution or exploitation, for example disturbed or destroyed ecosystems, interruptions to ecological life-support cycles, the dispersal of humanly and ecologically toxic substances in the environment.

It has become commonplace to refer to ecological goods and services as deriving from existing stocks of 'natural capital,' and increasing attention is, correspondingly, being placed on prudent management of and investment in the maintenance, regeneration, and enhancement of natural capital. This suggests an important role for physical, biological, and ecological sciences to furnish the knowledge base for this management. However, the extension of scientific and management concerns from the domain of produced national capital and the benefits (flows of goods and services) that can be obtained from them, to the much larger domain of *natural* or *ecological* capitals, brings some important changes of emphasis. The focus on economic and ecological sustainability implies a shift in focus from expansion of a commodity production vector (GDP growth) to the reproduction and resiliency of our planetary 'system of natural capitals' (Daly 1994; O'Connor 1994a). Whereas economic commodity production involves instrumental exploitation of an "external" environment as source and site of activity, the "side-effects" of commodity production and consumption are uncontrolled ramifications through the entire biosphere, emerging only over long periods of time and across widely dispersed spatial domains.

The scientific uncertainties combined with political choice requirements translate into indeterminacies of cost-benefit incidence. It becomes extremely difficult to estimate with any reliability the incidence across societies (present and future) of ecological costs and benefits of different resource management actions. Although the materials associated with environmental change (such as pollution discharges) are measurable in physical terms like volume, weight, concentration, or quantified in some respects such as area of forest, we remain a long way removed from a full specification of the services actually or potentially furnished in support of economic or non-human life. For example, it is not possible to describe exhaustively or to evaluate quantitatively the eventual significance in human welfare terms or in biodiversity terms, of a destroyed forest ecosystem, or of changes in rainfall patterns that may result from deforestation. A *fortiori* it is impossible to predict with any certainty, or to quantify in monetary terms, the severity of possible small and large-scale climate and (perhaps) ocean current changes relating to enhanced greenhouse gas emissions. For ecological goods and bads, the identities of the relevant agents and interested parties (the respective producers and receivers) are often unclear, and access or imposition is not well governed by established norms—for example people suffering from health problems induced by or aggravated by urban pollution or carcinogenic substances, or future generations that may be affected by accumulation of toxic wastes.

EPISTEMOLOGICAL AND SOCIAL BASIS FOR MANAGING ENVIRONMENTAL UNCERTAINTY

Environmental problems display a variety of features of uncertainty, irreversibility and complexity. The interaction between these three elements constitutes, as Vercelli (1995) has observed, an "explosive mix" for decision making in environmental economics. This implies a reversal of the generally held view in economics towards decision making, moving away from "substantive rationality" where decisions are made by reference to calculated outcomes or statistically expected outcomes, towards some sort of "procedural rationality" which acknowledges the three features mentioned above. In order to make plain the way that uncertainty enters both as a problem of knowledge (epistemology) and as a problem for decision making (rationality), we examine briefly the limits of the stochastic (probabilistic) environmental decision making approaches relying on Bayesian theory. Being based rigidly upon a substantive rationality hypothesis, such an approach cannot really take into consideration environmental uncertainty. This critique establishes the rationale for the approaches that we will propose in later sections, for the use of scientific knowledge in decision-making analyses based upon the idea of procedural rationality.

The distinction between substantive rationality and procedural rationality has its origins in the work of Herbert Simon (1976, 1982). In the case of substantive rationality, the concept of rational choice refers exclusively to the results (or expected outcomes) of the choice, independently of the manner in which the decision is made. In the case of procedural rationality, the concept or norm of rational behavior refers to the decision-making process itself. The dominant theories of rational decision making in economics are variants of substantive rationality, typically formulations of "optimal choice under constraint" (Favereau 1989). For the most part these refer to money values or individual utility associated with possible outcomes, the emphasis being either on individual choice (consumer or firm) or on a 'social choice function' that defines the way in which trade-offs are assessed between individuals. Then, as an extension to situations of *risk*, the same choice paradigm may be elaborated in terms of constrained maximization of expected values of outcomes based on application of probability theory. The avowed intention of the 'risk analysis' approaches has been to represent real-world situations where incomplete information on outcomes is an important feature. However, the sole change is that, instead of being associated with a unique certain outcome, each possible action is now associated with a known distribution of potential outcomes. The decision-making task is converted into making a decision (selecting an action) whose outcome probability distribution is, in some statistically defined sense, judged preferable. In the simplest versions of Bayesian decision theory, for example, it is assumed that the decision-making agents know the probability distribution for the complete set of possible outcomes, and that they act to maximize an "expected value" of the outcome. These are very strong assumptions, and obviously open to criticism. In a relaxation of the informational assumption, it may be proposed that, rather than knowing all probability distributions, the decision maker makes a *subjective* estimate of probabilities attaching to each possible outcome. These subjective probabilities may differ from the true (objective) probabilities, and this discrepancy is seen as introducing the possibility of learning through time, following Bayesian decision rules.

Proceeding from this reference point, a typology of uncertainty can be made according to two criteria, the first relating to the supposed probability distributions of events, and the second to the reliability or confidence placed in the probabilistic knowledge propositions. As suggested in Figure 12.2, we can establish a classification from certainty through to what Keynes (1921) and Shackle (1955, 1969) refer to as near-ignorance: " we simply do not know". In what sense do we not know? The dimension of events in time becomes critical here. Ecosystem changes are largely irreversible, and continue to unfold through long periods of time, with a complex enchainment of interactions (cf. Morin 1980). Strictly speaking, probabilistic calculus applies only to events whose occurrence is random within the defined structure of outcome possibilities. The Bayesian expected-value-maximization decision theory thus adheres to a version of substantive rationality, where the Laplacian ideal of a knowable future reality is maintained in the modified sense of the proposition that there is a "right probability distribution" towards which economic agents might converge as a learning process. But, in the view of emergent complexity, the spectrum of future environmental effects unfolding over space and time is not specifiable in advance, and a probability distribution cannot meaningfully be identified. It is not that the probabilities are unknown or badly estimated; rather they are unknowable for the fundamental reason that they do not exist and will never exist to be known. This is where irreversibility, uncertainty, and complexity make an explosive mix. We must understand decisions in the sense that ecological-social-economic histories are being made and understood within an emergent process in time.

Under such circumstances, representation of a choice problem "as if" it involves expected value maximization (money value, individual utility, or a social welfare function) based on subjective probabilities constitutes an *a priori* theoretical straitjacket. This leads to an oxymoron. While in a purely abstract sense, the Bayesian representation maintains a form of substantive rationality — that is, choices are justified by reference to information (or postulated information) about the outcomes of the available choices—in practice the employment of the Bayesian approach amounts to adoption of an "empty box". Depending on the subjective probabilities and states of the world incorporated into

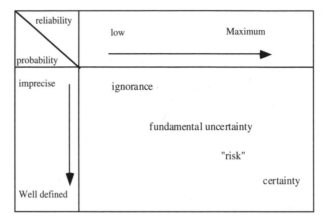

Figure 12.2. Modalities of uncertainty (adapted from Froger and Zyla 1996; Faucheux; Froger 1995).

the calculations, the procedure may serve to legitimate decisions that are substantially arbitrary. The actual outcomes unfolding in time may bear little connection with the expected values. Seen in this light, employing Bayesian calculations to guide decision-making amounts to an arbitrary choice of decision-making form, ironically masquerading as a substantive rationality.

In effect, 'expected-value maximization' involves gambling on a *risky* situation, where future generations (as well as members of current societies) are inescapably made participants in the gamble. Are those taking the decisions justified in imposing the gamble? As Perrings (1991) and Howarth (1996) have commented, when it is known that an action may cause profound and irreversible environmental damage that would permanently reduce the welfare prospects of future generations, it may be deemed unethical to impose that gamble. To act as if event probabilities were known amounts to exposing future generations to extreme dangers on the basis of rather arbitrary arithmetic. Examples are some cost-benefit analyses of new technologies making use of supposed statistical estimates of probabilities of serious accidents as with nuclear reactors or radioactive waste disposal, or with genetically modified organisms (for critical discussions see, for example, Funtowicz and Ravetz 1990, 1994c; Wills 1994).

For many economists, those who are often uncomfortable with making explicit distributional choices, the gamble is most easily justified if the decision-maker (or group) is in a position to insure all participants against adverse possible outcomes. But this may be out of the question if some outcomes, of unknown probability, may have a crucial and irreversible significance for the evolution of the system in question. So, we need an account of human rationality in economic and environmental policy decision making that gives weight, on the one hand, to the dimensions of our ignorance, and, on the other hand, to our ethical sentiments of joint responsibility.

Bringing ecological economics down to earth as a science of decision making means developing practices that give deep acceptance of fundamental uncertainty. This places ecological economics both socially and epistemologically on quite a different footing from old economics and from science oriented towards predictions. Our view of emergent complexity entails a rejection of historical and ontological determinism. There is no question of a complete specification of possible outcomes of human actions in their ecological setting. The question of what will constitute a satisfactory collective decision-making procedure will not depend on eliminating the uncertainties and dangers, nor masking over them. It will have more to do with how the risks are identified, discussed, and shared along the way—that is, with how agreements and compromises are reached, and how fears and losses are acknowledged and respected. This touches on questions of political legitimacy (e.g., van der Straaten 1993, 1996; Godard 1996) which we note but do not discuss in detail here. What we do want to emphasize is that the social acceptability of particular choices or proposals will depend very much on how the processes of scientific research and of decision making are conducted, and also on how people perceive the *fairness* of both the process and the outcomes of deciding the distribution of burdens, sacrifices, losses, and opportunities. So scientific research for sustainability must be planned and carried out in close relation with the emerging institutional frameworks for environmental policy formation and decision making.

We will now develop this perspective by discussing, its application to the selecting of priorities and standards in ecological and economic sustainability policies. These relate notably to matters of ecosystem conservation, maintenance of habitat quality (noise, toxicity, resilience), and provisions for renewable resource use within limits of regeneration capacity, etc. Then we will present a simple heuristic tool, the 'sustainability tree', designed to display the inter-relationships between different dimensions of sustainability decision-making and the specific criteria relating to each dimension. This furnishes an operating framework for employing procedural rationality to help decision-making for sustainability.

SUSTAINABILITY NORMS, PROCEDURAL RATIONALITY, AND POST-NORMAL SCIENCE

Sustainable development is now widely proclaimed as an objective of public policy, of environmental pressure groups, and even of many business enterprises. The term itself, however, evokes a diversity of objectives, or possible sub-goals, that are more or less difficult to reconcile to each other (Norgaard 1994). A straightforward procedure for an environmental decision-making context, one that for many people seems like common sense, may thus be described in the following terms: the implementation of *procedural rationality aimed at sustainability* must proceed through supplementing the general but non-measurable objective of sustainability with a set of intermediate objectives or intermediate sub-goals whose achievement (or not) can be observed and measured. The operational requirement is to identify an adequate set of these intermediate sub-goals, together with appropriate means of measuring and achieving progress towards them. It may be assumed that, generally speaking, these sub-goals may be *irreducible* in the sense that they define a situation of multiple decision criteria all of which must be considered simultaneously. Given the incommensurability of sub-goals for reasons of incommensurability, (e.g., based on distinct ethical or scientific premises), the decision-makers or decision making bodies are not in a position to solve the decision problem in the sense of an optimal choice. Rather, they must assess movements towards or in contradiction with the different intermediate sub-goals without being able to reduce the trade-offs to a common *numéraire*. The decision-making task is to search for and implement a course of action that is felt to be satisfactory taking into account the variety of economic, social, ecological, and other imperatives. This corresponds to a variant of Simon's 'satisfying principle'.

It has become commonplace to consider concerns for sustainability under the three broad headings of economic, social, and ecological. This distinction, which for the sake of exposition constitutes our primary sub-goal layer, refers partly to the nature of the system or feature being "sustained", but more particularly to the sort of concepts or units used in the description. In our view of emergent complexity, the three dimensions are, at root, inseparable. For example, the *economic* domain of commodity production and consumption can be deemed part of the *social* domain of activities establishing and renewing relationships and institutional forms; and the *social* category includes culture which bears on the ways that features of the *natural* world are classified and appraised. In both physical and cultural terms, the diverse features of the natural world are heterogeneous and incommensurate—for example appraisal of dangers associated with nuclear power cannot easily be placed on the same ethical, scientific or monetary planes as problems of NO_x emissions from thermal power stations.

The determination of appropriate environmental standards is often argued to be largely a matter of scientific research and its application. However, while scientific inputs are essential, there are irreducible social and political dimensions as well. The physical and biological sciences inform us about the world, and about the constraints and possibilities for a sustainable development: that is, they help us determine what is or may be feasible, and what is not. But such information merely sets the stage for the real policy process, which must respond to the question: How do we choose among the various particular economic and ecological outcomes that might be feasible within the framework of long-term sustainable activity?

All environmental measurements are subject to uncertainties of various intensities and types (Funtowicz and Ravetz 1990). These uncertainties augment the problems with commensurability—which show up in difficulties with making meaningful aggregation of different sorts of physical quantities and properties expressed in a variety of units. If emissions of CO_2 diminish while those of SO_2 rise, how can one decide whether the state of the environment has improved, got worse, or stayed the same? No single *numeraire* can capture the diversity of perspectives and valuations that are present in any issue concerning the environment (O'Neill 1993). People and groups may have commitments about their environment that are literally "beyond price", and in those cases attempts at quantification can be profoundly misleading (Funtowicz and Ravetz 1994b; Vadnjal and O'Connor 1994). In such cases, effective resolution of social conflicts becomes, in part, a matter of empathy and grief (O'Connor 1994d).

Without strong social commitments, there is no way that respect of principles or specific substance of ecological sustainability can be assured. This is one reason why, in our view, the environmental standards ought to be arrived at through a public participation process involving a wide range of social interests. In our post-normal science of emergent complexity, the decision process will thus have to conform to a sort of collective procedural rationality. Decision making and social evaluation takes place through an iterative process of identifying trade-offs and compromises with multiple criteria, ending up with a solution that is satisfactory in terms of economic, social, and ecological imperatives (Faucheux, Froger, and Munda 1994a, 1994b)—or, in other terms, which respects the actual distribution of economic and social power (see Martinez-Alier and O'Connor 1996). As Rittel (1982) suggests, in this process an analyst is more like a "midwife of problems" than a provider of tidy solutions. Decision making can be understood as an argumentative process, "one of raising questions and issues towards which you can assume different positions, and with evidence gathered and arguments built for and against these different positions (ibid.). Natural resource use and ecosystem management and conservation policies are, at root, matters of collective social choice that cannot be resolved by individualistic approaches to valuation, choice and resource ownership. Effective sustainability policy depends on putting in place political and communal processes for deciding on the mix of economic, community, and environmental interests, functions, and purposes that are to be fostered and sustained.

MULTI-CRITERIA DECISION ANALYSIS AND THE
SUSTAINABILITY TREE

Implementation of a procedural rationality implies, as we have said, the replacement of the global objective—in this case sustainable development or sustainability—with sub-goals that are amenable to measure and that, as such, can be considered in conjunction with each other. These primary sub-goals can be further characterized in terms of "intermediate sub-goals" in the form of standards or norms to be attained. A large variety of such sub-goals may be proposed. However these are not fixed immutably. They represent reference points to be worked with in an ongoing collective decision-making process.

The question is, how to bring together these multiple considerations represented by the sub-goals and their associated measures, and the attendant conflicts and incertitudes. In some situations, it may be practicable to define a linear sequence, where at each stage the concern would be to identify a "satisfactory" course of action according to an individual sub-goal, prior to considering the next policy sub-goal in the sequence. This is likely to be a workable approach where the goals are relatively weakly coupled and are not strongly antagonistic to each other. More typically, however, difficulties with simultaneous achievement of all sub-goals may be identified. Multi-criteria decision aid methodology, by definition, makes no *a priori* assumptions about the possibility (or not) of trade-offs between different dimensions or sub-goal achievements (Munda 1993; Munda, Nijkamp, and Rietveld 1995). In this respect, such methodologies aim to provide insight into the nature of the conflicts and the choices that, implicitly or explicitly, will have to be resolved through time. This can help the process of negotiated compromises in multi-group situations, so increasing the transparency of the decision process (Froger and Munda 1994).

We restrict our present discussion to examples of non-monetary 'indicators for sustainability' relating to economic and ecological dimensions, with measures using energy-based valuation techniques (see for example Slesser 1978; O'Connor 1991; Peet 1992; Faucheux 1994). Discussion should, in principle, be extended to consideration of other physical indicators such as direct and indirect needs of defined economic production and consumption processes for materials, land, water, or atmospheric space (as inputs, sites, or waste receptacles), and also to social dimensions (see for example Schultink 1992; O'Connor and Martinez-Alier 1996).

Work in ecological economics with energy-based measures proceeds on two quite different methodological levels. The first level relates to conceptual insights, and the principles of construction and use of generic measures characterizing economic and ecological systems, and their interactions, obtained on the basis of energy stock and flux accounting with defined thermodynamic potentials (enthalpy, entropy, free energy, essergy, etc.). The second level, is analytic and quantitative modeling work using an energetic *numeraire*, commonly known as applied energy analysis. The laws of thermodynamics furnish the basis for 'energy accounting' for exchanges between economic and ecological processes, and for quantitative analysis of the transformations (energy storages, conversions, dissipations) taking place within these processes.

(a) Considering energy inflows, the sources of energy in forms useful for economic purposes are limited in total availability to the quantities furnished exogenously on a flow basis as self-renewing fluxes (solar radiation, tides, geothermal heat, etc.), and the accessible stocks of fossil fuels and fission materials. Biomass may be considered as a dynamically renewable storage of solar energy. Energy analysis thus allows us to define opportunity costs, in energetic units, of exploitation of these stock and flux energy resources.

(b) Energy outflows from a given economic system to its environment may, depending on the system definition, be by-products or waste energy from the standpoint of the system or an output obtained purposefully for use outside that system. The physical conservation laws mean that mass and energy measures can always be used, in principle, for a systematic accounting of waste flows. In practice, this accounting can be quite an onerous task, due to the physical and chemical variety of these outflows and also to the fact that they are generally unwanted by-products.

(c) Thermodynamics also permits measures of physical transformations taking place within any chosen system. Any sector of commodity production, or household consumption, or an economy as a whole, can be considered as a transformation process in this sense.

In all three of these categories, one of the most valuable methodological functions of thermodynamic analysis is that it furnishes an input to economy-ecosystem modeling enabling it to "hold on to reality" in some clear-cut way (e.g., through incorporation of the physical conservation principles in description of transformation process or system constraints). At the same time, however, specific propositions about the significant features of such evolutions are embodied in any particular analytical paradigm or model, whether dealing with economic or ecological systems or both. We now illustrate by constructing a sustainability tree as a multi-criteria decision aid supporting a procedural rationality, and identifying the roles played by energy-based indicators for sustainability within the overall procedure. In the first phase, we build a static decision tree, representing a moment of analysis where the energy indicators are taken into consideration simultaneously. For illustration, in a simple way, we mention three energetic indicators, one corresponding to each of the categories above.

1. Primary energy requirements of a modern economy. Free (thermodynamically available) energy is necessary as an inflow to sustain all economic

(as well as ecological) production and self-maintenance processes. So the environmental sources of energy may be considered a category of 'critical natural capital' in the sense defined by Daly (1994) and others. It is crucial to consider the spatial distribution of energy availability as well as the temporal dimensions of depletion and renewability (Victor et al. 1996). Analyses may then be carried out by considering first of all the global constraints on energy availability, looking first at the biosphere as a single system, and thereafter at desired economic and ecological systems at any level of disaggregation based on defining spatial or organizational boundaries (e.g., nations or regions). For evaluation of opportunity costs, different types of energy must be aggregated in a coherent way. One method is *embodied energy analysis*, which aggregates direct and indirect energy requirements for a given economic output in a defined energy *numéraire*. If, for example, we use "solar energy equivalents" for embodied energy (that is, Odum's eMergy analysis conventions; see Faucheux and Pillet 1994), we can define for a national economy, an energy resources intermediate sub-goal called the:

National eMergy Surplus (NES). The National eMergy Surplus (NES), for a given time period, is defined as the difference between the amount of eMergy produced with natural resources from within the country, and the amount of eMergy consumed by this country's economy. If the concern is for natural resource self-sufficiency, then a criterion for national sustainability (ecologically sustainable development) is that NES $\geq$ 0, that is, extraction rates for primary energy resources (measured in eMergy units) not be higher than the overall renewal rate for energy natural resources. (For amplified discussions, see also Faucheux and O'Connor 1996).

2.   Pollution impacts on the environment. An accounting may be carried out using enthalpy or essergy (exergy) units of account, of the materials, heat, and work fluxes that are being discharged into an economic system's environment. On this basis, aggregate indicators may be constructed measuring the total enthalpy, essergy, or entropy flux associated with a given level and type of economic activity (for example, Ayres and Martinás 1995). These sorts of aggregate measures can provide some indicators about the potential scale of disruption, if comparisons are made of the orders of magnitude of energy and materials flows in the recipient systems. One example, relating to the objective of reducing pollution impact, is the:

Entropy degree. Let (Ne) be the actual entropy increase resulting from economic activity during a period of production, which is destined eventually to accrue as increased entropy in the environment. Let (Nm) be the minimum entropy production technologically possible (under the given state of knowledge) while achieving the same level of economic goods and services production.

The entropy degree for an economic system is defined as the difference (Ne - Nm). The higher is (Ne - Nm), the greater the impact on the environment per unit of production/consumption activity as measured in terms of induced environmental entropy increase, relative to what is technologically feasible. The reduction of Ne and/or of this difference, (Ne - Nm) —> 0, would, other things equal, signal a lessening of pollution impact through waste discharges.

3.   Technical efficiency of production. One important question is whether a given output level might be achievable with less total energy inputs, through technological changes or production efficiency improvements. Energy analyses based on first- and second-law considerations (energy conservation and irreversibility of entropy production) can be used to define a number of useful measures of thermodynamic efficiencies. Also, life-cycle analyses for capital and consumer products can be used to calculate direct and indirect energy (and other raw materials) requirements. Such analyses can be particularly important for integrated assessment at world, national, and sub-national region levels, of the impact of technological changes and of changes in social consumption patterns, for energy requirements and waste emissions of an economy. One example of such a measure, which is an indicator of the energy efficiency of an economic system, is the:

National Exergy Surplus. The National Exergy Surplus (NRS) is defined, for a given time period, as the difference between the exergy value (free content) of the inputs available for economic production, and the amount of exergy dissipated in a production or consumption process (or, depending on the system being analyzed, for the national economic system as a whole). For a time-trajectory of development to remain physically feasible, it is necessary to have NRS > 0, meaning that the economic system has available to it a surplus of exergy ("free energy") which may be used to undertake further expansion or development (that is, capital accumulation indicated in embodied exergy units). For a given level of energy resource input availability, technical improvements in energy use will mean a higher NRS and thus better growth and long-term economic sustainability prospects.

In a static decision-making perspective, the assessment of sustainability prospects is based on the simultaneous consideration of the various sub-goals, as is portrayed in Figure 12.3 (the sustainability tree). In terms of the three indicators we discuss, we would say that a nation satisfies designated requirements for sustainable development if:

1.   it produces an available eMergy surplus (NES 0);
2.   the quantity of entropy that it discharges tends towards the technologically minimum threshold (Ne - Nm)/Ne 0; and (3) it is characterized by a significant exergy surplus (NRS 0).

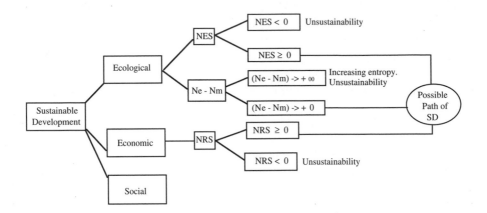

Figure 12.3. Sustainability tree for a "closed" economy in static perspective.

This exposition is merely illustrative; we do not suggest that these are the three best sustainability criteria! For example, it should be noted the entropy degree is a rather crude environmental pressure indicator, since the cumulative impacts of pollutants in ecological and other economic processes are not something that can, in general, be expressed in aggregate by well-behaved functions of a few variables, in this case, entropy increase (see O'Connor 1989, 1991, 1994c). Note also that, for a given nation, sustainability constraints may be relaxed through advantageous import-export relations (although clearly this sort of advantage cannot be obtained by all nations simultaneously). Imports of primary energy, for example, may permit a negative NES to be maintained, and may allow the NRS to remain positive despite high levels of energy consumption within the economy. Finally, while we have given examples of energy-based ecological-economic interface indicators measuring on the one hand aggregate economic system activity with respect to environmental constraints (NES, NRS) and environmental pressures due to a given level of economic activity (Ne and the difference Ne - Nm), it would be equally important to include social dimensions such as population and consumption patterns along with indicators of ecological distribution (see O'Connor and Martinez-Alier 1996).

The next issue to consider in our procedural rationality is the time dimension of progress towards sustainability sub-goals. Here we adopt a real-time dynamic perspective on prospects for a sustainable development. For example, there may be possibilities of technological progress, and of changes in production methods and changes in consumption patterns that would relieve pressures on natural resources and the environment and shift to greater reliance on

renewable environmental resources and life-support services. When we introduce these real-time evolutionary considerations into the sustainability tree,
we portray *a sequential and iterative appraisal process* which suggests possible policy-trajectories for implementing a sustainable development. First
we consider the global objective (sustainable development) which is to be appraised in terms of the three classes of sub-goals, ecological, economic and
social. Supposing that some of the chosen indicator levels are judged to be
unsatisfactory, policies to pursue a transition from the unsustainable towards a
long-term sustainable pattern of economic activity may be implemented. Such
a transition is not immediate, and the implementation of pro-sustainability
policies implies an iterative procedure with economic, technological, and ecological change over time.

We represent this iterative process by the decision and evaluation loops in
Figure 12.4 (adapted from Faucheux, Froger, and Munda 1994a, 1994b). For
example, technological progress may offer new possibilities for a country to
reach a sustainable production and consumption trajectory (at least under some
circumstances), yielding improvements relative to an initial situation where
the indicators have "unsatisfactory" levels. Technological improvements may
help alleviate a negative NES through improving efficiency of primary energy
use; or may improve a bad waste-entropy indicator (Ne - Nm) or a low NRS
through improving efficiency of energy use within the economy.

The dynamic sustainability tree portrays, in a schematic way, the application of two key characteristics of our procedural rationality: the identification
and appraisal of sub-goals, and the satisfying principle, worked with iteratively
through time. The framework does not give a method to solve a policy design
or choice problem in an optimizing manner. Rather, it is a conceptual tool to
help the decision making, through allowing information of a wide variety of
types to be brought together in an orderly and structured way. Constraints and
trade-offs measured in biophysical terms (such as energetic terms-of-trade, for
example) can furnish a backdrop for the analysis of social conflicts relating to
inequalities of access to natural resources and environmental benefits. In this
way too, the "social" is articulated to the "natural".

Numerous further amplifications of this perspective are possible. For example, in a simulation modeling framework, the decision maker can test different model trajectories exploring sustainable development policies and their effects under alternative assumptions about natural resource availability, population growth, technological change possibilities and consumer patterns, and environmental sensitivity to pollution and other stresses. The ECCO modeling
methodology (Slesser et al. 1994; Méral, Schembri, and Zyla 1994) is one example of such a technique, where the model user can explore scenarios in interactive and iterative ways. The modeling work by Duchin and Lange (1994)

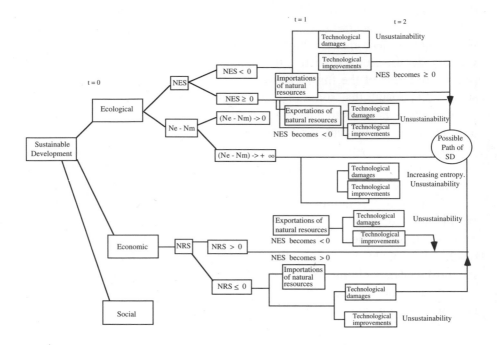

Figure 12.4. Sustainability tree in a dynamic perspective.

using dynamic Leontief-style input-output analyses to explore technological feasibility and world-regional implications of the Brundtland Report's sustainable development vision, is another. Exploration of unequal ecological exchange in terms of direct and indirect dependence of each nation's or region's production and consumption on land, energy, atmosphere and materials from other countries would be yet another.

The account in terms of procedural rationality is completed by the identification of procedures for appraisal of priorities in the case of non-achievement of several sub-goals. These may be real-time political processes (formalized or not), or specific analytical methods conceived as decision aids. For example Faucheux, Froger, and Munda (1994a, 1994b) explain how "fuzzy set" multi-criteria decision analysis (MCDA) can be used as a complementary tool to the dynamic sustainability tree. By incorporating veto criteria (minimum standards) as well as satisfying standards, it is possible to give a characterization of scenario outcomes as "near" or "far" from sustainability. Fuzzy set MCDA can also be used as a type of sensitivity analysis for policy prioritization depending on the levels decided for veto and satisfaction standards, and on the relative weightings given to different sub-goals.

CONCLUSION

Emergent complexity provides, we have suggested, a coherent and rich episte-mological framework through which ecological economics practice can tran-scend the restrictions imposed by the traditional disciplinary constraints of eco-nomics. The study of emergent complex systems necessarily cuts across tradi-tional scholarly disciplines. It is impossible to have an effective process inves-tigating problems of emergent complexity, where scientific understanding, so-cial goals, politics, and ethics are intertwined, while remaining within the con-fines of a single discipline or analytical paradigm. Our perspective on emer-gent complex systems allows that those aspects of economic activity that do resemble the behavior of atoms or steam engines, etc. can be studied along the "lower" dimensions of the total system. Equally, those aspects which involve structure and interactions among elements making up a functioning whole, (e.g., biological and ecological organization and intersectoral economic structure), are mapped in the middle dimensions, corresponding to ordinary complexity. But finally, those involving policy, where purposes, awareness, uncertainties, and ethics are involved, are recognized as belonging to the higher, emergent di-mensions. Work with the lower and middle dimensions of analysis must be grounded in a reflexive awareness of the emergent social processes that determine judgments of pertinence and urgency, and that contribute decisively to the ways that ecologi-cal and economic systems evolve and change.

Adoption of any single method in exclusion restricts the focus of research to a subset of the pertinent dimensions of enquiry. This is not a bad thing in itself. In this chapter, however, we have tried to emphasize how analyses along differ-ent dimensions of emergent complexity can be complementary, and mutually enriching. In this way, the principle of dialogue, expressed in post-normal science in relation to the policy stakeholders in an issue, applies as well for the disciplinary stakeholders, be they natural or social scientists, or decision makers in the policy process itself. The theory of emergent complex systems, locating each disciplinary approach within its appropriate dimensions, enables all of them to gain perspective, and thereby contribute to a genuine integration of knowledge.

ACKNOWLEDGMENTS

This chapter synthesizes research work carried out individually and jointly by the several authors. Some of it is a product of Research Project CT92-0084 undertaken in 1992–1994 on Application of Non-Monetary Procedures of Eco-nomic Valuation for Managing a Sustainable Development, funded by the Com-mission for the European Communities' DG-XII, and led by the C3E in Paris with participation by the Centre for Human Ecology at the University of

Edinburgh (Scotland), the Department of Economics and Economic History at the Autonomous University of Barcelona (Spain), and the Faculty of Economics at the University of Limburg (Netherlands). A full report on this research is forthcoming (Faucheux and O'Connor 1996). We thank colleagues at all these institutions, the two paper referees, and others who have provided hospitality in the spirit of scientific community.

REFERENCES

Ayres, R. U. and K. Martinas. 1995. Waste potential entropy: The ultimate ecotoxic? *Economie Appliquée* XLVIII No.2: 95–120.

Baudrillard, J. 1983. Les Stratégies Fatales. Paris: Grasset.

Castoriadis, C. 1975. L'Institution imaginaire de la société. Paris: Seuil.

Daly, H. 1994. Operationalizing Sustainable Development by Investing in Natural Capital. In Investing in Natural Capital: The Ecological Economics Approach to Sustainability, eds. A.-M. Jansson, M. Hammer, C. Folke, and R. Costanza. Washington DC: Island Press.

Duchin, F. and G. M. Lange. 1994. The Future of the Environment: Ecological Economics and Technological Change. New York: Oxford University Press.

Faucheux, S. 1994. Energy analysis and sustainable development. In Valuing the Environment: Methodological and Measurement Issues. ed R. Pethig. New York: Kluwer.

Faucheux, S. and G. Froger. 1995. Decision-making under environmental uncertainty. *Ecological Economics* 15 (forthcoming).

Faucheux, S., G. Froger, and G. Munda. 1994a. An Application of Multicriteria Decision Aid: the Sustainability Tree. Cahier du C3E, E, n° 94-19. Paris. Université de Paris I.

Faucheux, S., G. Froger, and G. Munda. 1994b. Des Outils d'Aide à la Décision pour la Multidimensionnalité Systémique: Une Application au Développement Durable. *Revue Internationale de Systémique* 8 (No.4-5): 495–517.

Faucheux, S. and M. O'Connor. eds. 1996. Valuation for Sustainable Development: Methods and Policy Indicators. Edward Elgar, Aldershot.

Favereau, O. 1989. Valeur d'option et flexibilité: de la rationalité substancielle à la rationalité procédurale. In Flexibilité, information et décision, eds. P. Cohendet, P. Llerena. Paris: Economica.

Froger, G. and G. Munda. 1994. Methodology for Decision Support: Procedural Rationality and Multicriteria Decision Aid. Cahiers du C3E, n° 94-20. Paris: Université de Paris I.

Froger, G. and E. Zyla. 1996. Decision-making for sustainable development. forthcoming In Sustainable Development: Concepts, Rationalities and Strategies, eds. S. Faucheux, M. O'Connor, J. van der Straaten. Dordrecht: Kluwer.

Funtowicz, S. O. and J. R. Ravetz. 1990. Uncertainty and Quality in Science for Policy. Dordrecht: Kluwer.

Funtowicz, S. O. and J. R. Ravetz. A New Scientific Methodology for Global Environmental Issues. In Ecological Economics: The Science and Management of Sustainability, ed. R. Costanza. New York: Columbia University Press.

Funtowicz, S. O. and J. R. Ravetz. 1992. The Good, the True, and the Post-Modern. *Futures* 24(10): 963–976.

Funtowicz, S. O. and J. R. Ravetz. 1993. Science for the Post-Normal Age. *Futures* 25(7): 735–755.

Funtowicz, S. O. and J. R. Ravetz. 1994a. Emergent Complex Systems. *Futures* 26(6): 568–582.

Funtowicz, S. O. and J. R. Ravetz. 1994b. The Worth of a Songbird: Ecological economics as a Post-Normal Science. *Ecological Economics* 10: 197–207.

Funtowicz, S.O. and J. R. Ravetz. 1994c. Uncertainty and regulation. In Scientific-Technical Backgrounds for Biotechnology Regulations, eds. F. Campagnari et alii. Netherlands.

Godard, O. 1996. Sustainable development and legitimation process in controversial universe. In Sustainable Development: Concepts, Rationalities and Strategies, eds. S. Faucheux, M. O'Connor, J. van der Straaten. Dordrecht: Kluwer.

Hollings, C. S. 1994. Simplifying the complex: The paradigms of ecological function and structure. *Futures* 26(6): 598–609.

Howarth, R. 1996. Sustainability, uncertainty, and intergenerational fairness. In Sustainable Development: Concepts, Rationalities and Strategies, eds. S. Faucheux, M. O'Connor, J. van der Straaten Dordrecht: Kluwer.

IÖW 1994. Distributional conflicts as a constraint for national implementation and International Harmonisation of Environmental Policy. Report on EC Research Project CT92-0139. Institut für Ökologische Wirtschaftsforschung GmbH. Berlin.

Keynes, J. M. 1921. A treatise on probability. Reprint as The Collected Writing of J. M. Keynes. Vol.8, 1971. London: Macmillan.

Knight, F. H. 1921. Risk, Uncertainty and Profit. Boston, Mass: Houghton and Mifflin.

Laplace, P. S. 1795. A Philosophical Essay on Probabilities (English translation). New York: Dover.

Latouche, S. 1984. Le Procès de la Science Sociale. Paris: Anthropos.

Martinez-Alier, J. and M. O'Connor. 1996. Ecological and Economic Distributional Conflicts. In Getting Down to Earth: Practical Applications of Ecological Economics, eds. R. Costanza, O. Segura, and J. Martinez-Alier. Island Press.

Maturana, H. R., and F. Varela 1980. Autopoiesis and Cognition: The Realization of the Living. Dordrecht: Reidel.

Meral, P., P. Schembri, and E. Zyla. 1994. Technological Lock-in and Complex Dynamics: Lessons from the French Nuclear Energy Policy. *Revue Internationale de Systémique 8* (No.4-5): 469–494.

Morin, E. 1980. La Méthode II: La Vie de la Vie. Paris: Seuil.

Munda, G. 1993. Fuzzy Information in Multicriteria Environmental Evaluation Models. Ph.D Thesis. Amsterdam: Free University.

Munda, G., P. Nijkamp, and P. Rietveld. 1995. Monetary and Non-Monetary Evaluation Methods in Sustainable Development Planning. *Economie Appliquée* XLVIII (No.2): 143–160.

Norgaard, R. 1994. Development Betrayed: The end of Progress and a Coevolutionary Revisioning of the Future. London: Routledge.

O'Connor, M. 1989. Codependency and Indeterminacy: A critique of the theory of production. *Capitalism Nature Socialism* 1(3): 33–57.

O'Connor, M. 1991. Entropy, structure, and organizational change. *Ecological Economics* 3: 95–122.

O'Connor, M. 1994a. On the Misadventures of Capitalist Nature. Is Capitalism Sustainable? New York: Guilford.

O'Connor, M. 1994b. Complexity and Coevolution: Methodology for a positive treatment of indeterminacy. *Futures* 26(6): 610–615.

O'Connor, M. 1994c. Entropy, Liberty and Catastrophe: The Physics and Metaphysics of Waste Disposal. In Economics and Thermodynamics: New Perspectives on Economic Analysis, eds. P. Burley and J. Foster. Boston/Dordrecht/London: Kluwer.

O'Connor, M. 1994d. Thermodynamique, Complexité, et Codépendance écologique: La Science de la Joie et du Deuil. *Revue Internationale de Systémique* 8 (No.4-5): 397–424.

O'Connor, M. 1995. La Réciprocité Introuvable: *L'Utilitarisme de John Stuart Mill et la Recherche d'une Ethique pour la Soutenabilité. Economie Appliquée* XLVIII (No.2): 271–304.

O'Connor, M. and J. Martinez-Alier Ecological Distribution and Distributed Sustainability. In Sustainable Development: Concepts, Rationalities and Strategies, eds. S. Faucheux, M. O'Connor, J. van der Straaten. Dordrecht: Kluwer.

O'Neill, J. 1993. Ecology, Policy and Politics. London: Routledge.

Passet, R. 1979. L'économique et le vivant. Paris: Payot.

Peet, J. 1992. Energy and the Ecological Economics of Sustainability. Washington DC: Island Press.

Perrings, C. 1991. Reserved rationality and the precautionary principle: Technological change, time and uncertainty in environmental decision making. In Ecological Economics: The Science and Management of Sustainability, ed. Costanza R. New York: Columbia University Press.

Rittel, H. 1982. Systems Analysis of the First and Second Generations. In: Human and Energy Factors in Urban Planning, NATO Advanced Study Institutes Series, eds. P. Laconte, J. Gibson, and A. Rapaport. The Hague: Martinus Nijhoff.

Schneider, E. and J. J. Kay 1994. Complexity and Thermodynamics: Towards a new ecology. *Futures* 26(6): 626–647.

Schultink, G. 1992. Evaluation of Sustainable Development Alternatives: Relevant Concepts, Resource Assessment Approaches and Comparative Spatial Indicators. *International Journal of Environmental Studies* 41: 203–224.

Serres, M. 1982. Genèse, Paris: Grasset.

Shackle, G. L. S. 1955. Uncertainty in Economics. Cambridge: Cambridge University Press.

Shackle, G. L. S. 1969. Decision, Order and Time in Human Affairs, Cambridge: Cambridge University Press.

Simon, H. A. 1976. From Substantive to Procedural Rationality. In Methods and Appraisal in Economics, ed. S. J. Latsis Cambridge: Cambridge University Press.

Simon, H. A. 1982. Models of Bounded Rationality. Cambridge, Mass: MIT Press.

Slesser, M. 1978. Energy in the Economy. London: Macmillan.

Slesser, M., J. King, C. Revie, and D. Crane. 1994. Non-Monetary Indicators for Managing Sustainability, Research Report. Scotland: Centre for Human Ecology. University of Edinburgh.

Stengers I. 1987. Complexité. In D'une Science à l'Autre. ed. I. Stengers Paris: Seuil.

Vadnjal, D. and M. O'Connor 1994. What is the Value of Rangitoto Island? *Environmental Values* 3 (December): 369–380.

Van der Straaten, J. 1993. Sustainable development: An institutional approach. *Ecological Economics* 7: 203–222.

Van der Straaten, J. 1996. Sustainable Development and Public Policy. In Sustainable Development: Concepts, Rationalities and Strategies, eds. S. Faucheux, M. O'Connor, and J. van der Straaten Dordrecht: Kluwer.

Vercelli, A. 1995. From soft uncertainty to hard environmental uncertainty. *SEconomie Appliquée* XLVIII (No.2): 251–270.

Victor, P., J. E. Hanna, and A. Kubursi. 1996. How Strong is Weak Sustainability? In Sustainable Development: Concepts, Rationalities, Strategies, eds. S. Faucheux, M. O'Connor, and J. van der Straaten. Dordrecht: Kluwer.

13 INTEGRATING SPATIALLY EXPLICIT ECOLOGICAL AND ECONOMIC MODELS

Robert Costanza

University of Maryland Institute for Ecological Economics
Center for Environmental and Estuarine Studies
University of Maryland
Box 38, Solomons, MD 20688-0038

Chesapeake Biological Laboratory
Center for Environmental and Estuarine Studies
University of Maryland
Box 38, Solomons, MD 20688-0038

Lisa Wainger

University of Maryland Institute for Ecological Economics
Center for Environmental and Estuarine Studies
University of Maryland
Box 38, Solomons, MD 20688-0038

Chesapeake Biological Laboratory
Center for Environmental and Estuarine Studies
University of Maryland
Box 38, Solomons, MD 20688-0038

Nancy Bockstael

University of Maryland Institute for Ecological Economics
Center for Environmental and Estuarine Studies
University of Maryland
Box 38, Solomons, MD 20688-0038
Department of Agricultural and Resource Economics
University of Maryland
College Park, MD.20742

OVERVIEW

Understanding and modeling the dynamics of linked ecological and economic systems, ranging in size from the biosphere as a whole to regional landscapes to local agroecosystems, is critical for designing a sustainable future. But integrated ecological economic systems have so far received only very limited direct attention. Several current approaches may be relevant to this problem and a cooperative synthesis among ecologists, economists, mathematicians, computer scientists, and others is essential.

This chapter reviews: (1) some of the key issues surrounding the modeling of complex ecological economic systems; (2) current and proposed approaches to modeling linked ecological economic systems; (3) some key research questions and issues for further study; and (4) an ongoing practical example of integrated ecological economic modeling at the regional scale in the Patuxent River basin in Maryland.

INTRODUCTION

New understanding about system dynamics and predictability that has emerged from the study of complex systems is creating new tools for modeling interactions between human and natural systems. A range of techniques has become available through advances in computer speed and accessibility, and by implementing a broad, interdisciplinary systems view.

Systems are groups of interacting, interdependent parts linked together by exchanges of energy, matter, and information. *Complex* systems are characterized by:

1. Strong (usually nonlinear) interactions between the parts;
2. Complex feedback loops that make it difficult to distinguish cause from effect; and
3. Significant time and space lags, discontinuities, thresholds and limits; all resulting in
4. The inability to simply "add-up" or aggregate small-scale behavior to arrive at large-scale results (von Bertalanffy 1968; Rastetter et al. 1992).

Ecological and economic systems both independently exhibit these characteristics of complex systems. Taken together, linked ecological economic systems are devilishly complex.

While almost any subdivision of the universe can be thought of as a "system," modelers of systems usually look for boundaries that minimize the interaction between the system under study and the rest of the universe in order to make their job easier. The interactions between ecological and economic systems are many and strong. So, while splitting the world into separate economic and ecological systems is possible, it does not minimize interactions and is a poor choice of boundary.

Classical (or reductionist) scientific disciplines tend to dissect their subject into smaller and smaller isolated parts in an effort to reduce the problem to its essential elements. In order to allow the dissection of system components, it must be assumed that interactions and feedbacks between system elements are negligible or that the links are essentially linear so they can be added up to give the behavior of the whole (von Bertalanffy 1968). Complex systems violate the assumptions of reductionist techniques and therefore are not well understood using the perspective of classical science. In contrast, *systems analysis* is the scientific method applied across many disciplines, scales, resolutions, and system types in an integrative manner.

In economics, for example, a typical distinction is made between partial equilibrium analysis and general equilibrium analysis. In partial equilibrium analysis, a subsystem (a single market) is studied with the underlying assumption that there are no important feedback loops from other markets. In general equilibrium analysis, on the other hand, the totality of markets is studied in order to bring out the general interdependence in the economy. The large-scale, whole economy, general equilibrium effects are usually quite different from the sum of the constituent small-scale, partial equilibrium effects. Add to this the further complication that in reality "equilibrium" is never achieved, and one can begin to see the limitations of classical, reductionist science in understanding complex systems.

Economic and ecological analysis needs to shift away from implicit assumptions that eliminate links within and between economic and natural systems, because, due to the strength of the real world interactions between these components, failing to link them can cause severe misperceptions and indeed policy failures (Costanza 1987). Since reductionist thinking fails in the quest to understand complex systems, new concepts and methods must be devised.

To achieve a comprehensive understanding that is useful for modeling and prediction of linked ecological economic systems requires the synthesis and integration of several different conceptual frames. As Levins (1966) has described this search for robustness: "we attempt to treat the same problem with several alternative models each with different simplifications... Then, if these models, despite their different assumptions, lead to similar results we have what we call a robust theorem which is relatively free of the details of the model. Hence our truth is the intersection of independent lies."

Existing modeling approaches can be classified according to a number of criteria, including scale, resolution, generality, realism, and precision. The most useful approach within this spectrum of characteristics depends on the specific goals of the modeling exercise. We describe a few examples of how one might match model characteristics with several of the possible modeling goals relevant for ecological economic systems, and claim that a better appreciation of the range of possible model characteristics and goals can help to more optimally match characteristics and goals.

Complex systems analysis offers great potential for generating insights into the behavior of linked ecological economic systems. These insights will be needed to change the behavior of the human population towards a sustainable pattern, a pattern that works in synergy with the life-supporting ecosystems on which it depends. The next step in the evolution of ecological economic models is to fully integrate the two fields and not just transfer methods between them. Clark's (1976, 1981, 1985) bioeconomics work was the start of this recognition of the importance of linking the mutually interacting sub-parts. But much work remains to be done to bring the two fields and the technology that supports them to the point where their models can adequately interact. Transdisciplinary collaboration and cooperative synthesis among natural and social scientists and others will be essential (Norgaard 1989).

COMPUTERS AND MODELING

Until computers became available, the equations that described the dynamics of systems had to be solved analytically. This severely limited the level of complexity (as well as the resolution) of the systems that could be studied, and the complexity of the dynamics that could be studied for any particular system. Table 13.1 shows the limits of analytical methods in solving various classes of mathematical problems in general.

As Table 13.1 shows, only relatively simple linear systems of algebraic or differential equations can, in general, be solved analytically. The problem is that most complex, living systems (like economies and ecosystems) are decidedly *non-linear,* and efforts to approximate their *dynamics* with linear equations have been of only limited usefulness. In addition, complex systems often exhibit discontinuous and chaotic behavior (Rosser 1991) that can only be adequately represented with numerical methods and simulations using computers.

We differentiate here between the use of linear systems of equations to model complex system *dynamics* (which does not work well) versus the use of linear systems to understand system *structure* (which may work reasonably well). Integrating these views of structure and dynamics is a key item for research on complex ecological economic systems.

In recent years, computers have become not only faster, but also much more accessible. This has allowed researchers to develop methods to allow adaptive, evolutionary, dynamic solutions. For example, Holland and Miller (1991) describe how recent computer and machine learning (a form of artificial intelligence) advances have spawned "artificial adaptive agents," computer programs that can simulate evolution and acquire sophisticated behavioral patterns. In these programs, individual agents (processes, elements, pieces of computer code) in networks of interacting agents reproduce themselves in the next

Table 13.1. The Limits of Analytical Methods in Solving Mathematical Problems (after von Bertalanffy 1968). The thick solid line divides the range of problems that are solvable with analytical methods from those that are very difficult or impossible using analytical methods and require numerical methods and computers to solve. "Systems" problems are typically nonlinear and fall in the range that requires numerical methods. It should be noted that while some special problems that fall in the areas labeled "impossible" in the table are actually possible to solve using analytical methods (frequently requiring special tricks), in general one cannot depend on a solution being available. Computers have guaranteed that a solution can be found in all the cases listed in the table.

	Linear			Nonlinear		
Equations	One equation	Several equations	Many equations	One equation	Several equations	Many equations
Algebraic	Trivial	Easy	Difficult	Very Difficult	Very Difficult	Impossible
Ordinary differential	Easy	Difficult	Essentially Impossible	Very Difficult	Impossible	Impossible
Partial differential	Difficult	Essentially Impossible	Impossible	Impossible	Impossible	Impossible

time period based on some measure of their performance in the current time period. The system exhibits changing group behavior over time and mimics evolution. To exhibit this adaptive behavior, the actions of the agents must be valued, and the agents must act to increase this value over time. Algorithms like these can provide a realistic representation of ecological and economic processes.

Another useful technique is 'metamodeling,' in which more general models are developed from more detailed ones. Richard Cabe, Jason Shogren, and colleagues (1991) have developed this technique to link models of agricultural production and economic behavior that could not normally be used together because, for one, they run at different time and space scales. Their models, which cover the entire midwestern farm belt of the U.S., provide a method for a quick and cost-efficient evaluation of ecological economic policies.

Computer hardware advances such as CRAY supercomputers and Connection Machines (massively parallel supercomputers) facilitate the modeling of complex systems using advanced numerical computation algorithms (such as finite difference and finite element routines, cellular automata algorithms, and emerging methods that employ at least a modicum of artificial intelligence).

For example, parallel computers make high spatial resolution, regional and global ecological economic models computationally feasible (Costanza et al. 1990; Costanza and Maxwell 1991), and allow the types and resolution of evolutionary and metamodeling approaches to expand dramatically. These new capabilities, linked with a more realistic and pluralistic view of the various roles and limitations of models in understanding and decision making, can dramatically increase the effectiveness of modeling.

Purposes of Models

Models are analogous to maps. Like maps, they have many possible purposes and uses, and no one map or model is right for the entire range of uses (Levins 1966; Robinson 1991). It is inappropriate to think of models or maps as anything but crude (but in many cases absolutely essential) abstract representations of complex territory, whose usefulness can best be judged by their ability to help solve the navigational problems faced. Models are essential for policy evaluation, but are often also misused since there is "...the tendency to use such models as a means of legitimizing rather than informing policy decisions. By cloaking a policy decision in the ostensibly neutral aura of scientific forecasting, policy makers can deflect attention from the normative nature of that decision..." (Robinson 1993).

In the case of modeling ecological economic systems, purposes can range from developing simple conceptual models, in order to provide a general understanding of system behavior, to detailed realistic applications aimed at evaluating specific policy proposals. It is inappropriate to judge this whole range of models by the same criteria. At a minimum, the three criteria of *realism* (simulating system behavior in a qualitatively realistic way), *precision* (simulating behavior in a quantitatively precise way), and *generality* (representing a broad range of systems' behaviors with the same model) are necessary. Holling (1964) first described the fundamental trade-offs in modeling between these three criteria. Later Holling (1966) and Levins (1966) expanded and further applied this classification. No single model can maximize all three of these goals, and the choice of which objectives to pursue depends on the fundamental purposes of the model. Several examples in the literature of ecological and economic models demonstrate the various ways in which trade-offs are made between realism, precision, and generality.

High-Generality Conceptual Models

In striving for generality, models must give up some realism and/or precision. They can do this by simplifying relationships and/or reducing resolution. Simple linear and non-linear economic and ecological models tend to have high generality but low realism and low precision (Clark and Monroe 1975; Brown and Swierzbinski 1985; Kaitala and Pohjola 1988; Lines 1989, 1990b). Examples include Holling's "4-box" model (Holling 1987), the "ecological economy" model of Brown and Roughgarden (1992), most conceptual macroeconomic models (Keynes 1936; Lucas 1975), economic growth models (Solow 1956), and the "evolutionary games" approach. For example, the "ecological economy" model of Brown and Roughgarden (1992) contains only three state variables (labor, capital, and natural resources), and the relationships between these variables are highly idealized. But the purpose of the model was not to create high realism or precision, but rather to address some basic, general questions about the limits of economic systems in the context of their dependence on an ecological life support base.

High-Precision Analytical Models

Often, one wants high precision (quantitative correspondence between data and model) and is willing to sacrifice realism and generality. One strategy here is to keep resolution high, but to simplify relationships and deal with short time frames. Some models strive to strike a balance between mechanistic small-scale models, which trace small fluctuations in a system, and more general whole-system approaches that remove some of the noise from the signal but do not allow the modeler to trace the source of system changes. The alternative some ecologists have devised is to identify one or a few properties that characterize the system as a whole (Wulff and Ulanowicz 1989). For example, Hannon and Joiris (1987) used an economic input-output model to examine relationships between biotic and abiotic stocks in a marine ecosystem and found that this method allowed them to show the direct and indirect connection of any species to any other and to the external environment in this system at high precision (but low generality and realism). Also using input-output techniques, Duchin's (1988, 1992) aim was to direct development of industrial production systems to efficiently reduce and recycle waste in the manner of ecological systems. Large econometric models (Klein 1971) used for predicting short-run behavior of the economy belong to this class of models since they are constructed to fit existing data as closely as possible (at the sacrifice of generality and realism).

High-Realism Impact Analysis Models

When the goal is to develop realistic assessments of the behavior of specific complex systems, generality, and precision must be relaxed. High-realism models are concerned with accurately representing the underlying processes in a specific system, rather than precisely matching quantitative behavior or being generally applicable. Dynamic, non-linear, evolutionary systems models at moderate to high resolution generally fall into this category. Coastal physical-biological-chemical models (Wroblewski and Hofmann 1989) that are used to investigate nutrient fluxes and contain large amounts of site-specific data fall into the this category, as do micro models of behavior of particular business activities. Another example is Costanza et al.'s (1990) model of coastal landscape dynamics that included high spatial and temporal resolution and complex non-linear process dynamics. This model divided a coastal landscape into 1km^2 cells, each of which contained a process-based dynamic ecological simulation model. Flows of water, sediments, nutrients, and biomass from cell to cell across the landscape were linked with internal ecosystem dynamics to simulate long-term successional processes and responses to various human impacts in a very realistic way. But the model was very site-specific and of only moderate numerical precision.

Moderate-Generality and Moderate-Precision Indicator Models

In many types of systems modeling, the desired outcome is to accurately determine the overall magnitude and direction of change, trading off realism for some moderate amount of generality and precision. For example, aggregate measures of system performance such as standard GNP, environmentally adjusted net national product (or "green NNP"), which includes environmental costs (Mäler 1991), and indicators of ecosystem health (Costanza et al. 1992a) fit into this category. The microcosm systems employed by Taub (1989) allow some standardization for testing ecosystem responses and developing ecosystem performance indices. Taub (1987) notes, however, that many existing indicators of change in ecosystems are based on implicit ecological assumptions that have not been critically tested, either for their generality, realism, or precision.

SCALE AND HIERARCHY

In modeling complex systems, the issues of scale and hierarchy are central (O'Neill et al. 1989). Some claim that the natural world, the human species included, contains a convenient hierarchy of scales based on interaction-minimizing boundaries; scales ranging from atoms to molecules to cells to organs to organisms to populations to communities to ecosystems (including economic, and/or human dominated ecosystems) to bioregions to the global system and beyond. By studying the similarities and differences between different kinds of systems at different scales and resolutions, one might develop hypotheses and test them against other systems to explore their degree of generality and predictability.

The term "scale" in this context refers to both the resolution (spatial grain size, time step, or degree of complication of the model) and extent (in time, space, and number of components modeled) of the analysis. The process of scaling refers to the application of information or models developed at one scale to problems at other scales. In both ecology and economics, primary information and measurements are generally collected at relatively small scales (i.e., small plots in ecology, individuals or single firms in economics) and that information is then often used to build models at radically different scales (i.e., regional, national, or global). The process of scaling is directly tied to the problem of aggregation, (the process of adding or otherwise combining components), which in complex, non-linear, discontinuous systems (like ecological and economic systems), is far from a trivial problem (O'Neill and Rust 1979; Rastetter et al. 1992).

For example, in applied economics, basic data sets are usually derived from the national accounts, which contain data that are linearly aggregated over individuals, companies, or organizations. Sonnenschein (1974) and Debreu (1974) have shown that, unless one makes very strong and unrealistic assumptions about the individual units, the aggregate (large scale) relations between variables have no resemblance to the corresponding relations on the smaller scale.

Rastetter et al. (1992) describe and compare three basic methods for scaling that are applicable to complex systems. All of their methods are attempts to utilize information about the non-linear small-scale variability in the large-scale models. They list:

1. Partial transformations of the fine-scale mathematical relationships to coarse-scale using a statistical expectations operator that incorporates the fine-scale variability;
2. Partitioning or subdividing the system into smaller, more homogeneous parts (i.e., spatially explicit modeling); and
3. Calibration of the fine scale relationships to coarse scale data, when this data is available.

They go on to suggest a combination of these methods as the most effective overall method of scaling in complex systems.

A primary reason for aggregation error in scaling complex systems is the non-linear variability in the fine-scale phenomenon. For example, Rastetter et al. (1992) give a detailed example of scaling a relationship for individual leaf photosynthesis as a function of radiation and leaf efficiency to estimate the productivity of the entire forest canopy. Because of non-linear variability in the way individual leaves process light energy, one cannot simply use the fine-scale relationships among photosynthesis, radiation, and efficiency along with the average values for the entire forest to get total forest productivity without introducing significant aggregation error. One must somehow understand and incorporate this nonlinear fine-scale variability into the coarse-scale equations using some combination of the three methods mentioned above. Method 1 (statistical expectations) implies deriving new coarse-scale equations that incorporate the fine-scale variability. The problem is that incorporation of this variability often leads to equations that are extremely complex and cumbersome (Rastetter et al. 1992). Method 2 (partitioning) implies subdividing the forest into many relatively more homogenous levels or zones and applying the basic fine-scale equations for each partition. This requires a method for adjusting the parameters for each partition, a choice of the number of partitions (the resolution) and an understanding of the effects of the choice of resolution and parameters on the results. Method 3 (recalibration) implies simply recalibrating the fine-scale equations to coarse-scale data. It presupposes that coarse-scale data are available (as more than simply the aggregation of fine-scale data). In many important cases, however, this coarse-scale data is either extremely limited or is not available. Thus, while a judicious application of all three aggregation methods is necessary, from the perspective of complex systems modeling, the partitioning approach (Method 2) seems to hold particular promise, because it can take fullest advantage of emerging computer technologies and data bases.

From the scaling perspective, hierarchy theory is a potentially useful tool for partitioning systems in ways that minimize aggregation error. According to hierarchy theory, nature can be partitioned into "naturally occurring" levels that share similar time and space scales, and that interact with higher and lower levels in systematic ways. Each level in the hierarchy sees the higher levels as constraints and the lower levels as noise. For example, individual organisms see the ecosystem they inhabit as a slowly changing set of constraints and the operation of their component cells and organs is what matters most to them. However, Norton and Ulanowicz (1992) suggest that what appears to be "noise" at a lower level could be turned into significant perturbations on the higher level. This can happen when a critical mass of components participate in a "trend," a behavioral pattern, which affects the slower processes at the higher level. The rapid and extensive human uses of fossil fuels could be seen as such a trend, causing perturbations at the global atmospheric level, which might feed back and radically alter the framework of action at the lower level.

Shugart (1989) explains the relationship between scales: "Clearly, natural patterns in environmental constraints contribute substantially to the spatial pattern and temporal dynamics of particular ecosystems ... these patterns, especially temporal ones, may resonate with natural frequencies of plant growth forms (i.e., phenology and longevity) to amplify environmental patterns." The simplifying assumptions of hierarchy theory may ease the problem of scaling by providing a common (but somewhat generalized) set of rules that could be applied at any scale in the hierarchy.

FRACTALS AND CHAOS

The concept of fractals (Mandelbrot 1977) can be seen as another related approach to the problem of scaling, based on the fundamental principle of "self-similarity" between scales. This concept implies a regular and predictable relationship between the scale of measurement (here meaning the resolution of measurement) and the measured phenomenon. For example, the measured length of a coastline is an increasing function of the resolution at which it is measured. At higher resolutions, one can "see" and measure more of the small-scale bays and indentations in the coast and the total length measured increases.

The relationship between length and resolution usually follows a regular pattern that can be summarized in the following equation:

1. $$L = k s^{(1-D)}$$

where:

L = the length of the coastline or other "fractal" boundary
s = the size of the fundamental unit of measure or the resolution of the measurement
k = a scaling constant
D = the fractal dimension

Phenomenon that fit Equation 1 are said to be "self-similar" because as resolution is increased one perceives patterns at the smaller scale similar to those at the larger scale. This convenient "scaling rule" (Equation 1) has proven to be a very useful in describing many kinds of complex boundaries and behaviors (Mandelbrot 1983; Turner et al. 1989; Olsen and Schaffer 1990; Sugihara and May 1990; Milne 1991). One test of the principle of self-similarity is that it can applied to produce computer-generated shapes that have a decidedly natural and organic look to them (Mandelbrot 1977).

Certain non-linear dynamic systems models exhibit behaviors whose phase plots ($x(t)$ vs. $x(t-dt)$) are fractals. These "chaotic" attractors, as they are called, are one of four possible pure types of attractors that can be used to classify system dynamics. The other three are:

1. Point attractors (indicating stable, non-time varying behavior);
2. Periodic attractors (indicating periodic time behavior); and
3. Noisy attractors (indicating stochastic time behavior).

Real system behavior can be thought of as representing some combination of these four basic types.

The primary questions about the range of applicability of fractals and chaotic systems dynamics to the practical problems of modeling ecological economic systems are the influence of scale, resolution, and hierarchy on the mix of behaviors one observes in systems. This is a key problem for extrapolating from small scale experiments or simple theoretical models to practical applied models of ecological economic systems.

RESOLUTION AND PREDICTABILITY

The significant effects of non-linearities raise some interesting questions about the influence of resolution (including spatial, temporal, and component) on the performance of models, in particular their predictability. For example, the relationship between the degree of complication (the number of components included) and the predictability of models is an important input to model design. Hofmann (1991) discusses this concern in the context of scaling coastal models to the global scale. The difficulty of using aggregate models that integrate over many details of finer resolution models is that the aggregated models may not be able to represent biological processes on the space and time scales necessary. Hofmann suggests that coupled detailed models (where the output of one model becomes the input for another) may be a more practical method for scaling models to larger systems.

Costanza and Maxwell (1993) analyzed the relationship between spatial resolution and predictability and found that while increasing resolution provides more descriptive information about the patterns in data, it also increases the difficulty of accurately modeling those patterns. There may be limits to the predictability of natural phenomenon at particular resolutions, and "fractal-like" rules that determine how both "data" and "model" predictability change with resolution.

Predictability (Colwell 1974) measures the reduction in uncertainty about one variable given knowledge of others using categorical data. One can define spatial *auto-predictability* (P_a) as the reduction in uncertainty about the state of a pixel in a scene, given knowledge of the state of adjacent pixels in that scene, and spatial *cross-predictability* (P_c) as the reduction in uncertainty about the state of a pixel in a scene, given knowledge of the state of corresponding pixels in other scenes. (P_a) is a measure of the internal pattern in the data, while (P_c) is a measure of the ability of a model to represent that pattern.

Some limited testing of the relationship between resolution and predictability, (by resampling land use map data at different spatial resolutions) showed a strong linear relationship between the log of (Pa) and the log of resolution (measured as the number of pixels per square kilometer). This fractal-like characteristic of "self-similarity" with decreasing resolution implies that predictability, like the length of a coastline, may be best described using a unitless dimension that summarizes how it changes with resolution. One can define a "fractal predictability dimension" (D_p) in a manner analogous to the normal fractal dimension, that summarizes this relationship. D_p allows convenient scaling of predictability measurements taken at one resolution to others.

Cross-predictability (P_c) can be used for pattern matching and testing the fit between map scenes. In this sense it relates to the predictability of models versus the internal predictability in the data revealed by P_a. While P_a generally increases with increasing resolution (because more information is being included), P_c generally falls or remains stable (because it is easier to model aggregate results than fine grain ones). Thus we can define an optimal resolution for a particular modeling problem that balances the benefit in terms of increasing data predictability (P_a) as one increases resolution, with the cost of decreasing model predictability (P_c). Figure 13.1 shows this relationship in generalized form.

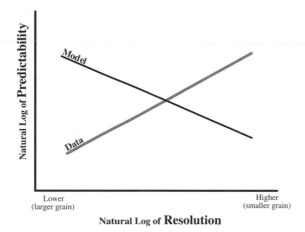

Figure 13.1. Hypothetical relationship between resolution and predictability of data and models, plotted on log-axes (from Costanza and Maxwell 1993). Data predictability is a measure of the internal pattern in the data (for example the degree to which the uncertainty about the state of landscape pixels is reduced by knowledge of the state adjacent pixels in the same map). Model predictability is a measure of the correspondence between data and models (for example the degree to which the uncertainty about the state of the pixels is reduced by knowledge of the corresponding state of pixels in model of the system). In general data predictability rises with increasing resolution (because more internal patterns are perceived) while model predictability falls (because it becomes more difficult to match the high-resolution patterns). Particular types of models and data sets would fall on different lines, and certain types of models would require certain types of data. An "optimal" resolution occurs where the data and models predictability lines intersect.

These results may be generalized to all forms of resolution (spatial, tempo-ral, and number of components) and may shed some interesting light on "cha-otic" behavior in systems. When looking across resolutions, chaos may be the low level of model predictability that occurs as a natural consequence of high resolution. Lowering model resolution can increase model predictability by averaging out some of the chaotic behavior, at the expense of losing detail about the phenomenon. For example, Sugihara and May (1990) found chaotic dynamics for measles epidemics at the level of individual cities, but more pre-dictable periodic dynamics for whole nations.

EVOLUTIONARY APPROACHES

In modeling the dynamics of complex systems it is impossible to ignore the discontinuities and surprises that often characterize these systems and the fact that they operate far from equilibrium in a state of constant adaptation to chang-ing conditions (Rosser 1991; Holland and Miller 1991; Lines 1990; Kay 1991). The paradigm of evolution has been broadly applied to both ecological and economic systems (Boulding 1981; Arthur 1988; Lindgren 1991; Maxwell and Costanza 1993) as a way of formalizing understanding of adaptation and learn-ing behaviors in non-equilibrium dynamic systems. The general evolutionary paradigm posits a mechanism for adaptation and learning in complex systems at any scale using three basic interacting processes:

1.   Information storage and transmission;
2.   Generation of new alternatives; and
3.   Selection of superior alternatives according to some performance criteria.

The evolutionary paradigm is different from the conventional optimization paradigm popular in economics in at least four important respects (Arthur 1988):

1.   Evolution is path dependent, meaning that the detailed history and dy-namics of the system are important;
2.   Evolution can achieve multiple equilibria;
3.   There is no guarantee that optimal efficiency or any other optimal per-formance will be achieved due in part to path dependence and sensitiv-ity to perturbations; and
4.   "Lock-in" (survival of the first rather than survival of the fittest) is pos-sible under conditions of increasing returns.

While, as Arthur (1988) notes "conventional economic theory is built largely on the assumption of diminishing returns on the margin (local negative feed-backs)" life itself can be characterized as a positive feedback, self-reinforcing, autocatalytic process (Kay 1991; Günther and Folke 1993), and we should expect increasing returns, lock-in, path dependence, multiple equilibria and sub-optimal efficiency to be the rule rather than the exception in economic and ecological systems.

Cultural vs. Genetic Evolution

In biological evolution, the information storage medium is the genes, the generation of new alternatives is by sexual recombination or genetic mutation, and selection is performed by nature according to a criteria of "fitness" based on reproductive success. The same *process* of change occurs in ecological, economic, and cultural systems, but the elements on which the process works are different. For example, in cultural evolution the storage medium is the culture (the oral tradition, books, film or other storage medium for passing on behavioral norms), the generation of new alternatives is through innovation by individual members or groups in the culture, and selection is again based on the reproductive success of the alternatives generated, but reproduction is carried out by the spread and copying of the behavior through the culture rather than biological reproduction. One may also talk of "economic" evolution, a subset of cultural evolution dealing with the generation, storage, and selection of alternative ways of producing things and allocating that which is produced. The field of "evolutionary economics" has grown up in the last decade or so based on these ideas (cf. Day and Groves 1975; Day 1989). Evolutionary theories in economics have already been successfully applied to problems of technical change, to the development of new institutions, and to the evolution of means of payment.

For large, slow-growing animals like humans, genetic evolution has a built-in bias towards the long run. Changing the genetic structure of a species requires that characteristics (phenotypes) be selected and accumulated by differential reproductive success. Behaviors learned or acquired during the lifetime of an individual cannot be passed on genetically. Genetic evolution is therefore usually a relatively slow process requiring many generations to significantly alter a species' physical and biological characteristics.

Cultural evolution is potentially much faster. Technical change is perhaps the most important and fastest evolving cultural process. Learned behaviors that are successful, at least in the short term, can be almost immediately spread to other members of the culture and passed on in the oral, written, or video record. The increased speed of adaptation that this process allows has been largely responsible for *Homo sapiens'* amazing success at appropriating the resources of the planet. Vitousek et al. (1986) estimate that humans now directly control from 25%–40% of the total primary production of the planet's biosphere, and this is beginning to have significant effects on the biosphere, including changes in global climate and in the planet's protective ozone shield.

Thus, the costs of this rapid cultural evolution are potentially significant.

Like a car that has increased speed, humans are in more danger of running off the road or over a cliff. Cultural evolution lacks the built-in long-run bias of genetic evolution and is susceptible to being led by its hyper-efficient short-run adaptability over a cliff into the abyss.

Another major difference between cultural and genetic evolution may serve as a countervailing bias, however. As Arrow (1962) has pointed out, cultural and economic evolution, unlike genetic evolution, can at least to some extent employ foresight. If society can see the cliff, perhaps it can be avoided.

While market forces drive adaptive mechanisms (Kaitala and Pohjola 1988), the systems which evolve are not necessarily optimal, so the question remains: What external influences are needed and when should they be applied in order to achieve an optimum economic system via evolutionary adaptation? The challenge faced by ecological economic systems modelers is to first apply the models to gain foresight, and to respond to and manage the system feedbacks in a way which helps avoid any foreseen cliffs. Devising policy instruments and identifying incentives that can translate this foresight into effective modifications of the short-run evolutionary dynamics is the challenge (Costanza 1987).

Evolutionary Criteria

A critical problem in applying the evolutionary paradigm in dynamic models is defining the selection criteria *a priori*. In its basic form, the theory of evolution is circular and descriptive (Holling 1987). Those species or cultural institutions or economic activities survive which are the most successful at reproducing themselves. But we only know which ones were more successful *after the fact*. To use the evolutionary paradigm in modeling, we require a quantitative measure of fitness (or more generally *performance*) in order to drive the selection process.

Several candidates have been proposed for this function in various systems, ranging from expected economic utility to thermodynamic potential. Thermodynamic potential is interesting as a performance criteria in complex systems because even very simple chemical systems can be seen to evolve complex non-equilibrium structures using this criteria (Prigogine 1972; Nicolis and Prigogine 1977, 1989), and all systems are (at minimum) thermodynamic systems (in addition to their other characteristics) so that thermodynamic constraints and principles are applicable across both ecological and economic systems (Eriksson 1991).

This application of the evolutionary paradigm to thermodynamic systems has led to the development of far-from-equilibrium thermodynamics and the concept of dissipative structures (Prigogine 1972). An important research question is to determine the range of applicability of these principles and their appropriate use in modeling ecological economic systems.

Many dissipative structures follow complicated transient motions. Schneider and Kay (1993) propose a way to analyze these chaotic behaviors and note that, "Away from equilibrium, highly ordered stable complex systems can emerge, develop and grow at the expense of more disorder at higher levels in the system's hierarchy." It has been suggested that the integrity of far-from-equilibrium systems has to do with the ability of the system to attain and maintain its (set of) optimum operating point(s) (Kay 1991). The optimum operating point(s) reflect a state where self-organizing thermodynamic forces and disorganizing forces of environmental change are balanced. This idea has been elaborated and described as "evolution at the edge of chaos" by Bak and Chen (1991) and Kauffman and Johnson (1991).

The concept that a system may evolve through a sequence of stable and unstable stages leading to the formation of new structures seems well-suited to ecological economic systems. For example, Gallopín (1989) stresses that to understand the processes of economic impoverishment "...the focus must necessarily shift from the static concept of poverty to the dynamic processes of impoverishment and sustainable development within a context of permanent change. The dimensions of poverty cannot any longer be reduced to only the economic or material conditions of living; the capacity to respond to changes, and the vulnerability of the social groups and ecological systems to change become central." In a similar fashion Robinson (1991) argues that sustainability calls for maintenance of the dynamic capacity to respond adaptively, which implies that we should focus more on basic natural and social processes, than on the particular forms these processes take at any time. Folke and Berkes (1992) have discussed the capacity to respond to changes in ecological economic systems, in terms of institution building, collective actions, cooperation, and social learning. These might be some of the ways to enhance the capacity for resilience (increase the capacity to recover from disturbance) in interconnected ecological economic systems.

PRACTICAL APPROACHES TO MODELING REGIONAL SYSTEMS

We are attempting to apply integrated ecological and economic modeling and analysis in order to improve our understanding of regional systems, assess potential future impacts of various land-use, development, and agricultural policy options, and better assess the value of ecological systems. Starting with an existing spatially articulated ecosystem model of the Patuxent River drainage basin in Maryland, we are adding modules to endogenize the agricultural components of the system (especially the impacts of agricultural practices and crop choice) and the process of land-use decision making. The integrated model will allow us to evaluate the indirect effects over long time horizons of current policy options. These effects are almost always ignored in partial analyses, although they may be very significant and may reverse many long-held assumptions and policy predictions. This section is a progress report on this modeling effort, indicating our motivations, ideas, and plans for completion.

An Overview of the Patuxent Modeling Project

Recognizing the need for improvements in understanding how ecosystems function, how humans interact with ecosystems, and how ecosystems are valued, the following objectives were identified for this project:

1. To increase our understanding of and our ability to model the interactions between human behavior and ecological processes;
2. To increase our understanding of and our ability to model the effect of the regulatory environment on human behavior; and
3. To develop through the above exercises a better understanding of the role of ecological processes in society's well-being, thus improving our methods for valuing ecosystem configurations and our ability to assess the benefits and costs of regulatory consequences.

To fulfill these three objectives, a pilot ecological-economic model is being developed to examine functions and processes of ecosystems, clarify relationships between human actions and ecosystems, and provide detailed information that will enable improved ecosystem valuation.

The model consists of interrelated ecological and economic models that employ a landscape perspective, for this perspective captures the spatial and temporal distributions of the services and functions of the natural system and human-related phenomena such as surrounding land-use patterns and population distributions. Configuration and reconfiguration of the landscape occurs as a result of ecological and economic factors, and these factors are closely intertwined.

The ecological part of the model is based on the Patuxent Landscape Model (PLM), one of several landscape-level spatial simulation models currently under development by Costanza and others at the University of Maryland (Costanza 1990; Fitz et al. 1993; Fitz et al. 1994). The PLM is capable of simulating the succession of complex ecological systems using a landscape perspective. Economic models are being developed to reflect human behavior and economic influences. The effects of human intervention result directly from the conversion of land from one use to another (e.g., wetlands conversion, residential development, power plant siting) or from changes in the practices that take place within specific land uses (e.g., adoption of agricultural best management practices, intensification of congestion and automobile emissions, change in urban water and sewer use, and storm run-off).

The Patuxent River Watershed, which includes portions of Anne Arundel, Calvert, Charles, Howard, Montgomery, Prince George's, and St. Mary's counties, is the study area (Figure 13.2). The ecological model is currently being calibrated for this area. In this phase of the project the economic models will characterize land use and agricultural decisions, and capture the effects on these decisions of institutional influences such as environmental, zoning, transportation, and agricultural policies. The integration of the two models provides a framework for regulatory analysis in the context of risk assessment, non-point source pollution control, wetlands mitigation/restoration, etc.

As part of this exercise, the ease (and cost-effectiveness) of generalizing the model to other regions will be assessed. It is expected that the modeling approaches will remain fairly constant over applications, although the particular behavioral models and ecological processes emphasized, as well as the actual parameters of the models, would differ. Because the models are designed to depict specific processes and ecosystems and to evaluate specific management strategies, they require a significant amount of site-specific data. However, the integrated

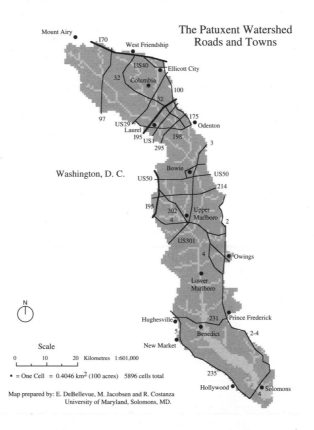

Figure 13.2. Towns and highways of the Patuxent watershed.

model will illustrate the circumstances under which human actions set in motion processes that can have far-reaching effects that play out over a broad geographical range and over time. These illustrations will help policy makers define the relevant questions to be asked and effects to be anticipated in other regional settings.

An overview of the components of the integrated modeling system is depicted in Figure 13.3. The major components of the system are the spatially explicit, dynamic models for the ecological system and the economic decisions, and the mechanism for exchange of information between the two. The results of the interrelated processes produce a new landscape and a new array of values associated with the landscape. Some of these become signals to private individuals and public agents in future decisions.

The Ecosystem Model

The starting point of the modeling effort, the Patuxent Landscape Model (PLM), is an outgrowth of the coastal ecological landscape spatial simulation (CELSS) model developed by Costanza et al. (1990). This modeling approach has been applied in two previous studies. The model was first implemented in the Atchafalaya Delta Area of coastal Louisiana, where it was developed to model

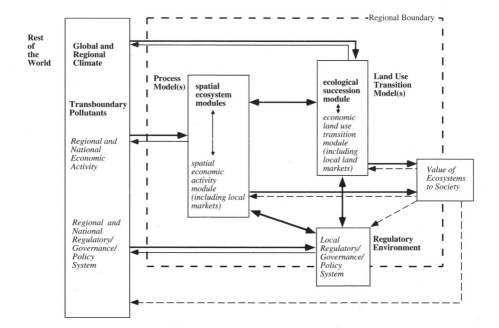

Figure 13.3. Integrated ecological economic modeling and valuation framework. Modules in bold are already included in the Patuxent Landscape Model (PLM). Modules in italics are to be added as part of ongoing projects.

spatial ecosystem processes, succession, and land loss problems and used to evaluate the impacts of management strategies and specific projects designed to alleviate coastal erosion problems (Costanza et al. 1990). A more sophisticated version of the model is currently being implemented in the Water Conservation Areas and Everglades National Park in Florida to examine the repercussions of management strategies on elements of the ecosystem such as water levels, nutrients, and plant successional patterns (Fitz et al. 1993).

The PLM uses an integrated, spatial simulation approach to model ecological processes. Central to the PLM is a General Ecosystem Model (GEM) (Fitz et al. 1994, see Figure 13.4) that is replicated in each of the grid cells that compose the study area (Figure 13.5). The GEM unit models are linked together and to a Geographical Information System (GIS) database using the Spatial Modeling Workstation (SMW) (Maxwell and Costanza 1994, see Figure 13.6). In addition to linking flows between cells, the spatial configuration superimposes the river network on the grid of cells allowing better simulation of river flow processes across the landscape.

The GEM unit model simulates fundamental ecological processes, with hydrology as its core. The hydrologic sector of the model simulates the availability of water and its vertical and horizontal movements, based on topography, geology, land use, and other characteristics within each cell. Characteristics of each cell's habitat type translate to parameters of physical, chemical and biological equations that are used to simulate such processes as primary production, nutrient fluxes, organic/inorganic sediment suspension and deposition, basic "consumer" dynamics, and decomposition. The dynamics of various ecological processes are expressed as the interaction between state variables (stocks) and flows of material, energy, and information. After the vertical or within cell dynamics have been simulated, the results of the unit model are processed by the spatial modeling program. In linking the stocks and flows, the model predicts the exchange of matter between cells (horizontal fluxes) and simulates the resulting temporal changes in water availability, water quality, and habitat/ecosystem type. The landscape model employs an algorithm for determining the habitat type of each cell at all times during the simulation. The habitat switching algorithm redefines the habitat/ecosystem type of cells as conditions change and selects parameter sets as necessary.

Data is collected to calibrate or initialize the model for a given set of ecosystems and a particular landscape. Effort is then devoted to simulating past behavior of the landscape. This allows for calibration of the functions of the model against actual historical data. For the Patuxent project, historical land use and geographic data (GIS) have been acquired from the Maryland Department of Natural Resources (DNR), Maryland Department of Environment (MDE), and the U.S. Geological Survey (USGS). Maps indicating land use

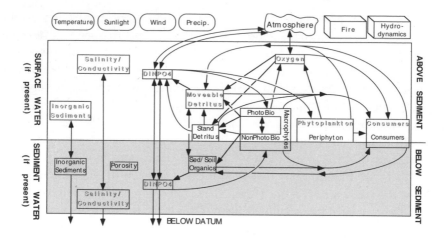

Figure 13.4. Summary diagram of the Patuxent Landscape Model's (PLM) unit model
(GEM) showing state variables and mass fluxes of the unit model, excluding hydrology. The model is run within one cell and parameterized for the
cell's habitat. State variables are enclosed within rectangles, and matter that
can flux vertically and horizontally with water movement is shown in outline type.

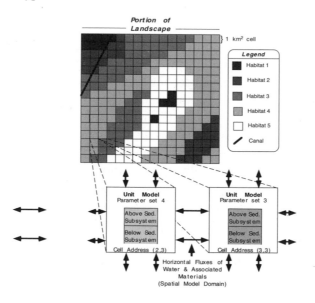

Figure 13.5. The cellular structure of the PLM. Each cell has a (variable) habitat type,
which is used to parameterize the unit model for that cell. The unit
model simulates ecosystems dynamics for that cell in the above-sedi-
ment and below-sediment subsystems. Nutrients and suspended materials in the surface water and saturated sediment water are fluxed between
cells in the domain of the spatial model.

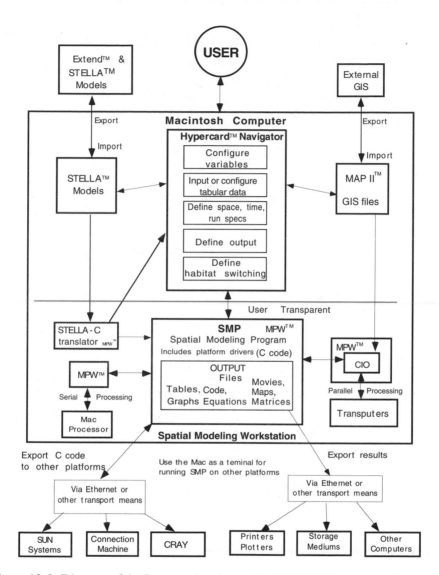

Figure 13.6. Diagram of the Patuxent Landscape Model (PLM) implementation archi-
tecture. The PLM is programmed and simulated in the Spatial Modeling
Workstation (SMW). The SMW consists of : STELLA™ unit models for
execution of ecosystem dynamics; MAP II™ program for storage and
manipulation of GIS data files; the Spatial Modeling Program (SMP) that
executes the interchange of flows among unit models on the computers,
and imports spatial (GIS) data; the Hypercard Navigator (under development) that is used to guide the user through configuration of models, data
sets, execution platforms and output files; and an Apple Macintosh™ computer with transporters installed, or a users terminal interface to other computer platforms.

estimates for 1973, 1981, and 1985 (with 1991 now available), as well as mappings of the watershed, streams, soils, slopes, contaminants, highways, marinas, railroads, water quality, and wetlands have been acquired. The PLM contains about 6,000 spatial cells each of about 100 acres and each containing a GEM with 21 state variables. The model will be calibrated with land use, stream flow, water quality, and other data from 1973 and 1985. The intent is to run scenarios to the year 2020.

The spatial resolution of the PLM allows evaluation of impacts from changes in land-use type or practices for particular groups of cells in the watershed. Our aim is to be able to estimate selected indicator variables that will describe processes of interest in the Patuxent River watershed. For example, fertilizer applications and mechanical soil manipulation (e.g., tillage) influence the total loadings of nutrients and sediment which are carried by surface and sub-surface waterflow off a given land parcel. The flow path of that water over various land types will determine its nutrient and sediment load when it reaches a wetland or stream. The combined effect of multiple land parcels then influences vegetative growth processes in wetlands within the Patuxent estuary. As plant biomass changes, nutrient uptake, evapotranspiration, and sediment retention rates change. The simulation of these multiple interrelated processes, allows the PLM to estimate general effects of such practices as vegetative buffers and retention ponds on urban and agriculture lands on total loadings to the estuary and ecosystem types of undeveloped land.

Future additions to the ecological model include adding estimates of fish and wildlife populations based on the pattern and productivity of the landscape elements. At this stage these estimates will not feed back to affect the ecosystem dynamics. Rather, they will be more on the order of "habitat suitability" indicating the type and quantity of various species that could be expected in a given landscape, rather than modeling the populations endogenously.

Economic Models of Human Decisions

The two notable aspects of the ecological modeling approach—its dynamic nature and its ability to spatially disaggregate—are also important dimensions for the economic sectors that interact with the ecosystem. The human activities of importance form an interrelated, dynamic, spatially distributed system in their own right. Economic models that reflect these dimensions are being conceptualized and estimated. Ensuring the necessary feedback between the two systems will require an integration characterized by exchange of information between the models at an appropriate time and space scale.

Human decisions that determine land-use designation, as well as those that affect flows/extractions from the system conditioned on the land use designation, will affect the configuration of the landscape. The existing PLM, like other ecological models, ignores the effect of the landscape on humans. In addition, human effects on the landscape, whether through changes in the land use of the cells or through the emissions assumed for any land use, are imposed exogenously, rather than modeled as part of the process. The economic considerations are important because human decisions are influenced by the characteristics of the ecosystem landscape, and the landscape changes as a result of the decisions. For ecological reasons, the effects of a single action taken at a given point in time will continue to play out over time and will affect more than just the cell where the action took place. Additionally, that action will have been influenced by the characteristics of the given cell, the characteristics of surrounding cells, and the expectations of changes in those cells.

Perhaps the most important type of economic behavior that requires modeling is land conversion because of its impact on the ecosystem at the whole range of scales from local to global. Since the ecological processes that are modeled in the generic ecosystem model are conditioned on land use, scenarios are driven by the land-use designation of the cells in the landscape at each period of time. The land use conversion model will endogenize those human decisions.

Conditioned on a cell's land use designation, the cell is programmed to undergo certain processes. But human decisions will affect these processes and may not be predetermined. In fact, they may be affected by feedback from the ecological system, and most surely will be affected by changing policy environments. In the first phase of this project, one such behavioral model, conditioned on land use, will be developed—a model of agricultural practices. Additional behavioral models, conditioned on land use, will be added in the future. An obvious candidate is a transportation model.

Land-Use Conversion

Economists have tried to explain land values and land-use decisions for some time, but generally in a static context and rarely incorporating features of the local ecosystems. Most frequent in this literature are hedonic models of residential transactions prices as functions of local amenities and housing characteristics (e.g., Diamond 1980; Beaton and Butcher 1989). Additionally, some models seek to explain conversion of agricultural land to residential and urban use as functions of profitability of alternative land uses (e.g., Alig and Healy 1987; Fishchel 1986; McMillan 1989). Data limitations have restricted these applications to cross-sectional analysis at one point in time.

Our proposed approach relies on spatially disaggregated data from digitized maps and allows dynamic analysis of micro-level changes that can be observed over time. Because the data reside in a geographical information system, it is easy to relate activities on individual parcels of land with local ecological and economic features of the landscape that might be driving these activities.

The land-use conversion decision is modeled probabilistically. This involves estimating the transition probabilities that a given parcel of land, set in a landscape configuration of given ecological/economic description, will be converted from its current state to any other state (including no change). The conversion probabilities are based on the value of the land in alternative uses. As surrounding landscape conversions take place, the probability of conversion of a given parcel changes.

Here we are interested in considering the discrete and finite set of alternative land uses. The set of uses in the Patuxent watershed for which we have data is listed in Table 13.2. Depending on the state of the parcel at the time of the decision, some uses may be precluded, at least for realization within a limited time period (of a year or shorter). For example, if the land is already in residential development, it is probably infeasible to return it to forest in one year. Federal laws such as wetland and coastal zone management will also affect the likelihood that land parcels switch uses as legislation often prohibits certain land uses and/or makes these uses significantly more costly. Again, the GIS system is useful because many of the land use restrictions and potential scenarios have been digitized in GIS maps and can be merged with the ecological and economic digitized geographic information.

This type of probabilistic model is appealing because it allows for variations over individual decision makers facing the same factors, and variation of the factors affecting the decision with spatial location and proximity to centers of economic activity, transportation networks, and ecological features. Thus it predicts the likelihood of each type of transition rather than predicting deterministically one type of conversion for all land of a certain ecological/economic description. These transition probabilities can be interpreted as the percentage of land of a given type that is converted to each alternative land use (including the percentage that remains unconverted) and are functionally equivalent to the transition probabilities in a Markov analysis.

Because the differential in economic returns among commercial, residential, agricultural, and open land uses differs depending on the state of the regional economy, the explanatory model will reflect these exogenous forces and the scenarios will incorporate predictions of these cycles. An existing county-based regional model for Maryland will provide predictions of the "macroeconomic" exogenous factors to be used in the simulations.

Agricultural Practices

The first step of the PLM modeling dynamics is to designate a cell as a given land use. Together with prior information, the economic land-use conversion model and the ecosystem succession model, these designations are made for each "round" of the model's calibrations. However, the land-use designations

Table 13.2. Relative Land Use for the Patuxent Watershed for 1973 and 1985

LAND USE DESCRIPTION	% 1973 Area	% 1985 Area	% change
URBAN	10.7	14.9	4.2
Low Density Residential	3.7	6.2	2.5
Medium Density Residential	2.9	3.5	0.6
High Density Residential	0.7	1.0	0.3
Commercial	1.1	1.5	0.4
Industrial	0.2	0.2	0.0
Institutional	1.2	1.2	0.0
Extractive	0.3	0.3	0.0
Open Urban Land	0.6	1.0	0.4
AGRICULTURAL	34.2	31.6	-2.6
Cropland	29.6	26.6	3.0
Pasture	4.6	4.5	-0.1
Orchard	0.2	0.1	-0.1
Feeding Operations	0.0	0.1	0.1
Row and Garden Crops	0.2	0.3	0.1
FOREST	48.1	46.0	-2.1
Deciduous Forest	31.4	27.6	-3.8
Evergreen Forest	1.4	1.6	0.2
Mixed Forest	14.3	14.8	0.5
Brush	1.0	2.0	1.0
WATER	5.3	5.5	0.2
Fresh Open Water (Plankton)			
Fresh Open Water (Benthic)			
Brackish Open Water (Plankton)			
Brackish Open Water (Benthic)			
WETLANDS	1.2	1.4	0.2
Salt Marsh			
Fresh Marsh			
Swamp			
BARREN LAND	0.1	1.2	1.1
Beaches	0.0	0.4	0.4
Bare Exposed Rock	0.0	0.0	0.0
Bare Ground	0.1	0.8	0.7
TOTAL	100. 0	100.0	0.0

are broad categories, with agricultural uses specified as either cropland, pasture, or orchards. It is important to know more about the agricultural land use, in order to understand the impact this land use has on the ecosystem. The agricultural practices model attempts this, and in so doing serves as an example of micro-level economic behavior models that capture human decisions that influence the environment, conditioned on a given land use. This economic model will accept information from the "outside world" (including existing policy) and the ecological world (such as topographical information) and will attempt to predict the cropping/livestock patterns, as well as the farming practices that serve as parameters in the model for the subsequent cropping season.

As with the land-use conversion model, the economic model of farming behavior will be probabilistic. That is, it is the probabilities of various alternative decisions that will be generated by the model. These probabilities will need to be interpreted as predicted proportions of similar farming land that is used for given crops/livestock and, conditioned on that choice, is subject to different best management practice (BMPs).

Models of agricultural crop/livestock choice are numerous, but few are conceived at as "micro" a scale as this project should be able to achieve. Profitability from different farming choices will drive the decisions, but profitability is conditioned, not only on relative output and input prices, but factors of the landscape that affect the production function for different crops (e.g., hydrology, slopes, soil types, etc.). In the Patuxent watershed there is an interesting added consideration. In Maryland, farmers often sell hunting rights on their lands. These rents can be a major source of income for farmers and affect not only how much land stays in agriculture but also crop and livestock decisions. Depending both on farmers' decisions and the ecological characteristics of the land, the amount and composition of wildlife will differ, endowing the land with differing hunting value.

In addition to models of crop choice, numerous behavioral studies of BMP adoption in the United States have examined the influence of factors ranging from topography and erodibility to human capital factors (e.g., age and experience) to farm operation characteristics (e.g., cropping patterns, scale, and scope and tenure status). A few generalizations can be drawn from the findings of these empirical studies. Adoption is more likely and expenditures on BMPs are greater on more erodible land and on larger operations. Older, more educated and more experienced farmers are more likely to adopt. Farmers with more off-farm income and greater risk aversion are less likely to adopt. Farmers are more likely to adopt if they perceive erosion to be more of a problem, attach greater importance to conservation and environmental quality or have conservation plans. Cash grain farmers are less likely to adopt (Ervin and Ervin 1982; Lee and Stewart 1983; Saliba et al. 1986; Shortle and Miranowski 1986; Norris and Batie 1987; Lynne et al. 1988; Nielsen et al. 1989). Although these generalizations are revealing, there is no study which comprehensively examines the adoption of numerous, but specific BMPs in a spatially explicit context linked to ecosystem characteristics.

The choice by farmers among farming practices that could alter their pollution emissions, conditioned on crop/livestock choice, is a difficult one to model, but one that has considerable importance for policy formation. Through provision of technical and financial (cost-sharing) assistance, federal and state agencies have attempted to address these problems by subsidizing the use of BMPs, defined as farming practices that reduce soil and nutrient losses at reasonable cost (U.S. Department of Agriculture). Adoption of new agricultural technologies depends on a variety of economic and behavioral factors, including scale and scope of operations, topography and other natural factors, human capital or skill considerations, relative prices, attitudes toward risk, and perceptions about the extent of erosion or leaching problems and about returns to adoption (for a survey, see Feder et al. 1985). These factors will be pursued in the agricultural decision model.

Integration of Components and Resolution of Modeling Inconsistencies

At present, the ecological model runs 14 sectors, tracks 21 state variables, estimates horizontal and vertical fluxes of water, nutrients, sediments, and biomass, and simulates ecological succession over the landscape. For the purposes of the economic model, two types of interactions between humans and natural resources will be of significance: (1) decisions that determine land-use designation of a cell, and (2) decisions that affect flows/extractions from the system conditioned on the land use type of the cell.

An interrelated model would capture how the distribution of human activities (farming, electric power generation, commercial and residential development, recreation, wastewater treatment, highway construction, fishing) affect the ecosystem. Such a model would also capture the effect of the ecosystem landscape on the quality and value of goods and services (e.g., recreation, wildlife enjoyment, water quantity and quality, housing, environmental aesthetics, etc.) and therefore, on human decisions. The model must also be able to reflect how human activity and its impact on the ecosystem may differ under different regulatory regimes and under alternative regulations.

Our approach will *not* be to meld both ecological and economic models into one "super-model," using one consistent time and space resolution. Instead, the two types of models will exist in parallel and will proceed at their own levels of specificity, but will exchange information on ecological and economic elements generated by the other. Because appropriate choices on time step, geographical scale, and level of aggregation differ in the ecological and economic models, there are several potential inconsistencies that may arise in this information exchange.

By design, the PLM model establishes physical boundaries. Activity is modeled in the area bounded by the top of the trees, the drainage basin boundaries, and the bottom of the groundwater. The choice of physical boundaries encompasses the dynamics of the ecosystem. The physical definition of the boundary of the Patuxent River Basin region will coincide with relevant economic boundaries, if the region is a price-taker in markets that extend beyond the boundaries of the region. That is, for markets that extend beyond the Patuxent River Basin Region, the region must not significantly influence the actions of others (i.e., it does not produce or demand a significant amount relative to other trading partners). For the Patuxent watershed, this is likely to be approximately correct and thus no serious inconsistencies with respect to "boundaries" are likely to arise. However, in other applications of this modeling approach, the definition of boundaries could well be conflicting.

The model is structured to simulate a desired level of ecological complexity and resolution. Modeling with greater levels of disaggregation is possible, but this would be costly and require a significant amount of additional research, data, and programming. The behavioral interactions will largely involve the water, nutrients, macrophyte, and consumer sectors. Although these state variables are linked with habitat types, much finer distinctions of the landscape will be necessary for the economic model, as human behavior is likely to depend on more detailed information. In our approach, the details will be introduced exogenously by distinguishing different sub-groups of macrophytes and consumers and associating these different sub-groups with different land uses. The model will include markers and detailed rules for species loss, treating habitat evaluation as a side calculation. Clearly, there are qualitative distinctions between different composition and phyla. A function will be developed that will indicate the likelihood of game species and other forms of wildlife in particular habitat types. This function allows for the provision of additional complementary information without increasing the level of disaggregation of the unit model.

The ecosystem model operates on a time scale of a day or less. Yet, given data availability, the economic models are most easily estimated on an annual basis. The intra-year timing of the agricultural decisions will be easy to predict, however, since these are governed by seasons. Land conversions pose a different problem, however. They can be predicted only on an annual basis, but their timing is important because construction costs can have different immediate ecosystem impacts depending on the season. Independent data on building starts and construction durations will be used to forecast seasonal impacts of construction.

The geographical scale of resolution between the two models will also differ. Land parcels modeled in the land-use conversion model will not correspond to cell boundaries in the ecosystem model. The latter divides the study area into 5,896 cells with each cell representing approximately 0.364 km² or 90 acres. The cell size in the ecological model was selected to balance the desired complexity and resolution of the ecological landscape. The fact that the economic model will produce probabilistic estimates may actually help to resolve the differences in geographical scale, as the probabilities can be interpreted as percentages of land of a given description that is put to a given land use. However, the transition probabilities may still "fracture" cells. The PLM model has the ability to assign to cells split land-use designations, allowing heterogeneity within a cell. Devising weights to monitor what is happening in cells, thresholds can be set so that cells could go from homogeneous to heterogeneous units and vice versa. This additional detail will also allow the model to make inferences on a wider variety of land use restrictions (i.e., agricultural policies, zoning policies, and environmental protection policies).

In resolving this array of modeling inconsistencies, sensitivity tests will be used to assess the importance of level of detail in both models. Sensitivity games are used now to accommodate uncertainty over elements such as rainfall patterns over time. By generating several patterns for the future and running these different patterns as distinct scenarios, the significance of the uncertainty can be revealed.

CONCLUSIONS

Improving our ability to model linked ecological economic systems in an integrated way is essential to the goal of effective regional management for long-term sustainability. While these integrated models are large, complex, and loaded with uncertainties of various kinds, our abilities to understand, communicate, and deal with these uncertainties are rapidly improving. It is also important to remember that while increasing the resolution and complexity of models increases the amount we can say about a system, it also limits how accurately we can say it. Model predictability tends to fall with increasing resolution due to compounding uncertainties (Costanza and Maxwell 1993). What we are after are models that optimize their "effectiveness" (Costanza and Sklar 1985) by choosing an intermediate resolution where the product of predictability and resolution (effectiveness) is maximized.

We also need to see the modeling process as one that involves not only the technical aspects, but also the sociological aspects involved with using the process to help build consensus about the way the system works and which management options are most effective. This consensus needs to extend both across the gulf separating the relevant academic disciplines and across the even broader gulf separating the science and policy communities, and the public. Appropriately designed and appropriately used integrated ecological economic modeling exercises can help to bridge these gulfs.

ACKNOWLEDGMENTS

This chapter summarizes results and progress on a number of ongoing projects at the Beijer International Institute of Ecological Economics in Stockholm, Sweden, and at the University of Maryland International Institute for Ecological Economics, including: (1) the research program on Complex Ecological Economic Systems Modeling at the Beijer Institute; (2) a cooperative agreement with the USEPA, No. 07-5-25196-3734 titled: Ecological Economic Modelling and Valuation of Ecosystems. Michael Brody and MaryJo Kealey project officers, Nancy Bockstael, Robert Costanza, Ivar Strand, and Walter Boynton, principal investigators; (3) Modeling Landscape Dynamics in the Everglades Basin. Cooperative Agreement with the South Florida Water Management District. Robert Costanza PI, and (4) Ecological Landscape Models for Evaluating the Interactive Dynamics of the Patuxent River Watershed and Estuary; Maryland DNR, Robert Costanza PI.; and (5) Landscape Modeling: the Synthesis of Ecological Processes over Large Geographic Regions and Long Time Scales, NSF, Robert Costanza co-Principal Investigator (with F. Sklar, SFWMD). We especially thank Carl H. Fitz and Thomas Maxwell for their valuable input and feedback on this chapter. Sandra Koskoff provided editorial assistance. We thank Ed DeBellevue, Carl Fitz, Marla Markowski, and Enrique Reyes for their contributions to the research effort, and Marjan van den Belt for helpful comments on earlier drafts. Parts of an earlier draft of this chapter appeared as: Costanza, R., L. Wainger, C. Folke, and K.-G. Maler. 1993. Modeling complex ecological economic systems: Toward an evolutionary, dynamic understanding of people and nature. *BioScience* 43: 545–55.

REFERENCES

Alig, R. J. and R. G. Healy. 1987. Urban and built-up land area changes in the United States: An empirical investigation of determinants. *Land Economics* 63(3): 216–26.

Arrow, K. 1962. The economic implications of learning by doing. *Review of Economic Studies* 29: 155–173.

Arthur, W. B. 1988. Self-reinforcing mechanisms in economics, 9–31. In The Economy as an Evolving Complex System, eds. P. W. Anderson, K. J. Arrow and D. Pines. Addison Wesley, Redwood City, CA.

Bak, P. and K. Chen. 1991. Self-Organized criticality. *Scientific American* 264 :46.

Beaton, C. H. and W. R. Butcher. 1989. The impact of regional land-use controls on property values: The case of the New Jersey Pinelands. *Land Economics* 67(2): 172–94.

Berkes, F. and C. Folke. 1994. Investing in cultural capital for a sustainable use of natural capital. In Investing in Natural Capital: An Ecological Economics Approach to Sustainability, eds. A. M. Jansson, M. Hammer, C. Folke, and R. Costanza. Washington DC: Island Press.

Bockstael, N., R. Costanza, I. Strand, W. Boynton, K. Bell, and L. Wainger. 1995. Ecological economic modeling and valuation of ecosystems. *Ecological Economics* (in press).

Boulding, K. E. 1981. Evolutionary Economics. Beverly Hills, CA: Sage.

Bouzaher, A. 1993. CEEPES: An Evolving System for Agroenvironmental Policy. Presented at The Integrating Economic and Ecological Indicators Symposium, Resource Policy Consortium. May Washington, DC: World Bank.

Brown, G. M. and J. Roughgarden. 1992. An ecological economy: notes on harvest and growth. Beijer Discussion Paper Series No. 12. Beijer International Institute of Ecological Economics. Stockholm, Sweden.

Brown, G. M. and J. Swierzbinski. 1985. Endangered species, genetic capital and cost-reducing R&D, 111-127. In Economics of Ecosystems Management, eds. D.O. Hall, N. Myers and N.S. Margaris. Dordrecht: Dr. W. Junk Publishers.

Cabe, R., J. Shogren, A. Bouzaher, and A. Carriquiry. 1991. Metamodels, response functions, and research efficiency in ecological economics. Working paper 91-WP 79. Center for Agricultural and Rural Development, Iowa State University, Ames.

Clark, C. W. and G. R. Munro. 1975. The Economics of Fishing and Modern Capital Theory: A Simplified Approach. *Journal of Environmental Economics and Management* 2: 92–106.

Clark, C. W. 1976. Mathematical Bioeconomics. New York: John Wiley and Sons.

Clark, C. W. 1981. Bioeconomics of the ocean. *Bioscience* 31: 231–237.

Clark, C. W. 1985. Bioeconomic Modelling and Fisheries Management. New York: Wiley and Sons.

Colwell, R. K. 1974. Predictability, constancy, and contingency of periodic phenomena. *Ecology* 55: 1148–1153.

Costanza, R. 1987. Social traps and environmental policy. *BioScience* 37: 407–412.

Costanza, R. and T. Maxwell. 1991. Spatial ecosystem modeling using parallel processors. *Ecological Modeling* 58: 159–183

Costanza, R. and T. Maxwell. 1993 Resolution and predictability: An approach to the scaling problem. *Landscape Ecology* 9: 47-57

Costanza, R., B. Norton, and B. J. Haskell. eds. 1992a. Ecosystem Health: New Goals for Environmental Management. Washington DC: Island Press.

Costanza, R., C. H. Fitz, J. A. Bartholomew, and E. DeBellevue. 1992b. The Everglades Landscape Model (ELM): Summary of Task 1, Model Feasibility Assessment Report. Center for Environmental and Estuarine Studies, University of Maryland, August.

Costanza, R. and F. H. Sklar. 1985. Articulation, accuracy, and effectiveness of mathematical models: A review of freshwater wetland applications. *Ecological Modeling* 27: 45-68

Costanza, R., F. H. Sklar, and M. L. White. 1990. Modeling coastal landscape dynamics. *BioScience* 40(2): 91–107.

Costanza, R., L. Wainger, C. Folke, and K.-G. Maler. 1993. Modeling complex ecological economic systems: Toward an evolutionary, dynamic understanding of people and nature. *BioScience* 43: 545–55.

Day, R. H. 1989. Dynamical systems, adaptation and economic evolution. MRG Working Paper No. M8908, University of Southern California.

Day, R. H. and T. Grove. eds. 1975. Adaptive Economic Models. New York: Academic Press.

Debreu, G. 1974. Excess Demand Functions. *Journal of Mathematical Economics* 1: 15–23.

Diamond, D. B. 1980. The Relationship Between Amenities and Urban Land Prices. *Land Economics* 56(1): 21–32.

Duchin, F. 1988. Analyzing structural change in the economy. In input-output analysis: Current developments, ed. M. Ciaschini. London: Chapman and Hall.

Duchin, F. 1992. Industrial input-output analysis: Implications for industrial ecology. *Proc. Natl. Acad. Sci. USA*. 89: 851–855.

Eriksson, K-E. 1991. Physical foundations of ecological economics. In Human responsibility and global change, eds. L. O. Hansson and B. Jungen. Göteborg, Sweden: University of Göteborg Press.

Ervin C. A. and D. E. Ervin. 1982. Factors affecting the use of soil conservation practices: Hypotheses, evidence and implications. *Land Economics* 58: 277–92.

Feder, G., R. E. Just, and D. Zilberman. 1985. Adoption of Agricultural Innovations in Developing Countries: A Survey. *Economic Development and Cultural Change* 33: 255–98.

Fitz, H. C., E. B. DeBellevue, R. Costanza, R. Boumann, T. Maxwell, and L. Wainger. 1994. Development of a General Ecosystem Model (GEM) for a Range of Scales and Ecosystems. *Ecological Modelling* (in press).

Fitz, H. C., R. Costanza, and E. Reyes. 1993. The Everglades Landscape Model (ELM): Summary Report of Task 2, Model Development. Report to the South Florida Water Management District, Everglades Research Division.

Gallopín, G. C. 1989. Global impoverishment, sustainable development and the environment: A conceptual approach. *International Social Science Journal* 121: 375–397.

Günther, F. and C. Folke. 1993. Characteristics of nested living systems. *Journal of Biological Systems* (in press).

Hannon, B. and C. Joiris. 1987. A seasonal analysis of the southern north sea ecosystem. *Ecology* 70: 1916–1934.

Holland, J. H. and J. H. Miller. 1991. Artificial Adaptive Agents in Economic Theory. *American Economic Review* 81: 365–370.

Holling, C.S. 1964. The analysis of complex population processes. *The Canadian Entomologist* 96: 335–347.

Holling, C.S. 1966. The functional response of invertebrate predators to prey density. *Memoirs of the Entomological Society of Canada* No. 48.

Holling, C. S. 1987. Simplifying the Complex: The Paradigms of Ecological Function and Structure. *European Journal of Operational Research* 30: 139–146.

Kaitala, V. and M. Pohjola. 1988. Optimal recovery of a shared resource stock: A differential game model with efficient memory equilibria. *Natural Resource Modeling* 3: 91–119.

Kauffman, S. A. and S. Johnson. 1991. Coevolution to the edge of Chaos: Coupled fitness landscapes, poised states, and coevolutionary avalanches. *Journal of Theoretical Biology* 149: 467–505.

Kay, J. J. 1991. A nonequilibrium thermodynamic framework for discussing ecosystem integrity. *Environmental Management* 15: 483-495.

Keynes, J. M. 1936. General Theory of Employment, Interest and Money. London: Harcourt Brace.

Klein, L. R. 1971. Forecasting and policy evaluation using large-scale econometric models: The state of the art. In Frontiers of Quantitative Economics, ed. M. D. Intriligator. Amsterdam: North-Holland Publishing Co.

Lee, L. K. and W. H. Stewart. 1983. Landownership and the Adoption of Minimum Tillage. *American Journal of Agricultural Economics* 65: 256–64.

Levins, R. 1966. The strategy of model building in population biology. *American Scientist* 54: 421–431.

Lindgren, K. 1991. Evolutionary phenomena in simple dynamics. In Artificial Life, SFI Studies in the Sciences of Complexity, vol. X, eds. C. G. Langton, C. Taylor, J. D. Farmer and S. Rasmussen. New York: Addison-Wesley.

Lines, M. 1989. Environmental noise and nonlinear models: A simple macroeconomic example. *Economic Notes* 19: 376–394.

Lines, M. 1990. Stochastic Stability Considerations: A Nonlinear Example. *International Review of Economics and Business* 3: 219-233.

Lucas, R. E. 1975. An equilibrium model of the business cycle. *Journal of Political Economy* 83: 1113–45.

Lynne, G. D., J. S. Shonkwiler, and L. R. Rola. 1988. Attitudes and farmer conservation behavior. *American Journal of Agricultural Economics* 70: 12–19.

Mandelbrot, B. B. 1977. Fractals. form, chance and dimension. San Francisco, CA: W.H. Freeman and Co.

Mandelbrot, B. B. 1983. The Fractal Geometry of Nature. San Francisco, CA: W.H. Freeman and Co.

Maxwell, T. and R. Costanza. 1993. An Approach to Modelling the Dynamics of Evolutionary Self-Organization. *Ecological Modeling* 69: 149–161.

Maxwell, T. and R. Costanza. 1994. Distributed Modular Spatial Ecosystem Modeling. *International Journal of Computer Simulation* (in press).

McMillan, D. P. 1989. An Empirical Model of Urban Fringe Land Use. *Land Economics* 65(2): 138–45.

Milne, B.T. 1991. Lessons from applying fractal models to landscape patterns. In Quantitative Methods in Landscape Ecology, eds. M. G. Turner and R. Gardner. New York, NY: Springer-Verlag Ecological Studies 82.

Nicolis, G. and I. Prigogine. 1977. Self-Organization in Non-Equilibrium Systems. New York: John Wiley and Sons.

Nicolis, G. and I. Prigogine. 1989. Exploring Complexity. New York: W. H. Freeman.

Nielsen, E. G., J. A. Miranowski, and M. J. Morehart. 1989. Investments in Soil Conservation and Land Improvements: Factors Explaining Farmers' Decisions. Agricultural Economic Report No. 601, Economic Research Service, U.S. Department of Agriculture. Washington, DC.

Norgaard, R. B. 1989. The case for methodological pluralism. *Ecological Economics* 1: 37–57.

Norris, P. E. and S. S. Batie. 1987. Virginia farmers' soil conservation decisions: An application of tobit analysis. *Southern Journal of Agricultural Economics* 19: 79–90.

Norton, B. G. and R. E. Ulanowicz. 1992. Scale and biodiversity policy: A hierarchical approach. *Ambio* 21: 244–249.

O'Neill, R. V., D. L. DeAngelis, J. B. Waide, and T. F. H. Allen. 1986. A Hierarchical Concept of Ecosystems. Princeton, NJ: Princeton University Press.

O'Neill, R. V., A. R. Johnson, and A.W. King. 1989. A hierarchical framework for the analysis of scale. *Landscape Ecology* 3:193–205.

O'Neill, R. V. and B. Rust. 1979. Aggregation Error in Ecological Models. *Ecological Modeling* 7: 91–105.

Olsen, L. F. and W. M. Schaffer. 1990. Chaos versus noisy periodicity: Alternative hypotheses for childhood epidemics. *Science* 249: 499–504.

Prigogine, I. 1972. Thermodynamics of Evolution. *Physics Today* 23: 23–28.

Rastetter, E. B., A. W. King, B. J. Cosby, G. M. Hornberger, R. V. O'Neill, and J. E. Hobbie. 1992. Aggregating fine-scale ecological knowledge to model coarser-scale attributes of ecosystems. *Ecological Applications* 2: 55–70.

Robinson, J.B. 1991. Modelling the interactions between human and natural systems. *International Social Science Journal* 130: 629–647.

Robinson, J. B. 1995. Of maps and territories: The use and abuse of socio-economic modelling in Support of Decision-Making. *Technological Forecast and Social Change* (in press).

Rosser, J. B. 1991. From Catastrophe to Chaos: A General Theory of Economic Discontinuities. Amsterdam: Kluwer.

Saliba, C., B. Bromley and D. W. Bromley. 1986. Soil management decisions–How they should be compared and what factors influence them. *North Central Journal of Agricultural Economics* 8: 305–17.

Schneider, E. D. and J. J. Kay. 1993. Life as a manifestation of the second law of thermodynamics. *International Journal of Mathematical and Computer Modelling* (in press).

Shortle, J. S. and J. A. Miranowski. 1986. Effects of risk perception and other characteristics of farmers and farm operations on the adoption of conservation tillage. *Applied Agricultural Research* 1: 85–90.

Shugart, H. H. 1989. The role of ecological models in long-term ecological studies. In Long-Term Studies in Ecology: Approaches and Alternatives, ed. G. E. Likens. New York: Springer-Verlag.

Solow, R. M. 1956. A Contribution to the Theory of Economic Growth. *Quarterly Journal of Economics* 70: 65–94.

Sonnenschein, H. 1974. Market excess demand functions. *Econometrica* 40: 549–563.

Sugihara, G. and R. M. May. 1990. Nonlinear forecasting as a way of distinguishing chaos from measurement error in time series. *Nature* 344: 734–741.

Taub, F. B. 1987. Indicators of change in natural and human impacted ecosystems: Status. In Preserving Ecological Systems: The Agenda for Long-Term Research and Development, eds. S. Draggan, J. J. Cohrssen and R. E. Morrison. New York: Praeger.

Taub, F. B. 1989. Standardized aquatic microcosm—development and testing. In Aquatic Ecotoxicology: Fundamental Concepts and Methodologies, Vol II., eds. A. Boudou and F. Ribeyre. Boca Raton, FL: CRC Press.

Turner, M. G., R. Costanza, and F. H. Sklar. 1989. Methods to compare spatial patterns for landscape modeling and analysis. *Ecological Modelling* 48: 1–18.

Vitousek, P., P. R. Ehrlich A. H. Ehrlich, and P. A. Matson. 1986. Human Appropriation of the Products of Photosynthesis. *BioScience* 36: 368–373.

von Bertalanffy, L. 1968. General System Theory: Foundations, Development, Applications. New York: George Braziller.

Wroblewski, J. S. and E. E. Hofmann. 1989. U.S. interdisciplinary modeling studies of coastal-offshore exchange processes: Past and future. *Prog. Oceanog* 23: 65–99.

Wulff, F. and R. E. Ulanowicz. 1989. A comparative anatomy of the Baltic Sea and Chesapeake Bay ecosystems. In Network Analysis of Marine Ecology: Methods and Applications, eds. F. Wulff, J. G. Field, and K. H. Mann. Coastal and Estuarine Studies Series. Heidelberg: Springer-Verlag.

14 ECOLOGICAL ECONOMICS: THE SECOND STAGE

Faye Duchin
Institute for Economic Analysis
New York University
269 Mercer Street
New York, NY 10003

OVERVIEW

According to this chapter, the first stage of ecological economics is about to end. It was characterized by the creation of a new approach to describing and working toward sustainable development and of a professional society of substantial size. Herman E. Daly's work defined the unique positions that came to characterize the first stage of the field: commitment to development rather than growth and to community over efficiency. But now it is necessary to provide motivation and conceptual grounding for the quantitative analysis that will hopefully be one of the strands elaborated in the second stage.

The author argues that the second stage will focus on building concrete, situation-specific strategies for sustainable development and an analytic framework for evaluating the environmental, social, and economic trade-offs among them. Structural economics is described as a theoretical and methodological extension of Wassily Leontief's input-output economics and is presented as a framework that can be used to make substantial progress toward sustainable development through its attention to physical phenomena as well as costs and prices, the activities and requirements of different kinds of households, and the ability to incorporate qualitative information into an integrated, formal evaluation framework.

ACCOMPLISHMENTS OF THE FIRST STAGE

Turning Point for Ecological Economics

The International Society for Ecological Economics (ISEE) is a relatively young professional organization which has experienced impressive growth under the leadership of Robert Costanza, the founding president. Over a thousand people participated in the third biennial conference of ISEE in Costa Rica in October, 1994. The Society publishes a journal and a quarterly Bulletin, a number of books about ecological economics are in print with more in preparation, and courses about the subject are taught at universities around the world. While few members were formally trained in the field, still many identify as ecological economists.

The ambition of ecological economics is to provide guidance for achieving sustainable development—economic development without environmental destruction. Like other economists, ecological economists are involved in the evaluation of trade-offs among alternative courses of action. Ecological economists are different from environmental economists because the former do not espouse economic growth as a general social objective and because of the importance they accord in social decision making to non-economic phenomena. These differences, along with a substantial commitment to collaboration across disciplines, are the most important defining characteristics of the first stage of ecological economics.

The administration of ISEE is now undergoing decentralization as regional chapters are established with agendas that reflect their distinctive concerns. This important development initiates the second stage in the life of the society. A parallel second stage is required in the intellectual development of the field. The second stage will depend on the elaboration of several distinct focuses built mainly around economics, biology, and public policy. This chapter describes structural economics as one of these focuses.

Ecological economics is "issue-oriented" (Silvio Funtowicz and Jerome Ravetz 1993) in that its agenda responds to the requirements of sustainable development. Ecological economists share a loose consensus about desirable development objectives and about the importance of government and citizens, individually and in groups, as well as the marketplace. To evaluate alternative development strategies, we need a theory that can situate economic activities and social actors within the natural world in a concrete and useful way. The theory needs to serve as a framework within which quantitative calculations can be made since the trade-offs among strategies require an empirical analysis and not just an application of abstract principles. Unfortunately, there has been a substantial disjuncture between verbal description about the role of quantitative analysis within ecological economics and the way in which it is actually carried out. The main reason is that quantitative techniques are often selected out of habit or for their availability, convenience in use, and respectability, sometimes at the expense of their relevance. Ecological economists now need to bridge the gap between verbal theory and formalism by producing models and databases for common use and encouraging further theoretical and practical developments by social scientists and natural scientists.

This chapter tries to motivate and sketch a conceptual structure that can help organize one part of the community of ecological economists. This is a necessary step because overcoming the fragmentation of our research agenda is a cumulative enterprise that requires collegial exchange and support. Too much energy is wasted when each study is based on its own illustrative model, small database, and simple scenarios. Some of our colleagues will prefer more general kinds of theory-building, simulation models and games, policy formulation and activism, or journalism. This kind of differentiation, along with both the stimulation and the tensions that accompany it, need to be welcomed rather than avoided.

The Contributions of Herman E. Daly

In their important history of ecological economics, Juan Martinez-Alier and Klaus Schlupmann (1987) describe the central role of Nicolas Georgescu-Roegen (1966, 1971) in focusing economists' attention on the creation of livelihood through the dissipative use of energy and materials. Kenneth Boulding's early paper about "spaceship earth" was also influential, providing a powerful, motivating metaphor for ecological economics (Boulding 1966). But I believe that it is the "macroeconomics of the environment" of Daly, which reflects the fundamental importance he accords to appropriate or even optimal scale rather than unlimited growth, and to the preservation of community over the increase in efficiency, which has provided the defining theoretical structure for the first stage of ecological economics (Daly 1991). Following their incisive critique of neoclassical environmental economics, John Gowdy and Peg Olsen (1994) cite Daly's work as their foremost example of the alternative represented by ecological economics. The sharp focus and incisiveness of Daly's reasoning, paired with his clarity of expression and skillful use of metaphors, account for the fact that his work is influential among non-economists as well as ecological economists. His contribution has been central to the building of the field, but it has to be recognized that it does not provide an operational theory of how an economy works.

Daly accords the highest importance to the determination of scale even though he acknowledges that scale, or throughput, cannot be measured (pers. comm). Daly has proposed a revised measure of gross national products (GNP) which is extremely popular—although Daly himself considers it to be of secondary importance (remarks at ISEE Conference, 1994)—and he supports natural resource accounting to provide the information needed to quantify adjustments to GNP. Daly endorses the split between macroeconomics and microeconomics and considers neoclassical microeconomics an adequate description of how a society does and should allocate resources in the interest of efficiency. The policy goals that follow from Daly's economic theory are:

- Determine the optimal scale for a particular economy,
- Identify the constraints that need to be imposed on the market in cases where the interests of the environment or of community would justify a sacrifice of efficiency, and
- Leave markets to assure the efficient achievement of the goal under these constraints.

Rather than being impressed by the strong interdependencies among policies and their effects, he believes that one generally needs "a separate policy instrument for each separate policy goal" (Daly 1994). Some of the policy positions that have been argued on the basis of Daly's work are opposition in principle to free trade and to opening borders (notably those of the U.S.) to immigration.

My conviction is that in its second stage, ecological economics needs to assert its independence from neoclassical economics even far more thoroughly than Daly has done. But the new theoretical foundations need to have an analytical orientation. Their formulation will require a different style of theorizing from Daly's, one based less on abstract arguments and more on models, data, and empirical analysis.

Metaphors and Models: The Two Cultures

Funtowicz and Ravetz have described the emergence of post-normal science, an issue-oriented version of normal science characterized by both new social practices and new intellectual structures. The common objective of post-normal sciences, according to them, is to "remedy the pathologies of the global industrial system" (Funtowicz and Ravetz 1993). Despite the fact that it shares this objective, they do not consider ecological economics as we know it to be a fully developed example (pers. comm.), and rightly so.

One obstacle to creating a coherent post-normal science within ecological economics has been our failure to recognize the roles and, at times, cross purposes of two different cultures, the cultural divide between scientists and literary intellectuals of which C.P. Snow (1956) made us aware. Some members of ISEE would situate ecological economics within the humanities rather than the sciences while others want to make use of the power of science for the further development of the field. Scientists develop tentative explanations of phenomena based on both induction and deduction, and they refine and sometimes replace these explanations on the basis of detailed measurements and other kinds of information that are systematically organized and documented. The scientific approach has undeniably been dramatically successful at achieving many of its objectives, but the objectives are often very narrowly defined and the side effects are sometimes unfortunate. A post-normal science of ecological economics can take advantage of the power of science while avoiding some of its traditional shortcomings. A holistic approach to problems can powerfully offset the characteristic reductionism of science, and acknowledging the value-laden nature of the work promotes taking responsibility for its effects.

Daly's contribution does not provide the basis for a science of ecological economics. It is instead in the literary tradition, based on the power of metaphors. Unfortunately, his metaphors only extend the scope of neoclassical economics, adding scale and community as criteria, while leaving its analytic core untouched. A scientific approach to ecological economics needs to provide a deeper understanding of how the global economy does and could function, on the basis of theory that can be made operational through quantitative analysis.

A striking example of the metaphorical use of analytic concepts is the so-called IPAT equation:

$$I = P \times A \times T$$

These symbols state that environmental impact (I) is equal to the product of three separable influences: population (P), affluence (A), and the effects of technology (T). (Ehrlich and Holdren 1974; Goodland et al. 1994).

Population can be measured by counting people. Conventions exist for measuring affluence in money units (e.g., consumption per capita, or capital stock per capita). "Technology" enters the equation at a deeper level of symbolism, as there is no reasonable or even conventional measure of the state of technology, let alone its effects. It is customary to approximate the expression (A x T) by per capita energy use.

IPAT succeeds not as an analytic expression but as a symbolic device that highlights in a memorable way the importance of population growth, along with consumption and energy use, for sustainable development. The variables appear to be measurable, especially because they are put in the form of a mathematical equation, but like scale they are what Wassily Leontief would call implicit index numbers.

The Contributions of Wassily Leontief

While ecological economics cuts across the concerns of a number of academic disciplines, it is clear that those ecological economists who are grounded in economics have a privileged role to play. However, we also face the substantial challenge of rethinking the roles played by theory and practice both in conventional economics and in the first stage of ecological economics.

Wassily Leontief's critique of "implicit theorizing" and non-operational theory was directed initially at the "Cambridge economists," including Keynes (Leontief 1937), and later at neoclassical economics in general (Leontief 1971) but would seem to apply equally to Daly's macroeconomics. What is at issue is not only the content of the theory but especially the form of analysis, or methodology, that follows from it. Leontief would call Daly's concept of scale a "theoretical index number" (1937). It is an evocative metaphor, a short-cut description of a complex reality. But scale (like affluence or technology in the IPAT equation) is not an operational variable. Rather than providing a conceptual framework for analyzing the underlying reality, Daly as theorist is putting the burden of interpreting what scale really means in any concrete situation on the empirical analyst.

Leontief's creation, input-output economics (1966a, 1966b, 1977), describes an entire economy in terms of its interdependent parts. It succeeds in bridging the micro/macro gulf and provides general interdependency as an alternative to general equilibrium, with the almost exclusive importance that the latter attributes to the determination of prices. Input-output theory is operational in that it is expressed in terms of stocks and flows translatable into variables and parameters that are well defined for empirical analysis.

The basic input-output table for a particular economy in a given year is a familiar object: using double-entry accounting conventions, it tracks all transactions involving goods and services. The interdependence among the different sectors is established by a representation in which one sector's outputs are the inputs to other sectors. This tabular format has been firmly institutionalized over the past several decades: input-output tables are part of the United Nations System of National Accounts, and statistical offices in over 100 countries compile tables, ranging in size from a few dozen to a few hundred sectors, on a periodic basis.

Official input-output (IO) databases (i.e., tables and related data produced by government agencies) have been used for empirical analysis in literally thousands of studies around the world. They have relied upon Leontief's famous matrix equation, $(I - A) x = y$, relating outputs of goods and services (the vector, x) to final deliveries (y) through a concise description of the technologies in use in an economy. The mathematical "dual" of this equation, $(I - A') p = v$, is an equally simple and powerful representation that relates prices of goods and services (p) to factor costs (v). The technology of a given sector is represented by the vector of inputs per unit of output (a column of the A matrix), which in turn is derived in a straightforward way from the input-output table. Values of output are computed on the basis of alternative assumptions about changes in technology or in final deliveries, and changes in unit prices are computed on the basis of alternative assumptions about changes in technology or in factor costs. It is also straightforward to calculate other quantities, like amount of employment or use of a particular material. Some of the extensions of this simple static model are described in the discussion of structural economics.

IO models are used widely by ecological economists (and by economists who build empirical models of the economy of virtually any type). The representation of production in IO economics appealed to Nicholas Georgescu-Roegen, who made an original mathematical contribution in this area (1951), and to Daly himself who used the IO formalism to illustrate the interdependence between human activities and the natural world (1968). An important generalization of the IO framework was made by Robert Ayres and his colleagues for the explicit representation of material balances (Ayres and Kneese 1969; Ayres 1978). Bruce Hannon and his colleagues made equally important extensions for the representation of energy balances (e.g., Herendeen and Bullard 1975). Of these four pioneers, only Hannon—like Leontief—actually carried out empirical analyses of alternative scenarios, for example to evaluate the energy savings that might be associated with the use of buses rather than cars (Hannon and Puleo 1975). Recently Ayres produced figures quantifying detailed material balances for several materials (e.g., Ayres 1994), but he has not yet integrated them in an empirical analysis of production and consumption. Hannon and colleagues have recently proposed an IO type of framework for describing ecological systems (Hannon et al. 1991).

Input-output economics has been used extensively over the past few decades, but most applications have applied the basic, static equation to new sets of data. Because of this relatively mechanical use of the framework, IO has often been relegated to a status (like "applications," "National Accounting data," or "computer modeling") that buries its theoretical content and its roots in classical political economy. This is unfortunate because IO has a special and under appreciated role in ecological economics as the basis for structural economics. The realization of this potential requires a fundamental questioning of major pillars of conventional economic thinking.

Leontief has taken a number of pioneering positions that are further developed in structural economics. He achieves an intimate relationship among verbal theory, empirical information, and the mathematical language used in drawing quantitative conclusions and he provides a framework that can be used to evaluate alternative scenarios. Structural economics takes up the challenge of extending the framework and using it to analyze scenarios about sustainable development.

STRUCTURAL ECONOMICS IN THE SECOND STAGE

Scenarios and Valuation

Making operational the popular, but only vaguely defined, concept of sustainable development involves two important components.

- Coming up with concrete strategies about ways for people to make their livelihoods (discussed in the final section) in particular physical and cultural settings, and
- Creating a framework and tools for evaluating alternative strategies from environmental, economic, and social points of view.

Mainline economists, of course, have been active in both areas. Development economists produce development strategies, but these have been mainly concerned with removing barriers to the automatic functioning of markets in order to enhance growth. Economists have generally taken positions of principle about encouraging industries that can substitute for imported goods (now out of favor) or ones that can be expected to produce for export.

Operating under a different conception of the development process, Japan has had the custom of formulating strategic economic and technological objectives rather than idealizing market mechanisms or aiming merely for growth. This approach, in recent years sometimes called the Asian development model, depends not only on a substantial role for government in a market economy but also on the creation of "visions" about alternative future objectives. The most serious shortcoming of the Japanese approach is that it does not reflect the requirements and concerns of the ordinary people who are stakeholders in a particular setting. The challenge for researchers is to set the stage for broader participation by demonstrating what example scenarios might look like. The Japanese approach to economic strategy can be helpful for this purpose.

Cost-benefit analysis is an economist's approach to evaluating the trade-offs among alternative ways of proceeding. Because of the conceptual framework in which it is embedded, it is suited for evaluating small projects that make a marginal contribution to an economy. Substantial generalization of the approach is needed to apply it to ambitious projects that affect the entire fabric of an economy, such as alternative scenarios for sustainable development. Structural economics can provide this generalization.

The standard cost-benefit framework requires putting a money value on any characteristic that is to be taken into account, and it is regularly called into service to evaluate projects that have substantial social and environmental as well as economic implications. In the effort to include these effects, neoclassical environmental economists have defined new valuation categories—for example, so-called existence values, option values, or precautionary value—and techniques for assigning money values to them.

The subject of scenarios has received inappropriately little attention, even within ecological economics. Scenarios have a relatively short history of use in the social sciences and usually take a simple form in which only one or a few variables are assigned a high, medium, or low value. A neoclassical economist does not need detailed scenarios because in a general equilibrium framework, virtually all outcomes are determined by the mathematical model (i.e., by the clearing of markets). In the applied, partial equilibrium world of cost-benefit analysis, the project options do have to be specified, but this task is not the responsibility of the analyst. For these reasons, the development of scenarios is largely uncharted territory.

Valuation, on the other hand, is heavily trodden terrain. It is central to the neoclassical economist's conceptual framework in which money prices serve as the common denominator for reconciling values of all sorts. Individual money values that are determined analytically, rather than in markets, are combined with market values not only in cost-benefit studies but also in the compilation of various index numbers like "green GNP." Even many ecological economists lend at least half-hearted support to the enterprise of calculating a monetized bottom line—in large part for tactical reasons, to capture and maintain the attention of busy decision-makers and the presumably unsophisticated public.

With the move from evaluation of individual resources or characteristics, individual projects, and individual index numbers to evaluation of alternative scenarios for sustainable development, the temptation to reduce all values to money values for tactical purposes is substantially reduced. If the scenarios are of sufficiently compelling interest, stakeholders will be frustrated by the absurd prospect of obscuring the social, environmental, and economic implications of a given course of action by reducing them to a single, more or less arbitrary number. An understanding of the outcomes requires, at the very least, a set of numbers, only some of which are in money terms, and opens the door to incorporating important but often unquantifiable characteristics of outcomes based on the value of biological diversity and ethical behavior and not only the economist's notion of monetizable instrumentality.

Structural Economics

The objective of structural economics is to provide a conceptual model of the interdependent parts of an economy and a valuation framework in the form of a formalized, mathematical version of the conceptual model. Scenarios about alternative ways of making a livelihood can be represented and evaluated within the framework. Input-output economics is a powerful starting point for structural economics because it is formulated in terms of physical stocks and flows as well as costs and prices; units of analysis like the sector and the household which are larger than the basic units of mainstream microeconomic analysis, the individual business firm and the individual consumer; actions taken by governments and citizens as well as market transactions; and the interdependence between the economy and the physical world through the ease of representation of energy, materials, water, and so on, and the generation of pollution and other forms of environmental degradation. The principal challenges for structural economics are to provide a more detailed description of environmental and social phenomena, and a better integration between them and the economic core of the framework. Methods for the integration of qualitative along with quantitative description also need to be given a high priority.

It has proven popular among economists to extend the IO framework by incorporating the basic static matrix equation into general equilibrium models and into macroeconomic econometric models of the economy. These two categories of models are governed by neoclassical economic theory, and the IO portion is used as a practical means of assessing sector-level trade-offs among marginally different courses of action.

My colleagues and I have taken a different direction in the development of structural economics. The efforts at the Institute for Economic Analysis have been aimed at theoretical improvements to the model and substantial enhancement of its empirical content and usefulness for the evaluation of alternative scenarios about livelihood. Four areas of work are discussed next.

First, we have developed an operational, truly dynamic IO model to represent changes in the structure of an economy (Duchin and Szyld 1985; Duchin 1988). The dynamic, multi-sectoral analysis is superior to any form of static analysis, including so-called multiplier analyses and those summarizing future outcomes in a discounted present value, because the effects of changes are detailed and spread out over time. The dynamic model represents changes in capital stocks and stocks of resources, and it incorporates projections about technological changes; it is used in most of our empirical studies.

Second, we have attempted to build detailed scenarios about how things might be different in the future from the past. One of the major efforts is related to the future form of computer-based automation and its impact on labor requirements in households and in the production of goods and services (Leontief and Duchin 1986); another is about the changing use of energy and materials in homes, factories, and offices (Duchin and Lange 1994). In both cases, the underlying assumptions about structural change are documented in detail.

The IO Case Study methodology was developed at the Institute for Economic Analysis to facilitate the utilization of a great deal of fragmentary information in the construction of scenarios and their representation. It provides for a systematic way to record quantitative information, using standard classifications and units, as well as qualitative information which is used in qualifying and interpreting results.

Third, we have incorporated into the analytic framework a representation of the use of energy and materials, land, and water; technologies such as cogeneration of electricity or energy conservation, substitution and recycling of materials, and industrial reuse of water; and degradation of the environment in the form of erosion, water pollution and gaseous emissions to the air. Natural resource accounting provides a structure for collecting some of these kinds of information in a base year.

Natural resource accounting is less well-defined than other areas of accounting for two fundamental reasons. The first is that the appropriate scope for the accounts is unlimited and, consequently, what to include as a resource in constructing a particular set of accounts is arbitrary. Second, the accounts are generally prepared in money units only since their principal use is to quantify "green GNP". (For a critique of resource accounting and recommendations for a more strategic orientation, see Lange and Duchin 1994). In our work, base-year flow information is collected in physical units; an example for Indonesia is presented in (Lange, in press).

For use in analysis, the accounting information provides the basis for calculating parameters, which are projected to the future under the alternative scenarios; see Duchin et al. (1993) for such scenarios about the Indonesian economy. In early work in this area, all parameters were measured as mass of pollutant per unit of output. More recently, improved representations have been realized for some resources; see, for example, the representation of sulfur emissions (which depends not only on the volume of output but also on the choice of fuel and its sulfur content) and nitrogen emissions (dependent on the temperature of combustion) in Duchin and Lange (1994).

Finally, we are developing an approach to substantially improve the representation of roles of households, and especially of consumption, in development scenarios. Social accounting matrices (SAMs) provide a formal framework for quantifying exchanges among all institutions, including different categories of households. Social accounting is less well-known among ecological economists than natural resource accounting although it is ultimately equally important. In virtually all work to date, social accounting is used to quantify the distribution of income only; therefore, households are generally classified in terms of income categories, and all flows are recorded in money units only (Keuning 1994). Through the development of a household classification scheme based on several criteria simultaneously, and the use of physical as well as money units, we are attempting to integrate the content of anthropological studies into a generalized social accounting structure. (See the design for a case study of Indonesia in Duchin and Lange 1995.) This expanded representation should make it possible to distinguish how different kinds of households make their livelihoods, as a basis for creating scenarios about changes in their practices.

Scenarios about Livelihood

Individuals in all societies live in households with other adults and children, or alone. Each household's needs for food, shelter, health care, recreation, and so on, are satisfied through the efforts of the household members, both directly and through exchanges for goods and services produced by members of other households. Dozens of categories of households can be distinguished in each society in terms of their distinctive patterns of work and consumption. For example, as marketing analysts know, two urban households in the U.S. with two professional working parents and two children under the age of six will have similar patterns of consumption and work activities compared to a 4-person rural household where all members work on the family farm—even if total household income is the same in all cases. The prospects for changes in the patterns of livelihood in the two cases will also be very different. These kinds of differences are even starker in many developing countries where the difficulties of the transition from traditional to modern ways of living pose a fundamental social challenge. In fact, most of the social accounts that have been constructed are for countries undergoing rapid modernization.

The work of household members involves the production of agricultural products, processed foods, cooked meals, the construction of buildings, furnishing and cleaning them, providing health-care services and products, paper and electronics, books and television sets. Much of this work is done not in the home but in business establishments like wheat farms, paper mills, restaurants, and banks. While it is sometimes arbitrary to distinguish production from consumption activities, the latter refers to the use of these goods and services.

By the livelihood of a particular category of households I mean what its members value, what they produce and consume, and the techniques they use. Decisions affecting livelihood are taken in households and business establishments, as well as in government agencies, and these decisions affect resource use and environmental degradation.

I believe that it is necessary to develop scenarios about livelihood in order to make the concept of sustainable development operational, but very little work has been done in this area in part because sustainable development is still a relatively new idea, and the household is a relatively unaccustomed unit of analysis for economists. Building a scenario of this sort is a work of synthesis spanning the knowledge, experience, and the concerns of many stakeholders. Before people will commit their time to this task, it is necessary to demonstrate its feasibility and value.

Will people living in different kinds of households be interested in imagining—and experimenting with—lifestyles that could be comfortable and satisfying but that put less stress on the environment than those of today's affluent classes? Could less work, less consumption, and more leisure be more attractive than the "work and spend" cycle? For more on this issue, see Schor (1991) and her work in progress on consumption). Can a better choice of technologies support the production that makes these lifestyles possible while putting less stress on the environment than many of today's production processes? Will both kinds of changes combined be enough to make a substantial difference?

The creation of alternative technologies regarding the use of energy and materials is underway in the engineering community where there is an abundant literature about it. The kinds of considerations entertained in the new field of Industrial Ecology are described in (Duchin et al. in press). The idea of using a systems approach to create libraries of technologies is periodically mentioned in this community.

There is a large literature on lifestyles and consumption patterns. Anthropologists and other social scientists have provided qualitative description about the lifestyles and patterns of work and consumption of many categories of households in different societies, and economists have implemented SAMs as part of the national accounting systems of a number of countries including Indonesia, Thailand, Botswana, a few Latin American nations, and the Netherlands. But the idea of using a systems approach to organize the descriptions of the actual livelihoods of different categories of households, and to make projections within this framework about important kinds of changes, is unfamiliar, to say the least.

Scenarios can be described for the world as a whole (in response to global problems), for individual regions of the world, for countries, or for small areas within single countries. A scenario might cover many inter-related issues, as in the case of a national energy strategy, or it might be more narrowly focused, for example on the management of a mangrove swamp or the provision of credit to a specific set of women farmers. We need to develop concepts and a vocabulary for describing and classifying such scenarios so that we can consolidate, and build cumulatively upon, an enormous amount of fragmentary and essentially qualitative work of this type. Perhaps this is best accomplished by launching a coordinated set of studies of strategies for sustainable development in several specific geographic regions. The first round of work can be expected to provide a basis for subsequent generalization.

Ecological economists need to focus on the relation between people's livelihoods and the environment. If on the basis of our analyses the social and environmental priorities and preferred ways of achieving them can become better understood, then incentive schemes of various sorts can be designed for promoting these objectives. No environmental policy can achieve narrowly defined objectives without substantial side effects: It matters from both an environmental and a social—not to mention economic—point of view whether a carbon tax encourages more nuclear power plants or less use of cars. These interconnections need to be analyzed, not replaced by simpler exercises like the construction of "green GNP" or the design of green taxes. The most important policy message from the scientists among ecological economists is: We cannot afford to accept simplistic answers to complex questions; the stakes are too high. Hopefully, the policy analysts and journalists among us will be willing and able to demonstrate the importance of this message, and our literary colleagues can incorporate our concerns into their powerful metaphors.

ACKNOWLEDGMENTS

I am extremely grateful to Herman E. Daly, John Ehrenfeld, Richard England, John Gowdy, and Charles Hall for their extensive critiques of an earlier draft of this chapter. I also thank Virginia Abernethy, Robert Ayres, Peter Fleissner, Silvio Funtowicz, Jerry Ravetz, and Tom Teitenberg for their comments and criticisms. Naturally, none of the above are responsible for the views expressed in the chapter or for any remaining errors.

REFERENCES

Ayres, R. 1978. Resources, Environment, and Economics: Applications of the Materials/Energy Balance Principle. New York: John Wiley.

Ayres, R., and L. Ayres. 1994. Chemical industry wastes: A materials balance analysis. Working Paper, INSEAD. France: Fontainebleau.

Ayres, R., and A. Kneese. 1969. Production, consumption, and externalities. *American Economic Review* 59(3): 282–97.

Boulding, K. 1966. The economics of the coming spaceship earth. In Environmental Quality in a Growing Economy. Resources for the Future. Baltimore, MD: Johns Hopkins Press.

Boulding, K. 1973. Spaceship earth revisited. In Economics, Ecology, Ethics, ed. H. E. Daly. San Francisco, CA: W.H. Freeman and Company.

Daly, H. E. 1968. On economics as a life science. *Journal of Political Economy* 76(3): 392–406.

Daly, H. E. 1991. Elements of environmental macroeconomics. In Ecological Economics: The Science and Management of Sustainability, ed. R. Costanza. New York: Columbia University Press.

Daly, H.E. 1994. Reply. *Ecological Economics* 10(2): 90–91.

Duchin, F. 1988. Analyzing structural change in the economy. In Input-Output Analysis: Current Developments, ed. M. Ciaschini. London: Chapman and Hall.

Duchin, F. and G. Lange. 1994. The Future of the Environment: Ecological Economics and Technological Change. New York: Oxford University Press.

Duchin, F. and G. Lange. 1995. Households and eco-restructuring: The social dimension of ecological and development economics. Report on work in progress to the United Nations University, Tokyo. Institute for Economic Analysis, New York University.

Duchin, F. and D. Szyld. 1985. A dynamic input-output model with assured positive output. *Metroeconomica* 37: 269–282.

Duchin, F., C. Hamilton, and G. Lange. 1993. Environment and development in Indonesia: An input-output analysis of natural resource issues. Final report prepared for BAPPENAS (Indonesian Ministry of Planning), Natural Resource Management Project of USAID, and the Environmental Programming Support Services Project of CIDA. Institute for Economic Analysis, New York University.

Duchin, F., G. Lange, and G. Kell. (In Press) Technological change, trade, and the environment. Ecological Economics.

Ehrlich, P. and J. Holdren. 1974. Impact of population growth. *Science* 171: 1212–1217.

Funtowicz, S. and J. R. Ravetz. 1993. Science for the post-normal age. *Futures* 25: 739–755.

Georgescu-Roegen, N. 1951. Some properties of a generalized Leontief model. In Activity Analysis of Production and Allocation, ed. T. C. Koopmans. New York: J. Wiley and Sons.

Georgescu-Roegen, N. 1966. Analytical Economics: Issues and Problems. Cambridge, MA: Harvard University Press.

Georgescu-Roegen, N. 1971. The Entropy Law and the Economic Process. Cambridge, MA: Harvard University Press.

Goodland, R., H. Daly, and J. Kellenberg. 1994. Burden sharing in the transition to environmental sustainability. *Futures* 26(2): 146–155.

Gowdy, J., and P. Olsen. 1994. Further problems with neoclassical environmental economics. *Environmental Ethics* 16(Summer): 161–171.

Hannon, B. and F. Puleo. 1975. Transferring from urban cars to buses: The energy and employment impacts. In The Energy Conservation Papers, ed. R. H. Williams. Cambridge, MA: Ballinger.

Hannon, B., R. Costanza, and R. Ulanowicz. 1991. A general accounting framework for ecological systems. *Theoretical Population Biology* 40(1): 78–104.

Herendeen, R. and C. Bullard. 1975. Energy costs of goods and services. *Energy Policy* 3: 268–278.

Keuning, S. 1994. The SAM and beyond. *Economic Systems Research* 6(1): 21–50.

Lange, G. In press. Strategic planning for sustainable development in Indonesia using natural resource accounts. In Economy and Ecosystems in Change: Analytical and Historical Approaches, eds. J. van den Bergh and J. van der Straaten. Washington, DC: Island Press.

Lange, G. and F. Duchin. 1994. Integrated Environmental-Economic Accounting, Natural Resource Accounts, and Natural Resource Management in Africa. Washington, DC: Winrock International Environmental Alliance.

Leontief, W. 1937. Implicit theorizing: A methodological criticism of the neo-Cambridge school. *Quarterly Journal of Economics* 51(2): 337–51.

Leontief, W. 1966a. Essays in Economics (Vol. I): Theories and Theorizing. New York: Oxford University Press.

Leontief, W. 1966b. Input-Output Economics. New York: Oxford University Press.

Leontief, W. 1971. Theoretical assumptions and nonobserved facts. *American Economic Review* 61(1): 1–7.

Leontief, W. 1977. Essays in Economics (Vol.II): Theories, Facts, and Policies. White Plains, New York: International Arts and Sciences (now M.E. Sharpe, Inc.).

Leontief, W. and F. Duchin. 1986. The Future Impact of Automation on Workers. New York: Oxford University Press.

Martinez-Alier, J. and K. Schlupmann. 1987. Ecological Economics. Oxford: Basil Blackwell.

Sack, R. D. 1992. Place, Modernity, and the Consumer's World. Baltimore: Johns Hopkins University Press.

Schor, J. 1991. The Overworked American: The Unexpected Decline of Leisure. Basic Books.

Snow, C. P. 1956. The two cultures. New Statesman. October.

15 MODELING THE DYNAMICS OF RESOURCE DEPLETION, SUBSTITUTION, RECYCLING, AND TECHNICAL CHANGE IN EXTRACTIVE INDUSTRIES

Matthias Ruth

Center for Energy and Environmental Studies
and Department of Geography
Boston University
675 Commonwealth Avenue
Boston, MA 02215

Cutler J. Cleveland

Center for Energy and Environmental Studies
and Department of Geography
Boston University
675 Commonwealth Avenue
Boston, MA 02215

OVERVIEW

Various counteracting factors determine the availability of natural resources for the economy. As extraction proceeds, resource quality and quantity tend to decrease. The move to lower quality resources creates the potential to divert energy, materials, and labor to the extractive sectors. As a result, depletion raises the cost of extracting the next unit of the resource. On the other hand, recycling, the use of substitutes and technical change may drive down the unit cost of extraction, opposing the forces of resource depletion. It is impossible to judge *a priori* which of those factors predominates trends in the availability of a particular natural resource. However, dynamic computer modeling can help assess the relative strength and timing of the factors that determine availability of natural resources. Towards this end, we develop a model of the important feedback processes among mineral and fossil fuel extraction industries, and apply that model to U.S. copper production. The study distinguishes itself from previous analyses by its extensive use of empirical and engineering information within the context of a nonlinear dynamic model.

INTRODUCTION

A principal goal of modeling in ecological economics is to develop quantitative, pluralistic, and integrated models that effectively deal with the inherent uncertainty in complex systems (Jansson et al. 1994; Costanza et al. 1993). One area where this approach needs to be applied is the use of natural resources in economic systems. For more than three decades, dynamic models have been used to assess the adequacy of natural resources to meet human needs. Many models focus on the relative strengths of positive and negative feedback processes that influence the availability of natural resources. Most notable is the question whether technical change, the use of substitutes, or recycling can compensate for a decrease in the quality or quantity of an essential resource. As extraction proceeds, resource quality and quantity tend to decrease. It may be more costly to extract, for example, a ton of metal or a barrel of oil from an increasingly depleted resource. Recycling, use of substitutes and technical change, on the other hand, may drive down the unit cost of extraction, opposing the forces of resource depletion. The relative strength and timing of these forces are difficult to specify *a priori* (Norgaard 1975; Walker and Young 1986; Cleveland 1991a), leading some analysts to assess the path of extraction cost with empirical dynamic models. Detailed analysis and extensive use of empirical and engineering information is required to measure the interconnections and feedbacks among depletion, recycling, substitution, and technical change.

This chapter develops a model of the important feedback processes among mineral and fossil fuel extraction industries, and applies that model to U.S. copper production. The study distinguishes itself from previous analyses by its extensive use of empirical and engineering information within the context of a nonlinear dynamic model. The chapter is organized as follows. In the next two sections we discuss various approaches used to assess the use of natural resources in economic systems. We then outline several challenges of modeling complex, dynamic systems, describe the structure of the model, and provide the empirical basis for the model specification. The results are presented and discussed, followed by a brief set of conclusions.

MODELING NATURAL RESOURCE USE: THE ECONOMIC APPROACH

Economic models that attempt to capture feedback processes in extractive industries are increasingly ambitious. Early economic models of natural resource use were highly theoretical and focused on the optimal path of resource extraction given a set of assumptions about the behavior of resource-extracting firms (Gray 1913, 1914; Hotelling 1931). Advances within economics take the form of introducing into these theoretical models aspects of alternative market structures, such as monopolies (Kay and Mirrlees 1975; Stiglitz 1976; Sweeney

1977; Pindyck 1978), decisions under uncertainty (Hoel 1978; Loury 1978; and Pindyck 1979), uncertain future resource prices (Weinstein and Zeckhauser 1975), and uncertain future demand (Dasgupta and Heal 1974; Long 1975; Lewis 1977). As Norgaard (1989) notes, these changes have not produced any major theoretical advances in the half century since Hotelling, with improvements largely taking the form of interesting but secondary caveats to Hotelling's original assumptions. Empirical tests of the neoclassical model are scant (Eagan 1987; Watkins 1992), and those available give mixed results about the validity of the model's assumptions.

The second pillar of the neoclassical model of natural resource use is the empirical analysis of resource scarcity by Barnett and Morse (1963) who found that, with the exception of forestry resources, extractive resources in the U.S. did not become more scarce from 1870 to 1957. In updates of the original study, Barnett (1979) confirms that result, Smith (1979), in contrast, rejects it on statistical grounds. Slade (1982, 1985) incorporates exogenous technical progress and endogenous change in ore quality into an optimal control model of resource depletion. Slade concludes that long-term price movements exhibit a U-shaped path that reflects the diminishing ability of technical change to overcome the effects of physical depletion. Hall and Hall (1984) also find evidence for increasing scarcity of some resources in the 1970s.

MODELING NATURAL RESOURCE USE: THE BIOPHYSICAL AND SYSTEM DYNAMICS APPROACH

The energy and environmental events of the 1970s spurred development of new modeling approaches and expanded the modeling of natural resource use. These approaches fall into the general categories of the biophysical and system dynamics approach. In one way or another, these approaches focus on the flow of energy and materials in economic systems, the physical and technological aspects of resource availability and transformation, and how changes in the cost, quality and availability of resources affect the economy. Thermodynamics provides the starting point for many of these models because it tells us where we are with respect to a fixed reference point in terms of the physical quality of the resource base, and in some cases, the technologies used to extract and upgrade resources to a useful state (Ruth 1993, 1995a; Ruth and Bullard 1993).

The biophysical approach defines the resource transformation process as one that uses energy to upgrade the organization of matter to a more useful state (Ayres 1978; Cook 1976; Gever et al. 1986; Hall et al. 1986; Cleveland 1991; Ruth, 1993). By definition, lower quality resources require more energy to upgrade to a given state. The same fundamental relationship exists for renewable and nonrenewable natural resources (Hall et al. 1986). Just as more energy is required to isolate copper metal from a lower grade ore, more energy is required to pump oil from deeper and smaller fields, harvest food from less fertile soil, and catch fish from smaller and more remote areas.

A second tenet of the biophysical model emphasizes the role that energy plays in technical innovation in the extractive sector. Technical improvements that boost labor productivity have taken the form of using more energy per laborer, often in the form of more powerful energy converters (Georgescu-Roegen 1975). Empirical research demonstrates a significant relationship between labor productivity, the quantity of installed horsepower (Maddala 1965) and fuel use (Hall et al. 1986) per worker in the U.S. extractive sector. Energy converters have also evolved towards the use of higher quality forms of energy. Animate energy converters such as human labor and draft animals were replaced by inanimate energy converters burning wood and coal, then oil and natural gas, and eventually electricity.

The move to lower quality resources creates the potential to divert energy, materials, and labor to the extractive sectors. The diversion is generated by a positive feedback relationship between the depletion of nonrenewable resources and the depletion of fossil fuel resources (Ayres 1978). Large amounts of fossil fuels are used to extract minerals and fossil fuels themselves. Cumulative depletion of a metal, such as copper, and a fuel, such as oil, increase the energy cost of extracting a unit of each. As the quality of copper ore declines, more oil is used to extract a ton of metal. The increase in the energy cost of copper increases the cumulative depletion of oil, which in turn increases the energy cost of oil, and so on. A positive feedback is established in which the depletion of fossil fuels and other minerals feed on each other. One possible result of the interdependency of fuel and mineral depletion is that an increasing fraction of available energy supply is diverted to the extractive sectors to supply the economy with the same amount of extractive output.

These feedbacks have important environmental implications. More energy per unit of extracted or refined product generates more waste heat and waste materials. For example, the decline in quality of the U.S. oil resource base has increased the energy cost of oil extraction. In turn, this has increased the amount of CO_2 released by the fuel burned to extract the oil, and the amount of water used per barrel of oil (Cleveland 1993). In surface metal and coal mines, a decline in resource quality increases the stripping ratio and hence the amount of waste produced per unit of the product (Gelb 1984).

Several factors can mitigate the spiral of energy costs and environmental impacts. Improvements in the efficiency of the energy converters in the extractive sector can offset the increase in energy use caused by cumulative depletion (Ruth 1995b). Technical improvements can reduce energy costs in other sectors of the economy faster than energy costs increase in the extractive sector. Recycling is a type of backstop technology that mitigates direct energy cost because the energy cost of producing a unit of metal from recycled scrap is significantly less than from primary sources (Gaines and Stodolsky 1993). Similarly, technical improvements can reduce the release of waste heat and materials per unit of product (Yoshiki-Gravelsins et al. 1993a, 1993b).

A number of techniques are used to model the interconnections among resource quality, energy and material use, technology, the economy, and the environment. Dynamic simulation models were popularized by The Limits to Growth (Meadows et al. 1972) and Beyond the Limits (Meadows et al. 1992) models. These models were the first ambitious attempts to conceptualize and measure at least some of the interrelationships among depletion, technical change, substitution and economic development. The models are frequently criticized for their lack of specific, detailed empirical information that actually describe and measure those interrelationships, and for their lack of market-driven negative feedbacks that could mitigate resource and environmental degradation. The furor over the projections of the models obscured their pathbreaking and powerful heuristic value.

The dynamic models in Beyond Oil (Gever et al. 1986) use a much richer empirical base to simulate the interconnections among the depletion of fossil fuels, the degradation of the agricultural resource base, energy efficiency, population growth, and the standard of living in the U.S. They project that per capita GNP will rise until the turn of the century, when it levels off and then drops until again leveling off in 2025. The principal driving forces in their models are the depletion of resources and diminishing returns to technology. Taming the Future (Watt 1992) develops dynamic simulation models of the interaction between the depletion of fossil fuels and key economic variables such as new investment and consumer prices. Watt argues that a few key relationships determine the behavior of entire economies, and he uses their historical values to forecast crude oil prices, oil production, business cycles, consumer prices, and population growth. Watt predicts that by 2010, the effects of fossil fuel depletion will be so severe that "talk of either population growth or economic growth will be a distant memory".

THE CHALLENGE OF MODELING COMPLEX, DYNAMIC SYSTEMS

With the popularization of computer models for natural resource policy-making attention is now directed at a number of closely related issues that potentially dilute the effectiveness of those models in decision-making (Smil 1993). First, all models are abstractions from reality and, therefore, incomplete. As Costanza et al. (1993) note, it is inappropriate to think of models as anything but crude, although in many cases absolutely essential, abstract representations of reality. What to include or exclude from a model depends on the goal of the model and is a choice that is ultimately made within a cultural, socioeconomic, and scientific context. As a result of the diversity in perceptions and aspirations of modelers with different cultural and scientific backgrounds, there are a large number of different methods for modeling resource use in economic systems, each of which has a unique set of strengths and weaknesses.

Second, unlike models of physical systems that are based on invariant rules, models of human systems are prone to misspecifications of the complexities of human behaviors. The context-dependence of human activities together with the variability in rules used to make decisions limit the applicability of models for descriptive and predictive purposes. The predictive ability of models is further reduced by the possibility of the occurrence of previously unencountered constraints on, and development possibilities for, the systems. The latter is frequently subsumed under the notion of novelty, and most prominent in the case of technological breakthroughs or discoveries of new deposits of a resource.

Third, models of natural resource use tend to become larger and more complex as modelers and decision-makers ask to include aspects of the system that have previously been treated as exogenous to the model. There is an increased tendency to "close" models, (i.e., to minimize the number of exogenously specified parameters and relationships). However, with increasing scale and model complexity only experts, frequently only the creators of the models themselves, can interpret the structure, dynamics, and results of the model.

Fourth, complex systems are characterized by substantial uncertainty that must be addressed as a central part of the model building and evaluation process, not relegated to the sidelines as is commonly the case (Funtowicz and Ravetz 1994). The task is to manage the uncertainty of each model in order to gain the highest quality information from it. The enormous uncertainty in the relationship between the economy and the environment calls for a plurality of modeling approaches and perspectives.

Given the number and complexity of models developed to assess issues of natural resource use, decision-makers frequently are faced with the following dilemma. If they choose one model over another, decision makers effectively transfer part of their power to the modeler. By using a number of models on which to base their decisions, the non-expert policy-makers are left to reconcile the different assumptions underlying the models, thus opening themselves up for criticism irrespective of the value of their decision. Many modeling exercises are full of hyper-precise numerical data, specious sophistication about uncertainties, and unsupported hunches and loaded rhetoric (Funtowicz and Ravetz 1994), leaving policy-makers with little hope of sorting through the various approaches.

Not surprisingly, the call for more transparent, flexible, yet more comprehensive models is common (Meadows and Robinson 1985). Some promote a revolution in systems thinking that furthers the democratization of the modeling process (Hardin 1980; Hannon and Ruth 1994). In this chapter we contribute to these goals by developing a template for, and example of, a flexible, comprehensive, yet transparent, model for the assessment of natural resource use in economic systems. We employ a systems approach to the analysis of resource depletion, substitution, recycling and technical change in extractive industries. The model extends traditional system boundaries, typically chosen to encompass the processing stages of a single resource, to subsume the dynamics of processes in related extractive industries.

The assessment of resource use can be done in monetary or physical terms. We choose to concentrate on calculating the energy cost of resource extraction to assess the dynamics of resource extraction and economic adjustment for the following reasons. First, unlike market prices, energy costs are less sensitive to small changes in the socio-political system. For example, prices of mineral resources are frequently guided by expectations about future extraction, which in turn are dependent on changes in technologies, consumer preferences and institutional arrangements. As a result, price changes may occur without any relationship to changes in the physical resource base. Second, not only prices for the output of extractive industries but also prices for inputs are prone to market fluctuations independent of changes in the resource base or technologies. Price changes of inputs affect the monetary cost of production, and thus the price of minerals and metals. Consequently, the monetary cost of resource extraction, too, may not be a good indicator of the availability of natural resources. Third, assessing resource use in energy terms rather than monetary terms enhances integration of engineering information into models of resource use, and at the same time, facilitates communication of model results to decision makers without being forced to solely rely on market based data. Additionally, it is typically easier to build models on the physical workings of the system and then express the resulting effects in monetary units than vice versa.

MODELING THE DYNAMICS OF NATURAL RESOURCE USE

Models of the relationship between resource depletion and technical change frequently neglect the interdependencies among resources. For example, extracting copper ore and processing it to yield metal requires significant energy use at each stage of the process. Models that assess the energy cost of resource extraction are incomplete if they only account for the extraction of the ore and neglect the energy cost of producing the metal. Furthermore, the energy necessary to bring about a change in state in copper at various processing stages itself has to be extracted from coal mines and oil wells. Energy extraction, in turn, requires energy. Consequently, a comprehensive assessment of the energy cost of copper production requires that energy cost of energy extraction and supply are properly accounted for, along with the energy cost of mineral extraction and processing.

Extraction of minerals typically proceeds from high to low quality sources. As ore grades decrease and as wells and mines are depleted, the energy cost of extracting the next ton of ore, barrel of oil or cubic feet of gas tends to increase. Lower quality resources also tend to generate more wastes and pollution per unit extracted (Ayres 1978; Cleveland 1991a). The changes in the physical characteristics of the resource base are accompanied by economic adjustments that mitigate depletion and environmental constraints (Ruth 1993). The four most important adjustments are: technical change, which increases the effectiveness of resource extraction and processing; recycling, which reduces pressure on the mineral resource base; substitution of one energy or material resource for another; and discoveries of new deposits of the resource. Technical change, recycling, the provision of substitutes and the exploration and development of new deposits, in turn, require energy that must first be extracted.

A fundamental issue in natural resource scarcity is whether technical change, recycling and substitution enable economies to free themselves from resource constraints, and, most importantly, whether economies can continue to do so in the future. The debate on this issue continues to be controversial. We contend that a model designed to give meaningful answers to this question must fulfil at least the following requirements:

- The model must be dynamic, rather than comparative static;
- Qualitative, physical changes in material and energy reserves must be captured;
- Interdependencies among depletion of fuel and material resources must be identified;
- Important technological features of resource extraction and processing industries must be incorporated;
- Recycling, substitution, and technical change must be endogenous to the model since none of them are self-generating;
- The specification of recycling, substitution and technical change must be constrained by the physical laws that govern efficiencies of all transformation processes;
- The relationships among system components must be based on empirical observation rather than *ad hoc* and unsubstantiated assumptions about forces that drive the real systems. Crucial assumptions and important areas of uncertainty must be explicitly justified and documented.

The model developed in this study is part of an ambitious effort to incorporate all these requirements into a comprehensive model of several major U.S. mineral industries. Since we present here the findings for only one metals industry we cannot effectively endogenize substitution among different metals. By the same token, copper recycling rates are given exogenously. However, we endogenize the fractions of different scrap types that are being recycled.

The model consists of a set of modules that communicate information with each other. The relationships among model components are illustrated in Figure 15.1. To illustrate the model, we only deal in this chapter with a single metal—copper—and five energy sectors—oil, natural gas, coal, uranium, and electricity.

A primary feature of the model is the transparency of the linkages between modules that communicate the use of data and functional relationships. Energy is used to mine, smelt, refine and recycle metal products for consumption. Further, energy is used to extract energy sources and to generate electricity for use in other mineral industries. Output of each subsector of the economy is determined by the demands in the other sectors of the model. The principal exogenous input is a forecast of apparent metal consumption for each metal.

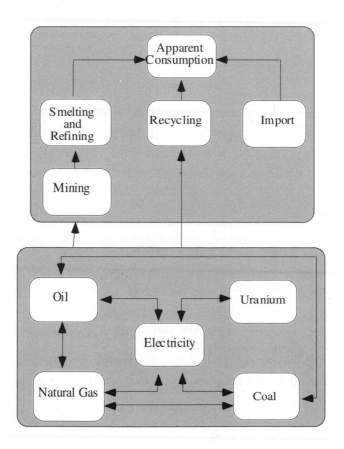

Figure 15.1. Modules of, and linkages among, metal and energy sectors.

The dynamics of each module and the linkages among them are captured in a systems dynamics model. The functional relationships within and among modules are specified with deterministic equations derived from economic theory and engineering studies. The parameters of each equation, and thus the relative strengths of feedback processes, is provided by statistical and econometric analyses of past system behavior, and by engineering studies.

The use of historical data to estimate parameters embodies a critical assumption: there will be no major structural changes in the extractive industries in the forecast period extending from 1987 to 2037. This is a reasonable assumption for the following reasons. First, U.S. mineral and fuel extracting industries use mature technologies that are not likely to significantly change in the 50 year period forecast by the model (Chapman and Roberts 1983). Extractive sectors that have a high ability to further adopt new technologies are likely to also have done so in the past. For example, in the US oil industry rotary rigs completely replaced turbo drills within a relatively short period of 10–20 years. Such relatively rapid changes are reflected in the time series data for the respective industry.

Second, the ability to substitute some major metals for each other seems exhausted, as it is apparent in the case of copper and aluminum (Kaufmann and Drury 1987). Third, even if major technological changes took place, new technologies diffuse gradually and thus will be in operation only after a considerable time lag (Slade 1985). Finally, once implemented, new technologies will be used jointly with present technologies, thereby dampening, on an industry-wide level, the overall effect of a technological breakthrough. The tendency to use capital equipment of different vintages is widespread in the mineral extracting and processing industries that utilize large-scale technologies to realize economies of scale.

The development of the model is done with the graphical programming language STELLA II® (Richmond and Peterson 1994; Hannon and Ruth 1994). The entire modeling process is open and highly interactive. It enables adaptations of general models to particular problems and linkage with other dynamic models. Modifications of both structure and parameter values occur simultaneously as new information is acquired that affects the model. For large-scale, interdisciplinary modeling efforts it is of paramount importance to maintain transparency and enable experts who contribute to the model to identify with, and keep track of, their contribution.

The dynamics of the model are determined by the specification of the workings of each module and their interrelationships. These are discussed in the following section.

MODEL SPECIFICATIONS

Changes in Resource Quality

Consistent with economic theory we assume that extraction proceeds from higher to lower grade ore deposits. The change in copper ore grade $g_c(t)$ over time is represented as a function of cumulative copper mine production $Q_c(t)$ and mine production rate $Y_c(t)$.

(1)
$$g_c(t) = \beta_{1c} \, Q_c(t)^{\beta_{2c}} Y_c(t)^{\beta_{3c}}$$

The parameters $\beta_{1c,}$ β_{2c} and β_{3c} are constants that are estimated from historical time series using regression analysis.

Changes in uranium ore grade $g_u(t)$ are specified as a function of cumulative uranium extraction $Q_u(t)$, the rate of production $Y_u(t)$, and parameters $\beta_{iu,}$ (i =1:3)

(2)
$$g_u(t) = \beta_{1u} \, Q_u(t)^{\beta_{2u}} Y_u(t)^{\beta_{3u}}$$

Changes in the quality of fossil fuel resources are measured by the quantity of energy used to extract them. As in the case of ore grade, cumulative production is assumed to diminish the quality or quantity of energy reserves. The energy intensity $\varepsilon_i(t)$ of oil, natural gas and coal (i = o, n, c), measured in Btu of energy input per Btu extracted, is expected to increase with cumulative depletion:

(3)
$$\varepsilon_i(t) = \alpha_{1i} \, e^{\alpha_{2i} Q_i(t)} \quad (i = o, n, c)$$

a_{1i} and a_{2i} are parameters and $Q_i(t)$ is cumulative extraction in the respective sector.

Technical Change

Although continued extraction is likely to decrease ore grades and increase the energy cost of energy extraction, technical change may overcome those adverse trends. Technical change is modeled endogenously with learning curves that relate improvements in the energy efficiency of a process to the experience of executing that process. Experience is represented as cumulative production (Yelle 1979). The functional form for the learning curves used in the modules calculating the energy cost of extracting metal from ore is:

(4)
$$\left(e_i(t) - e_i^*(t)\right) = \gamma_{1i} \, Q_i(t)^{\gamma_{2i}} \quad (i = m, s)$$

Here, $e_i(t)$ is energy use per ton of output, is $e_i^*(t)$ the physically determined minimum energy requirement extracting the metal from the ore, and γ_{1i} and γ_{2i} are parameters. Cumulative production is easily calculated from published data, and energy requirements are available from engineering studies. For the model, learning curves are estimated for copper mining (i = m) and copper smelting and refining (i = s) stages of the production process.

Combined Effect of Changes in Resource Quality and Technology

The combined effect of a decrease in ore grade and an increase in the efficiency of copper mining results in a particular energy demand at each point in time. Fuel use in mining, $e_m(t)$ is equal to the energy requirement for mining and milling ore of a given grade with a given technology, $\bar{e}_m(t)$, divided by the efficiency $\eta_m(t)$ with which fuels are used at that ore grade. Thus, fuel use per unit output in mining is defined by:

(5) $$e_m(t) = \frac{\bar{e}_m(t)}{g(t)\,\eta_m(t)}$$

Similar to the mining sector, fuel use per ton of copper from smelting and refining $e_s(t)$ is defined as the ratio of energy requirement $\bar{e}_s(t)$, and energy efficiency $\eta_s(t)$:

(6) $$e_s(t) = \frac{\bar{e}_s(t)}{\eta_s(t)}$$

Unlike the mining sector, ore grade is not a determinant of fuel use in smelting and refining since the minerals supplied by the mining and milling operations typically are of uniform quality.

Following Chapman and Roberts (1983) the energy efficiencies of the mining and smelting sectors each are defined as the ratio of minimum to actual fuel use:

(7) $$\eta_i(t) = \frac{e_i^*(t)}{e_i(t)}\,, \quad (i = m, s).$$

where $e_m^*(t)$ is the thermodynamic minimum amount of energy required to extract metal from ore of a particular grade and $e_s^*(t)$ is the thermodynamic minimum energy required in smelting and refining the metal.

Equations (4) to (7) can be combined to yield aggregate fuel use for mining and smelting (Chapman and Roberts 1983; Cleveland and Ruth in press)

$$(8) \quad e(t) = \bar{e}_m \, Q_c^{\beta_{2c}} \left(\gamma_{1m} Q_m^{\gamma_{2m}} + 1 \right) + \bar{e}_s \left(\gamma_{1s} Q_s^{\gamma_{2s}} + 1 \right)$$

The constants β_{2c}, γ_{1i} and γ_{2i} ($i = m$, s) are derived from equations (1) and (4). Values for cumulative extraction and production $Q_c(t) = Q_m(t)$, and $Q_s(t)$ are derived from historical data. The constants $\bar{e}_m(t)$ and $\bar{e}_s(t)$ are defined by (5) and (6).

Recycling

Recycling processes are well developed for many metals. Recycling dimin-ishes the feedback between decreasing ore grades in the metal industries and increased fuel requirements for metal production from virgin ores. Although recycling typically is less energy intensive than production from virgin ores, energy consumption in the metal recycling industry is significant and distinct in the type of fuels used, as it is evident in the case of copper (Table 15.1).

Copper recycling rates since 1978 fluctuated around a mean rate of 26.8% with standard deviation of 6.6%. Forecasting future recycling rates requires detailed forecasts on economic variables such as relative prices of copper from virgin ore and scrap, which is outside the scope of this model. In contrast, forecast of changes in the relative fractions of copper scrap types can be made more reliably, based on observations of rates of scrap consumption by smelters and cumulative smelter consumption.

We distinguish four different scrap types of copper metal: No. 1 scrap, No. 2 scrap, brass and bronze scrap, and low grade scrap. Various functional forms to explain fractions of scrap types have been explored and those with the best statistical fit have been chosen. In the model, the fractions $f_i(t)$ of the various scrap types are specified as:

$$(9) \quad f_i = \alpha_i \, Y_i^{\beta_i}, \quad (i = \text{No. 2, brass and bronze})$$

$$(10) \quad f_{\text{low grade}} = \alpha_{\text{low grade}} \, Q_R^{\beta_{\text{low grade}}}$$

with Y_i as the rates of scrap consumption by smelters and Q_R as cumulative low grade scrap consumption by smelters. In the model, the fraction for No. 1 scrap is set such that all fractions sum to one.

Table 15.1.   The Mix of Fuel Use in the Extraction of Crude Oil, Natural Gas, Coal, and   Uranium, in the Generation of Electricity, and Copper Scrap Recycling. Unless Otherwise Noted, Values are for 1987.

Sector	Coal share	Oil share	Natural Gas share	Electricity share	Renewables share	Nuclear share
Uranium extraction	0	.15	.35	.50	NA	NA
Copper extraction	0	.28	.20	.52	NA	NA
Coal extraction	.0	.55	.01	.37	0	NA
Crude oil extraction	0	.16	.74	.10	NA	NA
Natural gas extraction	0	.16	.74	.10	NA	NA
Electricity generation						
1990	.52	.04	.13	NA	.12	.19
forecast for 2010	.52	.04	.18	NA	.12	.14
No. 1 scrap recycling	.01	.13	71	.15	NA	NA
No. 2 scrap recycling	.02	.38	.04	.56	NA	NA
Brass and bronze scrap recycling	.04	.05	.79	12	NA	NA
Low grade copper scrap recycling	.51	.14	.01	34	NA	NA

NA = not applicable. Data for the extractive sectors from the Bureau of Census (1987). Data for electricity generation from the Department of Energy (1992). Data for scrap recycling from Department of the Interior, Bureau of Mines (1978).

Fuel Mix

The extraction of the fuels and the metals in the model requires different types of energy. For example, the extraction of oil uses large quantities of gas, while the mining of copper uses large quantities of oil and electricity. The mix of fuels and electricity required to extract oil, gas, coal, uranium, and copper are based on Bureau of Census (1987) data. The Census reports the quantities of each type of fuel used to generate electricity. The fuel mix in each of the extractive sectors and copper recycling in 1987 and in the generation of electricity is shown in Table 15.1.

Electricity Generation and the Demand for Uranium

We assume that the demand for electricity that is calculated by the model is generated by the same average fuel mix as in the U.S. economy (Table 15.1). This assumption ignores the fact that the extraction of each resource occurs in regions where the fuel mix of electricity generation is different than the U.S. as a whole. However, it does provide a reasonable aggregate measure of the demand for various fuels to generate electricity.

Imports

We assume that all demand for energy generated by the model comes from domestic resources of fossil and uranium fuels. Of course, the U.S. imports large amounts of oil and uranium fuel. But the purpose of our model is to demonstrate the feedback between the depletion of copper and the depletion of fossil fuels, so forecasting import dependence adds a layer of complexity to the model that is not necessary to investigate our main point. Furthermore, the import dependence especially on copper, oil, and uranium is itself due in part to the high cost of domestic production caused by depletion.

The forecast period extends beyond the time when conventional domestic resources of oil will be significantly depleted (Cleveland and Kaufmann 1991; Kaufmann 1991). Domestic oil production will be replaced by substantial imports of oil and/or by switching to different fuels. One could argue that imports of copper, for example, are not "energy free" because energy is used in the U.S.A. to manufacture goods that are traded for copper. A logical extension of this model will be to account for oil imports and the substantial energy cost associated with producing the goods and services that the U.S. trades for oil. Indeed, the energy return on investment for oil imports also has decline because higher energy prices require more goods and services (and hence more energy) to be used to trade for a barrel of oil (Hall et al. 1986).

Data Sources

Energy use per ton of output in copper mining and metal production is derived from Census of Manufacturers (Bureau of the Census, various issues) and Minerals Yearbooks (Bureau of Mines, various issues). Minimum energy requirements are estimated based on physical laws and engineering information provided by Argonne National Laboratories (Gaines 1980). For details of the calculations see Ruth (1995b).

Data on the net generation of electricity by fuel and the thermal efficiency of fossil fuel power plants are from the Department of Energy (1991). We use the Department of Energy (1992) forecast of changes in the fuel mix in electricity generation through 2010. During the next 20 years, the Department of Energy forecasts that coal will continue to generate about one-half of total electricity, the contribution of nuclear power will decline, gas will increase, and oil will decline. After 2010 we hold the fuel mix constant at its 2010 value, since there are no reliable forecasts after that date. The quantity of each fossil fuel used to generate electricity is based on the efficiency of fossil steam electric plants, which we hold constant at its 1987 value of 10,253 BTU per kilowatt hour. This assumption is consistent with the relatively constant thermal efficiency of power plants over the past 30 years (Department of Energy 1991).

The demand for electricity from nuclear power plants is used to calculate the quantity of uranium ore that must be extracted to produce the enriched nuclear fuel. This calculation is based on the efficiency of converting ore to enriched fuel, the thermal efficiency of nuclear power plants and their gross-to-net power ratio, and the efficiency of uranium mills (Laurence Sanders, Department of Energy, pers. comm.). We make the simplifying assumption that all of the uranium fuel is produced from domestic uranium mines, ignoring for the moment our substantial reliance on imports of uranium.

Econometric Results

The econometric estimates of the functions specified above are listed in Table 15.2. As expected, increases in cumulative production and production rates drive down ore grades of copper and uranium. Similarly, increases in cumulative extraction of fossil fuels increases their energy cost of extraction. As consumption of scrap increases, so does the fraction of No. 2 scrap, indicating that more medium quality scrap will be used. Brass and bronze scrap as well as low grade scrap, in contrast, decline in their importance as a supplier of copper mainly because higher quality scrap types are likely to be collected more efficiently and made available for the economy.

Table 15.2. Results of Economic Equations (t values in parentheses).

Copper extraction
ln (ore grade) = .82 - .013 (cumulative metal extraction) - .39 (rate of metal extraction)
            (9.1)   (5.2)   (3.1)
time period: 1907 - 1989
adjusted R^2 = .91
DW = 1.6

Uranium extraction
ln (ore grade) = -1.2 - .0009 (cumulative metal extraction) - .004 (rate of metal extraction)
            (4 2.6)   (2.9)   (16.7)
time period: 1947 - 1985
adjusted R^2 = .92
DW = 1.7

Table. 15.2. Continued.

Crude oil extraction

Energy use per Btu = .06 + .37*10^{-19} (cumulative oil extraction)

         (23.8)   (3.4)

time period: 1954 - 1987

adjusted R^2 = .43

DW = 1.3

Natural gas extraction

Energy use per Btu = .01 + .62*10-20 (cumulative gas extraction)

              (26.6)   (3.6)

time period: 1954 - 1987

adjusted R^2 = .46

DW = 1.4

Coal extraction

Energy use per Btu = .005 + .62*10-20 (cumulative coal extraction)

        (11.4)   (4.6)

time period: 1954 - 1987

adjusted R^2 = .53

DW = 1.2

No. 2 scrap

ln (f$_{No. 2}$) = -8.67 + 0.56 ln (smelter scrap consumption rate)

            (-4.3) (3.8)

time period: 1978 - 1993

adjusted R^2 = .47

DW = 1.8

Brass and bronze scrap

ln (f$_{brass and bronze}$) = 12.27 - 1.01 ln (smelter scrap consumption rate)

                (-4.1) (-4.5)

time period: 1978 - 1993

adjusted R^2 = .56

DW = 2.2

Low grade scrap

ln (f$_{low grade}$) = 4.47 - 0.38 ln (cumulative smelter scrap consumption rate)

           (2.1) (-2.8)

time period: 1978 - 1993

adjusted R^2 = .42

DW = 1.7

Learning in copper mining and refining

ln (e-e*) = 12.59 - 0.21 ln (cumulative mine production rate)

        (220.3) (-2.0)

time period: 1958 - 1981

adjusted R^2 = .11

DW = 1.9

Learning in copper smelting

ln (e-e*) = 22.74 - 1.09 ln (cumulative smelter production rate)

        (3.7) (-2.8)

time period: 1931 - 1987

adjusted R^2 = .84

DW = 1.7

DYNAMIC MODEL RESULTS

The computer model of feedback processes among copper mining, metal production from virgin ores, fuel extraction, qualitative changes in the resource base, technical change and recycling utilizes the relationships outlined in the previous section. The model is initialized with published data for the mineral industries (Bureau of Census, Bureau of Mines, Argonne National Laboratories) for the year 1987. The initial conditions for the model are listed in Table 15.3.

Due to a lack of detailed information, the fuel mix of the recycling industry is specified with 1978 data. The fraction of apparent consumption that is met by copper recycling is set at its observed 1987 value of 35%. Forecasts are calculated for 50 years, using the Bureau of Mines projected growth in apparent copper consumption and two scenarios for the behavior of the rate of copper recycling. The first scenario assumes that the copper recycling rate can be maintained at the historically high level of 35% observed in 1987. The second scenario assumes a doubling of the recycling rate to 70% over the 50 year time frame. The base year fractions of copper recycled from No. 1 scrap, No. 2 scrap, brass and bronze scrap, and low grade scrap are, 16%, 43%, 17% and 24%, respectively and change over time as described in the previous section.

Table 15.3. Initial Conditions of the Model.

		Production Rate	Ore Grade	Energy Cost
Primary Copper	1.43	[million short tons]	.46 %	
Uranium	.19	[million pounds]	.21 %	
Coal	60	[trillion BTU]		.00809 [BTU/BTU]
Oil	27	[trillion BTU]		.07036 [BTU/BTU]
Natural Gas	30	[trillion BTU]		.01256 [BTU/BTU]

Under the assumption of a constant recycling rate, copper ore grade decrease from 0.43% in 1987 to 0.17% in the year 2037. Over the same time, an increasing amount of apparent copper consumption is met by No. 2 scrap while the fractions of brass and bronze and low grade scrap types decrease steadily. The fraction of No. 1 scrap temporarily increases because the rate of increase in the No. 2 scrap recycling fraction is initially lower than the decrease in lower grade scrap types (Figure 15.2). This is consistent with economic theory and intuition as the higher quality scrap is less energy intensive to recycle, yet limited in supply.

As a result of substitution, recycling and technical change the energy cost of copper production from virgin ore decreases temporarily until technical change can no longer mask decreases in ore grades (Figure 15.3). Energy cost of smelting and refining, in contrast, are not affected by changes in ore grade and, thus, continue to drop over the next 50 years. The combined effect of temporary decreases in energy cost of copper extraction and long-term decreases in smelting and refining lead to an increase in energy cost of primary copper. A similar trend is present for secondary copper production due to the anticipated shift towards lower grade scrap types.

With the exception of natural gas, the temporary decline in energy cost of copper production leads to a temporary decline in demand for energy (Figure 15.4). In the long run, coal remains the dominant energy source, followed by natural gas and oil. This result is not fundamentally changed if recycling rates double over the 50 year time frame of the model. What changes, however, are the relative amounts of fuel used to produce a ton of copper. As No. 2 scrap becomes more important in meeting apparent consumption, oil and electricity become increasingly important in producing copper. Consequently, energy costs are driven up in the oil sector due to the direct impacts of an increase in demand for oil, and in all energy sectors due to the indirect impacts of an increased demand for electricity. Energy costs of fossil fuel extraction increases 14.4% for oil, 13.5% for coal, and 10% for natural gas over the case with constant recycling rates. The overall result is an increase in total demand for primary energy by approximately 12% by 2037 (Figure 15.5).

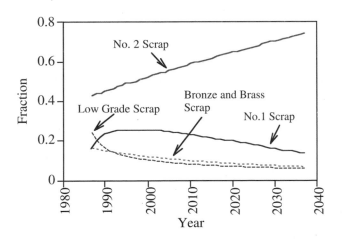

Figure 15.2. Fractions of scrap types recycled.

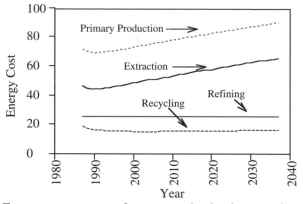

Figure 15.3. Energy costs per ton of copper production in extraction and refining, and total energy cost for primary and recycled metal per unit output (10^6 BTU per short ton).

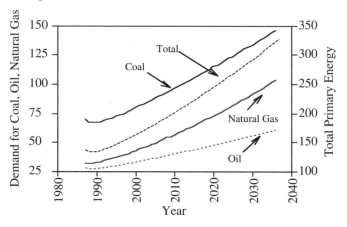

Figure 15.4. Total energy demand in the model at constant recycling rate (10^{12} BTU).

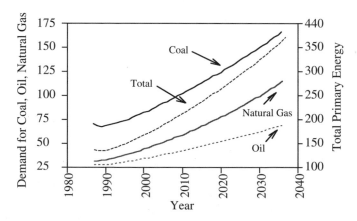

Figure 15.5. Total energy demand in the model for a doubling recycling rate by 2037.

CONCLUSION

The sections above outlined a comprehensive yet simple model of mineral extraction, metal production and energy use to assess system-wide effects of resource depletion. The modular structure of the model highly facilitates data collection, analysis and assessment of resource depletion, recycling, substitution and technical change in a dynamic context. The model captures a number of positive and negative feedback processes that govern the dynamics of, and interactions among, a variety of system components. It is initialized with widely published data and run to forecast energy cost of copper metal and fuels.

The model results indicate that from an energy perspective it may not necessarily be advantageous to increase copper recycling rates if increased recycling requires disproportionally large amounts of energy from sources that already exhibit significant depletion effects. Rather, increased recycling may drive up energy costs of energy production even though the direct energy consumption per ton of copper drops. Not considered here, however, are issues of pollution released in mining, smelting and refining copper from virgin ores and pollutants released by the energy sectors. These issues may lead society to favor strategies that are disadvantageous purely from an energy perspective. We deal with these issues in a separate study.

The system-wide increase in energy cost has several far-reaching implications for the analysis of resource scarcity and for policy decision making. First, the interdependencies that exist among mineral industries must be captured in models of natural resource use so as to not underestimate depletive effects of one sector on another. Second, high rates of substitution, recycling and technical change in one metal industry, though impressive from a technological perspective, may by themselves not be sufficient to determine long-run availability of that metal or its close substitutes. Depletion of fuels may make those metals prohibitively expensive. Third, policy making with regard to research and development of new metal extraction, processing, and recycling technologies must view the supply of metal as inherently linked with the developments in related industries and changes in the physical resource base. Fourth, even in sectors that, if taken by themselves, show promising rates of substitution, recycling and technical change, these rates may on a system-wide level be insufficient to overcome resource constraints if demand for the sectors' output continues to increase. Increases in demand may nullify the technical achievements. Fifth, all processes on Earth are bounded by fundamental physical laws that cannot be overcome by technical change. Thus, even if technical change is not restricted to incremental efficiency improvements, as assumed in the model, but can occur in leaps, there are limits to those leaps. Furthermore, even large improvements in individual processes will have small effects on the overall system performance as long as industries are limited in their adoption of new technologies. The latter will always be the case, especially in the mineral and metal industries.

REFERENCES

Ayres, R. U. and S. B. Noble. 1978. Materials/energy accounting and forecasting models. In Resources, Environment, and Economics - Applications of the Materials/Energy Balance Principle. New York: John Wiley and Sons.

Ayres, R. U. 1978. Resources, Environment, and Economics: Applications of the Materials/Energy Balance Principle. New York: John Wiley and Sons.

Barnett, H. J. 1979. Scarcity and growth revisited. Scarcity and Growth Reconsidered, ed. V. K. Smith. Baltimore: Johns Hopkins University Press.

Barnett, H. J. and C. Morse. 1963. Scarcity and Growth: The Economics of Natural Resource Availability, Resources for the Future. Baltimore and London: The Johns Hopkins Press.

Bureau of Census. 1987. Census of Mineral Industries - 1987. Washington, DC: Government Printing Office.

Chapman, P. F. and F. Roberts. 1983. Metal resources and energy. London: Butterworths.

Cleveland, C. J. 1991. Physical and economic aspects of resource quality: The cost of oil supply in the lower 48 United States 1936–1988. *Resources and Energy* 13: 163–188.

Cleveland, C. J. and R. Kaufmann. 1991. Forecasting ultimate oil recovery and its rate of production: Incorporating economic forces into the models of M. King Hubbert. *The Energy Journal* 12: 17–46.

Cleveland, C. J. 1993. An exploration of alternative measures of natural resource scarcity: The case of petroleum resources in the U.S. *Ecological Economics* 7: 123–157.

Cleveland, C. J. and M. Ruth. (in press). Interconnections between the depletion of minerals and fuels: The case of copper production in the U.S. *Energy Sources.*

Cook, E. F. 1976. Limits to the exploitation of nonrenewable resources. *Science* 210: 1219–1224.

Costanza, R., W. M. Kemp, and W. R. Boynton. 1993. Predictability, scale, and biodiversity in coastal and estuarine ecosystems: Implications for management. *Ambio* 22.2-3: 88–96.

Dasgupta, P. and G. M. Heal. 1974. The Optimal Depletion of Exhaustible Resources, Department of Energy. Annual Energy Outlook. Washington, DC: Government Printing Office.

Department of Energy. 1991. Annual Energy Review. Washington, DC: Government Printing Office.

Department of Energy. 1992. Annual Energy Review. Washington, DC: Government Printing Office.

Eagan, V. 1987. The optimal depletion of the theory of exhaustible resources. *Journal of Post Keynsian Economics* 9: 565.

Funtowicz, S. O. and J. R. Ravetz. 1994. The worth of a songbird: Ecological economics as a post-normal science. *Ecological Economics* 10: 197–207.

Gaines, L. 1980. Energy and Material Flows in the Copper Industry. Argonne, IL: Argonne National Laboratories.

Gaines, L. L. and F. Stodolsky. 1993. Mandatory Recycling Rates: Impacts on Energy Consumption and Municipal Solid Waste Volume, Energy Systems Division. Argonne, IL: Argonne National Laboratory, ANL/ESD-25.

Gelb, B. 1984. A look at energy use in mining: It deserves it, eds. J. P. Weyant and D. B. Sheffield. San Francisco: International Association of Energy Economists.

Georgescu-Roegen, N. 1975. Energy and economic myths. *Southern Economic Journal* 41: 347–381.

Gever, J., et al. 1986. Beyond Oil: The Threat to Food and Fuel in the Coming Decades. Cambridge: Ballinger.

Gray, L. C. 1913. The economic possibilities of conservation. *Quarterly Journal of Economics* 27: 497–519.

Gray, L. C. 1914. Rent under the presumption of exhaustibility. *Quarterly Journal of Economics* 28: 466–489.

Hall, C. A. S., C. J. Cleveland, and R. Kaufmann. 1986. Energy and Resource Quality: The Ecology of the Economic Process. New York: Wiley-Interscience.

Hall, D. C. and J. V. Hall. 1984. Concepts and measures of natural resource scarcity with a summary of recent trends. *Journal of Environmental Economics and Management* 11: 363–379.

Hannon, B. and M. Ruth. 1980. Dynamic Modeling. New York: Springer-Verlag.

Hardin, G. 1980. Global resources: Perspectives and alternatives. Baltimore: Baltimore University Press.

Hoel, M. 1978. Resource extraction, uncertainty, and learning. *Bell Journal of Economics* 9: 642–645.

Hotelling, H. 1931. The economics of exhaustible resources. *Journal of Political Economy* 39: 137–175.

Jansson, A. M., et al., eds. 1994. Investing in Natural Capital, The Ecological Economics Approach to Sustainability. Washington DC: Island Press.

Kaufmann, R. 1991. Oil production in the lower 48 states: Reconciling curve fitting and econometric models. *Resources and Energy* 13: 111–127.

Kaufmann, T. D. and R. C. Drury. 1987. Aluminum and Copper are no longer substitutes. *Natural Resources Forum* 11: 373–377.

Kay, J. A. and J. A. Mirrlees. 1975. The desirability of natural resource depletion. The economics of natural resource depletion, eds. D. W. Pearce and J. Rose. New York: John Wiley.

Lewis, T. R. 1977. Attitudes towards risk and the optimal exploitation of an exhaustible resource. *Journal of Environmental Economics and Management* 4: 111–119.

Long, N. V. 1975. Resource extraction under the uncertainty of possible nationalization. *Journal of Economic Theory* 41: 127–145.

Loury, G. C. 1987. The optimal exploitation of an unknown reserve. *Review of Economic Studies* 45: 621–636.

Maddala, G. S. 1965. Productivity and technological change in the bituminous coal industry, 1919-1954. *Journal of Political Economy* 73: 352-365.

Meadows, D. H., D. L. Meadows, and J. Randers. 1992. Beyond The Limits. Post Mills: Chelsea Green.

Meadows, D. H., et al. 1972. The Limits to Growth. New York: Universe Books.

Meadows, D. H. and J. M. Robinson. 1985. The electronic oracle: Computer Models and Social Decisions. New York: John Wiley and Sons.

Norgaard, R. 1989. Economic Indicators of Natural Resource Scarcity. Department of Agricultural and Resource Economics, University of California at Berkeley.

Norgaard, R. B. 1975. Resource scarcity and new technology in U.S. petroleum development. 15: 265–295.

Pindyck, R. S. 1978. The optimal exploration and production of nonrenewable resources. *Journal of Political Economy* 86.5: 841–859.

Pindyck, R. S. 1979. Uncertainty and the Pricing of Exhaustible Resources. Energy Laboratory Working Paper, #EL79-021WP: Massachusetts Institute of Technology.

Richmond, B. and S. Peterson. 1994. STELLA II User's Guide. Hanover, New Hampshire: High Performance Systems, Inc.

Ruth, M. and C. W. Bullard. 1993. Information, production and utility. *Energy Policy* 21: 1059–1067.

Ruth, M. 1993. Integrating Economics, Ecology, and Thermodynamics. Dordrecht: Kluwer Academic.

Ruth, M. 1995a. Information, order and knowledge in economic and ecological systems: Implications for material and energy use. *Ecological Economics* 13: 99–114.

Ruth, M. 1995b. Thermodynamic implications for natural resource extraction and technical change in U.S. copper mining. *Environmental and Resource Economics.*

Slade, M. E. 1982. Trends in natural-resource commodity prices: An analysis in the time domain. *Journal of Environmental Economics and Management* 9: 122–137.

Slade, M. E. 1985. Trends in natural-resource commodity prices: U-shaped price paths explored. *Journal of Environmental Economics and Management* 12: 181–192.

Smil, Vaclav. 1993. Global Ecology, Environmental Change and Social Flexibility. London, New York: Routledge.

Smith, V. K. 1979. Natural resource scarcity: A statistical analysis. *Review of Economics and Statistics* 61: 423–427.

Smith, V. Kerry, ed. 1979. Scarcity and Growth Reconsidered. Baltimore: Johns Hopkins University Press.

Stiglitz, J. E. 1976. Monopoly and the rate of extraction of exhaustible resources. *American Economic Review* 66: 655–661.

Sweeney, J. L. 1977. Economics of depletable resources: Market forces and intertemporal bias. *Review of Economic Studies*: 125–142.

Walker, D. J. and D. L. Young. 1986. Assessing soil erosion productivity damage. Soil Conservation—Assessing the National Resources Inventory, ed. National Research Council. Washington, DC: National Academy of Sciences.

Watkins, G. C. 1992. The Hotelling Principle: Autobahn or Cul de Sac? *The Energy Journal* 13: 1–24.

Watt, K. E. F. 1992. Taming the Future, A Revolutionary Breakthrough in Scientific Forecasting. Davis, California: The Contextured Web Press.

Weinstein, M. C. and R. J. Zeckhauser. 1975. The optimal consumption of depletable natural resources. *Quarterly Journal of Economics* 89: 371–392.

Yelle, L. E. 1979. The learning curve: Historical survey and comprehensive survey. *Decision Sciences* 10: 302–334.

Yoshiki-Gravelsins, K. S., J. M. Toguri, and R. T. C. Choo. 1993a. Metals production, energy, and the environment, Part I: Energy consumption. *JOM* 45: 15–20.

Yoshiki-Gravelsins, K. S., J. M. Toguri, and R. T. C. Choo. 1993b. Metals production, energy and the environment, Part II: Environmental impact. *JOM* 45: 23–29.

PART III

IMPLEMENTATION

16 INSTITUTIONAL CHANGE AND DEVELOPMENT TOWARDS SUSTAINABILITY

Johannas B. Opschoor
Institute of Social Studies
The Hague Netherlands
ISS, POBox 29776, 2502 LT The Hague

OVERVIEW

Most economic analyses of unsustainability look at market and government failure. In this chapter the conceptual framework is broadened to: transaction failure, empowerment failure, and government failure. This allows for the inclusion of elements such as: social mobilization (failure) or (inadequacy of) countervailing power, and lack of public authority due to inadequate mandate given by society to its governments, missing markets, preference failure, integration failure. The market system gives rise to cost shifting, facilitated by 'distance-related distortions', related to different types of distance (i.e., distance in time, space, and scale). The standard approach to these is to put in place some combination of instruments such that prices reflect the true cost of production and consumption, and the polluters/users of the environment pay for their pollution/use. However, this is a rather restricted approach. One has to realize more structural changes and systems' reforms: rights, responsibilities, and power relationships, such that environmental quality claims and existence rights (of species), etc. are recognized, coupled with compensations to be made by those inflicting upon those rights. There is a need for institutional change and reforms in the areas of: (1) redirecting growth, (2) curbing growth, and (3) creating new institutions and instruments capable of achieving the necessary entitlements and powers. Areas in which institutions or mechanisms appear to be lacking include: (1) redistribution of wealth and access to the environmental utilization space (EUS), (2) regional and global resource management, and (3) changing patterns of production and consumption

INTRODUCTION

Sustainable development is: "... a process of change in which the exploitation of resources, the direction of investments, the orientation of technological development and institutional change ... enhance both current and future potential to meet human needs and aspirations" (WCED 1987). Thus, institutions have an important role to play and this chapter takes its cue from that point.

Sustainability is related to the continuing existence of conditions favorable to life, human life in particular. It also has to do with fairness or equity, and to the integrity of natural systems and processes as perceived by *Homo sapiens*. The predominant institutions influencing decision making are market forces and market-based mechanisms. These are geared towards efficiency almost to the exclusion of other values such as sustainability and equity. Thus, there is a tension between the on-going process of enhancing the domain of market forces and the process of sustainable development.

Before giving operational meaning to the notion of sustainability, several important issues must be addressed.

1. Some agreement has to be reached on what the substance is of this notion: what elements in reality does it refer to? What are the "dimensions" of sustainability and how can we capture this multidimensional concept?

2. How can societies or economies move towards (more) sustainable states? Will individual decision makers be moving towards more sustainable ways of using natural resources automatically? Are changes necessary in payoff mechanisms and incentive systems? Is the international economic and institutional "environment" conducive to, and sufficient for achieving sustainability?

3. What are the costs and benefits of a business-as-usual type of development versus a sustainability-oriented development? What are the sacrifices in terms of income and consumption, to whom, and when?

4. Are the main driving forces behind unsustainability being addressed in our strategies to realize sustainability? What are these driving forces?

Within this 'agenda for sustainability' this chapter provides one attempt to further the debate about the institutional conditions that prevail and how institutional change might foster sustainable development and development towards sustainability. That is, especially the second and parts of the fourth issue listed above will be discussed. We cannot, however, proceed without a minimum amount of attention to the notion of sustainability itself.

SUSTAINABILITY

The systems and processes that operate in the physical environments of society, enable the environment to provide society with a range of functions or services, including the self-regulation of these systems and processes, the production of materials, and carrier functions (de Groot 1992). Reduced to their most basic essentials, one could conceive of these as made up of the following four elements:

1. A renewable resource that is harvested by society,
2. Its underlying regeneration process,
3. Environmental pressure, and
4. An absorption process.

Effective regeneration (or the productivity of the regeneration system) can be assumed to depend on environmental quality which, in turn, is a function of environmental pressure and the scale and rate at which absorption processes in the environment buffer that pressure. Harvesting from the environment and putting waste into it (elements 1 and 3 above) represent the ways society utilizes the environment. Regeneration and absorption and other processes such as regulatory ones, together form the so-called " life support" function of the environment; they can be referred to as the ecological infrastructure (James et al. 1989; IUCN et al. 1991; Opschoor and Perrings 1994).

If one analyzes environmental utilization in this simple framework, the result is literally a space, the boundaries of which represent environmental use patterns (in terms of combinations of resource stock levels, environmental quality and resource extraction rates) that can be maintained as long as the underlying ecological infrastructure remains intact. This space has been called the environmental utilization space (EUS) (Siebert 1982; Opschoor 1987; Opschoor and Klaassen 1991): the locus of all feasible combinations of environmental services that represent steady states in terms of levels of relevant environmental quality and stocks of renewable resources.

The notion of an environmental space of given magnitude still allows for the adoption by society of a wide range of more or less attractive, steady state positions. For example, more attractive steady state positions can be reached at the cost of temporary sacrifices in terms of reductions in environmental idolization. Moreover, social and technological change may expand (in real terms or virtually) the environmental space, and society can deliberately invest in that. And even if further expansion of the environmental space would eventually become impossible, this would only pose a limit on environmental utilization or "material throughput" (Daly 1972) and not necessarily on economic development or economic growth in welfare terms. Disregarding cross boundaries dependencies of an environmental and economic nature, one could say that societies have to identify and move towards a feasible and acceptable level of environmental utilization that it wishes to enjoy sustainability—if such a level that is both acceptable and sustainable exists.

"Weak" or "Strong" Sustainability

It is conceivable that one natural resource replaces the other (e.g., sugar cane as a substitute for fossil energy). When resources can thus be replaced, the unsustained use of a particular resource may not pose a problem in terms of economic survival of the activities using that resource. As long as the natural resource base in total is preserved, there is no question as to the sustainability of using it.

Substitution options might also exist between natural resources and non-natural ones, such as produced capital, knowledge and know-how. And technological development or innovation may even lead to an expanded range of perceived options for substitution of one resource for another. It may thus appear to be more advantageous to sell or burn up a given fossil energy resource or cut a forest, and invest the revenues in the development of alternative natural resources or even of artificial ones, than to preserve the resource. Economists often transform into one aggregate economic value natural resource stocks as well as produced capital (such as equipment and roads) and human capital (e.g., Solow 1992). In this approach, degrading environmental features is then considered acceptable as long as: (1) this is compensated by some form of increased produced capital, or enhanced intellectual capabilities, and (2) the welfare potential of the overall capital base remains intact. In this view, development can be regarded as sustainable while at the same time the environmental space is allowed to diminish. This is called 'weak sustainability' and one finds it reflected implicitly in the WCED definition and in World Bank positions (World Bank 1992).

Opposed to this is the view that this faith in the substitutability of human-made processes for natural processes, may be unwarranted, and that accepting the promise of technological innovation cannot balance environmental degradation. Both prudence considerations and preservation considerations based on the rights to existence and development of non-human species and natural systems, may lead to a choice in favor of what has been called strong sustainability. For renewable resources this "strong" approach entails that: (1) the stock levels to be maintained must be high enough to safely ensure a sustainable offtake at least the current level, and (2) the quality of the regenerative systems instrumental in regrowth processes be maintained beyond safe minimum levels of environmental standards. Environmental pollution and waste would then be allowed only insofar as prudently or risk-avertingly assessed absorptive capacities are not surpassed and/or accumulation is checked or prevented. Non-renewable resources would be allowed to be exploited as long as proven reserves are sufficient to provide for consumption over a predetermined minimum time span. Biological diversity would not be allowed to deteriorate by human interventions and safe minimum habitats and populations should be preserved.

In other words, strong sustainability is compatible with at least preserving the ecological infrastructure and thus maintaining some amount of environmental space, or even with enlarging it, where weak sustainability would require only the total capital base to at least remain equal over time. From a welfare maintenance perspective as is implied in the WCED definition of sustainability, staying within the EUS is a sufficient, but perhaps not a necessary condition for sustainability. Adding to sustainability the precautionary approach may imply that staying within the EUS becomes a necessary condition as well.

Unsustainability has often been related to processes such as economic growth and population expansion. Other factors mentioned include the diffusion of inappropriate technology, and poverty. Behind these forces, there are some more structural factors that economic expansion helps to spread globally, such as Western cultural world views (including views of humankind-nature relationships) and institutional failure to accommodate to the emerging environmental realities. This chapter looks at the latter factor in particular.

INSTITUTIONS, ECONOMICS, AND SUSTAINABILITY

The notion of 'institutions' is used here to indicate consolidated patterns of behavior (formal and informal ones), as well as social conventions and organizations influencing human behavior

In this sense institutions include both the organizations that give force to social conventions (such as markets and administrative settings) and the less tangible social structures governing particular aspects of human behavior (such as values, customs, and forms of moral suasion). As the degradation of the environment is the product of the independent decisions of billions of individual users of environmental resources, the underlying causes of environmental degradation accordingly lie in the determinants of those individual decisions, such as preferences and institutional elements like property rights, cultural, religious, and legal restrictions on individual behavior, and economic aspects such as relative prices. We begin by making some observations on value-related issues and then proceed to institutions as such.

In an institutional or evolutionary approach to assessing the performance of the economic process one refers not only to static values such as efficiency and equity, but also to very fundamental values such as: the recreation or regeneration of the community, and the continuity of human life. These two values imply as a corollary environmental compatibility or 'coevolutionary sustainability' (Swaney 1987). This in fact implies ecological sustainability, as otherwise the economy's material base will be insecure and cause future incompatibility. Taking a system's point of view, compatibility, or viability appears to be the overall concept. I postulate that these ulterior social values are accepted in themselves, and are taken to—in some ulterior sense—have precedence over short term interests or private interests. The continued existence of species and ecosystems may be in this category of societally relevant items where individual preferences or priorities for them remain low. This may, at the collective level, give rise to explicit *a priori* policies on nature conservation etc., on non-economic grounds. All these arguments support the position that the environment is a "merit-good" not to be decided upon by aggregate individual economic values attached to it (Opschoor 1974; James et al.1978). In terms of standard analysis, this means that I suggest a third and a fourth criterion in addition to efficiency and (intragenerational) equity, namely that of coevolutionary sustainability (see above), and interspecies equity (a societally accepted element of care for the prospects of other species insofar as humankind can affect these prospects).

We now proceed to institutions, in an endeavor to identify: (1) institutional causes of environmentally unsustainable behavior, and (2) interventions to modify that behavior. Most economic analyses looks at environmental problems as the results of "market and government failures" (Frey 1983, OECD 1992). Market imperfections had to do with deviations in reality from the theoretical preconditions for perfect competition on markets (including monopolistic tendencies, externalities and public goods features, rigidities and immobilities) and with socially undesirable market process outcomes such as a too skewed distribution of income. These led to government or policy interventions in the market process. Meanwhile, the effectiveness as well as efficiency of policy interventions had increasingly become subjects for analysis and discussion, and hence the notion of market failure was complemented by that of "government or intervention failure". Below, these notions shall be elaborated put in a wider and deeper context.

Market Failures

In market economies the decisions of resource users are coordinated by market forces: behavior driven by cost minimization or utility maximization, and competition. Market failure can be defined as the inability of the market to lead the economic process towards a social optimum. One main aspect of this is failure to encapsule in costs and prices the external effects, or reductions in utility and profits that economic agents inflict on others. In relation to environmental goods and services one may point at the externalities related to pollution, resource exploitation, and ecosystem intrusion. Button (OECD 1992) distinguishes two broad types of market failure: internal market failure and external market failure. The former are failures in the market system which lead to inefficiencies even in the absence of environmental considerations and include the market imperfections referred to above. The latter are related to the phenomenon of environmental externalities; they are outside the cost functions as perceived by the producers or consumers of the goods that "convey" the externalities. Externalities are the result of intended or unintended 'cost shifting' or 'displacement of costs' (Kapp 1969; Opschoor 1987; Pearce and Turner 1989); that is, (part of the) adverse consequences of one actor's decision are passed on to others to bear (see below).

Intervention Failures

Button defines intervention failures as: "...internal and external market failures which result from inappropriate actions (whether deliberate or not) of government" (OECD 1992). He then divides these intervention failures into: inadequacy in correcting market failure, and inappropriate policies in other sectors of the economy. In more practical terms, that is, looking at the operational mechanisms applied, intervention failures could be categorized into 'economic intervention failures', 'regulation and control failure', and 'administrative failures'. Past sectoral policies (e.g., in the field of energy, agriculture and transportation) have often been decided upon primarily with the sectoral interests in mind, at best with some consideration for tradeoffs *vis-a-vis* other sectors. Environmental concerns have not—or not yet—been appropriately internalized. Moreover, decision makers have limited time horizons and/or discount future consequences of present decisions. Thus, policy formation may suffer from biases towards stronger (in terms of economic and political power or significance) sectors and against interests that cannot manifest themselves on current markets and in today's political arena, such as future generations' interests. Sectoral policy failure often results in the subsidization of sectoral activities. In resource related sectors such as agriculture, water, timber, and energy, this leads to artificially low resource prices. In such cases, users of the products of these sectors are paying less than the social costs associated with their use; they thus are induced to consume more than would be the case were the price corrected for social costs. Prices then give the wrong signals and the sector may expand to levels beyond what is socially desirable.

The notion of administrative failure refers to a range of problems within the organization of government at the various levels, leading to inadequate policy implementation. Examples include: rigidities due to entrenched traditional divisions of labor within administrative organizations (very often along sectoral lines), insufficient integration between agencies and departments, lack of instruments or mandates sufficiently strong to achieve policy objectives, lack of instruments or powers to ensure policy implementation within the economic processes.

BEYOND MARKET AND INTERVENTION FAILURE

Transaction Failure, Empowerment Failure, and Government Failure

The range of environmentally relevant social interactions is not fully captured by the market as an institution. Outside the market there are all kinds of transactions with environmental and economic significance, such as barter and other informal exchange and distributive practices. Beyond transactions is social organization itself, either non-governmental or governmental. Social forces are among those that influence transactions, whether market transactions or non-market ones, and social empowerment in the form of formal or informal "counter-vailing power" is to be considered in an institutional analysis of economy-environment interactions.

My most fundamental point is, that we must replace the market-government distinction by a trichotomy: transactions-empowerment-government (Table 16.1). Inadequacies at any of these three levels to achieve a social optimum (in our case taking sustainability into account) can be labeled institutional 'failures'. Market failure thus becomes one element of transaction failure, which in itself is one component of institutional failure.

We have at least three kinds of transaction failure.

1.   Market system failure which includes both inefficient markets (or market failure in the strict sense) and absence of markets (as in the case of many environmental goods),
2.   Negotiation failure for nonmarket transactions, covering the situation where not all stakeholders are represented and the one where they suffer from bargaining power imbalances, and
3.   Preference failures, due to inadequate knowledge and information, or in relation to merit goods (see above).

Empowerment failure may occur at two levels: the non-governmental and the governmental. There may be a lack of social mobilization to enable negotiation or for demand-side market manipulation. Countervailing power at the non-governmental level is then inadequate. There may also be a lack of mandate at the government level to exert countervailing influence through policies, which should be addressed through political processes of authorization leading to enhanced or more explicit mandates. Finally, government failure should include at least three categories.

1.   Failures by government in formulating policies (either of intervention or of social mobilization) to address unsustainability,
2.   Failures in the intervention itself, which may have to do with inappropriate target setting, lack of instruments or an inadequate mandate, and with more traditional features such as failures related to policies in other sectors, and
3.   Administrative failure.

Causes of Market and Preference Failure

At their very best, markets coordinate in an efficiency-oriented way the decisions of billions of economic agents on how to allocate the resources they can decide over. They have as wide a horizon in time, space and scale, as these economic agents themselves. They are, therefore, not inherently geared to overall systems' performance in terms of distributional aspects and sustainability.

Table 16.1. A Classification of Environmentally Relevant Types of Institutional Failure.

Transaction Failure

---

1. Market System Failure
     Missing Markets
     Market Performance Failure
2. Negotiation Failure
     Missing Parties
     Asymmetries in Bargaining Power
3. Preference Failure
     Missing Knowledge / Information
     Incomplete Preferences
     Time Preferences Bias

Empowerment Failure

---

4. Social Mobilization Failure
     Missing / Inadequate Countervailing Power
5. Authorization Failure
     Missing / Inadequate Remit / Mandate

Government Failure

---

6. Correction Failure
     Missing Policies (environmental)
7. Intervention Failure
     Environmental Policy Failure:
          • Targeting Failure (inadequate objectives)
          • Instruments Failure (quantitative, qualitative)
          • Entitlement Failure
     Other Policy Failures (sectoral and macro-economic)
8. Administrative Failure
     Integration Failure (horizontal)
     Intervention Level Failure
     Enforcement / Implementation Failure

Source: Adapted from Opschoor et al. 1994: Managing the Environment. OECD, Paris

Inequity and scale issues may easily arise out of an economic process that is driven by market forces such as, economic growth under such circumstances will push the economy outside the environmental space (Daly 1992). Without corrective or preventative policies, the market system gives rise to cost shifting.

The practice of cost shifting is facilitated by what could be labeled as 'distance-related distortions'. There are three such distortions, related to different types of distance: distance in time, space, and scale. The consequences or effects of environmental degradation in relation to economic activities manifest themselves at often large distances from the source or agent causing them. This may be a distance both in terms of space and time (e.g., DDT in polar ice caps chemical time bombs and climate change). Effects of environmental degradation are thereby shifted onto other people, to future people and even to other species. There is a third type of distance involved, namely that between the level of one's individual influence and the level at which a problem must be addressed for its solution. One could refer to this as distance in scale or in decision-level. Single actors in a multi-actor context may face situations where their privately optimal behavior may lead to socially or collectively undesirable overall outcomes. Examples are countries sharing a common river basin, or individual fishermen exploiting a shared fish population. The absence of control and intervention leads to an irrational level of exploitation of a shared or common property resource, to ongoing and excessive pollution, etc. (the prisoners' dilemma in the case of very few actors, or the tragedy of the commons in the case of many actors).

Where such distance factors prevail and the party on which the burden is shifted cannot counteract this distance by pressing his interest, government intervention may be needed. Reasons why these external interests are not adequately internalized, include the absence of legally based property rights or access rights protecting the damaged party, or of liability/accountability regulations enforceable upon the causal agent; and the absence of means to exert countervailing power through the political system (lack of voting power as in cases of transboundary cost shifting, or intertemporal cost shifting, or cost shifting onto other species), or through the market place (i.e., lack of purchasing power). Reasons why this situation is not easily changed by installing more appropriate institutions or legislation, include shortcomings in political systems in responding to these failures. Governments and bureaucracies also suffer from time preference (whereby future effects and future interests are discounted away), and may be oversensitive to present purchasing or voting power and thus to the predominant economic and political forces. Many European governments, for instance, were and are incapable of addressing the environmental problems agricultural development gives rise to due to strongly voiced sectoral interests. Both absence of rights and means to exert countervailing power are present in situations of 'missing markets'. This term describes situations where there is scarcity in a long-term perspective for a particular environmental component which, factually, is dealt with as a free good; often, future demand for environmental goods is not reflected, property and access rights are not specified so as to lead to claims, etc. 'Missing parties' include situations where allocational decisions are taken without all stakeholders represented. Here again, future generations may be the most convincing example, but in fact other species could also be regarded as stakeholders in many of the decisions now taken in the economic process. Even if all parties with an interest can go to an appropriate market or negotiation table, they may be inadequately informed or suffer from "defective telescopic faculty" (Pigou) or "weaknesses in human imagination" (Ramsey) as manifested by our time preference; this is captured by the category of preference failure. Preference failure leads to questions on the relevance of notions such as consumer sovereignty as underlying Paretian welfare economics and the alleged superiority of market allocations even if otherwise market structures are perfect. For other causes of preference failure I refer to the comments on value hierarchies made above.

Government Failure

Failure to correct (i.e., to intervene in the face of transaction failure or empowerment failure) is the first type of government failure. At the most fundamental level, government could "go back" to society to renegotiate its own mandate, thus seeking correction of any kind of delegation failure that may have become manifest. Given an adequate mandate, however, governments may show correction failure in the sense that they fail to come up within this case, an environmental or sustainable development policy.

But if governments decide to have environmental policies, these may fail in several respects: intervention failures and administrative ones. Intervention failure can be divided into cases of environmental policy failures and other policy failures. At the level of objectives, governments may fail in adequately expressing sustainability considerations; they may fail to safeguard the preservation of an adequate 'portfolio' of environmental assets (or ecological infrastructure) for future generations. An important next element is that of the (re)definition and allocation of property rights (both collective and private rights) and rights of access and use, in the face of environmental scarcities. This could mean establishing entitlements over environmental resources, liabilities for environmental damages, etc., with beneficiaries at all relevant levels: individuals, communities and groups, regions, governments themselves (e.g., as custodians of ecological infrastructure for future generations, international agencies, etc).

At the instruments level, governments may fail in selecting appropriate instruments (i.e., they may have biases for or against economic instruments or command—and control approaches, or for voluntary agreement and consensus—approaches, like in the Netherlands).

Often prevalent policies relating to sectors other than environmental and resource management are based on decisions in which ecological or environmental considerations were given insufficient weight. Examples are policies in the areas of agriculture, energy, transportation. And also there is the case of macro policies without due consideration of sustainability issues. We restrict ourselves here to macroeconomic policies. Current macroeconomic policies may suffer from potential policy failure insofar as long-term environmental effects are ignored. The risk is that the global society will be confronted with environmental costs that are either irreversible (e.g., species extinction) or very costly to redress (e.g., the impact of pollution in Northern Bohemia or deforestation in tropical zones). From a long-run perspective the levels of economic activities may have to be controlled and redirected to ensure a more timely correction of this policy failure. This might be the case if changing the technologies or locations of our activities would not provide sufficient responses to the ecological challenge.

Finally, there is administrative failure. The most fundamental problem here is that of an approach at an inappropriate level of intervention: either too low (e.g., attempts to solve the greenhouse issue by one small country alone) or too high. In a way, intervention level failure may reflect empowerment failure, as is often the case with international, transboundary environmental problems where sovereignty and subsidiary become relevant considerations. But even if appropriate administrative levels exist, they may not be used correctly. A second type of administrative failure is that of lack of (horizontal) coordination or integration leading to spillovers in the form of externalities to other compartments or sectors. Finally, and at a very practical level, all impediments to appropriate enforcement and implementation have been incorporated here.

Looking at Table 16.1, it is easy to observe that a full scale approach to the causes of unsustainability in terms of institutional failure requires going far beyond market (performance) failure and policy failure as traditionally understood. This richer analysis may help in finding more appropriate answers to the question posed above: What are appropriate institutional settings from a sustainability perspective?

INTERVENTION: THE STANDARD APPROACH

Market forces will not automatically move the economy towards a socially optimal allocation. Standard economic analysis has suggested two basic paths along which one might proceed: (1) private negotiations and legal action, or (2) policy intervention directly aiming at an alteration of market prices (e.g., through charges), or redefining and altering the structure of property rights (e.g., by licensing, zoning, standards etc).

In the case of the first pathway, private actions, the point of departure normally taken is Coase's theorem on bargaining. He has suggested that a bargaining approach might suffice to reach a social optimum. Polluters and victims of environmental degradation are assumed to negotiate about the optimal level of environmental degradation or of economic activity giving rise to it, on the basis of their marginal damage costs and abatement costs. The social optimum is where the marginal profits are equal to the marginal damage due to the pollution. If the victim has legal rights to an unpolluted environment, then the polluter might wish to compensate the victim. The 'Coase Theorem', in fact, claims that regardless of who holds the property right, there is an automatic tendency to approach the social optimum via bargaining. If this mechanism could be trusted to operate adequately in real world situations, then government regulation of externalities would be redundant. A number of criticisms of and complications with the Coasian approach have been identified and testify to the need for policy intervention (Pearce and Turner 1989). These include the lack of realism of various assumptions underlying the analysis such as the alleged market perfection, the level of transactions costs in actually achieving negotiation and bargaining on the level of pollution, and difficulties in identifying and mobilizing the relevant polluters and sufferers. There are thus many reasons why bargains do not, and cannot easily, occur.

In the absence of bargains, there is a case for government intervention as addressed by the second pathway. In fact, environmental policies by governments can be regarded as remedies for situations with high transaction costs and compliance/enforcement costs in the absence of such policies. Possibilities for policy interventions include: direct regulation via standards or zoning, taxes/charges, trading approaches, negotiation for agreements. We discuss them below.

Charges and Standards

Pigou has advocated government intervention through the imposition of a tax on polluters based on the marginal (external) damage costs and the marginal abatement costs. The tax should induce polluters to automatically move to a socially optimal situation in terms of production and pollution abatement. However, in most cases it is impossible for an environmental agency to tax the pollution precisely at the appropriate level due to lack of adequate information on damage. The Pigouvian solution has thus proven to be impracticable. "Proxy solutions" to this problem have been proposed, such as emissions charges aimed at realizing some specified level of reduction of emissions (Baumol and Oates 1988). Charges then would at least equalize the level of marginal pollution abatement costs among firms, and thus provide an incentive for the most cost-effective total investment in pollution clean-up. One could regard the Baumol and Oates charge as a second-best alternative to the Pigouvian charge: government is making an assessment of where the socially optimum emissions reduction objective might be located, based on an implicit social valuation of (marginal) environmental damages, but this can be a proxy only.

Tradeable Rights or Quota

Marketable permits for emissions offer the same promise of efficiency as Baumol and Oates charges. By giving the polluters a chance to trade their pollution emission/discharge permits, the total cost of pollution abatement to some predetermined acceptable level, is minimized. As long as polluters have different costs of abatement there is an automatic market-low-cost polluters selling permits and high-cost polluters buying them. The same reasoning applies to quotas for exploiting a natural resource within some preestablished (sustainable) total yield. Trading ensures a cost-effective total abatement result. For emission permit markets to function well, they have to meet a number of conditions (Opschoor and Turner 1994). This may explain why they are applied less widely than seems indicated by the enthusiasm one finds in the academic literature on them.

Voluntary Agreements

One other form of intervention is that of negotiation between government or the environmental agency, and (representatives of) polluters. This may take the form of so-called "voluntary agreements" negotiated between the environmental agency and sectors of society (e.g., industries, consumer organizations, etc). The agreement will be on short and medium term changes in patterns of investment, energy or water conservation measures, emissions reduction, technological change, consumption, waste treatment, etc). These voluntary agreements may at first sight resemble Coasian negotiation and bargaining as described earlier, but there are important differences. First, this type of negotiation does not normally involve the exchange of environmental quality against financial transfers. Second, the damaged or potentially damaged parties do not participate in the negotiations. One could regard the role of governments in these voluntary agreements as taking place on behalf of society at large including the sufferers from environmental degradation; as in the case of the Baumol and Oates charge, government might be assumed to seek to approximate a social optimum on the basis of some estimate of the marginal external damage costs. This voluntary agreement is a second-best proxy only, but still one that could be better, from a point of view of effectiveness as well as efficiency, than that of no intervention.

Any of these approaches are seen as better (in the sense of more efficient and perhaps even more effective) than the traditional one of command and control-policies resorting to direct regulation, standards, permits, zoning, re-defining and allocating property rights, etc.

INTERVENTION RECONSIDERED

From a theoretical perspective one could say that an intervention strategy based on economic instruments would imply a restricted, economic process oriented approach, rather than a broad one addressing the institutional foundations.

For example, the approach is rather narrow and theoretical, it is borne out by empirical observations (OECD 1994). First, economic analyses do not al-ways convincingly reflect economic realities. Real markets do not always work as theory assumes—as in the case of the response of car drivers to higher en-ergy prices and other disincentives to private transportation. The efficiency and effectiveness arguments associated with economic instruments are not al-ways applicable, as in the case of many applications of emissions trading schemes and even fish quota. Second, non-economic instruments may perform equally well or even better than economic incentives, especially in terms of effective-ness, as is borne out by many cases of permitting and zoning to restrict the use of environmental resources. Hence, combinations of legal and economic ap-proaches may turn out to be more promising (e.g., Shogren et al. 1993; Zweifel and Tyran 1994). Third, economic analyses and recommendations often ignore or play down realities typical of the political "arena" in which (environmental) policy is shaped in reality. One aspect of this is the issue of the distributional implications of environmental policy and instruments choice. A recent example is the watered-down version of an incentive charge on energy in the Nether-lands, which, due to considerations related to competitiveness and income dis-tribution was reduced to a charge on small energy consumers only, with very intransparent and potentially adverse compensatory measures attached, such as an enhanced premium on births.

Additionally, there can be no single generally valid optimal intervention strategy, due to two sets of institutional or contextual aspects:

1. Differences in the structures (environmental, economic) in which the intervention is to operate (the application context), and
2. Socio-political and cultural structures (the policy context).

Situation-specific characteristics relevant to the choice of instruments in-clude source-related aspects such as the availability of substitutes, elasticity, the potential for technological innovation, differentiation in abatement costs, competitiveness, market structure related features; they also include impact-re-lated issues such as the seriousness of environmental damage, local and temporal variation in linkages between emissions and impact, etc. As one example, it may make more sense to approach SO_2-reduction via permits and agreements due to the relatively small number of sources, but NO_x could be more effectively reduced through standards and charges, due to the manifold and diffuse sources.

Moreover, governments' choices of policy instruments have a strong political basis and may be governed by a variety of considerations, some more rational than others. Acceptability is an important one, next to the economically more obvious effectiveness and efficiency considerations. Acceptability is defined here as the extent to which the instrument can be properly implemented and enforced without running into problems of non-concordance with existing regulations, principles, and policies, or of resistance by target groups or indirectly affected agents, on the basis' of allegedly unfair or unproportional burden-sharing implications (equity considerations). Yet, the preference for a regulatory approach as the foundation of a system of environmental policy instruments is understandable from the point of view of political feasibility. One can see this as the result of dominant motives with several of the main groups of actors: government, industry, environmental organizations. Assuming rent-seeking behavior, there is a rationale for regulatory approaches at least from the perspectives of industry and governments, possibly at the expense of consumers. Policy analysis shows that there may be grounds for assuming that the policy arenas, in which, instruments for water and air quality policies were shaped, might not be conductive to incentive based approaches, but might rather favor regulatory measures as these are less likely to lead to unsettling conflicts between the parties involved. These arguments show that political, institutional and even cultural developments may influence the process of articulation of environmental policy objectives and strategies, and of instruments selection.

Given the deep-rooted causes of unsustainability (see above), I doubt whether altering the stringency with which existing quantitative instruments would be applied, or even whether adding to that set of quantitative instruments, are sufficient interventions in terms of achieving sustainability. Basically, what is implied in the analysis so far, amounts to an argument in favor of alterations at the level of rights, responsibilities, and power relationships, such that environmental quality claims and existence rights (of species), etc. are recognized, coupled with compensations to be made by those inflicting upon those rights. Such recognitions and compensations could result from, as a start, an extension of the set of environmental policy principles (such as the polluter pays principle and the precautionary principle) and an appropriate set of policy institutions and non-governmental powers, at all levels. This has implications for economic valuation aimed at underpinning optimal levels of resource exploitation and pollution as well (Faber and Proops 1993).

INSTITUTIONAL IMPROVEMENTS TOWARDS SUSTAINABLE ECONOMIC DEVELOPMENT

There will be a need for redirecting growth; curbing growth, at least where it is becoming ecologically inviable (Daly 1972); and creating new institutions and instruments capable of achieving the necessary entitlements and powers.

Redirecting Economic Growth

Societies need to prevent or reduce cost shifting tendencies so that prices reflect (marginal) social costs and thereby provide appropriate and correct signals to decision-makers in the economic and political process. This requires an institutional reduction of the impact of distances between cause and effect in space, time, and decision level.

- Proper pricing policies may make remote or distant (in time, space, and in scale) environmental repercussions of economic behavior count in decision-making here and now; examples include direct price-oriented interventions such as charges and (the removal of) subsidies.

- The use of safe minimum standards will be an essential part of any environmental policy supporting sustainable development and will indirectly result in prices reflecting environmental costs, if the standards are implemented and maintained (James et al. 1989).

- New or extended legal arrangements for liability and accountability will have to be introduced by changing the structure of property rights in environmental resources and environmental effects. This may be particularly appropriate where the problem is one of local degradation.

- Distance in time needs to be overcome by lifting the veil of time preference and by altering the preoccupation in the public sector with matters of immediate urgency. One form this could take is the adoption of some type of 'legacy principle', whereby countries agree to pass on to the next generation an environmental quality and environmental resource stock at least as large as the one they found. Institutionally, this would have to be complemented by installing some authority or body to represent and defend future generations' interests (e.g., an Ombudsman-type organization for this specific purpose).

- The problems created by the distance in scale, or between decision levels can be overcome by creating platforms or authorities at levels high enough to cope with the problem at hand; that is at least to negotiate, and preferably to have some authority over the joint resource or environment and their uses. Many of these problems are manifest at the international level (see next page).

- There is a need to review taxation policies and their foundations. Insofar as scarcity is one justification for choosing tax bases, most current systems turn labor into an over-expensive factor of production and this reinforces tendencies towards unemployment. Ecotaxes are based on differences in environmental pressure or resource claims, and may be a very useful addition to the set of fiscal instruments, to replace other types of taxes (as on labor or value added) so that more labor intensive and less environmental resource intensive production processes are favored in a fiscally neutral way.

Managing Economic Growth

This may be needed when, even with the interventions and institutions discussed under "redirection", economic growth would still lead to an overall environmental pressure beyond the EUS. Economic activities likely to bring societies near or beyond their EUS would have to be scrutinized for their environmental impacts. If these are unacceptable, and if there is no scope for reducing them by further technological innovation, then it may be necessary to restrict the level of economic activity in that particular sector (volume-oriented or scale-oriented policies). For example, this might be accomplished by allowing that activity to expand only insofar as critical loads or safe emission standards are not exceeded. This may ultimately result in changes of the overall patterns of production. Thus, there will be cases (especially in the more intensively industrialized countries) where direct regulation of economic behavior will be warranted or even preferable (e.g., from an efficiency or effectiveness point of view). Environmental policy thus inevitably requires extensions of the powers of the state into areas (e.g., economic planning, pricing policy, sectoral or volume-oriented policies, etc.) from where it is, in fact, currently seen to withdraw.

Depending on how effective these growth-curbing policies are, more basic strategies might be needed. As we have seen, growth tendencies are triggered by structural elements such as poverty or inequality; insecurity in a competitive and dynamic context; wrongly oriented technological innovation. First then, society can stimulate technological innovation oriented towards:

- Reducing the environmental burden of economic activities (dematerialization, decoupling),
- Enhancing the environment's capacity to generate economic inputs (environmental productivity) and
- Improving the ecological infrastructure.

Second, poverty alleviation at the global level would both directly and indirectly reduce long-term environmental pressure. Third, the most profound policy to prevent growth would be that of reducing market insecurity and competition. As this comes close to the very essence of our economic system, one cannot but hope that the environmental crisis can be resolved without having to consider changes as fundamental as these.

Basically what has been recommended above, amounts to an alteration of rights such that environmental pressure is recognized as a new type of claim on livelihood, existence rights (of species), etc. to be compensated for by those laying that claim, to those on whom the claim is being laid. Compensation will have to follow new regulations on rights of property over (and/or access to) environmental resources, accountability and liability. This could be in the form of an extension of the 'polluter pays principle' to not only the measures prescribed by environmental policy, but to damage costs (including ecological damage) in general. It might also entail developing a 'user pays principle', and a practically operational precautionary principle. Each of these principles would have to be worked into the mandates and regulations of the major national and international institutions and new institutions would have to be created to ensure the interests of those stakeholders that have hitherto been neglected: those groups (in the present generation) with little purchasing power and political clout, future generations, and other species.

Such fundamental reversals in legal status of polluters *vis-a-vis* pollutes, will not easily come about and may require political mobilization and coalition formation between various NGOs and interest groups.

INTERNATIONAL INSTITUTIONS AND SUSTAINABILITY

A special set of problems has to do with the regulation of access to resources in which there is no clear central authority. These are frequently referred to as the problems of the global commons. Access to every public good involves a political process, in the course of which users cede rights to some decision making regulatory authority. This is most difficult in the case of ecological services that extend across a number of juridical boundaries: such as a number of biogeochemical cycles, the upper atmosphere or biodiversity. Prevailing inequalities and persistent tendencies of production growth in all societies, lead to an accelerated and unabsorbable growth push bringing the global economy beyond the levels of effective metabolism that the biosphere can sustain. Thus, globally and in a long-term perspective, the situation is one of inherent insecurity and unsustainability. Necessary (perhaps not even sufficient) steps to alter this include the establishment of: effective global redistributive mechanisms and institutions. Sustainable global development implies international institutions capable to change prevailing distributions of incomes and current distributions of access to sources of income and wealth, including environmental resources and world markets. This, therefore, is a question not just of aid, but also of trade and technology. In the area of the establishment of fair shares in future carbon emissions, distributional issues prove to be tremendous stumbling blocks. Most work on strategic behavior of parties to international negotiations over common property resources indicates the importance of transfers as instruments of international environmental policy. This raises a number of practical issues concerning, for example, the precise role of international institutions, such as the World Bank, and UNEP, in the process. It also raises the issue of conditionality. Certain forms of transfer are already linked to the adoption of environmental reforms (e.g., 'debt for nature swaps'). One of the most promising suggestions is that relief be offered on debt servicing obligations in exchange for a range of reforms, the principal being written off only as specific targets are fulfilled. Other forms of 'green conditionality' are now commonly attached to development assistance, and the World Bank has used its leverage in a number of countries to promote the development of Environmental Action Plans.

Effective resource management and enforcement facilities are also needed. In cases of internationally shared environments or commonly used environmental resources, legal and administrative institutions may be needed for more appropriate management, and for resolving disagreements about actual use. This often means establishing new types of jurisdiction at high administrative levels. The International Rhine Committee is an example of such a new institution (but one without enough authority), and so are the North Sea Conferences. This point leads to questions related to sovereignty and jurisdiction. Transfers of sovereignty to international institutions in the area of natural resources and environmental management, will be necessary both in view of global problems and with regard to regional and sub regional components of the biosphere. They will also take the form of engagements in agreements and conventions on the use of global resources and ecosystems, on biological diversity, on the rights of future generations and on the rights of other species.

There should also be an international environmental authority (within the UN system) with a mandate, the competence and the instruments to effectively implement a global sustainability oriented policy. This authority (whether vested in UNEP, in a special security organization, in ECOSOC, or elsewhere) is to:

- Coordinate multilateral work in the areas of environmental quality, natural resources and biological diversity,
- Set international standards and have the power to monitor and even enforce adherence and,
- Settle disputes between nations on transboundary environmental and resource problems.

Another necessary step involves reforming multilateral development structures. Sustainability oriented mechanisms are needed for price setting on world markets. In cases where environmental effects are redistributed via the world market mechanism (international trade and investment), these effects have to become known and visible, and (where needed) to be transferred into changing regulations on international trade (e.g., GATT/WTO-rules, international price regulation, etc). This will especially be the case when North-South trade results in unsustainable patterns of production in developing countries, or where developing countries (e.g., as a consequence of international debt servicing obligations) are forced to sell out natural resources on the world market. The 'polluter pays principle' (extended to: 'user pays') should be a central principle in the new WTO charter, and so should be the notion of minimum sustainability standards, to be translated into process standards by governments. The World Bank and IMF-mandates and structures may also require revision in the light of sustainable development. The World Bank has moved far along this road in theory, but this needs to be entrenched in the realities of bank-sponsored operations. IMF is beginning to give environmental matters some thought, but this is far from adequate. Accepting the necessity of development but underlining that development is to be sustainable, one must question the Bank's and Fund's strategy of fostering unrestricted trade liberalization and export-led growth that is implicit in WB and IMF interventions. Strengthening economies by developing domestic and regional markets might even be prudent from a sustainability point of view.

A last necessary step to be discussed is that institutions and mechanisms for changing global patterns of production and consumption, and poverty alleviation at the global level will come about only via economic development and growth, implying additional environmental burdens in the short run. Poverty alleviation without changing the quality of economic growth, is a *cul-de-sac*. Given the present distribution of per capita environmental claims as well as welfare levels, it is obvious that there are to be quantitative changes as well, and that these have to come in the West first: qualitative changes in East and South will only come about insofar as the consumption patterns in the West will manifestly reflect new environmental values and if there is an explicit willingness on the side of the richer countries to assist the poorer countries in accomplishing this reorientation in their production patterns while guaranteeing them rising material per capita welfare levels. This requires a drastic reorientation (sometimes reduction) of consumption and production in the North, new lifestyles and ecologized production patterns. There is no institutional structure in place to ensure that effective and equitable reconsideration and change of patterns of production and consumption will take place; it is here that I see the major shortcoming in the multilateral institutional structure.

CONCLUSIONS

The main question addressed in this paper is: What institutional conditions and changes might foster sustainable development and development towards sustainability?

Sustainability refers to the maintenance of the ecological infrastructure. This gives scope for society using the "environmental utilization space" (EUS). Societies have to identify and embark upon a feasible and acceptable level of environmental utilization that they wish to enjoy sustainably—if such a level that is both acceptable and sustainable exists. From a welfare maintenance perspective, as is implied in the WCED-definition of sustainability, staying within the EUS is a sufficient, not perhaps a necessary condition for sustainability. Adding to sustainability the precautionary approach may imply that staying within the EUS becomes a necessary condition as well. Normally in economic policy, attention is focused on issues of efficiency, and (to a lesser degree) of equity. Environmental or ecological economics cannot be satisfied with that, if the EUS is to be respected as presenting an ecological constraint on long-term economic development. A third and even a fourth criterion are needed: coevolutionary sustainability and interspecies equity: a societally accepted element of care for the prospects of other species, insofar as humankind can effect these prospects.

Typically, economic analyses of environmental problems and the response to these, look at them from the perspective of "market and government failures". In this chapter the conceptual framework is broadened to: transaction failure, empowerment failure and government failure. Outside the market structure there are all kinds of multilateral and bilateral transactions. Beyond that, and even underlying the level of transactions, is social organization itself, either non-governmental or governmental. I propose we incorporate into the analysis elements such as social mobilization (failure) or (inadequate) countervailing power, and lack of public authority due to inadequate mandate given by society to its governments, as two main categories of "empowerment failures".

Inequity and scale issues may easily arise out of an economic process that is driven by market forces (e.g., economic growth under such circumstances will push the economy outside the EUS). Without corrective or preventative policies, the market system gives rise to cost shifting. This is facilitated by 'distance-related distortions', related to different types of distance, (i.e., distance in time, space and scale). The standard approach to these is to put in place some combination instruments such that prices reflect the true costs of production and consumption, and the polluters/users of the environment pay for their pollution/use. However, this is a rather restricted approach. Moreover, there can be no single generally valid optimal intervention strategy, as policies have to operate in different settings: (1) differences in the structures (environmental, economic) in which the intervention is to operate (the "application context"), and (2) socio-political and cultural structures (the "policy context").

Given the deep-rooted causes of unsustainability one must doubt whether altering the stringency with which existing quantitative instruments are applied, or even whether adding to that set of quantitative instruments, are sufficient interventions in terms of achieving sustainability. One has to realize more structural changes and systems' reforms: rights, responsibilities and power relationships, such that environmental quality claims and existence rights (of species), etc. are recognized, coupled with compensations to be made by those inflicting upon those rights.

There is a need for institutional change and reforms in the areas of: (1) redirecting growth, (2) curbing growth (at least where it has become ecologically inviable), and (3) creating or expanding institutions and instruments capable of achieving the necessary entitlements and powers. Institutions are required that are capable of safeguarding that the economic process stays within the environmental utilization space (safe standards, zoning, etc.) will have to be applied and enforced. Environmental agencies will have to be empowered to take structural or volume-oriented measures wherever this is needed. Ombudsman-type institutions may be required to represent and defend future generations' interests, and perhaps other species' interests. Proper pricing in a framework of appropriate entitlements, liabilities, and responsibilities will have to back this up and enhance society's efficient use of its environmental space. Tax reform and financial accountability ("polluter" and "user-must-pay") can achieve that. Institutional reform must ensure that basic driving forces of unsustainability are addressed (e.g., effective reductions in poverty and insecurity) or neutralized (e.g., appropriate technological innovation). This has repercussions for existing international institutions (GATT/WTO, World Bank, IMF, etc), but a number of areas have been identified in which institutions or mechanisms appear to be lacking (e.g., the redistribution of wealth and access to EUS; regional and global resource management; and changing patterns of production and consumption).

REFERENCES

Baumel, J. and W. E. Oates. 1988. The Theory of Environmental Policy. Cambridge, Mass: Cambridge University Press.

Daly, H. 1972. Steady State Economics. San Francisco: Freeman and Cie.

Daly, H. 1992. Allocation, distribution and scale: Towards an economy that is efficient, just and sustainable. *Ecological Econ*omics 6(3): 185–194.

Faber M. and J. R. L. Proops. 1993. Natural resource rents, economic dynamics and structural change. *Ecological Econ*omics 8(1): 17–44.

Frey, B. S. 1983. Democratic Economic Policy: A Theoretical Introduction. Oxford: Martin Robertson.

de Groot, R. S. 1992. Functions of Nature. Groningen: Wolters-Noordhoff.

IUCN, WWF and UNEP. 1991. Caring for the Earth: A Strategy for Sustainable Living. Gland: IUCN.

James D. E., H. M. A. Jansen, and J. B. Opschoor. 1978. Economic Approaches to Environmental Problems. Amsterdam: Elsevier Scientific Publisher.

James D. E., P. Nijkamp, and J. B. Opschoor. 1989. Ecological Sustainability and Economic Development. In Economy and Ecology: Towards Sustainable Development, eds. F. Archibugi and P. Nijkamp. Dordrecht: Kluwer Academic Publishers.

Kapp, W. 1969. On the Nature and Significance of Social Costs. *Kyklos* 22(2): 334–347.

OECD. 1992. Market and Government Failures in Environmental Management: The Case of Transport. Paris.

OECD. 1994. Managing the Environment: The Role of Economic Instruments. Paris.

Opschoor J. B. 1974. Economic Valuation of Environmental Degradation (in Dutch). Meppel: Boom.

Opschoor J. B. 1987. Duurzaamheid en Verandering (Sustainability and Change). Inaugural Address. Amsterdam: VU-Boekhandel.

Opschoor J. B. and G. A. J. Klaassen. 1991. Economics of sustainability or the sustainability of economics: Different Paradigms. *Ecological Economics* 4: 93–115.

Opschoor J. B. and C. Perrings. 1994. The loss of biological diversity: Some policy implications. *Environmental and Resource Econ*omics 4(1): 1–13.

Pearce D. W. and R. K. Turner. 1989. The Economics of Natural Resources and the Environment. New York/London: Harvester Wheatsheaf.

Shogren J. F., J. A. Herriges, and R. Govindasami. 1993. Limits to environmental bonds. *Ecological Economics* 8(2): 109–134.

Siebert H. 1982. Nature as a life support system: renewable resources and environmental disruption. *Journal of Economics* 42(2):133–142.

Solow, R. 1992. An Almost Practical Step toward Sustainability. Washington DC: Resources for the Future.

Swaney J. A. 1987. Elements of a Neoinstitutional Environmental Economics. *Journal of EconomicIssues* XXI(4): 1739–1781.

WCED (World Commission on Sustainable Development). 1987. Our Common Future. Oxford: Oxford University Press.

World Bank. 1992. World Development Report 1992. Oxford: Oxford University Press.

Zweifel P. and J. R. Tyran. 1994. Environmental impairment liability as an instrument of environmental policy. *Ecological Economics* 11(1): 43–56.

17 CREATING THE INSTITUTIONAL SETTING FOR SUSTAINABILITY IN LATIN AMERICA

Marc J. Dourojeanni
Chief, Environment Protection Division
The Inter-American Development Bank
Washington, DC

OVERVIEW

While not being self evident that new institutions are required for sustainability there is explicit recognition that the following principles are requisites to achieve it: decision making based on consultation, public access to information, capacity of the population to use information, a different social ethics and discipline, new tools for conflict resolution, redistribution of authority and, a more realistic legislation. In Latin America, despite some recent progress, it is clear that the institutional setting is not yet in place even for the most conventional forms of development. The most notorious progress has been achieved by Bolivia and Costa Rica, respectively with the establishment of a Ministry of Sustainable Development and the launching of a National Sustainable Development Strategy. Overall, despite these and other progress, the capacity of the region to undertake sustainable development is still embryonic. The role of the private sector is considered important but limited, especially because its lack of willingness to open participation and consultation. The international institutions also require changes, especially simplification, clearer definition of roles, and separation of functions among agencies. The multilateral development banks need to be able to provide cheaper money for smaller projects and longer periods of execution for sustainable development.

INTRODUCTION

The discussion that follows tries to establish some key components of an institutional setting for sustainability and sustainable development, the latter being understood as a style of development able "to meet the needs of the present without compromising the ability of future generations to meet their own needs".[1] Of course, these two concepts sustainability and sustainable development—are far from being solidified, widely understood or even fully accepted. As a matter of fact there are as many interpretations of what sustainable development implies, in practical terms, as people thinking about how to apply it. That being the case, it is obviously difficult to discuss what institutions are necessary to promote and, especially, to apply these evolving concepts.

Sustainable development promises a better life in the future but, in exchange, requires that a long list of hard changes and sacrifices be made in the present, particularly by influential, powerful, better-off nations and groups within nations. Among these changes are greater social equity, clearly meaning that the richest members of global and national society will have to share more and to have less by adopting new patterns of consumption; heavy investments today to obtain environmental benefits tomorrow; stabilization of the population at a level consistent with the capacity of the earth; acceptance of the existence of a global commons or, in different words, a revisitation of classical concepts of national heritage. In many ways the fundamentals of sustainable development are not very different from those of the old French Revolution: "*liberte, egalit, et fraternit*", and are certainly not any easier to achieve.

WHAT ARE INSTITUTIONS FOR SUSTAINABLE DEVELOPMENT?

Obviously, it is possible to argue that there are no basic differences between the institutions for development and those necessary for sustainable development. In principle, institutions that are efficient in promoting development should also be able to efficiently promote sustainable development. Were this true, it would only be necessary to modify their mandates or the policies they apply.

Others would disagree, arguing instead that the institutions needed for sustainable development must be entirely different than those we have now. Many existing institutions have been captured by groups whose interest is in exploitation, not sustainability. Others reflect an obsolete paradigm of development which, because it is based on a conception of economic growth and social change that is too narrowly circumscribed, does not require the degree of personal commitment and self denial that is necessary for sustainable development.

Both arguments are arid in the abstract. Which line of thinking (adapting current public and private institutions, developing new ones, or, more likely, a combination of both) may be better or somehow more correct is less relevant than the explicit recognition that there are certain fundamental principles or main requisites that must be satisfied to achieve development that is more sustainable. Some ideas along these lines, particularly in the Latin American context, follow.

Decision Making Based on Consultation and Participation

Sustainable development means that society and each of its citizens must continually choose between long-term benefits and short-term sacrifices. Therefore, open consultation and full participation are essential for its successful application.

Democracy as we understand it in Latin America today is not enough to achieve sustainable development. It is necessary to pursue the concept of participatory democracy at the grassroots level to supplement and nourish representative democracy at the state and national levels where participation is delegated to a few individuals over long periods of time. While there are a few encouraging examples of institutions achieving participatory decision-making processes at the local level, the institutional mechanisms to achieve the kind of large scale participation required for sustainable development are yet to be designed.

Public Access to Information

A necessary prior condition for the achievement of a more sustainable development path is the provision of more and better information to the public. In Latin America, despite a sharp increase in public information about environment and development, the level and quality of information are still very low. The public is not motivated to pay attention to news regarding environment; information provided by the media is frequently inaccurate or heavily biased.

Capacity of the Population to Use Information for More Effective Participation

Sound decision-making requires more than the timely provision of good information. The public must be able to understand and interpret the data being provided. This can only be achieved through education or, occasionally, through short-term training. Currently, with few exceptions, public education in the region falls far short of what is needed to build an environmentally sound public opinion.

Environmental Social Ethics and Discipline

Sustainability goes far beyond avoiding environmental damages caused by public and private development activities. Above all other considerations, sustainable development means that a majority of individuals in a society accept and respect an agreed environmental ethic and the policies and legislation embodying it. This directly implies the exercise of a much greater degree of individual self control, especially the commitment by every citizen to apply this ethic in daily life, even in the privacy of home. Possible behavior modifications range from family planning and changes in family consumption patterns to more responsible home waste disposal and energy saving.

Conflict Resolution

Even today decisions are often taken without much attention to long-term environmental considerations in Latin America. More explicit and frequent attention to common long-term social interests is likely to create more open disagreements and confrontations than has previously been the case. Therefore, sustainable development may require better arrangements for conflict resolution.

Conflict resolution can be accomplished through participation and also through a more participative public administration. However it is obvious that a growing number of cases dealing with environmental damage are going to reach the judiciary which, in most countries of the region, is totally unaware of and unprepared for these sorts of problems.[2] Therefore it is essential to mount an effort to adapt the Region's judiciary systems to matters pertaining to the environment and, in general, to sustainable development. A great part of this effort would consist in improved monitoring and enforcement—(i.e., filling the gap between the scientific data related to the management (or mismanagement) of the environment and the legal and judiciary processes).

Decentralization and Redistribution of Authority

To achieve participation it is also necessary to decentralize and delegate functions in the decision making process. The transfer of responsibilities and means for action (i.e., tariffs, taxes, and other fees) from the central government to regional and local authorities is an essential part of this goal. Also, to make participation possible it is not enough to have the institutions and the legal mechanisms in place. As emphasized above, it is also necessary that the population be really motivated or interested to participate in the decision making for development and that they be sufficiently educated to do so in a socially profitable manner, including their capacity to request, interpret and utilize the information existing on the issues to be addressed.

Adequate Legislation

A very serious effort is needed in Latin America to develop more adequate legislation. At present, environmental legislation, in addition to its very general character, overlaps, and sectoral contradictions, is too theoretical, making it is almost inapplicable to local conditions. Environmental legislation in the region is often a poor copy of legislation in developed countries, consequently disregarding the national reality in terms of enforcement capacity, ecological conditions and the economic costs of its application. The principle of the carrot and the stick is rarely applied, most laws being essentially punitive. If incentives are included in the laws, they are rarely implemented.

The practice of having very general laws and very detailed regulations is the cause of several additional problems. In effect, it is common that the regulations, which are prepared by the executive branch, do not correlate well with the law which gives rise to them. In some cases the several regulations arising from a law leave gaps but, even worse, in other cases they depart from the spirit of the law. In general, especially when dealing with pollution problems, they do not set enforceable standards or, if they do, these are based on standards from other latitudes.

Authority and Law Enforcement

Despite being essential, participation cannot be used as an excuse for the weakening of public authority in environmental and natural resource matters. Rather, the exercise of authority will be strengthened to the extent that it is legitimized and empowered by participation. No real development is possible without the equitable enforcement of regulatory measures, much less sustainable development, which often will require the imposition of severe restrictions on traditional behaviors that damage the environment.

Higher Technological Capacity

Sustainable development institutions must have modern technological tools to supervise, monitor and evaluate the status of the environment and, also to inform the public. This is, again, rarely the case in Latin America where environmental institutions are usually poorly equipped and where the staff is not adequately trained.

THE SITUATION OF PUBLIC INSTITUTIONS IN LATIN AMERICA TODAY

General Overview

When reviewing the current situation of public and private national institutions in Latin America, despite some recent progress, it is clear that the institutional setting is not yet in place even for the most conventional forms of development. Progress has been made in reducing the size of the state by transferring public services and so called strategic industries to the private sector, creating more appropriate regulatory frameworks for private investments. Also, some responsibilities have been decentralized to regions and municipal authorities. However, in most countries this reduction of the size and duties of the state has not improved the ability of public institutions to carry out even their newly reduced responsibilities. Pervasive problems such as very low salaries, lack of equipment, and other budgetary constraints continue. In some countries, reductions in the size of public institutions responsible for the environment and natural resources have been so drastic that essential tasks in the field are simply not being executed, such as maintenance of critical protected areas or monitoring of air and water pollution. Research and extension services are also severely limited due to budgetary restrictions, both in governmental institutions and universities.

New Trends in Public Environmental Institutions

During the past twenty years there has been progress in establishing new environmental institutions in the region. Currently there are ministries, secretariats or vice-ministries or sub-secretariats of the environment in many countries, including Argentina, Bolivia, Brazil, Colombia, Costa Rica, Mexico, Nicaragua, and Venezuela. There are national environmental commissions with policy and planning functions, among other functions, in Chile, Ecuador, El Salvador, Guatemala, Honduras, Panama, and Uruguay. Other countries, such as Paraguay and Peru, have announced their intention to establish such commissions in the short-term. Countries where there are only national environmental commissions usually have environmental units in each public sector agency. In addition, most countries have long had one or more national institutes in charge of the administration of natural resources. Federal countries, such as Brazil and Argentina, have environmental secretariats or environmental commissions in most states or provinces. Some states, such as Sao Paulo in Brazil, even have environmental units and committees at the municipal level.

Both the Inter-Americian Development Bank (IDB) and the IBRD have been very active providing financial and technical support to build or strengthen institutions for environment and sustainable development in Latin America.[3] However, while environmental institutions are indispensable, sustainable development will not be achieved solely by improving them. Sustainable development needs every institution in a country to participate in the task of making it a reality as an integral part of their mandate. In the last two years, two countries have moved in that direction. In Bolivia, a new Ministry of Sustainable Development has been established and, more recently, Costa Rica has launched a well-designed sustainable development strategy. There are also several regional institutional arrangements for environment and sustainable development, the most important being a regional Alliance for Sustainable Development among the Central American countries. In most other countries sustainable development, if mentioned in public documents, remains a vague concept worthy of mention essentially because it is in vogue.

Overall, despite significant progress, the capacity of Latin American countries to undertake sustainable development initiatives is still embryonic. Of course, institutional weakness in the region (and elsewhere) is not exclusive to sustainable development, but, the implications of this weakness are more serious than they are for more traditional areas of public sector activity because of the relative newness of the concept, knowledge about ways to put in practice, and a basic absence of political will to implement it. This lack of political will is caused by an array of situations ranging from ignorance and indifference to, in a growing number of cases, a conscious and active opposition to the reforms that sustainable development implies.

Additional Challenges for the New Public Institutions

Public institutions for sustainable development, in addition to what has been already mentioned, also need to be adapted to new situations and perspectives. It has become increasingly evident that many environmental concerns are global or regional in nature because of transboundary effects (benefits or damages resulting from one nation's actions which accrue to other nations). The complex issues and interdependencies involved clearly transcend the usual tasks of ministries of foreign affairs.

National policies are today as affected by international public opinion as by domestic opinion. The amazingly complex net of international environmental treaties and agreements demands a very special effort on the part of public agencies. Global environmental issues which have to be resolved through a greater global governance capacity require unique coordination efforts among agencies in each country and among the countries of a region in order to face demands or pressures exerted by coalitions from other regions. This ability clearly does not exist in Latin America where it is still common to see an enormous divergence of official opinion on transcendental affairs among agencies within a given country.

This lack of coordination sometimes shows up in international fora as drastic changes of national positions in function of the agency—and in some cases the person- representing the country. Regional coordination to defend common interests is also limited and sporadic.

The future will bring more and more environmental "emergency" situations. These are usually national in magnitude, but they are increasingly international, as in the case of oil spills, acid precipitation, or erosion processes in shared watersheds, among so many others. It is necessary that the new public institutions be able to respond to these emergencies in an efficient manner.

THE GROWING ROLE OF PRIVATE INSTITUTIONS

In part as a consequence of government's lack of efficiency in undertaking development, especially sustainable development, an array of private institutions, including businesses as well as non-profit organizations, have taken in hand several of the functions and obligations of public institutions. This growing trend has both positive and negative aspects.

Business and the Environment

In comparison with public sector enterprises, the private sector has several positive attributes, including more efficiency and rapidity, faster introduction of new technologies, lower costs and, to some extent, greater accountability. Public environmental regulatory institutions evidently do better in controlling the private sector than they do public sector enterprises; there is little doubt that the private sector does better than government establishments in pollution abatement.

There are limits to the social benefits we can expect to be produced through private action. One overriding characteristic of the private sector is its fundamental interest in profit, and its consequent tendency to disregard the external effects arising from business activity in the absence of mandatory public revelation of damaging activities and/or environmental regulations. The private sector in Latin America often carries out activities having negative implications for sustainable development and the environment because the regulatory framework is not appropriate or because there is no serious enforcement of those regulations that do exist.

Of course the profit motive can sometimes be used advantageously through the application of economic instruments that yield environmental benefits (e.g., environmental taxes). On the other hand in some cases governments of the region are transferring obligations to private sector management which are incompatible with the aims of sustainability because they establish real conflicts of interest between the private profit motive and social welfare, more broadly defined. Examples of this are existing proposals in several countries to transfer the management of public protected areas to tourism or eco-tourism enterprises or the transfer of agrochemicals licensing to private laboratories without any real governmental capacity to supervise the process. Similar negative consequences are to be expected from the privatization of previously state owned forests or the establishment of competitive markets for water rights unrelated to land rights. In both cases, the services provided by these natural resources may be denied to large segments of the population, especially the poor majorities, and also negatively affect the provision of global environmental services such as carbon fixation, biodiversity conservation and others.

It is also important to underline the fact that the private sector, in dealing with sustainable development or environment, is even less in favor of consultation and participation than are current forms of national, regional or local governments. From this perspective the private sector's role in promoting sustainable development would appear to be limited.

Non-Profit Private Organizations

Grass roots, intellectual and other non-governmental organizations (NGOs) have experienced an explosive increase in their activities related to sustainable development. Today there are several thousand of these institutions. In Brazil alone, there may be 3-4,000 NGOs claiming to deal with the environment and sustainable development. The objectives of relatively traditional NGOs, dedicated to environment or to social affairs, have migrated toward sustainable development much faster than the transformation of the states and private enterprises, an exception in this last group being the consulting business. Their impact have been important in terms of raising public and political awareness, promoting changes in international institutions, and in developing actions in the field, especially pilot programs in many countries. The so-called environmental law institutions have been particularly successful promoting the passage of new legislation and the signing of international agreements and, more recently, in putting pressure on the judiciary systems to get better enforcement of legislation pertaining to environment and sustainable development.

It is evident, however, that the NGOs cannot and should not replace governments and, also, that as time goes on, the NGOs tend to exhibit some of the same problems that characterize public institutions, especially a lack of peoples' representation and participation in decisions. Several NGOs, especially in Latin America, have no broad constituency or membership; rather they are run by a very small group of well-intentioned and motivated persons who simultaneously act as board members and as executors (in some cases also as beneficiaries) of the monies they collect for their projects. This is particularly the case of the so-called centers, institutes and foundations, but it is also true for many associations and societies.

Another major problem most Latin American NGOs have is that they cannot sustain themselves. This is, in part, a consequence of their small membership and, when they do have members, it is because these do not pay. It is amazing to discover that, with few exceptions (i.e., Foundation Boticario, in Parana, Brazil) the foundations have no funds to administer and provide to others and that, instead, they work solely by requesting funds from real foundations, international agencies or governments to execute projects. To complicate a scenario which is already difficult, some of the important international NGOs have established offices in Latin American countries where they compete, with their vast experience in fund raising, against the truly native NGOs.

Finally, far too much importance has been provided on the so-called "intellectual" NGOs to the detriment of the "grassroots" NGOs that group farmers, workers, indigenous people, neighbors and other social sectors by forming associations, federations, unions, cooperatives or communities. To some extent there are today too many small and inefficient "intellectual" NGOs, each one with its own "micro-bureaucracy", competing for scarce resources and usually for the same ideas. Competition, little loyalty, and enormous overlaps among them add to the problem. Agencies involved in international cooperation fomented this situation, partly because it is obviously easier to work with environment and development with high level professionals who are fluent in English than with common people. Nevertheless, it is important to keep as top priority the gradual empowerment of local people to care for the earth. The "intellectual" NGOs should mostly be facilitators, promoting environmental goals that are as attractive to local people as they are to them.

INTERNATIONAL INSTITUTIONS FOR SUSTAINABLE DEVELOPMENT

Situation of the United Nations and Regional Systems

The situation of the international institutions to promote sustainable development is somewhat better than national institutions. They have, despite current financial difficulties, much more human and technical resources than institutions of the Latin American countries and, of course, their role is easier as they do not deal with enforcement. Since Stockholm, a growing number of agencies and other bodies have been established or empowered to handle environment and promote sustainable management.

However, these institutions also face deep troubles because they are overcommissioned and underfunded. Intending to do too much with very little results in many insignificant actions which, in addition, usually overlap or compete with equivalent actions of other institutions. This is characteristic of the United Nations (UN) system where, in addition to its notorious fragmentation, there is no single organization that is not dealing with environment in addition to its regular functions. Forests are a good example of this overlap; in addition to FAO, most other important UN agencies are also involved. Of course, very little money effectively reaches the forests. Forests are a good example of another problem typical of international organizations; too often they use the tactic of solving a lack of efficiency of existing institutions by building new ones instead of fixing existing institutions. Interagency or international commissions and committees are established to carry out specific tasks but often are not dismantled after completion; instead they endlessly invent new duties.

International institutions are also fond of spending excessive effort in launching new concepts while disregarding the effective application previously invented concepts, often as valid or at least equivalent to the new. This propensity to reinvent the wheel has given us a bewildering array of concepts ranging from 'conservation' to 'human sustainable development', passing through 'ecodevelopment' and 'sustainable development'; from 'environmental profiles', to 'environmental action plans' passing through 'environmental issues papers' and 'conservation strategies'; and from 'national parks and equivalent reserves' to 'protected areas', passing through 'conservation units' and 'biosphere reserves' or, again, from 'multiple use of forests' to 'sustainable forest management' passing through 'extractive reserves' and 'forests for people'. These are only a few examples of this problem in taxonomy which certainly is not helping countries to find their way. Of course, these "new" terminologies and concepts serve as a convenient pretext for countless and costly consultations and meetings, resulting in mountains of paper which directly and indirectly hamper actions in the field.

A reorganization of the UN system is necessary, involving simplification, clearer definition and separation of functions among agencies, better funding accompanied by much more accountability and increased and more effective participation of governmental and non-governmental organizations.

These agencies should be very careful when launching new concepts, making sure before embarking on such ventures that the concept has content, validity and makes a contribution to our understanding, rather than being just another buzzword.

The Multilateral Development Banks

The multilateral development banks have been instrumental in promoting sustainable development by:

- Improving the environmental quality of the projects they prepare,
- Promoting policy and legal changes in the borrower countries,
- Providing grants for technical cooperation, very often to NGOs and,
- Particularly, lending a very significant portion of their annual total lending for "brown" or "green" environment.

The building, or strengthening, of environmental and sustainable development institutions in the borrower countries has been a major area of work through policy driven lending, environmental loans, environmental components in other projects, and technical cooperation. This special effort is a response to the fact that, in the past, the main difficulty for these banks in applying their policies, procedures and guidelines has been that most countries in the region had no visible responsible institutions for environment and/or no real enforcement of existing legislation. This is why the so-called Pelosi Amendment, of the U.S. has done more for environmental consciousness in these banks than most other forms of pressure or outcry. This law requires that the executive directors representing the U.S. on the boards of the multilateral development banks abstain from voting in favor of projects for which an environmental assessment has not been submitted to them 120 days in advance of board consideration. This legislation allowed the Inter-American Development Bank to insist on environmental assessments of projects as an unavoidable requisite.

Despite these and other substantial achievements, there is still a very long way to go before every action of these banks is clearly in favor of sustainable development. Many operations, despite all the environmental reviews being done, still pose serious risks for the environment and many more still cannot be considered sustainable development operations. The new trends in economics, especially privatization and liberalization, as well as free trade, are certainly opportunities for sustainable development but also, simultaneously, introduce new hard to predict dangers for which there are no simple written recipes for avoidance or damage control.

There are a few options for the banks to do more in environment and sustainable development if some measures are taken. Among these measures those mentioned in the following paragraphs are the most important.

Financial Institutions for Sustainable Development Lending

Lending that addresses sustainable development, environmental or to financing "green" or "brown" conditionalities attached to projects should be available at interest rates and other conditions that make them really attractive to borrower countries. This is rarely the case today and, due to this, governments may find the utilization of commercial loans without conditions of sustainability more attractive than those provided by the multilateral development banks. To really promote sustainable development operations, the international finance institutions should be allowed to provide special lending terms (interest rate grace period, amortization period) for an introductory trial period of at least ten years in consideration of the inherent risk to the borrower posed by the often novel, untested nature of projects whose demonstrated purpose is sustainability. This period would be sufficient to demonstrate ex-post the social, economic and environmental benefits of sustainable development operations.

Smaller Projects, Longer Periods of Execution, Very Careful Preparation, and Intensive Supervision of Execution

The banks only reluctantly provide small and even mid-size amounts of funding that environmental or sustainable development projects usually require because the cost of preparation of such projects is higher per dollar loaned. Likewise, borrowers obviously prefer large projects prepared quickly with low development costs and encumbered with only minor conditionality. On the other hand, the developed countries providing the funds—often called "donors"—also want more large projects in which their consulting, contracting and supply enterprises can do good business. As a result of these convergent pressures toward bigness and hardware, projects dealing with environment or sustainable development are often made larger than necessary (i.e., overdimensioned). If they are properly dimensioned and their cost is modest, they are not given priority by the countries and, very often, by decision makers in the banks.

It is by now well known (for the previously mentioned reasons), that the banks have been practicing a so-called 'culture of approval' in opposition to a "culture of high project quality". Quality projects of course take longer time to prepare and are much more expensive to execute and supervise. By the same token, technical cooperation funding is not the main interest of the banks. Very often a relatively small grant takes as much effort for preparation as a large loan. Limited staff time is almost fully allocated to investment and sector loan preparation. They are given top priority because it is the most practical way to meet lending targets given staff constraints.

Finally, it is worth noting that many projects aiming at sustainability have to be executed over a longer period of time than the usual four to five year disbursement period customarily used by the banks. Allowing more flexibility in specifying the execution period of projects is important, especially when the substantive participation of affected populations is a necessary ingredient for project success (e.g., technology transfer to small farmers).

CONCLUSION

Developing an institutional setting for sustainable development will be a long, long march. The march will be worthwhile if the concept of sustainable development endures long enough to permeate into peoples' minds and governmental actions. This march means revolution. Let us hope that the revolution achieves a sustainable result.

NOTES

1. Our Common Future, report of the World Commission on Environment and Development, 1987.
2. For a particularly illuminating account of one judge's efforts to promote environmental education, form a task force to uncover environmental and public health violations, and enforce the law see Daniel Hugo Llermanos, "Environmental Agony: My Experience as an Argentinian Judge" Proceedings: Third International Conference on Environmental Enforcement, Oaxaca, Mexico, April 25–28, 1994.
3. The IDB considers a top priority the strengthening of environment and sustainable development institutions. This Bank loaned US $133 million in 1992 and 1993 for environmental institution building and provided 44 technical cooperations from 1990–1993 amounting to $ 21 million for the same purpose. However, institutional strengthening for environment is also carried out as component of a large number of "non-environmental" operations, meaning that much more money is really directed to that purpose. There are several other projects under preparation for 1994 and 1995 which may bring close to $120 million for environmental institution building in the region.

18 APPLYING AGROECOLOGY TO IMPROVE PEASANT FARMING SYSTEMS IN LATIN AMERICA: AN IMPACT ASSESSMENT OF NGO STRATEGIES

Miguel A. Altieri
College of Natural Resources
University of California, Berkeley
1050 San Pablo Avenue, Albany, CA 94706

Andres Yurjevic
Institute of Social Studies
Consorcio Latino Americano Sobre
Agroecología y Desarrollo (CLADES)
Casilla 97 Correo 9, Santiago, Chile

Jean Marc Von der Weid
Assesoría e Servicios a Proyectos un
Agricultura Alternativa (AS-PTA)
Rua Bento Lisboa 58-13% Andar
Catete, Rio de Janeiro, Brasil

Juan Sanchez
Centro de Investigación,
Educación y Desarrollo (CIED)
Apartado 11-0104, Lima 11, Peru

OVERVIEW

NGOs are the new actors of rural development in Latin America. Many have embraced the agroecological approach as a basis to devise new alternatives to the problems of small farm productivity. This chapter analyzes several case studies of NGO agroecological interventions in various rural areas of Latin America, assessing to the extent possible, given limitations in data availability, their impact in terms of production, enhanced food security, improved income and better conservation of the natural resource base. In order to better capture resource costs of various production technologies a specific study of wheat production systems in Chile using a natural resource accounting technique, demonstrates the economic viability of agroecological technologies when soil depreciation is considered.

INTRODUCTION

In the 1980s, "the lost decade", Latin American economies went through a major economic crisis with extraordinary social and environmental costs. Despite numerous international– and state–sponsored development projects, poverty, food scarcity, malnutrition, health deterioration, and environmental degradation continue to be widespread problems (LACDE 1990). As Latin American countries are pulled into the existing international order and change policies in order to serve the unprecedented debt, governments increasingly embrace neo-liberal economic models that promote export-led growth. Despite the fact that in some countries such as Chile and Brazil, the model appears successful at the macroeconomic level, deforestation, soil erosion, industrial pollution, pesticide contamination, and loss of biodiversity (including genetic erosion) proceed at alarming rates and are not reflected in the economic indicators. So far, there is no clear system to account for the environmental costs of such development models.

The crisis has demonstrated that conventional development strategies are fundamentally limited in their ability to promote equitable and sustainable development (Altieri and Masera 1993). The deficiencies of conventional agricultural development strategies in Latin America have demanded a broader approach to rural development, one that is centered around an ecological understanding of agricultural systems and that takes into account the social, cultural, and economic dimensions of development. A selected group of NGOs organized under the umbrella of the Latin American Consortium on Agroecology and Development (CLADES) have endorsed and implemented such an approach (Altieri and Yurjevic 1991).

Using agroecology as a new technological paradigm, NGOs have actively promoted the idea of alternative agricultural development. As such, they represent a step forward in technological innovation and new development styles that move beyond the rhetoric and are more connected to the cultural traditions and resource endowment of each region (Altieri 1992). Though formal and detailed evaluations are lacking in many NGO projects that emphasize this agroecological approach, there is strong evidence that many NGOs have generated and adapted technological innovations that have resulted in tangible benefits for the local peasant population by increasing peasants' food security, strengthening subsistence production, generating income sources, improving use-efficiency of local resources and regenerating the natural resource base. They have achieved these impacts through innovative technologies and institutional arrangements as well as through novel methodologies for working with rural communities. This is commendable given the formidable socio-economic and biophysical constraints prevailing in the rural environments where NGOs work (Redclift and Goodman 1991). Despite the many advances, bottom-up grassroots development efforts in poverty alleviation have met with mixed success. A key reason is that they are attempting to counteract an environment in which their constituents have little access to political and economic resources and in which institutional biases against peasant production prevail. Grassroots development is difficult to implement where land-ownership is very skewed or where institutional arrangement (i.e., credit, technical assistance, etc.) and factor markets favor the large farm sector.

Though adequate methodologies for weighing the results of these efforts are still lacking, there are hundreds of NGO initiatives that hold great promise for the development of more sustainable ways of growing food. As already noted, appropriate means for evaluating the impact of such programs, and a satisfactory set of indicators to judge their viability, adaptability and durability, are in short supply. However, some progress has been made using multidisciplinary assessment methods such as rapid rural appraisal (RRA) and natural resource accounting (NRA). RRA techniques emphasize the informal gathering and presentation of information, to foster a participatory process between local people and researchers. Technologies are evaluated through very general criteria, addressing environmental, economic, and social concerns expressed by residents. NRA techniques incorporate environmental factors in conventional cost-benefit analyses, and can be used to measure the real profitability of alternative systems, including their effects on the natural resource base. Despite the availability of these analytical tools—which may not be perfect but at least provide a starting point—to assess the virtues of agroecological interventions, little has been done by academic and research institutions in the region to try to quantify the impacts of agroecological strategies.

The NGOs themselves, meanwhile, are action, rather than research oriented and must operate with minimal funds. Nevertheless, several have engaged in modest research efforts, yielding important information, as this chapter shows. Needless to say, these attempts at incorporating sustainability concerns into the rural development process is proving to be a complex task.

AGROECOLOGICAL ELEMENTS OF A SUSTAINABILITY EVALUATION FRAMEWORK

A definition of sustainability in the context of Latin American rural development includes at least four criteria:

1. Maintenance of the productive capacity of the agroecosystem (productive capacity);
2. Preservation of the natural resource base and functional biodiversity (ecological integrity);

3. Social organization and reduction of poverty (social health); and
4. Empowerment of local communities, maintenance of tradition, and popular participation in the development process (cultural identity).

An important attribute of agroecological technologies is that they must maintain a non-declining crop yield over time, within a broad range of environmental conditions and avoid degradation of fragile and marginal ecosystems. The challenge of small farm development is that agricultural production requires ecosystem modification and resource utilization, while environmental protection requires some acceptable level of resource conservation. This balance must be achieved in the context of overcoming rural poverty (Altieri 1995). Thus monitoring of productivity, ecological integrity, and social equity must go beyond quantification of food production and monitoring of soil or water status to include levels of peasants' food security, social empowerment, and economic potential and independence or autonomy. Table 18.1 lists some indicators actually being used by some NGOs to evaluate the impact of their programs on agricultural productivity and ecological integrity. The idea is to transcend the tendency to monitor agricultural systems by merely focusing on quantifying food production, but to include an assessment of the status of soil and water resources, biodiversity levels, status of critical components and processes of the agroecosystem, as well as the status of the social and cultural fabric, and how each indicator interrelates. Given that many aspects of agricultural sustainability are difficult to categorize and quantify, NGOs often assign qualitative values to each attribute listed in Table 18.1.

Table 18.1. Association Between Rural Development Assessment Points and Indicators of Sustainability Utilized by Several Latin American NGOs

Indicator	Productitive Capacity	Ecological Integrity	Social Health	Cultural Identity
Crop Productivity	X			
Soil Fertility and Nutrient Cycling Capacity	X	X		
Soil Erosion	X	X		
Crop Health (pest, disease incidence)	X			
Biodiversity Status (native germplasm, forest cover, etc.)	X	X		X
Landscape Health (watershed status, biological corridors, etc.)	X	X		
Health and Nutritional Status	X		X	X
Community Participation and Solidarity	X		X	X
Income and Employment			X	
Required External Inputs, Costs of Production	X		X	
Cultural Acceptability of Technologies	X			X

A PRELIMINARY ASSESSMENT OF NGO
AGROECOLOGICAL PROJECTS

The urgent need to combat rural poverty and to regenerate the deteriorated resource base of small farms simulated CLADES and other associated NGOs to actively search for new kinds of agricultural development and resource management strategies that, based on local participation, skills, and resources, enhance productivity while conserving the resource base. Local farmers' knowledge about the environment, plants, soils, and ecological processes regains unprecedented significance within this new agroecological paradigm (Altieri 1995). The central idea inspiring the work of NGOs is that agricultural research and development should operate on the basis of the "bottom-up" approach, starting with what is there already: local people, their needs and aspirations, their farming knowledge and their autochthonous natural resources. The resulting agricultural approximation to the peasant production process is radically different from that of the Green Revolution and other high-input approaches. It also tends to be more socio-culturally acceptable, since it builds on local tradition. Techniques are ecologically sound because they don't radically modify or transform the peasant system, instead identifying traditional and/or new management elements that, once incorporated, lead to optimal production. By emphasizing the use of locally-available resources rather than expensive or hard-to-obtain imported inputs, these technologies are also more economically viable.

In practical terms, NGO programs emphasize six key points.

1. Improving production of basic foods, including traditional food crops (*Amaranthus*, quinoa, lupine, etc.), and conservation of native crop germplasm.
2. Rescuing and application of peasants' knowledge and technologies.
3. Promoting efficient use of local resources (land, labor, agricultural by-products, etc.)
4. Increasing crop and animal diversity in the form of polycultures, agroforestry systems, integrated crop/livestock systems, etc., to minimize risks.
5. Improving the natural resource base through soil and water conservation and regeneration practices.
6. Reducing the use of external chemical inputs, by developing, testing, and implementing organic farming and other low-input techniques.

The array of agroecological technologies used by NGOs which include among others, crop diversification in time and space in the form of polycultures and rotations, animal integration, soil organic management, continuous soil cover, alternative biopesticides, and cultural pest control tactics, etc. result in substantial positive impacts on soil properties, crop health and productivity, and economic viability. Scientific documentation of such effects (Table 18.2) have provided many NGOs with increased confidence to continue using and expanding such technologies. Table 18.3 is a brief summary of a few projects run by eight NGOs in the region and provides a quick idea of the types of ecosystems and constraints that NGOs face as well as the various agroecological strategies they use to overcome production problems. A more detailed description of projects is provided later in the text. The following is a description and preliminary evaluation of NGO-led agroecological interventions across diverse biophysical and socioeconomic contexts of peasant agriculture throughout Latin America.

Table 18. 2.   Documented Effects of Agroecological Productive Strategies Implemented by NGOs in Latin America

---

Effects on the Soil
1.   Increase in the organic matter content stimulation and biological activity, increment in nutrient mineralization;
2.   Erosion decline, soil and water conservation, improvement of soil structure and general soil conditions;
3.   Improvement of retention and recycling of nutrients, positive nutrient balances; and
4.   Enhancement of mycorrhitic and antagonistic activity.

Effects on Pests, Diseases and Weeds
1.   Diversification affects insect pests, reducing herbivores and stimulating natural enemies;
2.   Multilines and mixed varieties reduce pathogens;
3.   High soil cover polycrops suppress weeds;
4.   Cover crops on fruit trees diminish insect and weed infestations; and
5.   Minimum tillage can reduce soil diseases.

Effects on Yields
1.   Yields per unit of area can be 5–10% less, but yields in relation with other factors (i.e., per unit of energy, of soil losses, etc.) are greater;
2.   Polycrops overyield monocultures;
3.   An initial loss of production can exist during the conversion to organic management but it can be minimized with input substitution production improves with time; and
4.   Yield variability is lower, yield stability is greater and there are lower risks involved.

Effects on Economic Aspects
1.   Low production costs;
2.   Low environmental costs (externalities), lesser soil depreciation, low contamination costs;
3.   Higher energy efficiency and lower total energy use; and
4.   The labor requirements are bigger for some practices and lower for others. A dilution or spreading effect of the labor needs exists during the season, avoiding peaks on labor demands.

Table 18.3. Agroecological Features of NGO-led Rural Development Projects in Latin America

NGO	Characteristics of intervened area	Agroecological and socioeconomic constraints	Goals of the agroecological strategy	Technical components of the strategy	Impacts and/or achievements
SEMTA (Bolivia)	Pacajes Province, Altiplano (3500-3800 m.a.s.l.) Potato, cereals, andean crops, bovine/ovine cattle, alpacas	Frost, low soil fertility, erosion, deforestation, drought. Generalized poverty, low access to credit, public services, and markets.	Slow environmental degradation process and regenerate productive potential	Organically managed mud-built greenhouses for vegetable production. Terracing, crop rotations for erosion control. Reforestation with native species. Improvement/management of native pastures.	Early production of vegetables under greenhouses resulted in premium prices in nearby La Paz markets, increasing income of participating farmers.
CIED (Puno-Peru)	Altiplano(3500 m.a.s.l.) Natural pastures (ichu), andean crops, potato, cattle, camelids	Frost, droughts, flooding, soil and genetic erosion, low productivity. Poverty and marginalization.	Food self-sufficiency, conservation of natural resource base, rescuing of traditional technologies.	Rehabilitation of waru-warus and terraces (andenes). Crop rotations. Reintroduction of alpaca. Improved cattle management and sanitation.	Waru-warus ensure potato production in the midst of frost, therefore reducing risks in food production.
IDEAS (San Marcos - Peru)	Inter-andean valleys of Cajamarca (18 C, 450 mm rainfall). Potato, maize, cereals, cattle.	Steep slopes, erosion, seasonal drought. Poverty, low access to good land.	Design of self-sufficient farming system. Rescuing and enriching traditional technology. Soil and water conservation.	Predial design with rotation and polycultures. Organic soil management. Management of small mammals and poultry.	Organic crop production has proved viable, stabilizing yields without use of toxic chemicals.
PTA/CT AQ (Brazil)	Northeastern Brazil, semi-arid tropics. Eight-11 dry months. Perennial cotton, maize, beans.	Rapid organic matter photo-decomposition, low biomass production, low soil fertility, hardpan, and salinity. Poverty, low access to land, marketing problems.	Improve traditional shifting cultivation system (rozado). Offer new productive options for vegetable, fruit, and animal diversification. Water harvesting and conservation. Improved management of animals, in-situ conservation of local germplasm.	Agrosilvopastoral management of catinga (xeric natural vegetation). Design of rotations, agroforestry schemes and polycultures.	Water harvesting techniques and design of drought tolerant cropping systems have enhanced productive potential in semi-arid areas.
CPCC (Paraguay)	Subtropical serrania (600-800 m.a.s.l.) Cassava, maize, peanuts, beans, cotton, sugarcane, and rice.	Seasonal drought (4-6 months), low soil fertility. Low income, small landholdings.	Design of agroforestry systems, soil conservation and diversification of production.	Community tree nursery. Forest enrichment, soil conservation in slopes, organic soil management.	Agroforestry systems have enhanced production of multiple resources and reverted deforestation processes.
CETEC (Colombia)	Southwest of Cauca Valley (1500 mm rainfall). Cassava, tropical fruit trees.	Acid and erosive soils, crop pests and diseases, weed interference. Low income, no access to credit or technical assistance. Low prices of agriculture commodities.	Diversify production with low-input technologies. Natural resources conservation. Alternatives to pesticides.	Improved cassava cropping systems. Soil conservation systems. Home gardens. Pest control with parasites and botanicals.	Soil erosion has been reduced and alternatives to pesticides are proving effective.
INDES (Argentina)	Dry subtropical area (600 mm). Cotton and subsistence crops (maize, squash, cassava).	Drought, high temperatures, wind erosion, low soil fertility. Poverty, unemployment, lack of credit.	Food self-sufficiency. Optimize use of local resources.	Rationalize cotton based rotations. Improve soil cover to avoid erosion. Use of adapted crop variety.	Diversification schemes have brought new crops into production, challenging dominance of cotton.
CET (Chile)	Chiloe Island Southern Chile (2000-2500 mm rainfall). Potato, wheat, pastures.	Frost, acid soils, phosphorous deficiency, overgrazing of pastures, genetic erosion. Poverty, marketing problems.	Improve and stabilize productive systems through diversification, use of local resources, rescuing of traditional varieties and technologies, and soil conservation.	In-situ potato genetic community conservation programs. Pasture-based crop rotations. Rotational grazing systems. Silvopastoral systems.	More than 100 traditional potato varieties rescued, with about 56 families involved in-situ conservation programs.

CONSERVING SOIL ON SLOPES

Central America

A major challenge in Latin America is designing hillside cropping systems that maintain yields while reducing erosion. Several NGOs have taken on the challenge, and Loma Linda in Honduras has developed a simple, no-till system for steep slopes (Altieri 1995).

Initially, weeds in a fallow area are simply cut with a machete or other tool and no soil is removed. Using a hoe or small plow, small furrows are made every 50 or 60 cm, following the contour. Seeds and compost and/or chicken manure are placed in the furrow and covered with soil. As the crop grows, weeds are kept mowed to avoid excessive competition, with the cut weed biomass left between rows as a mulch cover and source of organic nutrients. Excellent yields can be obtained this way without using chemical fertilizers and—more importantly—without significant soil loss.

In a similar project in Guinope, Honduras, the private voluntary organization World Neighbors began a development and training program to control erosion and restore soil fertility. It introduced such soil conservation practices as drainage and contour ditches, grass barriers and rock walls, and emphasized such organic fertilization methods as using chicken manure and intercropping with leguminous plants. In the first year, yields tripled or quadrupled from 400 1,200 to 1,600 kg/ha. This jump in per-hectare grain production has assured the 1,200 families participating in the program ample grain supplies for the ensuing year (Altieri 1992).

Increased per-hectare productivity means most farmers are now farming less land than before, allowing more territory to grow back to pine forest or be used for planted pasture, fruit, or coffee trees. The net result is that hundreds of hectares formerly used for erosive agriculture are now covered by trees, while production has not suffered.

Andean Region

In Peru, several NGOs as well as government agencies have programs to restore abandoned terraces and build new ones. In the Colca Valley of southern Peru, the Programa de Acondicionamiento Territoral y Vivienda Rural (PRAVITAR) sponsors terrace reconstruction by offering peasant communities low-interest loans or seeds and other inputs to restore abandoned terraces, up to 30 ha at a time. The advantages of terraces are that they minimize crop loss risk in times of frost or drought, improve crop yields, reduce soil losses, and amplify cropping options because of the micro-climatic and hydraulic advantages they provide. First year data from new bench terraces showed a 43%-65% increase in yield in potatoes, maize, and barley compared to yields grown on non-terraced slopes. A drawback of this technology is that it is labor-intensive. An estimated 2,000 worker-days would be needed to reconstruct one hectare in the Colca Valley region, although in other areas of Peru, terrace reconstruction has proven less labor-intensive requiring only 350 to 500 worker days/ha (Treacey 1989).

In Cajamarca, Peru, EDAC-CIED an NGO initiated together with peasant communities in 1983 an all-encompassing soil conservation project. In 10 years, they planted more than 550 thousand native and exotic tree species and constructed about 850 ha of terraces and 173 ha of drainage and infiltration canals. The end result is about 1,124 ha of land under conservation measures (approx. 32% of the total arable land), benefiting 1,247 families (about 52% of the total). Crop yields have improved significantly (for example potato yields went from 5 t/ha to 8 t/ha and Oca yields jumped from 3t/ha to 8 t/ha, lupine from 0.7t/ha to 1.0 t/ha and maize and beans from 0.6t/ch to 1.0 t/ha). Raising of cattle for fattening and alpaca for wool, and enhanced crop yields has increased the income of families from an average $108 per year in 1983 to more than $500 today (Sanchez 1994).

In the watershed, campesinos and their grassroots organizations have set up rotating funds for seed and small animals (such as guinea pigs, chickens, and rabbits), improving conservation quality and productivity. The germplasm of these rotating funds are a type of "credit-in-kind" supported initially by CIED and then maintained by the crop harvest or the animal offspring obtained later. Between 1983 and 1993, the rotating seed funds allowed a total of 1,594 families to cover 138.8 ha with different species of root crops, 234.7 ha of cereals and 57.8 ha of grains.

Dominican Republic

About 10 years ago, Plan Sierra, an ecodevelopment project, decided to break the link between rural poverty and environmental degradation in the Central Cordillera of the Dominican Republic. Its strategy involved developing less erosive production systems than the *conucos* used by local farmers. Controlling run-off would not only stop erosion, but could also make use of hydroelectric potential and make possible the irrigation of up to 50,000 ha of land in the downstream Cibao Valley.

The specific objective were to allow farmers to make more efficient use of soil moisture and nutrients, crop and animal residues, natural vegetation, and genetic diversity, as well as family labor, in order to satisfy their need for food, firewood, construction materials, medicinals, and cash income. From a management viewpoint, the strategy consisted of a series of farming methods integrated in several ways.

- Soil conservation practices such as terracing, minimum tillage, alley cropping, use of living barriers, mulch, etc;
- Use of leguminous trees such as *Gliricidia, Calliandra, Cajanus, and Acacia* spp., planted in alleys, for nitrogen fixation, biomass production, green manure, forage production, and sediment capture;
- Use of organic fertilizers based on optimal employment of plant and animal residues;
- Adequate combination and management of polycultures and/or rotations planted along the contour and at optimal crop densities and planting dates;
- Conservation and storage of water through mulching and water harvest techniques; and
- Integration of animals.

Since more than 2,000 farmers adopted at least some of the improved practices, an important task of Plan Sierra was to determine the erosion reduction potential of proposed system. This was difficult because most methods of estimating erosion aren't applicable to farming systems managed by resource-poor farmers under marginal conditions. Devising a simple method using measuring stakes, field data from 1988–1989 showed that the alternative soil conserving systems recommended by Plan Sierra exhibited substantially less soil loss than the traditional shifting cultivation, and the cassava and guandul monocultures. The improved *conuco* positive performance seems related to the continuous soil cover provided by intercropping, mulching and rotations, as well as by the shortening of the slope and sediment capture produced by alley cropping and living barriers (Altieri 1995).

IMPROVING FOOD SECURITY AND INCOME IN MEDITERRANEAN AGROECOSYSTEMS

Since 1980, CET, a Chilean NGO, has engaged in a rural development program aimed at helping peasants reach year-round food self-sufficiency while rebuilding the productive capacity of their small landholdings. The approach has been to set up several 0.5 ha model farms which consist of a combination of forage and row crops, vegetables, forest and fruit trees, and animals. Components are chosen according to crop or animal nutritional contributions, their adaptation to local agroclimatic conditions, local peasant consumption patterns and, finally, market opportunities. Most vegetables are grown in heavily composted raised beds (5x1m each) located in the garden section, each of which can yield up to 83 kg of fresh vegetables per month. The rest of the 200m^2 area surrounding the house is used as an orchard, and for animals, (a Jersey, a Holstein cow, ten laying hens, three rabbits and two Langstroth beehives). The rest of the vegetables, cereals, legumes, and forage plants are produced in a six-year rotational system within a 4,200 m^2 area adjacent to the garden. Relatively constant production is achieved (about six tons per year of useful biomass from 13 different crop species) by dividing the land into as many small fields of fairly equal productive capacity as there are years in the rotation. The rotation was designed to produce the maximum variety of basic crops in six plots, taking advantage of the soil-restoring properties and built-in biological control features of the rotation (Figure 18.1).

Throughout the years, soil fertility in the farm has improved (P_2O_5 levels, which were initially limiting, increased from 5–15 ppm) and no serious pest or disease problems have been noticed. Fruit trees in the orchard and around rotational plots produce about 843 kg of fruit per year (grapes, quince, pears, plums). Forage production reaches about 18 tons per 0.21 ha /yr. Milk production averages 3,200 L/yr, and egg production reaches a level of 2.531 units. A nutritional analysis of the system based on its production components (milk,

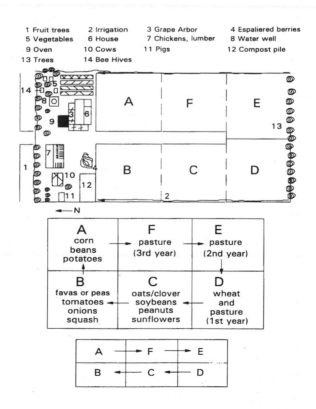

Figure 18.1. Model design of a self-sufficient farming system based on a seven year rotational scheme adaptable to Mediterranean environments (adapted from CET 1983).

eggs, meat, fruit, vegetables, honey) shows that it produces a 250% surplus of protein, 80% and 550% surpluses of vitamins A and C, respectively, and a 330% surplus of calcium. A household economic analysis indicates that, given a list of preferences, the balance between selling surpluses and buying pre-ferred items is a net income of US $790. If all of the farm output is sold at wholesale prices, the family could generate a net monthly income 1.5 times greater than the monthly legal minimum wage in Chile.

In Tomé, a depressed industrial-textile town in southern Chile, CET assisted unemployed workers satisfy subsistence needs through an urban agriculture program reaching 400 families. The model includes a 62 m^2 production unit in which the following can be grown or raised:

Intensive, raised bed for vegetable production	40.5 m^2
32 chicken	6 m^2
38 rabbits	7 m^2
4 bee hives	4 m^2
bread mud-oven	1 m^2

This production unit allows of the production of about 354 kgs/year of veg-etables , rabbits (53.4 kgs), eggs (40.1 kgs), chicken meat (28.8 kgs), honey (66 kgs) and bread (453.7 kgs). This production covers 66% of the protein require-ments of the family and about 35% of the caloric requirements. Due to the fact that the various food items are produced and not purchased, savings can reach up to $736 per year per family. These levels obviously substantially enhance the family's nutrition and overall economic well-being (Montero and Yurjevic 1993).

ASSESSING WHEAT PRODUCTIVITY IN PEASANT SYSTEMS USING NATURAL RESOURCE ACCOUNTING

In Chile 71% of the farms are smaller than 5 ha. Farmers working small par-cels produce 22% of Chile's wheat, 32% of its beans, 59% of its potatoes, and 38% of its lentils. About 58% of the small farmers are located on marginal lands where modern agricultural technologies adopted by peasants have proven inappropriate and have led to low productivity and erosion.

An attempt to compare profitability, productivity, input use and soil produc-tivity in peasant wheat farming under conventional management as promoted by government extensionists and under agroecological management as advised by NGOs, was done using a two-sector linear programming model developed by a multidisciplinary research team (Altieri et al. 1993a). Evaluated alterna-tive cropping practices included the use of wheat undersown with a red clover living mulch, fertilized with 15 metric tons of manure per ha as opposed to monoculture with pesticides and fertilizers.

The organic management system showed lower estimated cumulative soil losses than monoculture after 30 years which kept yields relatively high over the long run (Figure 18.2a and 18.2b). Conventional wheat monoculture exhibited higher rates of soil loss which caused significant yield declines with time. According to the model, for peasants the adoption of resource-conserving practices depends on labor availability and on the existence and knowledge of new agroecological technologies and on an appropriate participatory extension system to disseminate them. The model showed a total shift to organic farming practices for wheat in the rainfed areas of Chile, when peasants had enough knowledge about the practices and labor to use them, and when they had significant awareness to not ignore or underestimate the importance of natural resource degradation.

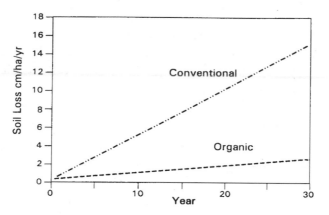

Figure 18.2a. Cumulative soil losses in wheat production systems under conventional and organic management.

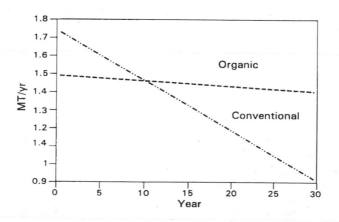

Figure 18.2b. Wheat yields as a function of soil losses in two peasants wheat cropping systems.

CONCLUSIONS

The challenges of Latin American agriculture are socio-economic and environmental, as well as technical. In this decade, they include two crucial dimensions: the ecological management of peasant agricultural resources, and the transformation of peasant communities into actors in their own development. Many NGOs have already adapted to these imperatives.

Examination of NGO projects applying agroecological concepts indicates that many of their proposed technologies and designs are highly productive and sustainable, as well as socio-economically and culturally compatible. In marginal environments, especially, they appear to be capable of greatly improving the resource base, along with the well-being of farm communities.

This chapter has highlighted some promising NGO-led local experiences among the rural poor in Latin America, assessing the impact of agroecological interventions on food security, resource conservation, crop productivity and income generation. The use of simple indicators in the evaluation of technological adoption by peasants is providing NGOs with a sufficient level of confidence in the agroecological approach to rural development.

More sophisticated and integrated methodologies and indicators are needed, and this could be a productive role for researchers interested in sustainability issues and a fruitful way for them to create partnerships with NGOs actively involved in field work within communities of resource-poor farmers throughout a range of farming conditions in Latin America.

REFERENCES

Altieri, M. A. and A. Yurjevic. 1991. La agroecologia y el desarrollo rural sostenible en America Latina. *Agroecologia y Desarrollo* 1: 25–36.

Altieri, M. A. 1992. Where the rhetoric of sustainability ends, agroecology begins. *CERES* 134: 33–39.

Altieri, M. A., C. Benito, A. Gomez-Lobo, P. Faeth, T. Tomic, and J. Valenzuela. 1993. Wheat farming in central Chile. In Agricultural Policy And Sustainability: Case Studies From India, Chile, Philippines, and The United States, ed. P. Faeth. Washington, DC: World Resources Institute.

Altieri, M. A. and O. Masera. 1993. Sustainable rural development in Latin America: Building from the bottom up. *Ecological Economics* 7:93–121.

Altieri, M. A. 1995. Agroecology: The Science of Sustainable Agriculture. Boulder: Westview Press.

LACDE (Latin American Commission on Development and Environment). 1990. Our Own Agenda. Washington, DC: Interamerican Development Bank-UNEP.

Moreno, A. and A. Yurjevic. 1993. Invest in the poor to allow them to create wealth. *Journal of Learnings* 1: 14–26.

Redclift, M. and D. Goodman. 1991. Environment And Development In Latin American. United Kingdom: Manchester University Press.

Sanchez, J. 1993. A seed for rural development. *Journal of Learnings* 1: 8–17.

Treacey, J. M. 1984. Agricultural terraces in Peru's Coca Valley: Problems and problems of an ancient technology. In Fragile Lands of Latin America, ed. J. O. Browder. Boulder: Westview Press.

19 PROPERTY RIGHTS, PEOPLE, AND THE ENVIRONMENT

Susan S. Hanna
*Department of Agricultural and
Resource Economics
Oregon State University
Corvallis, OR 97331-3601*

OVERVIEW

This chapter discusses the role played by property rights regimes in the interaction between human and natural systems. Property rights regimes are the arrangements which people devise to control their use of natural resources, and comprise property rights, bundles of entitlements defining owners' rights and duties in the use of the resource, and property rules, the rules under which those rights and duties are exercised. Property rights regimes differ by the nature of ownership, the rights and duties of owners, the rules of use, and the locus of control. They contain the incentives and disincentives to limit expectations and control use. They are necessary but not sufficient conditions to resource sustainability. The way property rights regimes are designed and used in a particular context determines whether natural and human systems are linked in complementary or conflicting ways. Current property rights regimes over natural resources are often inadequate to prevent resource degradation and overuse. Even more important, property rights regimes fail when overwhelmed by increases in both absolute population growth and per capita demand for resources. How property rights regimes function depends on three fundamental components: the principles of design on which they are based, the mechanisms by which they link the human system to the natural system, and the mechanisms by which they coordinate across jurisdictional boundaries. This chapter summarizes results of research on the structure and function of property rights, and identifies information still needed in these areas.

INTRODUCTION

This chapter is about the institutional dimension of environmental sustainability as reflected through arrangements that specify rights, rules, and obligations for the use of natural resources. The arrangements are called property rights regimes, and include two components: 1) property rights, the bundles of entitlements defining owners rights and duties in the use of the resource; 2) property rules, the rules under which those rights and duties are exercised (Bromley 1991). People interact with their environment through property rights regimes embedded in social, political, cultural, and economic context. The nature of that interaction affects both the quality and quantity of environmental resources (Hanna and Munasinghe 1995a, 1995b). Once in place, property rights regimes embody expectations about claims to resources (Bromley 1989), and as such serve as a link between human systems and natural systems. Property rights regimes generally evolve over time through incremental change (North 1990), but are sometimes emerge abruptly through radical change.

A problem with many of the property rights regimes under which natural resources are currently managed is that they do not specify claims to the full range of goods and services provided by an ecosystem. Property rights in industrialized economies focus on commodity production to the detriment of less direct uses of the ecosystem. The lack of full specification means that it is unclear who can claim rights of use, or how rights may be used. For example, in natural resource systems such as marine fisheries, rights and rules may apply to the extraction of fish for sale, but may ignore other services provided by those stocks of fish. The rights of non-human predators to prey, the rights of the species' population to genetic diversity, and the rights of the ecosystem to biodiversity are generally left unspecified. The rules under which those rights might be protected may also be unclear. As a result, the number of claimants to the services of the fish stock are narrowly defined as the population of human users. Those claimants' expectations about their rights and obligations are not necessarily consistent with the full spectrum of claims within the ecosystem.

It is becoming increasingly clear that economic development depends on institutions that can protect and maintain the environment's carrying capacity and resilience (Arrow et al. 1995). But attention to the importance of well-specified property rights regimes is often missing in national and international environmental policies (Hanna and Munasinghe 1995a, 1995b). Existing property rights regimes often represent an old frontier vision of resource use. Under this vision, resource degradation or depletion could be accommodated by abandoning one area and moving on to another resource frontier (Hanna 1995). Claims to indirect ecosystem services such as contributions to reproduction and the claims of non-human species to ecosystem goods could both be ignored because layers of unexploited frontiers lay in wait.

The frontier vision of resource use has not been sustainable. By now we are very accustomed to talking about the 'tragedy of the commons', using that phrase to represent the outcome of unspecified ownership and uncontrolled use (Scott 1955; Hardin 1968). Although there are many flaws in the 'tragedy' model as originally presented (Ciriacy-Wantrup and Bishop 1975; Cox 1985;

McCay and Acheson 1987; Berkes 1989; Feeny et al. 1990; Hanna 1990), its acceptance into common currency has served to focus attention on the fact that for many natural resources, property rights regimes have been inadequate to prevent overuse within a range of technological patterns, production techniques, cultural styles and ecosystem conditions. We tend to spend the natural capital of ecosystems at rates far greater than the systems' abilities to renew themselves. Marine fisheries are only one example of many natural systems in which it is becoming increasingly obvious that sustainability is more of an idea than a reality. This is evidenced in both the North and the South, in developed and developing countries.

THE STRUCTURE OF PROPERTY RIGHTS

Beyond being the rights, duties, and rules for using natural resources, property rights regimes take on a larger meaning as they connect natural systems—plants, animals and their biophysical environments—to human systems—constructions of economics, culture, and technology. Property rights regimes contain the incentives and disincentives to limit expectations and control use. They are where issues of sustainability get "down to earth".

The way property rights regimes are designed, assigned, and used in any particular context determines whether the two systems—the natural and the human—are linked in complementary or conflicting ways. The challenge is to build property rights regimes which reflect the specific ecological-human context and which create and maintain a compatibility between ecological dynamics and human nature. The history of industrialized economies is one which tends to emphasize short-term values of the human system at the expense of long-term impacts on the natural system. The history is also one in which claims to tangible commodity values are placed above claims to intangible "ecosystem service" values.

Property rights regimes differ by the nature of ownership, the rights and duties of owners, the rules of use, and the locus of control. Table 19.1 presents a simple taxonomy of four types of property rights regimes with their associated rights and duties (McCay and Acheson 1987; Berkes 1989; Bromley 1989; Feeny et al. 1990; Ostrom 1990). The regime types are ordered loosely along a spectrum of ownership.

Private property, *res privatae*, assigns ownership to named individuals (including legal "individuals", such as corporations), guaranteeing to those owners control of access and the right to a bundle of socially acceptable uses (Black 1968). It requires of the owners that they avoid specified uses which are deemed socially unacceptable, such as fouling the water of streams. Common property, *res communes*, is owned by an identified group of people who have the right to exclude non-owners and the duty to maintain the property through constraints

Table. 19.1. Types of Property Rights Regimes with Owners, Rights, and Duties

Regime Type	Owner	Owner Rights	Owner Duties
Private Property	individual	socially acceptable uses control of access	avoidance of socially unacceptable uses
Common Property	collective	exclusion of nonowners	maintenance constrain rates of use
State Property	citizens	determine rules	maintain social objectives
Open Access (non-property)	none	capture	none

placed on use (Ciriacy-Wantrup and Bishop 1975; McCay and Acheson 1987; Berkes et al. 1989; Stevenson 1991). Public property, *res publicae*, is owned by citizens of a political unit who assign rule-making authority to a state agency (Black 1968). The agency has the corresponding duty to ensure that rules promote social objectives. Citizens have the right to use the resource within the established rules. Open access, *res nullius*, has no ownership assigned, and is property open to all (Black 1968; Ciriacy-Wantrup and Bishop 1975; Berkes 1989; Bromley 1989; Stevenson 1991). Claims to resources are realized at the point of capture, and owners have no specified duty to maintain the resource or constrain use.

An early and widespread response to the 'tragedy' argument was to propose that natural resources be privatized, the argument being that only under sole ownership would people have the incentive to maintain the flow of resource services into the future. The idea was that private ownership would protect the resource user from the trap of the 'prisoner's dilemma' in which ignorance about the behavior of fellow users leads to resource overuse (Scott 1955; Luce and Raiffa 1957). The assumption underlying this argument was that only two types of ownership were possible for natural resources: private or open access (often mistakenly called common property). Since those early proposals for privatization, a rapidly expanding body of research (cf., National Academy of Sciences 1986; McCay and Acheson 1987; Berkes 1989; Berkes et al. 1989; Martin 1989; 1992; Feeny et al. 1990; Ostrom 1990; Bromley 1992) has demonstrated that the either-or choice of property rights is overly restrictive. Empirical evidence has undermined the argument for private property as the single solution for resource problems and has led to the following conclusive findings.

First, property rights regimes do not exist as two opposing types but rather as combinations along a spectrum from open access to private ownership. For example, property rights to some marine fisheries are held by the state, managed through centralized decision making. Property rights to other marine fisheries are held jointly by the state and fishery interests, and are "co-managed" through cooperative decision making. In yet another marine fisheries variation, fishery users hold private property rights to fish in the form of individual transferable quotas (ITQ's), but are subject to regulation by the state.

Second, no single type of property rights regime can be prescribed as a remedy for problems of resource degradation and overuse. Both effective control and ineffective control can exist under a variety of arrangements. The key attributes of an effective property rights regime is that it is context-specific, reflecting environmental, economic, social, and political conditions. For example, common property regimes are sometimes appropriate for marine fisheries when a specific group of owners can be identified, when the boundaries of the natural system can be defined, when a tradition of collective decision making exists, and when monitoring and enforcement are possible. In another context, as where fisheries cross biophysical or political boundaries or where users are fluid and ill-defined, the same common property regime may lead to fishery destruction (cf., Ostrom 1990; Schlager and Ostrom 1992).

Third property rights regimes create necessary but not sufficient conditions for resource sustainability. They are necessary because without specified rights to resource benefits ownership is realized only upon capture, creating the incentive to take as much as possible as soon as possible. If the assurance to future claims to resource benefits is absent, limiting current use can be irrational (Runge 1984). Property rights regimes are not sufficient because they cannot in themselves prevent resource depletion, even when configured as private property. For example, in a fishery managed under a regime of private rights, if the price of fish is very high and if the invested earnings from the sale of those fish earn a higher return than the fish "owners" can expect to recoup from future harvests, the holders of private rights may choose to liquidate their natural capital and fish out the entire population (Clark 1973).

In sum, property rights regimes exist in many types and combinations, are context specific, and are necessary but not sufficient conditions for sustainability. Part of the problem with sustainability is that it is a concept that has a wide range of meanings in different disciplines and different world views. To some extent sustainability is a human construct, based on a desire to maintain a flow of ecosystem services. But which services are to be maintained? Humans use natural resources for a range of objectives, including subsistence, value-added production, aesthetic pleasure, and indirect ecosystem services. These objectives have their basis in the desire to sustain human life, enhance standards of living, maintain a culture, and protect environmental quality for generations to follow. The different objectives for ecosystems lead to different expectations as to what is to be sustained, who has claims to ecosystem services, and how ecosystem use is to be controlled.

A major complication that follows from diverse objectives is that expectations may be, and probably will be, inconsistent with one another and impossible to meet simultaneously. Once levels of human use reach the point where ecological surpluses are diminished, all use of natural systems involves trade-offs between system components. Another complication is that people have conflicting objectives for natural systems. Human values vary with respect to the appropriate resource mix to sustain. People are often internally inconsistent as well, acting as consumers in ways which do not coincide with their science or philosophy.

A property rights regime which reflects the attributes of both the natural and human systems is the basis for sustainable use. An example that is often cited is that of informal property rights regimes in the Maine lobster fishery based on the geographical territories within which harvesters fish and the semi-sedentary lobsters live. Now being formalized through institutional evolution, the arrangement reflects both the cultural territories of the lobstermen and the biological territories of the lobster (Acheson 1989). The attributes of natural and human systems will not always be so well balanced. In some cases the property rights regime will be weighted toward modification of the human system, as is happening now with the end of "frontier" thinking about the use of publicly owned natural resources. In other cases the property rights regime will be weighted toward modification of the natural system, as in the production of food through agriculture or aquaculture.

If the property rights regime coordinates the human and natural systems in a complementary way, if it contains feedbacks through which they interact, and if the time horizon is long enough, natural systems can be maintained. Conversely, if the structure and function of the natural and human systems are unrepresented in the property rights regime, if feedbacks between them are absent, or if people discount the future heavily, the resulting pattern of resource use will only accidentally maintain both human and natural systems. The more likely outcome is the short-term contribution to human systems, and a long-term contribution to neither.

RESEARCH IN PROPERTY RIGHTS AND THE ENVIRONMENT

For any given problem related to natural resources there are accompanying pathologies in the structure or function of the property rights regime under which people use those resources. These pathologies are often related to one of three fundamental components: the principles of design on which a property rights regime is based; the mechanisms by which a property rights regime links the human system to the natural system; or the mechanisms by which a property rights regime coordinates across jurisdictional boundaries. The work of many applied property rights scholars has established several known attributes of property rights regimes as they relate to design, principle linking mechanisms, and coordinating mechanisms.

Design Principles

Objectives for long-term use of the resource must be specified. These objectives must reflect not only the owners at the management level, but also the sustainability objectives at the more general societal level (Bromley 1989; Daly and Cobb 1989; Ostrom 1992). The property rights regime must have clearly defined boundaries and within that regime rights are fully specified and the "community" of legitimate users defined (Ostrom 1990; Bromley 1992; Ostrom et al. 1993; Young 1992). For example, coastal fishery management must define a management area, specify how fishing may take place, and identify who may legitimately fish. It must protect rights to claims so that there is assurance about the current behavior of others and the future availability of resources. Those who invest in sustainability must receive its benefits (Bromley 1989; Young 1992).

Management must take place at a scale consistent with the natural boundaries of the ecological system; for example, watershed-level management instead of stream-level management (Costanza and Daly 1992; Gunderson et al. 1994; Folke and Berkes 1995). Decision rules must be consistent with ownership. For example, collectively owned resources are best managed through collective choice arrangements rather than by individual decision-makers. There is also, on the part of the owners, an expectation of long-term tenure which protects from the tyranny of short-term decisions (Jentoft 1989; Pinkerton 1989; Ostrom 1993). Property rights regimes must perform certain functions of limitation, coordination, response. How they perform these functions is sensitive to transactions costs; those costs of coordination, information gathering, monitoring, and enforcement (Eggertsson 1990; Hanna 1994).

Several important aspects of design principles for property rights regimes remain unknown. One of these is the appropriate determinant of management boundaries once natural systems have been fragmented by cultural or political division. For example, ocean fisheries are often managed in a context of overlapping jurisdictions over habitat, harvest and environmental quality. Although it is recognized that fragmented jurisdiction is a detriment to ecosystem management, it is difficult to define and implement more appropriate boundaries. Another unknown is the appropriate method of identifying and vesting the "interests" (claimants) of natural systems and accommodating their heterogeneous objectives. There are probably economies of scale in property rights regimes, but the size limits to effective control are unknown, as is an understanding about whether those limits change with the type of natural system or human system. Co-management systems seem particularly sensitive to questions of appropriate scale. And finally, a continuing design problem is how to produce cost-effective systems of sanctions against rule violations.

Linking Mechanisms

The rules of resource use must be simple and flexible enough to adapt to changes in environments or markets at local and larger scales (Ostrom 1990). Environmental variability is the rule, not the exception, and an array of signals from the ecological system must be monitored (Folke and Kåberger 1991; Holling 1986). Rules must be enforced, offenses punished, and conflicts resolved (Ostrom 1990; Young 1992). Human actions must be monitored and constrained because freedom of action is possible only when one activity does not affect another. As population pressure increases, spillover effects increase, and rules must increase in complexity and intensity. In the development of rules to constrain behavior, "local" (nontechnical) knowledge can complement scientific knowledge (Berkes et al. 1994; Ruddle 1994a, 1994b).

Except when resources are in surplus, trade-offs in natural system components are inevitable and must be explicitly recognized. The different growth rates and life spans of different species make it impossible to simultaneously use an ecosystem's services and protect all components at "virgin" levels. In making these trade-offs, uncertainty works at cross purposes in natural and human systems. In natural systems, uncertainty dictates a precautionary approach to cover contingencies. In human systems, uncertainty creates incentives for accelerated rates of use due to the lack of assurance that resources not used in the present will be available in the future (Gardner et al. 1990; Bromley 1991; Runge 1984).

Governance can be sustained only up to some threshold ratio of population to resource base. As necessary but not sufficient conditions for sustainability, property rights regimes are limited in their ability to constrain human action and can be overwhelmed by consumption (Costanza and Daly 1990; Bromley 1992). The growth in demand for resources either through increases in population (increases in total consumption) or increases in standards of living (increases in per capita consumption) can undermine the property rights regime's ability to keep human actions in bounds (Jodha 1985). No property rights regimes can hold in the face of human desperation.

An important aspect of establishing an effective linkage between human and natural systems is to ensure that the properties of both systems are reflected.

This leads to the question of how to reconcile the scales of natural and human systems so that the property rights regime covers the full range of rights and the full range of ecosystem goods and services. There is a trade-off between simplicity and diversity for a property rights regime, and both attributes may be important in determining the outcome. Simplicity promotes flexibility of decision making and oversight while diversity promotes resilience in the face of variability. Monitoring the performance of the property rights regime requires the definition of ecological and human system indicators which can adequately represent their respective systems. And finally, there is an ongoing issue of how best to combine scientifically generated knowledge with "local" anecdotal or experiential knowledge to provide the most complete information for decision making (Berkes et al. 1994; Ruddle 1994b).

Coordinating Mechanisms

Multiple geopolitical boundaries and legal systems add a great deal of complexity to the specification and coordination of property rights regimes. Because of the multiple jurisdictions, internalizing environmental benefits and costs is difficult (Dasgupta and Mäler 1992; Barrett 1993; Young 1982). Property rights regimes which are nested within larger institutional jurisdictions must ensure compatible incentives at several levels (Young 1982 1994a; Ostrom 1990). A variety of sustainability goals may and probably does exist between different political entities, and the goals are likely to be inconsistent with one another (Jentoft 1989; Pinkerton 1989). Coordinating human use is difficult because of the number of "games" being played simultaneously by different political entities. The multiple dimensions of conflicts add complexity to their resolution (Barrett 1993; Ostrom et al. 1993).

Both "scaling up" small-scale system properties to large-scale systems and "scaling down" international environmental agreements to local levels are problematic (Young 1982; 1994b). System properties, the motivations of actors, monitoring processes, and compliance are qualitatively different at different levels. The design, linking and coordinating components of property rights regimes entail transactions costs of organization, information gathering, monitoring, and enforcement. Transactions costs are important to the design of a particular property rights regime and vary with the scale of coordination. It is possible to create a system which is so costly to implement that it overwhelms the benefits to be gained from control and falls under its own weight. Attempts to reduce transactions costs are often the basis of movements to change property rights regimes.

There are two important attributes of coordinating mechanisms about which little is known. The first is how to scale up from local property rights regimes to regional, state, or international levels, and down from international property rights regimes to local levels in ways which keep compatible incentive systems in place (Young 1994b). The second is how to represent and reconcile conflicting goals for sustainability, particularly at the international level.

CONCLUSION

This chapter has presented a condensed picture of the interaction of property rights, people and the environment. Because they connect a particular human system with a particular natural system, property rights regimes are specific to context in all its ecological, economic, social, cultural, technological, and political dimensions. That is why there is almost infinite variety in the types of property rights regimes, that is why they fall continuously along a spectrum from open access to private property, and that is why no single type of property rights regime can be prescribed as a remedy for problems of resource degradation and overuse. Property rights regimes are a necessary but not sufficient condition for the sustainability of natural systems. Property rights regimes have failed in the past and are continuing to fail in the pursuit of short-term profits, rapid technological change, cultural change, high levels of absolute population growth, increased per capita demand for resources, and inappropriate government policies (Goodland et al. 1989; Ruddle 1994).

Despite the great deal that is known about property rights regimes and environmental resources, there are also important attributes the structure and function of property rights that remain unknown. A research program on property rights and natural resources at the Beijer International Institute of Ecological Economics is examining a variety of aspects related to humans and their natural environments. In pursuing this research, we are finding great benefits from collaboration between natural and social scientists. The field of property rights research has been the traditional domain of social scientists, with a focus on humans as "managers" of natural systems. The natural system itself has been left in the background as provider of services and the recipient of impacts. Similarly, the field of natural resource management has been dominated by biological scientists, with a focus on a species of concern, usually a single species at a time. They have tended to view humans as peripheral to the system's function, as intruders. Evidence surrounds us that the failure to account for the full complexity of both natural systems and human systems in property rights regimes has hindered our capacity to sustain the resource base. Social scientists working with natural scientists in the area of property rights and natural resources have a unique opportunity to contribute to the pressing scientific and policy problems which surround the human interaction with the environment.

ACKNOWLEDGMENTS

This research was sponsored by the Beijer International Institute of Ecological Economics, The Royal Swedish Academy of Sciences, Stockholm, Sweden, with support from the World Environment and Resources Program of the John D. and Catherine T. MacArthur Foundation and from the World Bank. The research was conducted as part of the research program Property Rights and the Performance of Natural Resource Systems.

REFERENCES

Acheson, J. M. 1989. Where have all the exploiters gone? Co-management of the Maine lobster industry. In Common property Resources: Ecology and Community-Based Sustainable Development, ed. F. Berkes. London: Belhaven Press.

Arrow, K., B. Bolin, R. Costanza, P. Dasgupta, C. Folke, C. Holling, B.-O. Jansson, S. Levin, K. G. Mäler, C. Perrings, and D. Pimentel. 1995. Economic growth, carrying capacity, and the environment. *Science* 268: 520–521.

Barrett, S. 1993. Managing the international commons. In Resource and Environmental Economics, eds. G. Brown and V. K. Smith. Cincinnati: South-Western Publishing.

Berkes, F., ed. 1989. Common property Resources: Ecology and Community-Based Sustainable Development. London: Belhaven Press.

Berkes, F., D. Feeny, B. J. McCay, and J. M. Acheson. 1989. The benefits of the commons. *Nature* 340: 91–93.

Berkes, F., C. Folke, and M. Gadgil. 1994. Traditional ecological knowledge. In Biodiversity Conservation: Problems and Policies, eds. C. A. Perrings, K- G. Mäler, C. Folke, C. S. Holling, and B.O. Jansson. Dordrecht: Kluwer Academic Publisher.

Black, H. C. 1968. Black's Law Dictionary, Revised Fourth Edition. St. Paul, Minnesota: West Publishing Co.

Bromley, D. W. 1989. Economic Interests and Institutions: The Conceptual Foundations of Public Policy. Oxford: Basil Blackwell.

Bromley, D. W. 1991. Environment and Economy: Property Rights and Public Policy. Oxford: Basil Blackwell.

Bromley, D., ed. 1992. Making the Commons Work: Theory, Practice, and Policy. San Francisco: ICS Press.

Ciriacy-Wantrup, S. V. and R. Bishop. 1975. Common property as a concept in natural resources policy. *Natural Resources Journal* 15: 713–728.

Clark, C. W. 1973. The economics of over-exploitation. *Science* 181: 630–34.

Costanza, R. and H. E. Daly. 1992. Natural capital and sustainable development. *Conservation Biology* 6(1): 37–46.

Cox, S. J .B. 1985. No tragedy on the common. *Environmental Ethics* 7:49–61.

Daly, H. E. and J. B. Cobb, Jr. 1989. For the Common Good. Boston: Beacon Press.

Dasgupta, P. and K. G. Mäler. 1992. The Economics of Transnational Commons. Oxford: Clarendon Press.

Eggertsson, T. 1990. Economic Behavior and Institutions. Cambridge: Cambridge University Press.

Feeny, D., F. Berkes, and B. J. McCay. 1990. The tragedy of the commons twenty-two years later. *Human Ecology* 18:1–19.

Folke, C. and F. Berkes. 1995. Mechanisms that link property rights to ecological systems. In Property Rights and the Environment: Social and Ecological Issues, eds. S. Hanna and M. Munasinghe. Washington: World Bank.

Folke, C. and T. Kåberger, eds. 1991. Linking the Natural Environment and the Economy: Essays from the Eco-Eco Group. Dordrecht: Kluwer Academic Publishers.

Gardner, R., E. Ostrom, and J. Walker. 1990. The nature of common pool resource problems. *Rationality and Society* 2(3): 335–358.

Goodland, R., G. Ledec, and M. Webb. 1989. Meeting environmental concerns caused by common-property mismanagement in economic development projects. In Common property Resources: Ecology and Community-Based Sustainable Development, ed. F. Berkes. London: Belhaven Press.

Gunderson, L. H., C. S. Holling, and S. Light. 1994. Barriers and Bridges to Renewal of Ecosystems and Institutions. New York: Columbia University Press.

Hanna, S. 1990. The eighteenth century commons: A model for ocean management. *Ocean and Shoreline Management* 14: 155–172.

Hanna, S. 1994. Co-management. In Limiting Access to Marine Fisheries: Keeping the Focus on Conservation, ed. K. L. Gimbel. Washington, DC: Center for Marine Conservation and World Wildlife Fund.

Hanna, S. 1995. The new frontier of American fisheries governance. *Ecological Economics* (in press).

Hanna, S. and M. Munasinghe, eds. 1995a. Property Rights in a Social and Ecological Context: Case Studies and Design Applications. Washington, DC: World Bank.

Hanna, S. and M. Munasinghe, eds. 1995b. Property Rights and the Environment: Social and Ecological Issues. Washington DC: World Bank.

Hardin, G. 1968. The tragedy of the commons. *Science* 162: 1243–1248.

Holling, C. S. 1986. Resilience of ecosystems: Local surprise and global change. In Sustainable Development of the Biosphere, eds. W. C. Clark and R. E. Munn. Cambridge: Cambridge University Press.

Jentoft, S. 1989. Fisheries co-management: Delegating responsibility to fishermen's organizations. *Marine Policy* 13(2): 137–154.

Jodha, N. 1985. Population growth and the decline of common property resources in India. *Population and Development Review* 11(2): 247–264.

Luce, R. D. and H. Raiffa. 1957. Games and Decisions: Introduction and Critical Survey. New York: John Wiley and Sons, Inc.

Martin, F. 1989. Common Pool Resources and Collective Action: A Bibliography. Workshop in Political Theory and Policy Analysis, Indiana University, 513 North Park, Bloomington, Indiana.

Martin, F. 1992. Common Pool Resources and Collective Action: A Bibliography, Volume 2. Workshop in Political Theory and Policy Analysis, Indiana University, 513 North Park, Bloomington, Indiana.

McCay, B. J . and J. M. Acheson, eds. 1987. The Question of the Commons: The Culture and Ecology of Communal Resources. Tuscon: University of Arizona Press.

National Academy of Sciences. 1986. Proceedings of the Conference on Common Property Resource Management. Washington, DC: National Academy Press.

North, D.C. 1990. Institutions, Institutional Change and Economic Performance. Cambridge: Cambridge University Press.

Ostrom, E. 1990. Governing the Commons: The Evolution of Institutions for Collective Action. Cambridge: Cambridge University Press.

Ostrom, E. 1993. The evolution of norms, rules, and rights. Beijer Discussion Paper No. 39, Beijer International Institute of Ecological Economics, The Royal Swedish Academy of Sciences, Stockholm, Sweden.

Ostrom, E., R. Gardner, and J. Walker. 1993. Rules, Games, and Common-Pool Resources. Ann Arbor: University of Michigan Press.

Ostrom, E. 1992. Crafting Institutions for Self-Governing Irrigation Systems. San Francisco: ICS Press.

Pinkerton, E., ed. 1989. Cooperative Management of Local Fisheries: New Directions for Improved Management and Community Development. Vancouver: University of British Columbia Press.

Ruddle, K. 1994a. External forces and change in traditional community-based fishery management systems in the Asia-Pacific region. *Maritime Anthropological Studies* 6(102): 1–37.

Ruddle, K. 1994b. Local knowledge in the folk management of fisheries and coastal marine environments. In Folk Management of Marine Fisheries: Lessons for Modern Fisheries Management, eds. C. L. Dyer and J. R. McGoodwin. Niwot: University Press of Colorado.

Runge, C. F. 1984. Institutions and the free rider: The assurance problem in collective action. *Journal of Politics* 46(1): 154–181.

Schlager, E. and E. Ostrom. 1992. Property rights regimes and natural resources: A conceptual analysis. *Land Economics* 68: 249–262.

Scott, A. D. 1955. The fishery: The objectives of "sole ownership." *Journal of Political Economy* 63:116–124.

Stevenson, G. G. 1991. Common Property Economics: A General Theory and Land Use Applications. Cambridge: Cambridge University Press.

Young, M. D. 1992. Sustainable Investment and Resource Use. Man and the Biosphere Series Volume 9, Parthenon Press.

Young, O. R. 1982. Resource Regimes: Natural Resources and Social Institutions. Berkeley: University of California Press.

Young, O. R. 1994a. International Governance: Protecting the Environment in a Stateless Society. Ithaca: Cornell University Press.

Young, O. R. 1994b. The problem of scale in human/environment relationships. *Journal of Theoretical Politics* 6: 429–447.

20 WILL NEW PROPERTY RIGHTS REGIMES IN CENTRAL AND EASTERN EUROPE SERVE NATURES CONSERVATION PURPOSES?

Tomasz Zylicz

Warsaw Ecological Economics Center
Warsaw University
Warsaw, Poland

OVERVIEW

In this chapter an example of the conflict between conservationists and Piecki, a rural municipality in Northeastern Poland, is analyzed in order to illustrate how changing property right regimes have influenced the social context of nature protection. The municipality resists establishing the Mazurian National Park, whose presence would imply certain economic restrictions. The pattern emerging from this case study is a complex one. On the one hand, any development constraints are perceived as more severe now than before when there was little private entrepreneurship around. On the other hand, however, the enforceability of law has improved as a result of increased transparency of public decision making. This includes the enforceability of environmental regulations. Thus the fate of nature protection crucially depends on the ability of conservationists to demonstrate economic benefits from investing in natural capital rather than letting it be degraded. A project is under way to identify local sustainable development options and to show that land-use restrictions, when combined with a larger package of social and economic improvements, can turn out to be an asset rather than a liability. The project is used by conservationists to seek support of the local population for the national park idea.

NATURE PROTECTION IN POLAND

The pre-1989 political regimes in Central and Eastern Europe were notorious for their poor environmental performance and thus worked against conservation measures at least indirectly. There is an impressive network of well-managed national parks there. Many of them, nonetheless, have suffered from excessive pollution originating from inefficient local economies. The collapse of the old political and economic system has already proved environmentally beneficial once some of the worst polluters went bankrupt and pollution in-spectors started to exercise control over the growing private sector in a way that respect the state-owned industrial dinosaurs they could not. All this works towards curbing indirect (industrial pollution) pressures on national parks and other ecologically valuable areas. At the same time, however, these are under the increasing direct pressure from individuals wishing to exercise their property rights. This manifests in three ways. First, parts of national parks are being claimed by previous land owners who feel they were not reimbursed fairly. Second, there are private or communal enclaves left within parks' boundaries which created a lot of ambiguity about their status. Third, even where the state ownership of a park's land and its integrity are not challenged, the neighboring land owners protest against development constraints implied by the park's existence.

Poland's environmental problems inherited from the past are immense. At the same time, because the communist industrialization concentrated in areas of traditionally high intensity of production, vast regions remained largely un-derdeveloped. These regions and their almost intact natural capital represent an asset which is becoming increasingly scarce in Europe. However, because of the prevailing cliché of disruption, not only average citizens, but also those environmentally concerned are not fully aware of the value of their natural heritage (Zylicz 1994).

In Poland experts estimate that about 8.5% of the area of the country re-mains relatively unscathed by development. Commercial forests and farms operating within sustainable and ecologically acceptable principles include about 19% of the Polish territory. Hence, over a fourth of Poland represents an asset that many areas of Europe no longer have. Poland's biological diversity is high, particularly with respect to forest and bog communities. According to a recent study (Andrzejewski et al. 1992), in the last 400 years, the Polish verte-brate fauna has lost 15 species (2.5%), including 3 mammals, 11 birds and 1 fish species. At the same time, the Polish flora has lost 31 species of vascular plants. Sad as they are, these figures, however, turn out to be much less alarm-ing than in other, more developed, European countries in the same biogeo-graphical zone. For instance, a sister study for Germany found that—appar-ently due to the longer and more intensive industrialization period—the biodiversity loss has been much more acute. In the last 150 years, 28 species of vertebrates (6%) have become extinct, comprising 7 mammals (8%), 19 birds (8%), and 2 fishes, along with 58 vascular plant species.

The ecological value of Poland's natural capital has been internationally recognized. Most of its 20 national parks are on the IUCN list, as they meet all the criteria for this highest degree of protection. Three of them have been included by UNESCO in a network of biosphere reserves representing typical, well preserved examples of the world's ecosystems. One of them—the

Bialowieza National Park (whose natural extension in Belarus has enjoyed the status of a national park too) has been declared an object of exceptional importance to the World Heritage, as the last remaining area of the characteristic Central European lowland primeval forest. Also a number of smaller objects, "nature reserves", were found to be of international importance, some of them being protected under the Ramsar Convention on wetland ecosystems. Table 20.1 presents the development of national parks in Poland in recent years. Between 1988–1994 their number grew from 14 to 20. The total area more than doubled which was achieved both by adding new parks and augmenting some of the old ones.

Table 20.1. National Parks in Poland

	1988	1989	1990	1991	1992	1993	1994	1995
Number of national parks	14	15	17	17	17	19	19	20
National park area, 1,000 hectares	127	141	166	177	179	244	249	275

Source: Ochrona (1989–1994) and files of the National Park Board. Data for 1995 as of Nov. 1.

Apart from the network of national parks, covering the area of 275,000 ha (0.9% of the country area), Poland has an even larger system of "landscape parks". In 1993 there were 91 such parks comprising as much as 1,726,809 hectares (5.5% of the country area). The difference between a national and a landscape park is in the scope of protection as well as in the legal authority. While the former is established by a decree of the Council of Ministers (the central government), the latter is enacted by a decision of a regional administrator (there are 49 such administrative regions in Poland). The former is financed from the central budget directly. The financial status of the latter is more complex. Even though most subsidies that landscape parks receive originate from the central budget, regional administrators are supposed to contribute to their accounts too. However, the most crucial difference between the two types of parks is that only the national ones have the authority to issue regulations, within well-defined legal limits, which otherwise fall within competence of regional administrators. In particular, directors of national parks have the right to license economic activities carried out within the park boundaries and to influence land use patterns in their parks' buffer zones.

Most examples of the country's unique and unspoiled ecosystems have been already given the status of a national park (Nowicki 1993). There are only few areas—usually protected as landscape parks—which are considered candidates for national parks. The Mazurian Landscape Park is the site of a major conflict between conservationists, who urge for turning it into a national park, and a part of the local population, who fear that the new status will make them worse off. The opposition comes from Piecki (pronounced Pee-etzkee), one of the three rural municipalities where the Mazurian Landscape Park is located. The conflict reveals in a transparent form what can be found in the existing national parks in a more or less latent form and its successful resolution can thus be instructive for other areas in Poland.

Quite paradoxically, the natural capital which survived several decades of the communist mismanagement is now under the serious threat of a new sort of development. Even though the logic of market economies is likely to lead to a more efficient resource use, at the same time, it exposes these resources to new pressures resulting from their opening up to large scale international tourism and international real estate markets. The ecologically valuable areas—especially those in Western and Northern Poland—are reported to experience tourism pressure which increased rapidly after the collapse of the Berlin Wall.

CONSERVATION AND PROPERTY RIGHT ISSUES

At first glance, nature conservation seems to have been easier under the central-planning regime. Even though most of the land was always in private hands in Poland (unlike in other Central and Eastern European countries), the non-democratic governments that ruled in 1945–1989 had little respect for owners' rights. Establishing a nature reserve or a national park was thus just a matter of an administrative decision. As a result, many patches of private property within national park boundaries were left. State policy towards buying these pieces of land was inconsistent, and quite often real estate owners could neither sell nor develop their lots. This contributed to tensions between park managers and the local populations.

Table 20.2 Land Ownership in National Parks in Poland (status December 31, 1992)

Land-use category	Total area	Of which private or communal property
	hectares	% of total[a]
All categories	178,764	12,955	7.2
of which:			
Forest	130,058	5,757	4.4
Agricultural land	13,014	6,485	49.8
Water	15,388	21	0.1
Other	20,304	692	3.4

[a] As percent of the total area of a given land-use category

Source: Files of the National Parks Board.

Table 20.2 presents ownership structure of the Polish national parks in 1992. As seen from the table, state property accounts for over 93% of the total area mainly because of the high share of the forest land in the parks. Most of the non-state enclaves are farms whose operators still hold ownership title to the land. The most typical conflicts include crop damages done by game animals, for which the parks serve as safe havens, constraints on the use of chemicals, and unclear prospects for the future. What could have been hushed up under the communist regime emerged as an open conflict after 1989. Thus national park directors started to face serious problems despite the fact that the agricultural land accounts for a minor fraction of the total area.

Another, perhaps an even more serious conflict exists where the agricultural enclaves are left as a communal property. Here park directors are challenged not by individual farmers but rather by strong collectives with a long tradition and the sense of self-identity. This type of conflict has been best known from the Tatra Mountains National Park located on the border with Slovakia (where the other part of the range, also protected as a national park, is situated). The park was established in the first—most brutal—decade of the communist rule in Poland. This fact has been often recalled in order to portray the conflict merely as the heritage of an insane political regime. The conflict, however, cannot be simply solved by compensating the original owners. The true struggle is not for a reimbursement for victims of unfair administrative decisions. What is at stake here is who will control the local assets which can generate decent revenues in the long-run if well managed, and enormous yet unsustainable short-term profits.

The predicament resembles much of the tragedy of the commons. In fact, the community went through this in the 19th century. One of the fertile valleys (Dolina Jaworzynki) was overgrazed. Once green slopes were turned into a barren rock. The community did not want to acknowledge its contribution to the erosion process and, until recently, insisted on increasing the number of sheep allowed in the national park. It keeps insisting on "recommunalization" of some of the valleys. For the time being the limit set at 1,000 sheep is seen by the park as ecologically safe and preserving the historical landscape. The culture of the region, which is one of the most popular in Poland, has been closely linked to pastoralism and to the gorgeous diversified landscape which depends on the land use (without sheep all the foothills, now being a major floristic attraction, would be covered by forest).

The grazing conflict should not be overemphasized in Poland of the 1990s any more. After all agriculture provides an ever decreasing share of the local incomes. The commons facing the tragedy now is the ecological integrity of the Tatra range. The region is of top tourist attractiveness. The local population has been known for their entrepreneurial skills, and the supply of capital is not a constraint; almost every family has at least one member who earns income in the USA (mainly in construction business) either temporarily or permanently. There is a strong pressure to invest money in creating sport and tourist infrastructure modelled after the Alps ski resorts. What is overlooked in these plans is the scale of the Tatra mountains. The entire range (less than 30 km long) could be contained in one of the many Alpian valleys some of which were developed into large recreation factories and some of which preserved. Building roads, luxury hotels and a system of cable cars—as envisaged by local leaders—would give investors high short-term revenues but only at the cost of an irreversible degradation of the Tatra ecosystem. In the long-run, such a scenario would seriously reduce attractiveness of the region for visitors and thus undermine the local economy.

It is a pity that the conflict affects a region where both natural and cultural capital are so rich and outstanding. Besides, they had seem to successfully co-evolved until the middle of the 20th century (with one exception of an over-grazing incident in the 19th century). This co-evolution and creative co-existence is considered to be a key element of a sound management of landscape and biodiversity resources (Berkes and Folke 1992; Nelson and Serafin 1992). It does not even help much that the present director of the Tatra National Park, who holds a Ph.D. in ecology, was born in one of the best-known and respected shepherd families in the region. The director faces a real danger of physical attack on himself and his estate. Apparently, the stakes are so high that they do not let the parties calm down and cooperate.

The lesson learned from the Tatra National Park experience is fourfold. First, it proves that the establishment of some parks by the old political regime stigmatized them permanently with the image of an external intrusion which makes rational cooperation difficult. Second, no realistic compensation scheme for the previous owners of assets protected by a national park is likely to solve some of the conflicts. Third, encroaching on the park land gradually becomes of a lesser importance (even though local poachers can be a serious problem in some places); the main conflict is over the pattern of development in the park neighborhood with or without taking advantage of the continued presence of its natural assets. Fourth, co-management (McCay 1993) understood as a regime entailing a mixture of local governance with an external authority based on mutual trust and recognition of each other's role in preserving resources is the only viable form of control.

A practical lesson learned from this experience is that carrying out a successful conservation project calls for cooperation of conservationists and the local population from the outset. Otherwise the project may be doomed to a lasting conflict, and its conservation objectives will be difficult to achieve.

McKean (1993) observes that "public ownership may be the most preferred form when a resource system is so threatened, so abused that (or so close to that point) most uses and harvesting must be prohibited for the time being." Indeed, in Poland in some instances the predicament of the natural capital assets calls for public ownership. At the same time, however, the local pressure on the resource system calls for "the cooperation of local people so that they become co-enforcers with the government, rather than perpetual encroachers" (ibid). Thus co-management emerges as a preferred form of control once again.

THE CASE OF PIECKI

When the initiative of establishing the Mazurian National Park in lieu of the existing Mazurian Landscape Park was first officially discussed in 1993, it met with various reactions. Two out of three municipalities involved decided to support it. The representatives of the third one, Piecki, announced that they would not let their municipality be included in a national park. Several informal consultations were held yet without any effect on the municipality's position. Facing such a strong local opposition, the Ministry of Environment asked the Warsaw Ecological Economics Center for assistance in discussing with the local leaders costs and benefits from having the national park. The following summary is based on the assessment (Kaczanowski et al. 1994) prepared in response to that request.

The assessment starts with general characteristics of Piecki and with the municipality's list of development constraints and other adverse effects expected from the national park's presence.

General Characteristics

The municipality of Piecki is located in the northeastern part of the country referred to as "The Green Lungs of Poland" because of the abundance of forests and diversified, near-pristine ecosystems. It belongs to the Great Mazurian Lakes district and it is adjacent to Sniardwy, Poland's largest lake. The area of Piecki is 31,500 ha and its population (as of the end of 1993) is 7,766 which gives average density of 25 persons/km² (i.e., 1/5 of the country average and 1/2 of the density recorded in the district). The sparse population and the lack of large enterprises are reflected in the breakdown of the municipal budget (Table 20.3).

In 1993, the municipal budget revenues in Piecki were 2,060,000 PLZ per person whereas the average number for Poland was 2,513,000 PLZ (the approximate exchange rate in mid-1993 was 17,500 PLZ / $). Thus the municipal revenues in Piecki can be estimated at $120 per person, which is 82% of the national average and corresponds to 6% of Gross Domestic Product per capita (estimated at somewhat less than $2,000).

Table 20.3. Breakdown of Municipal Budgets: Poland's Average and Piecki (1993)[a]

Revenue category	Poland	Piecki
All categories	100.0	100.0
of which:		
Real estate tax	14.8	17.0
Agricultural taxes and fees	3.8	4.7
Forest tax	0.3	8.3
Share in personal income tax[b]	21.8	36.8
Share in corporate tax[c]	3.6	0.3
Administrative fees	5.0	2.0
Grants from the state budget	16.7	14.2
General subsidy from the state budget	11.4	2.9

[a] Main revenue items providing 86.2% of revenues for the Piecki municipal budget.
[b] Municipalities receive 15% of the personal income tax the rest being claimed by the state budget.
[c] Municipalities receive 5% of the corporate income tax the rest being claimed by the state budget.

Source: Kaczanowski et al. (1994).

The composition of Piecki's budgetary revenues reflects the importance of the forestry as well as the relative importance of personal incomes *vis à vis* corporate profits. Despite low revenues per capita, nevertheless Piecki was considered more self-sufficient than average as reflected in the low "general subsidy" which serves a redistributive function and which is based on a complicated formula encompassing municipalities' socio-economic characteristics.

Agriculture gives more jobs than any other sector in Piecki. There is a growing number of firms in the service sector but their exact contribution to the local employment is not certain because of a far from perfect reporting system. Table 20.4 gives employment figures for sectors covered by regular reporting. The number of people employed in agriculture, which is dominated by small family farms, is probably underestimated. In addition, of the 303 registered service firms, 78 operate in commerce, 45 in tourism business, 34 in forestry, 33 run small restaurants, 30 operate in transport, and 28 in construction business. Most of them are one-person enterprises, and their contribution to the local employment yields to that of industry.

Table 20.4. Employment in Piecki in Selected Sectors, 1993

Sector	Employment
Agriculture	800
Saw-mills, wood processing and furniture production	467
Forestry	190
Food industry	40

Source: Kaczanowski et al. (1994).

Arguments Against the Park

The primary local argument against the Mazurian National Park is the loss of the forestry tax which accounts for 8.3% of budgetary revenues. The forestry tax, which is a flat rate payment based on the quality of the forest land rather than actual yields was conceived as an instrument to stimulate an optimal use of the land. The tax, which is indexed by the price of timber, is collected by municipalities. The tax is waived if the forest is classified as a protected one. National park forests certainly belong to this category. However, the Minister of Environment can classify an area as protected, if the forest plays an important role in controlling erosion, water table, climate, local habitats etc. In fact, a vast majority of protected forests are outside national parks.

No commercial hunting is allowed within national park boundaries. To the extent that some species may breed excessively while the local ecological system is not in a natural equilibrium (e.g., for historical reasons), hunting can be permitted but only under a direct supervision of park authorities. No foreign visitors are allowed to hunt. Even though the latter issue was never raised by park opponents openly, conservationists believe that the loss of incomes linked to foreign hunting business is nevertheless the main cause of the opposition. However, only few families were involved in foreign hunting activities. Typical tips for assisting in a successful shooting of a deer range from 100 to 200 Deutsche Marks (DM). Given the number of hunts, one can estimate the local income loss at no more than 10,000 DM per year. Under the central planning, with an average monthly salary worth $20 at the black market exchange rate, a 100 DM tip was a fortune. Now that an average salary is worth $300, the same tip is a pleasing addition to households' incomes, but its value has decreased 15-fold. Certainly it does not contribute to the municipal budget at all, as it never enters official records.

Other arguments against the park include expected denial of building permits, constraints on selling real estate, reduced attractiveness of the area for tourists, and no perspectives for the development of industry and agriculture. Under closer scrutiny, it can be demonstrated that all these concerns are inappropriately linked to the national park's presence.

Actually regulations which affect building permit procedure and real estate markets are totally independent from the park's existence. A house or a summer cottage can be built if the lot was designated in the municipal spatial development plan for this purpose. Also real estate can be bought and sold subject to regulations which have nothing to do with the national park. Perhaps a tacit assumption is often made that illegal construction or real estate transactions which were tolerated or "overlooked" in the past will be prosecuted when the national park officers are around, and the region is an object of general interest. Fortunately for conservationists, it can be demonstrated that enforcement improved dramatically after the

1989 (i.e., not as a result of the national park's presence, but rather because of the change of the political system). For instance, it was almost impossible in the past to enforce regulations against illegal construction. Since 1989 there have more than a dozen objects erected without a valid building permit and, torn down in Piecki.

Not all of the municipality's area is planned for inclusion in the Mazurian National Park, but only 15,300 ha, (i.e., slightly less than a half). Only 1,112 inhabitants (1/7 of the total number) would live within the park boundaries, and only 678 ha of agricultural land (out of 9,500 ha) would be included. Thus licensing economic activities by the park director will affect only a fraction of the local economy. In particular, all the existing industries operating in the municipality have valid pollution permits and their presence does not interfere with the national park objectives. Moreover the local spatial development plan, which is the main constraint for bringing new industries into the region, designates a number of sites for potential (small scale) industrial plants outside the park. Establishing businesses on these sites will not be hindered by the park's existence.

To some extent agriculture will be affected by the park's presence. Currently the use of chemical inputs is minimal and close to the country average (60 kg NPK/ha in mineral fertilizers, and 0.4 kg/ha for pesticide use). It is several times lower than in Western Europe and does not interfere with the park objectives. Problems may arise if in the future farmers would wish to apply Western input levels. However, the potential income loss is difficult to assess since alternative low input options may prove attractive as envisaged in the study of benefits from the national park's presence.

To sum up, the only demonstrable loss related to the establishment of the Mazurian National Park is a decreased municipal revenue from the forestry tax. Since not all the forest would be included in the park, the loss affects not the entire tax (i.e., the sum of 1,300 million PLZ, but only 900 million PLZ approximately $50,000). The municipal budget will suffer a loss of 6%. Tips left by foreign hunters are another quantifiable loss. It does not exceed 10,000 DM (approximately $7,000). Since this is a loss of a non-reported income, it does not affect the municipal budget.

Benefits from the Park's Existence

It proved to be fairly easy to demonstrate immediate local benefits from the park's existence in the form of additional employment and contracts. Most of the planned 160 employees of the Mazurian National Park will be recruited either from the existing landscape park administration or from the state forestry service; none of the present employees in these organizations will lose a job as a result of establishing the national park. On the contrary, the park will offer 17 new positions. This implies additional annual incomes on the order of 1,000 million PLZ, in 1993 prices (i.e., $57,000 - the sum exactly equivalent by a pure coincidence) to financial losses identified in the section on arguments against the park. The park will also employ additional part-time workers, thus creating incomes on the order of 400 million PLZ (i.e., $23,000). Investment expenditures of the Mazurian National Park on tourist infrastructure are planned at the level of 800 million PLZ (i.e., $46,000) for the first year.

In the long-run, indirect benefits from the park's presence are expected to play an increasingly important role. They include the following three broad benefits categories:

1. Increased demand for high quality tourist services,
2. A potential specialization in supplying "ecological farming" products, and
3. Attracting attention to the existence value of assets protected by the park.

The region is attractive for various types of tourists. It provides excellent opportunities for backpacking, sailing, kayaking, rafting, swimming, bird-watching etc. Despite local concerns, the establishment of the national park will not reduce the attractiveness of the region. The interest in the region will almost surely increase. According to a recent assessment of the 'carrying capacity' of Piecki, the number of tourists can increase without adversely affecting the local ecosystems. It depends only on the ability to provide tourists with services they desire to have this increased demand translated into new jobs and additional incomes. In a few years, further growth of the number of visitors may become constrained by what can be accommodated without degrading the natural capital or losing due to congestion. By licensing services offered, the national park will keep their supply within sustainable limits. This does not necessarily imply lower incomes (even in the short-run). By controlling supply and promoting high quality services rather than those aimed at consumers who expect less and pay less, it is possible to earn more than under an open access regime (Lanza and Pigliaru 1993). The latter assertion, however, depends on demand elasticities and should be empirically validated in each particular case.

Farmers in Piecki, especially those operating in the national park or its buffer zone, may find it profitable to specialize in high quality "ecological" products and services. There are a growing number of "ecological" grocery stores who claim that their products are pesticide free etc. While the demand for such commodities is uncertain, there is no doubt that customers will be increasingly choosy in selecting stores, brands and/or producers they trust. Hence products attested in one way or another by a national park will be trusted more than ordinary ones. Again, however, this is an empirical question and no firm conclusions about the Piecki farmers' revenues can be made at this moment. Another interesting option is agro-eco-tourism, a new type of services combining accommodation on an environment-friendly family farm with purchasing high quality farm products, perhaps hand-picked by tourists themselves. There is a European Association of Agro-Eco-Tourism which publishes catalogues of farms that offer such services. Location in a national park or its buffer zone is an additional asset a farm can demonstrate.

Both high quality tourist services and "ecological" farming involve arguments which are hypothetical and may be not convincing for the local community. One indirect benefit from establishing a national park that is tangible and certain is attracting attention to the existence value of protected assets. Existence values can materialize in many ways including wealth transfers to those who steward the natural capital supporting these assets. While some of such transfers are hypothetical as well, one can point at concrete mechanisms or funding sources that are available for national parks.

In Poland there are several institutions whose charter activities include providing support for national parks. The most important one is the National Fund for Environmental Protection which finances almost 25% of the country's environmental investment expenditures. The Fund has formal project selection procedures which favor investors located in national parks or their buffering zones. Thus establishing a park increases the likelihood of receiving support for an environment-related investment. Upgrading and expanding tourist infrastructure in Piecki will require investment in sewage treatment plants, environmentally friendly heating systems etc. With the National Fund support these (mainly private) projects will be much easier to undertake. There are also other domestic and international sources for project financing favoring national park sites Piecki can be referred to. In fact, the municipality was offered free services to prepare project proposals (addressed to banks or funding institutions) already now at the park planning stage.

SUMMARY

The direct financial benefits provided by the Mazurian National Park, should it be established, outweigh any quantifiable losses by a wide margin. Nevertheless, two qualifications must be added here. First, despite a demonstrable net increase in local revenues, there will be a net loss to the municipal budget (caused by the forestry tax loss), since 85% of personal income taxes and 95% or corporate profit taxes are claimed by the state budget. One way of responding to the municipality's concern is to argue that the forestry tax would have been lost anyway, since ministerial decisions are already prepared to increase the area of protected forest in the Great Mazurian Lake District. Even though this is a valid argument, it does not serve conflict resolution well and should be avoided. Second, there will be several households definitely worse off because of the loss of foreign hunters. In order to weaken their opposition to the park idea it is possible to offer them financial support (e.g., from sources like the National Fund for Environmental Protection) for investment in infrastructure to capture expected benefits from the park's presence.

It turns out that enclaves of private property within the park boundaries or in its buffer zone should not pose serious management problems. On the contrary, it is expected that private entrepreneurship can be channelled into high quality tourism and "ecological" farming providing sustainable revenues for the municipality. The national park logo attached to products and services provided by businesses licensed by the park authorities is a source of advantage Piecki can enjoy over competitors located elsewhere.

CONCLUSIONS

Nature protection under the old non-democratic regime was easier only formally. Actually, the neglected property right issues were a source of tensions in the past and still are now. The Tatra region conflict shows how bad things can become even though in most cases they do not. A more typical conflict entails a bit of poaching, illegal construction of small scale objects in the park's buffer zone, controversies about carrying out agricultural activities on private land in the park, and the general lack of interest in taking advantage of the protected natural capital in the neighborhood.

The respect for private and communal property rights reestablished under the post-1989 regime makes the position of national park authorities more difficult. From now on they must prove the legality of all decisions taken. At the same time, however, they have an opportunity to become local community leaders by demonstrating development options linked to the preservation of natural capital. There was no demand earlier for such a role to be played by conservationists, since little entrepreneurship was allowed, economic decision-making was heavily centralized and development was seen as a matter of bringing industry into the region. Many ecologically valuable regions in Poland happen to be located in economically depressed areas without clear perspectives for attracting external investors. It is here where a skilled national park manager can win local support for conservation measures when they bring jobs, visitors, and capital.

As Eggertsson (1993) points out, in designing institutions for the control of natural assets one has to face the universal problem of non-exclusivity. The latter term means that none of the actors such as private owners, local community, and the government can ever enjoy the full control of resources they own or care for. A socially optimal use of resources requires that a balance is kept between the cost of governance (i.e., internal control) and the cost of exclusion (i.e., control against encroachers). One extreme case is an actor's attempt to control an asset completely by excluding all other potential users. On the other extreme there is a fully cooperative arrangement allowing for a controlled access for all potential users. There is no universal rule on how to optimally allocate effort between governance and exclusion, and the problem has to be solved in each particular case. Nevertheless, it is obvious that neither of the extremes is a good model for managing ecologically valuable resources such as those protected in national parks.

Co-management seems to be the only viable strategy for integrating diversified interests of local communities and other social groups having stakes in protecting the natural capital in question. This capital entails not only traditional resources such as grazing land, fisheries, etc., but entire ecosystems and their life-supporting functions too. It is unlikely that communities themselves would be able to arrive at optimal let alone effective models of local resource control in the case of assets of national or international importance. A mix of local management with an external support in the form of standards, enforcement and funding will serve nature conservation best.

New property right regimes in Poland mean reestablishing respect for private and communal interests and mutual trust in economic relations between private and public entities (which, by the way, is a long process rather than a one-time event). This new situation implies certain problems for a number of national parks which struggle with the conflicts inherited from the communist rule, which carelessly manipulated ownership titles and private rights. For new parks this situation creates a level playing field where interests of various groups can be articulated and taken into account in the institutional design phase.

The case of the Mazurian National Park provides an interesting example of an experiment in designing a model for an effective cooperation between local communities and representatives of "public interest". The study referred to in this chapter identified opportunities for local sustainable economic development based on the natural capital protected by the park. As of 1995, the conflict between conservationists and the municipality of Piecki has not been resolved. There is, however, a firm economic foundation for a compromise, since the net outcome of establishing the park is positive beyond any doubt. Hence there are no fundamental reasons precluding a mutually satisfactory agreement. If the park is finally established with local support, the question raised in the title can be answered positively. Interim results from the negotiation process suggest that a co-management regime has been emerging with a somewhat smaller park size accepted by both sides as a key element of the final compromise.

ACKNOWLEDGMENTS

This research was sponsored by the Beijer Institute, The Royal Academy of Sciences, with support from the World Environment And Resources Program of the John D. and Catherine T. MacArthur Foundation and the World Bank. The research was conducted as part of the program Property Rights and the Performance of Natural Resource Systems. And the case study received funding from the Pew Scholar Program in Conservation and Environment.

REFERENCES

Andrzejewski, R. et al. 1992. Krajowe studium bioróznorodnosci. Raport polski dla. National biodiversity study. Poland's report to UNEP. UNEP, Warsaw.

Berkes, F. and C. Folke 1992. A systems perspective on the interrelations between natural, human-made and cultural capital. *Ecological Economics* 5: 1–8.

Eggertsson, T. 1993. Economic Perspectives on Property Rights and the Economics of Institutions. Beijer Discussion Paper Series No. 40. Stockholm: The Beijer International Institute of Ecological Economics.

Kaczanowski, F., E. Lapinska, J. Spyrka, Z. Szkiruc, and T. Zylicz. 1994. Bilans kosztów i korzysci-gminy Piecki zwiazanych zutworzeniem Mazurskiego Parku Narodowego. Warsaw Ecological Economics Center, Warsaw University (An assessment of costs and benefits for the municipality of Piecki resulting from the establishment of the Mazurian National Park).

Lanza, A. and F. Pigliaru 1993. Specialization in Tourism Based on Natural Resources in the Presence of a Trade-off between Quality and Quantity. Milan: Nota di lavoro della Fondazione ENI Enrico Mattei.

McCay, B. J. 1993. Management Regimes. Beijer Discussion Paper No. 38. Stockholm: Beijer International Institute of Ecological Economics.

McKean, M. A. 1993. Empirical Analysis of Local and National Property Rights Institutions. Beijer Discussion Paper No. 42. Stockholm: Beijer International Institute of Ecological Economics.

Nelson, J. G. and R. Serafin 1992. Assessing Biodiversity: A Human Ecological Approach. *Ambio* 21(3): 212–218.

Nowicki, M. 1993. Environment in Poland. Issues and solutions. Kluwer: Dordrecht.

Srodowiska, O. 1989 ... 1994. Glówny Urzad Statystyczny. Warsaw (Environmental Protection Yearbook 1989 ... 1994).

Zylicz, T. 199. In Poland, it's time for economics. *Environmental Impact Assessment Review* 14: 79–94.

21 VALUING SOCIAL SUSTAINABILITY: ENVIRONMENTAL RECUPERATION ON FEVELA HILLSIDES IN RIO DE JANEIRO

Peter H. May
*Program in Ecological Economics
and Agrarian Policies Federal Rural
University of Rio de Janeiro
Av. Presidente Vargas, 417 - 8o. andar
20071-003 Rio de Janeiro, RJ, Brazil*

Marília Pastuk
*ECO-ECO - Brazilian Society for
Ecological Economics
R. Senador Vergueiro, 232/1801*

OVERVIEW

Sustainable cities represent a challenge in the application of ecological economics principles to developing country problems. Unequal access to land due to unfair distribution of income and power forces poor urban migrants to occupy fragile and inhospitable sites, subjecting themselves and others to serious environmental and health risks, a problem common in Rio de Janeiro, Brazil. This study evaluates a municipal project for reforestation of hillside squatter settlements (favelas) in the Rio de Janeiro metropolitan region that aims to partially avert such risks. The evaluation took into account a project's social sustainability, considering not only the benefits and costs of environmental recuperation, but also the socio-political forces and local perceptions that condition efforts to reconcile environment and equity. While reforestation partially ameliorated environmental risks faced by community members, their own perception of the benefits brought by this project was colored by the extent to which investments were integrated with urban services and sanitation, and by a false image of prosperity engendered by arborization of denuded slopes. In this sense, it can be concluded that community engagement in defining and acting upon local environmental priorities is an essential prerequisite to social sustainability.

URBAN POVERTY AND SOCIAL SUSTAINABILITY

Progress toward the macro goals of global and national sustainability can be made only if there is equivalent progress toward building local and regional alternatives to current patterns of resource degradation and human squalor (ICED 1992). Successful efforts in this direction have arisen through societal learning and empowerment, that enable communities to define and act on problems through a discursive co-evolutionary process (Norgaard 1994). The experience gleaned from such endeavors leads to knowledge applicable toward a range of problems whose resolution in turn depends on locally relevant social and political processes. To balance the uncertain facts and competing values paradigmatic in socio-environmental conflict, "extended peer review" (Funtowicz and Ravetz 1994) must reach beyond the realm of science itself to include the communities that are the subjects of policy and intervention. These precepts are particularly valid in the developing world, where social inequities are brutally juxtaposed with environmental problems (Environment and Development Commission 1990).

In evaluating one case of public intervention to allay socio-environmental conflict in a developing country setting, this study reflects a concern with social sustainability. Such an approach considers not only the benefits and costs of investments but also the social and political forces and the local perceptions which condition efforts to reconcile environment and equity in developing countries.

Coming to grips with poverty in the developing world means confronting urban problems. Urbanization has assumed significant proportions in many developing nations, particularly in Latin America's southern cone, where an average of 75% of the population now lives in cities (World Bank 1992). Rural households whose labor has become superfluous to an increasingly mechanized agribusiness complex have been drawn to the cities by the possibility of access to schools and health care, and the magnetism of industry and service employment. But many soon discover that urban land is scarce and expensive, forcing them to seek unoccupied spaces that are invariably subject to environmental hazards and are rarely equipped with the services that initially attracted them.

FAVELAS IN RIO

The city of Rio de Janeiro is no exception to the pattern of explosive urban growth experienced by most developing nations. Compressed in a narrow strip between the seashore and the steep granite slopes of the Atlantic coastal range, Rio's spatial occupation reveals a stark social stratification that contrasts with its physical beauty. Those better-off live on urbanized lowlands well-equipped with infrastructure and services. The poor, on the other hand, live primarily in flood-prone shanty towns or in hillside slums known as favelas, a generic term which refers to improvised housing on lands lacking well-defined property rights or public services. In 1993, there were 570 favelas scattered throughout the Rio de Janeiro metropolitan region, serving as home to about one million people (over 10% of the regional total). Inhospitable terrain and immoderate densities combine with poverty and violence to make these settlements the blight of rapid urbanization.

Rio's historical pattern of development resulted in an obliteration of natural forest cover, that declined from an estimated 97% of state land area in the era of colonization to 12% by the end of the 1980s (SOS Mata Atlantica 1992). Efforts to curtail detrimental downstream effects of deforestation occurred in two phases. In the 18th Century, coffee cultivation had laid waste to steep slopes surrounding the city, causing lowland floods and landslides. The Imperial government of the mid-19th Century successfully reforested and protected slopes in the Tijuca Forest, assuring natural forest regeneration.[1]

In a second phase, with rapid urban growth in the mid-20th Century, decimation of natural cover on hillsides and widespread construction of roads and housing in favelas led to increased surface runoff and sedimentation. Despite engineering solutions that channelled streams into culverts and canals, the city again became prone to frequent flooding, a problem further exacerbated by inadequate sewerage and solid waste collection. Areas that had been forested were converted over time into degraded pastures of aggressive elephant grass (*Panicum maximum*) that easily caught fire in the dry season, a cause of high mortality in tree seedlings that struggled to gain a foothold on the steep slopes. The failure to define limits to settlement expansion or to encourage natural forest regeneration soon brought calamity, threatening lives and property.

Up to the 1950s, public authorities responded to these land use conflicts by razing slums and constructing cement slope buttresses. Yet, it became clear that the forced relocation of slumdwellers simply transplanted urban problems to other parts of the city. Expanded urbanization made the housing deficit ever more acute. Public housing projects were decried by a growing squatter movement as destructive to community values. Movement participants presented such projects as counterproductive in that those removed from the favelas were usually unable to afford even the subsidized cost of public housing payments, forcing them to swell squatter populations elsewhere in the metropolis. By the 1980s, municipal governments began to accept that the favelas should be treated as an integral and vital part of the urban fabric, and vowed to allocate resources toward making them more livable (Kreimer et al. 1993).

Despite this new orientation on the part of public authorities, hillside communities, which count for half of Rio's favelas, remained vulnerable to natural disasters. In 1988, a brutal storm left hundreds of hillside homes crushed by rockslides, many died and thousands were left homeless (Munasinghe et al. 1990). As is often the case, crisis finally led to action on the part of the municipal government. This study evaluates one of the responses to socio-environmental conflict that emerged in Rio in the wake of the 1988 storm.

COMMUNITY REFORESTATION PROJECT

In the aftermath of the storm, a team of foresters and social service workers in the city government of Rio de Janeiro conceived the Community Reforestation Project (Mutirao/Reflorestamento, hereafter the "Project"). The Project aims to recover forest cover on degraded hillsides located above favela communities, at a low cost. Sites selected for this effort were defined according to the following criteria:

1.   Deforested hillsides with steep slopes, subject to landslides or rockfall;
2.   Areas prone to flooding, sedimentation of rivers or drainage channels;
3.   Subject to patterns of human occupation that constitute risks; and
4.   Having some measure of community organization.

This Project, thus has a clear social connotation, not only due to its target population and sites, but also because it involves local community members in its implementation. Reforestation and drainage works are carried out by local residents named by community associations and remunerated by the city government for their role in the Project. Aiming to reduce costs associated with natural disasters, the Project would be of benefit to the public purse, to populations located in the area of influence of the affected hillsides, and to those who live on the hillsides themselves. Since its first pilot efforts in 1988, the municipal government expanded the range of Project actions into over 27 favelas throughout the metropolitan area.

The approach toward environmental recuperation involved the planting of native species in patterns that would mimic natural succession of tropical forests. Species were selected for their rapidity of establishment and root spread to maximize soil protection and retention, as well as for their rusticity which would ensure survival on the hazardous hillside environment. They include nitrogen-fixing legumes, and a number of fruit trees were also typically included to further stimulate community interest in protecting the reforested area.[2]

In examining the Project in one beneficiary community, the research reported below assessed features of the actions undertaken and the role of involved stakeholders, to consider the potential contribution of its design and outcomes toward sustainable cities in the developing world.

COMMUNITY PROFILE

Actions under the Community Reforestation Project were initiated through pilot investments in the favela Morro Sao Jose Operrio in Jacarepagu district in

Rio de Janeiro, where residents had been severely harmed by storms. Degraded, deforested, with unstable rock outcroppings and steep slopes averaging 46%, Sao Jose Operrio had also been the site of a clandestine granite quarry which further placed the population at risk. Access roads were cut and soils disturbed by stone cutting, dynamiting, and transport that provoked gullying and sedimentation.

Project interventions were focused on a micro-watershed covering 32 ha, whose lower half is densely occupied by hundreds of residents' shacks. Many of these houses lack foundations and are situated on risky sites; due to the hillside's steep incline, they are threatened by rolling boulders and landslides.

On this hillside, the Project aimed to stabilize slopes, thus avoiding risk of accidents, and to reduce erosion and sedimentation that obstructed drainage channels and had caused floods on residential streets lying at the base of the hill. As related objectives, it was hoped that the watershed would be preserved and replenished, and that inappropriate occupation would be avoided by restricting the expansion of the community in the risk-prone area.

According to results of a survey conducted for this study, Sao Jose Operrio is socially stratified according to the location of shacks on the hillside. To buy a home of two or three rooms, residents pay on average about $1,000.00[3] a value which can double for those located "from the church on down", the community's most accessible sites. Those situated near the hilltop are even cheaper than the average home price, not only due to difficult access, but also because they lack basic sanitation. These families must individually pipe their own water supplies from springs on the hilltop, which—due to lack of watershed protection—had been prone to dry-up, making it necessary to carry water to the home from a more distant standpipe. The community in collaboration with the municipal water authority had built and maintained a pumping system distributing water to remaining favela dwellings from a tank halfway up the slope.

Residents' incomes of about $110/ household /month for the average family of five is barely enough to purchase a basic food basket consisting primarily of rice, beans, and cassava flour. Household heads are employed in civil construction or in odd jobs, while women usually find work as domestic servants often far from the community. There is one primary school on the hillside, but residents must descend to the neighboring community to obtain health care.

Table 21.1 summarizes the principle factors that had caused degradation in the local ecosystem, and the negative impacts of these factors on both ecosystem and the resident community. It also describes interventions carried out by the community with technical and financial support from the municipal government in an effort to revert the problems that have arisen.

ENVIRONMENTAL VALUATION

The valuation procedure applied by the study first characterized the extent to which the Project averted risks faced by local residents, and then quantified these benefits in monetary terms. This represents an incremental-net-benefits approach (Squire and Van der Tak 1975) assessing social costs associated with environmental degradation before and after the project was implemented. This approach treats a reduction in costs as a benefit from the intervention, net of reforestation and associated direct costs.

The principal natural capital investments made by the project involved establishment of over 80 species of native and exotic fast-growing trees, as well as the maintenance of the reforested areas and of drainage works installed. Hillside reforestation—including wages, tools, inputs and transport costs—totalled $2,308/ha reforested and $4,611/ha/yr during the three year maintenance phase, for an overall gross cost of $16,143/ha. These relatively high main-

Table 21.1. Sources of Degradation, Environmental Effects Receptors, and Municipal Interventions in Sao Jose Operrio, Rio de Janeiro, Brazil

ORIGIN	EFFECTS
Inadequate	Deforestation / Burning / Grass invasion
hillside	Erosion / Sedimentation
Occupation	Lowland flooding
Granite mining	Risk of rockfall / Mudslide
Lack of basic infrastructure	Health costs
	High cost of service provision
	(Water supply, Waste disposal)

RECEPTORS	INTERVENTIONS
Local population	Reforestation with native fast-growing species
Ecosystem / Watershed	Mining prohibition
Collective infrastructure	Containment of hillsides and
Homes / Improvements	Rock outcroppings
Downstream community	Drainage works
Local population,	Storm sewerage works
Particularly children	Paving
(high diarrhoea incidence)	Trash removal / Recycling

Note: The first two columns represent processes that jointly affect Receptors in the local human and natural environment. Interventions were designed to combat problems identified in receptor ecosystems and facilities in concert.

tenance costs can be explained by continued payment of salaries to the local six person reforestation crew over the latter period, to ensure adequate seedling protection and community engagement in the process. The estimated cost of construction of the 1,000 m of drainage works installed was $17,311 under-taken during the first project year. Overall costs of the project, involving refor-estation of 9.8 ha and installation of drainage channels, were thus $175,412 spread over a four year period.

Benefits identification reflects the perceptions of municipal employees and community members, as well as residents of the adjoining bottomland streets. Consistent with the aims of the Project, these benefits include the reduction of risk from flooding and rockslides, reduced costs of clearing debris from stormwater channels, adjustment in real estate values, assurance of reliable springwater flow, and expanded space available for community recreation. The procedure for estimation of monetary benefits is sensitive to the fact that sedi-ment reduction and related risk could not be alleviated until tree cover had fully taken hold, and that environmental risks will never be completely eliminated as long as the community occupies this precarious slope. Thus, the analysis esti-mated that no benefits accrued until after the initial four year planting, replant-ing and maintenance period. However, to simplify assessment and due to un-availability, as of this writing, of soil loss data that is being gathered through ongoing research at the Project site, an average based on the Universal Soil Loss Equation (USLE) was calculated, rather than rely on uncertain projection of progressively declining erosion rates.

Benefits estimation took into account the following components:

- *Sediment reduction* Prior to the Project, based on USLE estimates, an average of 40 t of sediment and solid wastes were deposited to streets below the hillside during torrential storm events, approximately once each year, making necessary their removal in dump trucks by the mu-nicipal government—these loads were reduced to about 14 t /yr by the Project, thus cutting municipal expenditures by $873/ yr;
- *Reduced flood loss* Periodically, about every 10 yr, a catastrophic storm flooded a 23 ha area lying at the foot of the hillside, damaging the 2,000 homes situated there—these property damages were reduced by the reforestation project by $100/household, for a total benefit of $200,000. In addition, working members of these households would no-longer lose work days due to the difficulties caused by these cata-strophic floods, an incremental benefit valued at $14,000;
- *Reduced rockfall risk* Fifty homes lay in the path of potential rockfall, mapped from aerial photographs, constituting risk of complete destruc-tion and associated danger to life and property—the Project averted a great deal of this risk with reforestation complemented by minor civil

works to secure unstable boulders; these investments were estimated to bring reduced property losses of $50,000 that were projected at intervals of five years, beginning 10 years after Project initiation;

- *Property revaluation.* Reduced sedimentation and a safer living environment have resulted in a 20% improvement in property values, principally in the area "from the church on down", occupied by about 500 homes, for a total value of $100,000 accruing on a one-time basis on attainment of young forest cover five years after project initiation;

- *Springflow stabilization.* Some 40 houses located on the slope above the community's water distribution tank are now assured of a more even flow of water from springs on the hilltop, due to greater infiltration in reforested areas (calculated based on differential groundwater recharge rates for altered vegetation cover conditions on the soils and slopes in question); this thereby reduced the frequency with which residents had to descend steep paths to obtain tapwater or pay others to deliver it, a benefit valued on the basis of municipal water service charges on a volume basis at $12,348/yr beginning in the fifth year after Project initiation; and

- *Recreation site provision.* Due to the provision of shade and fruit trees, the community now possesses a recreation area that reduces costs incurred previously by residents in visiting other open areas for leisure pursuits, valued on the basis of bus transport costs for a monthly visit by 500 families whose four members were directly benefited by the Project, totalling $16,800/ yr beginning five years after project initiation.

The results of this simple benefit/cost analysis, summarized in Table 21.2 suggest that the benefits of environmental recuperation, despite a conservative estimation approach, were considerably superior to their associated costs. Using a relatively high real cost of capital of 12% commonly applied as a cutoff rate by multilateral financial institutions, the discounted benefits stream attains a value that is more than double that of the initial public investment. These results argue that the benefits the community obtained from these investments more than justify the public expenditures involved, when viewed from the limited perspective of public finance.

EQUITY EFFECTS

With regard to distributive issues, as the funds applied toward investments in Sao Jose Operrio were public in origin, the incidence of revenues between social groups and firms is of concern. Since municipal revenues in Brazil are derived primarily from value-added taxation and from property taxes, the tendency is for their incidence to be regressive in relation to taxpayers' income. This is true because the marginal tax rate for consumer goods is not differentiated

Table 21.2. Present Value of Direct Costs and Benefits on Hillside Reforestation in Sao
Jose Operrio, Rio de Janeiro, Brazil

COSTS AND BENEFITS	PRESENT VALUE[a]
COSTS	
Reforestation establishment/maintenance	$ 117,098
Drainage works	$ 15,456
Subtotal	$ 132,554
BENEFITS	
Sediment reduction	$ 3,869
Reduced flood loss	$ 91,087
Eliminated rockfall risk	$ 30,417
Housing revaluation	$ 56,743
Springwater stabilization	$ 54,728
Recreation site provision	$ 74,459
Subtotal	$ 311,302
Net Benefits	$ 178,748
Benefits/Costs	2.35

[a] Costs and benefits in current US dollars discounted over 20yr at 12%/yr. Full details on assumed cash flows available on request from the authors.

between consumers, and property tax rates do not increase with property values. In this sense, the directing of benefits toward those social groups having least purchasing power might compensate partially for the regressive origin of investment funds.

However, of the benefits assessed, a substantial share was found to be in the improved value of property, in the protection of material possessions and in the gained worktime that would have been lost due to flooding that affected those members of the community who reside on the streets at the base of the hillside, and not specifically to those who reside on the hillside itself. Since the former have incomes superior to those on the hillside, this result characterizes an investment whose benefits are distributed inequitably. One compensatory factor in this sense is the fact that the works were concluded through remunerated community self-help, and the majority of "costs" reverted directly to the community in the form of wages to individuals who reside in Sao Jose Operrio.

Some community members were opposed to the interdiction of clandestine granite quarrying, on the argument that this enterprise stimulated the local economy and provided investments in community facilities. The granite miners had purportedly made financial contributions to the local residents' association, but employed no community members directly. Furthermore, as a clandestine operation, the miners paid no taxes on output or sale, and made no effort to observe environmental safeguards that require mined land to be restored. In social sustainability terms, retention of economic activity may be desirable should greater control over environmental degradation and employment associated with the enterprise be assured. However, there was no legal recourse available to the community to avert environmental risk caused by clandestine mining short of its embargo.

COST-EFFECTIVENESS

Besides evaluating incremental benefits, the study assessed the cost-effectiveness of the Sao Jose Operrio investment, comparing the costs of environmental recuperation with alternative measures that could have been used to meet these objectives. These alternatives included:

1. Use of cement slope retention to secure against rockfall,
2. Reforestation carried out by third party firms and,
3. The complete relocation of slumdwellers and prohibition of hillside occupation.

Civil works to retain slopes, which would cost somewhat more than reforestation, nevertheless represents only a partial solution. The full range of additional benefits generated by the Community Reforestation approach such as sediment reduction, shade and recreational opportunities would not be provided through an engineering approach. However, the complementary nature of minor civil works with reforestation reinforced the benefits derived from the former investments.

Reforestation by third parties, besides being more expensive, has failed generally to be effective in meeting objectives in Brazilian cities due to inadequate attention given to tree protection and maintenance after planting (Pastuk 1995). To be effective, reforestation on favela hillsides requires that local communities commit themselves to manage reforested areas over the long-term.

As for the ultimate solution contemplated, relocation would not only represent a major financial burden, but has also become politically unacceptable. As previously described, communities that had disintegrated in the wake of prior actions to remove squatter settlements successfully challenged this approach. Favelas are now treated as a legitimate part of the urban fabric.

SOCIO-POLITICAL ASSESSMENT

The concept of social sustainability implies that people in general will have their basic needs satisfied not only through a fair income distribution and an equal access to services and facilities provided by the State, but also through an equal opportunity to participate in the political arena as subjects of public policy design and implementation. For this to occur, the needs and interests of the poor must first be considered legitimate.

Thus, in the framework of social sustainability adopted for this study, options for environmental protection investment should also be considered in the light of the perceptions of target groups regarding the relative importance they attribute to these options among concerns affecting their cultural and natural environment.

In the Sao Jose Operrio community reforestation project, unfortunately, this process did not occur. Based on in-depth follow-up interviews, the postulated benefits were, in fact, only partially perceived by community members. No further losses were registered in homes or improvements after the works were implemented and many springs had indeed began to flow more copiously and with greater regularity, benefiting the residents located near the reforested area. On the other hand, the homes in this area did not increase in value as had initially been imagined they might. For this to occur it would have been essential for them to have access to basic sanitation services and for residents to have an easier climb to their homes. Nevertheless, the works resulted in improved valuation to the shacks situated lower down the hillside, where such services and ease of access already existed.

With regard to the homes located at the base of the hill, reforestation and drainage investments reduced losses that had previously arisen due to flooding and sediment deposits, but these continued with lesser intensity, owing to the solid wastes accumulated on the hillside that continued to obstruct stormwater drains when carried down the slope by torrential rains. Even for the downstream community, therefore, the benefit was perceived as only partial in scope.

Regarding the Project itself, it was only valued favorably by community members interviewed to the extent that it was accompanied by other actions they considered as local priorities, such as drainage and, more recently, the tying-in of sewerage connections to stormwater drains. In fact, water, sewerage, and trash collection are always present when the community made its own accounting. Solicited to indicate the most urgent problems facing them, only 10% of its members mentioned reforestation as an issue, while 90% mentioned lack of basic sanitation services. It can thus be concluded that a reforestation project would have greater success from the favela community's point of view had it been accomplished in articulation with other projects that its members defined as priorities.

Through this analysis, it became clear that, the more integrated the public intervention in a determined community, the more effective that action can be from the community members' point of view. This fact, however, would contradict the political strategy or logic at play. From this perspective, a logic based on traditional power structures of clientelism and the "ideology of favors", the more dispersed are public actions among the greatest possible number of communities, the more these will feel they have benefited from this action, which will bring more votes and political adhesion for the proponent.

Therefore, it may not be that important whether such actions in fact have positive socio-environmental repercussions, but rather, that some attention has been dedicated by public figures to community problems in a widespread, visible way.

As a further hypothesis, it was initially suggested in this study that as a result of community members' involvement in the Project, greater local organization would ensue, thus increasing local capacity to mobilize around priority works in future. This hypothesis cannot be considered confirmed, however, for two reasons. Firstly, although the municipality hired indigent local residents that had been selected by the residents' association to act as remunerated workers on the Project, broader community involvement was not guaranteed by this strategy.

Furthermore, Sao Jose Operrio, like most favelas in major Brazilian cities, faced serious difficulties throughout the Project's implementation due to local interference from drug traffickers. This led to a prevalent mood of fear and insecurity among residents, now no longer due to risk of accidents from natural causes but rather to violence. Warily, they keep the "law of silence", and all problems seem of little importance when confronted with the threat of death from the crossfire to which they are constantly exposed. As can be imagined, further community mobilization that could have been spurred by involvement in environmental recuperation has been stymied as a response to this new social risk.

It is important to emphasize another aspect that called attention as a result of this study. Few members of the community understood the nature of the government project; most did not know they were living in a risky situation and showed surprise when it was mentioned. This perception makes evident the lack of information favela residents possess about the cumulative and sporadic risks that arise from their settlement condition. Some even declared that it was a pity that the squatter housing area could not continue to expand as they had wished, because the more visible the favela, the more obvious its problems, and hence the greater flow of public funds that might eventually ensue. Reforestation for these people created a false image of prosperity in the eyes of the outside world.

CONCLUSIONS

This analysis has revealed a number of important themes that permeate investigation of socio-environmental conflict in developing societies. In the first place, the role of local stakeholder engagement in defining priority investments has become an evident necessity in the light of innumerable cases of misguided public policies and projects. On the other hand, the evident contradiction between locally perceived values and sheer physical risk urge the need for an interactive process of project planning that includes initially empowering residents to become more capable of diagnosing the environmental features and problems they face daily. For this, nonformal environmental education becomes a crucial tool.

A second related issue is that of the mechanisms for contribution by poverty-stricken communities to local investments aimed to safeguard environmental values. On the one hand, an active contribution is considered to engender commitment to protection and maintenance, crucial to the recuperation of degraded landscapes, particularly on favela hillsides vulnerable to wildfires and vandalism. On the other, the poor are seldom able to divert time they could be using to secure basic economic necessities toward sweat equity for community needs. The solution applied in the Community Reforestation Project of remunerating workers selected by the residents' association from among local indigent households may be perceived as paternalistic, but the return of most reforestation costs to the community in the form of employment surely helped to guarantee project success. Nevertheless, such employment must be seen not as an end in itself, but as a tool to stimulate community participation and greater mobilization for needed services and investments.

Finally, the paradox of desirably integrated investment versus politically motivated dispersion is a ubiquitous tension not easily reconciled with demands for efficient public resource allocation. The importance of coordination among complementary institutions in unifying efforts to solve complex urban problems has been reinforced by this study.

As has become evident in the preceding analysis, the assessment of social sustainability is an essential complement to economic valuation of environmental investments in developing nations. Insofar as it reveals both the potential and the fragility of traditional cost-benefit analysis, further opportunities are needed to define concepts and methods that can make ecological economic analysis pertinent to decision making in the transition toward sustainable cities.

ACKNOWLEDGMENTS

This study arose from a didactic exercise (May et al. 1995) used in training the growing number of professionals and graduate students in Brazil eager to apply concepts and tools of ecological economics, counteracting the absence of case study materials available in Portuguese related to the urban environment. Original research involving fieldwork in Sao Jose Operrio was an integral part of training; the authors acknowledge the contributions of 12 course participants during the initial fieldwork. Further on-site fieldwork, institutional interviews and benefits estimation were undertaken by an interdisciplinary team including, besides the authors (a natural resource economist and an environmental sociologist), other specialists in watershed management, forestry, soil science, biology, and political science. The authors thank the municipal government of Rio de Janeiro, particularly Celso J. Santos and Marcia Garrido for logistical assistance and project documentation. Support from the Jessie Smith Noyes Foundation, the Rockefeller Foundation and the Conservation, Food and Health Foundation is gratefully acknowledged, as are valuable comments made on a previous version by Karl Steininger and Marc J. Dourojeanni. For any errors that remain, the authors assume the full burden of responsibility.

NOTES

1. The Tijuca Forest is now considered a marvel of urban parkland, that literally envelopes the sprawling metropolis of Rio de Janeiro, adding to the city's tropical exuberance. Drummond (1988) offers a chronicle of the massive reforestation effort using native species, undertaken over more than a decade by a handful of slaves under the direction of the intrepid Major Archer.
2. A partial listing of species used and further details regarding successional principles that guide the Project are provided in Pastuk (1995).
3. Values used in this study refer to current nominal prices converted to U.S. dollars at the tourism rate, an approximation for the border exchange rate. This conversion does not represent purchasing power equivalent which, in Brazil, has fluctuated considerably as a result of monetary policies. At the time the study was conducted, purchasing power parity was considerably higher than exchange rate equivalency. Since the Plano Real in 1994, however, purchasing power has declined dramatically. Inflation stabilization achieved by this plan has nonetheless been popular insofar as real earnings of low-income groups improved.

REFERENCES

Drummond, J. A. 1988. O jardim dentro da maquina; breve historia ambiental da floresta da Tijuca. *Estudos Historicos* (Rio de Janeiro) 1: 276–298.

Environment and Development Commission for Latin America and the Caribbean, 1990. Nuestra Propria Agenda. New York: IDB/UNDP.

Funtowicz, S. and J. Ravetz. 1994. The worth of a songbird: Ecological economics as a post-normal science. *Ecological Economics* 10: 197–208.

ICED (Inter-Parliamentary Conference on Environment and Development), 1992. Draft Final Document. Brasìlia: Inter-Parliamentary Union.

Kreimer, A., T. Lobo, B. Menezes, M. Munasinghe, R. Parker, and M. Preece. 1993. Rio de Janeiro - the search for sustainability. In World Bank, Towards a Sustainable Urban Environment: The Rio de Janeiro Study. Washington, DC.

May, P., A. de Andrade, and M. Pastuk. 1995. Custos e beneficios de recuperacao ambiental em morros favelados: o Projeto Mutirao-Reflorestamento em Sao Jose Operrio. In Economia Ecologica: Aplicacoes no Brasil, ed. P. May. Rio de Janeiro: Editora Campus.

Munasinghe, M., B. Menezes, and M. Preece. 1990. Case study: Rio flood reconstruction and prevention project. In Managing Natural Disasters and the Environment, eds. A. Kramer and M. Munasinghe. Washington, DC: World Bank Environment Department.

Norgaard, R. 1994. Development Betrayed: The End of Progress and a Coevolutionary Revisioning of the Future. London: Routledge.

Pastuk, M. 1995. Urban and Peri-Urban Forestry in the Rio de Janeiro Metropolitan Area. Rome: Consulting report to FAO Forestry Department.

SOS Mata Atlantica. 1992. Mapeamento dos Remanescentes da Mata Atlantica. Sao Paulo, Brazil.

Squire, L. and H. Van der Tak. 1975. Economic Analysis of Projects. Baltimore, Maryland: Johns Hopkins University Press.

World Bank, 1992. Development and the Environment (1992 World Development Report). Washington, DC.

22 RESOURCES PLANNING SHOULD INTEGRATE CONSERVATION AND DEVELOPMENT NEEDS: THE CASE OF TEGUCIGALPA'S WATER REQUIREMENTS

Carlos A. Quesada-Mateo
*Director: Centro de Investigaciones en
Desarrollo Sostenible (CIEDES)
Universidad De Costa Rica*

OVERVIEW

Planning of resource development projects tend to leave out the concept of integrated resources management and to fall short in incorporating broader social, economic and environmental issues. Lack of holistic perspectives is true of many of the so called "master plans" for infrastructure development such as in water resources, energy, transportation, etc.

Narrow project conception and formulation condition the evolution of the overall project under consideration, such as the planning process, the type of data collected and of the analysis performed, the solutions chosen, the implementation procedures and the follow up mechanisms.

The case study presented in this paper deals with Tegucigalpa's water supply problems and the way in which the Potable Water Master Plan project was conceived to meet the potable water requirements for the year 2010. This plan constituted the official framework document in 1986, at the time in which the author participated as a consultant to evaluate the role of La Tigra National Park in terms of its contribution to Tegucigalpa's potable water system and the need for the Park's Cloud Forest protection and conservation. The narrow focus with which this master plan was conceived has not changed significantly at the way water supply, or other infrastructure resource development projects, are normally addressed in many developing countries and therefore constitute a good case study from which lessons could be learned.

A critical review of Tegucigalpa' master plan shows the urgent need to incorporate more holistic approaches to the planning processes, so that the analysis may address the future resource requirements to meet broader social and economic development needs along with the conservation and sustainable management of the natural systems from which those and other interdependent resources ultimately depend.

An environmental appraisal of the opportunity costs of La Tigra National Park to the present water supply system, is made. It is evident that the degradation of the cloud forest will irreversible affect the quality and the amount of water it contributes to the distribution system. Recommendations regarding adequate biophysical and economic assessment of land use options are presented in order to incorporate a multiple resource use approach and to internalize the costs required for the sustainable management of soil and water conservation and the pollution prevention and abatement of the scarce and valuable water resources.

If the natural environment of the watersheds surrounding Honduras' capital city can not accommodate the expected population growth and the water supply needs for the broader requirements associated with that future demographic and socio-economic growth, so that the majority of the people can meet their basic needs without irreversibly degrading the environment, deconcentration alternatives must be explored outside the present geographic area of influence of Tegucigalpa.

INTEGRATED RESOURCE MANAGEMENT IN WATER RESOURCE PLANNING: ISSUES RELATED TO LAND USE IMPACTS

Setting

With a population of only 56,000 in 1945, the city of Tegucigalpa reached near 375,000 by 1980. It was projected to reach 1,100,000 by the year 2000 and over 1,800,000 by the year 2010, as shown in Table 22.1 (SANAA 1982).

This accelerated growth has taken place by a series of push and pull factors, which has caused the city to grow almost twice as fast as the national average, largely due to rural migration of poor peasants. Under these circumstances there has been little time to plan or allocate scarce financial resources to satisfy housing and potable water needs, among others social demands.

By mid-1980, 65% of the population lived in slums and 15% in low cost housing. By 1986 only 40% of the population had water connections in their homes. The projections from the master plan estimate that by the year 2000 58% of the urban dwellers will be living in slums and 28% in low income housing. These percentages are assumed to remain the same for the year 2010. Even if all the projects considered in the master plan were successfully executed for a total of 380,000 m³/day, there would still be severe water shortages, since the projected demand for the year 2010 was of 550,000 m³. (SANAA 1982).

Figure 22.1 shows a map of Tegucigalpa and its surrounding watersheds from which present and future water resources need to be tapped, included the La Tigra Cloud Forest which was established as a national park in 1980. By 1990, Tegucigalpa had two major sources of water, which jointly contributed about 90% of the supply. One is the 186 km² Guacerique River watershed where Los Laureles reservoir is located, a few km east of the city. The other is the 75 km² La Tigra National Park, with 25 minor intakes and very small dams collecting water, which is transported by gravity to El Picacho treatment plant.

Table 22.1. Population Projection According to Socio-Economic Class (1980-2010)

Years	Slum Type A		Low Class Type B		Middle Class Type C		High Class Type D		Commercial Neighborhood	
	Pop /	%	Pop /	%	Pop /	%	Pop /	%	Pop /	%
1979										
1980	243.655	65	56.228	15	33.737	9	14.994	4	26.240	7
1990	400.749	60	158.873	24	61.318	9	24.095	4	19.965	3
2000	656.094	58	318.532	28	109.122	10	37.529	3	14.723	1
2010	1088.811	58	516.284	28	194.210	10	57.942	3	20.762	1

NEIGHBORHOOD TYPE

Total Population per year	
1979-1980	373.854
1990	665.000
2000	1.136.000
2010	1.868.000

Source: SANAA.

Tegucigalpa Region

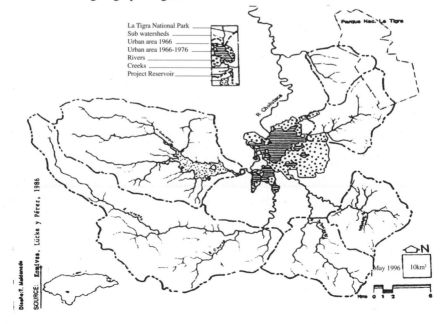

Figure 22.1. Location of Tegucigalpa in relation to neighboring watershed and La Tigra National Park.

The Guacerique River Watershed

Land use changes over time in the Guacerique River basin have increased the areas of overuse dedicated both to agriculture and pasture lands, largely at the expense of thicket and forest cover, leading to a continued degradation of the watershed and negatively affecting its water resources. The darker areas in Figure 22.2 show the overuse in the watershed and the arrows along its border indicate land invasions to the headwaters through the divide, mostly by small scale farmers, many of whom take advantage of the water availability and climate, to grow horticultural crops under irrigation in the hillsides. In the short period between 1975–1982 agriculture and pasture lands increased by 8% each, while thicket and forest decreased by 11% and 5% respectively. An assessment of actual versus land use capability in the watershed utilizing 1982 data, showed overuse in 38% of the watershed (Komives et al. 1986).

Hillside agricultural practices and irrigated agriculture have not been the only factors affecting water quality. Untreated raw sewage from army barracks and a religious seminary, waste dumps from chicken farms and a few slum dwellings in the lower reaches of the watershed, all located near or along the Guacerique river banks, were among other important negatively impacting activities found during the field visits.

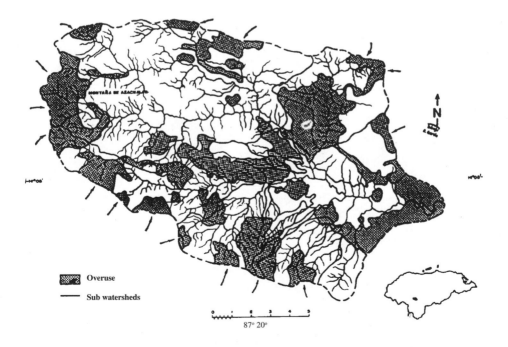

Figure 22.2. Land overuse in the Guacerique watershed (Adapted from Komives et al. 1986; Brenes 1986).

Because of its elevation, the Laureles reservoir and its nearby treatment plant can not reach by gravity those housing developments located in the hills of Tegucigalpa, in which growing numbers of slum dwellers have been settling, and costly pumping will be required to meet their needs. New, large-scale, low-cost housing projects upstream of Los Laureles reservoir were approved, with potential negative environmental consequences for the existing and future water supply systems.

Because of its accessibility, the demographic and economic pressures for land occupation, timber extraction, and water for irrigation will keep increasing over time. All this will mean more cumulative negative impacts for the already degraded water resources, unless consistent long-term integrated resource management planning approaches are defined and implemented as soon as possible to prevent further irreversible damages in the watershed.

La Tigra National Park

In contrast, located 16 km North East from Honduras' capital city, the magnificent 7500 ha. Cloud Forest of La Tigra National Park generates, by far, the cleanest, cheapest, and most reliable water supply for Tegucigalpa. El Picacho Treatment Plant, located at an elevation of 1,310 m serves by gravity most high elevated planned settlements connected to the water supply grid. However, population pressures and competing land uses also threaten this unique cloud forest ecosystem, which constitutes a living and tangible example of the meaning of environmental sustainability, providing valuable free services to the communities, such as the regulation of the spring and stream flows and the preservation of its water quality.

The water from this mountain forest comes mostly from the cloud interception and the high rate of rain percolation through the permeable forest floor. These conditions make the tree stands and the forest litter vital parts of a fragile ecosystem since, in its natural state, its permeable protected soils favors water infiltration and storage as well as its slow releases to many mountain springs and small catchments within the Park. Thus, La Tigra Mountain performs the function of a "water reservoir without dams" which could be irreversibly damaged by deforestation. In fact, 25 individual small water intake structures collecting water from micro-watersheds and springs, constitute a precious part of Tegucigalpa's water supply network, delivering by gravity close to 50,000 m³ /day of water of extremely good quality.

Other actual and potential benefits of La Tigra National Park include biodiversity, scenic values and eco-tourism opportunities. Direct benefits related to water are flow regulation, offering better distribution options during the dry season, minimizing storage infrastructure and avoiding costly pumping costs. In terms of quality, the economic benefits associated only to water treatment costs where assessed for 1985 to be 23 times less than that of the Guacerique watershed (Table 22.2). Thus, the preservation of La Tigra's Cloud Forest just in water quality terms makes economic sense and should be treated as an issue of resource security for a capital city facing chronic water crisis.

Conflicting Land Uses

The escalation of Tegucigalpa's watershed degradation will make existing and future water resources development projects more expensive to operate over time. Although reservoir sedimentation is an issue, the impacts of changes in the streamflows, particularly decreases of low flows during the dry season, may prove to be even more critical in meeting firm supplies (Quesada 1979). The causes of these impacts are mainly due to more intensive land use changes, with little or no planning, and which temporary relieve the pressures of the growing needs for food production, fuelwood, urbanization, and timber supply of a rapid expanding population. The long-term consequences of these short-term needs have not been addressed, although the qualitative analysis of cause and effect leads to conclude that they will be severe, some of them irreversible, restricting the options for sustainable development.

The situation described above, makes La Tigra's water opportunity cost grow over time, since alternative options for new reservoirs or groundwater projects are much higher, both in construction, pumping, and water treatment costs. On the other hand, the explosive socio-economic conditions prevailing in the Tegucigalpa region mean a real threat to the Park's conservation. Potential land invasions and with it, the eventual destruction of its cloud forest and the loss of an irreplaceable source of water, are impacts that can only be prevented by a coherent long-term plan of action aimed at the permanent protection of the Park.

Ongoing irrigation activities for agricultural production in some watersheds and the future water needs to sustain a moderate industrial basis to create jobs for the present and future generations were not considered in the master plan. Thus, while no water was allocated to meet present or future irrigation requirements, only 3% of the future water supply was considered for industrial development for the year 2010, when the human population is expected to reach 1,868,000 (Table 22. 3). This table shows that the percentages of water by use category tend to remain very similar over time. Thus while in 1980, 3% of the water was allocated to small industry, that percentage is basically retained for all type of industry for the year 2010.

Water for irrigation is important issue since it is a consumptive use and it is an on going activity easily observed in Guacerique and other watersheds. Obviously, such omissions in the planning process are unrealistic, since humans do not live from potable water alone.

An important consideration is that future water projects will come from more distant places and will tend to be more costly, given the length of the supply lines, as in the cases of the Zinguizapa and El Chile projects located at radii beyond 40 km from the City. Others sources located at radial distances larger than 20 km, like those of Río Hondo y Amarateca, will require pumping from groundwater sources. Preventive actions of these future water sources through adequate land management and zoning should be taken at once to avoid the mistakes of the past, as in the Guacerique watershed. Complementary approaches for the effective protection of the already existing water supply sources need to be considered as part of a comprehensive, sustained watershed management effort.

Table 22.2. Production Costs for Different Water Sources (1985)

Treatment Plant	Production (m^3)	Al SO_4 (Kgs)	Ca CO_2 (Kgs)	Cl (Kgs)	Polymers (Kgs)	Sodium Hypochloride (Kgs)	Water Treatment Cost (Lempiras /m^3)
Los Laureles							
(Guacerique)	12.707.696	674.805	163.090	120.385	1.875	1.000	0.23
Picacho							
(La Tigra)	17.347.690	—	—	34.705	—	45	0.01
Loarque	715.825	31.670	1.360	5.520	—	590	0.28
Miraflores	668.807	6.150	115	2.250	—	—	0.10

Source: Personal Communication with Engineers Francisco Zepeda and Robert Medrano. Tegucigalpa, March 1986.

Table 22.3. Average Water Demand in L/per capita/day (LCD)

Category	Years				
	1980	1990	2000	2100	
Domestic	132	176	198	212	79.4%
Commercial	21	26	27	29	10.9%
Small Industry	5	6	5	5	1.9%
Other Industry	—	1	3	3	1.1%
Public	11	14	15	18	6.7%
TOTAL	169	223	248	267	

Source SANAA 1982.

A final remark about the Tegucigalpa's master plan has to do with the fact that the planning process was focused on expected population growth and its water requirements over time, following a simplistic demand and supply approach for potable water requirements. Little consideration was given to the investment in the conservation of the existing supply sources, particularly La Tigra or the need to take specific preventive actions for future projects through watershed management techniques that enhance soil and water conservation. Issues related to water saving alternatives and water efficiency utilizing best available technologies to promote water conservation were also left out, and may prove to be a major option for the future, given the unbalances between future demands and the existing supplies in the region.

CONCLUSIONS

The obvious differences in the flow regimes and in the water quality characteristics derived form contrasting watershed land uses between Guacerique and La Tigra National Park offer tangible evidence of the importance of the natural systems to provide long-term, free services to society and the value to invest in their protection so that future generations may permanently enjoy those vital services.

Population annual growth rates in the order of 6% for Honduras' capital city are well above the 3% national average. Presently, population pressure on existing forest resources causes continue deforestation in critical watersheds since over half of the population still depends on fuel wood for cooking and timber demands tend to go up as construction needs go up. Other natural resources, particularly land, are also affected by people pressing for the expansion of the agriculture frontier or urbanization growth, at the expense of less intensive land uses. Most of these ongoing competing resource uses will directly or indirectly affect future water availability and quality requirements over time and space, but were not given the attention they deserve in the mater plan.

An integrated resource management approach would have given due consideration to other resource demands and allowed to compare them on the basis of the opportunity costs associated with desired watershed land uses and ecosystem protection objectives. Also, this approach would have related the impacts of those potential uses to the potential tangible benefits and costs associated to water availability and water quality over time.

A rapid assessment of the present and projected water demands for Tegucigalpa under the "business as usual" alternative considered in the master plan indicate that drastic institutional and individual changes are needed to promote technological innovation in soil and water conservation, including the adoption of water efficient technologies at the end use level. Options to deconcentrate the present unsustainable growth of the human settlements of Honduras capital city and to mitigate the present migratory trends need to be seriously considered.

RECOMMENDATIONS

Major steps to minimize the conflicts and maximize the opportunities for natural resources development under the vision of sustainable development strategies, will require important changes in the way master plans and terms of references for major infrastructure development projects are drafted. These efforts need to be complemented with the ways and means for financial resources allocation to promote long-term management and protection of the natural resource base as a necessary investment in the future quality of life.

Master or sectorial plans should be designed and analyzed from a broader, systems perspective, looking at the cumulative impacts and the interactions of present and future major local and regional developmental activities with the sectorial resource being planned for.

Integrated watershed management plans for the Guacerique and the Rio Grande basins must be taken or strengthen without delayed since both the existing Los Laureles reservoir and the newer Concepción water project in the Rio Grande are subjected to a series of pressures to intensify land uses and to promote further resources extraction which will negatively affect the hydrologic regime.

A long-term, integrated management plan must be implemented for La Tigra National Park, while undertaking its immediate protection.

Since financial resources are very limited in Honduras and water is a precious, irreplaceable resource for the Capital City, a cost-effectiveness strategy to set priorities of both prevention and corrective measures to enhanced water resources protection and conservation must be defined and implemented. Thus, the costs associated to watershed management and ecosystem protection should be properly weighted and internalized in the overall, long-term master plan analysis.

Planning based just on extrapolation of present trends may be misleading and conducive to self-fulfilling prophecies and impossibility situations when all things are considered. In the Tagucigalpa's Master Plan, for example, population is expected to grow unchecked, with no consideration to employment options towards the future or their future living conditions. Normative planning should be part of the analysis by presenting alternative futures scenarios of human settlements and expected quality of life within the region, so that realistic paths can be defined based on feasible targets set with a sense of human dimension and environmental direction.

Policies regarding present and potential land uses must be defined on multiple objectives and ecological economic analysis should weight the relative value of the water resources and their watersheds protection to the overall development options of the region considered. Competing or complementary resources uses with water quality and availability should be adequately valued and assessed as part of an integrated resource management approach.

The integral development of society should be viewed from an holistic social, economic, cultural, and biophysical perspective. If the conditions are such that future probable scenarios of population growth and the required multiple use of resources, water included, are not positive for the human and the natural environment, alternative options of decentralization should be considered, such as creating new or complementary poles of development to Tegucigalpa.

REFERENCES

Abarca, F. 1986. Aspectos hidrológicos sobre la región de cabeceras. Información presentadaen el Primer Seminario Taller sobre Abastecimiento de Agua para Tegucigalpa. Tegucigalpa, Honduras.

Blair, M. A. 1986. Propuesta para manejo y conservación de cuencas. Asociación Hondureña de Ecología. Información presentada en el Primer Seminario Taller sobre Abastecimiento de Agua para Tegucigalpa. Tegucigalpa, Honduras.

Brenes, L. G. 1986. Interpretación morfodinámica preliminar del área de subcuencas del río Choluteca, región metropolitana de Honduras. Turrialba, Costa Rica: CATIE.

Campanella, P. et al. 1982. Honduras. Perfil ambiental del país. Un estudio de campo. McLean, Virginia, U.S.A: AID/JRB Associates.

Eckholm, E. P. 1976. Losing ground. New York, U.S.A: W.W. Norton and Company, Inc.

Hernandez, H. 1983. Plan preliminar de ordenación y manejo de la subcuenca del río Guacerique. Tegucigalpa, Proyecto de Manejo de Recursos Naturales.

Honduras Ministerio de Recursos Naturales. 1984. Proyecto de Manejo de Recursos Naturales. Plan de Manejo de las Cuencas de los ríos Choluteca y Sampile/Guasaule.

Komives, R., O. Lucke, and R. y Perez. 1986. Agua potable para tegucigalpa: Estudio de uso de la Tierra. Turrialba, Costa Rica: CATIE.

Larios, E. N. 1986. Exposición presentada en el Primer Seminario Taller sobre Abastecimiento de Agua para Tegucigalpa. Tegucigalpa, Honduras.

Perez, J. R. 1981. Plan de trabajo tentativo para la ordenación y manejo de la cuenca "Los Laureles". Tegucigalpa: COHDEFOR.

Quesada, C. A. 1979. Effect of reservoir sedimentation and streamflow modification on firm power generation. Ph. D. Dissertation, Colorado State University. U.S.A.

Quesada, C. A. 1985. El Seguro Nacional de Conservación: una necesidad impostergable. Primer Congreso Ambiental de Costa Rica. Turrialba, Costa Rica: Universidad de Costa Rica. CATIE.

Quesada, C. A. 1986. La problemática demográfica-ambiental de Tegucigalpa y su relación conel abastecimiento y costos de agua potable. Memoria Seminario sobre Agua Potable para Tegucigalpa. Tegucigalpa: AHE-CATIE-UICN.

Reiche, C. E. 1985. Abastecimiento y mercado de la leña en América Central: Estudio de Casos, Turrialba, Costa Rica: CATIE.

Rodriguez, M. J. 1986. Diseño hidráulico del sistema primario y periférico del agua potable para Tegucigalpa. Tegucigalpa, Honduras: Universidad Nacional Autónoma de Honduras.

SANAA. 1975. Informe Final de diseño. Plan de emergencia "Proyecto Los Laureles". Servicio Autónomo de Acueductos y Alcantarillados. Banco Centroamericano de Integración Económica. Tegucigalpa, Honduras.

SANAA. 1982. Proyecto "Plan Maestro para Tegucigalpa, D.C." Servicio Autónomo Nacional de Acueductos y Alcantarillados. XVII Congreso Interamericano de Ingeniería Sanitaria y Ambiental EXPO-AIDIS. Panamá, agosto.

Segovia, J. L., P. Hearne, and A. y Lewandowski. 1985. El Programa de Monitoreo de la Calidad del Agua en la Cuenca del Río Guacerique. Tegucigalpa, SANAA/PRMN. Honduras.

UICN. 1980. Estrategia Mundial para la Conservación - La conservación de los recursos vivos para el logro de un desarrollo sostenido. Suiza: UICN, PNUMA y WWF.

U.S. Agency For International Development. 1986 Honduras: Natural Resources Management Project. Second Evaluation Report. AID Project 522–0168. Tegucigalpa, Honduras.

23 THE POLITICAL DIMENSION OF IMPLEMENTING ENVIRONMENTAL REFORM: LESSONS FROM COSTA RICA

David Kaimowitz
Center for International Forestry Research (CIFOR)
P.O. Box 6596, JKPWB Jakarta
10065 Indonesia and Masters Program in Economic Policy

National University (UNA) of Costa Rica
Apartado 264-3000, Heredia
Costa Rica

Olman Segura
National University (UNA) of Costa Rica
Apartado 264-3000, Heredia
Costa Rica

OVERVIEW

This chapter analyzes how the adoption and success of policies in Costa Rica related to deforestation, pesticides abuse, and air pollution have been influenced by interest groups, the economic impact of these policies, and the institutional capacity to carry them out. It concludes that environmental policies are more likely to be implemented when they: are supported by broad international and domestic coalitions, are not opposed by strong entrenched domestic interest groups or international financial institutions, and open new economic opportunities or do not pose a major threat to important existing activities. Environmental policies which threaten key economic sectors are unlikely to be adopted, even when interest groups apply substantial pressure to do so. On the other hand, without such pressure governments will be slow to implement effective environmental policies, even when they do not threaten any fundamental interests. While the Costa Rican government has been committed to implement environmental policies, it has generally succeeded in developing the institutional capacity to do so, although due to technical considerations some policies have proved more difficult to implement than others.

INTRODUCTION

Work on ecological economics has grown rapidly over the last few years. Thousands of economists, ecologists, and other professionals are now actively analyzing the interactions between economics and the environment. Most of them are trying to figure out what economic policies and new technologies are suitable for limiting environmental degradation while at the same time achieving other social goals.

These efforts have concentrated on what theoretically should be done rather than what is politically and institutionally feasible in any given circumstance. Ecological economics cannot come "down to earth" and be applied, however, without addressing issues related to policy formulation and implementation. To design policies with a good chance of being adopted and effective and strategies to make that happen, we must improve our understanding of how environmental policy is made and implemented.

Key aspects which influence whether a given environmental policy will be carried out are.

- The pressure interest groups apply to support or oppose the policy.
- The policy's potential impact on the profitability of major economic activities.
- The institutional capacity to implement the policy.[1]

This chapter analyzes how these aspects have helped determine which policies have been adopted and how successful they have been with respect to three specific environmental problems in Costa Rica: deforestation, pesticide abuse, and air pollution. In each case, the chapter first presents the problem and to what extent it is improving or worsening and then examines how different interest groups, economic considerations, and institutional factors have affected government policy and the degree of progress. It concludes that environmental policies are more likely to be implemented when they: are supported by broad coalitions, including both domestic and international groups, are not opposed by strong entrenched domestic interest groups or international financial institutions, and open new economic opportunities or do not pose a major threat to the most important existing activities. Where these conditions exist, the necessary institutional capacity to carry out the policies in question is likely to be developed, although different policies require different levels of institutional capacity, and policies which require more institutional capacity are less likely to be implemented. This chapter makes no pretense of presenting all the details of each case, but rather uses the cases to illustrate general lessons regarding the political dimension of environmental policy reform.

The three problems analyzed are among Costa Rica's most pressing environmental concerns and cover a diverse range of interest groups, economic sectors, institutional frameworks, and outcomes. Costa Rica itself was chosen as a context in which to examine these issues because it has gained a wide spread international image over the last few years as a country committed to environmentally friendly policies that has already achieved certain significant successes and has recently helped to establish The "Alliance for Sustainable Development" involving all the governments of Central America.

The current president of Costa Rica, José María Figueres, has made sustainable development a centerpiece of his administration and has emphasized the concept on many occasions. As the following analysis shows, however, he is more likely to achieve tangible results with respect to certain problems than with others.

DEFORESTATION

Half a century ago, three quarters of Costa Rica was covered with forests. But by 1984 only about a third of that forest remained (Boyce et al. 1994). During the 1970s, between 30,000 and 60,000 hectares of forest were cleared each year, mostly by ranchers and farmers interested in expanding their pastures and crop lands (Peuker 1992). This deforestation led to increased soil degradation, loss of valuable forest products and biodiversity, and the sedimentation of dams and waterways, and contributed to global warming.

During the last ten years this situation has improved. After 1987, annual deforestation dropped to 18,000 ha, and by 1993 had fallen to 8,000 ha (Lutz et al. 1993). Forest plantations now cover 90,000 ha, compared to less than 30,000 ha in the late 1980s. In addition, the area in secondary forest has increased by some 150,000 ha (Nuñez 1993). Forest clearing is still a major problem, but is no longer as severe as it once was.

The government's most effective policy to reduce deforestation has been to establish protected areas, such as national parks, forest reserves, and Indian reservations. Protected areas became important in the mid-1970s and now cover approximately 28% of Costa Rica's territory (Peuker 1992). Two thirds of the country's forests are located in protected areas (Boyce et al. 1994). Despite great efforts, the government has been unable to fully control forest destruction in protected areas, but deforestation would certainly have been much higher in recent years if the areas did not exist.

The government has promoted reforestation through incentives such as tax credits, direct payments, and subsidized credit. These incentives began in the late 1970s, operated at a low level for several years, and then expanded rapidly after 1986 (Peuker 1992).

At the same time, lower public support for livestock credit and agricultural colonization and more secure property rights that allow land owners to protect their property without having to deforest to maintain their ownership have reduced pasture and crop expansion (Lehmann 1991). Unfavorable market conditions for cattle production, new alternative investment opportunities in other economic activities, and the reality that little forest remains in Costa Rica outside protected areas have also helped reduce land clearing.

The shifts in government policies affecting deforestation reflect changes in the relative influence of different interest groups. During the 1950s, 1960s, and 1970s, politically powerful, large ranchers associations lobbied successfully for government support for livestock and against restrictions on forest conversion (Edelman 1992). The World Bank and the Inter-American Development Bank (IBD) supported the livestock sector to promote economic growth by increasing beef exports. Pressure for public agricultural colonization programs came from land-poor rural families, large landowners who considered the programs a substitute for agrarian reform, and urban sectors interested in maintaining low food prices (Jones 1992).

In recent years, however, social forces interested in forest preservation and reforestation have emerged and traditional opponents to these efforts have become weaker or changed their positions. The public has become more aware about the environment and foreign funding agencies have begun to provide money and technical assistance to support conservation and forestry projects.[2] The country's first major environmental organization, the Costa Rican Conservation Association (ASCONA), was formed in 1972 and within ten years attracted 2,000 members. Since then, the number of environmental groups has grown from 31 in 1984 to 89 in 1991 (Boyce et al. 1994).

The IDB and World Bank have stopped supporting subsidized agricultural credit in general and livestock credit in particular and begun to fund environmental projects. Small farmer organizations now focus less on land distribution, and in recent years have successfully struggled to broaden and adapt the incentives for reforestation to allow small farmers to benefit. Lumber interests have become concerned with decreasing timber supplies and have begun to consider forest plantations as a possible alternative (Jones 1992). Even many large ranchers are now less enthusiastic about cattle production, which has become less profitable, and have started to reforest or allow secondary forests to regrow.

Groups favoring subsidies for livestock still have influence. During the mid-1980s, cattle ranchers succeeded in getting a law passed which allowed them to reschedule and reduce their debts, and through those mechanisms obtain subsidies worth US$ 49 million (World Bank 1994). Similarly, legal challenges to restrictions on land use and the expropriation of land for national parks have greatly complicated government efforts in these areas. Nonetheless, these groups are no longer as powerful as they once were.

Another factor favoring conservation and reforestation policies has been that cattle and timber production and other activities traditionally associated with deforestation are no longer central to the Costa Rican economy. During the early 1980s, beef exports provided 6%-8% of Costa Rica's foreign exchange earnings, but they now account for less than 2%. During the same period, the participation of livestock in the country's Gross Domestic Product (GDP) fell from 2.3% to 1.7% (Masis and Rodriguez 1994). The real value of forest production fell by 50% between 1976 and 1985 (Peuker 1992). Hence, the Costa Rican economy is no longer likely to suffer greatly from any policy which restricts these activities.

At the same time, economic sectors which stand to benefit from policies that promote greater forest coverage have become very important. Thanks in part to government subsidies and tax exemptions, tourism has gone from being a marginal activity only a few years ago to generating 685 million dollars in 1994, one fourth of the country's foreign exchange earnings (Noguera 1995).

At present, tourism is the country's number one source of foreign exchange earnings. And given that 75% of the 400,000 tourists who came in 1992 visited the national parks, the parks' existence is key to the industry's viability (Boyce et al. 1994). As previously noted, large amounts of money have also come into the country to support conservation activities and increasing numbers of ranchers and lumber companies have been attracted by the public incentives for reforestation.

Over the last few years, there has also been a substantial improvement in the government's capacity to carry out forestry policies. The development of this capacity is especially notable given the government's almost complete inability to regulate the use of forest resources prior to the mid-1980s.

The most important steps taken to improve the effectiveness of the government's forestry policy have been:

- The creation of a National Park Services in 1977 and a new Ministry of Natural Resources, Mines, and Energy (MIRENEM) in 1986, which brought together most forestry-related activities in one institution,
- Increased spending and the establishment of innovative financial mechanisms to fund conservation and reforestation, such as a quasi-public National Parks Foundation, "debt for nature" swaps, high entrance fees at national parks, and public incentives for reforestation aimed at small producers, and
- Attempts at greater decentralization of park management and local participation in environmental projects (Umaña and Brandon 1992). At the same time, numerous Non Governmental Organizations (NGOs) have arisen, which provide valuable services in research, information dissemination, training, and protected area management.

Within this general context, it is noteworthy that the National Parks Service has achieved a much greater institutional capacity than has the MIRENEM's forestry division (DGF) responsible for regulating forest reserves and lands outside protected areas. This disparity in resources and effectiveness reflects the stronger political constituency and economic interests promoting the national parks than those that exist for forest protection in general. This disparity has also led the Costa Rican government to consider combining the two agencies and MIRENEM's Wildlife Division in a single National Service for Conservation Areas (SENAC).

PESTICIDE ABUSE

Many Costa Rican farms use large amounts of hazardous pesticides which intoxicate farmers and agricultural workers, cause health problems for consumers, kill animals and plants, and may even increase pest problems by eliminating natural predators and inducing the appearance of pesticide—resistant organisms (Hilje et al. 1987). Per capita pesticide use in the country is eight times the world average and it has been estimated that almost one out of every twenty agricultural workers suffers from pesticide poisoning each year (Wesseling et al. 1993). Approximately 6,500 ha had to be completely abandoned for almost thirty years due to damage from copper-based fungicides (Thrupp 1991).

Moreover, unlike the situation with deforestation, the problem of pesticide abuse has not improved much over the last fifteen years, and may have gotten worse. Between 1980 and 1991, net pesticide imports increased 66%, from US$24.6 million to US$40.8 million and the volume of pesticide imports rose from 8.3 million kg in 1985 to 12.5 million kg in 1993 (J. F. Chaverri, pers. comm.).[3] There is now less use of certain pesticides widely criticized for their negative effect on the environment, such as the organochlorines and lead-based fungicides; but they have been largely replaced by other pesticides such as the organophosphates, which while less persistent are more acutely toxic (Boyce et al. 1994). And while some farmers have converted to organic agriculture or adopted practices of Integrated Pest Management (IPM) which allow them to use less pesticides and switch to less hazardous products, most have not.

On balance, Costa Rican government policies have worsened the pesticide problem, rather than solved it. Since the mid-1980s, the government has offered major tax benefits and other incentives to produce bananas and non-traditional agricultural exports, such as flowers, ornamental plants, and pineapples. These crops use extremely high levels of pesticides and probably account for over half of the pesticides used in the country. Had the government supported instead the production of basic foodstuffs, which use much less pesticides, these problems would not have been so great.

Pesticides problems are particularly serious in the case of flowers and ornamental plants because there are no maximum limits on the amount of pesticide residues in the exported products and many of them are produced in green houses and covered areas with little ventilation. Between 1982 and 1992, exports of these crops increased 138%, and the pesticides used for their production probably grew proportionally (Banco Central de Costa Rica 1992; Kaimowitz 1992). As a result of broader policies favoring trade liberalization, the government has reduced tariffs and taxes on pesticide imports and made it easier for agrochemical companies to introduce new pesticides. During the period of low international coffee prices between 1989 and 1993, the government also provided coffee growers with subsidized credit and other incentives specifically designed to facilitate agrochemical use for that crop.

At the same time, public agricultural extension and plant health services have encouraged IPM and safe pesticide use through media campaigns, training events, and visits to farmers. The government has prohibited 18 pesticides and restricted the use of several others and the country now has better facilities to test for pesticide residues (Trivelato and Wesseling 1992). Nevertheless, the work on IPM has been largely limited to a few foreign—financed projects focusing on vegetable production and many hazardous pesticides are still freely available on the market.

Misuse of pesticides was first seriously questioned in Costa Rica in 1979, when 800 workers from a Standard Fruit banana plantation sued that company and the Shell and Dow Chemical Companies for having caused them and 700 other workers to become sterile as a result of contact with a nematicide known as DBCP. This case was well publicized and remained in the courts until 1992, when the workers received US$15.4 million in compensation in an out-of-court settlement (Boyce et al. 1994).

Throughout the 1980s, researchers from Costa Rican and foreign universities and environmental organizations produced a steady stream of studies documenting the damage caused by pesticides to human health and the environment; many of which were widely covered by the press (Hilje et al. 1987; Vega 1991). Bilateral agencies such as the United States Agency for International Development (USAID) and the German and Danish foreign aid agencies began financing projects which discouraged misuse of pesticides. Incidents in which certain Costa Rican products were not allowed to enter the United States or Europe because of excessive pesticide residues also helped raise consciousness in the country regarding the problem.

In the 1990s, the rapid expansion of banana production in Costa Rica's Atlantic Coast brought about major social and environmental problems; one of which was excessive and unsafe pesticide use. In response, church organizations, labor unions, and environmentalists formed a coalition aimed at pressing the banana companies and the Costa Rican government to address these problems.

These groups demanded, among other things, the prohibition of highly toxic pesticides, increased support for the use of pest resistant banana varieties, greater control over aerial fumigation, and the monitoring of soils and waterways for pesticide residues. Around the same time, the Association for Watershed Protection (ADCH) accused the Standard Fruit Company before the International Tribune of Waters of having seriously damaged the environment in the Estrella River through misuse of pesticides.

Nevertheless, as discussed above, these activities in favor of limiting pesticide use have produced only modest results. One reason for this is the lack of sufficient practical alternatives to hazardous pesticides. More important still are the economic importance of the crops involved, the political influence of the groups favoring the status quo, and the weaknesses of the institutions charged with addressing the issue.

Unlike the deforestation issue, where the productive activities involved have lost economic importance, most of the crops which now rely heavily on pesticides, such as bananas, coffee, flowers, fruits, and ornamental plants are at the very heart of the current Costa Rican economic model of "outward-oriented" growth. These crops currently provide approximately 35% of the country's foreign exchange earnings, and both the Costa Rican government and the international financial institutions on which the country depends perceive them as being fundamental components for the country's development. Thus, neither group has been willing to support strong measures to control pesticide abuse which could potentially limit these crop's competitiveness.

In addition, politically powerful interest groups, such as the banana companies and the agro-chemical industry have lobbied strongly against restrictions or taxes on pesticide use. In certain cases these industries have sought to deflect criticism by initiating their own programs for controlling pesticide abuse such as the "safe pesticide usage campaign" led by the National Chamber Importers, Producers, and Distributors of Agricultural Inputs and the Environmental Commission for Bananas (CAB) created by the banana industry. These efforts, however, have had little practical impact and have been overshadowed by the huge resources which many of these same companies dedicate to encouraging pesticide sales.

The agencies in the ministries of agriculture and health assigned to regulate and monitor pesticide use and provide technical assistance in IPM lack effective policy instruments, are understaffed and poorly motivated, have little contact with the export sectors where most pesticide use is concentrated, and are highly dependent on foreign funding. Two reasons for this are the lack of political will to discourage the use of hazardous pesticides and the Costa Rican government's broader concern with reducing public spending.

AIR POLLUTION

Air pollution affects human health, corrodes building materials, and contributes to global warming (Grutter 1994). In many areas of San José, Costa Rica's capital, air pollution levels often rise above the standards established by the Panamerican Health Organization (Alfaro 1994).

As a result, residents of that city frequently report suffering respiratory problems, eye irritations, nausea, dizziness, headaches, and concentration problems. This increases health care costs and lowers worker productivity and the quality of life. Acid rain caused by air pollution is also a major reason for the deterioration of Costa Rica's National Theater and other historic buildings and monuments (Alfaro and Aguilar 1989).

Between 1975 and 1989, total air contaminants increased 158%, from 33,119 tons to 85,673 tons (Arcia et al. 1991). This increase was a direct result of rapid growth in the number of cars, buses, and trucks, which almost doubled between 1984 and 1994 from 217,824 to 406,288 (Alfaro 1994; Ramirez 1994). Currently, these vehicles generate over 70% of the air pollution in the country (Alfaro 1994). Moreover, pollution levels in 1993 and 1994 were even higher than might be expected given the magnitude of the growth in vehicles because the vehicles' average age has risen and older vehicles produce higher emissions (Alfaro 1994).

One reason why the number of cars circulating in San José has grown so rapidly is that the city's population and per capita income have both risen. Nevertheless, government trade liberalization policies, which have dramatically reduced the taxes on car imports, has been the most important factor. Since the mid-1980s, tariffs and taxes on car imports have been reduced from above 300% to 100% of the car's value.

Largely as a result of these policies, the average number of cars imported annually rose from 11,777 in the 1980s to 30,518 during the first five years of the 1990s (National Registry 1995 pers. comm.). These same tax policies have also contributed to the rise in the average age of Costa Rica's vehicles because they have favored the importation of used vehicles over that of new vehicles.

The implementation of trade liberalization policies such as the reduction of car import taxes has been one of the main conditions placed on the Costa Rican government by the World Bank, the IDB, the International Monetary Fund (IMF), and USAID in exchange for access to loans and donations. The Costa Rican middle class, some of which have been able to purchase a car for the first time, has also widely, though passively, supported lower car import taxes.

In contrast, the concern about air pollution is diffuse and largely limited to occasional complaints by individuals or small local community groups.[4] There is no specific constituency particularly affected by the problem, which itself is not that visible and has only recently been quantified. Organized pressure on the government regarding the issue has largely come from a handful of scientists and small projects, whose findings have received attention in the local media.

Given this situation, it is not surprising that the government has moved slowly to remedy the air pollution problem. In 1982, it issued an initial set of regulations limiting toxic emissions from vehicles but these were never enforced. Then, in 1986, the Ministry of Public Works and Transportation (MOPT) created a "smoke and noise unit" which monitored air pollution levels in several points in San José; but after a brief flourish of activity this unit practically disappeared. Three years later, the government issued a decree requiring the public petroleum refinery (RECOPE) to sell unleaded gasoline, but the decree was apparently never applied.

In fact, the government did not take any effective action with respect to air pollution until 1993, when it passed a new Traffic Law with stricter regulations controlling vehicle emissions and higher fines for vehicles which fail to comply with those regulations. This was followed in 1994 by a set of regulations issued jointly by the MOPT, the Ministry of Health, and MIRENEM which require all cars imported after January 1, 1995 to be equipped with catalytic convertors, as well as regular vehicle inspections. Catalytic convertors only work with unleaded gasoline and the government has now started to lower the levels of lead in the gasoline it sells and has announced that it will soon begin to sell completely lead-free gasoline, which it has publicized as 'ecological gasoline' (Pastor 1995). Transit police have begun to fine some car owners for having excess emissions and the public national training institute (INA) has initiated a project with Swiss support to train car mechanics, transit police, and others regarding aspects of vehicle maintenance related to air contamination.

Nevertheless, the problem is likely to persist. Even though, the Ministry of Health has a clear responsibility for air quality, the ministry's environmental control department is small and has little capacity to implement solutions and the different agencies involved do not coordinate much. The MOPT has taken some initiative regarding the problem, but continues to give it low priority. There are only eight machines in the entire country for measuring vehicle emissions, and of these only three are in San José (Proyección Institucional MOPT 1995).

Pollution from urban buses is a particularly sensitive issue. These buses pollute more than most cars because they use diesel fuel and most are quite old. Government officials admit informally, however, that they are reluctant to take action when it comes to the buses because almost two thirds of the urban population uses them regularly and any strong steps to control bus emissions could disrupt the transportation system and cause serious economic problems.

CONCLUSION

Costa Rica has advanced a great deal towards reversing the decline in forest area, has a mixed record regarding hazardous pesticide use, and has only recently begun to make modest efforts to control air pollution (see Table 23.1). The emergence of strong economic interests favoring forest protection and plantations and the declining importance of the activities associated with deforestation in the first case, compared to the powerful economic sectors tied to pesticide use in the second, are at least one reason for these different outcomes.

With regards to air pollution, few major economic interests are tied to the increase of the number of vehicles per se, but there are enormous interests at stake in the broader issue of trade liberalization, of which vehicle imports form part. The need to maintain public transportation services in San José to avoid economic disruptions has also been important in keeping the government from restricting emissions from buses.

Interest groups such as trade associations, environmental groups, international financial institutions, bilateral funding agencies, religious groups, small farmer organizations, trade unions, scientists, and the media, have greatly affected the outcomes in each of the three cases. In the first case, the emergence of powerful new groups favoring increased forest area combined with changes in the positions of certain groups which had previously supported forest clearing and the weakening of others has been key in getting the Costa Rican government to modify its policies affecting forests. Numerous groups have pressed for reductions in pesticide use but they have been less successful, in part because of the power of the groups opposing such measures and the potential economic risks involved in taking strong actions. In the case of air pollution, the lack of any strong cohesive constituency concerned about the issue has probably been the most important factor keeping it from the public agenda.

To a certain extent, the institutional capacity to solve these problems is related to the specific technical aspects of each case as well as more general aspects of public administration in Costa Rica. Clearly one reason for success in the forest case has been the invention of various innovative mechanisms for obtaining resources, organizing the necessary tasks, and providing incentives to landowners. In contrast, in the case of pesticides few new institutional mechanisms have been developed and it has been difficult to find technological alternatives attractive to farmers. The government's control over petroleum refining and vehicle imports has facilitated the shift to lead-free gasoline and the use of catalytic convertors. The government's broader efforts to cut public spending in order to reduce the fiscal deficit has tended to weaken all the public agencies concerned with environmental policy.

Table 23.1. Factors Affecting the Implementation and Success of Environmental Reforms in Costa Rica

Factor	Deforestation	Pesticide Abuse	Air Pollution
Strength of groups favoring reforms	High. International and domestic. Important productive sectors favor reforms.	Medium. Mostly domestic, with a few foreign financed projects. No important productive sector favors reforms	Low. Dispersed domestic public opinion.
Strength of groups opposing reforms	Medium. Ranchers and some lumber interests are opposed, but their opposite has weakened	High. Agricultural exporters and agrochemical companies are strongly opposed, with the implicit support of the international financial institutions	Medium. International financial institutions and the middle class favor trade liberalization for vehicles. Transport sector is opposed to reforms.
Economic costs of reforms	Medium. Some lumber and cattle interests would be affected, but tourism and forest plantations gain	High. Exports of bananas and non-traditional agricultural exports could be greatly affected.	Medium. Raises transportation costs.
Institutional capacity to carry out the reforms	Medium. the National Park Service is strong and the Forestry Department is moderately effective. Many NGOs carry out activities	Low. Ministry of Agriculture is weak. Several institutions have small projects	Low. Several ministries have small dispersed efforts.
Technical difficulties with implementing reforms	Medium. Innovative mechanisms have been developed to protect forests and promote reforestation	High. In some cases there are no profitable substitutes for pesticide use and the technology is hard to disseminate.	Low. Technology exists. The government controls the refineries and car imports.
Outcome	Substantial success. Deforestation has decreased and reforestation increased.	Moderate success. Pesticide use has risen, although use of some of the most toxic pesticides have largely been eliminated. Some farmers use integrated pest management.	Minimal success. Air pollution has increased. Some catalytic convertors and lead free gasoline in use

Nevertheless, the country's institutional capacity to solve these problems is also directly related to the political will which to face these issues. It is not surprising that the Costa Rican government has been successful in finding institutional mechanisms for supporting protected areas, less successful at developing mechanisms for restricting pesticide use, and so far has largely failed to create the capacity to control contamination by vehicles. The cases discussed in this chapter also show that when the government has really been interested in ensuring significant results within a short time period it has tended to use subsidies, taxes, and restrictions. However, when there has been only a weak interest in making serious progress it has relied almost exclusively on educational activities and persuasion.

In summary, environmental policies which threaten key economic sectors are unlikely to be adopted, even when interest groups apply substantial pressure to do so. On the other hand, without such pressure governments will generally be slow to implement effective environmental policies, even when they do not threaten any fundamental interests. While organizational and management issues certainly affect whether a country has the institutional capacity to formulate and carry out environmental policies, the strength of the government's real commitment to such policies is equally important in that regard.

ACKNOWLEDGMENTS

The authors are grateful for comments by F. Duchin and C. Kiker.

NOTES

1. Other factors such as the nature of the political regimes involved, the specific procedures for policy making, and the sequencing of the steps required for approval are also important, but could not be addressed in this chapter due to space limitations.
2. Between 1989 and 1992, the Costa Rican government received or obtained commitments for 45 million dollars for environmental projects from foreign agencies (Boyce et al. 1994). Non-governmental organizations and international agencies also received large sums of money for this purpose.
3. Net pesticide imports are a fairly good indicator of total pesticide consumption in Costa Rica since the country imports all its pesticides. In any given year, however, net imports may differ slightly from consumption due to changes in inventory levels.
4. The authors were only able to identify one case where a neighborhood group has organized around the issue of air pollution; in 1992 the residents of the Amon neighborhood of San José formally complained to the Ministry of Health regarding excessive air and noise pollution caused by vehicles. There have been, however, a small number of formal complaints by groups about air pollution caused by industries.

REFERENCES

Alfaro, R. 1994. Contaminación del aire en el area metropolitana. *Tecnología MOPT* 2(3): 1–2.

Alfaro M. R. and A.Y. Aguilar. 1989. Efectos de la contaminación del aire sobre el Teatro Nacional. San José: Estudio Técnico.

Arcia, G., L. Merino, and A. Mata. 1991. Modelo Interactivo de Población y Medio Ambiente en Costa Rica 1990. San José: Asociación Demográfica Costarricense.

Banco Central de Costa Rica. 1992. Principales Estadísticas sobre las transacciones internacionales de Costa Rica. San José.

Boyce, J. K., A. Fernández González, E. Furst, and O. Segura Bonilla. 1994. Café y desarrollo sostenible: del cultivo agroquímico a la producción orgánica en Costa Rica Heredia: Editorial Fundación UNA.

Edelman, M. 1992. The Logic of the Latifundio, The Large Estates of Northwestern Costa Rica since the Late Nineteenth Century. Stanford: Stanford University Press.

Grutter, J. 1994. Control de emisiones de gases, motores a gasolina. San José: Programa ecológico de Centroamérica / Swiss Contact.

Hilje, L., L. Castillo, L. A. Thrupp, and I. Wesseling. 1987. El uso de los plaguicidas en Costa Rica. San José: Editorial Universidad Estatal a Distancia.

Jones, J. R. 1992. Environmental Issues and Policies in Costa Rica: Control of Deforestation. *Policy Studies Journal* 20 (4): 679–694.

Kaimowitz, D. 1992. El apoyo tecnológico necesario para promover las exportaciones agrícolas no tradicionales en America Central. Serie documentos de programas #30 San José: IICA.

Lehmann, M. P. 1991. After the Jungleburger: Forces Behind Costa Rica's Continued Forest Conversion. *Latinamericanist* 26 (2): 10–17.

Lutz, E., M. Vedova, H. Martinez, L. San Ramon, R. Vasquez, A. Alvarado, L. Merino, R. Celis, and J. Huising. 1993. Interdisciplinary Fact-Finding on Current Deforestation in Costa Rica. Environment Working Paper No. 61, Environment Department. Washington DC: World Bank.

Masis, G. and C. Rodríguez. 1994. La inserción del campesinado en un proceso de modernización no incluyente. In La agricultura campesina en Costa Rica, eds. G. Masis and C. Rodríguez. San José: IDEAS.

Noguera, Y. 1995. Turismo, principal fuente de divisas. *La Nación*. February 12: 18A.

Nuñez Olivas, O. 1993. Deforestación en Costa Rica: la pesadilla y la esperanza. *Esta Semana,* April 13-19: 11-12.

Pastor, R. 1995. Eliminan plomo de gasolina regular. *La Republica* February 2: 8a.

Peuker, A. 1992. Public Policies and Deforestation: A Case Study of Costa Rica. Latin America and the Caribbean Technical Department, Regional Studies Program, Report No. 14. Washington DC: World Bank.

Proyección Institucional MOPT. 1995. Informe de prensa, MOPT será riguroso en control por emisión de gases y particulas.

Ramirez, E. 1994. Vehiculos arruinan aire de San José. December *Seminario Universidad* 2: 3.

Thrupp, L. A. 1991. Long-term losses from accumulation of pesticide residues: A case of persistent copper toxicity in soils of Costa Rica. *Geoforum* 22 (1): 1–15.

Trivelato, M. D. and C. Wesseling. 1992. Utilización de plaguicidas en cultivos no tradicionales en Costa Rica y otros países centroamericanos: aspectos ambientales y de salud ocupacional. In Promesa o espejismo: Exportaciones agrícolas no tradicionales del istmo centroamericano, eds. A. B. Mendizabal and J. Weller. Panama: CADESCA.

Umaña, A. and K. Brandon. 1992. Inventing Institutions for Conservation: Lessons from Costa Rica. In Poverty, Natural Resources, and Public Policy in Central America, ed. S. Annis. New Brunswick: Transactions Publishers.

Vega, S. 1991. El impacto de los organofosforados en las aves. *Ciencias Ambientales* No. 8: 98–105.

Wesseling, C., L. Castillo, and C. G. Erlinder. 1993. Pesticide poisonings in Costa Rica. *Scandinavian Journal of Work and Environmental Health* 19 (4): 227–235.

World Bank. 1994. Costa Rica Forest Sector Review. Report No. 11516–CR. Washington DC: World Bank.

24 ENVISIONING SUSTAINABLE ALTERNATIVES WITHIN THE FRAMEWORK OF THE UNCED PROCESS

Alicia Bárcena
Earth Council
Apartado 2323-1002
San José, Costa Rica

Diomar Silveira
Earth Council
Apartado 2323-1002
San José, Costa Rica

OVERVIEW

The United Nations Conference on Environment and Development (UNCED), which took place in Rio de Janeiro in June 1992, and was a landmark for envisioning sustainable alternatives. The UNCED process represented a unique opportunity to initiate the major shift needed to get out of our inertia and to put us on the pathway to a more secure, equitable, and sustainable future. Many hopes existed on the "road to Rio", but for many analysts Rio was a missed opportunity, as the concept of sustainable development is still seen more in terms of its environmental component.

The real path towards sustainability requires a balance in four important dimensions: social equity, ecological integrity, change of the economic paradigm, and the participation of society in the decision-making process. Each of these dimensions need to be seen and analyzed in terms of the system as a whole and not separate parts, so that the policies established reflect the real world we are faced with.

INTRODUCTION

The third meeting of the International Society for Ecological Economics chose as its theme "Down to Earth: Practical Applications of Ecological Economics" to demonstrate how much the international community is claiming for actions rather than rhetoric when dealing with the broad issue of sustainability.

It has been more than two years now since governments and civil society of all the world met in Rio de Janeiro with the purpose to establish a new set of principles, decisions, programs, and projects which could shape our destiny towards a more secure and equitable path on Earth.

It is our intention in this chapter to show briefly the main results of this important gathering, the trends in the international scenario since then and a proposition for tackling the issue of sustainability in terms of four macro issues. In the last part we list a series of recommendations that we hope may serve as a guidelines for action when envisioning sustainable development.

UNCED: THE TWO SIDES OF A PROCESS

The United Nations Conference on Environment and Development (UNCED), more commonly known as the Earth Summit, was undoubtedly a landmark for envisioning sustainable alternatives, since it represented an opportunity where more than 120 Heads of State and more than 180 governments together with around 14,000 representatives from the civil society gathered in Rio de Janeiro to advocate for a sustainable development.

UNCED represented a unique opportunity to initiate the major shift needed out of our inertia to put us on the pathway to a more secure, equitable, and sustainable future. However, it was a missed opportunity since what came out of the process was that social and economic issues received less emphasis than environmental issues. This is clear in the Agenda 21, where much stress was put on its section II, "Conservation and Management of Resources". Section IV, on the other hand, where themes like financing and technology transfer were not indeed treated in depth. From the institutional and structural point of view, there was also the expectation that UNCED could be an opportunity to evaluate and assess the current international order (Bretton Woods Institutions, the United Nations System, the transnational corporations, and the International Court of Justice).

There is no doubt that major milestones were reached in Rio during the UNCED process. Historic inter-governmental agreements on basic principles, incorporated in the Rio Declaration, a comprehensive and far-ranging program of action in Agenda 21 and the Conventions on Biodiversity and Climate Change, established a baseline for future behavior and action. In the process, governments addressed issues and concerns many had hoped to avoid. Such as the need for new and additional resources, technology transfer, and new approaches to trade. However in terms of financing the ODA has diminished by 10%; the conclusion of the Uruguay Roundtable has not considered at all the provisions contained in Agenda 21 and today more than ever technology transfer is out of the control of governments.

The governmental agreements were not the only outcome of Rio. There was an unprecedented level of involvement of those outside government that provided the political will and impetus for this. The "peoples summit" at the global forum which accompanied the official conference, produced its own initiatives and "treaties". This unprecedented combination of the largest gathering ever of heads of government together with the voices of the people assembled at Rio and those throughout the world whose attention was engaged through the media produced the basic elements for a new global partnership to secure the future of our planet and its people.

TRENDS TOWARDS GLOBALIZATION AND THE RIO AGREEMENTS

In Rio de Janeiro many elements came to the surface as evidences of the globalization process we are faced with. Among them, we can list the following:

1. The North-South debate is more a gap than a debate. The real confrontation is nowadays between rich and poor. Each developing country has its little north and each developed country has its little south in it. This is even more clear in the access to information, transfer of technology, etc.

2. In the last four years the world has changed from an ideological and geo-political framework to a geo-economic one in which the trading blocks are playing a leading role. This has severed consequences in the social field in developing countries since they being obliged to orient their economies towards exports at any price that could be seen as a "social price".

3. Capital, technology, and knowledge are dividing the world into those that are excluded and those that are included. Global financial regime and world economy has mushroomed as a result of the globalization of industrialism and technology, information telematics, transnational corporations. This globalized economic apparatus with its some $4 trillion daily financial flows swamping real investment and trade now, is driving most of other human institutions, policies and activities. However, the flows of capital occur in those countries that are communicated electronically and basically among the megacities of the world with the marginalization of traditional societies and cultures, the restructuring of work and production and the widening of poverty gaps.

4. The changing nature of money, a very useful invention that is now globally changing from gold, coins, and paper to information. Money and information have become almost equivalent and interchangeable if you have the one you can have the other. The gap is therefore growing wider between poor countries and rich and technological ones. The same information revolution is fostering the growth of civil society at the global level through e-mail, Internet and many other electronic devices.

5.   This scenario is now playing out on a global stage, with unexpected results: services sectors are automating worldwide and corporations to stay competitive, are searching for cheaper labor and unprotected resources and environment to exploit and degrade. The borders have been open to capital and information flows and discriminatory for labor flows.

6.   The organizations that were really empowered after Rio were the transnational corporations, the World Bank, the International Monetary Fund, and in general, the tendency towards privatization and free trade. These were the real winners of the Rio process. Democratization of international negotiations is at stake. The United Nations multilateral system (one vote-one country) versus the Bretton Woods system (one dollar one vote). The lack of political decision to democratize the security council.

7.   Paradoxically to the $4 trillion of daily financial flows, in Rio we were fighting for $60 billion to implement Agenda 21. Although in Rio it was approved that international development assistance should be doubled from .3% of GNP of developed countries to .7% of GNP this has been diminishing almost 10% in the last two years. Most of the assistance has been reoriented towards humanitarian help and the Agenda for Peace of the United Nations.

8.   The origin of military conflicts are no longer between countries but between ethnic groups and religious groups that are fighting for scarce resources as in former Yugoslavia, Rwanda, Somalia, and soon in other countries of Africa. We are moving from military wars to trade wars in search of consumers markets.

9.   The radical change to the concept of human security ranging from crime, drugs, plagues, environmental global threats, etc.

10. Democracy is growing but peoples choices are not. The ignorance of their entitlement, their inability to purchase what is available and the new rules.

11. Double codes of standards and ethics. Free trade. Protectionism from the North while forcing the South to open up to capital and foreign investment while not opening the borders to labor for example.

12. Trade, consumption, financing, and technology were all at the center of the debate. Everybody agreed to change the future but the North did not agree to give up any bit of their current pattern of consumption and status quo or to change the patterns of trade and technology transfer much less to devote new and additional resources to sustainable development.

13. Globalization versus universality in which the predominance of the Agenda of G-7 is the name of the game more than a real democratic agenda that includes the views of all countries. In an interdependent world the weak will lose.

14. The astounding results of Marakesh. The unequal terms of creation of WTO for non industrialized countries. The non-industrialized countries see the GATT and Marakesh as a betrayal to Agenda 21. More market access, technology funding, and various forms of assistance including a serious analysis of debt issues within a more democratic and just governance of the World Bank, the International Monetary Fund, and WTO.

A PATHWAY TOWARDS SUSTAINABILITY: THE 4 E'S

The legacy of the Brundtland Commission in 1984 was basically the conceptualization of sustainable development as that development that satisfies the needs of present generations without compromising the options of future generations.

The Legacy of Rio was that it provided a programmatic approach to the concept of sustainable development that could desegregate this concept into projects and actions. The concept of sustainable development as agreed in Rio entails respecting the equilibrium of four dimensions: the social equity, the ecological integrity, the change of the economic paradigm, and the participation of society in the decision-making processes. None of the four should be sacrificed in terms of the other.

It was recognized then that the origins of the ecological and social crisis lie deep within the assumptions of our commercial and economic systems. The compelling nature of this crisis is, however, its evolutionary nature. As the concept of sustainable development evolves we are moving more and more towards a profound change of values, the celebration of diversity and the economics for community. This will overcome the concept of development as linked to overconsumption and growth.

This will take time since it requires a profound change of paradigms of the magnitude of the one generated by Copernicus in his time when he proved that the Earth was not the center of the Universe.

We are facing global symptoms of local problems. The array of choices and problems that face us call for a profound change in paradigms. However, many of the proposed global solutions to environmental degradation arise from the same industrial paradigm that caused them. Such as more growth, more technology, money and environmental remedies that aim at strictly national issues arising from political pragmatism.

As Daly and Cobb stated in 1989, the first step towards redirection must be a widespread recognition that something is wrong and that the present policies, economic system does not work. Second is a widespread recognition that most of the problems faced by humanity today are interconnected and indeed have a common source and a diversity of solutions. Third that humanity has still the possibility of choosing a livable future for themselves and their children.

Both ecology and economics are needed to find the solutions. Economists need to recognize that environment and ecology could offer solutions and not only be considered as externalities and the cause of trouble. Ecology is a science that studies facts, interlinks phenomena, and helps to understand nature. Economics is a discipline that tries to accommodate facts into a world of assumptions. Economists cannot do their work without simplifying assumptions.

Some possible alternatives towards a sustainable development future can be described ordered under four variables called by Maurice Strong the "E-4 scheme": equity, economics, ecological integrity, and empowerment. The four need to be in equilibrium and none should be sacrificed by the other.

1. In terms of equity the alternatives are:
    - Access to global commons and redefinition of property rights;
    - Social access to nature;
    - Social equity in the present;
    - Intergenerational justice and equity;
    - Distribution of Income; and
    - Community versus private.

2. In terms of economics the alternatives are:

    a) Changes in trade policies, involving:
    - The need to review the balance of payments and reconsider trade;
    - Review the balance of payments accounting by reclassifying transactions in a way that converts a country's balance of trade from a surplus to a deficit when the exports are unsustainable since they are based on the export of depleted natural capital like petroleum or timber cut beyond sustainable yield;
    - Urgency to identify measures to rectify the inconsistencies between the current global trade agreements and sustainable development. Such as the prominence given to eco-labelling. The principle is correct but the agreed scheme is highly discriminatory against the production modalities of developing countries. The expansion of intellectual property rights regimes is another area that requires revision; and
    - Structural change of preventive nature such as innovative and creative trading arrangements, global taxation, joint implementation.

    b) Fiscal policies, involving:
    - Tax labor and income less, and tax resource throughput more;
    - Remove distortionary subsidies and perverse incentives;

- Brown taxes and Green subsidies;
- System of National accounts towards greening the GNP;
- Discrepancies between GNP and economic welfare. GNP is a measure of production and not consumption, whereas economic welfare is a matter of consumption. Reclassify health and education as capital investments;
- Count user cost as part of the opportunity cost of projects that deplete natural capital; and
- Demand side management to reduce the incremental resource requirements.
- Redeployment of existing financial resources.

3.   In terms of ecological integrity the alternatives are:

- What ecology offers is a way to examine all present economic and resource activities from a biological rather than a monetary point of view, including the impact that our present lifestyle will have on generation henceforth;
- Ecology is not here to endorse capitalism, free market, and trade but to put caution on these policies to get back to ethics, equity, and common values. To provide an organizing principle. The concept of carrying capacity for example is the maximum level of species or population that can be steadily and consistently supported by the resources that they coated. The key word is consistency; and
- The importance of ecological economics thought as Paul Hawken states in his book The Ecology of Commerce, is that in permits to propose three approaches guided by the example of nature:

    First, eliminate waste by rearranging our relationship to resources from linear to a cyclical one. Instead of organizing systems that efficiently dispose of or recycle our waste, we need to design systems of production that have little or no waste to begin with. This is to focus on the efficiency of the processes rather than only on the end of the pipe technologies.

    Second, change from an economy based on carbon to one based on hydrogen and sunshine. This is what we call the energy transition and can be achieved by reversing the historical incentives surrounding the production and consumption of energy, away from the cheapest combustion towards the most enduring production. It does not matter how many hundred years of supply we have of coal and oil, because if we burn it, we will rise the levels of CO_2 eight to ten times higher than normal and this will be disastrous in terms of global warming, ozone loss and destruction of forest due to acid rain.

Third create a system of feedback and accountability that support and strengthen restorative behavior, whether they are in resource utilities, green fees on agricultural chemicals or reliance on local production and distribution. Ecology offers the possibility to question how our present economic system consistently rewards short-term exploitation while penalizing long-term restoration and then eliminate ill-placed incentives that allow small sectors of the population to benefit at the expense of the whole.

4.   In terms of empowerment and democracy the alternatives are:

• The need for a fresh start that will challenge the existing inertia, honor differences and create mechanisms that are not about power but about aspiration, that aim at including people, that should be recognized by politics but not politicized, that build consensus, recognize diversity and encourage constructive change;

• Reconstruction of the common would insure that once again life is celebrated on Earth. This means to take a position in the debate. The traditional economists think that the solution to market failure is to clearly define property rights and are in favor of private property. The ecological economists take the view of strong sustainability and concern to promote and enhance communities capacity to manage sustainable development;

• Rethinking consensus building. Link and bring together the global networks to initiate a global intersectoral dialogue between: economists, ecologists as today, local authorities, consumer unions, trade unions, parliamentarians, universities, and mobilize broad constituencies for sustainable development; and

• Global versus universal. The benefits of global expansion are highly concentrated in the Northern countries and in the hands of corporations and their owners. Privatization is now of global dimensions.

CONCLUSIONS AND RECOMMENDATIONS

1.   Empower people: change will not come from governments. Establishment of new alliances among networks of consumers, parliamentarians, universities, producers, entrepreneurs, etc.

2.   Break the alliance between the mass media and the Transnational Corporations. There is a need for an alliance between these global networks for example between consumers unions and the media as a tool to empower people instead as a tool to promote wasteful consumption and enrich Transnational Corporations. Consumers and media are powerful mobilizers of values. A new powerful alliance that needs to be

built in the system with the other mobilizers of values are the mass media, the spiritual groups, and the schools.

3. Reinforce public accountability. For that, access to information is the key factor. For example the Rio Agreements are not yet in the hands of people as well as many other results from international negotiations that affect their livelihood.

4. Target the public goods and explore the new forms of trade. This is in relation to tradeable emission quotas or permits. This comes from the climate change convention. This opens new avenues for capitalization of developing countries. The CO_2 emissions and the tropical forests in the South. The possibility of opening a carbon stock market. It has to be carefully regulated to avoid corruption or paying to pollute. Twenty dollars per ton of CO_2 with technological devices. With forests the cost will be five times less.

5. Lobby to open the borders not only to capital, information and technology, but to labor. Market is interested in consumers. NAFTA for the 90 million Mexicans as consumers but not as a working force.

6. Orchestrate a world lobby towards the democratization, transparency and accountability of the Bretton Woods Institutions, including the newly formed WTO and the Transnational Corporations.

7. Build alliances with the small entrepreneur. Link the local realities with the global priorities taking advantage of the growing tension between the small entrepreneurs and the Transnational Corporations.

8. Open avenues for arbitration of conflicts at the local, national, and international levels. There is a need to ensure a recourse to address the grievances of communities when caused by transnational actors. Many of the existing ombudsman of the world are already facing transboundary conflicts of environment and development nature. The cases of pesticides dumping by Dow Chemical in Central America, Ston Forestal, Shell, etc.

9. Prepare an assessment and a set of indicators to distinguish between environmentally sound, greening of trade, and sustainable development. They are not synonymous. Analysis of the consequences of TREMS, PPMS, property rights and its impact on biodiversity, local production, etc.

10. A final note can be said about Costa Rica and Central America. This is the home of the Earth Council and a region that is challenging their present and future and bringing together peace and sustainable development. Small countries that are becoming the super powers of sustainable development in the world by putting people first. Many things can be learned from these countries as the basic ingredients found here are: culture, ethics, tradition, and community values. Costa Rica our host today is an example.

INDEX

Accountability, public 11
Accounting, integrated 8
Acid rain 25, 447
Administrative failure 333, 338
Agenda 21 144, 455, 457
Agenda for sustainability 328
Agricultural 206
   development alternatives 366
   development strategies 366
   practices 274, 430
   technologies 277
Agriculture 445
Agro-Eco-Tourism 406
Agroecological technologies 368
Agroecology 366
Agroecosystems, Mediterranean 374
Alliance for Sustainable Development
   441
Altieri, Miguel A. 10, 365
Analysis 7
Applied energy analysis 239
Appropriated ecosystem area (AEA)
   206
Arrow-Debreu equilibrium 171
Asian development model 292
Association for Watershed Protection
   (ADCH) 446
Atchafalaya Delta 268
Atmosphere 21
Authority
   decentralization 354
   redistribution 354
Auto-predictability 260

Back-casting 20
Baltic Sea 203
Banks, multilateral development 361
Bárcena, Alicia 11, 455
Barnett and Morse 53
Bayesian expected-value-maximization
   theory 233

Beijer International Institute of
   Ecological Economics 390
Best management practice (BMPs) 276
Bioaccumulation 30
Biodiversity 19, 35, 80, 92, 97, 367,
   382, 431, 441, 455
Bioeconomics 83
Biological diversity 93, 396
Biosphere 21
Bockstael, Nancy 249
Boulding, Kenneth 55
Bretton Woods system 457
Brundtland Commission 41, 458
Business 357

Capital stocks 55
Carrying capacity 107, 159, 215,
   382
Central America 372
Central Europe 10
Change 112
Chaos 259
Chile 374
Class struggle 162
Cleveland, Cutler J. 9, 301
Climate change 455
   global 102
Coase Theorem 339
Coastal ecological landscape, spatial
   simulation 268
Cobb 458
Communal property 399
Complexity 62, 112, 227
   averse 63
   cultural 65
Conflict resolution 353
Conservation 98, 154, 395, 398, 428,
   442
   soil 372
   strategies 360
Conservationist 80

Consumption 50, 55, 58, 131, 190
Convention on International Trade in
    Endangered Species 144
Copper 307
Cost-benefit analyses 137, 234, 292
Cost-benefit incidence 231
Cost-effectiveness 420
Cost shifting 336
Costa Rica 10, 440
Costanza, Robert 1, 9, 249
CRAY supercomputers 253
Cross-predictability 260
Cultural capital 400
Cultural diversity 92
Cultural evolution 263
Cultural vs. genetic evolution 263

Daily, G.C. 19
Daly, Herman E. 4, 19, 27,
    49, 287, 458
Decentralization of authority 354
Decision analysis 238
Deforestation 67, 413, 441
Democracy 461
Deposits 22
Development 187
    urban 10
    strategies alternatives 286
Discount rate 108, 132, 173, 174
Dissipative structures 265
Distance-related distortions 336
Distribution 81
    wealth 7
Diversity 112
Dominican Republic 373
Dourojeanni, Marc 10, 351
Duchin, Faye 9, 285

E-4 Scheme 458
Earth Council 462
Earth Summit (UNCED) 455
Ecological
    degradation 79

distribution 160, 161, 230
economy 255
ethics 109
integrity 11
management 230
scarcity 215
Ecological economic accounting 8
Ecological economics 3, 78, 118, 216,
    225, 286, 440
Ecological footprint 8, 216
Ecology 459
    productive 85
Economic
    development 67, 286
    distribution 159
    growth 5, 186, 343
    growth management 343
    redirection 343
    values 103
Economics 331, 459
    neoclassical 61, 287, 161, 169
    resource 130
    Sraffian 159, 161
    Structural 9, 291, 293
Ecosphere 21
Ecosystem protection 10
Ecosystems
    forest 209
    marine 210
Ecotechnological productive process 85
Ecotechnological productivity 85
Ecotourism 431
Ecotourists 159
Ecotoxicity 30
Ecuador 156
Ehrlich and Holdren equation 190
Ehrlich equation 186
Ehrlich, P. R. 19
Ekins, Paul 129
Embodied energy analysis 240
Employment 404
Empowerment failure 9, 335
Energy 315
    analyses 241
    consumption 191

efficiency 36, 196
  production 191
  solar 66, 71, 240
  use 289
Entropy 57
Environment 57, 80
Environmental
  degradation 82
  economics 7, 135
  externalities 129
  impact 190
  justice 160
  legislation 354
  planning 43
  policies 382, 440
  protection 421
  racism 160
  regulations 398
  research 386
  risk-taking 144
  sustainability 141
  uncertainty 232
  valuation 416
Environmental change, global 5
Environmental Commission for Bananas
    (CAB) 446
Environmental utilization space (EUS)
    329, 348
Environmentalism 80
Environmentalists 118
Envisioning 6, 122
Equity 81
Eriksson, Karl-Erik 4, 17
Ethical values 96
Ethics 103
  environmental 353
  social 353
Ethno-agricultural 97
Ethnomedicinal 97
Everglades National Park 269
Evolution 262
  biological 263
  cultural 263
  genetic 263
Evolutionary approaches 262

Evolutionary paradigm 262
Exergy 20
Existence values 134
Expected-value maximization 234
Externalities 135, 161

Faucheaux, Sylvie 8, 223
Figueres Olsen, José María 441
Financial institutions 362
Fishers, Irving 56
Folke, Carl 8, 201
Food
  consumption 203
  security 374
  supply 140
Food-for-work program 95
Forestry tax 403
Fossil fuel 33, 73, 315
Fractals 259
Froger, Géraldine 223
Fuel mix 314
Funtowicz, Silvio 8, 223
Future Contamination Index 33

Gallopín, Gilberto C. 7, 185
Geographical balance accounts 35
Global
  change 62, 70
  trade agreements 459
  warming 52, 137, 441
Globalization 456
Gore, Al 58
Government
  failures 9, 335, 337
  intervention 339
Grass-roots movement 82, 97
Green GNP 292
Green Revolution 369
Gross domestic product (GDP) 183, 443
Gross national product (GNP)
    52, 187, 287, 459
Gross world product (GWP) 138
Growth, urban 412

Guacerique River 430
Gupta, Anil 5, 91

Hanna, Susan S. 10, 381
Harvesting rate 133
Hawken, Paul 460
Health
    care system, U.S. 68
    human 447
Hierarchy 256
Holdren, J. P. 19
Holling, C. S. 255
Holmberg, John 4, 17
Honey Bee Network 99
Hotelling's Rule 130
Humansphere, 21
Hydrosphere 21
Hypercard Navigator 271

IBRD 356
Implementation 117
Imports 315
Impoverishment 265
Income 374
Index of Sustainable Economic Welfare
    (ISEW) 38, 58
Indigenous knowledge 99
Individual transferable quotas (ITQ's)
    385
Industrial Revolution 67
Industrialism 67
Information
    gathering 118
    public access to 353
    reformation 50
Input-output economics 290
Institutions 331
    environmental 356
    international 360
    private 357
    public 355
Integrated Pest Management (IPM) 72,
    444

Integrated resource management 434
Integrated watershed management 435
Intensity of use 195
Inter-American Development Bank
    (IBD) 356, 442
Inter-temporal valuation 174
International Society for Ecological
    Economics (ISEE) 285, 454
Intervention, failures 333
Intra-household risk adjustments 106
Investment strategy 43
IPAT Equation 289

Jacobs, M. 19, 28

Kaimowitz, David 10, 439

La Tigra Cloud Forest 428
La Tigra National Park 428, 431
Land grazing 208
Land use 27, 272, 432
    changes 432
    conversion 273
    forest 403
    management 433
    planning 37
Larsson, Jonas 8, 201
Latin America 10, 79, 352, 366, 412
Law enforcement 355
Lawrence Summers' principle 157
Leff, Enrique 5, 77, 91
Leontief, Wassily 289
Limits to growth 225
Lithosphere 21, 34

Macro-economics 289
Mal-development 188
Manmade Capital 54
MAP II™ 271
Marginal net private benefit (MNPB)
    135

Marine
  ecosystems 214
  fisheries 382, 385
Market economy 154, 333
Market failure 168, 333
Marketable permits 340
Marshal, Alfred 50
Martinez-Alier, Juan 1, 7, 153
Matter
  high-quality 23
  low-quality 23
Matter/energy 53
Maximum sustainable yield harvest 134
May, Peter H. 10, 411
Mazurian Landscape Park 397, 401
Mazurian National Park 401
Meadows, Donella 6, 71, 117
Metamodeling 253
Ministry of Natural Resources, Mines,
  and Energy 443
Ministry of Public Works and
  Transportation (MOPT) 448
Modeling 8, 252
  inconsistencies 277
  integrated ecological economic 9
  natural resource use 303
  Neo-Ricardian 162
Models 7, 118
  conceptual 254
  general ecosystem (GEM) 269
  high-generality conceptual 254
  high-precision analytical 255
  high-realism impact analysis 255
  input-output (IO) 294
  landscape 269
  moderate-generality precision 256
  Patuxent landscape (PLM) 268
Montreal Protocol 143
Multi-criteria decision analysis (MCDA)
  244
Multilateral development banks 10
Munda, Guesippe 8, 223

National eMergy Surplus (NES). 240

National Exergy Surplus 241
National Fund for Environmental
  Protection 406
National Park Services 443
National parks 396
National Service for Conservation
  Areas (SENAC) 444
Natural capital 54, 162, 400, 459
  depletion 5
Natural resource accounting (NRA)
  294, 367, 376
Natural resource
  scarcity 308
  use 303
Natural Step Foundation 4, 44
Natural subsidy 54
Nature protection 395
Negative externalities 105
Negentropic
  economy 83
  process 84
Neo-Ricardian approach 168
Non-governmental organizations
  (NGOs) 10, 358, 366, 443
  grassroots 359
Nitrogen emissions 295
Non-profit private organizations
  358
Nordhaus, William 52
Nuclear energy 34, 146
Nuclear industry 33
Nuclear power 34, 316

Occam's Razor 63
O'Connor, Martin 7, 8, 153, 223
Open system 53, 84
Opschoor, Johannas B. 9, 327
Optimal
  depletion 131
  scale 55
  use 134
Optimum stock level 133
Option values 134
Organic management system 376

Overlapping generations (OLG) general equilibrium models 172
Ozone
  depletion 143
  layer 26

Pareto-efficient equilibria 173
Pastuk, Marília 10, 411
Patuxent River 9, 265
Peru 372
Pesticides 444
Phosphorus 33
Piecki 401
Pigouvian tax 136
Pigouvian charge 340
Pigouvian solution 339
Planck, Max 68
Planck's Principle of Increasing Effort, 68
Plimsoll line 30
Poland 395
Policy 118
  public 230
Political
  distribution 159
  ecology 82, 159
Polluter Pays Principle 344
Pollution 29, 80, 135, 198
  air 447
  control 267
  industrial 396
  permits 404
  point source 202
  tradeable quota 338
  vehicles 447
Population 67, 289, 353
  data 206
  growth 50, 67, 193, 289, 432
Post-normal science 8, 225, 288
Poverty 79, 95, 265, 369
  urban 412
Precautionary principle 134, 342
Predictability 260
Preservation 442

Price analysis 161
Production 53, 80, 190
Property
  common 383
  private 383
  rights 10, 108, 111, 154, 161, 383, 398, 412, 459
Property rights regimes 10
Proxy solutions 337

Quality of life 8
Quesada-Mateo, Carlos A.   10, 427, 439

Rapid rural appraisal (RRA) 367
Rawls, John 40
Recycling 304, 313
Redistribution of authority 354
Reforestation 414, 441
Regeneration 100
Relative stock 28
Resolution 260
Resource
  conservation 104
  depletion 307
  efficiency 196
  extraction 9
  management 112, 387
  quality 311, 312
  renewable 203
  substitution 328
  use 27
Resource economics 7
Resources 67
  natural 95, 383
  natural flow 22
  non-renewable 28, 132, 143, 303
  non-substitutable 29
  renewable 28, 132, 143, 214, 303
  renewable substitutable 29
  water 431
Ricardian land 162
Rio de Janeiro 10, 412, 455
Rio Declaration (UN) 41

Rio Summit 144
Risk analysis 232
Risk-assessment 26, 267
Robèrt, Karl-Henrik 4, 17
Roegen, Georgescu 83
Roman Empire 66
Ruth, Matthias 9, 301

Sanchez, Juan 365
Sao José Operrio community
    reforestation project 421
Scale 256
Scarcity 147
Schumpeter, Joseph 3
Segura, Olman 1, 10, 439
Senge, Peter 119
Silveira, Diomar 11, 455
Simultaneity 112
Social accounting matrices 295
Social welfare rule 172
Society for Research and Initiatives for
    Sustainable Technologies and
    Institutions (SRISTI) 101
Socio-ecological principles 19
Sociosphere 21
Soyinka, Wole 40
Spatial Modeling Program (SMP) 271
Sraffian joint production theory 155
Static sink life 32
STELLA II® 310
STELLA™ 271
Steward, Julian 63
Stocks 56
Strong sustainability 330
Sulfur emissions 295
Sustainability 3, 8, 40, 70, 80, 98,
    117, 170, 186, 216, 328, 367,
    383, 458
  coevolutionary 331, 346
  international institutions 345
  social 412, 420
Sustainability Tree 8, 225, 238
Sustainable
  alternatives 146

development 24, 27, 56, 79, 186, 199,
    235, 243, 291, 325, 455
economic development 343
harvest 132
harvesting 143
institutions 352
national income (SNI) 174
society 4, 36
world 124
yield 132
Sweitzer, Julie 8, 201
Systems analysis 251

Tainter, Joseph A. 5, 61
Tatra mountains 400
Technical
  change 311
  improvements 304
Technological
  change 329
  progress 243
Technology 192, 214, 289, 303, 355
Technosphere 21
Tegucigalpa 428
Tegucigalpa's master plan 434
Thermodynamics 4, 19, 53, 239, 264,
    303
Third Industrial Revolution 198
Thurow, Lester 52
Tourism 443
Trade 216, 447
Trade liberalization policies 447
Tradeable rights quota 340
Transaction failures 9, 331

Under-development 187
United Nations (UN) 360
United Nations Conference on
    Environment and Development 11,
    455
United States Agency for International
    Development 445
Universal Soil Loss Equation (USLE)
    417

Uranium fuels 315
Urbanization 217, 412
User cost 53

Valuation 292
Valuations of statistical lives (VOSLs)
    137
Value added 51, 57
Vision 2, 119
Voluntary agreements 340
Von der Weid, Jean Marc 365

Wainger, Lisa 249
Waste
    disposal 80
    flow 28
    stock 28
Water quality 430
Watershed management 433

Weak sustainability 330
Weak sustainability criterion 174
Welfare 55
Wetlands 272
    restoration 267
White, Leslie 63
Willingness-to-accept (WTA) 157
Willingness-to-pay (WTP) 136, 157
Wilson, E. O. 109
Wolfle, Dael 68
World Bank 344, 446
World Biosphere Reserves 144
World Resources on Diskette Database
    (WRI) 206

Yurjevic, Andres 365

Zylicz, Tomasz 10, 395